# GUIDING CHILDREN'S SOCIAL DEVELOPMENT

# GUIDING
# CHILDREN'S
# SOCIAL
# DEVELOPMENT

## THIRD EDITION

Marjorie J. Kostelnik, Ph.D.
Laura C. Stein, M.S.
Alice Phipps Whiren, Ph.D.
Anne K. Soderman, Ph.D.
MICHIGAN STATE UNIVERSITY

## Delmar Publishers

*an International Thomson Publishing company* I(T)P®

Albany • Bonn • Boston • Cincinnati • Detroit • London • Madrid
Melbourne • Mexico City • New York • Pacific Grove • Paris • San Francisco
Singapore • Tokyo • Toronto • Washington

## NOTICE TO THE READER

Cover Design: Brucie Rosch

**Delmar Staff**
Publisher: William Brottmiller
Administrative Editor: Jay Whitney
Associate Editor: Erin O'Connor Traylor
Project Editor: Marah Bellegarde
Production Coordinator: James Zayicek
Art and Design Coordinator: Timothy J. Conners
Senior Editorial Assistant: Mara Berman

COPYRIGHT © 1998
By Delmar Publishers
an International Thomson Publishing Company

The ITP logo is a trademark under license.

Printed in the United States of America

For more information, contact:

Delmar Publishers
3 Columbia Circle, Box 15015
Albany, New York 12212-5015

International Thomson Publishing Europe
Berkshire House
168-173 High Holborn
London, WC1V 7AA
England

Thomas Nelson Australia
102 Dodds Street
South Melbourne, 3205
Victoria, Australia

Nelson Canada
1120 Birchmount Road
Scarborough, Ontario
Canada, M1K 5G4

International Thomson Editores
Campos Eliseos 385, Piso 7
Col Polanco
11560 Mexico D F Mexico

International Thomson Publishing GmbH
Konigswinterer Strasse 418
53227 Bonn
Germany

International Thomson Publishing Asia
221 Henderson Road
#05-10 Henderson Building
Singapore 0315

International Thomson Publishing—Japan
Hirakawacho Kyowa Building, 3F
2-2-1 Hirakawacho
Chiyoda-ku, Tokyo 102
Japan

3  4  5  6  7  8  9  10  XXX  04  03  02  01  00  99  98

**Library of Congress Cataloging-in-Publication Data**

Guiding children's social development  /  Marjorie J. Kostelnik . . . [et al.].—3rd ed.
          p.    cm.
     Includes bibliographical references and index.
     ISBN 0-8273-7690-1
     1. Child development.  2. Socialization.  3. Social skills in children.  I. Kostelnik, Marjorie J.
HQ767.9.G85   1998
155.4' 18—dc21
                                      97-27007
                                        CIP

# ▼Contents

*I have come to a frightening conclusion. I am the decisive element in the classroom. It is my personal approach that creates the climate. It is my daily mood that makes the weather. As a teacher, I possess tremendous power to make a child's life miserable or joyous. I can be a tool of torture or an instrument of inspiration. I can humiliate or humor, hurt or heal. In all situations it is my response that decides whether a crisis will be escalated or de-escalated, and a child humanized or dehumanized.*

*—Haim Ginott*

*A person's a person, no matter how small.*

*—Horton of* **Horton Hears a Who**
*Dr. Seuss*
*Random Books*

Six-year-old Seth was telling his mother about the substitute teacher in his class.

Seth: She wasn't very nice, Mom. She was real loud and frowny all the time.

Mom: Mmm, doesn't sound good.

Seth: Us kids talked about it on the playground.

Mom: What did you say?

Seth: Carl said she was mean. Lizabeth said maybe she didn't like kids. Maressa said it was like she didn't even respect us.

Mom: Respect, that's a pretty big word. What do you mean, respect?

Seth: (After a long pause) Well, Mrs. Gomez (the children's regular teacher), she respects us. She treats us like she *likes us* . . . and . . . like *we have possibilities.*

Children as young as Seth can easily distinguish adults who truly enjoy being with children and who are supportive of their development. Our hope is that after reading this third edition of *Guiding Children's Social Development* you will be better able to demonstrate the kind of respect for children that Seth was talking about.

Our original purpose in writing this book was to do something to improve the quality of life for children and their families and to contribute to the professional development of practitioners in training. That continues to be our aim. We believe that helping professionals have a primary role in providing emotional support and guidance to the youngsters with whom they work. This includes helping children develop positive feelings about themselves, increasing their ability to interact effectively with others, and teaching them socially acceptable means of behavior. We have also come to know that this type of learning is facilitated when children view the adult as a wellspring of comfort and encouragement as well as a source of behavioral guidance. How proficiently adults perform these roles is affected by the extent to which they understand child development, their ability to establish positive relationships with children, and their grasp of principles related to behavior management. Therefore, it is our premise that helping professionals must first learn about children's social development and then become adept in relationship-enhancement skills and behavior-management techniques.

Unfortunately, in the literature and in practice, a dichotomy often is assumed between relationship enhancement and behavior management. For example, approaches that focus on the former teach students how to demonstrate warmth and respect, acceptance and empathy, but leave them to their own devices in figuring out how to deal with typical childhood behaviors such as spitting, hitting, teasing, or making friends. Conversely, approaches that focus on behavior control address the latter circumstances but often neglect to teach students how to build rapport with children, how to help children develop coping strategies, or how to assist them in better understanding themselves and others.

We have decided to tackle these issues by including research, information, and skills associated with both relationship enhancement and behavior management. We have pulled together a unique blend of organismic and mechanistic theory and practice that establishes common ground between the two while maintaining the integrity of each. In doing so, we demonstrate that there is a factual knowledge base that can be brought to bear on how aspiring professionals think about children's social development and how they respond to it.

Additionally, too often, we have encountered students and practitioners who treat their interactions with children as wholly intuitive. They rely on "gut-level" responses, adhering to no explicit or comprehensive principles. These adults frequently view child guidance as a series of tricks that they use indiscriminately to meet short-range objectives, such as getting a child to stop interrupting. They have no purposeful or integrated set of strategies that address long-range goals, such as teaching a child to delay gratification. Other adults have more knowledge about broad principles regarding relationship building and behavior management but have difficulty integrating those principles into a systematic, consistent plan of action. Most distressing to us are those adults whose lack of training leads them to conclude that the normal behaviors children exhibit as they engage in the socialization process somehow are abnormal or malicious. These people also fail to recognize the impact of their own behavior on their interactions with children. As a result, when children do not comply with their expectations, they view condemnation, rather than teaching, as appropriate for the situation.

*Guiding Children's Social Development* has been written to address these shortcomings. It is our goal to eliminate much of the guesswork and frustration experienced by professionals in the field as well as to improve the conditions under which children are socialized in formal group settings. To accomplish this, we have provided a solid foundation of child-development information. In addition, we have shown how to translate that information into related skills and procedures that support children's social development.

## New to This Edition

The third edition of *Guiding Children's Social Development* has been extensively updated. Based on feedback from our readers, we have also added several new segments to the book. Readers will note that there is increased attention to professional ethics, both in the content of Chapters 1 and 15, as well as through the inclusion of ethics-related discussion questions at the end of every chapter. Material focusing on infants with special needs has been added to Chapter 2. Stressors for families of the 1990s and helping children in crisis are featured in Chapter 6. The theoretical portion of Chapter 10 has been completely reorganized to provide a clearer entree to the topic of self-discipline. Chapter 12 introduces a new section on bullying behavior, as well as ways to work with both bullies and their victims. Chapter 14 includes expanded coverage of children with special needs, especially children displaying characteristics of attention deficit disorder and attention deficit/hyperactivity disorder; advanced and precocious children; and differences in children's temperament. In various chapters, new figures and charts have been added to underscore key points and to make concepts easier for readers to visualize.

Readers familiar with the previous editions of *Guiding Children's Social Development* will note that the order of the chapters has been reconfigured. We have placed like-chapters in closer proximity to one another, allowing for better bridges between one chapter and the next. For instance, Supporting Children in Stressful Situations now follows Responding to Children's Emotions. This placement allowed us to introduce basic skills in the chapter on emotions and more advanced, but related skills in the stress chapter. Similarly, the chapter entitled Supporting Children's Friendships has been moved directly following Enhancing Children's Play. These two chapters share many common elements, and the skills introduced in the play chapter lead to those presented in the one on friendship. Perhaps the most significant change has been the elimination of a single chapter devoted to working with parents. This deletion does not reflect a decreased emphasis on the importance of families. Rather, we found that putting parental issues in a separate chapter isolated the topic in the minds of readers. Moreover, although parents are important, other family members also play a significant role in children's social development. To better address the reality of modern children's lives and to make family matters more pervasive throughout the text, we have included a family communication feature in every chapter. The family communication feature includes chapter-related strategies that professionals can use to interact more effectively with family members. Two-way communication is emphasized, as is respect for differences among families.

All of these revisions are meant to address current issues in child development and early intervention. Their inclusion should better prepare students to face the realities of working with young children on a day to day basis.

## Presentation

Taken altogether, the chapters in this book comprise a thorough picture of children's social development and the classroom practices professionals use to enhance child development and learning. We have been careful to include traditional areas of study such as self-esteem, aggression, routines, rules, and consequences. We also have addressed more current topics of interest such as infant communication, stress, friendship, superhero play, and prosocial behavior. Considered individually, each chapter offers an in-depth literature review in which findings from many fields have been integrated (psychology, physiology, education, medicine, sociology, home economics, personnel management, interior design). Thus, even within the confines of a single subject, there is breadth. The sequence of chapters also has been thoughtfully planned so that each serves as a foundation for the next—simple concepts and/or skills precede more complex ones; chapters that focus on relationship enhancement come before those that discuss behavior management.

Throughout the text, we have tried to establish a lucid, straightforward style, which we hope makes the book easy to read and interesting. Although many research findings have been cited, we have purposely used parenthetical notation rather than constantly referring to the researchers by name. We want students to remember the *concepts* those findings represent rather than to simply memorize names and dates. In addition, we have made liberal use of real-life examples to illustrate concepts and related skills. This is to assist students in making the connection between what they read and "flesh-and-blood" children. Furthermore, we have described many different settings in which adults find themselves working with children so that regardless of their professional intents, students can relate to what we have written. Another reason for multiple-setting scenarios is to demonstrate that the content is not situation bound and that the knowledge and skills can be generalized from one setting to another.

Our scope of study encompasses the social development of children from birth to twelve years of age. We have targeted this period of childhood because it is during the formative years that the foundation for all socialization takes place. Furthermore, the skills taught have been specially designed to take into account the cognitive structures and social abilities particular to children of this age.

Because children live and develop within the context of a family, a community, a nation, and a world, they are constantly influenced by, and in turn affect, the people and events around them. Thus, our perspective is an ecological one in which children are viewed as dynamic, ever-changing beings in an equally dynamic, ever-changing milieu. This ecological perspective is incorporated into each chapter in the literature review and in many of the examples provided. Additionally, in most chapters, at least one and sometimes more of the discussion questions raise these issues for students to think about.

It has been our experience that students learn professional behavior best when they are given clear, succinct directions for how to carry out a procedure. Defining a procedure, offering examples, and giving a rationale for its use are necessary, but not sufficient. Thus, our approach to skill training is to point out to the student research-based strategies

related to chapter content. We then break those strategies down into a series of discrete, observable skills that students can implement. We have been direct, rather than circumspect, in articulating the specific steps involved. This forthrightness should not be taken to imply that our directions are immutable or that there is no room for students to use the skills creatively. Rather, we anticipate that students will internalize and modify skills according to their own needs, personality, interaction style, and circumstance once they have learned them. In addition, we recognize that an important component of using skills correctly is determining which alternatives from the entire available array are best suited for a given situation. Hence, knowing when to use a particular skill and when to refrain from using it is as important as knowing how to use it. For this reason, we discuss these issues throughout each chapter, both in the body of the text and in the pitfalls section at the end. We also have incorporated specific guidelines for how the skills can be adapted for use with youngsters of varying ages and differing cultural backgrounds. Finally, Chapter 15, Making Judgments, has been included to further help students make these decisions.

**Learning aids.** This book incorporates a number of features aimed at enhancing student learning:

Each chapter is introduced by a statement of objectives, which tells students what they should know on completion of that segment of the book. This alerts them to the major foci of that chapter.

All chapters open with a discussion of theory and research related to a particular social-development topic. Implications of the research for both children and adults also are described.

A major portion of each chapter is devoted to presenting the professional skills relevant to the topic under discussion. Each skill is broken down into a series of observable behaviors that students can learn and instructors can evaluate directly. This section also makes extensive use of examples to further illustrate the skills under consideration. Strategies for use with children as well as family communication techniques are offered.

Near the end of each chapter is a description of pitfalls or common mistakes students make when first learning to use the skills. Suggestions for how to avoid these difficulties are provided.

All chapters include a summary that gives a brief overview of the material presented. This is a useful synopsis for student review of important concepts.

An added feature of each chapter is a listing of topics for discussion. These are thought-provoking questions aimed at helping students synthesize and apply, through conversations with classmates, what they have read.

Each chapter concludes with a suggested list of field assignments students may use to practice and perfect the skills described. These assignments may be carried out independently or under the direction of the instructor.

## Supplementary Materials

In addition to the textbook, we have designed an instructor's manual for the teacher and an electronic student activity guide to help students master the skills presented in the textbook.

**Student aids.** An electronic student activity guide is available on diskette to help students understand and master the skills presented in the textbook. The guide includes modules that correspond to each chapter in the textbook. Every module contains performance objectives, a rationale for the skills, an outline of key points regarding skill performance, a review of key terms, and a series of exercises focused on skill development. The guide enables students to practice and apply, in both hypothetical and real situations, skills they have learned. Skills are broken down into manageable segments and are presented in a sequence ranging from simple to more complex. In addition, students can gauge their own progress via an answer key. All of these features increase students' ability to incorporate the skills into their professional behavior. Note that a prototype of the student activity guide has been extensively field tested with college students and practitioners (Kostelnik, 1978, 1983; Peters and Kostelnik, 1981). Data from those studies show that students who complete the guide significantly increase their ability to use the skills and to maintain them over time. Moreover, many of the items that have been included in this guide are ones that students have recommended.

The terms covered in the electronic student activity guide are set in boldface throughout the textbook. In addition, an icon of a computer diskette (Flash!) appears in the skills section of each chapter, designating skills covered in the guide.

**Instructor's manual.** A comprehensive instructor's manual further supplements the textbook. In it, we describe how to organize a course using the textbook; how to search out, select, and maintain appropriate field placements for students; how to model skills for students to imitate; and how to provide feedback to students assigned to field placements. In addition, we have included a series of rehearsal exercises, which are role-play activities meant to be carried out in class. They are aimed at acquainting students with how to use particular skills prior to implementing them with children and at clarifying basic concepts as they emerge during discussion or interaction. An extensive test bank also has been developed as part of the instructor's manual. Multiple-choice, true-false, short-answer, and essay questions are presented on a chapter-by-chapter basis. Finally, the instructor's manual contains a criterion-referenced observational tool, the PSI (professional skills inventory). This is a unique feature of our instructional package. It can be used by instructors and/or practitioners to evaluate the degree to which students demonstrate the skills taught.

## To the Student

This book will give you a foundation of knowledge and skills necessary for guiding children's social development in professional practice. We hope it will contribute to your enthusiasm about the field and to your confidence in working with young children and their families. Although what you read here will not encompass everything you will need to know, it will serve as a secure base from which you can begin to develop your own professional style.

You will have the advantage of learning, in one course, myriad information and strategies that otherwise might take many years to discover. Through examples, you will be able to accumulate a background of experience that you may not yet have had a chance to develop or learn by other means. Finally, you will be reading a book authored by people with extensive practical experience in working with children, engaging in research, and teaching this content to learners much like yourselves. As a result, we are well aware of the issues related to children's social development that are important to students, and we have focused on those. We also have anticipated some of the questions you might ask and some of the difficulties you might encounter in working with this material. Consequently, we have made a conscious effort to discuss these in relevant places throughout the book.

## Hints for Using the Materials

1. Read each chapter of the textbook carefully. Plan to read them more than once. Use the first reading to gain a broad grasp of the subject matter; then, read a second time, paying particular attention to the sequence of development presented. Identify major concepts regarding adult behavior, and focus on the actual procedures related to each skill. Use subsequent readings to recall the material in more detail.

2. Jot notes in the margin and underline points you wish to remember.

3. Go beyond simply memorizing terminology. Concentrate on how you might recognize the concepts you are studying in real children's be-

havior and how you might apply this knowledge in your interactions with children. Not only will this expand your understanding of the material, but both levels of information are likely to appear on quizzes and exams.

4. Ask questions. Share with classmates and the instructor your experiences in using the material. Participate fully in class discussions and role-play exercises.

5. Try out what you are learning with children. If you are in a field placement, are volunteering, or are employed in a program, take full advantage of that opportunity. Do not hesitate to practice your skills simply because they are new to you and you are not sure how well you will perform them. Persist in spite of your awkwardness or mistakes, and make note of what you might do to improve. Focus on your successes and your increasing skill, not just on things that don't go perfectly. Allow yourself to enjoy the children even as you are learning from them.

# ▼Acknowledgments

We would like to thank the following persons for their contributions to our work:

Louise F. Guerney, The Pennsylvania State University; Steven J. Danish, Commonwealth University of Virginia; Anthony R. D'Augelli, The Pennsylvania State University; and Allen L. Hauer, University of Massachusetts, were major sources of information regarding the philosophy and skills presented here.

Stephen R. Jorgensen, Texas Tech University, offered numerous suggestions and citations, which we incorporated throughout the book.

Our colleagues at Michigan State University generously assisted us:

Lillian A. Phenice expanded our understanding of children's development from a multicultural perspective and offered valuable insights into issues of ethnicity.

Verna Hildebrand gave numerous suggestions during the initial phases of this project.

Donna R. Howe contributed materials to the chapters on friendship and prosocial behavior.

Linda Nelson and Dennis Keefe made available important material regarding values and decision making.

Kara Gregory contributed to numerous chapters, providing valuable insights and resources. Her attention to each skill section was especially helpful. She also made important contributions to the instructor's manual and had primary responsibility for converting the original student activity guide to an electronic format. In addition, she added several new exercises to the electronic guide, making it more congruent with the third edition of the textbook.

The following reviewers provided valuable feedback throughout the revision process for this edition:

Judy C. Campbell
Parkland College
Champaign, Illinois

Dickson Carroll, Ed.D.
Georgia Southwestern University
Americus, Georgia

Sally Edgerton, Ph.D.
Saginaw Valley State University
University Center, Michigan

Helen E. Hagens, Ph.D.
Ohio University
Athens, Ohio

Jann James, Ed.D.
Troy State University
Goshen, Alabama

Margaret King, Ed.D.
Ohio University
Athens, Ohio

Marcia Rysztak
Lansing Community College
Lansing, Michigan

Olivia N. Saracho, Ph.D.
University of Maryland at College Park
College Park, Maryland

Jeffrey Trawick-Smith
Eastern Connecticut State University
Willimantic, Connecticut

Sharon T. Willis
North Harris Community College
Houston, Texas

Finally, over the years, we have worked with many students whose enthusiasm and excitement have invigorated us. Simultaneously, we have been privileged to know hundreds of children during their formative years. From them we have gained insight and the motivation to pursue this project. To them this book is dedicated.

# ▼Chapter 1

## Professional Involvement with Young Children

## ▼ OBJECTIVES

*On completion of this chapter, you will be able to describe:*

▼  Social competence in children.

▼  Basic principles of human development.

▼  How children learn.

▼  Contexts that influence child development and learning.

▼  How families function in children's lives.

▼  How formal group settings influence children's development and learning.

▼  What it means to be a helping professional.

▼  The overall structure and format of this book.

*Pease porridge hot, pease porridge cold.*
*Pease porridge in the pot, nine days old.*
Baby Rosalie chortles with delight as the adult pats her hands in rhythm to the words.

Three-year-old Ishien falls on the sidewalk, scraping the palms of her hands. She looks toward her mother, who gently picks her up, soothing the child with quiet sounds.

"Was too!" "Was not!" Jamie and Lucien are in a heated argument about who forgot to turn off the computer. Each insists it was the other's responsibility to carry out this job.

Robert is new to the Elm Street Saturday Morning recreation program. As the children rush outside, grabbing bats and balls, he asks another boy, "Can I play?"

Children are social beings. From the moment they are born, they begin a lifetime of interdependence and active engagement with other people. Through social interactions children gain knowledge of who they are and what they can do. They learn about human relationships, develop interpersonal skills, and come to know the rules and values of the society in which they live. Much of this learning occurs from infancy through the later elementary years. Indeed, it is during this time that children develop the social foundation upon which they build for the rest of their lives.

## ▼ SOCIAL COMPETENCE

To operate effectively in the social world, children must learn to recognize, interpret, and respond to social situations (Hendrick, 1996). They must also make judgments about how to "achieve personal goals through social interactions while simultaneously maintaining positive relationships with others over time and across situations" (Rubin and Rose-Krasnor, 1992:285). How well they do this is a measure of their **social competence.** In the United States, children are generally viewed as more socially competent when they are responsible rather than irresponsible; independent versus suggestible; friendly,

1

not hostile; cooperative instead of resistive; purposeful rather than aimless; and self-controlled, not impulsive (Baumrind, 1970, 1995). Other behaviors associated with social competence include giving and receiving emotional support, social awareness, processing information accurately, communicating, problem solving, and self-monitoring (Goleman, 1995). Thus, Art, who notices that Gary is unhappy and attempts to comfort him, is more socially adept than Ralph, who walks by unaware of his peer's distress. Dinah, who habitually blurts out whatever is on her mind the instant it occurs to her, is less socially mature than if she were able to wait without interrupting. When Chip uses verbal reasoning to persuade his friends to try his idea, he is demonstrating more social competence than classmates who rely on physical force to make their point.

## Benefits

Socially competent children are happier than their less competent peers. They are more successful in their interactions with others, more popular, and more satisfied with life. In addition, there is evidence that children's social relations greatly influence their academic achievement with more positive social relations being associated with greater success in school (Alexander and Entwhistle, 1988; Goleman, 1995). Consequently, socially competent children see themselves as worthwhile human beings who can make a difference in the world. Social competence does not happen suddenly or automatically. It is acquired over time and is affected by development as well as experience.

## Developmental Influences

As children mature, developmental changes occur in their thinking that increase their social capacity. Thus, social development becomes more complex and sophisticated as children's language memory, cognitive, and physical abilities expand. This progression is illustrated by the role that development plays in the strategies children use to elicit caregiving behaviors in the first few years of life (Bowlby, 1969). Initially, it is the infant's reflexes that contribute most to closeness with the caregiver—grasping, sucking, and rooting are all automatic, unconscious actions that draw the adult near. Gradually, as infants' cognitive structures change and the use of their bodies comes more into conscious control, they have a greater range of eliciting behaviors at their disposal. Soon, they vocalize, smile, and reach in order to gain adult attention and affection. Once babies become mobile, their expanded physi-

cal development allows them to actively seek out their caregivers, crawling after them, clinging to them, and scrambling into their laps. Older children, whose language and reasoning are more developed, quickly use such strategies as asking for a story or inviting Mom to play a game as ways to be close to adults.

## The Function of Experience

Practice and experience go hand in hand with development to expand children's social competence. Youngsters practice relevant skills, such as collaboration or more precise communication, through numerous interactions with others. Each small episode gives the child information about which behaviors to maintain, which to avoid, and which to try instead (Boneau, 1974). In this way, children learn social behaviors based on whether the outcomes of their interactions are rewarding or costly for them (Lamovec, 1989; Thibault and Kelley, 1959). Rewards result from interactions that are satisfying to children's needs; costs stem from negative social exchanges. Interactions that lead to acceptance, positive feedback, encouragement, or clarification are highly rewarding, and those that result in rejection, avoidance, or misinterpretation are costly. Children who experience mostly rewarding interactions and few costly ones feel better about themselves and become more socially competent than children for whom the reverse is true (Chaikin and Derlega, 1974; Seligman, 1995).

## The Role of Adults

Adults who work with children play a major part in their development of social competence. Every day adults are faced with social situations in which they must make judgments about how to support and guide children. These are challenging tasks. On any given day, adults may wonder:

Should I pick up the crying baby or should I let her cry it out?

What should I do about a child who bites?

When is it reasonable to expect children to know how to share?

How can children learn better ways to resolve their differences?

What is the best way to help a child who is rejected by other children?

Where can I turn if I suspect a child is being physically abused?

How adults answer questions such as these and what actions they take can be more or less helpful. Some responses may even be harmful. For instance, adult actions may enhance children's feelings of self-worth or detract from them. They may increase children's interpersonal abilities or leave children at a loss about how to interact effectively. What adults do and say may either promote or inhibit children's development of self-control. Effective professionals make decisions based on the following information:

▼ What they know about how children develop and learn
▼ What they know about the strengths, needs, and interests of individual children
▼ What they know about the social and cultural contexts in which children live

When adults take into account these factors, they are more likely to interact with children in ways that enhance their social competence. Such practices are described as being *developmentally appropriate* (Bredekamp and Copple, 1997). Developmentally appropriate practices are associated with high-quality childhood programs. Such programs promote the development and enhance the learning of each child served. Since developmentally appropriate practices provide a foundation for guiding children's social development, the first step in acquiring them is to understand basic principles of child development.

## ▼ PRINCIPLES OF DEVELOPMENT

Certain generalizations can be made regarding child development worldwide. These developmental principles help us to recognize commonalities among children and characteristics typical within age ranges. Although no two children are exactly alike, we know that three-year-olds are more like other three-year-olds than they are like seven-year-olds. Likewise, we recognize that certain abilities emerge at fairly predictable times. Most children talk somewhere between ten months and two years. First and second graders often tattle as they explore ways to obey school rules. Early adolescents shift their attention to peer relations, with greater emphasis than was placed during their preschool years. Knowledge of child development helps adults predict what strategies, materials, interactions, and experiences will be safe, healthy, interesting, achievable, and challenging to children (Bredekamp and Copple, 1997).

### Cognitive, Physical, Social, and Emotional Development Are Interrelated

All threads of development interweave and exist simultaneously. No one aspect of development occurs independently of the others. For instance, children's ability to make friends obviously relates to the social domain. However, friendship skills are affected by other developmental processes too. Language, memory, cognition, self-esteem, and physical development all influence how children approach others, how they adapt to social situations, and how they feel about their encounters with peers. Thus, making friends is a holistic process that taps all aspects of child development. The same is true for every attitude and action associated with social competence.

### Development Occurs in an Orderly Sequence

Development proceeds in a stepwise fashion that is relatively predictable (Case and Okamoto, 1996; Erikson, 1950). For example, before they learn to walk, children develop the skills to lift their heads, then sit up, then stand, and then crawl. Eventually they walk, then run. Although children spend differing amounts of time on each step and sometimes seem to skip some altogether, progression is seen in roughly the same order for everyone. Knowing developmental sequences provides a general framework for determining what is reasonable to expect of children as they mature. Such knowledge also influences the kinds of experiences adults plan to enhance children's social competence. For instance, in the sequence of learning to play a board game on their own, children must first understand turn taking. If you know that certain children are just learning this skill, you would play the game with them, offering support and guidance. You might help them decide who goes first, remind them who goes next, and soothe impatient players. You would also make sure the game is short. As children become better turn takers, you would gradually decrease the amount of your direct participation in their play. This process could take weeks or even months to achieve.

### Development Is Continuous

All development is based on a foundation; past, present, and future are related and build one upon the other in succession. Thus new phases of development evolve out of what is already there. For instance, children develop a sense of autonomy only after having established an adequate sense of trust (Erikson, 1950). Similarly, grade schoolers increasingly complex social understandings grow out of and incorporate the more basic concepts formed during their preschool years (Sroufe and Cooper, 1996). In this way, certain developmental threads are carried forward over time, providing continuity from one phase of development to the next.

## Rates of Development Vary within the Same Child and between Children

For all children, the different developmental threads are dominant at different times. For instance, height and weight increase dramatically during infancy, moderately during the preschool years, and slowly in middle childhood. During adolescence, the rate of growth again proceeds rapidly. On the other hand, expressive language development progresses quickly between the ages of two and five and then proceeds more slowly, although somewhat steadily. These are examples of *intrapersonal* variations—variations within the same child. Variations in developmental rates also occur *interpersonally*, that is, between children. Although the principle of predictable sequences still applies, the pace at which individuals go through the sequence differs. This explains why Ruth utters her first word at one year of age and Tony does not start talking until eighteen months of age. Both are exhibiting normal development, but the timing is different. Because children vary in their rates of development, we cannot expect all children to achieve skills like sharing or recognizing other people's emotions accurately at precisely the same age.

## There Are Optimal Periods of Growth and Development

There are certain times throughout development when children can benefit most from interactions with their environment (Begley, 1996). If children are denied the kinds of experiences that will enhance development at a critical stage, they may be unmotivated or unable to reach potential later.

For instance, if children in the early years have many opportunities to practice basic motor skills such as skipping, hopping, and jumping, they later combine these into the more complex skills necessary to ride a bike, play sports, or dance. Children with limited access to motor skill development during these years are less likely to become physically competent, to remain physically active, or to use physical activities for social purposes later in life. Therefore the early elementary years are an optimal period for developing fundamental motor skills (Gallahue, 1995).

Socially, the years from birth to age twelve are an optimal period for the development of many essential attitudes and behaviors, some of which include the following:

Trust
Self-awareness and self-esteem
Interpersonal communication skills
Prosocial attitudes and behaviors
Friendship dispositions and skills
Problem-solving strategies
Coping skills
Self-discipline

When these social processes are supported in early childhood, children's social competence is enhanced. If they are ignored, chances are less likely that children will become socially adept in adolescence or adulthood.

## There Is Continual Differentiation and Integration of Development

Behaviors first exhibit themselves in large, global patterns. From these, smaller, more specific behaviors emerge. This is the process of *differentiation*. Later, when *integration* occurs, these specific, smaller subpatterns combine into new, larger, and more complicated patterns. For instance, infants initially greet others with thrashing limbs, wiggling body, and general sounds. Out of this broad, undifferentiated array of behaviors, children gradually develop such specific actions as smiling, saying "Hello," or reaching out. At first, these behaviors may be displayed on separate occasions. Eventually, preschoolers put them all together, for example, running to another person, laughing, and shouting their greeting. School-age children display an even more sophisticated integration of greeting behaviors when they make judgments about whom to approach and what to say. Understanding the principle of differentiation and integration helps us appreciate the complexity of the behaviors related to social competence.

## Development Has Both Cumulative and Delayed Effects

An experience that has a minimal effect on a child's development if it occurs once in awhile may have a harmful influence if it happens often, over a long period of time (Katz and Chard, 1989). This is the principle of cumulative effects. For instance, being the target of occasional criticism is not likely to cause permanent damage to children's self-esteem. However, youngsters who are subjected to steady fault finding are likely to develop lasting feelings of inferiority and pessimism (Seligman, 1995). Likewise, seeing an aggressive character on television a few times does not automatically make children more aggressive. However, the long-term effects of observing television violence appear to be deep and enduring. Children who spend many hours watching violent programs on television or playing violence-oriented video games demonstrate increased levels of aggression in their day-to-day lives (Friedrich and Stein, 1973; Shaffer, 1994). Such cumulative effects are difficult to reverse.

In addition to these accumulated impacts, developmental outcomes may be delayed. That is, early experiences may influence children's functioning in ways that only appear much later in life (Wieder and Greenspan, 1993). For instance, children's development of self-discipline takes years to accomplish. The delayed nature of this process may cause adults to wonder if their early efforts to reason with children will ever yield positive results. However, research shows that children do eventually become better able to monitor their behavior without constant supervision when adults consistently provide reasons for rules and restrictions. This strategy must be used for a long time before children can reason on their own.

Knowing the principle of cumulative and delayed effects causes professionals to consider the long-range implications of their practices, as well as short-term outcomes. Quick solutions that counteract long-term goals are rejected. Thus, even though it is faster to simply tell children "No," practitioners take the time to talk to children about their actions. Both the cumulative and delayed effects of reasoning better support children's development of social competence.

### There Are Developmental Tasks Throughout Life

At different points in time, people work through different developmental issues (Berk, 1996). For example, one task that all individuals must deal with over the life span is that of achieving autonomy or an appropriate dependence-independence pattern. In infancy (birth to age two), this simply means establishing self-awareness as a separate person. In early childhood (ages two to seven), children become more physically independent, learning to eat, dress, and use the bathroom alone, and in later childhood (age seven to puberty), children's task is to free themselves from primary identification with adults and move toward greater interaction with a peer group.

The periods for accomplishing these tasks are not distinct. They often overlap, and there are variations in how dominant a particular issue is

at a given time. Behaviors characteristic of a new life task begin to appear as the preceding life task still is being resolved. Gradually, a person's effort and energy shift from the first task to the second until the latter is more dominant. Even so, traces of the first may still remain. People also may regress when they are under stress, displaying characteristics of an earlier period. Thus, Ellie who has long since achieved bladder control at night begins wetting the bed when she becomes upset about being bullied at school. Professionals who know the developmental tasks typical of childhood are better able to support children in dealing with those tasks. Also, they are more likely to recognize children who are experiencing difficulty. These understandings increase adult effectiveness.

Development plays a significant role in the extent to which children gain social skills. However, development alone does not ensure that each child will achieve social competence. Learning is also important.

## ▼ How Children Learn

Children are expected to learn a variety of social behaviors, such as to say, "Excuse me" when they bump into someone, to cross a street at a corner, and to derive pleasure from sharing with a friend. True learning in each of these instances occurs only when children make a relatively permanent change in their behavior as a result of practice or experience (Shaffer, 1994). Children who clean up, even when no one else is around, have learned. Children who remember a peer's name for 5 minutes and then forget it, have not learned. Certain universal principles describe children's learning from birth through early adolescence.

### Children Are Active Learners

Children have active bodies and active minds. They are not merely empty vessels passively waiting to be filled up with information and experiences determined by others. Instead, they strive to make sense of social experiences everywhere they go. Children do this by observing, acting on objects, and interacting with other people (Bredekamp and Copple, 1997). As a result of their experiences, children form hypotheses about how the social world works (e.g., "If I say please, Mohammed will give me the scissors right now."). Sometimes children's ideas are confirmed (Mohammed says, "Okay.").

Sometimes children encounter evidence that is contrary to what they believe (Mohammed says "No" because he still needs the scissors). By observing, experimenting, and reflecting on what happens, children gradually make adjustments in their thinking ("I will have to wait for the scissors, but I'll get them next."). Through hundreds of experiences like these, children construct ideas about what code of behavior to follow and what strategies to use (Piaget, 1952; Vygotsky, 1978).

## Children Have Multiple Ways of Knowing and Learning

There are many ways in which children perceive, learn, and process information. Howard Gardner has coined the phrase *multiple intelligences* to describe these multilearning capabilities. His research suggests that there are at least seven* ways of learning (Gardner, 1995), which include the following:

Linguistic: children learn by seeing, saying, and using language

Logical-mathematical: children learn by looking for patterns and relationships among objects and events

Musical: children learn through rhythm and melody

Spatial: children learn through visualizing

Kinesthetic: children learn through touch and movement

Intrapersonal: children learn on their own through self-paced activity

Interpersonal: children learn through relating to others and collaborating

All children have these intelligences, but each one is not developed equally. Thus children learn best when they have access to learning opportunities that match the mode of learning they favor. Because adults cannot always be sure which mode of learning suits an individual child best, children benefit when practitioners use a variety of modes in their teaching. For instance, some children may absorb lessons in helping through chances to talk about the helpful actions they observe or carry out; others may find it most useful to consider patterns that characterize helpful behaviors. On the other hand, a catchy song about helping may capture the interest of particular youngsters, whereas others may do better after reflecting on a helpful act that they have seen or heard about. Most likely, children will combine such experiences, extracting important information from the ones that match their preferred ways of learning.

## Social Learning Takes Time

Children are not born socially competent. From birth to age twelve and beyond, they continually experiment with various social strategies, seeking clues about what works and what does not. It may take a child eighty tries to learn how to appropriately comfort someone in distress, or twice that number to learn that the rule is "Walk, don't run." Another child may need far fewer or even more attempts to gain these same milestones. Because social learning evolves slowly, most children in formal group settings are novices at knowing all the rules of society and how to comply with them. In addition, they are just beginning to understand the complexities of interpersonal relationships and have much to learn in this regard. Thus, young children's social skills are relatively immature in comparison to those of most adolescents or adults. This means children need many opportunities to engage in social interactions and need support from adults to develop their skills. When providing that support, professionals should keep in mind the conditions of learning that positively affect children's social competence and conditions that have the opposite impact.

### Conditions of Learning

**Comfort and security.** Children learn best when they feel psychologically safe and secure (Bredekamp and Copple, 1997). For young children, this translates into being with people they like and trust. Security also comes from *consistent* relationships with loving adults, as well as predictable routines. Children who know that their mistakes will be tolerated and that their efforts to learn will be supported are more open to learning new things. On the other hand, youngsters who are frightened or suspicious are not likely to absorb social lessons of any kind. Finally, children are better able to acquire social learning when they are free of strong biological urges such as hunger or the need to go to the bathroom (Maslow, 1954).

**First-hand experiences.** Children are better able to understand and learn social behaviors when they

---

*In recent writings, Gardner speculates about the existence of an eighth intelligence, called the naturalist's intelligence—focused on recognizing flora and fauna (Gardner, 1995). However, he has not yet officially added that intelligence to the original seven he described.

experience those behaviors in meaningful situations. Simply being told about them is not as useful. This is why children become more skillful at sharing when they have chances to practice sharing with others in day-to-day situations. Figuring out how to divide the crackers at snack time, how two people can use the computer together, or how to fit an extra person around the table are tangible examples for children to consider. Children learn more from these real-life problem-solving activities than from talking about hypothetical situations.

**Relevant experiences.** Children are most open to learning things that are important to them at the time. Such relevant opportunities are sometimes referred to as "teachable moments." They explain why a youngster who wants a turn with the jump rope may be more willing to take in information about how to negotiate for it than she would have been were she less anxious to jump. Even when the information has been presented and the child has had an opportunity to use bargaining skills, it cannot be assumed that she has "learned" to negotiate. Instead, this one instance must be viewed as a practice episode, which should be repeated on other occasions in both similar and somewhat different circumstances. It will take many such experiences before the child will be able to demonstrate effective negotiation skills on her own (Wolfgang, 1995).

**Mastery and challenge.** Simply giving children access to social learning opportunities, through planned activities or by taking advantage of spontaneous events, is not enough. Adults also must monitor such situations to make sure they are manageable and stimulating for children. A youngster who is overwhelmed may be unable to understand or apply knowledge gained regardless of how potentially useful it may be. On the other hand, children who experience no challenges fail to progress in their understandings and abilities. Positive social learning is most likely to occur when children feel both successful and stimulated.

"Research shows that children need to be able to successfully negotiate learning tasks most of the time if they are to maintain their motivation to learn. Confronted by repeated failure, most children will simply stop trying" (Bredekamp and Copple, 1997:14). With this in mind, childhood professionals strive to fit their strategies and expectations to children's capabilities. At the same time, there is increasing evidence that children are highly moti-

vated to adopt concepts and skills that are slightly beyond their current level of independent mastery (Bodrova and Leong, 1996). That is, children are eager to learn what they nearly, but do not quite grasp, or they attempt what they can almost do but not quite carry out on their own. For example, a child is aware that another child needs help but is not sure how to assist. In this case, some on-the-spot coaching by an adult or more knowledgeable peer regarding potentially helpful strategies could facilitate the helper's learning a new skill. If the lesson is too complex or beyond the child's understanding, the child will not absorb it. However, if the child can simply stretch his or her thinking to encompass the new idea, higher order learning is possible. In such cases, the adult's role becomes that of assisting children to perform at higher levels of mastery than they might be able to manage on their own. Gradually, children learn the necessary skills to perform the task independently, and adult support fades into the background. In this way, children make gradual but steady progress toward increased social competence.

The principles of development and learning outlined here and the conditions under which optimal learning occurs are summarized in Table 1–1. In addition to applying these principles, adults wishing to support children's social competence must approach each child as an individual.

## ▼ CHILDREN ARE INDIVIDUALS

The children are visiting a farm. Walter runs to the fence, calling out, "Here horsey. Come over here!" Mareesa hangs back from the group, unsure of how close she wants to get to the big hairy creatures. Carlos moves to the fence with Ms. Lopez. He is happy to watch as long as she is nearby.

Three different children—three different reactions. Each calls for an individualized response by adults.

Every child who comes into this world is a unique being, the result of a combination of tens of thousands of genes inherited from his or her parents. Each child has a distinctive voiceprint, fingerprint, lip print, and footprint and a natural odor singular enough for a bloodhound to follow. Even the size, shape, and operation of a child's brain are slightly different from those of all other children. Children's temperaments are so distinct at birth that family

▼ **Table 1–1  Development and Learning**

**Principles of Development**

Cognitive, physical, social, and emotional development are interrelated.

Development occurs in an orderly sequence.

Development is continuous.

Rates of development vary within the same child and between children.

There are optimal periods of growth and development.

There is continual differentiation and integration of development.

Development has both cumulative and delayed effects.

There are developmental tasks throughout life.

**Principles of Learning**

Children are active learners.

Children have multiple ways of knowing and learning.

Social learning takes time.

**Conditions of Learning**

Children learn best when they are comfortable and secure.

Children learn best through first-hand experiences.

Children learn best through relevant learning experiences.

Children learn best when they experience both mastery and challenge.

members often make remarks like, "Lucida has been that way since she was a baby." These biological differences are complemented by experiential factors that further differentiate one child from another. The individual child in any group setting brings a backlog of experiences and understandings that influence social competence. A child who has had few group experiences will have different needs and strengths than a child who has been in group care since birth. Likewise, youngsters who have a certain game at home will be more capable of explaining the rules than children who have never played the game before. The kinds of experiences children have, the amount of experience they acquire, the quality of that experience, and its outcomes all combine to yield a different result for each child.

Thinking about children as individuals enables adults to adapt programs and strategies appropriately and to be responsive to the variations that exist among children (Bredekamp and Copple, 1997). Other factors that influence children's individuality

are the social and cultural contexts in which children live.

## ▼ THE CONTEXTS OF CHILDHOOD

Children develop and learn within many contexts, usually beginning with the family and then extending into the community. Both of these contexts are embedded in society at large, and all are interrelated and interdependent. To work effectively with children, helping professionals must consider how these forces combine to affect children's lives. Thinking about environments in this way is referred to as an ecological perspective (Bronfenbrenner, 1989, 1993).

An ecological perspective takes into account four distinct social/cultural systems—the microsystem, the mesosystem, the exosystem, and the macrosystem. These four systems exist in layers around the developing child, much like a set of nesting cups or a circle of rings around a bulls-eye. With the child at the center, microsystems are embedded within mesosystems, mesosystems are contained within exosystems, and exosystems function within macrosystems. This nested ecological environment is depicted in Figure 1–1 (Bronfenbrenner, 1989; Oppenheimer, 1989). Each of these systems interacts with the others and with the individual child in complex ways to influence child development and learning.

### Microsystems

The most basic social system is the **microsystem.** Microsystems include all the people, materials, activities, and interpersonal relationships experienced directly by children in face-to-face settings such as home or school. For instance, at various times in their lives, children may participate in the following microsystems:

- ▼ Family
- ▼ School
- ▼ Child-care program
- ▼ Head Start center
- ▼ 4-H group
- ▼ Church, synagogue, temple, or mosque
- ▼ Doctor's office
- ▼ Recreation center

Each setting is its own microsystem, offering a distinct context for child development and learning. However, this influence is not unidirectional. Not only are children affected by the people, relationships, resources, and activities in their microsystems, but they influence all these elements as well. For example, children serve as resources to families.

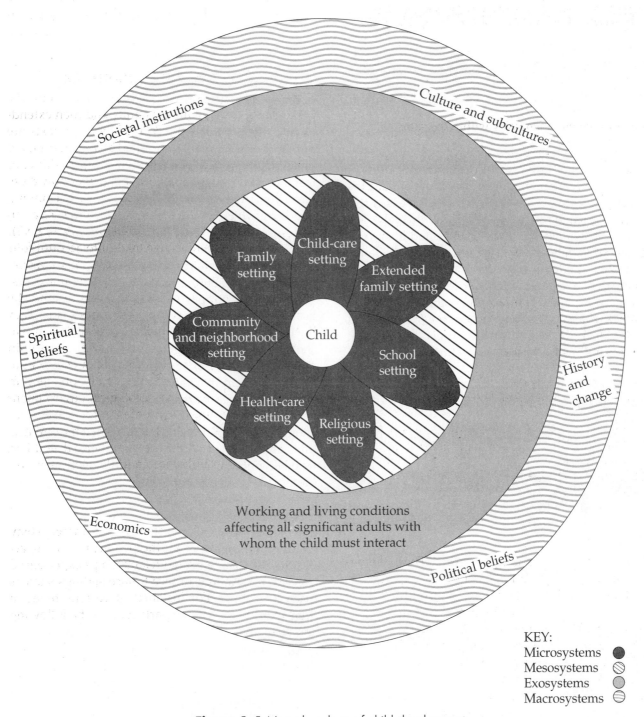

**Figure 1-1** Nested ecology of child development.

They can help with chores, provide needed information (What time is the basketball game? What are the names of ten dinosaurs?), and give family members a sense of continuity. In turn, children use up resources—money, space, and time are all reallocated within a household once a child arrives. Similarly, a chronically irritable child may prompt feelings of inadequacy or resentment from caregivers. If such feelings are communicated to the child, his or her negative demeanor may intensify. Examples such as these illustrate the dynamic interaction among all the elements within each microsystem.

### Mesosystems

All the different microsystems in which a child participates combine to form that child's **mesosystem.** Rachel may be involved in a mesosystem that includes home, school, peer group, after-school child care, synagogue, and grandma's house. Jason's mesosystem may include some of the same elements as well as other microsystems that are specific to him. In both cases, the children are influenced by multiple microsystems and the interaction among them. How well information flows from one part of the mesosystem to another and the degree of congruence among microsystem beliefs and standards influence children's social development. For instance, Rachel must learn to live by the rules of home, school, and synagogue. The more similar the expectations are in each microsystem, the easier it is for Rachel to adapt her behavior accordingly. The greater the gap between what is expected in one microsystem versus another, the greater the challenge for Rachel as she moves from one to the next. Current evidence suggests that children's development and learning are enhanced when there are strong supportive links among mesosystems (Shaffer, 1994). Generally, these links are formed by adults in the various microsystems who communicate with one another.

## Exosystems

**Exosystems** represent settings and relationships children do not experience directly but that ultimately affect them. One common exosystem for most children is their parent's workplace. What happens to Mom or Dad on the job affects children too. The parent's mood, level of stress, income, and time available for the child are exosystem-related factors that influence children at home. Some exosystem influences are even more distant. For instance, the child-care programs available to children are shaped by people and events in their community with whom children have no real contact, but which impact them profoundly. Thus, even when children are not directly involved in a particular microsystem, decisions and conditions must be considered, keeping in mind their potential impact on children's lives.

## Macrosystems

The larger context in which all other systems operate is the **macrosystem**. Macrosystems are depicted as the outermost ring in Figure 1–1. They are defined not by environments but by values, traditions, and beliefs shared by groups of people. Such groups may form around geography, custom, social class, income, or particular life events. Thus, people may share certain values, traditions, and beliefs because they:

Are Canadian
Can trace their roots to Rumania

Consider themselves middle-class
Are blue-collar workers
See themselves as part of the "X-generation"

These macrosystem elements shape the structure of the social institutions of a society including its legal, economic, religious, and political systems. Eventually, the impact of societal beliefs, laws, economic conditions, religious concerns, and political positions filters down to the microsystem level. For instance, the frequency of child abuse (a microsystem event) is high in societies such as the United States in which physical force and violence have widespread approval at the macrosystem level (Belsky, 1980). Child abuse is less likely to occur in societies in which physical force is taboo, like Sweden (Haeuser, 1997). Similarly, even children brought up "in a loving, supportive family within a strong, healthy community may be affected by the biases of the larger society such as racism or sexism, and may show the effects of negative stereotyping and discrimination" (Bredekamp and Copple, 1997, p. 12).

Macrosystem beliefs vary from society to society and within societies among various subcultures. Such variations include the way human beings relate to one another, the significance of time, what personality traits are highly prized, and fundamental notions of whether human beings are naturally good or bad (Berns, 1993). As a result of how different groups approach these issues, children learn different things. For instance, some children learn that competition is good; others learn to value cooperation more highly. One culture might interpret a child's loud behavior as a positive sign of independence, whereas another might translate that same action as disrespectful. In this way, macrosystems broadly define how people believe children should be treated, what they should be taught, and what goals they should strive to achieve (Shaffer, 1995). However, because there is so much variation, there is no one correct combination of beliefs. Instead, adults who work with children must recognize the legitimacy of multiple perspectives, including some that are different from their own. This understanding is essential for helping professionals to promote children's social competence in respectful, supportive ways.

A summary of all the social systems just described and related questions to consider are presented in Table 1–2.

## The Value of Maintaining an Ecological Perspective

The primary advantage of thinking ecologically is that it helps a person to obtain the "bigger picture" of factors influencing children's social develop-

▼ **Table 1–2    Social Systems Summary**

| SOCIAL/CULTURAL SYSTEM | DEFINITION | EXAMPLES | QUESTIONS TO CONSIDER |
|---|---|---|---|
| Microsystem | Settings in which children have direct contact with influential others | Family<br>School<br>Peer group<br>Child-care program<br>Church<br>Synagogue<br>Temple | Is the child viewed positively?<br>Is the child accepted?<br>Is the child rewarded for socially competent behavior?<br>Is the child exposed to diversity in roles and relationships?<br>Is the child given an active role in his or her learning? |
| Mesosystem | Combination of microsystems; the relationships and links between microsystems | Home and school<br>Home and temple<br>School, 4-H group, and neighborhood | Is there communication among settings?<br>Is there consistency among settings?<br>Is respect conveyed among settings? |
| Exosystem | Settings in which children do not participate directly but in which significant decisions are made affecting the child or adults who interact directly with the child | Parents' places of employment<br>School board<br>Local government | Are decisions made with the interests of children and families in mind?<br>How well do supports for families balance stresses for families?<br>How well do supports for helping professionals balance stresses for helping professionals? |
| Macrosystem | Overarching values, beliefs, and traditions shared by groups<br>Context that shapes the institutional life of a society | Ideology<br>Social policies<br>Shared assumptions about human nature, desirable traits, and standards of behavior | Are some groups valued at the expense of others?<br>Does the culture encourage individual or collective efforts?<br>Are people considered naturally good or bad?<br>Is violence a norm? |

Source: Data from Garbarino, J. *Children and Families in the Social Environment.* 2d ed. New York: Aldine de Gruyter, 1992; and Garbarino, J. *Raising Children in a Socially Toxic Environment.* San Francisco: Jossey-Bass Publishers, 1995.

ment. In this way, children are thought of in context, not in isolation. This holistic view prompts consideration of many dimensions when assessing children's behavior and determining appropriate methods of intervention. Sensitivity to multiple influences and varying perspectives demonstrates respect for children and families and increases the effectiveness of decision-making.

A second benefit of using an ecological approach is that it underscores the importance of communication among systems. No single microsystem in which children are included should operate as though the others did not exist. If Alfreda's mesosystem involves home, school, and after-school care, her development can be enhanced if the adults in those settings confer and periodically share information with one another. Furthermore, if Alfreda were to become involved in some additional intervention, such as play therapy or speech therapy, persons from those microsystems should also be included in the information loop. Professionals who think ecologically are likely to appreciate the importance of and facilitate such communication.

Third, an ecological framework helps you to understand that the influence of the micro-, meso-, exo-, and macrosystem is unique for each child. While some effects may be shared among a group of children, the total context for one youngster is unlike that of any other. This understanding will increase your sensitivity to the individual strengths, needs,

> You will:
>
> See children in context.
>
> Recognize the importance of communication among systems.
>
> Appreciate the unique circumstances experienced by each child.

**Figure 1–2** Benefits of maintaining an ecological perspective.

and interests each child brings to the formal group setting. Figure 1–2 summarizes the benefits of maintaining an **ecological perspective.**

Keeping an ecological framework in mind, we now turn to the two primary microsystems in which children are members—the family and the formal group setting. Together with other informal settings, these dominate the mesosystems of most children between birth and twelve years of age.

## ▼ CHILDREN AND THEIR FAMILIES

The majority of children in this country grow up in families, and there is no doubt that this microsystem has the primary influence on their social development. A family usually is made up of individuals related to one another through strong reciprocal affections. Family members share common goals, resources, and a commitment to each other over time (Bubolz and Sontag, 1993). Members enter through birth, adoption, or marriage, and leave only by death. Even when divorce or separation cause family members to be less available or to live in different places, they still are the child's family. Although families differ in configuration, size, life-style, available resources, history, traditions, and values, all families perform the same basic functions.

### Family Functions

Many of the functions the family once performed, such as educating the young, passing on religious faith, maintaining health, providing protection, and ensuring the economic survival of its members, have been altered considerably. Over the centuries, other institutions have taken over considerable re-

sponsibility for those functions: the educational system; the religious system; the health-care system; and welfare, legislative, and law enforcement agencies.

Beyond the family functions of procreation and provision for actual physical needs, the primary tasks of today's families have come to be the nurturance and socialization of its members (Goldsmith, 1996). Just as individuals have developmental tasks to perform over the life span, the family as a group has tasks it must accomplish in order to exist and have its members live in reasonable harmony (Havighurst, 1954). Some of the more important tasks for families with children from infancy to adolescence are the following:

1. Preserving family relationships during the demanding years of child rearing.
2. Meeting the changing needs of growing children for privacy, activities, friends, and wider social relationships.
3. Helping prepare children to make transitions to new roles.
4. Providing for family members' needs for privacy and quiet.
5. Continuing to establish basic values in a world that is continually changing.
6. Meeting expanded costs.
7. Maintaining the morale of the family.
8. Creating and maintaining adequate communication in the family.
9. Working out ways of sharing the tasks and responsibilities.
10. Fitting into community life as a family and as persons.

All of these activities take place through direct and indirect teaching in constructive and sometimes destructive ways, more or less successfully. Each of the environmental influences discussed earlier is channeled to some extent through the family. For instance, through the family children gain access to economic resources and learn the customs of their cultural group. The first attitudes toward other people, education, work, and society that children encounter are in the family. Parents arrange for out-of-home care and make initial school contacts on behalf of their children. They also promote or inhibit opportunities for peer and community contact. If families receive help or support from family, friends, or social institutions, the family microsystem may be enhanced. If families are stressed by the hardships of poverty, the uncertainty of losing a job, or the prospects of divorce, their ability to meet the needs of their children is weakened (Kostelnik, Soderman, and Whiren, in press).

## What Is an Ideal Family?

Each of us has a differing personal concept of what the ideal family might look like. We draw that ideal from remembered experiences within our own family of origin and from what we know about the families of our colleagues, friends, and neighbors. We also have become acquainted with "media" families, few of which realistically depict the wide variations possible in family life.

Competent helping professionals are those who avoid judging family worth based on stereotypical or familiar personal constructs. For instance, in the past several years, it has become popular to assume that intact family systems automatically function better than those in which not all adult family members are present (Boss, 1980; Hale, 1992). Yet, family members can be physically present but psychologically absent. For example, a parent may be so consumed with a work role or with personal problems that she or he is truly unavailable to a child, despite the fact that they both physically reside together. Conversely, a parent can be physically absent but play such a dominant role that he or she is a tremendously important psychological presence in the child's life. In addition, one cannot assume that families with multiple children are the same as those with one child or that families experiencing crises, such as the death or chronic illness of a member, divorce, or loss of a job, function in the same way as families not experiencing these events. Nor can we expect families who have a wealth of resources to behave in the same way as families who are experiencing scarcity. Because there is no one "correct" family form, value system, tradition, or lifestyle, it is best to remain flexible as to what constitutes normal family behavior and to perceive both children and their families within an ecological perspective.

From this discussion, it can be concluded that the family is the most significant microsystem in children's lives. As youngsters' mesosystems expand, they also become involved in the microsystems of any number of formal group settings.

## ▼ FORMAL GROUP SETTINGS

**Formal group settings** are microsystems in which children participate in organized programs of service for some portion of the day. Although some children receive these services in their own households, the majority do not. Common settings include those that provide informal education in the community, such as 4-H, YMCA, YMHA, and Scouts; those that offer formal education, such as public and private schools, preschools, Head Start programs, Chapter I programs, Home Start programs, child-care centers, and family daycare homes; those that supply health services, such as hospitals, outpatient clinics, and therapeutic nursery schools; those that offer recreational programs, such as camps, parks, and recreational centers; and those that involve residential care, such as group foster homes and residential treatment centers. Although each of these settings is different in its primary focus, all have a defined purpose and a predetermined structure and require specialized leadership. They often involve physical settings that contain materials purposely designed for use with children. Also, formal group settings all support the basic functions of the family but are, in fact, tangential to it. Many services frequently are delivered without adult family members being present. For example, in a child-care center, parents give and receive information about their children at arrival and pick-up and through other formal contacts, but the child-care provider cares for the children without the parents most of the time. Even in a cooperative nursery, in which parents work with the professional caregiver on a scheduled basis, an individual parent is absent more often than present as other parents participate in their rotation of duty. Thus, adults who work in these settings have continual responsibility for the children in their care and must repeatedly make program-related decisions regarding their welfare.

The formalized structure described here becomes evident when comparing an informal setting, such as a family household, with a formal setting, such as a family daycare home. In the informal setting, children might come and go as they please, play inside or out, and frequently play without adult supervision. The choice of activities is largely up to them, and family members often are occupied with household tasks. In the formal setting, however, the provider expects to receive and release children and know where they are at all times. Children are never unsupervised, and they participate in planned activities. The adult's primary function is to watch and interact with the children rather than become involved in tasks for maintaining the household. There are no licenses or contracts in the informal setting, but both may be present in the formal situation. These same kinds of comparisons could be made between informal and formal settings in the educational, recreational, and medical fields as well.

## The Atmosphere of the Formal Group Setting

Formal group settings consist of more than the organizational structures just described. In each setting, the interpersonal relations that exist among adults and children also are important and determine what is referred to as **program climate** or **atmosphere** (Bee, 1996). People talk about this dimension when they depict a program as being friendly or unfriendly, chaotic or busy, relaxed or uptight, pleasant or unpleasant, caring or impersonal. All these terms describe an emotional tone that may either promote or inhibit children's learning.

It is the adults in the setting who dictate its atmosphere (Anderson and Brewer, 1945; Kostelnik, Stein, and Whiren, 1988; Withall and Lewis, 1963). Their attitudes about the children with whom they work, what they say to them, and how they act toward them all determine the aura that prevails. For example, there is a noticeable difference between the climate that characterizes the Girl Scout troop at Adams School and the one at Springfield Elementary School. In the former, the leaders make it clear that "fooling around" will not be tolerated and that troop members are there for one purpose: to earn their badges. For the candle-making project, the goal is for all candles to look exactly alike. Children are told which materials they must use and the precise sequence of steps they are to follow. Youngsters are expected to work on their own, neither giving nor receiving help from friends. The room is generally silent as the leaders stand at the front calling out instructions. When Madeleine has difficulty unmolding her candle, she is admonished to be less clumsy in her work. When Carrie asks a question, an adult sighs in exasperation and tells her to pay more attention next time. Two other girls whose final products are lopsided and somewhat askew are told to melt their candles down and try again until they get it right.

A very different atmosphere exists at Springfield. The troop's project for the day also is making candles. Youngsters are given a wide array of materials from which to choose. They are told that each girl should decorate her candle in her own special way. They may either work by themselves or with a partner and are encouraged to lend assistance as necessary. The leaders circulate among the girls, praising their work and offering on-the-spot assistance. The room reverberates with laughter and chatter. When all the projects are finished, the adults urge everyone to applaud a job well done.

There is little doubt that the climate in the Springfield Scout program is more conducive to learning than the one at Adams School. At Springfield, children are comfortable and happy. Although youngsters are involved in a common activity, their individuality also is valued. They feel respected as human beings because the leaders treat them as competent and important. As a result, the girls view the adults as both supportive and capable of giving them clear guidelines for how to be successful. The Springfield Scouts feel good about themselves and their participation in the troop. This is not so for the Adams School Scouts. A tension pervades the setting that is a direct result of the adults' disparaging remarks and their obvious impatience with the girls. The children learn that their best efforts are not good enough and that failure is more likely than success. They also find that the adults are not sources of guidance. Rather, they are authorities to be avoided. These scouts come away each week feeling bad about themselves and their abilities.

**Climatic outcomes.** Program atmosphere has a major influence on children's opinions about themselves. In addition, it affects the social behaviors children acquire in the setting. Whether they learn to be cooperative or resistant, friendly or unfriendly, controlled or impulsive has much to do with how they are treated by the helping adults with whom they come in contact. For instance, poor social learning occurs when adults shame children, shout at them, coerce them, or physically hurt them. Youngsters subjected to such conditions often become destructive, hostile, and aggressive (Hoffman, 1983). They learn to be covert in their actions, continually looking for ways to avoid responsibility (Parke, 1977). In an effort to protect themselves, these children also become self-centered and have difficulty considering the needs of others. As a result, they are less likely to be helpful, cooperative, or kind. On the other hand, adults who convey respect for children through actions and words and who provide constructive guidelines for how children can succeed, generate a positive social climate. Children in such an environment are most apt to be responsive to others' feelings, cooperative, friendly, and eager to learn the rules of society.

Obviously, adults who work with children in settings such as these have a tremendous impact on social development. Such individuals are called helping professionals.

## What Is a Helping Professional?

**Helping professionals** use their skills and abilities to assist other people in improving the quality of their lives (Graves, Gargiulo, and Sluder, 1996; Katz, 1988). In this book we focus on helping professionals who are employed by families to provide services to children from birth through twelve years of age. Services rendered are those that families may find too specialized, too time consuming, too cumbersome, or too expensive to provide directly themselves.

Regardless of whether the helping professional's title is teacher, counselor, caregiver, leader, social worker, or childlife specialist, certain characteristics differentiate the professional from the nonprofessional. One major distinction is that professionals have access to a body of knowledge and skills not available to the general public. This is acquired as a result of prolonged education and specialized training (Katz, 1988). Life experience alone is not sufficient to provide the full range of technical know-how and professional skills necessary for maximum effectiveness on the job. People who do not have this background cannot perform the services as skillfully or support the development of children as well as those who have it, although in some settings they may be employed to do so.

Another means of distinguishing professionals from lay persons is that the former have to demonstrate competencies related to their field in order to enter the profession. The most formalized evidence of mastery requies earning a license or certification, which usually is governed by state or national standards. Slightly less formal monitoring involves having to take tests, pass courses, and demonstrate one's proficiency either in a practicum setting or on the job. All of these experiences take place under the supervision of qualified members of the profession.

Professionals also must perform their duties in keeping with standards of excellence generally accepted for the field. Such standards come about through research and professional discourse. They are enforced through self-monitoring within the profession as well as governmental regulation. In early childhood education, for instance, practices have been identified that support and assist children's physical, emotional, social, language, and intellectual development. Some of these include health and safety provisions that ensure children's well-being; staff-to-child ratios that enable frequent personal interactions between each child and staff member; requiring adults to have specific training in child development and early childhood education; stable staffing so children have chances to develop trusting relationships with adults; and programming that is appropriate for children's developmental levels and interests (Doherty-

Derkowski, 1995). Professionals who strive to maintain such standards are more likely to provide high-quality programs for the children in their care. Deviation from these standards has detrimental effects on children and is considered undesirable within the profession (Vandell and Corasaniti, 1990). Thus, professional standards provide a gauge by which members can assess their own performance as well as the overall quality of the services they offer children and families.

To keep up with the standards in their field, helping professionals participate in continuing education throughout their careers. They constantly upgrade their knowledge and skills both informally and formally. Such efforts might include attending workshops, consulting with colleagues, participating in professional organizations, reading professional journals, and pursuing additional schooling. Regardless of the means, professionals treat learning as an ongoing process from which they have much to gain.

Finally, professionalism implies adoption of an ethical code of conduct. Specific ethical codes govern professionals whose work involves children. Although the particulars may vary, such codes all aim toward ensuring confidentiality, providing safe and wholesome experiences, and treating people appropriately regardless of sex, race, or religion. One such code, prepared under the auspices of the National Association for the Education of Young Children (NAEYC) is presented in Appendix A. The NAEYC Code of Ethical Conduct resulted from a five-year collaboration among teachers, administrators, and policy-makers. It was first published in 1989 and has been reviewed periodically ever since.

An important part of this code is the affirmation of the following professional values that undergird all early childhood programs.

▼ Appreciating childhood as a unique and valuable stage of the human life cycle.
▼ Basing one's professional work with children on knowledge of child development.
▼ Appreciating and supporting close ties between the child and family.
▼ Recognizing that children are best understood in the context of family, culture, and society.
▼ Respecting the dignity, worth, and uniqueness of each individual (child, family member, colleague).
▼ Helping children and adults achieve their full potential in the context of relationships based on trust, respect, and positive regard.

In support of these values, the NAEYC Code of Ethical Conduct outlines ideals and principles in four areas of professional relationships: (1) children, (2) families, (3) colleagues, and (4) community and society. The ideals and principles identify acceptable and unacceptable professional behaviors. Thus, the code outlines what helping professionals should do and what they should refuse to do as they carry out their programs. In this way the code provides a guide for decision-making and a standard against which helping professionals can judge the appropriateness of their behavior over time.

Although most people attracted to the helping profession already bring with them strong character and high moral standards, knowing right from wrong in a professional sense requires more than intuition and good intentions (Katz, 1991). What makes common sense to an individual, may or may not be in concert with collectively agreed upon standards of professional behavior. Likewise, adults may have strong personal convictions, but as professionals, they cannot necessarily act on them. For example, an adult may have particular religious or political beliefs, yet in the professional setting, it is inappropriate to try to convert children or their families to a particular way of thinking. Furthermore, professionals may have personal knowledge about children and their families, but must refrain from gossiping about them. Only in child-abuse cases, for which states mandate reporting, is the confidentiality rule waived. Thus, professionals are obliged to protect the interests of children and their families regardless of personal biases.

Fundamentally, it is expected that helping professionals will act in ways that enhance the development of children and maintain standards of acceptable behavior. Thus, groups of professionals monitor the behavior of their own practitioners to ensure high-quality service. This monitoring system is not available to lay persons. The characteristics that differentiate a professional from a lay person are summarized in Figure 1–3.

## The Role of the Helping Professional in Relation to Children's Social Development

Although helping professionals in different settings may concentrate on particular developmental domains, such as physical well-being or intellectual accomplishments, they invariably also must support children's social and emotional development. For instance, children in hospitals are there for specific health reasons. Yet, no matter how ill they might be, their needs cannot be met by medical intervention alone. Nurturance, information, and communication continue to be important social di-

**Commitment to improving the quality of people's lives**

**Access to specialized knowledge**

**Prolonged education and training**

**Monitored entry into field**

**Standards of practice**

**Continuing education**

**Code of ethics**

**Figure 1–3** Characteristics that distinguish professionals from lay persons.

mensions that cannot be ignored if optimal health is to be achieved. For this reason, all helping professionals must be prepared to support their young clients emotionally as well as carry out the procedures dictated by their professional role. Thus, helpng has two dimensions: facilitation and action (Gazda, 1995).

**The facilitation dimension.** Children's social development is enhanced when they view the adults in their lives as sources of comfort and encouragement (Garbarino, 1995). Creating emotionally supportive relationships with children is the function of the **facilitation dimension.** Helping professionals communicate emotional support by demonstrating empathy, warmth, respect, acceptance, and authenticity toward the children with whom they interact.

*Empathy.* The single most important element of the helping process is **empathy** (Carkhuff, 1969; Goleman, 1995). Empathy involves recognizing and understanding another person's perspective even when that perspective is different from your own (Musson, 1994). An empathic person also responds to another's affective or emotional state by experiencing some of the same emotion (Damon,

1988). Empathy, therefore, involves the cognitive processes of examining and knowing, as well as the affective process of feeling. We describe this as "walking in someone's shoes," or "seeing the world through another person's eyes." When the third graders rush into his class, brimming with excitement over the frog they found outside, Mr. McBride conveys empathy by listening closely to their words and mirroring their excitement in his response.

*Warmth.* Showing interest in children, being friendly toward them, and being responsive to them are all aspects of **warmth** (Berk and Winsler, 1995). Early childhood professionals who are warm help children feel comfortable, supported, and valued. Ms. Bilenko is demonstrating warmth when she greets three-year-old Sarah by squatting down to the child's eye level, smiling, and touching her shoulder gently as Sarah tells her about last night.

*Respect.* **Respect** involves having faith in children's ability to eventually learn the information, behavior, and skills they will need to constructively function on their own. Having respect for children means believing that they are capable of changing their behavior and of making self-judgments. Helping professionals show respect when they allow children to think for themselves, make decisions, work toward their own solutions, and communicate their ideas (Goffin, 1989). Lack of respect is evident when adults tell children how to think and feel, ignore their points of view, or deprive them of genuine opportunities to grow and learn.

*Acceptance.* Closely related to respect is the concept of **acceptance**. Acceptance refers to every human being's need for self-confirmation from others. Without acceptance, constructive development is impossible. To be accepted fully means to be valued unconditionally. Adults who demonstrate acceptance toward children care about them regardless of their personal attributes, family background, or behavior. They do not require children to earn their caring through good grades, compliance, charm, or beauty. Rather, they believe that all children are worthy of acceptance simply because they are human. Thus, "acceptance does not judge" (Egan, 1994).

Unfortunately, acceptance is the component of facilitation that is most widely misunderstood. Some grown-ups assume that acceptance translates into condoning all child behaviors, even the antisocial ones. This is an inaccurate interpretation. As you will discover throughout this text, there are ways to communicate acceptance of each child's essential being, while at the same time guiding him or her toward the adoption of more appropriate behaviors. This dual agenda is illustrated by Olivia Chigubu when she moves quickly over to two children who are hitting each other with sticks on the playground. They are obviously angry. She communicates acceptance by acknowledging their anger. At the same time she makes it clear that hitting will not be permitted.

*Authenticity.* Positive adult-child relationships are also characterized by **authenticity** (Curry and Johnson, 1990). Authentic adults are genuine with children. That is, what they say to children is truthful, yet also reasonable and encouraging. As a result, youngsters receive balanced, informative, helpful feedback that enables them to more accurately assess their own ideas, values, and behaviors.

Authentic adults gain children's trust, because children know their words are believable. Mrs. Takashima demonstrates authenticity when she takes the time to point out something interesting about each child's painting rather than simply telling each child, "Good job."

All five components of the facilitation dimension—empathy, warmth, respect, acceptance, and authenticity—contribute to the relationship-building process. As such, they provide the foundation from which action can be taken. It is important for helping professionals not to take action before building a facilitative base, even if time is limited (Gazda, 1995). Even if only a few moments are available, facilitation should always precede action.

**The action dimension.** The **action dimension** of helping focuses on teaching children to maintain desirable behaviors and to change inappropriate ones to more acceptable alternatives. Action may be more or less directive, but it always focuses on helping children achieve certain standards of behavior. To do this, professionals must provide children with appropriate behavioral *cues.* These are verbal or nonverbal expressions, direct physical acts, or a combination of these aimed at helping children maintain or change their behavior. Some cues and cueing strategies work better than others. Effective cueing is dependent on two factors: concreteness and technical proficiency. Adults are *concrete* when they pinpoint and accurately label emotions, experiences, and behaviors. This means they are specific and use techniques that make children fully aware of what is expected. *Technical proficiency* is achieved when adults know when to use particular strategies and how to carry them out.

Expert practitioners blend the facilitative and action dimensions. They understand when and how to use each component and are skilled in effectively implementing them. At this point, you might ask how aspiring helping professionals attain such knowledge and skill.

## Becoming a Helping Professional

*That Jenny Taylor has a gift for working with children. She's a natural.*

*He must be good with children. He comes from a large family.*

*Well, working with children might wear you out, but they're so young you don't have to know much.*

Comments such as these often are aimed at people who indicate a desire to work with children on a professional basis. Such comments imply that effective helping professionals are born, not made, that productive helping behavior is a product of personality, and that, although working with children may be physically and emotionally demanding, it offers little intellectual challenge. Such notions are false. They are as wrong as thinking that pilots fly solely on intuition or maintain good safety records based on their charm, or that all that is required to be a pilot is a love of airplanes. Certainly, when passengers buckle up for takeoff, they expect the pilot to have more than instinct and desire to get them safely to their destination.

Although some people do have qualities and abilities that enhance their potential for success in a particular profession, all professions have specialized knowledge that must be learned and certain competencies that must be acquired. This is no less true for professions that focus on helping children.

**Knowledge and skills.** The knowledge base from which helping professionals work is derived from a combination of theories and empirical research related to child development and human intervention. It establishes relevant terminology, facts, principles, and concepts aimed at explaining why children behave as they do and providing clues as to helpful and nonhelpful modes of intervention. Although the knowledge base of any field is constantly changing as new information becomes available through research, the information that currently exists provides a framework from which to operate. Professionals cannot approach their work

haphazardly; they cannot simply react to children. Rather, they must respond rationally and purposefully, using theoretical and empirical information to guide their actions. Such knowledge also provides professionals working in widely divergent settings a common foundation from which to communicate with one another and work toward shared goals.

Once gained, knowledge must be translated into practice. It is not enough to simply recite textbook philosophy: you must also learn how to act in ways that accurately support and convey that philosophy. Thus, professionals must learn certain behaviors that represent effective helping (Gazda, 1995). These learned behaviors are called skills.

**Skills** consist of observable actions that, when used in combination, represent mastery of a given technique or communicate general attitudes. Thus, they can be seen, learned, and evaluated. For instance, a person who wants to convey the facilitative characteristic of warmth toward children will smile at them, establish eye contact, and stoop down to their level. All of these behaviors can be readily observed and identified.

In addition, a person who does not smile much can be taught to smile more; an individual who avoids eye contact can be trained to look at people's faces; someone who tends to tower over children can learn to bend or squat. Finally, it is possible to assess how often these behaviors are exhibited and how appropriately they are used. Because smiling, establishing eye contact, and stooping are observable, learnable, and assessable, they are skills.

Some skills, such as these, are simple to understand and easy to learn; others are more complex and difficult. In all cases, skill mastery requires the learner to know what to do, why to do it, and how to do it. Yet, even when all this is accomplished, true mastery is not attained until the learner uses the skill in the setting for which it was intended. It is not sufficient only to realize the importance of smiling or even to smile appropriately during a role-playing situation in a college class. You must also smile at children in the center, on the playground, or in the playroom. This transfer of training from practice situations to real-life encounters is the goal of skill learning.

## ▼ CHAPTER STRUCTURE

Based on the previous discussion, it is apparent that both knowledge and practice are essential elements in the training of helping professionals. Consequently, the following chapters each contain sections representing the information and skills related to a particular facet of social development. A statement of objectives precedes the chapter text and tells you what you should know after completing this chapter. This list also helps make clear the progression from knowledge to practice for that unit.

The objectives are followed by a discussion of the latest empirical findings and the theory pertinent to the topic of the chapter. This constitutes the knowledge base for the chapter. The skills section that follows describes specific techniques related to the topic. Also included are common pitfalls you may experience when first adopting the skills in your own interactions with children. All chapters conclude with a summary, which provides a brief overview of the topic just presented. Discussion questions have been developed to help you better assess your understanding of the material. Field assignments give you an opportunity to apply what you have learned.

## ▼ CHAPTER SEQUENCE

The next fourteen chapters are presented sequentially. Chapters that focus on relationship-building skills appear before those more commonly considered part of the action dimension of helping. This sequence is based on the idea that adult attempts to maintain or change children's behavior are successful only after bonds of trust and caring have been developed. The chapters build on one another: skills covered in earlier chapters lead to those that follow.

This initial chapter introduced the premises around which the rest of the book is structured. Included was basic information about how children develop and how they learn, as well as how adults influence these processes. Throughout this discussion, we have emphasized the interdependent nature of children and the environment. Finally, those characteristics that set helping professionals apart from lay people, as well as how helping professionals should function in guiding children's social development, were identified.

Because social relationships begin at birth, Chapter 2 discusses infant development and the methods by which adults can relate to even the youngest child. Although positive communication goals are fundamentally the same throughout the life span, techniques that are effective with children younger than two years of age are somewhat different from those used with older youngsters. Thus, Chapter 2 focuses entirely on the earliest period of childhood. All the following chapters deal primarily with children between the ages of two and twelve.

With this in mind, Chapter 3 discusses the nonverbal aspects of communication. How toddlers, preschoolers, and school-age children communicate nonverbally and how they interpret the nonverbal communication of adults are discussed. Ways in which adults manifest empathy, acceptance, respect, authenticity, and warmth through voice and action are also explained.

In Chapter 4, the emphasis turns to verbal communication. This chapter describes how adult words affect children's self-awareness and self-judgments about their competence and worth. Specific skills are introduced that, when implemented, positively influence children's development in these areas.

Recognizing and understanding emotions is another arena in which verbal communication plays an important role. How children develop emotionally and what adults should do to enhance children's emotional development is the subject of Chapter 5. Chapter 6 extends the affective theme by focusing on one of the strongest and most frequent emotional states with which children must cope— stress. Symptoms of stress, factors that contribute to stress in children, and specific strategies children can learn to reduce stress are described.

Chapter 7 deals with children's play. Why children play, how they play, and what role adults should take in enhancing play are discussed. Many of the play skills developed during childhood also contribute to children's ability to interact effectively with peers. Chapter 8 describes the value of children's friendships and how children's concepts of friendship change over time. This content provides a base for helping children learn effective ways to initiate and maintain friendly relationships with peers.

In Chapter 9, attention is turned to the influence of the physical environment on children's social development. In particular, techniques are emphasized that enhance children's ability to function independently and interact constructively with others. Ways in which adults can structure the environment to avoid problems altogether or address problem situations as they unfold are also described. Factors that contribute to the development of self-discipline in children and ways to formulate appropriate rules are presented in Chapter 10. Chapter 11 continues this topic by underscoring the developmental reasons for why self-control is not automatic, as well as how adults can use consequences to enable children to take more responsibility for regulating their own behavior. One of the most difficult behaviors for children to learn to control is their aggressiveness. For this reason,

Chapter 12 is entirely devoted to this subject. Why children are aggressive, variations in aggressive behavior, and how aggression changes with age are outlined. Tactics adults should avoid and those they should pursue are presented.

Chapter 13 focuses on prosocial behavior, which is a powerful countermeasure to aggression. This chapter explains what is meant by prosocial behavior and describes the evolving nature of such behavior throughout childhood. Techniques for teaching children kindness, both informally and through more structured experiences, are presented.

The last two chapters of the book build on all of the content and skills presented thus far. Chapter 14 includes both facilitation and action-oriented strategies aimed at helping professionals respond sensitively to children's burgeoning sexuality, racial awareness, and special needs. Personality differences among children are also discussed.

Chapter 15 emphasizes how to match the skills you have learned to the situations for which they are best suited. This chapter also discusses the circumstances in which you should seek outside intervention or consultation in dealing with children and their families.

## ▼ STUDENT OBJECTIVES

When used as a whole, the knowledge and skills presented in this book will provide aspiring and current helping professionals with comprehensive and systematic guidelines for promoting children's social development. When you have completed the book, you will know more about how to do the following:

1. Articulate the role of the helping professional in enhancing children's social development.
2. Integrate factual information with practical strategies for interacting with children individually and in groups.
3. Adjust your behavior with children to accommodate cultural and developmental needs.
4. Work cooperatively with families to enhance children's social development and learning.
5. Respond to children in a manner that the children interpret as supportive and predictable.
6. Identify the child's perspective within varying interpersonal and situational circumstances.
7. Talk to children in ways that promote positive adult-child relationships.
8. Extend children's understanding of their own emotions and the emotions of others.

9. Help children develop specific coping skills for a variety of situations.
10. Facilitate growth-enhancing play among children.
11. Help children learn specific strategies to enhance their relationships with peers.
12. Plan children's environments to promote independence, decision making, and harmonious relationships.
13. Express your emotions clearly and precisely to children.
14. Utilize rules and consequences that further self-discipline in children.
15. Assist children in developing specific prosocial behaviors such as helping and cooperating.
16. Identify multiple issues to be considered in adult-child interactions.
17. Provide child development–related rationales for choosing specific strategies when working with children and families.
18. Determine when children's behavior warrants additional consultation and referrals to other helping professionals.

## ▼ SUMMARY

Social competence refers to a person's ability to recognize, interpret, and respond to social situations in ways deemed appropriate by society. The acquisition of social competence begins in childhood and occurs as a result of both development and experience. As children develop greater language, memory, cognitive, and physical abilities, their capacity for social competence increases. This capacity also is affected by what children learn and how they learn it.

Social learning takes place within an interdependent network of systems—the microsystem, the mesosystem, the exosystem, and the macrosystem. Each system influences children and in turn is influenced by them. In addition, both the individual and the system are modified by the interaction. The understanding of all these concepts taken together contributes to what is called an ecological perspective. It is beneficial to maintain such a perspective because it enables you to see children and respond to their needs in context.

The most basic system within the ecological framework is the family. Families play a primary role in socializing the young. This function is effectively carried out by families whose structure and values differ widely. Thus, no one family form is considered preferable. As children mature, other systems, including formal group settings, play an ever-increasing role in their lives. In these settings, children receive a particular service from trained individuals. Such adults not only teach, counsel, lead, or supervise children, but also create a program atmosphere that can make children feel good or bad about themselves. Because these adults focus on helping children achieve positive growth, they are called helping professionals.

Professionals differ from lay persons in several important ways. As the result of prolonged education and training, professionals possess specialized knowledge and skills to which nonprofessionals have little access. Also, entry into a profession depends on each person's ability to demonstrate certain competencies. Continued membership requires the performance of your duties according to standards of excellence established within the field and continuing education throughout your career. Adoption of a professional code of ethics is an additional expectation of the helping professional.

Because the basis of all helping is emotional supportiveness, professionals who work with children must learn to demonstrate empathy, warmth, respect, acceptance, and authenticity. Only after these skills have been established can adults effectively help children change their behavior in ways that will increase their social competence. Becoming a helping professional requires both knowledge and skills. The structure of this book and the sequence of chapters within it are aimed toward teaching both in a systematic and comprehensive manner. In this way, you can learn to guide children's social development.

## ▼ DISCUSSION QUESTIONS

1. Define social competence. Discuss behaviors that could be described as evidence of social competence and those that illustrate lack of social competence.
2. Choose three of the principles of development and learning described in this chapter. Give examples based on children you know that illustrate each principle. Then talk about how knowledge of these principles would influence your work with children in a formal group setting.
3. With a partner, describe the microsystems and mesosystems of which each of you are a part. Discuss how they overlap and how they differ.
4. Imagine you are entering a children's group setting for the first time. Discuss the clues you could use to judge whether the atmosphere supports or inhibits children's social development.
5. Discuss the differences between professionals and nonprofessionals. Describe what steps you have taken in your pursuit of a helping profession.
6. Discuss the similarities and differences of formal and informal group settings. Choose two settings with which you are familiar to use as examples.
7. Describe the facilitative and action dimensions in terms of children's social development. Discuss their relationship.
8. In a small group of three or four, discuss your aspirations as a helping professional.
9. Read the following ethical scenarios. Refer to the NAEYC Code of Ethical Conduct presented in Appendix A. Find the sections of the code that provide insight into the professional responsibilities related to each one.
    a. The staff of the five-year-old classes is meeting for lunch at a local restaurant. One of the teachers mentions by name the children she is having trouble with in her class. She asks her co-workers for advice.
    b. Tyrone Murray, a teacher at the Andover School, has noticed that Marlene Smith, another teacher, frequently comes to work late. This makes it difficult for him to confer with her about plans for the morning. He discusses the problem with the cook who is his friend.
    c. Mrs. Gonzalez arrives at the program wishing to observe her child. She is turned away by the director, who tells her it is not convenient.
    d. Mrs. Akina, director of the Oakleaf Nursery School, receives a call from a parent whose child has been diagnosed as having attention deficit disorder. The parent is interested in enrolling his child in the program. Mrs. Akina invites him to come to the school to observe the program and puts a brochure and application in the mail for him that day.
    e. Lauren Winslow is newly hired as a teacher's aide in an infant/toddler unit. Before reporting to work the first day, she is given a copy of the center's personnel policies to review. She is told she will have an opportunity to ask questions regarding anything she does not understand during her orientation session with the director the next day.

## ▼ Field Assignments

1. List ten formal group settings in your community, the population of children or families they serve, and their goals.

2. Select two children from your field placement. Talk to your head teacher and other significant adults in the children's lives to figure out the micro-, meso-, and exosystem for each child. Depict these in a diagram. Add elements of the macrosystem as you understand it.

3. Identify three professional organizations in your community to which helping professionals belong. List the requirements for membership, benefits that members receive, and the procedures for joining each group.

4. Interview two helping professionals in your community. Ask them to describe their current position, their educational background, the requirements they needed to enter the profession, professional organizations to which they belong, how they continue their education over time, and what they believe are the most significant ethical issues in their field.

# ▼Chapter 2

## Initiating Social Relationships in Infancy

## ▼ OBJECTIVES

*On completion of this chapter, you will be able to describe:*

▼  The behavioral states of infants and how to soothe a crying infant.

▼  The sensory abilities of infants and how these relate to social behavior.

▼  The role of motor development in social interaction.

▼  The relationship of temperament to social interaction.

▼  The sequential steps of individuation, or becoming a separate person.

▼  The capacity of an infant for social interaction with peers and adults.

▼  The role of the professional with infants and toddlers who have special needs.

▼  Strategies that adults can use to support healthy social-emotional development.

▼  Strategies for interaction with parents of infants and toddlers.

▼  Pitfalls to avoid in interacting with infants and their families.

---

Now, don't spoil the baby.

Please shut that baby up!

Oh, babies are no trouble to me!

---

In a few years, you may be working professionally with infants and their families in a newborn nursery of a hospital, in a child-care center, or in a community-based infant development program. How social development begins and how it changes as the infant matures will be important information for you to know. You may even be asked to teach others how to provide the responsive, loving care that infants need in order to thrive.

When a baby is born, he or she immediately is a member of a social group: a family, who lives in a community, which is contained within a larger culture. Although newborns are not truly social in the beginning, their posture when held and reflexes are such that parents interpret their responses as social acts and modify their own behavior accordingly (Brazelton, 1974). Within two short years, the newly born infants will participate as full partners in social interactions within the family and with others they encounter outside the home.

The primary caregiver is central to the normal development of the infant. Although the primary caregiver usually is the mother in our society, others may fulfill this function. The relationship that develops between the primary caregiver and child during the first two years of life is the foundation on which all later development is based (Isabella and Belsky, 1991). Fortunately, other family members, friends, and helping professionals often participate in the early child rearing in ways that can support and enhance the efforts of parents.

This chapter focuses on abilities of newborns that enable them to become true social partners, typical behaviors that caregivers can expect during the first year, and the skills adults can learn to maximize infant social development.

## ▼ Infant Competencies

What does an infant look like? Newborns have large heads and trunks with relatively smaller arms and legs. They may or may not have much hair, but their heads smell nice. Their skin, in the beginning, may be discolored and wrinkly, but is always soft, and soon fills out. Eyes are large in a face that may be quite flat, and in the beginning, they have no tears. Rounded cheeks are characteristic of the first year. This cherubic appearance makes the infant cute and appealing to adults.

Newborns are small but grow rapidly during the first year, gaining in both length and weight so that a one-year-old seems heavy in comparison. Newborns are fairly still, moving only head and limbs, but by the sixth or seventh month of age, they become intrepid travelers. Thus, rapid change is the hallmark of infancy.

There have been two widely held views about the nature of infants. The first, and earliest, is that infants are not yet "real people," are largely unaware of their environment, and have few resources for interacting with it. The second view, based on later research and parental experience, is that the human infant is remarkably competent and is able to respond socially quite early in life. These views are illustrated by the behavior of Mrs. Roberts and Mrs. James, two women who shared a hospital room after giving birth for the first time. Mrs. Roberts kept her newborn with her, watching the baby's hands and feet move about while quietly talking to her. She told the baby how glad she was to have her, about her family, and what her room at home was like.

Mrs. James looked at Mrs. Roberts in surprise and asked, "Don't you know she can't talk? She can't do anything for a long time." Her own infant was brought in for feedings and promptly returned to the nursery.

Mrs. Roberts thought of her newborn as a person already capable of engaging in social interaction, whereas Mrs. James expected her infant to become a real person at some later date.

### Behavioral States

Infants do not behave in the same way all the time. The usual behavior alternatives are known as behavioral states (Wolff, 1966). The infant's current be-

havioral state influences how he or she perceives the world and responds to social encounters. For example, an infant who is sleeping or crying vigorously obviously is less able to attend to the environment than one who is quiet and watching what is happening nearby. There are seven different behavioral states, each of which is characterized by differences in respiration, muscle tone, motor activity, position of the eyelids, and alertness (Ashton, 1973; Dittrichova and Paul, 1971; Papousek and Papousek, 1977; Wolff, 1966). Newborns change states rapidly and irregularly and may not establish a routine pattern for several weeks. As infants mature, however, changes in state become more regular and infants establish their own routine *rhythm,* or predictable pattern of behavior (Prechtl and O'Brien, 1982). Adults who learn to recognize each of these states are better able to receive clues for responding to even the youngest child (Korner, 1974). The behavioral states of infants are summarized in Table 2–1.

**Sleep states.** Infants who are in any of the four sleep states should not be interrupted or stimulated. Only the infant who is waking up slowly from a long sleep and is still drowsy should be picked up. Infants should not be awakened to be changed, fed, or engaged in social interaction. For this reason, schedules fixed by the clock for adult conveniences rather than by the infant's cues are not appropriate.

Newborns spend much of their time sleeping (about 16 to 20 hours a day), with frequent episodes of wakefulness for feeding (Hutt, Lenard and Prechtl, 1969; Parmelee, Werner, and Schultz, 1964). The total amount of time the newborn sleeps drops off rapidly in the first few days and then declines gradually; babies sleep about 12 hours a day at six months of age, usually sleeping through the night.

**Aroused states.** In the quiet alert or alert inactive state, the infant may appear to stare and is more likely to be responsive to stimulation and social contact. States of quiet alert are both brief and rare initially but increase noticeably over the first few months.

Caregivers should take advantage of moments when infants are displaying alert inactivity by talking to them, touching them, and presenting objects for them to enjoy. Caregivers should not conclude that quiet infants will entertain themselves or do not require stimulation just because they are not obviously demanding attention. However, if the amount of stimulation is too great, the infant will increase its activity, cry, or go to sleep as a way to avoid overstimulation (Brazelton, 1976; Lewis, 1972).

▼ Table 2-1    Infant Behavioral States and Appropriate Adult Responses

| | RESPIRATION | FACIAL EXPRESSION | ACTION | ADULT RESPONSE |
|---|---|---|---|---|
| Regular sleep | Regular; 36 per minute | Eyes closed and still; face relaxed | Little movement; fingers slightly curled, thumbs extended | Do not disturb |
| Irregular sleep | Uneven, faster; 48 per minute | Eyes closed, occasional rapid eye movement; smiles and grimaces | Gentle movement | Do not disturb |
| Periodic sleep | Pattern varies | (Alternates between regular and irregular sleep) | | Do not disturb |
| Drowsiness | Even | Eyes open and close or remain halfway open; eyes dull/glazed | Less movement than in irregular sleep; hands open and relaxed, fingers extended | Pick up if drowsiness follows sleeping; do not disturb if drowsiness follows awake periods |
| Quiet alert | Constant; faster than in regular sleep | Bright eyes, fully open; face relaxed; eyes focused | Slight activity; hands open, fingers extended, arms bent at elbow; stares | Talk to infant; present objects; perform any assessment |
| Waking activity | Irregular | Face flushed; less able to focus eyes than in quiet alert | Extremities and body move; vocalizes, makes noises | Interact with infant; provide basic care |
| Crying | | Red skin; facial grimaces; eyes partially or fully open | Vigorous activity; crying vocalizations; fists are clenched | Pick up immediately; try to identify source of discomfort and remedy it; soothe infant |

Newborns spend most of their time awake being fed, changed, dressed, or bathed. As the amount of time spent in sleep decreases, a corresponding amount of time is available in the quiet alert and waking activity states for social encounters. Infants who have difficulty in establishing and maintaining a consistent pattern of state changes may be at higher risk than their more stable peers (Rosenblith, 1992).

## Crying and Soothing

Adults spend much time and energy in responding to infant cries, trying to determine what the infant needs, and soothing the infant.

Individual infants have recognizable voices; they also have characteristic cries for hunger, pain, and anger, which an be distinguished from one another by the pattern of pauses between bursts of crying, the duration of the cry, and by noticeable tonal characteristics (Vuorenkoski, et al., 1969, 1971; Wolff, 1967, 1969). The pain cry, for example, is a long, piercing wail. This cry is a peremptory signal that something is wrong and must be changed. It is quite different from speech sounds and is extremely effective as a communication signal in getting the attention of the caregiver (Lenneberg, 1964; Tonkova-Yampolskaya, 1962). Some parents may not be able to reliably distinguish their infant's cries initially (Donovan and Leavitt, 1985), but most increase in their ability to distinguish between the child's bid for attention and distress or pain over time (Boukydis, 1985). Likewise, caregivers familiar with individual infants learn to identify and respond appropriately to these cries.

Infants also may cry for a variety of other reasons, such as fright caused by a loud noise or a sudden change in light, exposure to cold, being undressed, or other physical discomforts, not just because of hunger or a wet diaper (Wolff, 1966). Infants about four months of age may cry because they have not been placed in the preferred sleeping position. Others in the second half of the first year may cry from rage or boredom. Once the source of distress is identified and attend to, the infant usually can be soothed and the crying stopped.

American babies tend to increase their crying during the first six weeks. If babies are carried in an upright position when they are not experiencing distress, this increase in crying does not occur. Apparently, the babies respond to the physical contact of the adult and the more varied and stimulating environment (Hunziker and Barr, 1986).

In recent years, caregivers have had increasing contact with infants who have experienced physical or emotional stress such as being born with drug addiction or displaying failure-to-thrive syndrome. Such infants do not display expected crying patterns. Adults who care for such children should seek specific information about each child's condition and crying patterns as some cry for long periods of time and others do not cry at all.

Normal, healthy infants may spend between 5 and 20 percent of their time crying (Berg, Adkinson, and Strock, 1973; Korner, et al., 1974). Infants cry more during the first three months of life, gradually becoming able to exert a little control. For example, a hungry four-month-old may stop crying when picked up and held while the caregiver gets the bottle ready. However, if put back down, this young infant may not be able to hold back the crying. A hungry six- or seven-month-old whose needs usually have been attended to promptly may stop crying when the caregiver is seen or heard approaching.

Occasionally, parents or other caregivers have tried to train very young infants not to cry by ignoring them, hoping that the crying will stop. This does not work (Bell and Ainsworth, 1972). Often, a newborn cannot control the crying because it has a physiological cause (Wolff, 1966). In general, the longer the infant has been crying, the longer and more difficult the soothing time.

The most effective way to calm infants is to pick them up and hold them upright at your shoulder (Hunziker and Barr, 1986; Korner and Thoman, 1970). Infants also can be soothed by any stimulation that is continuous and unchanging for some minutes (Brackbill, 1979). Swaddling, or wrapping a young infant firmly in a blanket, also is effective (Stone and Church, 1973) as are changes in position (Rosenblith, 1992). A pacifier will affect infant states, increasing the amount of time in quiet states and decreasing the frequency of transitions in state and overall activity as most parents have noted

(Rosenblith, 1992). In fact, the more senses that receive continuous stimulation, the calmer babies become (Brackbill, 1979). Thus, picking up crying babies, swaddling them, walking or rocking them, and singing lullabies continue to be effective. Older babies prefer the soothing strategy with which they are familiar so individual preferences may be influenced by cultural patterns.

Infants whose caregivers are most responsive to cries in the first few months of life cry least. These children also become more effective in noncrying communication later (Bell and Ainsworth, 1972). When adults use these strategies, infants learn that the environment is predictable and the caregiver can be counted on to respond to their signals of distress. This is an important element of trust that is developed early in life (Erikson, 1963).

## Sensory Ability and Social Interaction

Is it really possible to establish a social relationship with an infant? A social relationship requires the participation of at least two persons. Although the participation between an adult and a child is decidedly unequal and mostly dependent on the adult, babies are born with the capacity to receive information from the environment and to respond, although in a limited way. Thus, the foundations for social relationships exist from birth and are built up as the caregiver develops patterns of response to infant cues such as those discussed in the previous section.

When infants are in the alert inactive state, they are ready to interact with their environment. During the first two months, they usually are being held when they are in this state. Their first information about the world is based on sensations they receive while being handled. They smell the adult's hands, hair, and body. They taste his or her skin. They see the adult's face when being fed, bathed, clothed, and changed. They feel the caregiver's body directly as they are held close, so they sense muscular tension or relaxation as well as the rhythm of movement. Caregivers who are comfortable with their own bodies and can accept infants' ways of knowing about them through body exploration have taken the first step in establishing a relationship.

Perceptual abilities present at birth undergo a sequence of developmental changes during the first year of life (Lamb and Campos, 1982). Piaget (1962) has described how these processes are essential to cognitive development. Perceptual capacities also are critical to social development as the avenue through which babies come to know what it means to be a person.

An infant may be competent to use a sensory ability but may not perform a specific task (Chomsky, 1957; Flavell and Wohlwill, 1969). This distinction is important because caregivers sometimes think that an infant cannot do something simply because he or she did not do it when expected. One should not conclude that babies cannot see the pattern on the bumper guard simply because they do not look at it very often when the caregiver is at hand. For this reason, it is important for adults to understand the basic competencies that infants possess.

**Touch.** The sense of touch is well-developed at birth and may be almost completely developed at that time. It is perhaps the least studied of the senses. We do know that touch triggers many infant reflexes, such as sucking and grasping. In addition, extremes of temperature cause distress in babies. Temperature and humidity also affect infant sleep. Infants can be comforted by being swaddled, having a hand placed on the abdomen, changing position, or being held (MacFarlane, 1977). When caregivers are both firm and gentle during feeding, bathing, and diapering, silent messages of comfort, approval, and affection are conveyed. Rough or painful handling causes distress and may influence the infant's view of the environment as a risky place.

Infants also learn to identify objects through touch by the age of ten months (Soroka, Corter, and Abramovitch, 1979). This is why they may develop preferences for stuffed animals, blankets, or other objects. Preferred objects may assist older babies in controlling their crying or in soothing themselves when drowsy or distressed. Caregivers should recognize such attempts at self-regulation and show respect for infants' preferences by allowing them to keep such objects close at hand.

**Smell and taste.** Newborns have a well-developed sense of smell and can distinguish between pleasant and unpleasant odors (Engen and Lipsitt, 1965) as well as among certain food odors (Steiner, 1979). Babies quickly learn to recognize the smell of their mother's milk and bodies (Cernoch and Porter, 1985).

Infants also have a keen sense of taste, preferring sweeter flavors than are preferred by adolescents or adults (Desor, Maller, and Green, 1977). Nevertheless, caregivers must consider the nutritional needs of the infant as paramount and not offer sweetened water or other sweetened drinks to infants, even if they like them. Additionally, it should be noted that infants and young children are not able to distin-guish a poison by its taste or smell and have been known to consume noxious, lethal substances. Caregivers must make sure such substances are not available.

**Hearing.** Hearing is possible before birth, and newborns may be able to distinguish their own mother's voice from the voice of another female, even when most of their time has been spent in a nursery (Bernard and Sontag, 1947; DeCasper and Fifer, 1980). Also, most newborns will turn their heads in the direction of a shaking rattle (Muir and Field, 1979). They appear to prefer complex sounds rather than pure tones, soft sounds rather than loud ones, and those that have a longer duration rather than short, sharp sounds (Rosenblith, 1992).

Very young infants are sensitive to speech sounds. When the caregiver speaks to them, they will turn toward the sound. Between three and five months of age, infants can imitate the changes of pitch in an adult's voice, and when they are sung to, they can "sing" back (Kessen, Levine, and Wendrich, 1979).

Between three and six months of age, there is a sharp decrease in infants' auditory thresholds, making them much more sensitive to sounds around them (Hoversten and Moncur, 1969). This means they may startle at noises previously ignored. By the sixth month, infants recognize their parents or other caregivers by the sound of their voices alone. By eight months of age, infants recognize a variety of familiar sounds such as music boxes and sound toys.

**Vision.** Newborns do not see as clearly as adults. Babies' eyes can accommodate as well as an adult's by two months of age (Banks, 1980). They achieve visual clarity at about six months of age (Acredolo and Hoke, 1982; Dayton, et al., 1964) and develop the full range of visual competence at about twelve months (Cohen, De Loache, and Strauss, 1979). Initially, infants focus on objects between 8 and 10 inches away from them. Coincidentally, this is the approximate distance between an adult's face and that of a baby being held for feeding (Wickelgren, 1967). By the sixth week, babies appear to look directly at the faces of the caregivers, with eye brightening and eye widening, and by three months, infants can distinguish photographs of their parents from same-sexed strangers (Maurer and Heroux, 1980; Wolff, 1963). Infants prefer to look at people rather than objects during the first year (Sherrod, 1981) and by six months of age, recognize all the people with whom they have regular contact.

Using each of the senses independently, infants are able to recognize the important people in their lives. Using the senses together, they go further, establishing basic social relationships such as attachment to their parents and preferences for particular caregivers. As infants mature, their sensory competencies become more complex and support increasingly complex social behaviors.

## Motor Control and Social Interaction

With the gradual increase in control of the head, arms, and shoulders, infants are able to manipulate the amount of stimulation they receive. By three months of age, they use their head position and gaze as a means of influencing communication with the caregiver. Three early gaze directions are possible. In the face-to-face position, infants are fully engaged in gazing at their caregivers. When infants turn their heads slightly, they maintain contact but signal that the play may be too fast or too slow. When the head is fully turned and the gaze lowered, contact is completely broken (Beebe and Stern, 1977). When infants are completely overwhelmed by interactions that are too intense, they go to sleep, cry, or go limp. This behavior often is seen when infants are greeted by overly enthusiastic relatives. A summary of infant behaviors relating to head, gaze, and facial expression and corresponding typical meanings to the caregiver is presented in Table 2–2.

By the third month, infants are capable of tracking people as they move around the room. They stare at other people for long periods and, as they get older, will shift into a better position to watch what others are doing. For many sensitive caregivers, this is an invitation to conversation or play.

Once infants can sit up, between seven and ten months of age, they develop greater eye-hand coordination skills and a corresponding increase of interest in objects. They also may turn completely away from the caregiver to focus on an object. This is not a rejection of the caregiver, but is the exploration of the environment made possible by a comfortable relationship with a trustworthy adult.

## Temperament

Infants are not all alike. Temperamental differences are evident from earliest life and are thought to affect personality development (Thomas and Chess, 1977). Also, characteristics of the child's temperament influence interaction with the caregiver right from the beginning.

An infant may be timid or intrepid, quick tempered or slow to anger, passive or actively curious, rhythmic or irregular. Some infants respond to every event, whereas others ignore loud noises, bright lights, and other sensations. **Temperamental differences,** then, are differences in the degree, or intensity, of emotional behavior and in timing and duration of responses. Individual differences in temperament influence the organization of the child's personality and social relationships.

Other factors may affect infant behavior, such as drugs administered to the mother just before birth or given to the infant, malnourishment, or parents' interpretation of their child's personality (Brackbill, 1979; Murray, et al., 1981; Osofsky and Conners, 1981). However, all these factors can be changed by appropriate intervention, whereas temperamental differences are thought to be biologically based.

## Influence of Temperament on Social Relationships

Several kinds of individual differences in temperament have been identified as well as their influence

| ▼ Table 2–2 Infant Gaze and Social Meaning to Caregivers | |
| --- | --- |
| **POSITION AND EXPRESSION** | **TYPICAL INTERPRETATION** |
| Face to face, sober | Fully engaged, intent |
| Face to face, smiling | Pleased, interested |
| Head turned slightly away | Maintaining interest; interaction too fast or too slow |
| Complete head rotation | Uninterested; stop for awhile |
| Head lowered | Stop! |
| Rapid head rotation | Dislikes something |
| Glances away, tilts head up; partial head aversion | Stop or change strategy |
| Head lowered, body limp | Has given up fighting off overstimulation |

on the social relationship of the caregiver and infant. Emotionality, activity, sociability, impulsivity (Buss and Plomin, 1975), rhythmicity, approach-withdrawal, adaptability, intensity, distractability, attention span and persistence, and activity level all are dimensions that have been attributed to temperament (Thomas and Chess, 1977). The way these attributes are combined make the infant easy or difficult to care for and more or less pleasant and interesting to play with, and they influence the amount and quality of social interaction that the infant is likely to receive.

The caregiver is influenced by the nature of the baby as well as having an influence on the child (Crockenberg, 1981). Difficult temperaments at birth seem to require extreme amounts of patient, persistent caregiving skills from an adult who has little other stress and much time to devote to the baby. Consequently, not everyone is able to provide these optimal conditions, and the difficult baby seems to challenge the resources of overtaxed caregivers. Fortunately, some adults are able to overcome the barriers to social interaction with difficult infants (Belsky, Lerner, and Spanier, 1984) and provide the support, patience, and interaction necessary for good development.

Adults often find building a supportive relationship with some infants natural, easy, and satisfying. Establishing a similar relationship with another infant whose temperament is different requires self-discipline, patience, and perseverance from the caregiver (Klein, 1980; Soderman, 1985).

For example, two children who differ markedly in activity and impulsiveness elicit different responses from adults. Mike moves slowly, watches what is going on, seldom cries, and plays in his crib contentedly for long periods after awakening. Todd, on the other hand, is distracted by every movement or noise; moves quickly from one part of the room to another; always seems to be underfoot; cries vigorously, long, and frequently; and rarely is content to play in his crib after awakening. Both boys are eight months old. Mr. McIntyre, who takes care of them, interacts less frequently with Mike but finds him satisfying and restful, if slightly boring, to play with. Todd gets much more attention, although Mr. McIntyre frequently feels irritated with him. The only time Todd seems to settle down is when he plays with him. Mr. McIntyre is aware of his tendency to ignore Mike and pursue Todd, so he carefully remembers to check on Mike regularly and involve him in play.

As patterns of interaction between adults and children emerge and become habitual, each child's social context becomes unique, influencing the organization of personality. "Goodness of fit" between adult and child is important because both parties to the relationship have temperaments. The experience of an infant like Mike, who is somewhat inactive and not very sociable, with an adult who is impulsive, impatient, and expects quick social responses from him would be very different from his experience with an easygoing, patient adult who is willing to wait for him to respond in his own good time.

Sometimes the characteristics of an infant's temperament combine in such a way to produce a very shy child (Broberg, 1993). Such children seem to be notably unsociable early in life, tend to be very wary or fearful, and react more strongly to stressful events than their peers. They may be more inhibited in exploring the environment and suffer great distress when separated from the primary caregiver. It is the infant-caregiver relationship that is the cornerstone of all individual differences as the adult adapts to the specific needs and characteristics of each child (Sroufe, 1996). A responsive, supportive caregiver who provides consistent support in a predictable environment may enable this shy child to emerge into a competent, if slightly hesitant, member of his or her social community.

The goodness of fit between the infant, the caregiver's temperament and expectations, and the infant's general living environment may be more important to the long-term outcome for the child than temperament alone. Even infants with difficult temperaments can be happy and successful if their caregivers are easygoing, if the caregivers' expectations for the child are clear and suitable for the child's age, and if caregivers use skills that enable them to be sensitive and responsive.

## ▼ SOCIALIZATION AND INDIVIDUATION

Two functions of social development begin to operate during the first year of life. **Socialization** is the process that includes one's capacity to cooperate in a group, to regulate one's behavior according to society, and, in general, to get along the others. **Individuation** is the process by which the self or personal identity is developed and one's individual place in the social order is acquired. Individuation integrates the emerging perceptual, memory, cognitive, and emotional capacities to form a unified personality or self-identity in the young child. Both of these functions operate at the same time throughout childhood, and both are absolutely essential to successful adaptation to life.

The processes of socialization and individuation have long been of interest. Much of the work completed thus far focuses on how these processes operate and how they influence the behavior of children. Behavior can be observed, but the processes themselves are internal and must be inferred. For this reason, theories have been developed that help to explain the process and the outcome for the child.

The process of becoming a person and then becoming a member of a group begins in infancy. It occurs over a long time in a sequential manner and is dependent on a relationship between the infant and a loving adult. This adult may be a parent, grandparent, foster parent, or helping professional. What happens in infancy forms the foundation for later social-emotional development. It also influences all other aspects of the child's behavior. For infants to develop a sense of self, their physical needs must be met and they must enjoy a stable emotional climate (Ainsworth, 1973; Bowlby, 1969; Erickson, 1950, 1963; Mahler, Pine, and Bergman, 1975; Sroufe, 1996).

## Becoming a Separate Person Within a Social Group

Individuation differentiates the self from others and takes place in a social context. Individuation must occur if **attachment,** or preference for specific adults, is to take place. Table 2–3 summarizes the process of individuation, including infant capabilities; social actions that stem from these capabilities; and appropriate adult responses that support individuation.

**Phase I.** The infant does not psychologically differentiate self from parent and has no sense of time and place in the first phase of the process of individuation. He or she uses sucking, grasping, visual tracking, and cuddling to maintain contact with the parent. The infant's behavior is primarily reflexive or accidental in response to external stimulation. For example, grasping and bringing objects to the mouth, smiling, and simple thumb-sucking all are unintentional acts (reflexive).

**Phase II.** The second phase is characterized by the infant's internal notion of parent and self as one omnipotent unit (Mahler, Pine, and Bergman, 1975). Young infants are likely to be alert and ready to pay attention and learn information when they are picked up (Korner and Thoman, 1970, 1972). Because the caregiver is the most noticeable feature in the en-

vironment, infants are likely to learn first about people, particularly the parents, through their senses. Also, adults tend to act in response to infant behaviors. In this way, there is a beginning differentiation between self and objects, such as the blanket, bottle or toy, as well as between parent and objects, although not between parent and self. During this phase, the infant molds to the parent's body when held, engages in mutual cueing with the parent, is most easily soothed by the preferred adult, and responds to signals contingently with another. Contingent responses are like a conversation with turn taking, but using only gesture, facial expressions, touching, or playing, often with vocalizing.

In addition, infants eventually discover how to make interesting events last, and the beginnings of intentional behavior thereby emerge (Piaget, 1952). Even though infants cannot discover new ways to engage in social exchange or physical activity, such as getting a mobile going, they are capable of continuing an action that was discovered by accident (Frye, 1981).

**Phase III.** During the third phase of the individuation process, the preference for the primary caregiver (usually the mother) is clear, but the infant still has no self-awareness. Behaviors such as arching the back away from the parent, creeping away, focusing on objects, but regularly checking back on the parent are common (Mahler, Pine, and Bergman, 1975).

By this time, the infant has learned about social expectations. The distress-relief sequence contains all the components necessary for the infant to accomplish the following (Lamb, 1981):

Learn that relief quickly follows distress
Recognize the person who provides relief
Gradually develop a complex concept of the caregiver
Associate the caregiver with the pleasurable outcomes he or she produces

It is from these simple, everyday interactions that the infant develops the ability to engage in an affectively positive relationship, to generate expectations concerning the parent's responses, and to acquire a sense of power. Apparently, the more promptly parents respond, the more likely infants will learn associations between their own and another person's behavior. They are capable of learning and remembering positive social behavior from six months of age and are likely to show surprise if their caregivers behave unexpectedly (Tronic, et al., 1978). Infants in the third phase of individuation are able to use behaviors that they have previously learned in

▼ Table 2-3 The Individuation Process and Appropriate Adult Responses

| PHASE | AGE OF ONSET IN MONTHS | INFANT CAPABILITIES | SOCIAL OUTCOME | FUNCTION IN INDIVIDUATION PROCESS | ADULT BEHAVIORS THAT SUPPORT INDIVIDUATION |
|---|---|---|---|---|---|
| I | 0 | Sucking; visual tracking; grasping; cuddling; vocalizes | Reflexes | Proximity to mother | Observation of states; prompt basic care |
| II | 1–2 | More time quietly alert; sensory learning about people and objects; molding to caregiver's body; continues interesting activities; coos and goos | Mother–infant pair perceived as a unit; beginning social responsiveness; mutual cueing, gazing | Begins differentiation between self and objects; more ways of maintaining proximity | Provide objects; engage in turn-taking play; give prompt basic care; respond sensitively to different states |
| III | 4–8 | Sits, grasps; creeps; increased interest in objects; sensory learning: mouthing, manipulating, examining, banging; laughs, yells, and squeals; babbling | Recognizes familiar people; shows clear preferences among people; intentionality limited to previously learned actions; playful; social smile, laughter | No self-awareness; beginnings of social expectations; stranger fear; maintains proximity by following, checking back on caregiver after short excursions | Provide a safe environment for floor exploration; establish limits for child; respond predictably |
| IV | 9–12 | Walking, climbing, running; joyful exploration; curious, excited; beginning use of language and gesture; person and object permanence becoming clearer; trial-and-error problem solving; intentions conveyed by language, gesture, and action; makes requests; comprehends words; complex babbling | Strong desire for approval, inclined to comply; self-willed; increased self-control; variety of emotions; social play with adults; interest in events | Beginning to recognize that mother is not part of self; maintains proximity by following and calling mother; strong preferences for particular people; protests separation; uses mother as a "base of operations" and moves outward | Protect from hazards (child has mobility without judgment); respond promptly to communicative acts; set and maintain routines and limits; provide opportunity for independence; use language to comfort, explain; leave child with familiar adults; have patience |
| V | 15–24 | Increase of all motor tasks; skillful exploration of objects, events; rapid increase in language and nonverbal communication skills; likely to carry objects to preferred adults; object permanence achieved at end of phase V; pointing, says words then word combinations | Is likely to cling, then run away; plays "mother chase me!"; self-willed: "No" before compliance; considerable amount of self-control; may show sudden fear after departure from mother; may cry from relief at her return | Realizes mother's goals are not own goals; may be ambivalent about dependence/independence; can play happily in absence of preferred person; uses "gifts" of toys in seeking proximity, more language | Verbalize about departures, reassure; tolerate rapid changes in approach and withdrawal; use language to discuss events, relationships, objects, etc.; allow child to control some holding on, letting go; make social expectations clear over and over; have patience |
| VI | 24–30 | Good understanding of ordinary language; intentionality well developed; mental problem solving; ability to ask for help based on need; goal-directed behavior | Increasing interest in other children; peer play and communication stronger; mutually regulated social interactions; pretend play | Realistic sense of self and others; uses a wide array of techniques to maintain proximity (helping, conversation, play, stories); can cope well with separations | Continue to reassure, support, and provide affection; praise efforts at self-control and independent behavior; provide experience with another toddler |

order to pursue a goal. They creep after the parent when she or he leaves the room; they may cry in order to bring the parent close. Intentionality, however, is limited in that only previously learned behaviors can be used to bring about the desired end (Frye, 1981).

Fear or wariness toward adult strangers may appear about seven months of age. The age at which "stranger anxiety" occurs and the duration and intensity of the fear vary considerably among infants (Emde, Gaensbauer, and Harmon, 1976). Infants show less anxiety in the presence of the parent, in familiar surroundings, and when adult strangers give infants enough time before approaching closely or attempting to touch them (Sroufe, 1977; Trause, 1977). Some infants may show no noticeable stranger anxiety, and infants usually exhibit no fear of other children.

**Phase IV.** The accomplishment of separation from the primary caregiver, or the capacity to recognize that another human being is not a part of the self, is gradually acquired during the fourth phase of individuation. This ability becomes the basis for learning about others. To succeed, infants must understand that a person continues to exist when not in their presence.

During this phase, the infant is joyfully and actively engaged in exploration, using the parent as a secure base of operations. Starting from and returning to the parent, the infant investigates objects and events. The infant is practicing being a separate person and having a will, and is beginning to develop a sense of autonomy. Creeping and walking enables these older infants to experiment with new ways to achieve some desired goals. For this reason, this phase has been called "practicing" (Mahler, Pine, and Bergman 1975), and the child has been described as having a "love affair with the world" (Kaplan, 1978).

The exploits of this period require persistence and patience in adults. Barriers that previously protected children from falls are surmounted. Climbing makes forbidden objects high on shelves accessible. Saying "No!" is common at the end of this phase and is a means to exert self-will. The emergence of self-will is accompanied by the gradual development of enough physical self-control to enable the child to act, to do.

The child must learn when to hold on and when to let go (Erikson, 1963). From the necessity of controlling body movements emerges the sense of autonomy. Children feel that if they can control their own bodies, then they can exert their will over their own actions. However, children who are not permitted to exert control over their own movement will feel doubt about their ability to do so. This is probably why floor freedom and appropriate independence have been found to be related to the ability to internalize self-control (Stayton, Hogan, and Ainsworth, 1971). Playpens, which well-meaning adults use to control the movement of babies, may interfere with the related long-term goal of self-control if overused.

Children learn by imitating people important to them. Direct imitation of the routines of dressing, eating, eliminating body wastes, locomotion, and speech are primitive at first. Adults should expect mistakes as new skills are learned and not shame or scold the child for approximations of success.

During the fourth phase, infants have preferences for individuals and are capable of intentional behavior. They express a variety of emotions, including anger, rage, sadness, and despair. Seeking proximity to preferred adults, particularly parents, by crying, calling, pointing, and following can be expected. Parents can handle separations best by first allowing the child to become familiar with an alternative adult, then explaining that the parent is leaving soon, having the familiar adult help the child to start an activity, then quickly departing. Helping professionals must, of course, provide comfort and reassurance and support the child in exploration as soon as possible. Practices such as lying to or deceiving the child, encouraging parents to sneak out, or pulling a screaming infant from the parent's arms are to be avoided because the infant is quite capable of associating these terrifying and painful experiences with the caregiver as a person.

**Phase V.** Near the end of the second year, children begin to realize that their parents' goals and desires may be in conflict with their own. Having begun to think of themselves as separate persons, they begin to realize that parents are persons, too. No longer is the parent-infant pair one omnipotent being. Wanting to be self-willed and independent, children often are frightened by the accompanying sense of separateness and aloneness. Toddlers can hold *opposing* emotional feelings such as loving a caregiver while feeling angry at the same time. This beginning of *constancy* helps toddlers come to terms with their own and adults' wishes. They love and resent at the same time (Honig, 1992). This ambivalence of feelings often is observed in behavior: a child might cling one minute and dart away the next; he or she may show a toy or show off and then turn abruptly away.

Because older infants have developed a considerable amount of self-control and can maintain a mental image of the absent parent, they might be able to tolerate several hours of separation. However, because holding back crying still is difficult, they might burst into tears at the moment of return. Parents may need help to understand that the child contained the desire to cry as long as possible and that this behavior should not be misinterpreted as the infant not wanting the parent (Mahler, Pine, and Bergman, 1975).

**Phase VI.** During the last phase of individuation, toddlers engage in mutually regulated conversation, conveying their intentions and understanding well the verbalized intentions of others. They cope well with the loneliness and distress of separation and are capable of using a variety of behaviors to achieve closeness to preferred adults. Language plays an important role as they begin to attend to adult verbal reasoning as a guide to behavior. Goal-directed partnerships with adults are possible (Frye, 1981).

The presence and reassurance of the parent continue to be important. As the child reaches out into the neighborhood and community and meets the challenge of interacting with peers, behaviors seen in earlier phases are likely to reappear and be worked through again.

When children are away from parents for substantial periods of time, or when parents are under such stress that they are emotionally unavailable to the child, a helping professional may become the child's primary nurturer. Infant-child care provider attachments appear to be independent of infant-mother and infant-father attachments with the provider having a secure relationship with some infants whose relationships with their parents are insecure (Goossens and van IJzendoorn, 1990). Providers tend not to have any more insecure relationships with infants than do parents even though they may have several to care for at once. Apparently the urgent needs of infants can be met if the provider does not have too many infants at once (Goossens and van IJzendoorn, 1990). The attachment figure can be anyone, but it must be *someone* if healthy development is to occur. Therefore, caregivers should act as if they were the preferred adult with all their young charges. Children prefer a parent when exposed to several caring adults, so this does not entail competing with the family for the child's affection and loyalty.

The process of individuation is never really finished. The development of self-control, identity, and the place of the individual within the group continues to challenge each person as he or she is socialized as a member of the culture.

## Individual Differences in Outcome

Developing a wholesome sense of trust is central to the process of individuation (Erikson, 1963). If feelings from the sensory world are typically pleasant, the infant will develop a sense of trust. However, if sensory stimulation is harsh, the child will develop a sense of mistrust or a sense that the world is a dangerous place. The discomforts infants experience from hunger, gas, wet diapers, cold, or excessive heat are typical, as are the pleasures of being dry and warm and being fed, cuddled, or played with. Trust and mistrust are the endpoints of a continuum, with each child needing some of both.

Complete trust is as maladaptive as complete mistrust. On one hand, a completely trusting child may be oblivious to the real dangers of the world, such as rapidly moving cars, because of the inappropriate expectation that she or he will always be taken care of. On the other hand, a completely mistrustful child may be unable to interact with the world because nothing but pain and danger are expected.

The ideal is to have children on the trusting end of the continuum so that they can risk exploration and learn to tolerate frustration and delay gratification. Such children expect to be safe and comfortable most of the time, and their view of the world is hopeful. Trust is acquired through communication with the caregiver. The interaction between the infant's behavior and the caregiver's response is the basis of affective bonds, security, and the confidence on the part of the infant (Lamb, 1981; Sroufe, 1977). The consistent responsiveness of the caregiver to the child and the type of relationship that develops between them are important factors in determining the degree to which children thrive.

Another outcome of the process of socialization and individuation is the child's self-concept. If adults are available, responsive, and loving, children perceive themselves as endearing, worthy, and lovable. However, if adults are inaccessible, unresponsive, or unloving, infants perceive themselves as disgusting, unworthy, or unlovable. The adult's general pattern of expressing affection and rejection will influence how well a baby's strong need for affection and comfort are met (Tracy and Ainsworth,

1981). Most infants' world views and self-perceptions are a blend of these continua (endearing, disgusting; worthy, unworthy; lovable, unlovable).

From this discussion, it can be seen that no two infants emerge from the early individuation process alike. Differences in temperament, daily relationships with the parents and other caregivers, and the comparative amounts of pleasant or unpleasant experiences they accrue influence the degree of trust, the quality of attachment, and the perception of self they develop.

## Friendliness

Adults may not think of babies as being friendly with one another, but as more infants are experiencing group care, more of them have the opportunity for true peer interaction. It seems that infants acquire social styles and an enduring orientation toward other people from their parents (Lamb and Campos, 1982).

Like other aspects of development, social interaction with age-mates changes rapidly during the first year as the child's cognitive, motor, emotional, and linguistic abilities become increasingly complex (Campos, et al., 1983).

As mentioned earlier, babies show more interest than fear when strange babies approach. Prior experience with other infants helps when strange agemates are encountered. Babies initiate more interactions and more complex interactions with familiar peers (Field and Ignatoff, 1980). They cannot engage in complex play with more than one other child at a time, however.

Toddlers in a group setting use three types of social bids to initiate social interaction with their peers. Distal contact such as watching from more than 3 feet away, or glancing or smiling at another is used infrequently and rarely results in positive social engagement. Proximal nonverbal contact such as touching another child or leaning over to see what another is doing is often more successful, but rejections of such approaches do occur. Proximal contact combined with child verbalizations is about as effective as nonverbal contact for these youngest players in a group setting, although ignoring and rejecting are more common than a positive response (Honig, 1993). Sometimes when toddlers are attracted to an object or a person, they gather rapidly together, tumbling over one another in an effort to get near the person or obtain the object. This group approach has been described as "swarming" and is most frequently an unsuccessful social interaction.

Toys attract children and bring babies together, but they also may draw attention away from the other player (Mueller and Lucas, 1975). Toddlers usually can start a friendly approach, but they have difficulty keeping the interaction going. Those under eight months of age are not really capable of the intentional behavior necessary for more than a cursory friendly gesture (Frye, 1981). Toddlers fifteen to twenty months old are capable of engaging in an activity that involves taking turns, repetition, and imitation along with much smiling and laughing. Going around and around the table is a typical example. Typical early peer behavior is summarized in Table 2–4.

## ▼ COMMUNICATION

Social relationships are based on communication between people. Intimate communication with infants under two months of age is possible between a caring adult and a tiny infant as they gaze into each other's eyes. This shared attentiveness merges gradually into interpersonal engagement in which mutual affect is shared and is marked by social smiling, cooing, and babbling. At around six months of age infant-adult interactions become focused on joint object involvement. The children "request" objects by looking at them, pointing, verbalizing, and otherwise attempting to focus the adult's attention

| ▼ Table 2–4    Peer Relationships in Infancy | |
|---|---|
| **AGE** | **INFANT BEHAVIOR** |
| 0–2 months | Contagious peer crying; intense visual regard between familiar infants |
| 2–6 months | Mutual touching |
| 6–9 months | Smiling; approaching and following |
| 9–12 months | Giving and accepting toys; simple games: "chase," "peek-a-boo" |
| 12–15 months | Vocal exchanges with turn taking; social imitation; conflicts over toys; "swarming" may occur with groups of infants |

on the desired object. When adults talk to children of this age, they frequently do so around some referent object in the near environment: "You are ready for your bottle, aren't you?" At about thirteen months of age symbolic communication emerges, and toddlers and their partners become increasingly routinized and ritualized as they repeat and expand upon their ways to interact (Adamson, 1995). The flow of social interaction between infant and adult depends on regular contact, detailed observations of each of the partners, and the time and commitment for such engagements.

Even with regular, healthy interactions, misunderstandings occur when a message is misinterpreted. The social relationship between an infant and caregiver is no different in this regard. However, the adult participant must bear the burden of interpreting all the meaning from the array of signals that infants produce during the first year. At one time, it was thought that interpreting infant communication "came naturally" or was based on "maternal instinct." We now know that interpreting infant signals can be learned by anyone, and it is based on observation of infants and information about how infants gradually acquire adult communication skills.

## Making Contact

As mentioned earlier, looking toward a sound, gazing into another's face, and visual tracking indicate attentiveness. Other signaling behaviors such as crying, smiling, cooing, and babbling have the effect of drawing the caregiver closer. Following brings the infant closer to the caregiver. Although these signals are not intentional, they are part of the attachment system, which tends to ensure that an adult is present to provide for the basic needs of the infant (Bowlby, 1969).

In addition to communicating the need for proximity, infants effectively communicate emotional content (Sroufe, 1979). The pain cry of the newborn alerts every adult within hearing distance. Contentment is accompanied by silence or by grunting noises.

Newborns respond to human speech, showing a preference for vocalization over instrumental music, and respond to the rhythms of speech with their own body movements (Butterfield and Siperstein, 1972). Thus, infants learn elements of language early in life, although speech occurs much later.

Between three and six months of age, babies expand their array of communication skills. Pleasure

is expressed by smiling, and active laughter indicates delight. They seem to enjoy simple games such as "tug the blanket." Infants cry in rage when disappointed. When angry, the infant's eyes are open and vigilant and the facial expression reflects anger. Adults can easily distinguish rage from distress because the infant's eyes are closed during the distress cry (Izard, 1981). A baby may express wariness, a mild form of fear, by looking away, knitting the brows, and having a sober facial expression.

When control of the head and torso is achieved, infants become better able to signal when they want to engage or disengage in social interaction. They may turn their backs toward someone when they would rather focus on something else. An infant who is playing with a toy may glance at the caregiver and turn away to concentrate on the toy (Stern, 1977). This behavior should not be interpreted as dislike of the caregiver. Instead, it can be explained by the fact that infants cannot concentrate on several things at the same time. The focus is either on the adult or on the object.

## Maintaining Contact

Once contact is made, infants influence whether the communication proceeds by using a variety of options in gaze, head and body orientation, spatial positioning, distance from the adult, and posture. Caregivers can observe these behaviors and interact when the message is clear that the baby is ready for social activity. Forcing interaction when the infant is otherwise involved may lead to anger or fussiness.

Between birth and the end of their first month, infants make sounds such as grunts and moans that are not social in nature. During the second month the social smile and coos and goos emerge along with other vocalizations in response to people and things. At four months the infant may laugh, squeal, yell, or growl in a communicative context. Babbling, which is producing a lot of phonemes (basic component sounds) that occur in all languages, begins to develop. Soon babies drop those sounds not in their native language, and sometime between five and seven months the babbling sounds familiar to their caregivers (Adamson, 1995).

When caregivers reply to the infant's "talk" in a conversational manner, infants tend to increase the amount of their vocalization (Kagan, 1971). Babbling, which is a part of this kind of conversation, is different from the vocalizations heard when infants are alone or when they are in the same room with caregivers but not "talking" to them (Beckwith, 1971; Jones and Moss, 1971).

By the last quarter of the first year of life, infants have developed some alternative ways of handling certain emotions. They might appraise a new situation before responding to it instead of responding immediately. One means of evaluating a situation is called **social referencing.** In this process, the infant observes the caregiver's face and if the expression is neutral or smiling, the infant will respond by exploratory behavior. On the other hand, if the caregiver appears fearful or upset, the infant is likely to behave warily (Clymen, et al., 1986; Klinnert, 1981). As babies get older, they become more adept and more accurate in using their caregiver's nonverbal communications (Walden and Ogan, 1988).

The effective use of social referencing means that infants can observe and interpret some of their caregiver's nonverbal messages and are likely to act on the messages that come from a loving adult. The caregiver's tone of voice, muscular tension, and facial expression convey feelings of affection, anger, fear, and interest, which infants use as a guide to behavior. Even the opportunity to see their caregiver enables older infants to play happily and explore their environment more independently and more comfortably (Sroufe, 1996).

Caregivers also begin to label infants' feelings and act according to these interpretations, although the infants are not yet likely to understand these labels (Lewis and Michalson, 1982). Words and gestures have meaning for infants well before they begin to speak. The outstretched, open arms of a smiling adult, with a simple command, "Come here," usually is understood well before the child talks.

Recognizable speech begins early in the second year. Babies may imitate words such as "Haaaaachooo" and repeat them in a manner similar to repetitive babbling as early as eleven months of age. Words used by the baby are holophrastic: one word is used to communicate an idea. Adults use the context of the situation to interpret the meaning. Much shared experience with a specific baby is necessary to interpret the one-year-old's words. The words may have a unique meaning and may be composed of easily produced sounds, such as "Piti" for "That's interesting" (McNiel, 1970). Words such as "Mama" and "Dada" appear early and also are composed of easily produced sounds.

Beginning word use usually is accompanied by gestures that enhance the expression of the baby's intent, desire, or goal. When the baby says "Meh!" and points to the refrigerator, you can easily determine that hunger is being expressed, but whether the baby wants milk or a whole meal must be interpreted from your knowledge of that child's routine.

Early true words are about objects, actions, and locations (Bloom, Lifter, and Brazelton, 1981), with rapid increases in vocabulary occurring during the remainder of the second year. As babies develop a small vocabulary, they tend to overextend their word use. "Dada" may be applied to all male adults indiscriminately. However, when adults use only the correct names for objects and actions, babies soon learn to correct words (Gruendel, 1977). "Dada" will be applied to one important male adult and "Bompa" to the grandfather. Some sounds are more difficult to produce than others, and the baby will substitute sounds as necessary until skill in articulation is acquired. When adults consistently use precise words for objects or actions, that is, use "walk" or "run" instead of the more general word "go," babies will also use precise words by the end of the second year.

Between eighteen and twenty-four months of age, the infant learns to use both referential speech and expressive speech. **Referential speech** is about concrete objects, actions, and locations. **Expressive speech** is about emotional content, feelings, and social experiences. Less dependent on gestures to convey feelings, the baby uses words that express possession ("Mine"), negation or defiance ("No!"), and goals ("Want down"). Two-word sentences appear with little attention to details, such as "Me cookie."

With the increased competence of the baby to send and receive messages that can be understood by anyone, and the ability to mentally formulate intentions, the baby achieves a milestone in social relationships. By the end of the second year, the infant can function as a social partner and can communicate intentionally to influence the behavior of adults or other children.

## Infants and Toddlers with Special Needs

Up to this point, the discussion and description of infants and toddlers has been based on typically developing youngsters. Unfortunately, not all children are so favored. Some infants are identified at birth as having conditions that will alter the speed or the outcome in their growth and development. Some infants are identified as having high risk of not developing typically. Yet others have not been identified because the challenges they face may not become apparent until later. For example, children experiencing delays in language development generally are not identified until well into the second year or even later. All of the helping professionals who work with infants and their families have a responsibility to refer children for special services or to cooperate with the intervention team in providing optimal conditions for their development. Physicians and child-care workers are most likely to be among the first to identify irregularities in the child's developmental progress because they see children regularly during their first two years.

Early intervention has moderate and positive effects on the developmental progress of many children with disabilities under three years of age and their families (Shonkoff and Hauser-Cram, 1987). These services are free to the family if they meet one of the following criteria (Solomon, 1995, p. 40):

▼ Identifiable condition (e.g., Down syndrome, cerebral palsy)
▼ Physical disability (e.g., blindness)
▼ Developmental delay
▼ Need for early intervention indicated by clinical judgment

In some states infants and toddlers who are at high risk are also eligible for services. High risk is defined by the states but is likely to include infants born to chemically dependent mothers, abused and neglected youngsters, children who have had lead poisoning, and low birth weight infants.

**Professional roles.** Early childhood professionals who also have background in special education are usually involved directly in developing the early intervention plan for infants and their families. Caregivers in programs providing child care or other services to infants and their families are likely to encounter special needs children in the course of their practice. The role of the specialist is to devise and support the intervention plan around the special needs of the child. This plan, which is called the Individualized Family Service Plan (IFSP), is developed with parents, any professionals who can contribute specialized knowledge to implementing the plan, and those people involved in day-to-day work with the baby. However, the role of the general practitioner is to deliver a quality program typical for the age and development of a group of children, taking the intervention plan of the special needs child into ac-

count and cooperating as much as possible with the specialists.

General practitioners also have the significant role of surveillance of all the children in their programs. They must perform skilled observations of children, communicate with parents, and refer children for assessment when necessary. Consulting with the administrators of the program and sharing concerns with the family are necessary prerequisites for making a referral to the appropriate agency in the community. (Local public schools will be able to identify the specific agency in any community.) A referral means that someone with specialized skill will make a detailed assessment of a child. Some youngsters are on the "edge" of normal ranges and may not require specialized interventions, and other children may be missed because caregivers and families continue to think that the problem will correct itself in time.

**Problem recognition.** Caregivers can recognize when referral would be appropriate by identifying some of the cues. Table 2–5 lists guidelines that are based on language development, as it is the most frequent diagnosis for special intervention (Solomon, 1995). Table 2–6 is a listing of signs of emotional distress and/or mental health troubles of infants and toddlers (Honig, 1993). These signs are diffuse, and sometimes children do not get the help they need in this area in a timely manner because adults in their environment do not recognize the signals. When caregivers observe a clustering of characteristics of concern that persist over time and are not helped by high-quality responses, then they should seek assistance, first through supervisors and then with families and other professionals.

Many early child-care professionals do not recognize that the skills they have may be applied to special needs infants and toddlers. Many special needs are mild to moderate, and the children can fit into a program with typically developing peers with minimal alteration of the environment and strategies used to guide children. For example, children with Down syndrome learn more slowly than others. They will need more repetition and will achieve milestones of self-feeding and toilet learning later than their age mates. Often they are brought into a group of children younger than they are as the primary program adjustment. However, their social development will progress in the same direction, but more slowly.

▼ **Table 2–5    Referral Guidelines for Children with Speech Delay**

| | |
|---|---|
| 12 months | Exhibits no differentiated babbling ("bababa") or vocal imitation<br>Exhibits no recognition of familiar names or words ("mama, bye-bye") |
| 18 months | Exhibits no use of single words<br>Is not following simple commands ("Give it to me")<br>Does not wave "bye-bye" or point to familiar objects |
| 24 months | Has single-word vocabulary of less than ten words<br>Does not point to body parts when requested (eyes, nose, mouth, or ear)<br>Does not point to pictures in a book or when they are named |
| 30 months | Uses fewer than 100 words, shows no evidence of two-word combinations, is unintelligible<br>Does not follow simple directions ("Put it on the table," "Pick up the book," "Go get your shoes") |
| 36 months | Uses fewer than 200 words, has no use of telegraphic sentences, has clarity less than half the time |
| 48 months | Uses fewer than 600 words, has no use of simple sentences, has clarity less than 80 percent of the time |

Source: Data from Solomon, R. "Pediatricians and Early Intervention: Everything You Need to Know But Are Too Busy to Ask." *Infants and Young Children* 7, no. 3 (1995): 44.

▼ **Table 2–6    Signs of Emotional Distress in Infants and Toddlers**

| BODY CUES | SOCIAL CUES |
|---|---|
| Dull eyes without sparkle | Lack of fluency in the older toddler who is already verbal |
| Back arching and body stiffening as a regular response, especially in the latter third of the first year | Reverse emotions such as giggling hysterically when frightened |
| Eye gaze avoidance | Impassive or angry when peer becomes hurt or distressed |
| Pushing away rather than relaxed molding onto the adult | Lack of friendliness to loving adult overtures |
| Limp, floppy, listless body when without illness | Echoic verbalizations: Repeats the end of the adult statement or phrases rather than responding to what is said |
| Smiles are rare despite tender adult elicitation, after adjustment to the program | Fearful withdrawal or flinching when caregiver tries to touch or caress |
| Diarrhea or very hard stools, without infection present | Regular avoidance of or indifference to parent at pickup time |
| Difficulties in sinking into deep, refreshing sleep | Anxious "shadowing" of caregiver without letup |
| Regular rocking of body back and forth, even when rested | Continuous biting or hitting of others with no prior aggressive provocation |
| Inconsolable crying for hours | Strong aversion to limit setting and explanations of caregiver over time |
| Scattered attention rather than attention flowing freely between caregiver and baby during intimate exchanges | Little if any interest in peers or persons |

Source: Data from Honig, A. "Toddler Strategies for Social Engagement With Peers." Paper presented at the Biennial National Training Institute of the National Center for Clinical Infant Programs (8th), Washington, D.C., December, 1993.

| ▼ Table 2–6—continued    Signs of Emotional Distress in Infants and Toddlers | |
|---|---|
| **BODY CUES** | **SOCIAL CUES** |
| Head banging against crib persistently | Constant masturbation daily even when not tired or at nap |
| Grimaces of despair | Other children let toddler be strongly aggressive, in deference to the "disabled" status, but then mostly avoid this toddler in play |
| Frozen affect (apathetic look) | |
| Wild, despairing, thrashing tantrums | |
| Banging headlong into furniture or hurting self often, without turning to caregiver for comfort | |

## SKILLS FOR INITIATING POSITIVE SOCIAL RELATIONSHIPS IN INFANCY

You have read about the importance of being a responsive, loving adult in the lives of infants. Feelings of concern, affection, and attraction for infants seem to come naturally to many adults, but the skills to help infants grow and develop must be learned. Many of the skills first presented here will be more fully developed for older children in later chapters. All the skills focus on the quality of sensitivity.

How do people demonstrate sensitivity? Lamb and Easterbrooks (1981) have identified four sequential acts that, when used together, comprise sensitive behavior: perceiving the infant's signal or need; interpreting it correctly; selecting an appropriate response; and implementing it effectively. In addition, sensitive adults provide contingent, appropriate, and consistent responses to infants' needs.

 **Provide Prompt Basic Care**

**1. Respond promptly to infants' bids for aid.** When an infant six months of age or younger cries, pick up the infant quickly and attend to his or her needs. Older infants have an increased ability to wait and will respond to speech and other signs of attention while waiting for care, but their patience is limited. No child under a year of age should wait long

for routine care such as feeding, diapering, or being put to bed for a nap. Infants who cry a great deal, and conversely, infants whose caregivers do not wait for them to cry, do not associate their communication behavior with the caregiver's response. This leads to increased feelings of helplessness (Suomi, 1981). The pattern of prompt response to infant cries enables the infant to learn that adult help is an outcome of their distress signals.

**2. Establish a regular pattern in giving care when responding to infant signals.** Timing is important, so is developing a particular pattern of picking up, talking, soothing, changing diapers, feeding, or holding the infant. Consistent adult behavior allows children to learn through the adult's repetitious acts to expect a particular kind of response to their bids for aid. Although some general consistencies in common procedure among caregivers in the child-care center are highly desirable, infants are able to distinguish among potential caregivers with whom they are familiar and can develop preferences for specific individuals by six months of age.

**3. Confer with parents about the child's routine.** Exact duplication of the parents' caregiving routine is not necessary, but undue stress can be avoided if the caregiver knows

*continued*

## SKILLS FOR INITIATING POSITIVE SOCIAL RELATIONSHIPS IN INFANCY—continued

the child's particular pattern of sleeping, playing, and eating. In addition, caregivers should inquire about the preferred sleeping position and the preferred soothing strategy for infants over four months old. Ask simple, direct questions: "What do you usually do to soothe Terry when he cries?" or "Show me how you usually place Terry on the bed for sleeping."

*4.* **Handle infants gently but firmly, moving them so they can see your face or other interesting sights.** Infants will not "break" and should be held securely, with the head supported during the first weeks until head control is attained. Place them at your shoulder when walking so they can see the environment. Support them in the crook of your arm for feeding so they can gaze into your face. Carry older infants at your side with their backs supported so that when they pull away from your body, they will not fall backward out of your arms. At the end of the first year, some infants may protest at being carried at all. In such a case, if for any reason you must carry the child, hold her or him closely and firmly to your body, wrapping the arms and legs with your arms so the child does not strike you in the process of protesting. When held, an infant should be safe and secure, and should not experience falling, being squeezed too tightly, or other discomfort.

*5.* **Ensure that the infant experiences tactile comfort.**

a. Change wet clothing promptly. Babies who urinate several times before being changed get a painful rash. Some disposable diapers are designed to absorb substantial amounts of fluid before appearing wet; therefore, change diapers when damp.

b. Pat gently when burping the baby; a thump is not required.

c. Use caution when securing diaper pins. Place your hand under the diaper next to the skin to avoid pricking the skin. Place the pin so that it points across the abdomen. The baby then can bend without being jabbed with the closed head of the pin.

d. Wash the baby's skin as needed. Smeared food, feces, and mucus from the nose irritate the skin and should be promptly removed.

e. Caress the infant whenever opportunities arise. Loving touches are pleasurable to them. Back rubs or massage also may be effective in helping infants to relax.

 **Detect Individual Needs**

*1.* **Use all your senses to gain information about the children.** Scan all the infants under your supervision regularly. Look for signs of drowsiness, level of activity, degree of involvement with objects, potential opportunities for social engagement, and possible safety hazards. Listen to their vocalizations as well as their cries. Sometimes you can smell that an infant needs a diaper change or has spit up. Observing in detail is not enough because perception requires that you make some sense of what you see. However, intent observation helps you to become knowledgeable about an individual child and often facilitates understanding and even liking between adults and the children in their care.

*2.* **Write down the time and date of occurrences that seem to be descriptive of the child's development and behavior.** This may be an instance of a milestone such as the first step or of a behavior that concerns you, such as the appearance of apathy in an infant. Noting an infant's eating and elimination patterns are not as useful as noting changes or irregularities in such patterns. Describe specifics of the circumstances and how adults and children acted rather than writing your conclusions about such experiences. Cards that are lined and large enough (4 × 6 or 5 × 8) to record on are useful because they can be filed by the child's name and consulted over time in planning for the child and/or for parent conferences.

*3.* **Read the Individualized Family Service Plan for any child who has identified special needs.** Make note of any recommendations that

## SKILLS FOR INITIATING POSITIVE SOCIAL RELATIONSHIPS IN INFANCY—continued

you can implement in the daily routine of your program, and seek any information that you might need to carry out your part. Most children have a consultant who will work with you, especially in the beginning, so that the needs of a challenged child are being met.

**4. Use your knowledge of development and the infant's typical behavior to interpret behavior.** Your knowledge of all these can help you understand what children's behaviors mean. For example, Juan, four months old, awakened quietly and has been staring blank faced into distant space for the last 10 minutes. Saba, at eight months of age, has tossed all her toys onto the floor and is looking at them with an angry expression, waving her arms and vocalizing loudly. Alexis, ten months old, is rapidly crawling toward the discarded toys. Bridget, only one month old, is sleeping restlessly.

Miss Zimmerman knows that Juan usually takes a long time to become interested in exploration after he wakes up. She promptly removes Saba from the crib, offers a toy, and changes her diapers. Attending to another child, Miss Zimmerman did not know the reason for Saba's displeasure. Bridget's need obviously is to be left alone, and Alexis is clearly attending to his own needs to move in space and to explore objects. Finished with diapering Saba, Miss Zimmerman places her on the floor near Alexis, offers her a plastic bowl and balls, and moves to speak to Juan. This example demonstrates how knowledge of child development in general and of individual children in particular can enable adults to respond with greater sensitivity and skill.

**5. Take into account the temperament and experience of all the children in your care.** Be sure to provide adequate stimulation for the very quiet child as well as the fussy baby. If you are more comfortable with peaceful babies, do not ignore the frequent crying of infants whose responses are less satisfying to you. In working with infants, preferences are almost always inevitable. These feelings are legitimate, but should not alter your standards of professional practice. As a caregiver, you will have to exert self-control and self-discipline. You must distribute your attention among all the infants under your supervision.

**6. Keep pace with the changing needs of children as they mature.** During the first year of life, infants' abilities and interests change rapidly, and a response appropriate to an infant only a short time ago now may be somewhat outdated. Turning the head away when a new food is offered and promptly spitting it out is not unusual for an infant between four and six months of age who is just learning to eat pureed foods. The appropriate response is to continue offering the food if at the beginning of a feeding or discontinue if the child is at the end of a feeding. However, when the infant is only a few months older, head-turning, armwaving interference, and spitting may signal the infant's emerging motor competencies, and offering a curved-handled spoon for the infant's participation in the feeding process might be messier but more appropriate.

**7. Permit older infants to participate in their own care.** Adults can do practically anything faster and easier themselves, and infant participation usually is inefficient and messier. The purpose of participation is to support the infant's emerging concept of the self as an actor: a person who can do something and is not always done unto. For instance, an infant who can sit can participate in diaper changes, altering his or her body and leg position as necessary; one who can sit, reach, grasp, and let go can put at least one object into a storage container; an older infant who has sufficient eye and hand coordination to easily move objects to the mouth and who can sit independently may be ready to hold a bottle and later, a spoon.

Once basic finger control is achieved, undressing is possible. The removal of socks and shoes is common at about twelve months of age with other articles of clothing coming within the motor-skill range of the older toddler. Children need to learn the appropriate time and place to remove clothing, as they are likely to practice this interesting skill indiscriminately. Putting clothing back on usually is more difficult.

*continued*

## SKILLS FOR INITIATING POSITIVE SOCIAL RELATIONSHIPS IN INFANCY—continued

**8. Report new skills and abilities to parents as soon as they are observed.** This is particularly important to parents who are away from the infant all day. Parents may have little time with the infant while he or she is awake and may not have the opportunity to observe the new abilities as soon as the caregiver can. Help them understand each day's achievement.

 **Establish and Maintain Effective Communication**

**1. Respond to infants' signals in a way that is consistent with your interpretation of the meaning and appropriate for the developmental level of the child.** If a young infant is in the quiet alert state, provide something to look at such as your face, a mirror, a mobile toy or a leaf on the tree outside the window. If the same child becomes drowsy after a period of wakefulness, settle him or her for a nap. Immediately respond to a crying infant less than six months old. However, if a child nineteen months old cries in similar circumstances, she or he may be signaling for your attention and wanting to play. The need of the older child for social interaction is also legitimate, but can be delayed for a few minutes while the younger child's needs are attended to. The older child is capable of intentional behavior; the younger one is not. This means that the younger child is crying due to discomfort and the older one to attract attention. Explain your behavior to the older child: "It seems that you want to play, Hanna. I will come as soon as I change Billy's diaper."

The behavioral state the infant is in, the non-verbal cues of facial expression, pointing, and vocalization, and the typical behavior of the child are useful in determining appropriate responses.

**2. Talk to every baby of any age.** Words are never wasted on infants. Maintain a face-to-face position and eye contact while speaking. Use short, simple sentences or phrases. Use a higher pitched voice, emphasizing vowel sounds, and allow time for the infant to respond. To seven-month-old Brandy Marie, her caregiver said,

"Hel-l-o-o-o. Hel-l-o-o, Brandy, h-e-l-l-o little girl." Brandy smiled openly and waved her arms, "so you want to play . . . want to play." Brandy's caregiver continued in a lyrical tone of voice, repeating many phrases to the delight of the infant. To fifteen-month-old Kevin, the caregiver said, "Here's the ball. It's here, by the crib," pointing to the ball when he didn't find it: In a higher pitch she repeated "Look here (pointing). The ball is by the crib." Kevin responded by running unsteadily toward the ball. This language is sometimes called "Motherese" because of its notable differences from speech between adults. Imitate the infant's vocalizations, facial expressions, and gestures in play-like conversations. Once you begin to converse with a baby, she or he will respond with coos, smiles, laughter, babbling, and attentiveness, depending on the baby's age.

Pause for the child to respond in much the same way that you would carry on an adult conversation. Allow older infants enough time to respond to your speech with words or gestures.

**3. Talk during routine care about objects, positions, or actions that concern the infant and are immediately observable.** Use specific vocabulary. The following script is based on an interaction between a three-month-old and his caregiver.

Charlie begins to cry and Ms. Nu approaches. "Charlie, are you hungry? The bottle is warming." (She picks the infant up and walks toward the changing table.) "I'll bet you are wet . . . a diaper, yes . . . " (Charlie has stopped crying and appears to be watching her hands.) "Lay you down . . . now, unfasten this diaper . . . take it off, ooooff, ooooff." (She smiles and looks into Charlie's face as he wiggles his body and moves his arms.) Ms. Nu continues to tell Charlie what she is doing as she completes the diaper change, puts him in an infant seat near the sink, and washes her hands.

**4. Slow down or discontinue the interaction if the infant looks away for a few seconds, lowers the head, or cries.** A child who looks away, lowers the head, or cries may be experiencing overstimulation. Going to sleep or shutting the

**SKILLS FOR INITIATING POSITIVE SOCIAL RELATIONSHIPS IN INFANCY—continued**

eyes is another means for younger infants to terminate an interaction. Older babies may simply crawl or walk away.

**5. Use language to respond to older infants' gestures.** When a toddler points to a cookie, say, "Cookie?" Or, when an older infant bangs the cup after drinking juice, say, "Looks like you're finished." Name actions that the child is doing. For example, when Jeff was bobbing up and down while music was playing, his caregiver smiled and said, "Gee, Jeff, you're dancing!" Simple, short, direct statements are best.

**6. Wait for a physical response to key phrases for babies who don't talk yet.** Before toddlers begin to talk, they understand several words and phrases such as "Bye, bye," "So high," or "All gone." They may, however, take a little time to respond before waving the hand, putting the arms up, or looking into the cup.

**7. Tell infants and toddlers what you are going to do before you do it and wait a second or two before acting. Engage children in participating in their own care whenever possible.** Announce, "I am going to pick you up now" before you do it. Allow the baby time to reach for you. "It looks like your nose is runny. I will wipe it with a Kleenex." Then hold the tissue before the child's face, and then apply it to the nose. For babies seven months and older, "Lift up your legs now so I can put the diaper under you." In each case, provide opportunities for the child to participate as much as possible in the social event. Avoid quick, impersonal actions that treat the baby as an object rather than a social person.

**8. Repeat and expand toddler utterances.** At the end of the first year, infants may begin to say their first words. Simply use their word in a way that seems to make sense: "Mama!" exclaims Diedra.

Her caregiver responds, "Mama's gone to work."

Sometimes a baby's word is not readily recognized by people outside the family; parents must be consulted if the word is used regularly. "Manky" may mean a particular blanket; "Doe" may mean "Look at that." In either case,

respond with words such as "Do you want your blanket?" or "Blanket?" This skill is further developed in Chapter 4.

Encourage Exploration and Learning

**1. Provide play materials and interaction experiences that encourage infants to explore the environment.** Allow young infants to explore your body by touching your hair, skin, or by patting your clothing. Provide toys and materials that are within children's developmental range but that challenge their awakening interest in objects. Demonstrate how toys work, such as how a pull toy chimes when dragged across the floor. Place toys and materials where older infants can reach them. Periodically remove the clutter of toys on the floor and replace two or three so that children can more readily perceive them.

Give babies leisurely opportunities to explore toys as they wish and at their own tempo without intrusiveness. Entice slower developing babies into play with toys by offering them and demonstrating play yourself. Play impromptu interactive games such as peek-a-boo or "where's the toy" with young toddlers or "making faces" with younger infants.

**2. Praise each success.** Rejoice in the infant's accomplishments. Finding a toy that has rolled behind a box is a significant achievement for an eight-month-old. Getting food from the plate onto the spoon and into the mouth is a feat for a one-year-old. The first time to sit, to crawl, or to walk is the result of concentration, effort, and practice for the developing infant. Let children know you are proud of their successes. Laugh with them. Hug them. Talk to them. Let them know how glad you are that they can do something new.

**3. Encourage exploration by being physically available to children during play.** Infants not asleep or engaged in other routine care should be on the floor for play. Stay in close proximity as infants move out into the world of objects. Do not walk away as soon as they are engaged or leave them alone in a strange environment or with strange people without giving them a chance to acclimate themselves to the new situ-

*continued*

**SKILLS FOR INITIATING POSITIVE SOCIAL RELATIONSHIPS IN INFANCY—continued**

ation. Timid infants especially need patient support because to them, the world may appear to be a frightening, dangerous place. Be aware that older infants can "read" your fear, pleasure, anger, or joy from the tone of your voice, your facial expression, and your body tension. This social referencing helps the exploring baby to determine if he or she should cry after a fall or other painful event.

**4. Play with toddlers and organize playtime so that more than one adult at a time is sitting on the floor and interacting with toddlers in group settings.** Nothing is more appealing to a toddler than an adult who is doing something that they can play too. They hurry over to play, all of them, all at once. In their desire to engage they crawl over, squeeze between, step on, fall over, or push down their peers. This is sometimes called "swarming." Often a child is hurt or frightened, so the best prevention is to have more than one adult at a time prepared to sit on the floor to play.

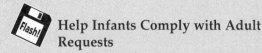 **Help Infants Comply with Adult Requests**

*1.* **Use simple, common verbs to make requests of older infants.** Say things like "Come here," "Look," and "Show me." A baby can understand and comply with these requests sometime between eight and ten months of age. Use a warm tone of voice that is relaxed and in your usual pitch and make requests or suggestions in a conversational volume, and children will be more likely to comply. Harsh voices and physical force are less effective.

*2.* **Show infants what to do.** Demonstrate the action that you wish the infant to perform. At the same time, describe it in words. For example, if you want an infant to place a toy in a storage box, then sit on the floor, pick up a toy, place it in the box, offer another toy to the infant, and, pointing to the box, ask him or her to put it in. Infants learn by imitation. They are likely to do what they see others doing. Do not expect infants to already "know how to behave." They are just beginning to learn social behavior and must experience

many appropriate interactions with adults who patiently demonstrate what is to be done.

**3. Repeat suggestions or requests.** Babies need to hear directions and see demonstrations more than once. Infants generally comply with requests for behaviors that are made with a warm voice by an adult who has taken into account their needs and interests (Honig, 1985). Children under the age of two cannot really stop an action in progress on their own, but a simple repetition of the request with a few moments delay is likely to be effective.

Sometimes older infants respond with "No!" when asked to do something. Wait a moment or so and repeat the request. This assertion of self is not the same as defiance, and many toddlers will happily comply a minute or so later.

Repeat suggestions or requests as often as is necessary for the child to learn what is expected. Try not to be impatient or convey urgency or hurry. All toddlers take many repetitions, and youngsters with special needs take even more.

**4. Distract an infant's attention by offering a substitute action or object.** Getting the child's attention is the first step. This usually is done by offering an alternative object or pointing something out that might be of interest. An exploring infant may readily give up a pair of glasses if offered an appealing toy. Use simple substitution; infants often let go of what they are holding in order to get something else. Verbal demands and pulling objects out of the infants' hands are less effective and lead to angry confrontations that need not occur.

Use *proactive controls* such as engaging the infant's attention, distracting her or him from less appropriate actions or objects, making suggestions about what to do, and showing how to do it. These will avoid power struggles and are likely to achieve compliant behavior.

**5. Physically pick up and move an infant who does not comply with your requests when safety or orderly function is at stake.** Never delay action when safety is involved! Simple, firm, friendly physical removal with appropriate redirection of the child's interest is both appropriate and effective. Quietly voiced explana-

## SKILLS FOR INITIATING POSITIVE SOCIAL RELATIONSHIPS IN INFANCY—continued

tions, such as "It's not safe for you outside all by yourself" or "you can play in the tub of water when it's out, not the toilet," should accompany the removal and be followed by helping the child into another exploratory experience.

**Support the Beginnings of Peer Relationships**

*1.* **Arrange social experiences between infants when they are comfortable and alert.** Place small infants in seats so they can see other children. Provide opportunities for creeping infants to explore objects in the same area. Usually, any social overtures between infants occur when there are only two children in close proximity and when each child is comfortable and unafraid. Even then, infants in the first twelve months of life will not be able to maintain an interaction for very long. Peer play skills are slowly acquired in the second year of life.

*2.* **Provide adequate space and material for older infants to use while playing together.** Toddlers are unable to stop quickly and often have poor balance as they acquire locomotor skills and therefore are likely to inadvertently lurch into other children. They should have enough uncluttered space to avoid getting into one another's way.

Duplicate play materials are useful in minimizing conflict over toys and for increasing social play. Sharing toys is unrealistic before the age of three. Older infants are just beginning to act on their own goals and are unable to comprehend that others also have goals.

Quick action that prevents interpersonal stress between infants supports the eventual development of more positive relationships.

*3.* **Demonstrate simple actions or words that can extend peer play.** One strategy is to "talk for the baby" or explain nonverbal play bids to the other child. "When Cassandra points to the dough, she is letting you know that she wants to play with some here beside you." In another instance Spencer walked into the housekeeping area and picked up a doll, looking at Austin. Their teacher said, "Austin, you are fixing food to eat. I think Spencer's baby might be hungry. Do you think that you could fix something good

for the baby to eat?" Austin brought the high chair to the table and began to prepare food as Spencer placed the doll in the high chair. The teacher observes carefully and expresses the toddler's wishes and intentions in words so the social exchange can get started or be maintained for a few minutes.

**Be Available to Interact with Infants**

Even though you know what to do and how to do it, there inevitably will be times when you are unavailable to respond promptly. You will experience time and energy constraints. Infants whose caregivers usually respond sensitively receive the beneficial effects of developing expectations of adults, acquiring a sense of effectiveness, and associating their own actions with the outcome. Being available is not always the same as being present.

*1.* **Do housekeeping chores when infants are asleep or when another caregiver is available to interact with the children.** Any task that diminishes your attentiveness to the children makes you unavailable.

*2.* **Limit the frequency and duration of adult-to-adult conversations.** People who are unfamiliar with infants sometimes consider them unsocial or uncommunicative and seek to engage other caregivers in conversation to meet their own affiliative needs. Helping professionals must focus their attention on the children and meet their own affiliative needs in other social contexts. Telephone conversations should be limited to short, essential messages and emergencies.

*3.* **Use techniques of efficient body movement to minimize fatigue.** Squat on the floor, bring a child toward your body, and then stand up rather than bending over to pick up a baby. This shifts the stress from the back to the stronger leg muscles. Adjust the mattress level of cribs so that lifting is minimized, ensuring that older infants who can sit or stand are still protected. Lifting tiny infants from a low crib is unnecessarily exhausting. Use a changing table or counter of comfortable

*continued*

## SKILLS FOR INITIATING POSITIVE SOCIAL RELATIONSHIPS IN INFANCY—continued

height for diapering rather than a crib, bed, or low counter. The repeated bending of the upper body necessary for changing several infants at a low height numerous times each day causes excessive fatigue for the caregiver. Select a comfortable rocking chair with arms to use when giving infants bottles and rocking them. The strain on the muscle of the upper arm and shoulder caused by using a chair without arms all day with a group of infants is likely to induce the inappropriate practice of propping bottles in cribs. A better alternative is to stack pillows on the floor to support the arm holding the infant. Caring for one infant is hard physical work; caring for several can create such fatigue and muscular aching that, if appropriate furnishings and efficient movement techniques are not used, the caregiver becomes effectively unavailable at the end of the day.

**4. Send long-distance cues to cruising babies that you are available for a hug, a lap, or general sharing of delight.** Smile at them from across the room. Hold your arms open to be run into outdoors. Clap your hands when you see a new accomplishment. Nod your head when they look up at you when they finish a task. Offer your lap for a rest spot after a quick run. All of these specific actions let the child know that you are there for them. You are present wholly for them.

**5. Limit the number of infants cared for by one adult.** The adult-to-child ratio should be established after taking into account the age distribution of the infants in the group, the skill of the caregivers, the physical setting, and other resources. For all practical purposes, an adult-to-child ratio of 1:3 or 1:4 would be needed to implement the skills previously described. Ratios as high as 1:8 are not recommended (Scarr, 1984).

When an adult is involved with one infant, he or she is essentially unavailable to all the others. The probability of giving adequate, sensitive, supportive nurturance necessary for healthy social and emotional development decreases as the number of infants for each caregiver increases.

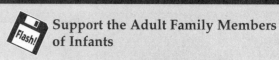 **Support the Adult Family Members of Infants**

**1. Listen to what parents tell you about their infant.** Adults who are caring for an infant full-time since birth know a lot about that particular baby. They will tell you about what the child can do at this point, what other professionals have said regarding the child's development, how well the baby sleeps or eats, and if there is a change in the baby's behavior. This information is very useful to caregivers to provide for the continuity of care and to affirm the parent's role.

**2. Write down pertinent information for other adults who provide care for the child in the program.** If a parent reports that a child has had a poor rest during the night or if stressful family events or other experiences have disrupted the tranquility of the home for the infant, make a note for other staff members who will be providing care when you leave for the day. Many infants and toddlers are in care for 9 or 10 hours. Be sure that private information is communicated only to those who need to know and is not discussed indiscriminately.

**3. Allow parents opportunities to talk about how they feel about leaving their infant or toddler with a caregiver.** Nearly all parents feel some misgivings and many are ambivalent about infant caregiving outside of the home. Mrs. Walinsak brought her seven-month-old son into the center looking a little worried. "I think he is feeling cranky," she commented, as she started to give him to the caregiver. Ms. Biggs took Kelvin and smiled. He reached out for his mother and began to howl. Mrs. Walinsak began to tear up, looking as if she were about to cry. She said, "Good-bye Kelvin" and hurried out the door as Ms. Biggs assured her she would let her know how Kelvin was doing. She went to her car, sat a moment, came back to a window to peek in. Kelvin was still whimpering but no longer crying so gustily. She hesitated, then went to the car and drove off.

Ms. Biggs waited for about 45 minutes before phoning Mrs. Walinsak at work: "I just wanted you to know that Kelvin started playing just af-

**SKILLS FOR INITIATING POSITIVE SOCIAL RELATIONSHIPS IN INFANCY—continued**

ter you left. He's rolling balls right now and laughing."

Mrs. Walinsak sighed, "I really need to work, but it is hard you know."

"Yes, most parents find it hard. You want to stay and go at the same time," replied Ms. Biggs.

"You can say that again!" responded Mrs. Walinsak.

**4. Provide opportunities for parents to talk privately, periodically.** Some centers have regularly scheduled parent conferences. Some offer the parents opportunities to schedule them based on their perceived needs. Generally speaking, major concerns should be addressed by the head teacher at a time when children are not competing for attention. If the major concerns about the child's development are addressed to program support people, they should follow through with arranging for the head teacher and the parent to talk. However, if parents ask if the child had a good day or slept well, any staff member could answer this question.

**5. Ask questions periodically so that parents will have an opportunity to share concerns or inquire about typical behavior.** Simple questions can be asked, such as: "What changes have you seen in Aida recently?"; "What are you finding most difficult about caring for Ian just now?"; "What are Kala's favorite play activities at home?"; or "Do you have anything that you are wondering about in regard to Sandra's development?"

When eliciting parental concerns, take their questions and answers seriously. Never deny their feelings or they will cease to share with you. For example, Mrs. Mir may indicate that Faizan is thirteen months old and has not started walking, but that her sister's daughter is younger and is already cruising the furniture. If you think that Faizan is doing well in motor development, then let the mother know that this is not unusual: "Toddlers start to walk sometime from nine months to about fourteen or fifteen months. Have you noticed that Faizan can pull himself up and stand for a few moments? Babies do that just before they begin to walk around things." Once reassurance is provided, make a note to tell the parent as the child acquires the new skill.

**6. Know resources for information about child development and parenting as well as community resources.** Most adults enter the parenting role with little information about being a parent, raising a child, or performing ordinary tasks like taking a temperature, changing a diaper, or spoon-feeding a baby. They frequently know even less about normal development or how to use this information to guide them in supporting their child's daily life. Various local, state, and government agencies and professional groups provide free or low-cost written materials that are very useful to parents. Sometimes commercial organizations such as insurance companies provide safety information. The child-care sections of local bookstores have many titles, some more useful than others. Increasingly, materials related to health and to concerns of parents are on the internet. Professionals who work with infants and toddlers should be able to refer parents to written materials suitable for their needs as well as provide information about basic development themselves.

Additionally, professionals should know the agencies that serve in the community, their addresses, phone numbers, and the scope of services that they provide so that parents have specific information when they need a referral.

## ▼ PITFALLS TO AVOID

Regardless of whether you are working with infants individually or in groups, informally or in structured activities, there are certain pitfalls you should avoid.

**Heeding the myths that urge the ignoring of infant cries.** Such notions as "Let him cry it out" or "Crying exercises their lungs" or "You'll spoil the baby if you pick her up when she cries" are not true and do not work. The infant continues to cry because crying is the only signal for pain, hunger, or distress that is available. Infants cannot be spoiled in the first six months of life (White, 1975; Santrock, 1996). Providing quick, responsive, sensitive care to infants is likely to produce a compliant, cooperative, competent infant rather than one with unacceptable behavior.

**Attributing intentionality to infants' behavior before age two.**   Infants don't cry to make you run; they cry because of some discomfort. Infants don't get into things to annoy you; they are exploring the environment and are mentally incapable of planning to aggravate an adult. In the second half of the first year, intentional behavior begins when the child notes the effects of his or her behavior on adults. Children stumble on these behaviors through trial and error, so ignoring whining or screeching and suggesting another alternative to get your attention is fine.

**Attributing moral characteristics to infants.** There are infants who are easy to take care of and infants who are very difficult or challenging to care for. These babies are neither "good" nor "bad." Sometimes, adults project their feelings onto a baby. An infant is born with a temperament not of his or her choosing. Colic is a painful condition that makes life as difficult for the infant as for the caregiver. A sunny, happy temperament does not make an infant an "angel," nor does an intestinal complaint make a baby a "perfect devil." The ability to make choices based on a value system is not acquired for several years. *Avoid the trap of "good child–bad child" by focusing on actual infant behavior and emerging competencies.*

**Focusing all your attention only on the attractive, cuddly, or responsive infants.**   Distribute attention to all children and be sure that infants who are slow to warm up or who are not cuddlers get reasonable and appropriate care. The more passive, less demanding infant should not be left alone in the crib for more than 15 minutes after awakening. Give this child the encouragement to explore and to socialize even if she or he appears content to do nothing at all.

**Assuming that nonspeakers cannot communicate.** Communication includes a wide range of verbal and nonverbal behaviors that allow us to send and receive messages. Speech is universally understood, but infants have an array of abilities to both send and receive information long before they develop speech.

**Ignoring cues that development is not progressing well and/or discounting parental concerns.** Nothing is less helpful than the phrase, "He will grow out of that." Infants and toddlers grow out of shoes and clothing with little intervention, but language, cognitive, motor, and social development usually require adjustments in adult behavior to facilitate improvement in problem behavior. Sometimes simple adjustments are not enough and children need more intensive intervention from specialists. No concern of a parent is trivial to the parent, so each concern should be treated respectfully. If concerns are treated as insignificant, parents will stop expressing them.

**Communicating important information or significant concerns about the child's behavior or development casually or in a hurry.**   Sometimes caregivers do not want to see parents become upset, and other times they are so busy with children that they have insufficient time to interact effectively with the parents. However, casual, fast communications that may be difficult or stressful for the parent to handle must be avoided. Think of how a parent would feel if the only thing you said was, "Mitchell had a bad day today. He bit four other children hard enough to leave tooth marks," and then went on to do something else. Instead, ask the parent to stay until you are free for about 15 minutes, try to set up an appointment, or arrange to talk to the parent by phone later. Rapid communications that are *positive*, "K.C. and Carl played in the blocks for a half hour today" or statements that affirm the parent, "The book you sent with Peter was really enjoyed by the other children," are always appropriate.

## ▼ Summary

Infants are born with the sensory systems that equip them to become independent members of society. Having the capacity to communicate their emotions and degree of alertness, they interact with caregivers and the environment from early life. All development is very rapid during the first two years. Some children encounter challenges from the beginning of life and may need the intervention of specialists as well as the cooperation of teachers of typically developing children to support their development.

Skills that will enable you to become a sensitive, responsive adult who can support the child's individuation process were presented so that children in your care may establish a system of maintaining proximity to you, of exploring the environment, of establishing an identity, and of beginning social relationships with adults and other children. Basic skills of communicating with the adult family members can support continuity and understanding between professionals and the home.

Using these skills, you can recognize individual differences among children and quickly perceive their needs, accurately interpret their signals, and select appropriate alternatives for action.

Integrating social interaction into the basic care of infants and using an array of communication skills will help you to nurture the infant's development of basic social relationships. Strategies for managing the environment to ensure true availability of caregivers, combined with strategies for influencing infant compliance, work together in establishing a harmonious relationship between you and the infants in your care as well as with their families.

Now that you understand some of the foundations of building a social relationship during the earliest part of life, you are ready to concentrate on building and maintaining positive relationships with children as they mature. You will begin by examining the role of nonverbal communication in the next chapter.

## ▼ DISCUSSION QUESTIONS

1. Why is it important for helping professionals who are concerned with social development to be able to distinguish the behavioral states of infants?
2. Describe the techniques that are most effective in soothing a crying infant.
3. How do the newborn's sensory capabilities influence the course of social interaction?
4. Describe how children with temperaments differing markedly in rhythmicity and activity might influence the same caregiver. What impact, if any, do you think this would have on the development of the child?
5. How does the way in which basic care is given to an infant influence the course of the child's development?
6. Describe the typical infant behaviors in each phase of the gradual individuation process in infancy.
7. What peer relationships can be expected of infants between nine and twelve months of age? Would you say that they could react to an experience as a group or simply as a collection of individuals? Why?
8. Describe how infants six, nine, twelve, and eighteen months of age are likely to communicate. How are they similar, how different?
9. What behaviors would you expect to see or not see in a twelve-month-old who has an undiagnosed language delay?
10. Steven has toddled over to the window where the poinsettia plant is sitting and is reaching out to grab it. What should you do first? How could this have been prevented?
11. Mary has just taken her first step from the table into the center of the room. Should you do anything? What?
12. Describe what you could do to help parents see you as a source of information.

## ▼ FIELD ASSIGNMENTS

1. Visit a child-care center or a family daycare home and observe how children respond to routine events of the day, such as being brought to the center and left by their parents, being fed, diapered, and put down for a nap. Record the caregiver communication to the child and the infant's responses in these situations.
2. Note at least two instances of infant crying. How did the caregiver respond? What cues were there as to the meaning or message of the cry? Sometimes adults have difficulty in interpreting a cry, and try several responses. If you observed this, note what the baby did in reaction to the adult behaviors on each occasion. What soothing techniques worked for each infant?
3. Describe incidents in which older babies responded to simple directions and gestures from the caregivers. Compare the instances of compliance and noncompliance. What strategies did adults use when the children did not comply? How did this vary with the age of the child?
4. Watch an older infant play with a toy and then play with the baby yourself. Take cues from the infant, imitate the baby, and then elaborate on what the child has previously done. Note what you say and do and how the infant responds to your behavior.
5. Select one toddler to observe intently during the day. Watch how the child approaches other children, under what conditions he or she just observes a peer play, how the toddler responds to the social approaches of other children and adults, and the duration and quality of social engagements with adults and peers. After the session, write three descriptions of the child engaging in some social or communicative event.

# ▼Chapter 3

## Building Positive Relationships Through Nonverbal Communication

## ▼ OBJECTIVES

*On completion of this chapter, you will be able to describe:*

▼ The channels of nonverbal communication.

▼ Cultural differences in nonverbal communication.

▼ The function of nonverbal communication in working with children.

▼ Adult abuses of nonverbal behavior.

▼ The means by which children acquire nonverbal skills.

▼ How nonverbal behaviors communicate messages about relationships between adults and children.

▼ Specific adult skills related to nonverbal behavior.

▼ Pitfalls to avoid in interacting nonverbally with children and parents.

---

*Don't look at me in that tone of voice!*

Shari, age five, clearly understood the message conveyed by her mother, who stood stiffly with feet apart, hands on hips, scowling from the doorway as she viewed a clutter of baking supplies spilled on the counters and shelves where Shari was playing. Like most children, Shari could quickly interpret the meaning of her mother's stance and facial expression.

---

Such nonverbal messages rarely are discussed but usually are understood by people sharing the same culture. Unlike spoken language, in which words are explicitly defined, nonverbal codes are implicit, with the meaning derived from the context of the situation and the flow of the interaction. For this reason, nonverbal messages may be ambiguous or confusing. However, they are a common way for people to convey their feelings.

**Nonverbal communication** is composed of actions rather than words. It includes facial expressions, hand and arm gestures, postures, positions in space, and various movements of the body, legs, and feet. In addition, nonverbal communication includes paralinguistic, or vocal, behaviors such as the frequency range of the voice, its intensity range, speech errors or pauses, speech rate, and speech duration (Mehrabian, 1971).

The meaning of all nonverbal communication is derived from the specific behaviors within a specific context. Thus, the same act in a new context may have a decidedly different communicative intent.

## ▼ FUNCTIONS OF NONVERBAL COMMUNICATION

Some of the functions of implicit behavior have been described by Ekman and Friesen (1969).

Gestures such as a handshake, nodding the head, or waving the hand are used as **emblems.** Such gestures can be directly translated into words but are efficient, meaningful signals by themselves.

Usually, emotional or evaluative content is conveyed nonverbally and is transmitted more accurately in this way than by verbal means. Feelings of pleasure, surprise, happiness, anger, interest, disgust, sadness, and fear are expressed in interactions and may be demonstrated with or without accompanying speech. However, words alone cannot convey the depth of meaning present in a verbal message enriched by nonverbal cues. For example, compare a written note with a telephone conversation, which has both words and intonations, and then with an interpersonal experience, in which words, intonations, and visual information are available simultaneously. The amount of meaning that can be derived from a message increases as the number of nonverbal behavioral cues increases, either complementing the spoken word or reinforcing it. Words alone may be the result of careful thought and may offer more possibilities for concealment or distortion. Maintaining a deception across all nonverbal channels is extremely difficult, however, so true feelings are likely to be revealed in face-to-face interactions.

Nonverbal communication acts as a regulator of social interaction. For example, turn taking in a conversation is indicated by changes in eye contact, voice pitch, and body position. The person speaking may involve the receiver in the communication by signaling a message such as "As you know," with the hands or acknowledging the listener's response with a nod to indicate "I see you understood me." Other gestures such as tapping the forehead are information-seeking gestures: "Now what is that person's name?" (Bavelas, Chovil, Coates, and Roe, 1995). Nonverbal cues may serve a **metacommunication** function, that is, may communicate about the message itself (Leathers, 1976). For example, facial expressions can convey a notion about the way the total message is to be interpreted, such as, "I'm only kidding" or "Now, seriously speaking."

Some nonverbal behaviors also may serve an adaptive need rather than function as a communication signal. For example, a person may scratch the scalp because the skin is dry and it itches, or the gesture may indicate bewilderment or confusion. Some actions related to satisfying body needs would, in other circumstances, indicate an emotional state. Nonetheless, unintended signals may be misinterpreted by the receiver.

Another function of nonverbal communication is the presentation of personality, and sometimes a person's role. This has been referred to as the process of impression formation and management. A person's clothing, posture, tone of voice, facial expressions, gestures, and so forth provide information to others about social position, temperament, disposition, and other characteristics of personality. However, it is difficult to interpret these nonverbal cues without understanding culture, race, and gender expectations (O'Hair and Ropo, 1994).

Nonverbal cues represent the most suitable vehicle for suggestion (Leathers, 1976). Because nonverbal cues are not explicit and can potentially be misinterpreted, they also may be denied. Adults may use these deliberately as they try to "act a part" in a socially uncomfortable situation. Such "acting" requires that the adult perform as though he or she is at ease in the situation. Clothing can be selected to suggest that an individual is a professional, a student, or a potential sexual partner. Older children who have learned to use nonverbal cues as suggestions may adopt an amazing look of innocence when a misdeed has been discovered. The "Who, me?" expression is not usually considered to be a falsehood, as a verbal denial would be.

A clear relationship exists between the level of development of an individual's social skills and his or her successful use and interpretation of nonverbal behavior (Feldman, White, and Lobato, 1982). Children become adept at nonverbal communication by interacting with skillful adults. In addition, children are more likely to learn from people who show them acceptance, genuineness, warmth, and respect and who show sincere interest in them. All of these attitudes are made tangible to children by nonverbal means.

## ▼ Channels of Nonverbal Communication

A **channel** of communication is one of the modes or types of nonverbal communication. For example, the tone of voice itself is one mode, or channel; posture and position in space are others. Each channel of nonverbal communication may function independently and may or may not be congruent with the verbal message sent. Under ordinary circumstances, nonverbal messages are not likely to be under conscious control.

Nonverbal communication is a major medium of communication in everyday life (Richmond and McCroskey, 1995). In interpersonal interactions, people may choose not to speak, but they still send and receive nonverbal cues. These cues influence the flow and outcome of human interactions. For example, a person may "look daggers" at another, "deliberately ignore" someone, or perhaps give the appearance of mental abstraction or boredom. On a more subtle level, the relationships of people interacting in a group can be discerned by observation of nonverbal cues. The leader or speaker usually can be identified by noting the body orientations, head tilt, and arm gestures of all the group members. For example, in a group of children on the other side of the playground, one could pick out the leader by watching the children interact. One child is gesturing; her head is tilted up and she is looking at the others in sequence. The others in the group are looking and nodding in response to her gesturing. There is little doubt as to which child is the center of attention, even though the conversation cannot be heard.

In the following section, selected components of nonverbal behavior will be described as they relate to the helping professional's ability to deliberately send and receive messages while working with children.

## Position in Space

"Personal space," radiating from the center of the body, has specific boundaries. Comfortable distances for interacting with others are from 0 to 1½ feet for personal contact, from 4 to 10 feet for social or consultive contact, and 10 feet or more for public interaction (Hall, 1966).

Another description of personal space places the boundaries in relation to body parts or functions (Machotka and Spiegel, 1982). **Internal space** is the area between the inner core of the body and the skin and is the most intimate and personal of all spaces. Openings to the body, such as the mouth, ears, nostrils, anus, vagina, and urethra, all represent access to internal space. Internal space also is entered when the skin is broken in injury or when a hypodermic needle is inserted. **Proximal space** is the area between the body and its covering of clothing, hair, or ornament. Uncovered body parts, such as the face, are not physically restricted but are psychologically restricted. Casual acquaintances do not touch one another's arms, legs, or face, even though those parts are not covered by clothing. Some uncovered sections of proximal space, such as the hands, are freely accessible to entry unless otherwise protected by countermoves in axial space, such as crossing the arms or turning away. This means that, ordinarily, people do not touch portions of another's body that are clothed and limit touching the skin of others ex-

cept when invited, as in shaking hands or giving a hug. **Axial space** is bounded by the full extension of the arms and legs in all directions. Invitation to enter the axial space is indicated by open arms, in contrast to crossed arms or legs. **Distal space** is located between the axial boundary and the outer limits that the eye or ear can scan. The knowable world, the impersonal world, exists in distal space.

It is important for professionals to understand the implicit rules of interpersonal space for three reasons. First, violation of personal space generates negative feelings (Hall, 1966). These negative feelings may be only mild irritation, such as that experienced in overcrowded church pews or elevators. Adults in these situations carefully refrain from inadvertently touching one another. Children, however, may poke or shove, violating both the axial space and the proximal space of another. Negative feelings increase as successive boundaries of personal space are crossed. Young children defend themselves when they *perceive* that their proximal space has been violated, or they try to avoid the person or situation. For example, when crammed close together in a line, children are likely to push other children who unavoidably touch them, to leave the line, or to call for help because such experiences are interpreted as aggression. Rage and violent protest are common when internal space is entered without permission. Medical personnel can expect to meet with severe protest when patients have not accepted that nurses and doctors have special roles that permit them to invade internal space. People prefer to have only their most intimate companions, the ones they prefer the most, to have any access to internal space. In fact, this is why children want their mothers or preferred caregivers to take care of them when they are sick. Extrusions (feces or vomit) from internal space also are considered to be intimate.

The second reason for understanding the rules of personal space is that a message is considered more remote, impersonal, or inapplicable as the distance between the communicators increases (Machotka and Spiegel, 1982). For example, Phillip, a college student, entered a theater and saw someone across the wide expanse looking in his direction and beckoning. He looked around, noted numerous other people in his general vicinity, and ignored the signal, which he assumed was not meant for him. Similarly, Sally, age seven, was stirring the water in a mud puddle on the playground with the toe of her shoe. She looked up to see the playground attendant shaking her head and shouting "No!" while looking in her direction. Sally was aware that a lot of children were in her vicinity and ignored the signal. However, when the attendant walked up to her and suggested that she use a stick for playing in the water rather than her shoe, Sally willingly complied because she then knew the message was meant for her. The power or potency of a message is greater at lesser distances and more remote and impersonal at greater distances.

The third reason for understanding the concepts of personal space is that the definitions of intimate space, personal space, and general social or public space vary by culture and subculture. Children learn the rules of interpersonal space from their parents, and helping professionals must recognize cultural differences as they interpret children's behaviors. Adults may misinterpret the meaning of a behavior because it is different from their cultural expectations. Although cultural differences exist for all channels of nonverbal communication, variations in the distance factor may be the most apparent. For example, a child who stands very close to an adult, speaks in a slightly louder voice than is usual, orients the body in a face-to-face position, and maintains eye contact longer than expected may be considered by a teacher of European ancestry to be pushy, brassy, or aggressive, when the behavior actually is rather typical for an Arabic male child. Another child, who also stands close to the adult while conversing, but maintains less eye contact than expected and speaks in a softer voice, may inaccurately be considered clingy or dependent. Such behavior reflects simple courtesy in Asian cultures.

## Body Motion

People do not remain stationary. They move through space toward or away from others. An approach into one's axial space may be met by accepting it, either by standing still or by extending the hands or arms. An approach may be reinforced by a mutual approach, with each person moving toward the other. However, an approach may be refused by moving away slightly, by simply avoiding the person approaching, or by closing the axial space by folding the arms.

An unwanted approach into another's axial space may be enforced by grasping the person, who may respond by submitting to the undesired contact, remaining immobile and passive. There is no reciprocity in this passive resistance. The alternative is averting the grasp by throwing it off, shaking it off, or pushing the person away.

When unfamiliar adults make contact, the asserting and accepting movements usually are ritualized, such as a handshake, a salutation, or other for-

mal introduction or greeting. Frequently, adults are much less polite to children, particularly when the children are in a group. Children may experience being shoved into a line by a strange adult or may be patted on the head, pinched on the cheek, or chucked under the chin. Often, children correctly interpret these as hostile invasions of proximal space and attempt to avoid the approach or avert the contact as best they can. Then, the child is sometimes chastised for improper behavior!

A termination of interaction may be met by accepting the separation and moving away simultaneously or by one person moving while the other remains still. On the other hand, a separation may be refused by advancing while the other retreats. When a separation is desired by one person but not another, pushing the person away may be the only choice. To avoid a separation, a person may slow down his or her retreat, turn and stand, or show defiance against the other's intentions by facial expression or posture. Sometimes, forced separations are accepted by a rapid retreat.

Difficulties in separation often are seen as parents leave their very young children with caregivers. This particular situation was discussed in the preceding chapter. Older children frequently experience exclusion from other children. For example, Mike, age six, was listening to older boys talk about their marbles. Mike had some marbles, too; so, when the others decided to play a game, he bent down to join them. They told him that he was too little and didn't know how to play. Mike stood up, in the way of the other players. One of them pushed him slightly. Mike moved a step back. The older boys formed a circle with Mike on the outside. Mike took a step back and watched for a while before going to join other children on the climber. In this case, Mike tried to refuse the separation, then accepted it.

## Body Orientation

The position of the front of the body in relation to the front of the body of another conveys meaningful information. The face-to-face position is the most confronting **body orientation.** This is the position used in greeting, comforting, fighting, and conversing intimately. Avoidance of this position usually indicates evasion or the desire to conceal. When people are facing the backs of others, they are proceeding in turn, following, or chasing. The side-by-side position implies companionship, togetherness, or a united front. The back-to-back position is associated with disengagement that is not simple separation, that is, hostility, or protection in a hostile situation. Rotating the body around is simply a display. Slight turns of the body usually are a transition from one position to another, but may convey no interest or distrust or indicate impending separation (Machotka and Spiegel, 1982).

The relationship between body orientations of people who are interacting also has a vertical dimension. The term *one-upmanship* is descriptive both visually and in meaning. The position of being higher, or on the top, denotes status, authority, or power. The position of being lower denotes incapacity, humility, or servility. In the natural course of things, adults are big and powerful and children are small and weak. Movement to diminish the vertical space between adults and children signals that an important message is about to be conveyed. This leveling can be done by squatting to the child's level or by lifting the child into a face-to-face position with the adult, as is commonly done with babies and very young toddlers. Between adults, leveling may be accomplished by sitting down, as height differentials among adults are usually in the legs. Squatting down may indicate friendliness or a willingness to interact on a cooperative basis (Machotka and Spiegel, 1982).

Body orientation also has other dimensions. Leaning toward another implies interest or regard, and leaning away suggests interpersonal distancing, offense, or no interest. An *inclusion,* in which the axial space of a person is surrounded by another, usually is either an emotionally positive experience, such as an embrace, or a negative one, such as a struggle. Professionals who work with children use inclusion in giving affection or comfort or when they use their bodies to keep children from harming themselves or others. The intersecting of the axial spaces of two persons indicates togetherness or friendship, but this also occurs in fighting. When two children are angry with each other, one child approaching the other within two child-sized arm lengths usually indicates that physical battle is about to begin.

## Gesture

Movements of the hands, arms, and body accompany speech and may be used to illustrate a word, such as moving the hands apart to show how large a fish was; to emphasize a statement, such as bringing the fist down on the table; and to replace speech, such as pointing to where the missing truck went. Gestures may be used as insults such as in raising the middle finger from a clenched fist, or as terms of endearment, such as a caress (Lee and Charlton, 1980). They also convey attitudes of the speaker

about the content and about the listener (Feyereisen and DeLannoy, 1991). Most gestures occur in the axial space of the sender and may be made without speech at all. For example, Steffan slumped his shoulders, lowered his head so his face could not be seen, and inched along, scuffing the toes of his shoes on the sidewalk. Clearly, this child's gestures alone communicated his dejection. Communication problems occur whenever a person's gestures suggest a different meaning than the verbal message (O'Hair and Ropo, 1994).

People in lower social positions gesture more, and more vividly, than people of higher social status in all cultural groups. There are, however, distinct differences between ethnic groups in the amount and expansiveness of the gestures commonly used. The English probably use the fewest and the least expansive gestures, and people from southern Europe use larger gestures and use them more frequently (Lee and Charlton, 1980). Some gestures are widely used and understood, such as the finger click or snap for attention, whereas others such as the fingers in a claw position (contempt in Saudi Arabia) are used only in one country.

## Touch

Situations in which touching occurs may be the most intimate, loving experiences, or the most hostile, angry, or hurtful ones. Situations in which touching is least likely to occur also are the most emotionally neutral. The probability of touch occurring is implied in the discussions of position in space (nearness to one another) and body orientation (face-to-face encounters).

The skin is both a communication sender and receiver (Geldhard, 1960; Brown, 1974). The role of touch in soothing and stimulating infants was discussed in Chapter 2. Other affective messages also can be conveyed. Feelings related to mothering, fear, detachment, anger, and playfulness can be conveyed between adults by touch alone (Smith, 1970). Although little research has been done with children, gentle strokes, cuddling, caresses, and pats of affection are associated with nurturance or mothering. Games of walking fingers up a child's arm or "buzzing the bee to the tummy" illustrate playful touches. Slaps, kicks, pinches, and pokes that hurt are clearly understood by even young children as being hostile.

Two factors influence the quality of tactile communication: the quantity (how much touching takes place) and the region of the body where one is touched (Leathers, 1976). People touch and are touched by friends and family more than by casual acquaintances. People tend to touch peers or younger persons more than those older than themselves (Hall, 1996). Touching is more likely to occur in less formal situations with higher status individuals using more relaxed and affectionate strategies and lower status persons using more formal strategies such as handshaking (Hall, 1996). The accessibility of the body to touch is limited by age, relationship, and gender. Obviously, infants must be changed, fed, and otherwise handled extensively by caregivers of either sex. As children mature, direct touch of the skin between the chest and the knees is taboo. In adulthood, most direct touching of the skin is limited to the hands, arms, neck, and face for parents and same-sexed friends (Jourard, 1966). Mothers, followed by other close relatives, are more likely to touch children than are other people. However, caregivers who have established a relationship with a child also have more freedom to touch or be touched by a child. Touching the clothed body of a child in an appropriate public situation is acceptable for caregivers of either sex. For example, lifting a child so that a climber can be reached, putting an arm around a child who has suffered a mishap, or cleaning a cut are acceptable regardless of the age and sex of child or adult. Men initiate touching with the hand more frequently than women, such as backslapping and handshaking, but the regions of the body that are acceptable to touch are more limited (Richmond and McCroskey, 1995). Women touch both children and other adults more frequently as well as receive more touching from them. The touching behavior of children less than six years is prevalent but decreases steadily through later childhood with marked sex differences emerging gradually until adult patterns are reached in adolescence. The channel of touch may be the primary mode of establishing a sense of identity in the first three years, and physical contact may be necessary for the development of satisfactory interpersonal relationships (Burgoon and Saine, 1978). Therefore, appropriate physical contact with adult caregivers, especially for children under six, should be available to them.

Touch is an important means for establishing personal regard. The concept of "being touched" by a story implies emotional involvement. Being "close" to someone implies being close enough to touch, as well as having strong affectionate bonds.

## Facial Expression

Facial expression is the most obvious component of body language. It also is the component most read-

ily brought under conscious control and therefore may be confusing or used for deception.

Many dimensions of meaning can be communicated by facial expression (Leathers, 1976). The face communicates evaluative *judgments,* the degree of *interest* in the environment, and the *intensity* or degree of involvement in a situation through pleasant and unpleasant expressions. Although the face can clearly convey specific emotions, such as happiness, surprise, fear, anger, sadness, disgust, contempt, and interest, it is very mobile, and combinations of affect also may be displayed (Ekman, Friesen, and Ellsworth, 1972). Children display affect through facial expressions from early infancy onward. Pouting is a well-known expression of displeasure, and sticking out the tongue is a widely known expression of insult in Western cultures. Wrinkling of the nose when smelling an unpleasant odor and the disgust displayed when children taste new or different foods are readily understood. More subtle expressions, such as surprise quickly followed by interest or anger, sometimes are more difficult to detect.

The smile is one of the earliest facial expressions acquired. The simple smile, the broad, open smile, and the grin convey different meanings and use different muscles (Key, 1975). When the smile is broad and lines form at the corners of the eyes, the person is amused or very pleased. A grin frequently is associated with mischief, and may also indicate pleasure with oneself. A simple smile sometimes called a *social smile,* is the gesture of slight pleasure, greeting, and appeasement. It may be used to avert aggression or to indicate submissiveness. The simple smile with an otherwise neutral expression is called a *mask smile* (Key, 1975) because it is used to hide unpleasant or unacceptable feelings. The mask smile often has been described as being "painted on the face" or "plastered on" and has a rather immobile quality.

Some middle-class women have been socialized to perform a traditional role that is warm and compliant, so the smile may be a habit or role defined rather than an indicator of pleasure. The combination of a mask smile or a habitual smile and either very serious or emotionally negative verbal content is particularly offensive to children (Bugental, Love, and Gianetto, 1971; Bugental, et al., 1970). This insincere smile lacks warmth and feeling. Adults who have developed this pattern of behavior in other social contexts will have to alter their typical pattern so that they smile genuinely when giving praise, when amused, or when making a friendly gesture toward a child and do not smile at all when they are very serious or angry.

The cultural meaning of the smile varies. For example, children of western European descent traditionally smile when greeting another person, and Japanese children offer greetings with a sober face. As with other nonverbal communications, cultural variations in the use of the smile are modified as children interact in the context of the larger society (Klineberg, 1935).

Use of the *mask face,* or the face with no expression at all, makes communication with children more difficult. This expression, sometimes called the corporate face or poker face, conceals feelings, as any student who has used it while attending lectures well knows. The nonexpressive face, if used with children, may be interpreted as lack of interest, lack of caring, or phoniness, and may become a serious hindrance to real communication. Unsuccessful attempts at using a mask face result in a display of an expression that represents neither what the sender feels nor what they want people to perceive. Usually this comes across as a blend of emotions and frequently misleads and confuses the receiver (O'Hair and Friedrich, 1992).

Finally, adults must be careful in interpreting children's facial expressions as well as in using their own expressiveness to highlight the message they intend to convey. For example, a young child may smile when a person slips on the ice and falls because the movements of the arms and legs are unusual, not because the child is amused that someone has been hurt.

**Eye contact.** Eye contact between two persons is a special kind of communication that can rapidly move an interaction to a personal or intimate level even though considerable physical space may separate the communicators. The *eye lock,* or prolonged gaze, implies a more intimate holding or communication. The very long gaze between an infant and an adult is normal communication, but a similarly long eye lock between an older child and an adult is a glare and may be interpreted as hostility or aggression (Key, 1975).

The glance also holds meaning between persons who know each other well. A shared moment of eye contact may mean anything from "Have you ever seen anything so ridiculous?" to "Let's go!" Culturally appropriate eye contact denotes interest and the willingness to engage in social contact.

Eye aversion also is used to indicate turn taking in normal conversation. In Western cultures, people tend to look more when listening than when speaking (Kenden, 1967). Speakers glance away briefly at

the end of an utterance, then return the gaze to the other (Kenden, 1976); they expect the listener to be looking at them at this point. This pattern is essentially reversed in African cultures and modified in mixed racial interaction (La France and Mayo, 1976). In mixed racial interaction, black listeners gaze less at the speaker than do white listeners. In fact, black Americans consider eye-to-eye gazing as rude, a put-down, or a confrontation (Scheflen, 1972). The pattern of looking down to show respect also is common to Japanese, Puerto Ricans, and Mexican-Americans (Johnson, 1971). Unfortunately, adults sometimes become very angry when a child violates the rules of establishing rapport through eye contact and may not recognize that the child is behaving correctly within a different set of culturally defined rules. There are normal variations among families as well as regional variations in the same cultural group.

## Paralinguistics

**Nonlexical sounds,** or sounds that are not words, are produced by everyone and can serve all the functions of nonverbal speech. Physiological acts such as coughing, clearing the throat, sneezing, spitting, belching, sucking the teeth, hiccuping, swallowing, choking, yawning, and sighing can be used solely as adaptive mechanisms or to demonstrate affect. For example, the cough, besides clearing the throat, may be used to communicate tension, anxiety, criticism, doubt, surprise, a prompting to pay attention, or recognition of one's own lies while talking (Feldman, Jenkins, and Popoola, 1979). Several familiar sounds are used as emblems, in place of words, such as "Uh uh" (no), "Ah, ah" (warning), "Mmhmm" (yes), "Mmmmmmmm" (good!), "Psst" (look here), and "Ugh!" (how unpleasant!). Intonation is used to denote the end of a sentence, an exclamation, or a question and serves as an indicator in conversational turn taking.

In addition, much of the affective content of a message is conveyed by particular vocal qualities expressed simultaneously with speech. These include rhythmicity, intensity, volume, pitch, and tone (Ostwald, 1963).

The rhythm of speech is composed of differential stress on words, the length of time sounds are held while speaking, and pauses. The stress given to each part of a sentence can determine its meaning. For example, when different words are stressed in the following sentence, the meaning of the pure lexical, or word, content is altered. "*Philip* is sharing the book with Harriet" implies that it is truly Philip, not someone else, who is interacting with Harriet.

However, "Philip is sharing the *book* with Harriet" indicates that the book is the focus of attention.

In the English language, the lengthening of consonants gives a terrifying or dramatic effect. *"Runnnnnnn!"* is a serious, urgent, frightened demand for haste. Adults are likely to lengthen consonant sounds for dramatic appeal when reading stories to children. Variations in the lengths of vowel sounds, though, simply may reflect dialectal patterns.

Hesitations, or pauses in speech, allow the speaker to retain the floor or a speaking turn while gathering the next thought. People may pause for mental deliberation when they have been interrupted or as a reaction to an external disturbance such as a slamming door. Pauses may be filled with verbalizations such as "Er," "Um," or "Ah," nonlexical sounds such as a cough, or nonverbal expressions such as swallowing. Major pauses in children's speech to adults usually occur because the child needs time to organize his or her thoughts. The tempo of a child's speech may be fast or slow, and the total rhythm smooth, jerky, or abrupt. Adults should allow plenty of time for children to complete their thoughts, should refrain from jumping in to finish the sentence for them, and should suppress the urge to take a talking turn prematurely. Such restraint shows respect for the child.

An increase in intensity, the force and volume with which something is said, usually is associated with strong feelings such as excitement, joy, eager anticipation, terror, rage, and coercion. However, how loud is "too loud" in normal speaking usually is situationally and culturally determined. For example, speaking intensely and loudly may be perfectly appropriate in a gym or on the street, but speech of the same volume would be inappropriate in a classroom or movie theater. High-volume speech in situations that call for moderate-to-low volume is considered by adults to be boorish, inappropriate, and annoying.

Whispering or simply mouthing words may be interpreted as attempts at secrecy or intimacy. When a voiced utterance dwindles to a whisper, it may be embarrassment being expressed (Key, 1975). In any case because a whisper lacks pitch and volume, a listener must attend to it more intently than to regular speech to receive the message.

Silence, the absence of sound when sound is expected, also is a powerful communicator. Deliberate silence in response to a question may be an insult or a provocation or may indicate resistance. Silence may also be used selectively in an attempt to be polite, to avoid an imposition on another, or to allow someone else to avoid embarrassment (Sifianou, 1995). Silence

also stresses the utterance following it, making the message stand out as being of extreme importance.

Variations in pitch and tone convey a variety of emotional messages. High-pitched voices are associated with strong emotions such as great excitement or panic. Fluctuations in pitch are characteristic of the angry tone of voice. The pitch and tone of the voice are difficult to control; therefore, subtle interpersonal attitudes and emotions can "leak through" (Bugental, Caporeal, and Shennum, 1980; Zuckerman, et al., 1981). The quality of the voice itself conveys meaning to the listener, often adding emotional content to the message. Voice quality can be described as follows (Key, 1975:61):

| | | |
|---|---|---|
| raspy | heavy | gruff |
| shrill | dull | full |
| resonant | gravelly | reedy |
| squeaky | soft | moaning |
| deep | rough | thin |
| harsh | smooth | breaking |
| guttural | groaning | singing |

In an emergency situation, an adult who is distraught may speak rapidly in a shrill, fluctuating tone. Such speech is not likely to instill confidence in his or her ability to handle the problem. On the other hand, an adult's voice that is within the normal range of speech tone and volume enhances the message that the adult can cope with the circumstances (Mehrabian, 1972).

## ▼ Adult Abuses of Nonverbal Behavior

There are some forms of paralinguistics, body motion, and gesture that are not appropriate for adults who work professionally with children. The use of these behaviors communicates that adults cannot be trusted or that they do not like or care for the child.

### Baby Talk

*Baby talk,* a stylized form of adult speech, does not imitate any developmental stage of infant speech. It is used to establish an intimate relationship, a status relationship, or a nurturant relationship or is used to control behavior. It is produced by puckering the lips, which alters the sounds of the words, and using either a falsetto voice, a high pitch, or an unusually low pitch. Use of the diminutive form of words is common (doggie, dolly, horsie), as are sound substitutions ("twain" instead of train). The plural first-person pronoun is used improperly. For example, a nurse might say:

"How are we today?" or "Did we shower yet?" Other pronouns either are not used or are used improperly: "Is you going bye-bye?" (Are you going outside?); "Let teacher carry Davie" (Let me carry you) (Key, 1975).

Adults often use baby talk when talking to pets, children, persons considered inferior in status, mentally incompetent persons, and sick persons. Professionals should not use baby talk in interacting with children because it is insulting to the child and confuses meaning. For example, the statement "We must put away the toys" can legitimately be interpreted to include the adult speaker. Particularly offensive is the habit of adults to fix diminutives on personal names, such as "Ralphie" instead of Ralph or "Annie" instead of Ann, particularly when the family uses the regular form.

### Yells

Screams, shouts, roars, howls, bellows, squeals, shrieks, or screeches have unique qualities of volume, pitch, and tone that demand attention (Key, 1975). Adults who work with children may hear these frequently in the course of play as children express their exuberance. However, adults should never scream or yell at children. Shouting across a room for children to be quiet, although common, is particularly ineffective and inappropriate. When these unique paralinguistic forms are used by an adult, children surmise that the adult has lost self-control and is potentially dangerous or, at best, ineffectual.

### Hurtful Touching

Adults should never physically injure children. Yanking children by the arms, dragging them by the legs, pulling their hair, twisting their arms or wrists, biting, pinching, kicking, or even chucking them under the chin, or otherwise causing the child bodily pain or injury, are always inappropriate. In many states, such behavior is illegal. Because adults provide guidance and support to children, they should never abuse the authority they have. Sometimes strong adults unintentionally hurt children by grabbing them firmly to restrain them.

## ▼ COMMUNICATING ABOUT THE RELATIONSHIP

People communicate specific messages nonverbally in the course of everyday interaction. In addition, through a combination of various nonverbal channels, people convey impressions about their overall relationships with others. Messages that communicate authority, warmth, and caring, or the relative importance of another person, are mostly nonverbal.

### Time

Many social expectations are based on the shared meaning of time. Helping professionals must be aware of their own concept of time so that they can more easily understand their responses to children's behavior. In addition, they must learn how others, particularly people of different cultural backgrounds, interpret time. Otherwise, misunderstandings about time between adults and children will be inevitable. An adult may interpret that an eight-year-old is late for a Cub Scout meeting because the child arrived several minutes after the scheduled meeting time. However, the child may consider himself "on time" because he arrived before the major activities that were important to him had begun.

Children must learn a complex set of rules for the use of time in American culture. Children from Native American and Hispanic cultures may perceive clock time as less important than subjective time, which may cause additional misunderstanding (Hall, 1981). *Subjective time*, in contrast to clock time, is ambiguous. It is based on an internal feeling of the people using it. Native American adults attending a powwow may know the dancing will be done on a particular weekend, but it may be at any hour during that period.

Many Americans treat time as a material resource: it can be bought, saved, wasted, and segmented. Time is future oriented, but very short. The focus is on the minutes, hours, and days, not on months, seasons, or generations. The control of time is an indicator of status. This means that adults are likely to become angry with children who are slow, who dawdle, or who use what the adult perceives as too much time for a task. On the other hand, adults get angry with children who are impatient and do not wait for them for "just a minute." In American culture, being fast is equated with being intelligent or being efficient. For example, a seven-year-old announced that she had finished her sentences before the others. Her paper had a period on each of the lines but no words on the page. Clearly, she had understood that speed was important, and she had, indeed, put on the finishing touch!

Adults who take the time to listen to a child demonstrate that the child is important and the conversation is interesting. Adults who interrupt children, who are obviously ready to leave the interaction at the first opportunity, or who are excessively distracted by the events around them demonstrate a lack of interest. Attending to children promptly, keeping appointments or commitments, and taking the time to observe the child's work or play communicate to the child that she or he is important. On the other hand, adults must keep in mind that although children understand these cues in others, they are just learning to adopt such actions in their own behavior. As a result, their own use of time to convey respect and interest is not fully developed.

## Warmth

How do children know that you like them? Only a small portion of the message of liking a child is conveyed by words; much more of the message is communicated by vocal characteristics and most by facial expression (Mehrabian, 1972). Warmth is communicated entirely nonverbally (Gazda, Childers, and Walters, 1982). Adults who want to communicate caring and concern are more likely to approach the child and interact close to them. They will maintain frequent but not continuous eye contact and will face the child directly, keeping their head at about the same level as the child's. They may lean or reach toward the child while gesturing or speaking. Smiling and a relaxed facial expression and body also indicate warmth and interest. Speech is at normal pitch, speed, and volume, and the tone is relaxed and melodious. The overall impression is smooth, comfortable, and relaxed.

Coolness, aloofness, or the absence of warmth is communicated by fidgeting, turning away, a mask expression, a sharp tone of voice, or standing up and looking or moving far away. Maximum coldness can be communicated by crossing the arms or legs and either staring or failing to maintain normal conversational eye contact. The overall impression is either tense or carelessly offhand. Unfortunately, adults who are unsure of themselves or who are afraid of doing the wrong thing also may behave in this manner. Children and other adults may misinterpret this behavior as uncaring and uninterested.

## Power

Fortunately, adults have the legitimate power, or authority, to provide for the safety, security, and well-being of the children in their care. Obviously, adults control the resources needed for survival such as food, clothing, shelter, and medicine. Perhaps less obvious is the fact that adults also provide for the order, safety, and feeling of security that children need. Much of this sense of authority is conveyed to children nonverbally. Adults demonstrate their *assertiveness* when they interact in close physical proximity, maintain eye contact, and use a firm, even, confident tone of voice. They may need to grasp a child firmly to prevent an injury to the child or someone else. *Aggressiveness* implies the addition of excessive force or hostile feelings to assertive behavior. *Nonassertiveness* implies lack of control of the situation or unwillingness to act responsibly. Both of these are communicated nonverbally, and even very young children can detect the fluctuating, intense, loud voice of anger and the weak, waivering, hesitant voice of nonassertiveness. As a result, they are likely to respond to these aspects of that adult message rather than to the words that are used.

Young children appear to display status and power through arguments with one another. Dominant children are more successful in getting other children to do what they want them to do, and submissive children tend to avoid arguments in favor of using more polite requests. The strategies that appear to work for the dominant child to gain power include leaning close to the other or invading the play area; standing up while the opponent is sitting and exerting superior strength while pulling or struggling; or offering empty compromises (Meyer, 1992). Such interchanges do not necessarily lead to violence or personal injury and may be necessary for children to learn how to deal with the social system in which individuals have incompatible goals. For example, Rudy entered the block area that he had left 15 minutes previously and asserted, "I didn't say you could move these blocks," as he moved in closely and loomed over the players. David, Devan, and Forrest initially tried to ignore him. Rudy moved forward, scowled, and said, "Put those back, over there . . . Don't you hear me?" as he grasped one of the offending blocks and moved it. Devan protested and told Rudy that he had left and they were building. Rudy responded in a firm, loud voice, "I left and came right back." More softly and casually he continued, "You can do it when I am not here." Since Rudy is rarely absent, this compromise offer is essentially meaningless. The play continued with Rudy directing, asserting, and demanding, and the other three complying. This is essentially a collaborative arrangement between the ones who dominate and the ones who submit, as all the children know that adults would intervene if a vigorous altercation took place. Very young children learn how to exert power over their peers using nonverbal strategies in conjunction with verbal ones.

The normal nonverbal behaviors of adult males also are the nonverbal behaviors of power (Henley, 1977). This may present problems to adults who work with older children, particularly ten- to twelve-year-olds. In adopting the correct "male behavior," boys also adopt assertive behavior. This often is considered a "discipline problem" when their interaction is with adult women. General behaviors considered "tough," "all boy," "smart-alecky," or belligerent usually are of this type and should be distinguished from actual disobedience. Many women are infuriated when their legitimate authority is challenged in this way by a child. The problem is especially difficult because typically feminine nonverbal behavior is submissive. Women need to assert authority when necessary. To do so, they must distinguish between true infractions of expectations, such as direct noncompliance with stated directions or breaking of group rules, and an inappropriate use of assertive behavior. In older boys, this might be throwing the head back and rolling the eyes when asked to comply, or swaggering and grinning at the adult when complying. The boy may comply, but the adult is likely to feel angry. The adult should focus on the actual act or behavior rather than the way it is carried out.

## ▼ THE IMPACT OF MIXED MESSAGES

Unspoken messages are transmitted by one or all channels of nonverbal communication. In addition, it is possible to communicate one message in one channel of communication, such as facial expression, while communicating something quite different in another channel, such as the tone of voice. Neither of these may correspond to the meaning of the actual words spoken, resulting in a **mixed message.** For instance, an adult may smile and say, "Sure, have another helping," at the same time display a rigid posture, a tense voice tone, and a clenched hand, which clearly demonstrate disapproval. Discrepant messages can be detected from what is said as well as being linked to four nonverbal processes: control, arousal, negative affect, and cognitive complexity. The untruthful communicator tends to select words carefully and use grammar differently than when being truthful. In addition, the voice is more controlled while the body is more tense, and unnecessary detail is frequently added. Apparently, it is much easier to be an accurate, honest communicator (Zuckerman, Driver, and Guadagno, 1985).

There is evidence that by nine months of age infants can both interpret discrepant affect and apply its meaning to a social context (Blanck and Rosenthal, 1982). Children of preschool age are sensitive to and wary of messages when the facial expression and tone of voice do not match (Volkmar and Siegel, 1982). When modalities are discrepant, young children tend to trust the tone of voice more than gestures or facial expressions. The qualities of what they hear are more important than what they see when they are young (Blanck and Rosenthal, 1982). Children as young as one year of age are capable of weighing and interpreting discrepant affective messages. Research supports the folk wisdom that little children seem to know who really likes them and who does not.

As children get older, they show greater accuracy in decoding facial expressions. The dominance of depending on what they hear to interpret the meanings of the message gradually gives way to the increasing dominance of facial expression, but without losing their previously developed skills. As they become more skilled, children are able to extract more subtle emotional messages from the nonverbal communications, and their dependence on the words that people use is decreased. They are less easily fooled, more accurate, and more competent in receiving the totality of the communication.

However, children with learning disabilities are substantially less accurate in interpreting emotions in others. Boys particularly may not use facial cues to judge another's feelings, relying instead on motion cues (large gestures and movement through space). Although the trend of greater accuracy is maintained over time, many of these youngsters may be still confused as they enter adolescence (Nabuzoka and Smith, 1995). This can be especially serious; for example, a smiling child who is running fast toward another who is disabled in this way may be seen as an aggressor rather than a potential playmate. Nearly all social interactions will pose potential problems of misinterpretation for children who are playing with their more skilled age-mates.

*Sarcasm* combines negative lexical (word) content and a scathing tone of voice with a pleasant facial expression. Adults perceive this markedly mixed message as funny or a joke. Young children are disturbed by it because the words and tone of voice are both strongly negative, and these are the cues they rely on to interpret the affective meaning of a message. Preadolescents interpret such humor as negative in tone or a bad joke (Blanck and Rosenthal, 1982; Bugental, 1974; Bugental, et al., 1970). Even between parent and child, sarcastic "joking" by the adult is perceived as ridicule by the child (Bugental, Kaswan, and Love, 1970).

## ▼ Children's Acquisition of Nonverbal Communication Skills

Nonverbal communication skills are acquired gradually by children from the adults in their families, schools, and neighborhoods. Content of nonverbal messages as well as style and degree of expressiveness are socialized by families from birth to adulthood (Halberstadt, 1991). This means that by imitation children learn the specifics of the communication strategies of their families and their immediate neighborhoods. It also means that from the earliest years, children pick up the nonverbal behaviors typical of their gender and cultural group. Not surprisingly, Americans vary systematically by racial groups, cultural heritage, gender, and even region of the country (Richmond and McCroskey, 1995). In fact, though adults may speak the same language, the nonverbal patterns may be still closely linked to the country of origin of the family. For example, an individual may use the gestures more typical of Italians for families of Italian descent while speaking American English as a primary language. The same variations are true for Spanish speaking families. For example, though comfortable communicating distances are closer for all Latin nationals than for North Americans of northern European descent, they vary from country to country. Professionals who are aware that systematic differences in nonverbal communication exist should observe carefully the adults close to the child to pick up the typical nonverbal behavioral cues that they use. In this way, they will more quickly understand the total message that the child is communicating.

Children tend to imitate the patterns of behavior of adults with whom they interact. This means that youngsters who interact with skillful, expressive adults also will eventually become skilled in nonverbal communication. Also, children who have a cultural experience at home that differs from that of their mesosystem will modify their behavior when they encounter the larger culture at school or in other community settings. They become nonverbally bilingual. Adults share in the responsibility for learning the meaning of the child's nonverbal environment, particularly for children under six years of age.

Some rules of nonverbal behavior are pointed out by admonition. When adults see a child doing something that "everyone" finds inappropriate, like spitting on the floor, they respond with a strong statement such as "Don't you ever do that again." Formal traditions are learned when a child makes an error and is corrected. Americans have firm rules about nudity and all interactions with internal space. Children simply cannot urinate in public! Rarely are these nonverbal rules formally explained.

A third way children learn nonverbal behavior is through instruction. Adults may give children suggestions on how to "be friendly" or how to stand up for their rights. Family members may also provide scripts and coaching for younger children with cues as to nonverbal congruence: "Say, 'Thank you *very* much'" or "Tell him you are sorry if you *mean* it" (Halberstadt, 1991). Children receive formal instruction in English in schools and in caregiving settings. However, they seldom receive similar instruction for nonverbal behaviors except when they are engaged in theatrical experiences and must assume a role unfamiliar to them. Adults may give formal instruction as to nonverbal communications when children attend a performance ("Sit still. Don't whisper during the play."), when children attend an unfamiliar ceremony such as a wedding or a funeral, or when they are to be polite in an unfamiliar setting, such as eating unfamiliar food in someone's home.

The pattern of the development of nonverbal language is very similar to that of speech. Children become increasingly skillful as they get older. Their messages become more complex and come increasingly under their control. Understanding of discrepant messages becomes easier with age and experience, although children cannot send mixed messages (lies) that are undetectable by an adult until the age of eleven or twelve. Comprehension precedes expression, and children shift from reliance on the verbal channel to the adult pattern of major reliance on facial expression between seven and ten years of age.

Communication of emotional content also is influenced by social learning. Boys are less likely to spontaneously express their feelings as they get older, and girls are less likely to be aggressive or show an achievement orientation (Buck, 1982). Girls also are more likely to be tolerant of mixed messages or "white lies" than are boys (Blanck and Rosenthal, 1982).

## ▼ GUIDING CHILDREN WITH ADULT NONVERBAL BEHAVIOR

When adults use nonverbal communication that repeats, complements, or accents the lexical meaning of their messages to children, they clarify the total meaning of the message. Thus, children are more likely to understand and respond to what is being said. People usually display subtle differences in their styles of nonverbal communication, and an individual may communicate differently in varying circumstances. These differences in communication style also influence the flow of communication with children and affect the probability of them responding appropriately. The following guidelines will help you increase the effectiveness and accuracy of your nonverbal communication.

---

**SKILLS FOR BUILDING POSITIVE RELATIONSHIPS THROUGH NONVERBAL COMMUNICATION**

 **Tune in to Children**

*1.* **Observe the nonverbal behavior of the children in your care.** Observing your typical interactions with a child, those between the child and other children, and those between the child and other adults will help you acquire information about the meaning of various movements and gestures for that particular child. For example, Anne Janette's teacher checked for a fever when the child had been playing quietly by herself at the puzzle table. Ordinarily, Anne Janette was noisy, boisterous, social, and physically active. Her temperature was over 100°F. The teacher was alert to the *change* in the child's typical behavior.

*2.* **Recognize and learn cultural and family variations in children's nonverbal behavior.** With so many variations among cultural groups, only direct observation within an appropriate context will provide enough information to understand the meanings of particular behaviors. Does the child usually look toward the speaker or away from the speaker when listening? Does the quiet wriggling of a three-year-old when listening to a story mean that the child is uncomfortable, is bored, or has to go to the bathroom? Be alert for consistent sequences of behavior in individual children so you can eventually learn what these cues mean. Respect children's nonverbal indications of violations of personal space.

*3.* **Respect children's proximal space.** Pat children on the back; shake their hands; give them congratulatory hugs. Avoid absent-minded fondling or patting children on the head or buttocks. These gestures communicate patronization or disrespect.

*4.* **Use nonverbal signals to gain the attention of a group of children who are engaged in an activity or who are dispersed in space.** Indoors, signals such as playing a chord on a piano, flicking the lights on and off, singing a specific tune, clapping your hands, sitting quietly waiting for children to join you, or other signals are effective in getting the attention of the children. Then, you may signal for silence by putting a finger over your pursed lips or beckoning the children nearer with your hand. Outdoors, signals such as whistling, waving a hand or flag, holding an arm high with flattened palm toward the children, ringing a bell, or blowing a whistle are effective for getting children's attention.

Children cannot be expected to receive and understand spoken messages if they don't know that you are trying to communicate with them. You can tell that they have received a signal if they turn toward you or begin to quiet down. Your spoken message should begin after you have gained their attention. Very young children will need to be taught the meaning of nonverbal signals such as those mentioned in the preceding paragraph, as they are seldom used by families: "When I turn the lights on and off like this (demonstrate), stop what you are doing, stop talking, and look at me. Let's practice it once."

*5.* **Walk up to children with whom you want to communicate and orient yourself in a face-to-face position at their eye level.** Move your body into the axial space of the child to get the

*continued*

## SKILLS FOR BUILDING POSITIVE RELATIONSHIPS THROUGH NONVERBAL COMMUNICATION—continued

child's attention before trying to deliver a message. For example, Paul was concentrating on gluing together a model airplane. The recreation leader, standing about 10 feet away from him, said: "Put newspaper down on the table before gluing. That stuff won't wash off." Paul continued with his task, completely unaware that someone had spoken to him. The message would have been effective if the adult had walked over, stooped down, and looked directly at Paul when speaking to him.

Thus, when children are engaged in activities, move from child to child and speak to them individually. *You will have to squat down to achieve face-to-face communication with small children.* Children should be able to see your face. Verbal messages can otherwise go literally "over their heads"! Facial expressions that reinforce your words help children to understand what you are saying.

**6. Keep all channels of communication consistent when communicating about your feelings.** When expressing your feelings to a child, your words should match your behavior. During the course of working with children, you are likely to experience a variety of feelings such as joy, amusement, annoyance, anger, surprise, puzzlement, and interest. Communications that are consistent across all channels are authentic, genuine, and honest. You can achieve clarity and understanding by using all channels to convey one message. Multiple feelings can be expressed in rapid sequence and still be genuine. When adults try to suppress, mask, or simulate feelings, they are not being authentic, genuine, or honest. If you are angry, you should look and sound angry; if you are happy, your face, body, and voice should reflect your joy.

**7. Touch the child.** The younger the child, the more likely it is that he or she will find physical touching acceptable. Frequently, boys over eight years of age resent being touched. The adult must, of course, respect the child's preference. However, when trust has been established, touching or patting a child in a friendly or congratulatory manner is accept-

able regardless of age. When used appropriately, touch is soothing, comforting, and emotionally healing because it is a tangible link between you and the child. Something as simple as a nurse holding a child's hand while someone else is drawing a blood sample can reduce the child's anxiety.

 **Show Warmth and Caring**

**1. Stand, sit, or squat close to the child, not more than an arm's length away.** Don't allow furniture or materials to act as a barrier between you and the child.

**2. Sit or stand so that your head is at the same level as the child's.** This avoids the appearance of talking down to the child.

**3. Maintain frequent but not continuous eye contact.** This is normal listening behavior and demonstrates your interest in the child.

**4. Face the child so that your shoulders and the child's are parallel.** When your upper body is at an angle to another's you are in an unstable position that usually implies that you are going to move. Therefore, your upper body as well as your face should be in a front-to-front position with the child.

**5. Lean slightly toward the child.** Leaning toward the child communicates interest and also helps you hear what the child is saying. Maintain a relaxed body posture. Slouching or rigidity do not convey interest or concern. Your body should not appear "ready to leave immediately." The arms and legs should be open, not tightly closed or crossed.

Use movements that convey alertness. Nodding the head or using other gestures to indicate your understanding are appropriate. This should not be confused with fidgeting, which usually indicates lack of interest or boredom. Feet should be unobtrusive, not moving about. Mannerisms (hair flicking, lint picking, or table tapping) should be unobtrusive or absent. None

## SKILLS FOR BUILDING POSITIVE RELATIONSHIPS THROUGH NONVERBAL COMMUNICATION—continued

of your movements should compete with the child's words for attention.

**6. Convey a generally positive facial expression in neutral situations.** Smile when greeting the child. Relax and enjoy everyday interactions with the child.

**7. Respond as quickly as possible when spoken to, and take the time to listen.** Taking time to really listen to a child is sometimes very difficult to do. If you don't have time to listen to what a child has to say, let the child know that you are interested and will be able to attend more fully later. Then, be sure to do so. For example, Mr. Wardlich had begun reading a story aloud to the class when Carrie announced that she was going to Florida during spring break. Mr. Wardlich told her that she could tell him about it when the children were working on their penmanship, but that now it was time to read a story.

**8. Try to be understood by the children.** Take the child's abilities into account. Stick to the point and give neither too much nor too little information for the circumstances. Assume that the child is trying to understand what you are trying to convey. For example, the directions given to a child of twenty-four months may include all nonverbal channels, repetition, and demonstration with clear verbalization as you guide the child on how to climb a short ladder to go down the slide. You might say, "Put your hands here" while showing exactly where to put them, then, "Lift your foot up here and move one hand up." All this time the adult would be standing behind the child, perhaps grasping the waist as the climb progresses. "Now sit here and hold the sides. Wait and I will catch you." The adult then moves to the catching position. Avoid chattering between statements. Your presence, closeness, and attempt to truly communicate is sufficient to convey caring. To provide the same level of support to a typical nine-year-old would not convey the same meaning. Instead, the same behavior would likely be interpreted as demeaning by the older child. An adult would stand 3 to 9 feet

from the slide and might remind the children, "Allow the child ahead of you to sit down before you start to climb." Only if the child asked for assistance or the adult perceived a potential danger to the youngsters would a move in close physical proximity be appropriate.

**9. Use voice tones that are normal to soft in loudness and normal to low in pitch, and a voice quality that is relaxed, serious, and concerned.** Your voice should be clear, audible, and free of many filled pauses such as "Ah" or "Um." The speech should be regular and even in tempo, not impatient or excessively slow. Your speech should be fluent when answering simple questions or commenting on a topic rather than staccato or full of hesitations.

 **Demonstrate Authority and Security**

*1.* **Dress appropriately.** Clothing, grooming, hairstyle, and general appearance convey messages, particularly of power and authority. A person responsible for the supervision of children, especially those younger than the children's parents may be ignored. Unfamiliar young children won't approach you for assistance and the 10- to 12-year-old is likely to treat you as a peer if your appearance suggests a peer relationship. Since appropriate dress varies from setting to setting, the easiest guide is to observe the dress of the highest status adults in the group.

*2.* **Maintain a tone of voice that is firm, warm, and confident. The pitch should be even and the volume normal.** Tonal quality should be open (sound is full and melodious) and the speed steady. The desired tonal quality can be achieved by dropping the jaw, relaxing the throat, and projecting through the mouth rather than the nose. Variations in pitch during a sentence or very rapid speech give the impression of uncertainty. A weak, distant, wavering, or very soft voice is nonassertive and may convey the message "I am telling you to do this, but I don't think you will. And if you don't, I won't

*continued*

## SKILLS FOR BUILDING POSITIVE RELATIONSHIPS THROUGH
## NONVERBAL COMMUNICATION—continued

follow through." Adults whose normal voices are very soft or very high may need to add extra depth or intensity to their very important messages in order to be taken seriously.

**3. Look directly at the child when speaking and maintain regular eye contact.** Eye contact may be maintained for longer periods while speaking firmly to a child than is typical of usual conversation, but staring or glaring at a child usually is not necessary. A steady, firm look at a child who is misbehaving sometimes is sufficient to remind the child to redirect the behavior in question. Aversion of eye contact or a pleading look are nonassertive.

Because some adults are shorter than tall eleven- and twelve-year-olds, serious messages will be more effective if both child and adult are seated. Differences in height are usually differences in leg length. When a child towers over an adult, assertive messages are unusually difficult to deliver. Face-to-face interaction is more effective.

**4. Relax, maintain close physical proximity, and maintain arms and legs in either an open or semi-open position.** You are in a naturally authoritative position in regard to small children. It is unnecessary to display aggressiveness, as demonstrated by hands on hips, feet apart, and a tense body, to achieve compliance. However, having a stooped or dejected-looking posture or leaning on something for support certainly is not assertive and children may not comply with requests when they detect a nonassertive stance.

**5. Use your hands to gesture appropriately or if necessary, to grasp the child until the communication is complete.** Little children are quite capable of darting away when they don't want to hear what you have to say. They may also twist about, turn their backs toward you, or put their hands over their ears. The child can be held firmly and steadily without pinching or excessive force until the message is completed.

Gestures that enumerate points, that describe the meanings of the words used, or that indicate

position in space are appropriate. Fidgeting, restless hands, or even "clammy" hands are nonassertive.

 **Apply Nonverbal Communication Skills to Informal Interactions with Parents**

**1. Approach parents with a relaxed body posture and a smile of welcome.** Family members may come to the program for a variety of reasons. If the safety of children is not jeopardized by your doing so, walk up to the parents, greet them, and ask if you can be of assistance. Some beginning professionals may appear to be cold and indifferent when they are feeling a little shy or timid in initial interactions with parents, so remember that the professional role is to help parents feel at ease and comfortable.

**2. Orient your body for a face-to-face interaction in close proximity to the parent.** This is the normal pattern for personal interaction between adults and should be comfortable for both of you. However, if you are observing children at the same time, ask the parent to step further inside the room or position yourself so that you can continue to supervise children, and explain this to the parent.

**3. Maintain eye contact for brief interactions or alternate between child focus and adult focus.** For example, bend down so that you can look at the parent in a car while speaking. Shift your focus from the parent to the child as appropriate to maintain the interaction while assisting children to enter and leave the automobile. In a classroom, you might seat yourself while the parent is seated or stand as necessary to maintain eye contact.

**4. Use voice tones that are normal to soft in loudness and normal to low in pitch, and a voice quality that is relaxed, serious, and concerned.** The nonverbal communication strategies for warmth and respect are the same for

### SKILLS FOR BUILDING POSITIVE RELATIONSHIPS THROUGH NONVERBAL COMMUNICATION—continued

adults and children. Many relaxed, friendly encounters help to establish rapport between adult family members and the staff.

**5. When parents communicate, pay attention to their nonverbal behavior and maintain your nonverbal channels appropriately for their message to you and the message you wish them to receive.** For a worried parent, a look of confidence in the caregiver is reassuring. When someone is distressed or angered, a serious expression and a firm, quiet tone is appropriate; a nervous giggle or laugh would irritate them even more. A smiling face and general tone of friendliness are appropriate when a child tells a funny story but probably would not be appropriate if a parent of the opposite sex told an off-color joke at pickup time. The nonverbal messages that you send parents are much better communicators about your professionalism and your feelings about them than any other mode of communication.

## ▼ PITFALLS TO AVOID

Regardless of whether you are using nonverbal communication techniques with children individually or in groups, informally or in structured activities, there are certain pitfalls you should avoid.

**Giving inconsistent nonverbal messages or nonverbal messages inconsistent with the verbal content.** Don't smile when you are angry, stating a rule, or trying to convey an admonition or your displeasure. Don't use a loving tone of voice while giving an admonition, or use a cold, distant tone while expressing approval or affection. These classic double-bind messages result in confusion or distrust on the part of children.

**Hurting children.** Some nonverbal means of getting attention, such as rapping children on the head with a pencil, yanking them to get into line, or using excessive force to hold them in place so you can talk, are aggressive and inappropriate.

**Using baby talk.** Parents and intimates may use baby talk as a form of affection. Professionals who work with children must establish clearer communication based on respect for the child.

**Interrupting children.** Allow children the chance to speak. Don't complete sentences for them even if you think you know what they mean. Don't try to fill the normal hesitations of a child's speech with your own words. Allowing children time to speak their own thoughts shows respect. Interrupting children and finishing sentences for them is in-

trusive, patronizing, and disrespectful. Let children choose the words to use, and don't hurry them along. This demonstrates good listening skills, providing a positive example for children to follow.

**Shouting, bellowing, shrieking, or screaming at children.** More effective ways have been described for getting the attention of children. In addition, loud or shrill voices can be frightening. Such behavior in adults usually indicates that the adult has lost self-control.

**Calling to children across the room.** In neutral or positive situations, adults usually remember to walk over to children and speak to them directly. However, in emergencies or when danger threatens, this procedure often is forgotten. In such a situation, you may attempt to regulate a child by calling out a warning. Unfortunately, this usually is ineffective because children do not always know the message is directed toward them. In addition, they may startle and thereby get hurt. Take a few seconds and move toward the child to deliver the message.

**Placing your hand over your mouth, on the chin, or otherwise covering your face and mouth.** Your speech may be unclear or misunderstood. Your facial expressions may not be fully visible. Wearing hats such as baseball caps indoors may shadow your face so much that your expressions cannot be readily seen.

**Ignoring parents who are in reasonably close proximity.** When any adult approaches a caregiver, simple courtesy is always appropriate. Ignoring them gives the impression of indifference or of being rude. Adults may or may not be parents, so identifying them appropriately is also a safety issue for the children in your care.

## ▼ SUMMARY

People use nonverbal behaviors to efficiently and subtly communicate their feelings about a relationship as well as about the substance of the verbal message they are sending. Nonverbal messages usually are implicit and often fleeting and therefore can be denied or misinterpreted.

Each of the channels, or modes, of nonverbal communication can work independently of the others and can complement or contradict the lexical message. Messages that are consistent across all channels are more easily understood; in addition, the speaker sends the general message of honesty, genuineness, and integrity. Mixed messages—those that are not consistent across channels—are confusing to children, convey a general sense of deception or disinterest, cause children to distrust the adult, and are less likely to elicit the desired response.

Children learn to interpret nonverbal messages before they learn to deliberately send them. Most of their learning is based on imitation. Therefore, children exposed to effective communicators will themselves become more effective communicators. Infants are able to detect mixed messages, and they rely substantially on the paralinguistic features of the message. As children get older, they become more skillful in understanding and sending nonverbal messages. They also tend to rely more on facial expressions in decoding messages, except when they detect deception.

Adults who understand the meanings of nonverbal messages can deliberately use them to enhance their effectiveness in communication. Skills have been presented that will increase your ability to nonverbally convey warmth and concern as well as authority. Using these skills will help you to communicate clearly and develop positive relationships with children and their families built on respect and concern.

Pitfalls have been identified that should be avoided. These will, in the long run, either prove ineffective or interfere with building positive relationships with children.

Now that you understand some of the most basic components of communication with children, you are ready to explore ways in which these can be combined with verbal communication skills to facilitate the development of positive, growth-enhancing relationships with children and their adult family members.

## ▼ DISCUSSION QUESTIONS

1. Describe the functions of nonverbal communication and how each is used in ordinary interactions.
2. How does nonverbal communication regulate social interaction?
3. Why is it necessary to describe how the different channels of nonverbal communication operate when discussing building relationships with young children?
4. Imagine watching two ten-year-olds in a face-to-face situation in which one is thrusting a stick at the other. What would be your interpretation of this event if the children were 12 feet apart; 3 feet apart; quite close together? Why would you interpret these differently?
5. Answer Question #4 in relation to internal, proximal, axial, and distal space.
6. Why is it important to know something about the cultural heritage of children when interpreting the meaning of their nonverbal behaviors?
7. How do age, relationship, and gender affect nonverbal communication behaviors? Give examples.
8. Why should helping professionals use congruent verbal and nonverbal communications with children and strictly avoid incongruent messages?
9. Nonverbal communication, unlike language arts, is not taught in school. How do children learn about it?
10. How does your use of time in interactions with other people denote your social relationship to them?
11. Which nonverbal behaviors are most likely to convey warmth?
12. Which nonverbal behaviors are most likely to convey assertiveness?
13. How do the nonverbal communications of adults contribute to building positive relationships with children?
14. Describe how nonverbal skills for adults compare to those for children.

## ▼ FIELD ASSIGNMENTS

1. Observe two adults anywhere you can see them, but not hear them. This may be in a mall, grocery store, or restaurant. Watch them and describe what you see. Record what you think the emotional tone or content of the interaction is. Include a description of the setting, position in space of each participant, body motions and orientation, gestures, and facial expressions.

2. Reread the guides to behavior for warmth and caring as well as for demonstrating authority. Try each one out with one or two children in your field placement. Describe what you did and how the children responded. Evaluate how well you were able to use these skills.

# ▼Chapter 4

## Promoting Children's Self-Awareness and Self-Esteem Through Verbal Communication

## ▼ OBJECTIVES

*On completion of this chapter, you will be able to describe:*

▼ Self-awareness.

▼ How children develop a concept of self over time.

▼ What constitutes self-esteem.

▼ The origins of self-esteem.

▼ Characteristics of a negative verbal environment.

▼ Characteristics of a positive verbal environment.

▼ Adult communication strategies associated with a positive verbal environment.

▼ How to apply positive communication strategies to interactions with family members.

▼ Pitfalls to avoid in communicating verbally with children and their families.

If asked to respond to the question, "Who am I?" depending on his or her age, a child might answer:

"I am a boy with red hair."
"I live on Elm Street."
"I like to play baseball."
"I play the clarinet better than my brother."
"I am a perfectionist."

Statements like these describe how children perceive themselves and how they distinguish themselves from those around them. The combination of perceptions a person has about himself or herself is referred to as *self-concept*, that is, the sense of being a distinct individual who possesses a blend of attributes, values, and behaviors that is unique (Shaffer, 1995). A person's notion of self goes beyond the physical entity bounded by her or his skin;

it is a psychological construct in which the concepts of "me" and "not me" are defined (Maccoby, 1980). These distinctions emerge gradually, having rudimentary beginnings in infancy, and continue to evolve throughout adulthood.

## ▼ THE CHILD'S EVOLVING CONCEPT OF SELF

Awareness of self develops through children's interactions with objects and materials. It is linked with children's cognitive development, as well. The experiences youngsters have provide the framework within which knowledge of themselves grows. How they are able to think about and interpret these experiences is determined by their cognitive structures. The information children select and the way they integrate that information become part of their definition of self.

It is widely believed that newborns do not distinguish themselves from the surrounding environment and that psychologically they merge themselves with their caregiver, not knowing where one person begins and the other ends. Hence, it has been said that neonates begin life with no real concept of self (Mahler, Pine, and Bergman, 1975).

Gradually, as the process of individuation takes place, the beginnings of **self-awareness** appear. By about eighteen months of age, children clearly differentiate between themselves and others (Bertenthal and Fischer, 1978; Harter, 1983; Lewis and Brooks-Gunn, 1979). Part of this self-understanding involves recognizing that they have unique attributes that can be named and described with words (Clarke-Stewart, Friedman, and Koch, 1985). Thus, toddlers, realizing they are distinct from other people, are quick to verbalize "Mine" when claiming a favored possession and "Me" when referring to their image in a looking glass or photograph. They also are able to use personal pronouns such as "you," "he," and "she" when referring to others.

The way children view themselves changes over time. Throughout the preschool years, children think of themselves primarily in terms of physical attributes—whether they are boy or girl, their age, what they look like, what they possess, and where they live (Damon and Hart, 1982, 1988; Selman, 1980). Somewhat later, their self-definitions will focus on bodily attributes in comparison with another person (I am taller than she is; I have more computer games than he does).

Five- and six-year-olds extend the idea of the physical self to include activities as part of self-concept (I take gymnastics; I walk to the center) (Keller, Ford, and Meachum, 1978). This seems to indicate that once children have explored the physical boundaries of self, their interests and capabilities become noticeable to them. Although still observable, these attributes are less concrete and more abstract than those identified by younger children. Physical activities continue to be an important aspect of self-concept for several years, although the manner in which children think about them changes over time. Five-year-olds say, "I roller-skate"; nine-year-olds announce "I roller-skate better than my cousin" (Ruble, 1983). Just as with physical attributes, children initially describe what they themselves can do and then later make comparisons with others.

Such differentiations and eventual comparisons are quite logical when one considers that children younger than seven years of age focus much of their attention on organizing their world (Ruble, 1987). Age, gender, and material goods are convenient, observable features for grouping "me" and "not me." In addition, preschoolers concentrate on the here and now, making few references to past or future personal states (Mohr, 1978). Ideas about time, as well as nonobservable psychological traits, such as intelligence and ambition, are more difficult for them to think about because they are less concrete and more abstract. During this period, children do respond to questions about the "self." However, they combine the notions of self and body and treat the two as one and the same (Harter, 1990; Selman, 1980).

By the early elementary school years, children's physical view of the self starts changing. Eight-year-olds begin to show an understanding that the mind and body are not the same. Increasingly with age their answers to the question "Who am I?" now encompass both visible characteristics (I am a boy; I run fast) and psychological traits (I am dependable; I am a liberal person; I am moody) (Montemayer and Eisen, 1977). For the first time, youngsters' concept of the self includes internal states such as feelings, thoughts, beliefs, and knowledge. By the sixth grade, most youngsters no longer rely on the concrete, physical descriptors of the earlier years. Instead, their self-definitions focus almost entirely on those internal states that they consider most characteristic of them (Harter, 1986). This more sophisticated view also is more complex than before because their perceptions are influenced by what they have done in the past as well as by what they might do or be like in the future. Such descriptions often refer to patterns of behavior that have been established over time and that children perceive will continue (I am smart; I am shy; I am a hard worker). Thinking of the self in these terms represents a more abstract orientation, which has become possible through the child's increased experience and more advanced cognitive powers. At this point, youngsters perceive the self to be a purely psychological construct. Hence, they enter adolescence with much greater self-awareness than was possible at earlier points in their lives.

## Self-Esteem

As children gain self-knowledge, they begin to evaluate that knowledge, making positive and negative judgments about their self-worth. Their judgments are made in comparison to some internalized standard or expectation (Harter, 1990). For instance:

| | |
|---|---|
| I am good looking. | I am not very good looking. |
| I am someone people like. | I am not someone people like much. |
| I am smart. | I am not very smart. |
| I can do things well. | I can't do many things well. |
| I am agile. | I am clumsy. |
| I like myself. | I don't like myself. |

This evaluative component of the self is called **self-esteem.** Self-esteem has three broad dimensions: worth, competence, and control (Curry and Johnson, 1990; Marion, 1995). The extent to which people value and like themselves as well as perceive that they are valued by others is a measure of their **worth. Competence** involves the belief that one is able to accomplish tasks and achieve one's goals. **Control** refers to the degree to which individuals feel they can influence outcomes and events in the world. People who judge their competence, worth, and control mostly in positive terms are said to have high self-esteem, and those whose self-evaluations are primarily poor are described as having low self-esteem (Damon and Hart, 1982; Gecas, Colonico, and Thomas, 1974).

**The importance of self-esteem.** Whether people's self-esteem is generally high or low, favorable or unfavorable, has a tremendous impact on their ability to derive joy and satisfaction from life. It affects how they feel about themselves, how they anticipate others will respond to them, and what they think they can accomplish (Rutter, 1987; Hendrick, 1996).

Youngsters whose self-esteem is high feel good about themselves and evaluate their abilities highly (Isberg, et al., 1989). They consider themselves to be competent and likeable. They have a sense of control, believing that their own actions usually determine their fate. Thus they expect to do well and are able to prevail in challenging circumstances (Hrncir, 1985). In social interactions, they anticipate that their encounters with others will be rewarding and that they will have a positive influence on the outcome of the exchange (Coopersmith, 1967). These optimistic feelings make it easier for them both to give and to receive love (Fromm, 1956). Such children also have confidence in their own judgments. As a result, they are able to express and defend ideas they believe in, even when faced with opposition from others. When confronted with obstacles, they draw on positive feelings from the past to help them get through difficult times. In addition, they

tend to appraise their abilities and limitations realistically and can separate weaknesses in one area from successes in others (Rosenberg, 1979). For these reasons, high self-esteem is related to positive life satisfaction and happiness.

Low self-esteem, on the other hand, is often associated with depression, anxiety, and maladjustment (Damon, 1983; Harter and Marold, 1992). Children whose estimations of self-worth are entirely negative experience feelings of inadequacy and incompetence and fear rejection (Openshaw, 1978). They also are less likely to be objective about their capabilities. Theirs is not a balanced view but one that focuses primarily on failings. Such youngsters have little hope of influencing others and anticipate that most interactions will be costly for them. They see that what happens to them is governed largely by factors beyond their control and are convinced that no matter how hard they try, their efforts will mostly go unrewarded unless they're lucky. Consequently, children may hesitate to express their opinions, often lack independence, and tend to feel isolated or alone (Coopersmith, 1967). Their gloomy outlook often leads them to build elaborate defenses as a way to protect their fragile egos or to ward off expected rejection (Dreikurs, 1991). Typical means of self-protection include putting themselves down, keeping people at a distance, or building themselves up by tearing others down (Kaplan and Pokorny, 1969). Thus, having low self-esteem takes away from one's quality of life.

Although most of the research to date has treated self-esteem as a totally "either/or" concept, in reality almost everybody falls somewhere between the two extremes (Curry and Johnson, 1990). In addition, there are times in each person's life when he or she experiences temporary feelings of high or low self-esteem depending on the circumstance. These variations are in keeping with the dynamic nature of human development. Therefore, it may be most accurate to think of high self-esteem as involving predominantly positive self-judgments across many life areas, with some negative self-evaluations mixed in. Low self-esteem represents the opposite combination of personal perceptions.

**Influences on self-esteem.** Children continually gather information about their value as persons through interactions with the significant people in their lives—family members, helping professionals, and other children (Coopersmith, 1967; Shaffer, 1995). Through the accepting and rejecting behavior of these important people, children receive answers to the questions "Who am I?" "What kind of person am I?" "How valued am I?" (Vander Zanden, 1989).

All these people serve as mirrors through which children see themselves and then judge what they see (Maccoby, 1980). If what is reflected is good, children make a positive evaluation of self. If the image is negative, children deduce that they have little worth. Children are sensitive to the attitudes people have toward them and often adopt those opinions as their own (Openshaw, 1978; Moore, 1986). From the time they are born, all of children's experiences are important in influencing their assessment of themselves. These experiences add up as children mature and, thus, have a cumulative impact on self-esteem.

This explains why two children who seem very similar to an outsider may, in fact, differ considerably in their self-judgments. Take the case of Renato and Manuel. Both are nine-year-old boys in the same class at Marble School and have similar socioeconomic and cultural backgrounds. In a recent teacher-led discussion, time ran out before either boy was called on to express his ideas. Both were disappointed. Renato reasoned that the teacher might not have seen his hand waving in the air; Manuel assumed that the teacher deliberately ignored him because nothing he had to say would have been important anyway. Initially, one might wonder why the boys' reactions were so different. An analysis of their past experience would yield some clues.

The majority of Renato's interactions with his parents and teachers tend to be positive. They listen to what he has to say and often point out the merit of his observations. The message he receives is that he is a competent, valued person. Manuel's experiences tend to be more negative; frequently, he is cut off before he has finished speaking or told to be quiet. On numerous occasions, adults have dismissed his ideas as silly. His self-esteem mirrors the poor opinion others have of him. Based on what he has learned to expect, each child perceived the situation in a way that fit what he had already come to believe about himself. This incident also was added to their store of self-knowledge and will be used to interpret future social encounters.

The differences between Renato and Manuel are, in part, due to their interactions with adults who may approach their relationships with children quite differently. However, because people are contributors to their own microsystems, the boys also influence the milieu that is created. Thus, Renato may promote the favorable reaction he receives by thinking before he speaks, by waiting for others to make their point, and by acknowledging the value of other

people's opinions. Some of Manuel's negative interactions may result from his impulsive outbursts, which frequently have little relation to the topic; his constant interruptions; and his refusal to consider that others may have valuable ideas to share.

From this example, it can be seen that self-esteem is a product of one's social interactions. Both others and the person involved contribute to the picture that is projected to others and perceived by oneself. Moreover, the way children think and feel about themselves is important: Positive, accurate self-perceptions provide the confidence, energy, and optimism children need to master life's tasks. Feelings of high self-esteem are promoted by positive self-experiences (Curry and Johnson, 1990; Kontos and Wilcox-Herzog, 1997).

**The evolution of self-esteem.** Just as the development of self-concept follows a normative sequence, so does self-esteem. Toddlers and young preschoolers tend to make assessments of their self-worth that are all-encompassing (Harter, 1983). That is, they make no distinctions among the various aspects of the self (e.g., the cognitive self versus the physical self). Instead, they think of themselves as either competent or incompetent across all areas. Because their self-concept is rooted in the here and now, these assessments change as circumstances change. For instance, three-year-old Jessica, who has mastered opening and closing the screen door entirely on her own, may feel quite pleased with her new found prowess. She announces, "I can do anything." Yet moments later, she may be plunged into tears when her older brother says she's too little to join him in a game in the backyard. Her self-evaluation at that point may be "I can't do anything."

Older preschoolers and school-age children begin to compartmentalize their notions of self-worth. They make different evaluations of the self in different categories—social, physical, and intellectual (Harter, 1990). By age eight, most youngsters make essential distinctions about their abilities in each realm. From then on, self-esteem represents a multifaceted combination of perceptions (Curry and Johnson, 1990). Hence a child may have positive feelings about himself or herself in relation to physical activities, such as sports, while simultaneously feeling inadequate academically. However, simply recognizing perceived inadequacies in a particular realm does not automatically result in low self-esteem (Damon, 1991). The relative significance of a particular category to an individual child also factors into his or her self-judgment. Consequently, a child may truly conclude, "I'm not good at fixing things and that's okay."

As children garner a backlog of experiences their self-perceptions become more enduring. Rather than shifting dramatically from situation to situation, children begin to identify patterns related to their social, physical, and intellectual abilities and make self-judgments with that in mind. This is demonstrated when a child concludes, "I'm good at spelling. I have a hard time making friends." Such perceptions also serve as the basis for projecting a future/possible self as when the child states, "Probably they won't like me. I never have been good at making friends," or "I'm good at math. If I keep practicing, I should be able to do these problems" (Markus and Nurius, 1984). There is some evidence that such patterns of thinking tend to last and that they become difficult to change (Bee, 1996). For instance, a child who has high self-esteem at age ten is likely to have high self-esteem as a teenager and even as an adult. Likewise, low self-esteem in middle childhood is often predictive of negative self-judgments as a person matures. Having said this, it must also be noted that the evolution of self-esteem never really ends (Curry and Johnson, 1990). People's self-perceptions continue to be influenced by their interactions with one another and the environment throughout their lifetimes.

## ▼ HOW ADULT PRACTICES RELATE TO SELF-ESTEEM

Many adults believe self-esteem is something they grant to children by telling them they're wonderful (Hendrick, 1998). Others hope children will acquire high self-esteem by participating in "feel good" activities during time slots set aside in the day. This latter, direct instruction technique has been increasingly tied to the use of commercially prepared self-esteem programs in which children and helping professionals make their way through a prescribed set of experiences or a workbook (Beane, 1991). Neither of these approaches take into account the holistic, complex nature of child development. Instead, self-esteem is isolated from all other developmental domains and treated as something children acquire in doses rather than develop continuously over time.

Fifteen-minute activities or the adult's gushing remarks will not give children a sense of well-being or prevent negative self-perceptions. Because esteem-influencing experiences are vital parts of children's lives, authentic esteem-enhancing efforts must be ever present too. Some child advocates suggest that this means reshaping the total environment in which children live. At the macrosystem level, that would require changing conditions in the larger society that detract from children's self-esteem: poverty, sexism, racism, agism, violence, and so forth (Beane, 1991). At the microsystem level of the center or school, one would expect helping professionals to create a program atmosphere in which children's internal sense of self-confidence and worth are promoted throughout the day and in a variety of ways.

In such an environment we would observe children making, creating, and doing things; planning; making decisions; and carrying out projects. Self-discovery would be encouraged and children would learn new strategies to expand their abilities and opportunities. In addition, the nature of the adult's day-to-day interactions with children would be such that each child would receive the message that he or she was a valuable, competent human being. This latter condition is particularly important because, as was noted earlier, adults serve as mirrors through which children make assessments regarding their worth, competence, and control. The reflections children perceive are manifested through adults' behavior toward them. Certain adult actions are known to promote positive self-judgments in children, whereas others clearly contribute to negative ones. These key adult behaviors can be grouped into two major categories: guidance and nurturance. *Guidance* involves the discipline and instruction approaches adults use; *nurturance* refers to the types of relationships they establish with children.

**Guidance.** Generally, it can be said that adults who help children learn the skills they need to achieve personal goals contribute to the development of positive self-esteem in children. These are adults who have high standards for children's behavior, who consistently enforce reasonable rules, and who encourage children to participate in developing some of those rules. Adults who do little to increase children's sense of competence, who are harsh, who employ unreasonable rules, or who enforce no rules at all contribute to children's negative self-judgments (Coopersmith, 1967; Curry and Johnson, 1990). Exactly why this is so and what it means to helping professionals is fully explained in Chapters 10 through 15. For now we will focus on nurturance.

**Nurturance.** Adults who demonstrate warmth, respect, acceptance, authenticity, and empathy are most likely to foster positive self-judgments in children (Gecas, Colonico, and Thomas, 1974; Marion

1995). You will remember that these are the very qualities that mark the facilitative dimension of the helping relationship and that have been identified as the primary components of positive adult-child relationships. Adults exhibit these qualities when they show affection to youngsters, when they take an interest in what children are doing, and when they become actively involved with them (Cooper-smith, 1967; Kontos and Wilcox-Herzog, 1997).

On the other hand, children whose contacts are primarily with rejecting, uninterested, insensitive adults find it hard to feel good about themselves (Coopersmith, 1967; Curry and Johnson, 1990). Adults manifest these attitudes when they ignore children or when they are aloof, impatient, discourteous, or nasty toward them. If adults act in these ways, youngsters often conclude that because the authority figure finds them unworthy and incompetent, it must be so. This is exemplified in the extreme by abused children who perceive that their failings justify the treatment they receive from their parents.

**Relating nurturance to adult talk.** Whether adults convey esteem-enhancing or esteem-damaging attitudes frequently is determined by what they say to children and how they say it. In fact, adult verbalizations are a major contributor to the perceptions children form about themselves (Marion, 1995). Consider the following scenario.

**SITUATION:** You are invited to visit a program for children. When you arrive, you are asked to wait until the youngsters return from a field trip. As you survey your surroundings, you notice brightly colored furniture comfortably arranged, sunlight softly streaming through the windows, children's artwork pleasingly displayed, attractive materials that look well cared for, green plants placed about the room, and a large, well-stocked aquarium bubbling in a corner. You think to yourself, "What a pleasant place for children!"

Just then, a child bursts into the room crying. She is followed by an adult who snaps: "Rose, you're being a big baby. Now, hush." As the other youngsters file in, you hear another child say, "Look what I found outside!" An adult replies: "Can't you see I'm busy? Show it to me later." After a while, you overhear a child ask, "When do we get to take these home?" He is told, "If you'd been listening earlier, you'd know."

Your favorable impression is shattered. Despite the lovely surroundings, the ways in which adults are talking to children has made the setting unpleasant. Adult comments have caused you to question whether it is possible for children to feel good about themselves in this program and whether the adult-child relationships can be anything but distant and unfavorable. What you have overheard has made you privy to an invisible but keenly felt component of every program—the verbal environment.

## ▼ THE VERBAL ENVIRONMENT

The **verbal environment** encompasses all of the verbal exchanges that take place within a given setting. Its elements include words and silence—how much is said, what is said, how it is stated, who talks, and who listens. The manner in which these elements are used and combined dictates whether the environment is one in which children's self-evaluations are favorable or unfavorable. Thus, verbal environments can be characterized as being either positive or negative.

### The Negative Verbal Environment

Negative verbal environments are ones in which children feel unworthy, unloveable, insignificant or incompetent as a result of what adults do or do not say to them. You could readily identify the most extreme illustrations of these. Adults screaming at children, ridiculing them, cursing at them, or subjecting them to ethnic slurs are blatant examples. Yet there are less obvious, more common adult behaviors that also contribute to negative verbal environments, and hence detract from children's self-esteem. These are summarized as follows:

1. Adults show little or no interest in children's activities because they are in a hurry, busy, engrossed in their own thoughts and endeavors, or tired. Whatever the reason, they walk by children without comment and fail to acknowledge their presence. When standing near children, they do not talk with them and respond only grudgingly to children's attempts to initiate an interaction. In addition, grown-ups misuse time designated for interaction with children by talking more with each other than with the children. Children interpret these behaviors as signs of a lack of interest.

2. Adults pay superficial attention to what children have to say. Instead of listening attentively, they are absorbed in other thoughts. They communicate their preoccupation by asking irrelevant questions, responding inappropriately, failing to maintain eye contact, or cutting the child off in order to follow through on whatever was on their mind.

3. Adults are discourteous when speaking with children. They interrupt the child who is speaking to them as well as youngsters who are talking to each other. They expect children to respond to their requests immediately and do not allow them to finish what they are doing or saying. Their voice tone may be demanding, impatient, or belligerent, and they neglect such social niceties as saying, "Excuse me," "Please," and "Thank you."

4. Adults use sarcasm in talking with children. The negative impression conveyed has as much to do with the adult's voice tone as with the actual words they use. Their remarks often make children the butt of a group joke or otherwise establish the adult's superiority ("Hey everybody, listen to this! Erica thinks she's so smart she doesn't need to read page twelve. She already knows the answers").

5. Adults use judgmental vocabulary in describing children to themselves and to others. They may label the child as "hyper," "selfish," "greedy," "a motormouth," "grabby," or "klutsy." Typical demeaning remarks include "He's such a brat"; "She's so spoiled"; "You're always acting like a baby"; "She'll never learn"; "Well, Edgar, here, is not too bright. He tries hard, but he just doesn't get it." These comments sometimes are said directly to the child and sometimes to another person within the child's hearing. In either case, youngsters are treated as though they have no feelings or as if they were invisible.

6. Adults discourage children from expressing themselves. When children approach them with something to talk about, they say: "Hush," "Not now," or "Tell me about it later." The "later" often never comes.

7. Adults ignore children's interests in order to pursue their own. They do this in either of two ways. One is to come right out and tell children that what they are doing or saying is uninteresting or unimportant and that they should be doing or talking about something else instead. Thus, youngsters hear admonishments like: "I'm sick of hearing about your troubles with Rorey; find something else to talk about," or "You've had plenty of time to examine that butterfly; now come over here and help me pass out the books." Another tactic is for adults to pretend they did not hear what a child asked or said, pursuing their own agenda instead.

8. Adults talk to children primarily to give directions ("Sit in your chair," "Turn to page five,"

"Do your spelling first, and then begin the math assignment"), state rules ("No fighting," "Everybody get your coats off and settle down for lunch," "Only one person in the bathroom at a time"), and change behavior. This is the epitome of one-way communication—adults talking, children listening. Very few interactions are conversations.

9. Adults ask questions for which no real answer is expected or desired and are sarcastic. Typical queries might include: "What do you think you're doing?" "Didn't I tell you not to get your feet wet?" "Did you leave your brain at home today?" Regardless of how children respond, their answers are viewed as disrespectful or unwelcome. Children soon learn that these remarks are not real invitations to relate to the adult.

10. Adults use children's names as synonyms for the words "no," "stop," or "don't." They bark out "Keith" or "Andrea" as a reprimand, causing children to associate the most personal part of themselves, their name, with disapproval or rejection. When using this tactic, adults seldom take the time to describe the child's objectionable behavior or to clarify the reason for their angry voice tone. This leaves children with the impression that something is basically wrong with them and that they are unworthy, insignificant persons.

11. Adults belittle children's efforts and accomplishments. Their words focus on what children can't do, not on the strengths they display. These negative messages take two forms. The first is to deny children opportunities to increase their skills by constantly telling them they are "too little," "too young," "too unskilled," or "too dumb" to attempt a given task. Adults neglect to find ways to make tasks more manageable for children or to substitute similar but more suitable goals for children to pursue. The second way adults detract from children's positive self-judgments is to insist on perfection. Children's approximations of desired behaviors are ignored as are their attempts to succeed. Adults make fun of children for not doing things right or they scold children for not meeting their standards.

12. Adult praise is insincere or destructive. It is often used to manipulate children into doing what adults want. For instance, "You're so good at sitting. Can't you sit just a little while longer?" Complimentary remarks are always the same, "Good job" or "Nice," with no differentiation from child to child or situation to situation. Such

phrases are usually stated in an offhand or overly sweet tone. Sometimes, adults link positive statements to ones that also contain some sort of put down: "I'm glad you finally decided to behave" or "I'm pleased you remembered what comes next. With all that talking you were doing I thought you missed it." On other occasions, praise serves to build up one child at the expense of another. "Look at Jena. She's the best cleaner-upper in the room. Why can't the rest of you work as hard as she does?"

All of the preceding verbal behaviors convey to children adult attitudes of aloofness, disrespect, lack of acceptance, and insensitivity. They cause the program setting to be dominated by adult talk and make it clear to youngsters that adult agendas take precedence over their own. In addition, children quickly learn that their ideas, thoughts, and concerns are not valued, nor are the children important enough as persons to be afforded the courtesy and respect one would anticipate if held in high regard. The aversive encounters that occur in a negative verbal environment tend to make children feel inadequate, confused, or angry (Hoffman, 1963; Kontos and Wilcox-Herzog, 1997). If interactions such as these become the norm, then children's self-esteem is likely to suffer. A different set of circumstances exists in programs characterized by a positive verbal environment.

## The Positive Verbal Environment

In a positive verbal environment, children experience socially rewarding interactions with the adults present. Adult verbalizations are aimed at satisfying children's needs and making the children feel valued. At all times, when speaking to children, adults concern themselves not only with the informational content of their words, but with the affective impact their speech will have as well. Adults create a positive verbal environment by following these principles in their verbal exchanges with children:

1. Adults become actively engaged with children. They postpone nonessential housekeeping tasks and personal socializing to times when children are not present. Once the children arrive each day, the adults are fully available to interact with them.

2. Adults use words to show children they are interested in them and are aware of their activities ("You've been working hard on that dinosaur puzzle"; "You look like you're enjoying the 'Brain Teaser'"). The adults laugh with children,

graciously respond to their inquiries, and tell children they enjoy being with them. When children invite adults to participate with them, the adults accept the invitation enthusiastically ("That sounds like fun"; "Oh, good; now I'll have a chance to work with you").

3. Adults actively listen to what children have to say and concentrate on their words. They respond to children in an accepting and sensitive manner, not by refuting, criticizing, or brushing aside children's remarks.

4. Adults speak courteously to children. They refrain from interrupting children and allow them to finish what they are saying, either to the adult or to another person. The voice tone used by adults is patient and friendly, and social amenities such as "Please," "Thank you," and "Excuse me" are part of their conversation.

5. Adults avoid making judgmental comments about children either to them or within their hearing. Children are not labeled. Rather, children are treated as sensitive, aware human beings whose feelings are respected. Discussions about children's problems or family situations are held in private between the appropriate parties.

6. Adults plan or take advantage of spontaneous opportunities to talk with each child informally. In the course of a day, children have many chances to talk with adults about matters that interest or concern them. Eating, toileting, dressing, waiting for the bus, settling down for a nap and just waiting until the group is called to order are treated as occasions for adult-child conversation. Adults do not relegate such conversations to scheduled times only.

7. Adults use children's interests as a basis for conversation. They observe what children are doing and comment on it. They speak with them about the things youngsters want to talk about. This is manifested in two ways. First, they follow the child's lead in conversations. Second, they bring up subjects known to be of interest to a particular child based on past experience.

8. Adults encourage children to express their ideas. They elicit children's opinions and reactions throughout the day and invite children to talk about their observations. When a child becomes involved in an elaborate communication, which the adult doesn't have time enough to hear, he or she expresses regret, then explains the situation to the child. Making a promise to listen to the rest some time later in the day, the adult follows through as vowed.

9. Adults ask thought-provoking, varied questions for which genuine answers are desired. These inquiries tend to be open-ended in nature, allowing children to say whatever they are thinking. The adult uses such questions as a signal to children that their thoughts and opinions are welcome and important. Such questions also promote children's problem-solving skills, contributing to an increased sense of competence.

10. Adults use children's names in positive circumstances whenever possible to build children's good feelings of self. If corrective action is necessary, they approach children directly and communicate with them in ways that make the message clear but nonaccusatory. Children's names are never substituted for negative commands such as "no" or "stop."

11. Adults use words to encourage children, to relieve frustration, and to provide guidance to children as they pursue their aims. They acknowledge children's efforts as well as their gradual progress and find ways to make tasks manageable enough that children feel challenged but still successful.

12. Adults praise children in ways that are sincere and constructive. Their remarks expand children's self-recognition of competence and worth. Adult compliments are individualized and specific, varying from child to child and from one circumstance to another. Praise is never used to compare children or to make one child feel good at the expense of another.

**The importance of a positive verbal environment.** Positive verbal environments are beneficial to both the adults and children who participate in them. The principles outlined here provide concrete ways for adults to communicate warmth, respect, authenticity, acceptance, and empathy to children. This makes it more likely that youngsters will view adults as sources of comfort and encouragement. Demonstration of such attitudes also creates the facilitative base from which adults can more confidently take appropriate future action. Simultaneously, children gain because there are people in the program with whom they feel comfortable and secure. In addition, the adult-child interaction patterns enable children to learn more about themselves and to feel good about the self they come to know. Thus, a positive verbal environment is associated favorably with self-awareness and self-esteem.

**Establishing a positive verbal environment.** Helping professionals would not knowingly act in ways to damage children's self-esteem. Observations of early childhood settings, however, show that at times adults unintentionally slip into verbal patterns that produce the negative verbal environments described here (Kontos and Wilcox-Herzog, 1997; Kostelnik, 1987). When interviewed, daycare, Head Start, preprimary, and elementary school teachers identified four common reasons why this occurs:

▼ Adults underestimate the impact their words have on children.
▼ Adults get caught up in the hurried pace of the job and miss opportunities to have more positive verbal interactions with children.
▼ Adults sometimes react unthinkingly, saying things they don't really mean.
▼ Adults sometimes lack training in the most effective ways to talk with young children while guiding their behavior.

Over the years it has become increasingly clear that positive verbal environments do not happen by chance. Their creation is the result of purposeful planning and implementation. Adults pay careful attention to the principles just described. They incorporate, as part of their daily interactions, such simple but telling behaviors as making time for children, addressing children by name, inviting children to talk, speaking politely to children, and listening carefully to what children have to say. These basic actions convey fundamental attitudes of affection, interest, and involvement. Another strategy helping professionals can use to further communicate these same qualities is the behavior reflection.

## Behavior Reflections

**Behavior reflections** are nonjudgmental statements made to children regarding some aspect of their behavior or person. The adult observes a child and then comments to the child about her or his attributes or activities. Such statements do not express opinion or evaluation but are exactly about what the adult sees.

**SITUATION:** A child is coming down a slide on his stomach.

> *Adult:* You're sliding down the slide. (Or, either of the following: You found a new way to come down; You're sliding head first.)

**SITUATION:** Joe and Melissa are drawing a mural together.

*Adult:* You two are working together. (Or: Each of you has figured out a way to contribute to the mural; You're concentrating on what you are doing; That's a very involved project you're working on.)

**SITUATION:** A child arrives at a daycare center.

*Adult:* You're wearing your tennis shoes today. (Or: You look all ready to go; That bag you're carrying looks like a heavy load.)

**The value to children of using behavior reflections.** Behavior reflections are a powerful way to show interest in children. When adults reflect what children are doing, they talk about actions and experiences that have the most meaning for youngsters—those in which they themselves are involved. Verbal observations such as these increase children's self-awareness and make them feel valued because the adult notices them and takes the time to note aloud something they have done.

As a result, children learn that their everyday actions are important enough to be noticed and that extreme behavior is not needed to gain appropriate attention. This is an important concept for children to understand because they sometimes assume that adults will only notice behavior that is out of the ordinary (Dreikurs and Cassel, 1992). Youngsters' interpretations of "out of the ordinary" might include excelling in a particular area, or acting out. Such conclusions are not surprising because in many group settings, one has to be the birthday child, the one who gets all A's, or the child who pinches a lot in order to receive individual attention from adults. By reflecting, adults instead make note of such commonplace events as:

"You're sharing the paint with Wally."
"You're trying hard to tie your shoes."
"You noticed our math books are brand new."

Simple comments such as these say to the child, "You are important." Because each takes only a few seconds to say, these comments are particularly useful to helping professionals who must work with more than one child at a time. Thus, while helping Nakita with her coat, the caregiver also can attend to Micah and Leon by saying: "Micah, you have almost every single button done," "Leon, you wore your brown coat today," and to Nakita, "You figured out which arm to put in first." This spreads the attention around and helps Micah and Leon as well as Nakita feel that the adult has taken them into account.

Because reflections do not evaluate behavior, children learn not to feel threatened by adult attention. The nonevaluative nature of the reflection enables adults to actively and concretely demonstrate acceptance of children; youngsters interpret reflections as tangible efforts by adults to understand them better (Kostelnik and Kurtz, 1986).

Further, when used appropriately, behavior reflections call on adults to take the child's perspective within an interaction. Understanding what is important to a child about a particular activity by seeing it through the child's eyes sets the stage for adults to be more empathic in their responses to children (Rogers, 1957, 1961). Also, observing closely and taking cues from the children makes it more likely that youngsters feel good about the interactions that take place with the adult. Thus, an adult watching children dancing in a conga line might reflect: "You formed a really long conga line," or "Everybody's figured out a way to hang on," or "Everyone's smiling. You look like you're having fun." These are child-centered remarks that correspond to the youngsters' agenda in that situation rather than the adult's.

All too often, adults in group settings feel more comfortable supervising children than actually interacting with them. Within this mode, their remarks might have been: "What's that you're doing?", "That's a hopscotch outline, not a conga pattern," or "You forgot to put the kickstep in. It goes like this." Even if these observations were meant to show adult interest, they do not match the children's perception of what is important in their game. Such comments only disrupt the activity and tell children that the adult knows better. Neither outcome promotes favorable self-judgments in children or positive adult-child relationships.

Behavior reflections can also increase children's receptive language skills. This is because children learn word meanings from hearing the words used to describe their immediate experiences (Mattick, 1972; Sharp, 1987b). This type of contextual learning occurs when youngsters hear new words and new ways of putting words together to describe day-to-day events. For instance, young children who hear the daycare provider observe on different occasions:

"You are walking to the door."
"You and Jeremy walked into the coatroom together."
"We were walking along and found a ladybug."

will begin to comprehend the meanings of different verb forms based on their own direct involvement in each situation. Similarly, words children already know help them figure out the definitions of new words they hear (DiVesta, 1974). Thus, a child may realize that "gargantuan" means "big" because a helping professional reflects, "You found the most gargantuan dinosaur of all" as the child points to an Apatosaurus, which he already considers a large animal. New words add to children's store of knowledge about themselves and the world around them. Becoming better able to understand the words directed toward them contributes to positive self-esteem.

New vocabulary expands children's concepts as well as their language. For instance, an adult who describes the child's action in the following way: "Tonia, you are building with all the square blocks. You've figured out how to balance them on edge," adds the additional concepts of "square" and "balance" for Tonia to consider, if she is ready. Such scaffolding by the adult facilitates the child's competence at a higher level than would be possible without the adult's comments (Berk and Winsler, 1995). *Scaffolding* means to link what the child already knows or can do with new information or skills that he or she is ready to acquire. In cases where children are not prepared to move forward, they will simply ignore the new ideas.

An added benefit of using behavior reflections is that they may serve as an opening for children to talk to adults if they wish. Often, youngsters respond to the adult's reflections with comments of their own. Thus, a verbal exchange may develop that is centered around the child's interests. On the other hand, children do not feel compelled to answer every reflection they hear (Guerney, 1980). For this reason, reflecting does not interrupt children's activities or make them stop what they are doing in order to respond to an adult query. Even when youngsters remain silent, they benefit by being made aware of the adult's interest in them.

**When to use behavior reflections.** Behavior reflections can be used singly, in succession, and with other skills you will learn about in later chapters. When interacting with toddlers, preschoolers, youngsters whose primary language is not English, and children whose receptive language development has been delayed, it is appropriate to use a series of behavior reflections. For example, in a 10-minute interaction at the water table, the teacher might say: "You're pouring the water down the hose and watching it come out the other end," "You found a funnel to use," "You all remembered to put your smocks on," "Lucy, you're churning the water

with an eggbeater," "Mimi, you're getting the water to move with your hands." Such remarks could be addressed to one child, to more than one child, or to the group as a whole. Regardless of whether or not they answer, children of this age and ability appreciate knowing the adult is nearby and attentive.

School-age children, on the other hand, may feel self-conscious having that many remarks directed their way. For them, a single behavior reflection acts as an appropriate signal that the adult is interested in them and is available for further involvement if they wish it. Thus, out on the playground, children would consider it a friendly overture for an adult to say: "That was some catch!" or "You figured out the rules all by yourselves." In each case, if the child were to reply, the adult would have a clear invitation to continue the interaction. Were children to remain engrossed in their activity or direct remarks to others, this would be a cue to the adult that a prolonged interaction was not desired at that time.

Both children and adults benefit when helping professionals use behavior reflections in their repertoire of communication techniques. Most importantly, behavior reflections afford adults an excellent means to show children they care about them and are interested in their activities. Behavior reflections are particularly effective with young children, children who are just learning to speak English, children who are mentally impaired, and as an entree to more involved interactions with older youngsters. Yet, to build relationships with children over time, it is necessary to implement additional skills that eventually will lead to more prolonged verbal exchanges.

### Demonstrating Affection, Interest, and Involvement via Conversation

One of the most basic ways for adults to show their concern for and interest in children is to carry on conversations with them. Adult-child conversations contribute to children's positive feelings about themselves. When adults are attentive and respond meaningfully, they are demonstrating interest in the youngsters with whom they interact. Because adults represent authority figures, this clear sign of the adult's respect, caring, and acceptance conveys a powerful message to children about their value (Danish and Hauer, 1984; Kontos and Wilcox-Herzog, 1997; Sharp, 1987a, 1987b). Attitudes such as these increase children's self-respect and self-acceptance.

In addition, conversations that center around topics in which children are interested are more likely to produce spontaneous and lengthy discussions than those focusing on adult topics. In such an atmosphere, youngsters begin to feel more confident about expressing their own thoughts, ideas, and feelings. As adults become actively involved with children in this manner, children come to view them as people worthy of receiving their trust and as potential sources of information and guidance. Thus, the foundations for positive adult-child relationships are extended and built on.

Unfortunately, many adults inadvertently discourage conversations because they have difficulty engaging in the give-and-take necessary for communication to occur. Instead, they feel compelled to take charge of the exchange rather than allow the child to dictate its direction. They see their role as instructor or admonisher, not listener (Hendrick, 1996). This is manifested in any one of several ways.

### Conversation Stoppers

Adults communicate lack of interest, disdain, and intolerance for children when they do the following:

Brush aside children's comments
Interrupt children to correct their speech
Immediately supply a fact or render an opinion
Ask too many questions

All of these tactics inhibit conversation, inhibit self-awareness, and contribute to feelings of low self-esteem. In addition, they are barriers to the development of positive adult-child relationships.

**Missing children's conversational cues.** At times, children make comments that seem irrelevant or only vaguely related to the topic. Sometimes, when this happens, adults are tempted to ignore the child's remarks. For instance, several kindergarteners and Mr. Yakely, their teacher, found a robin's nest that contained an egg and began to examine it. As the teacher was pointing out characteristics of the egg, one child piped up: "I had eggs for breakfast. Mine were scrambled." Immediately, the others chimed in with comments about breakfast. Mr. Yakely ignored what he considered to be an interruption and continued his discourse on robins and their nests. (A variation on the teacher's disregard of the remark would have been for him to say, "That's nice" and then continue his own train of thought.)

Mr. Yakely missed an opportunity for a positive interaction with his pupils by passing over their remarks. The children had, in fact, found a way to connect the finding of the nest with something

relevant to them. By his verbal behavior, Mr. Yakely demonstrated to the children that the bird's nest was a more significant topic of conversation than any the children could initiate. The children felt brushed aside and unimportant because they did not have a chance to explain their own ideas.

**Correcting grammar.** In their attempts to convey ideas, children may make grammatical errors. In response, adults sometimes ignore the content of the child's speech and interrupt them by making them repeat the phrase correctly. This is ill advised. Most children do not change their grammar when corrected in this manner and in the process, may be offended. They feel overwhelmed, lose track of what they are saying, and have difficulty associating the correction with their actual words (DiVesta, 1974). None of these sensations are conducive to positive adult-child relations or feelings of high self-esteem. Rephrasing the child's message appropriately and conversationally is a better approach (Cazden, 1972; Sharp, 1987a). If LaDonna says, "I holded the record real careful," she would feel more accepted and heard and, incidentally, would learn more about grammatical sentence structure were the adult to reflect, "You held it very carefully so it wouldn't break" instead of admonishing, "Don't say 'holded,' say 'held'" (Nelson, 1977). In addition, LaDonna would be more likely to express her feelings to this adult in the future without fear of criticism. This could lead to a more constructive relationship between the two individuals.

**Supplying facts and giving opinions.** Adults sometimes stifle conversation by evaluating the content of the child's message rather than simply responding to it. Consider the following dialogues.

Carly: I bet Michael Jordon would love my dad's pumpkin pie. He would jump right out of the T.V. and get some.

Adult: Now, you know that can never happen. He's not really in the T.V.

Carly: (Walks away)


Carly: I bet Michael Jordon would love my dad's pumpkin pie. He would jump right out of the T.V. and get some.

Adult: Your dad must make great pumpkin pie.

Carly: Yeah, it's all orange and yummy and has whipped cream on top.

*Adult:* Mm-m! No wonder Michael would want some.

*Carly:* He would eat one whole pie all by himself.

In the first example, Carly's attempts at conversation were hindered by the adult's preoccupation with getting the facts straight. In the second, the adult used Carly's ideas and interests as a basis for prolonging the verbal exchange. The latter was more conducive to positive relationship building because the adult's verbalizations helped Carly to feel interesting and important.

**Advising.** When children approach older persons with a problem, it is natural for adults to try to help by offering solutions and advice. If this is done before the child has had sufficient time to talk out his or her ideas, two problems may result. First, the real issue may never emerge, so the solution the adult suggests may not suit the problem. Second, whenever an authority figure states what is best, it is difficult for the conversation to continue because children don't feel comfortable questioning an adult's judgments or telling them they don't like the idea. In either case, further elaboration by the child is unlikely (Gazda, 1995; Gordon, 1990). This prevents children from exploring ideas or increasing their own problem-solving abilities.

**Inappropriate questioning.** A common strategy adults use in conversing with children is to ask them questions. When used judiciously, questions can be an effective way to indicate interest in children and to gain needed information from them. However, questioning is a strategy that is often abused, which can result in fewer and shorter responses (Dillon, 1978). For this reason, constant probing interferes with relationship building (Gazda, 1995). Questioners become the dominant persons in conversations by taking the lead and dictating the direction the dialogue will go. This detracts from the respondent's feeling that she or he is a partner in the communication process. Moreover, a questioner may force a child into disclosing information that he or she prefers to keep private, at the same time giving the child no opportunity to say what he or she really wants to say (Dillon, 1981). For instance, a child is asked probing questions about his performance on a test and in the process reveals a low score he has hoped no one else would find out about. Time spent on this subject also preempts his opportunity to describe the weekend he spent with his cousins.

Another way that questions are so often misused is that many are accusatory statements rather than requests for information (Holzman, 1972; Parten, 1979). Samples include:

"What do you think you're doing?"
"Haven't you finished that project yet?"
"Don't you think you ought to get busy?"
"How do you expect us to be on time if you spend your whole day in front of the mirror?"

One study found that only 20 percent of the questions asked of children in group settings actually require them to think or to reply (Gall, 1971). In addition, adults may ask so many questions in such rapid sequence that children tune them out. For example, studies of teacher behavior indicate that, on the average, 60 percent of all adult-child interactions involved questions, with at least one question being asked every 72 seconds (Resnick, 1972). Some teachers asked as many as 150 questions in half an hour (Hyman, 1977). Other research has found that, on the average, children are allowed only 1 to 3 seconds to provide answers to questions (Rowe, 1974). As a result, approximately half of the questions that adults ask go unanswered and when children do respond, their answers tend to be brief. Most typically, answers consist of one word or a short phrase (Boggs, 1972). In fact, the more questions that are asked, the fewer words children use to answer them. This is particularly true when children are subjected to a series of questions (Boggs, 1972; Drake, 1972; Labov, 1970). For example, Enrico is at the easel and the adult asks:

"Why did you pick green paint?"
"Do you like green?"
"Is green your favorite color?"
"Can you think of anything that's green?"
"Are you going to use any other colors?"
"What's that shape you just made?"
"What other shapes can you make?"

It is probable that he will ignore most, if not all, of these queries. Additionally, the interaction that the helping professional hoped would be positive has turned into an unpleasant interrogation. Thus, when questions are used rhetorically, in succession, or too often, they are a poor means of prompting conversation and, hence, are poor relationship builders.

All of the preceding conversation stoppers should be avoided. Instead, adults can learn two techniques that are known to be effective ways to keep conversations going: paraphrase reflections and open-ended questions (Sharp, 1987b; Trepanier-Street, 1991).

## Paraphrase Reflections

A **paraphrase reflection** is a restatement, in an adult's words, of something a child has said. The adult listens carefully to what the child is saying, then repeats the statement to the child in words slightly different from those she or he had originally used. As with behavior reflections, paraphrase reflections are nonjudgmental statements. They are not vehicles through which adults express personal opinions about what the child is trying to communicate. Rather, they are a tangible means of indicating that the adult is listening attentively. Examples might include:

*Child:* Teacher, see my new dress and shoes!

*Adult:* You have a new outfit on today. (Or either of the following: You wanted me to see your new clothes; You sound pleased about your new things.)

*Child:* (At lunch table) Oh no! Macaroni again.

*Adult:* You've had more macaroni than you can stand. (Or: Macaroni's not your favorite; You thought it was time to have something else.)

*Child:* Is it almost time for us to get going?

*Adult:* You think we should be leaving soon. (Or: You're wondering if it's time to go yet; You'd like to get started.)

In each of the preceding situations, the adult first listened to the child, then paraphrased the child's statement or inquiry. You will note that there was more than one appropriate way to reflect in each situation. Although paraphrase reflections are all similar in form, the content of each depends on the adult's interpretation of the child's message. Thus, there is no one reflection that is most correct in every situation. Rather, any one of several alternate responses is possible.

**Why paraphrase reflections benefit children.** For true conversations to take place, it is important that adults listen to what children have to say. However, real listening involves more than simply remaining silent. It means responding to children's words with words of one's own that imply, "I hear you; I understand you" (Gordon, 1990). Paraphrase reflections are an ideal way to get this message across. Sometimes called active, reflective, or emphatic listening, paraphrase reflections are widely used in the helping professions to indicate positive

regard and involvement. People who employ this technique often are perceived by those with whom they interact as sensitive, interested, and accurate listeners (Gazda, 1995; Guerney, 1975). The result is that people talk more freely and that conversations are more rewarding for both participants. This favorable outcome occurs for several reasons (Gazda, 1995; Gordon, 1990):

1. Paraphrasing gives the message sender the impression that the listener is carefully considering his or her ideas and is trying to understand the sender's frame of reference. Hence, although the listener may not always agree with the other person's point of view, he or she manifests an awareness and a comprehension of it. Such understanding is critical if miscommunication is to be avoided.

2. Paraphrasing helps the listener to be more empathic toward the message sender. In order to accurately paraphrase another person's words, one must not only listen to them literally, but must take into account their underlying meaning. When both aspects of the message are considered, the listener gains a better understanding of how the message sender is seeing and interpreting his or her world. The ability to achieve this understanding is always beneficial, but it is particularly critical when the listener and the message sender have different opinions or goals within the interaction.

3. Paraphrasing may allow the message sender to state the original message in different words or phrases if the listener has not quite grasped the point, or to correct a mistaken reflection if the listener's interpretation was not accurate. Additionally, senders have a chance to elaborate and provide further information that they think is important for the listener to know.

4. Paraphrasing highlights what the message sender really said. Often, people are surprised to hear what someone else has understood by their words and are rewarded by a deeper insight into their own thoughts on hearing a reiteration of them.

5. Paraphrasing allows the message sender to control the direction of the conversation. She or he determines what to reveal and what channels to pursue. This is particularly advantageous to children because the nature of the instructional and socialization process often requires them to follow the adult's lead in a discussion rather than determining it themselves. Use of paraphrase reflections enables children to discuss topics adults might never think of or might consider too silly, too gory, or too sensitive to talk about.

6. Paraphrasing children's queries often prompts them to answer some questions or solve some problems on their own. Children are more likely to rely on their own ideas if the adult helps them clarify the issue via a paraphrase reflection rather than immediately furnishing a fact or solution (Hendrick, 1996). How this can work is illustrated in the following:

*Helene:* Is it snack time yet?

*Adult:*   You're not sure when we'll be having a snack.

*Helene:* Must be soon. There's the cups out already.

In this situation, Helene used the evidence available to her in the physical environment to determine that it was almost time for a snack. The adult's response prompted Helene to think more than if the question had been answered directly.

7. When used with children younger than seven years of age, paraphrase reflections can have a positive influence on their language development. This occurs when adults expand children's verbal messages. Expansion means to fill in or extend what the child is saying. This type of paraphrasing is slightly different from and more complex than the youngster's speech and has been shown to stimulate children to produce lengthier, more varied sentences (Kontos and Wilcox-Herzog, 1997; Sharp, 1987b). Between the ages of eighteen months and three years, simple expansions are best (Brown and Bellugi, 1964; Educational Products Inc., 1988).

*Child:* Kitty sleep.

*Adult:* Yes, the kitty is sleeping.

*Child:* Me eat.

*Adult:* You are eating a sandwich.

In each of these examples, the adult has expanded the child's telegraphic message to include appropriate connecting words in the same tense as the child's.

Children aged four and older profit from a more elaborate variation termed *recasting* (Nelson, 1977; Educational Products Inc., 1988). Recasting refers to actually restructuring the child's sentence into a new grammatical form:

*Child:* The cat is sleeping.

*Adult:* Snowball is asleep on the windowsill.

*Child:* This car goes fast.

*Adult:* Your car is going very fast around the track. Soon it will have gone the whole way round.

Recasting preserves the child's meaning, but rephrases it in a way that is moderately novel. Novelty can be introduced by changing the sentence structure, by adding auxiliary verbs, or by using relevant synonyms. This helps the child to notice the more complex grammatical form. Recasting works best when adults make modest changes in the child's words but do not alter them entirely. Overcomplication causes children to overlook the new grammatical or syntactical structure, making it unlikely that they will use it themselves.

The strategy of scaffolding can be applied when adults paraphrase two children, as in the following example: Jeffrey and Andy, both seven years old, are playing with some blocks and having a discussion about how to put the blocks in a particular configuration. Jeffrey is holding two flat, narrow boards, trying to make them stand on end. Each time he tries to balance them, they fall. "It won't stay up! My castle needs a pointy tower." Andy says, "Wait. If you put this other block there, they won't fall over," as he demonstrates how to make a tripod. Ms. Haas, who has been listening and watching, paraphrases, "Jeffrey, you were trying to make a tower. Andy, you figured out how to use a third block as a brace. That's one way to solve the problem." In this way, the teacher's words have reflected Andy's more sophisticated approach to solving the dilemma. These comments, to which Jeffrey has access, serve as a scaffold or a bridge between what he knows and what Andy has seen as a solution. If Jeffrey is ready to use the information, he can apply it to his building at the moment or in the future.

**Using paraphrase reflections.**   Paraphrase reflections can be used any time a child addresses a comment to an adult. They may consist of a simple phrase or multiple statements. Sometimes, a simple verbal acknowledgment of something a child has said is all that is required:

*Child:* I'm up to page fifteen.

*Adult:* You've gotten pretty far in a short time. (Child resumes reading)

On other occasions, program pressures preclude the feasibility of involved adult-child interactions. Again, a single paraphrase can indicate interest in the child while minimally interrupting the flow of events.

However, when time permits, paraphrase reflections are also excellent conversation starters and may be used to prolong an interaction once it begins. Consider the following two conversations. The first involves Chris, who is five; the second, his six-year-old brother, Kyle. Both discussions were spontaneous.

*Chris:* We got a new dog over the weekend!

*Adult:* You sound excited. Tell me more.

*Chris:* Well, he's got a flat nose . . . well, ah . . . he's been biting a lot . . . and, he's ah, he's cute . . . you know, he's ugly and homely. He's cute . . . and, ah . . . he's in a biting mood . . . you know, he has to chew on something a lot of times, he's just, he's going to be . . . ah, October . . . um, August seventh was his birthday! Not his real birthday. His real birthday was . . . what was his real birthday? His real birthday . . . was February seventh, I think.

*Adult:* Ah, but you celebrated his birthday at a different time even though it wasn't his real one.

*Chris:* August, uh huh, August. He's only six months old. Six months. . . .

*Adult:* Oh, he's only six months old. He's just a small dog.

*Chris:* No, he's not a small dog. He's about, you know, from here to here (child spreads arms to indicate size) . . . you know . . . he's. . . .

*Adult:* Oh, he's a pretty large dog.

*Chris:* Yeah. He's pretty large, all right! He's got a fat stomach and tiny legs! (Laughs)

*Adult:* (Laughing) He sounds comical, with a flat nose too.

*Chris:* Yeah, and . . . you know, he has knots on his head . . . and he has a face like he's real sad, and . . . um. . . .

*Adult:* Sad-faced.

*Chris:* Uh huh.

*Adult:* Sad-faced dogs are really cute sometimes.

*Chris:* Yeah.

*Kyle:* Know what? Our dog's really cute, and . . . we keep him in one of those kinds of pens where you keep like babies when you want to keep them from falling down the steps or something. Well, we . . . we keep him in one of those. We keep him in our laundry room and, uh . . . we got him from North Carolina. My dad says that he

was . . . he, his father, um, was registered as Nathan Hale. Well . . . he was the champion bulldog of the nation . . . and, uh . . . we got him for free, because we know the people, who know the owner of Nathan Hale.

*Adult:* Sounds like you were pretty lucky to get such a special dog.

*Kyle:* Yeah. We are. We got him from North Carolina.

*Adult:* He came from far away.

*Kyle:* Yeah. We, they took him . . . they took him on a trip for eight hours . . . and, he threw up about four times.

*Adult:* Four times, huh, in eight hours. That must have been a long trip.

*Kyle:* Yeah, when he got out, um . . . he just sorta layed there, and he was . . . he really looked sick, and um . . . this is the stage when he has long legs, but *you should see his stomach!*

*Adult:* It's really something else.

*Kyle:* Yeah.

As can be seen from the preceding conversations, youngsters may pursue the same topic in very different ways. Each child talked about the same dog, but chose a different feature to discuss. By paraphrasing, the adult was able to respond to Chris and Kyle individually. She also was able to key in on what interested them most. If she had led the conversation by asking a series of questions, such as:

"What kind of dog did you get?"
"How big is he?"
"What's his name?"
"What color is he?"
"Where did you get him?"

the two interactions would have been similar, rather than unique as they were. In addition, it is unlikely that the adult would have thought to inquire about the knots on the dog's head or how many times it threw up, important considerations to the boys. Note, too, that Chris felt comfortable enough to correct an inaccurate response. This occurred when the adult's interpretation that a six-month-old dog was small (meaning "young") did not match what Chris wished to convey. Because paraphrase reflections are tentative statements of what the adult thinks she or he heard, children learn that the reflections are correctable. Directing the conversation in these ways makes children feel important and worthwhile.

## Supporting Linguistically Diverse Children

*Hello* (English)
*Guten Morgan* (German)
*Karo* (Nigerian)
*Bonjour* (French)
*Chao Em* (Vietnamese)
*Konnichiwa* (Japanese)
*Halo* (Spanish)

Although English is spoken by many Americans, the population of people who speak English as a second language has been increasing over time. This group is most pronounced among children younger than age six (Center for the Study of Social Policy, 1992). Current estimates also indicate that more than 6 million school-age children in the United States speak a language other than English at home. This figure is expected to grow even more in the next century (U.S. Bureau of the Census, 1995). The term **linguistic diversity** is used to describe those children enrolled in educational programs who speak a language other than English at home and who are variously proficient in English (NAEYC, 1996). The notion of home language is also important for speakers of English who have regional or ethnic dialects or other distinct speech patterns. In every case, children's self-concept and self-esteem are strongly tied to their home language (McGroarty, 1992). Children whose home language is treated with respect feel valued. Those who receive the message that their home language is unimportant, or even worse, a "problem" are less likely to feel good about themselves. Thus, it is potentially harmful to deny children access to their home language in the formal group setting. This has sometimes been done in the mistaken belief that "English only" rules promote speedier acquisition. The research does not support this assumption. A more natural approach to second-language acquisition makes better sense. Such an approach is based on three major assumptions (Wolfe, 1992:144–145):

▼ If we want to help children develop a positive self-concept and a real sense of belonging, "We need to integrate the language and culture of each child in our classrooms." Children need many opportunities to encounter both their home language and English in their day-to-day interactions with adults, peers, and materials.

▼ "We must adopt a non-deficit perspective in relation to linguistic diversity." Children who are just learning to speak English, but are fluent in their home language have demonstrated strengths in language acquisition. Thus, a child may be Mandarin proficient with some English proficiency. Such youngsters are not simply limited-English speakers.

▼ Parents and community members are important resources for assisting children's transitions into the program. They can underscore the importance of the children's home language at the same time that children are learning to speak English as a second language.

Helping professionals can better support linguistically diverse children when they are sensitive to variations in how children acquire English as a second language.

Some children may experience a silent period (of six or more months) while they acquire English; other children may practice their knowledge by mixing or combining languages (for example, "Mi mama me put on mi coat"); still other children may seem to have acquired English-language skills (appropriate accent, use of vernacular, vocabulary, and grammatical rules) but are not truly proficient; yet some children will quickly acquire "real" English-language proficiency. Each child's way of learning language should be viewed as acceptable. (NAEYC, 1996:1)

One of the most concrete ways formal group settings demonstrate acceptance is to have people who speak children's home language on staff or as volunteers in the program. When staff are bilingual or when the staff includes both English-speaking members as well as persons who speak the children's home language, children have many opportunities to speak and hear speech that is familiar to them (Chang, Muckelroy, and Pulido-Tobiassen, 1996). In addition, they have the chance to hear languages other than their own. This increases children's involvement in learning and validates the importance of the children's home language as well as English (Berk, 1997). Other visible signs of acceptance include making available an assortment of multilingual story tapes, song tapes, books, wall hangings, signs, and posters. Singing and reciting in a variety of languages are additional strategies that convey the value of children's home languages. Additional ideas for celebrating the cultural and ethnic heritage of linguistically diverse children are presented in Chapter 14. In addition, it is advisable to learn a few key words in the children's own language, even if you are not fluent in that language. Words of greeting and farewell, words that describe family relations, and those that indicate basic needs, such as hunger, thirst and the need to use the bathroom, are all useful to know.

Exposing children to English in the formal group setting can be carried out through a combination of formal instruction and informal conversation. All of the skills outlined in this chapter are useful in the latter approach. Behavior and paraphrase reflections extend children's language skills and also indicate interest in and acceptance of all children. Behavior reflections are particularly effective when working with children who are in the early phases of English proficiency. Simple words and phrases, accompanied by gestures and demonstrations, help to get the message across. Teaching children simple scripts in English such as "my turn," "I'm next," or "show me" provide children with basic words they need to function socially. This contributes to children's feelings of competence and worth. Another skill that promotes such feelings is the effective use of questions.

## Effective Questioning

Earlier in this chapter, a strong case was made for limiting the use of questions in conversations with children. Questioning, however, is not entirely undesirable; but questions must be posed thoughtfully and skillfully. The kinds of questions adults ask dictate the quality of the answers they receive (Cassidy, 1989; Trepanier-Street, 1991). Thus, to stimulate verbal exchanges, the best questions are those that draw people out and prompt them to elaborate. These are sometimes called **open-ended questions** or *creative questions* (Heath, 1989; Hendrick, 1998; Schlichter, 1983). Open-ended questions are questions for which there are many possible answers and for which no single answer is correct. Their purpose is to get children to talk about their ideas, thoughts, and emotions, not to quiz them or test their powers of memorization. Using open-ended questions communicates acceptance of the child, thereby enhancing children's self-esteem and promoting positive adult-child relationships (Marion, 1995).

Conversations that begin with questions that do not meet these criteria and call for one-word answers ("Are you rooting for the Cubs?"; "Do you like grapes?"; "What kind of bird is this?") end when the response is given. These are examples of closed questions. Although their intent is to show interest in a subject presumably favored by the child, such probes give him or her little else to say.

On the other hand, questions that require children to reason, predict, make decisions, or describe their reactions encourage verbal interplay (Sharp, 1987b). Samples include:

"How do you think this will turn out?"
"Why do you think the bridge fell down?"
"What's your opinion?"

Open-ended questions ask children to:

▼ **predict** ("What will happen next?")
▼ **reconstruct a previous experience** ("What happened when you visited your grandma?")
▼ **make comparisons** ("How are these animals the same/different?")
▼ **make decisions** ("What do you think we should do after lunch?")
▼ **evaluate** ("Which story was your favorite? Why?")
▼ **imagine something** ("What would it be like if the dinosaurs were alive today?")
▼ **propose alternatives** ("What is another way you could cross the beam?")
▼ **apply factual knowledge** ("Where do you suppose we might find a caterpillar at this time of year?")
▼ **solve problems** ("What can we do to find out how many marbles are in this jar?")
▼ **generalize** ("Now that you saw what happened when we heated the ice cube, what do you think will happen when we heat this snowball?")
▼ **transform** ("How could we make muffins from all these ingredients?")
▼ **reason** ("How did you decide those went together?")

All of these questions are open to a wide variety of answers and allow children to express whatever is on their minds. As a result, children are able to choose in what direction the dialogue will go. This increases the likelihood that they will remain interested and involved in the give and take of true conversation. In addition, challenging, well-timed, open-ended questions promote children's thinking and problem-solving skills (Cassidy, 1989; Trepanier-Street, 1991). Refer to Table 4–1 for a comparison of closed versus open-ended questions.

The intent of using open-ended questions is to enhance children's sense of worth, competence, and control. Another strategy adults sometimes use to promote similar self-judgments is praise. However, as was mentioned in the verbal environment section

### ▼ Table 4–1    Comparison of Closed and Open-Ended Questions

#### CHARACTERISTICS

| Closed Questions | Open-Ended Questions |
| --- | --- |
| Require a nonverbal response or a one- or two-word answer from children | Promote multiword, multiphrase responses from children |
| Tend to have right or wrong answers | Have more than one correct answer |
| Are ones for which adults already know the answers | Are ones for which adults don't know what children's answers might be |
| Require a "quick" response | Allow children time to formulate and collect their thoughts |
| Focus on facts and similarity in thinking | Focus on ideas and originality in thinking |
| Ask for information | Ask for reasoning |
| Focus on labeling or naming | Focus on thinking and problem solving |
| Require the child to recall something from memory | Require the child to use his or her imagination |

#### EXAMPLES

| Closed Questions | Open-Ended Questions |
| --- | --- |
| What shape is this? <br> . . . Square. | What do you think will happen next? |
| How many cows did you see? <br> . . . None. | How else could we . . . ? |
| What street do you live on? <br> . . . Gunson. | What's your idea? |
| How are you? <br> . . . Fine. | How did you. . . . ? |
| Who brought you to school today? <br> . . . Mom. | What would happen if. . . . ? |
| Where is your knapsack? <br> . . . Home. | What do you think about. . . . ? |
| Do you know what this is? <br> . . . Yes. | What do you suppose would explain. . . . ? |

of this chapter, praise can have either positive or negative effects.

### Effective Praise

Everyone knows children need lots of positives (Briggs, 1987). Therefore, it's logical to assume that praise favorably influences children's self-esteem. But research throughout the past decade makes it clear that this is not always so. For instance, if teachers laud children indiscriminately, children discount the praise (Parsons, Kaczala, and Meece, 1982). Furthermore, certain kinds of praise actually have the potential to lower chil-

dren's self-confidence, to inhibit achievement, and to make children reliant on external rather than internal controls (Kamii, 1984; Stringer and Hurt, 1981). All these conditions contribute to low self-esteem. For this reason, educators have investigated the characteristics that distinguish **effective praise** from ineffective praise. A comparison of the two, along with relevant examples, are summarized in Table 4–2.

As you read through the examples of effective praise in Table 4–2, you probably noticed that most were either reflections or simple informational statements to children. None made any reference to

▼ **Table 4–2    Comparison of Ineffective and Effective Praise**

| INEFFECTIVE PRAISE | EFFECTIVE PRAISE |
| --- | --- |
| Evaluates children<br>"You draw beautifully." | Acknowledges children<br>"You used a lot of colors in your picture." |
| Is general<br>"Good job." "Nice work." | Is specific<br>"You worked hard on your painting." "You spent a lot of time deciding what to draw." |
| Compares children to one another<br>"You wrote the most interesting story of anyone." | Compares children's progress to their past performance<br>"You wrote two words in this story that you have never used before." |
| Links children's actions to external rewards<br>"You read three books. Pick a sticker from the box." | Links children's actions to the enjoyment and satisfaction they experience<br>"You read three books. You seem pleased to have read so many." |
| Attributes children's success to luck or to ease of task<br>"That was a lucky catch." | Attributes children's success to effort and ability<br>"You tracked that ball and caught it." |
| Is off-hand in content and tone | Is thoughtful |
| Is offered in a falsetto or deadpan tone | Is offered in a natural sounding tone |
| Is always the same | Is individualized to fit the child and situation |
| Is intrusive—interrupts the child's work or concentration | Is nonintrusive |

the teacher's feelings or evaluated the child in any way. Those kinds of remarks are reserved for the action dimension of the helping relationship and are described in Chapters 10 and 11.

A variety of techniques have been discussed that, when used in combination, contribute to the development of a positive verbal environment. These techniques have included fundamental strategies, such as greeting children and calling them by name, as well as the more complex skills of behavior reflections, paraphrase reflections, open-ended questions, and effective praise. Let us now examine ways to formulate and adapt these skills.

## SKILLS FOR PROMOTING CHILDREN'S SELF-AWARENESS AND SELF-ESTEEM THROUGH VERBAL COMMUNICATION

 **Use the Skills Associated with a Positive Verbal Environment**

**1. Greet children when they arrive.** Say "Hello" to youngsters at the beginning of the day and when they enter an activity in which you are participating. Show obvious pleasure in their presence through the nonverbal communication skills you learned in Chapter 3.

**2. Address children by name.** When speaking to children, use their names. This lets children know that you have remembered them from one day to the next; that you perceive them as individuals, unique from others in the group; and that your message is aimed especially at them. Take care to pronounce each child's name correctly; check with a family member or ask the child for the exact spelling and pronunciation if it is not known to you.

**3. Extend invitations to children to interact with you.** Use phrases such as: "We're making tuna melts. Come and join us," "There's a place for you right next to Sylvia," "Let's take a minute to talk. I wanted to find out more about your day," or "You look pretty upset. If you want to talk, I'm available." These remarks create openings for children to approach you or to join an activity and make it easier for shy or hesitant children to interact with you.

**4. Speak politely to children.** Allow children to finish talking before you begin your remarks. If you must interrupt a child who is speaking to you or to another person, remember to say, "Excuse me," "Pardon me," or "I'm sorry to interrupt." Remember also to thank children when they are thoughtful or when they comply with your requests. If you are making a request, preface it with, "Please." Use a conversational, friendly voice tone rather than one that is impatient and demanding.

**5. Listen attentively to what children have to say.** Show your interest through eye contact, smiling, nodding, and allowing children to talk uninterrupted. In addition, verbally indicate interest by periodically saying, "Mmm-hm," "Uh-huh," or "Yes." If the child has more to say than you can listen to at the moment, indicate a desire to hear more, explain why you cannot, and promise to get back to the child. Remember to keep your promise.

**6. Invite children to elaborate on what they are saying.** Prolong verbal exchanges with children by saying: "Tell me something about that," "Then what happened?" or "I'd like to hear more about what you did." Such comments make children feel interesting and valued.

**7. Think of some conversation openers in advance.** Before seeing the children each day, generate ideas for one or two topics that might interest them ("Tell me about last night's game," "How's that new brother of yours?" or "I was really interested in your report on Martin Luther King. Tell me what you liked best about him"). Comments or questions like these can be answered in any number of ways and have no right or wrong answers; thus, they are easier for children to respond to and serve as "door openers" for further communication.

**8. Remain silent long enough for children to gather their thoughts.** Once you have asked a question or made a remark in response to something a child has said, pause. Children need time to think of what they are going to say next. This is particularly true if they have been listening carefully to what you were saying, because their attention was on your words, not on formulating their subsequent reply. Adults who feel uncomfortable with silence often rush into their next statement or question. This overwhelms children and gives them the impression that the adult has taken over completely rather than becoming involved with them in a more participatory way. A pause that lasts less than 3 seconds is too short. Listen to yourself. If your pauses are too brief, consciously wait (or even count silently to five) before continuing.

**9. Take advantage of spontaneous opportunities to converse with children.** Look for times

*continued*

## SKILLS FOR PROMOTING CHILDREN'S SELF-AWARENESS AND SELF-ESTEEM THROUGH VERBAL COMMUNICATION—continued

when you can talk with children individually. Snack time, dressing, toileting, having lunch, waiting for the bus, settling down for a nap, wheeling a child to the X-ray room, or the time before the group is called to order afford excellent possibilities for communication. It is not necessary to wait for some special, planned time to initiate a conversation or respond to one.

**10. Refrain from speaking when talk would destroy the mood of the interaction.** Remember that silence is the other component of the verbal environment. Too much talk, inappropriate talk, or talk at the wrong time detracts from a positive verbal environment.

When you see children deeply absorbed in their activity or engrossed in their conversations with one another, allow the natural course of their interaction to continue. Keep quiet even if you think of a relevant remark. These are times when the entry of an adult into the picture could be disruptive or could change the entire tone of the interchange. Speak only when your comments would further the child's interests, not only your own.

In addition, there will be times when you find yourself interacting with a child in a comfortable silence. When this is the case, do not feel compelled to verbalize. The absence of talk in situations like these is a sign of warmth and respect.

**11. Provide verbal encouragement to children as they refine and expand their skills.** Do this by giving children relevant information such as, "Just one more piece and you'll have the whole puzzle complete." Also, make clear to children that you believe in them and have confidence in their abilities. "This project will be challenging, but I'm sure you can do it."

**12. Listen carefully to what you say and how you say it.** Consider how children may interpret your message. If you realize or others point out that you are using poor verbal habits, such as incorrect grammar, colloquialisms, highly idiomatic speech, or mispronounced words, correct yourself. Refer to a dictionary, as well as asking your colleagues to give you feedback about how you sound. Another strategy is to

carry a tape recorder with you for a short time as a means of self-monitoring.

 **Formulate Behavior Reflections**

**1. Describe some aspect of the child's person or behavior in a statement to the child.** After observing a child carefully, select an attribute or behavior that seems important to him or her and remark on it. At all times, focus on the child's perspective of the situation, not your own. Thus, an appropriate behavior reflection to Manny, who is tying his shoes, would be any of the following:

> "You're working on your left shoe."
> "You know how to make a bow."
> "Those are the new shoes Grandma bought you."

The following statements would not constitute behavior reflections:

> "I wish you'd hurry up."
> "I'm glad you're putting those on all by yourself."
> "If you don't hurry, we'll be late."

Although the latter remarks may be accurate statements of what is important to the adult in the interaction, they do not mirror the child's point of view.

**2. Phrase behavior reflections as statements.** Reflections should not be phrased as questions. Rather, they should be simple statements. Questions imply that children must respond; reflections do not. The goal of this skill is to enable adults to show interest in children without pressuring them to answer.

**3. Address behavior reflections directly to children.** Use the word "you" somewhere in your statement so that the child recognizes that your reflection is aimed at her or him. This makes each reflection more personal.

**4. Use descriptive vocabulary as part of your reflection.** Including adverbs, adjectives, and

## SKILLS FOR PROMOTING CHILDREN'S SELF-AWARENESS AND SELF-ESTEEM THROUGH VERBAL COMMUNICATION—continued

specific object names as part of the reflection makes them more meaningful and valuable to children. Children's contextual learning is more favorably enhanced when you say, "You put the pencil on the widest shelf" than when you say, "You put it on the shelf."

**5. Use nonjudgmental vocabulary when reflecting children's behavior.** Reflect only what you see, not how you feel about it. It does not matter whether your evaluation is good or bad; reflections are not the appropriate vehicles through which to express opinions. Therefore, "You're using lots of colors in your painting" is a reflection; "What a nice picture" or "You used too much grey" is not. This is because evaluations represent the adult's point of view; the reflection represents the child's. A painting the adult likes may be one with which the child is dissatisfied; a picture with more grey than the adult would prefer may fit exactly the child's perception of the blur made by a herd of elephants rushing by.

 **Formulate Paraphrase Reflections**

*1.* **Listen actively to the child's words.** Consciously decide to pay attention to the child's message. Actively involve yourself in this process by looking at the child and listening to his or her entire verbalization without interrupting. Concentrate. Momentarily set aside other thoughts; think more about what the child is saying than what you are going to say in response.

**2. Restate in your own words what the child has said.** Make sure that your rewording maintains the child's original intent. Neither introduce your own opinion nor add things you wish the child had included.

**3. Rephrase erroneous reflections.** At times, children give signs that your reflection was not in keeping with their intent. They may correct you directly by saying, "No" or "That's not what I meant." Other, more subtle cues are children repeating themselves, adding new infor-

mation, or sighing in exasperation. Be alert for these and, if they occur, try a variation of your statement. Do this conversationally, with no implication that the child was at fault for communicating inaccurately. This is not the time to insist that *you heard* correctly based on the child's words. Instead, focus on more acutely perceiving the child's frame of reference.

**4. Match your reflection to each child's ability to understand language.** Use simple, short reflections with toddlers. Construct these by adding one or two connecting words to the child's telegraphic utterances. Go beyond simple expansions, however, when working with children aged four and older. Recast the child's message by adding auxiliary verbs or relevant synonym phrases. Periodically, use multiple-phrase reflections when working with school-age children:

> *Child:* There's Webelos on Tuesday and all the guys are going. Me too.
>
> *Adult:* Sounds like you've got a special meeting coming up. Lots of your friends are going.

Be aware of how well children understand spoken English. Accompany your words with gestures and demonstrations if some children seem confused.

These adaptations demonstrate respect for children's varying communication abilities and make your reflections more interesting and comprehensible to them.

**5. Use a conversational tone when reflecting.** Use an expressive voice tone when reflecting either children's behavior or language. Adults who reflect in a monotone or singsong voice sound condescending and disrespectful. Children do not respond well when they perceive these attitudes.

**6. Summarize children's actions and words rather than reflect each individual behavior or idea expressed.** Formulate reflections that tie together a series of actions or statements. For instance, if Malcolm is playing with colored blocks, do not say, "You have a red block. You

*continued*

have a green block. Now you're picking up a blue block." Do say, "You're using many colors in your building." Similarly, if Katie announces, "I got a bear and a cake and a dress for my birthday," do not say, "You received a bear and a cake and a dress for your birthday." Say, "You got lots of gifts for your birthday."

**7. Select one idea at a time to paraphrase from the many a child may express.** There will be times when children spend several minutes describing a particular event or expressing their thoughts, ideas, or concerns. It is neither feasible nor desirable to reflect everything, because this would take too much time from the child, who might be anxious to say more. Instead, pick one main idea that stands out to you and reflect that. If this is not the child's major focus, he or she will indicate this discrepancy by correcting you or by rechanneling the conversation in the favored direction. An example of this was evident in the adult conversation with Kyle about his dog. Initially, Kyle made several comments regarding where the dog was kept and how his family got it. Based on his building excitement when describing the dog's championship lineage, it was this part of the description the adult reflected. Had Kyle wanted to talk more about the laundry room, he might have said: "Yeah, he's special. We keep him in the laundry room" as a way to return to his main interest.

**8. Add interest to your reflections by periodically phrasing them in a form opposite from that used by the child.** Thus, if Sue says, "I want the door open," it would be appropriate to say, "You don't want the door closed." If Mark announces, "I want another helping of everything," you could say, "You don't want to miss anything." If Beth whispers: "I have a headache. I wish everybody would be quiet." You could reply, "You hope no one gets too loud."

**9. Reflect first when children ask you a question.** Reflect children's wonder, uncertainty, confusion, or interest before offering an answer or solution to their queries. This helps children

clarify what it is they are really asking and gives them an opportunity to answer some questions themselves. If the child repeats the question, asks a second, more pointed question, or waits expectantly for an answer, provide it.

**Situation:** Miss Drobney is tenderizing meat with a meat pounder. Audrey approaches and asks, "What are you doing?" The adult reflects, "You noticed I'm using a special tool."

At this point, it is possible that Audrey might say, "It makes holes in meat." This provides an opportunity for Miss Drobney to reflect again. "You've figured out one thing this tool can do— it makes holes." This could be the beginning of a verbal exchange in which Audrey discovers for herself the various attributes of a meat pounder. On the other hand, it is also possible that when the adult reflects, "You noticed I'm using a special tool," Audrey would remain quiet, waiting for more, or would respond, "Yeah, what is that?" Miss Drobney would then have a choice of simply answering, "This is a meat pounder" or pointing out attributes of the tool that might help Audrey discover some of its characteristics on her own: "Look at the bumps on the end. See what they do when I pound the meat," or "See how it puts holes in the meat? That makes it easier to chew."

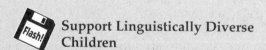 **Support Linguistically Diverse Children**

**1. Evaluate your sensitivity to children's use of home language.** Ask yourself the following questions:

Do I know what home languages are represented within the group of children with whom I am working?

Do I respond respectfully to children when they talk to me in their home language?

Do I feel confident interacting with children whose language I do not speak fluently?

If you find yourself answering "no" to any of these items, review the skills you have learned so far. Identify specific strategies you can use to

## SKILLS FOR PROMOTING CHILDREN'S SELF-AWARENESS AND SELF-ESTEEM THROUGH VERBAL COMMUNICATION—continued

interact more sensitively with linguistically diverse children.

**2. Learn relevant words in the home languages of the children in your group.** Look up such phrases or ask colleagues and parents to help you. Ask children to teach you a few key words if possible. Find poems, songs, and riddles in a variety of languages to share with children in the group. Refer to books, audiotapes, colleagues, or family members as necessary.

**3. If you are fluent in children's home language, monitor how you interact with the children using that language.** Ask yourself the following questions:

Do I use the children's home language for more than simply giving children directions?
Do I use the children's home language for more than simply correcting children's behavior?

If your honest answer to either of these queries is "no," review the skills associated with a positive verbal environment. Plan to incorporate those skills as you speak to children in their home language. Also make sure to use that language to provide positive reinforcement to children, to soothe and comfort them, and to simply engage them in enjoyable, supportive interactions. Adopt the skills you are learning in this chapter and others to the children's home language as well.

**4. Familiarize yourself with ways in which the formal group setting can be designed to better support children's linguistic diversity.** Observe ways in which the formal group setting encourages the use of home language by both children and parents. Notice ways in which the helping professionals in your setting provide opportunities for different languages to be used in day-to-day activities. Survey your setting for materials that reflect children's home languages. Think about how you might strengthen the program's support of linguistically diverse children and families. Discuss your ideas with colleagues and make a plan to put some of these into action.

 **Formulate Questions**

**1. Ask open-ended questions.** Monitor the questions you ask. Determine when you are asking questions for which you have a predetermined answer in mind as well as ones for which only a yes-no answer will suffice. In either case, rephrase the question so it allows for a variety of answers.

**2. Ask questions when you are truly perplexed.** Some questions are genuine requests for information rather than conversation starters. Questions such as "Who has to go to the bathroom?" "What time is your appointment?" "Who hasn't had a chance to bat yet?" are legitimate inquiries. At the same time, they are not designed to prompt a conversation, so none should be expected. Also, avoid empty questions. If you really do not want to know what time the appointment is or whose turn it is at bat, do not ask.

**3. Carefully choose when to ask open-ended questions.** Consider both the time available and the circumstances under which the question is to be asked. Pick an unhurried time, giving children ample opportunity to respond. Youngsters become frustrated when adults make inquiries knowing that children's answers will have to be rushed or terminated prematurely. If you catch yourself saying, "Okay, okay," "Fine, fine, fine," "That's enough," or "I get the idea" in the middle of a child's response, your question should have been saved for later.

Similarly, pose conversational questions during those parts of the day in which child-directed activities predominate rather than during activities that require a great deal of adult instruction or management. For instance, it would be inappropriate to initiate a prolonged conversation with a child while you are counting heads during a fire drill, proctoring a spelling test, or when the rest of the children are waiting for you to lead them in the next activity.

**4. Emphasize quality over quantity in using questions in conversations with children.** It is better to ask one or two open-ended questions

*continued*

## SKILLS FOR PROMOTING CHILDREN'S SELF-AWARENESS AND SELF-ESTEEM THROUGH VERBAL COMMUNICATION—continued

than to pose several of the yes-no variety in which neither you nor the children have much interest. Measure the effectiveness of the questions you ask by listening to children's answers in regard to both content and tone. If responses become monosyllabic or the child sounds weary of answering, stop. If answers are lively and lead to elaboration, continue.

 **Formulate Effective Praise Statements**

**1. Use behavior reflections to acknowledge children's efforts and accomplishments.** Make nonevaluative comments such as, "You've been working on that a long time," "You found a new way to make a tunnel," or "You did it." These statements show children you are aware of their expanding competencies while allowing them to judge for themselves the adequacy of their efforts. They also help children recognize that they can influence outcomes and events in their daily lives. This realization contributes to children's increasing sense of control, which promotes positive self-judgments.

**2. Note positive changes you've observed in children's abilities over time.** "Last time you climbed to the first platform. Now you've made it all the way to the top" or "You've been practicing a lot and now you can make it across the whole beam without falling off" or "You're getting a lot faster at matching those shapes."

**3. Point out to children the positive effects their actions have on others.** "You noticed Marcel was having a hard time getting the computer going. You gave him some help and now it's working fine."

**4. Focus on some positive aspect of children's efforts to do something, not simply the product they achieve.** It is better to say, "Look at how you made those brush strokes sweep across the page. You've worked for 10 minutes on that" than to say, "Nice picture."

**5. Be honest in your praise and offer children authentic feedback.** Again, behavior re-

flections are a good tool to help you achieve this. For instance, if Elliot has just struggled through reading a page aloud, it would be best to say something like, "You're learning to read some new words" or "You read that whole page by yourself." This is more honest than "Great reading" or "That was terrific." Elliot is probably quite aware that his reading is not yet fluent. The latter comments lack credibility and may sound patronizing to the child. Adult praise means more when it is believable. Since behavior reflections describe rather than evaluate the child's performance, they fit this criteria well.

 **Communicate with the Family**

**1. Apply the principles of a positive verbal environment in your interactions with family members.**

*Greet family members.* Take time to learn the names of the families in your program. Use adults' last names, unless you have a relationship outside of the program, as well as their appropriate title, such as Mr., Ms., or Mrs., when addressing them. This form of greeting is often viewed as a sign of respect by those receiving it. If you aren't familiar with family names, greet them as the parent/guardian/grandparent of their specific child. Then, introduce yourself. For instance, "You must be with Elise. I'm Ms._____." If the child is with his or her family, remember to greet him or her, as well. It is proper to speak about the child in this circumstance only if you include the child in the conversation. In other words, avoid talking "above the child's head."

*Get to know family members as individuals.* Treat family members as people whose lives are multidimensional. In addition to playing the role of parent or guardian, family members have other roles in life—worker, student, wife, animal lover, basketball player, shopper, church goer, and so on. Convey friendly interest in these facets of people's lives. Remember, in addition to talking about the child, comment on day-to-day living or on upcoming events that family members have mentioned to you.

## SKILLS FOR PROMOTING CHILDREN'S SELF-AWARENESS AND SELF-ESTEEM THROUGH VERBAL COMMUNICATION—continued

*Invite family members to enter the room, to watch their child, and to speak with you.* Use such phrases as, "You've come to see Jose. He's in the group area looking at books. You are welcome to join him there"; or "Welcome to the classroom. We're almost finished with story time. Here is a comfortable place to wait"; or "Thank you for coming in to speak with me. Let's watch Jose for awhile and then I'd be happy to answer any questions you have about his time at school."

*Speak politely at all times.* Parents and other family members, in their efforts to communicate with you, may not always express themselves calmly or politely or with good grammar. They may seem brusque, hurried, demanding, or timid. Furthermore, family members may speak in a manner that is comfortable for them but that sounds unfamiliar to you in terms of word usage or grammatical syntax. It is the professional's responsibility to decipher the intent of the message without necessarily responding in kind to its mode of delivery. Part of your role is to build relationships with every family member. Just as you do with children, allow these adults to finish their requests or comments before introducing your own. Remember to include everyone in the conversation, using appropriate eye contact and facial expressions. Use polite language, such as "please" and "thank you," and speak in an even, conversational tone, independent of the manner in which you are addressed.

### 2. Use paraphrase reflections and open-ended questions while interacting with family members.

*Adapt your use of paraphrase reflections to demonstrate respect for and interest in adults.* Paraphrase reflections can be very effective with adults when used carefully. First, mix your reflections with other verbal strategies. Second, make sure not to "mirror" an adult's words or exact style of speech. Vary your word choice using some of the techniques outlined earlier in this chapter, such as reversing the word order, saying the opposite of what the speaker has stated, and using multiple sentences. Although reflecting is suitable for all kinds of interactions, it is particularly useful when family members

are expressing concern. This strategy helps to clarify the information they are attempting to convey, so that you can respond to needs and desires more effectively. Rephrase the speaker's sentences to demonstrate your awareness of the message being delivered. Do not hesitate to correct yourself if the speaker indicates that you interpreted his or her intent inaccurately.

*Respond positively to the inquiries of family members regarding their children.* Use paraphrase reflections and open-ended questions as appropriate to obtain information and to indicate interest. If you do not know the information they are seeking, direct family members to a teacher or director in charge of the program. Offer to find that individual, if you are in a position to do so (that is, if you have no other responsibilities at the moment).

*Use commonly understood language.* An important element of verbal communication is that the participants feel acknowledged and respected. Use of jargon or a specialized "teacher" vocabulary is an impediment to effective and genuine communication. Examples of jargon or specialized talk include referring to aspects of the curriculum as "domains," speaking about "reflecting the child's point of view," or mentioning the child's "mesosystem." When speaking with family members, clearly describe the issue at hand in natural, unaffected vocabulary and sentences. Use the principles of good verbal and nonverbal communication to both talk and listen. If you sense a misunderstanding, find alternate words or phrases to clarify your meaning. If you think you have misunderstood what others are saying, verify your perception with phrases, such as, "What I think you are saying is . . ." or "It sounds as if you think . . ." In addition, it is best to avoid using evaluative or overly "gushing" language in talking with family members about their own children or in reference to other children.

*Allow sufficient time for family members to gather their thoughts.* It is not always easy for parents and other family members to come to a program to speak with professionals about their children. They may, therefore, be hesitant in their speech, fumble for words, or stammer. Be patient and refrain from finishing their sentences or interrupting them. Use all of your best verbal and

*continued*

nonverbal skills to indicate interest, warmth, caring, and respect while you wait for the person to complete his or her message. Use open-ended questions and continuing responses to encourage their verbalizations. Respond appropriately when they do tell you about their concern or interest.

**3. Use honest praise and authentic feedback to acknowledge family participation in the program.**

*Respond genuinely to family involvement.* When parents and other family members help on a field trip, bring something of special interest to share with the children, or simply assist in the classroom, acknowledge their efforts honestly and specifically. Use phrases such as, "Thank you for driving on the trip. Having you along made it possible for everyone to participate," or "The children really enjoyed the story you told about your mother's first days in America. It gave them a real understanding of what life must have been like for her at that time," or "I really appreciated your helping us work on the journal project. It meant that more of the children were able to write down their ideas."

**4. Collaborate with family members in supporting linguistically diverse children.** Ask family members to teach you some words and phrases that could be useful in interacting with their child. Invite family members to the program to tell stories, sayings, and riddles in their home language and to share other oral traditions typical of their family. Ask families to bring music, artifacts, or foods into the classroom to share and discuss. Have family members, who are literate in their home language, read storybooks aloud to the children or make audiotapes for children to hear at school or take home (Wolfe, 1992). Ask families to provide books, newspapers, and magazines that feature the home language in print for use in the classroom. When working with older children, provide ways in which family members can use their primary language to help their children with program-related assignments/activities at home. Create a school library that includes a variety of print materials written in families' home languages, which the children could borrow. Make clear the importance of the child's home language to the child, and therefore, to you. Stress that although children will be learning English in the formal group setting, such learning does not require children to abandon or reject the language of the home.

## ▼ Pitfalls to Avoid

Whether your words are aimed at demonstrating your interest in children, or whether you are using your speech to become more involved in children's activities, there are certain hazards to beware of.

**Parroting.** A common way in which adults paraphrase children is to respond by mirroring exactly the child's words and voice tone. Parroting is often offensive to children because it makes the adult sound insincere or condescending. Although parroting is a natural first step for people just learning how to paraphrase, adults should learn to vary their responses as quickly as possible. Several techniques can be used. One is to listen to children who are talking to one another and *silently* formulate paraphrases for statements they make. Although you are not actually say anything, this provides good mental practice. A second tactic is to listen to children talking or remember things they have said throughout the day, and then later, write down several alternate paraphrases. Finally, students have reported that it is helpful to practice paraphrasing family members and friends. In many cases, this involves paraphrasing adults, which may prompt the student to work harder at sounding original because mimicking someone's words is not part of natural conversation.

**Reflecting incessantly.** It is a mistake to reflect everything children do or say. The purpose of behavior and paraphrase reflecting is to give adults opportunities to observe children, to listen to them, and to understand their point of view. None of these goals can be accomplished if adults are talking nonstop. Using summary reflections is a good way to avoid overpowering children with excessive verbiage.

**Perfunctory reflecting.** Reflecting without thinking is not appropriate; it is another form of parroting. Adults who find themselves simply "going through the motions" or responding absentmindedly to children just to have something to say should stop, then intensify their efforts at attending more closely to what children are really saying or indicating through their actions. A good reflection increases children's self-understanding rather than merely serving as a placeholder in a conversation. Another form of perfunctory reflecting occurs when adults reflect children's questions but neglect to follow up on them. For example, Ralph asks Mr. Wu, "When are we going to have music?" Mr. Wu responds, "You're wondering when we're going to have music," and then immediately turns to talk to Alicia. In this case, his response was not wholly correct, because he did not attend to the entirety of the child's message. He should have waited to determine if Ralph was going to answer the question himself, or if he needed additional information. The best way to avoid such a dilemma is to think while reflecting and to pay attention to how children react to the reflections.

**Treating children as objects.** There are many times when adults speak to children in the third person. That is, they make comments about the child that they intend for the child to hear but that are not personally addressed to the child. For instance, Miss Long is playing with two-year-old Curtis in the block area. No one else is nearby. She says things like: "Curtis is building with square blocks. Curtis is making a tall tower. Oops, Curtis' tower fell." If other youngsters were close at hand, her remarks might be interpreted as information aimed at them. But, as the situation stands, her impersonal running commentary on his activity is not conversational and leaves

no real openings for a response from Curtis should he choose to make one. Miss Long's remarks could be turned into reflections by the insertion of "you" in each one: "Curtis, you're building with square blocks. You're making a tall tower. Oops, your tower fell."

**Turning reflections into questions.** Phrases such as "aren't you?"; "didn't you?"; "don't you?"; "right?"; or "okay?" tacked to the end of a sentence transform reflections into questions. A similar result occurs when the adult allows his or her voice to rise at the end of a sentence. When adults slip into this habit, the nature of their verbal exchanges with children changes from unintrusive interest and involvement to a tone that is interruptive and demanding. This is one of the most common misuses of the reflecting technique and occurs because adults would like some confirmation regarding the accuracy of their reflection. They want some sign from the child that what they have said is right. Yet, rarely does one hear:

> *Child:* I'm at the top.
>
> *Adult:* You're excited to be so high, aren't you?
>
> *Child:* You're right, Teacher.

The real confirmation of appropriate reflecting is that children continue their activity or conversation. If they stop or correct the adult, these are signs that the original reflection was not on target. Adults who find themselves questioning rather than reflecting must consciously work at eradicating this habit from their repertoire. If you notice that you have done this in conversation with a child, it helps to stop and repeat the reflection correctly.

**Answering your own questions rather than allowing children to answer.** Adults frequently answer many of their own questions. For instance, Ms. Cooper asks, "Who remembered to bring their permission slips back?" Without a moment's hesitation, she says: "John, you've got one. Mary, you've got one, too." Later, she inquires, "Why do you think birds fly south for the winter?" Before children have a chance to even think about the question, she supplies an answer: "Usually, they're looking for food." In both instances, Ms. Cooper precluded children answering by responding too quickly herself. Unfortunately, as this becomes a pattern, Ms. Cooper may well conclude that children are incapable of answering her questions, while the youngsters translate her actions as lack of interest in what they have to say. If you detect this habit in yourself, deliberately work to eliminate it. When you answer prematurely, verbally make note of it; then, repeat your question: "Oops. I didn't give you a chance to answer. What do you think about . . . ?"

**Habitually answering children's questions with your own.** Sometimes, when children ask a question, adults automatically echo the question back to them:

*Child:* Where do bears sleep in the winter?

*Adult:* Where do you think they sleep?

Echoing causes children to form negative impressions of adults. The question sounds like a put-down; youngsters translate it to mean: "You're dumb. You should know that," "I know and I'm not going to tell you," or "I'm going to let you make a fool of yourself by giving the wrong answer. Then, I'll tell you what the real answer is." Although this may not be the adult's intent, it is often the result. To avoid these unfavorable impressions, either supply the needed fact or reflect the children's questions and then help them discover the answer by working with them.

**Using ineffective praise.** When adults catch themselves praising children indiscriminately or falling back on overused, pat phrases, the best strategy is to stop talking, then refocus on what the child is actually doing. Rephrase your statement so it conforms to the guidelines for effective praise presented earlier in this chapter. If an on-the-spot correction seems too difficult, simply remember the situation and during a quiet moment later in the day, reconsider what you might have said. On another day, in a similar activity, see whether any of the alternatives you thought about might fit. If so, use one or a variation of it.

**Interrupting children's activities.** Reflecting or asking a question when a child is obviously engrossed in an activity or is absorbed in conversation is intrusive. At times like these, adults can exhibit interest in children by observing quietly nearby and responding with nonverbal signs such as smiles, nods, laughter at appropriate moments. When children are working very hard at something, an occasional re-

flection that corresponds to their point of view is appreciated; constant interruptions are not. Children who are speaking to someone else and give no indication of wanting to include the adult should not be reflected or questioned at all. If, for a legitimate reason, the adult must get the child's attention or enter the conversation, he or she should just say, "Excuse me."

**Failing to vary your responses.** It is common when learning new skills to find a tactic with which one is comfortable and then to use that to the exclusion of all others. For instance, after reading this chapter, you might be tempted to use a behavior reflection in response to every situation that arises. This would be a mistake; certain skills meet certain needs. When one skill is developed to the exclusion of others, the benefits offered by the other skills will not be available to children. In addition, overuse of one form of verbal communication becomes monotonous and uninteresting for adults and children alike. For this reason, it is best to utilize all of the skills presented thus far rather than only one or two.

**Hesitating to speak.** Individuals new to the helping professions, as well as those who have worked with children before, may experience awkward moments in which they find themselves fumbling for the right words when trying to implement the skills presented in this chapter. By the time they think of a response, the opportunity may have slipped by or the words that come out may sound stilted. When this happens, some find it tempting to abandon these techniques and revert to old verbal habits. Others stop talking altogether. Both of these reactions arise from adult efforts to avoid embarrassment or discomfort with unfamiliar verbal skills. Such experiences are to be expected, and every student goes through these uncertain times. Yet, the key to attaining facility with reflections, appropriate questioning techniques, and effective praise statements is to use them frequently so that they become a more natural part of your everyday interactions. In fact, in the beginning, it is better to talk too much than to neglect practicing these skills. Once the mechanics are mastered, you can turn your attention to appropriate timing.

**Sounding mechanical and unnatural while using the skills.** Implementing reflections and open-ended questions feels awkward and uncomfortable at first. Beginners complain that they do not sound like themselves and that they have to think about what they are saying more than they ever have in the past. They become discouraged when their responses sound repetitive and lack the warmth and spontaneity they have come to expect from themselves. Again, at this point some people give up, reverting to old verbal habits. As with any new skill, however, proficiency develops only after much practice.

Learning these techniques can be likened to learning to roller-skate. Beginning skaters have a hard time keeping their balance, shuffle along, and fall down periodically. They have enough trouble going forward, let alone going backward, doing turns, or making spins. Stopping also is a major hurdle. If people only roller-skate a few times, chances are they will continue to struggle and feel conspicuous. If these feelings cause them to give up skating, their progress is halted and they will never improve. However, should they keep on practicing, not only will their skill increase, but they will be able to get beyond the mechanics and develop an individualized style.

The process is the same for the skills taught in this chapter. When readers are willing to practice and continue working through the difficulties, noticeable improvement occurs. The artificial speech that marks the early stages of acquisition of verbal skills gradually gives way to more natural-sounding responses.

## ▼ SUMMARY

Self-concept is a descriptive set of ideas each person forms about himself or herself. A person's notion of self begins in infancy and evolves gradually throughout adulthood as a result of both cognitive development and experience. When babies are born, they do not yet have a concept of self. As children mature and gain experience in the world, they come to realize their distinctness from others. At first, toddlers and preschoolers identify themselves only in terms of physical attributes; later, they include activities in their self-descriptions as well. During the early elementary school years, youngsters incorporate psychological traits along with physical traits in their self-images, and by the sixth grade, they think of themselves entirely in terms of internal or psychological states.

Self-esteem is the evaluative component of the self and includes perceptions related with competence and control. Children who judge their worth, competence, and control positively have high self-esteem; those who do not have low self-esteem. Individuals with high self-esteem lead happier lives than those whose self-judgments are negative. The development of self-esteem follows a normative sequence, evolving from assessing oneself in the here and now as a preschooler to a more compartmentalized view of the self as a young grade-schooler to a general index of one's value as a person by middle-school age. This predominantly positive or negative view remains relatively constant throughout life.

Adult behaviors prompt children to make either positive or negative judgments about themselves. Self-judgments of competence, worth, and control are likeliest in children who interact with adults who demonstrate warmth, respect, acceptance, and empathy. What adults say to children conveys these or the opposite messages to children and therefore is a key factor in the degree to which children develop high or low self-esteem.

The atmosphere adults create by their verbalizations to children is called the verbal environment. It can be either positive or negative. Continual exposure to a negative verbal environment diminishes children's self-esteem, whereas exposure to a positive verbal environment enhances children's self-awareness and perceptions of self-worth. Behavior reflections are a specific verbal strategy adults can use to help create a positive verbal environment. Behavior reflections are nonjudgmental statements made to children about some aspect of their behavior or person. Using behavior reflections increases children's self-awareness and self-esteem; it helps adults look at situations from children's perspectives; it demonstrates interest, acceptance, and empathy for children; and it helps children increase their receptive language skills.

Conversing with children is another way for adults to demonstrate affection, interest, and involvement. Perception of these attitudes increases children's self-respect and self-acceptance. However, certain common errors, such as missing children's cues, correcting grammar, supplying facts and rendering opinions prematurely, advising, and using unnecessary or unskillful questioning act as conversation stoppers. On the other hand, paraphrase reflections, restatements in the adult's own words of something the child has said, are effective conversation sustainers. Paraphrase reflections help clarify communication, help the listener to be more empathic toward the message sender, allow the message sender to control the direction of the conversation, provide the message sender an opportunity to solve his or her own problems, and have a positive influence on the language development of young children. In addition, appropriate use of open-ended questioning and effective praise also adds to the creation of a positive verbal environment. Furthermore, it is possible and advisable to tailor these strategies in interactions with family members as a means of developing and maintaining positive relationships.

Finally, certain pitfalls are to be avoided, such as parroting, reflecting incessantly or perfunctorily, treating children as objects, using inappropriate questioning methods, interrupting children, and failing to vary one's responses. Hesitating to speak and sounding mechanical at first also are common problems encountered by individuals who are just beginning to learn these skills.

## ▼ DISCUSSION QUESTIONS

1. Describe the normative sequence of the development of self-concept in children from birth to early adolescence.
2. Describe an incident from your childhood that enhanced your self-esteem. Describe another that detracted from it. How did it enhance your self-esteem? What does it say to you about your behavior with children? Use the information in the chapter to assess this incident.
3. Review the characteristics of the positive and negative verbal environments. Discuss any additional variables that should be added to both lists.
4. Describe three ways in which you could improve the verbal environment of a setting in which you currently interact with children.
5. Refer to Appendix A: NAEYC Code of Ethical Conduct when responding to the following: One of your colleagues talks about "those children" when referring to youngsters who are just learning to learn English. Consider her point of view as well as what she is communicating to children.
6. Describe at least four benefits of using behavior reflections with young children.
7. Describe how the adult's use of paraphrase reflections affects children's self-awareness and self-esteem.
8. Describe the characteristics of an open-ended question, and discuss how the use of this technique relates to self-awareness and self-esteem in children.
9. Describe how interaction strategies that are used with children can be applied to interactions with adults.
10. Talk about the differences between effective and ineffective praise. Using examples from your past experience, describe times when you were praised effectively and/or ineffectively. What was your reaction at the time? What do you think about it now?

## ▼ FIELD ASSIGNMENTS

1. Identify three strategies you used with children that are associated with the creation of a positive verbal environment. For each situation, briefly describe what the children were doing. Summarize the strategy you used. (Describe it and quote the words you said.) Discuss the children's reaction in each case.
2. Keep a record of the behavior reflections and paraphrase reflections you use with children. When you have a chance, record at least four of your responses. Begin by describing what the child(ren) did or said that prompted your response. Next, quote the words you used. Correct any inaccurate reflections as necessary. Finally, write at least two alternate reflections that fit the situations you described.
3. Focus on using open-ended questions and effective praise as you work with the children. Describe at least four situations in which you used these skills. Begin by describing what the child(ren) said or did to

prompt your response. Next, write down your exact words. Finally, correct any mistaken responses by rewriting them. Finally, write at least two alternate ways of phrasing your remarks, regardless of their accuracy.

4. Describe an interaction you heard or observed involving a child's adult family member. Include positive verbal strategies that were used, including behavior and paraphrase reflections, open-ended questions, and conversation extenders. Give a summary of your assessment of the interaction.

# ▼Chapter 5

## Responding to Children's Emotions

## ▼ OBJECTIVES

*On completion of this chapter, you will be able to describe:*

▼ What emotions are and what functions they serve in people's lives.

▼ How emotions emerge over time.

▼ How children recognize and understand emotions.

▼ The emotional tasks of childhood.

▼ How children differ in their emotional development.

▼ Problems children experience in expressing their emotions.

▼ How adult behavior influences children's emotional development.

▼ Strategies for helping children cope more effectively with emotions.

▼ Family communication strategies.

▼ Pitfalls to avoid in responding to children's emotions.

---

A butterfly lands on Sean's hand—his eyes widen in amazement.

Paulo proudly announces, "I won honorable mention in the cooking contest!"

On her first day at the center, Maureen sobs miserably as her mother attempts to leave.

Emily makes a diving catch and is elated to find the ball in her mitt.

Tony is frightened by the escalating sounds of angry adult voices in the other room.

When Larry calls her stupid, Jennifer yells furiously, "No, I'm not!"

---

Children experience hundreds of different emotions each day. Emotions are linked to everything children do and are triggered by numerous happenings, both large and small. They are what cause children to be affected by the people and events around them. You may wonder, where do emotions come from? What role do emotions play in children's lives? What can adults do to support children's emotional development? This chapter is designed to answer those questions.

### What Are Emotions?

People in all cultures experience emotions. Joy, sadness, disgust, anger, surprise, love, and fear seem universal (Ekman and Davidson, 1994). Although there are obvious differences among these emotional states, they all have certain characteristics in common (Bukatko and Daehler, 1995). Each is triggered by internal or external events that send *signals to the brain* and central nervous system. As a result of these signals, people become aroused and their bodies respond with physiological changes. Their hearts may beat faster, their palms may sweat, or their throats might become dry. This is the *physical* part of emotion. Such sensations usually are accompanied by observable alterations in facial expression, posture, voice, and body movement. Smiling, frowning, or laughing are visible signs of how people feel. Actions like these represent the *expressive* side of emotion. As all this is going on, people interpret what is happening. Their interpretations are influenced by the context of the situation, their goals, and by past experience (Kagan, 1994). Considering all of these factors, people make a judgment about whether they are experiencing some degree of happiness, sadness, anger, or fear. This is the *cognitive* part of emotion.

Although scientists vary in their beliefs about the order in which physical sensations, expressive reactions, and cognitive interpretations occur, they generally agree that all three combine to create emotions (Fox, 1994; Lewis and Saarni, 1985). To understand how these elements might work together, consider what happens when Kitty, age eight, is called on to read her report aloud:

*Signals to Kitty's brain:* Teacher speaking Kitty's name, the other children's silence, a giggle from the back of the room.
*Physical response:* Kitty's mouth dries up, her pulse beats rapidly, her stomach contracts.
*Expressive response:* Kitty scowls, her shoulders slump.
*Cognitive response:* Kitty thinks about past difficulties in front of an audience as well as her desire to do well in class.
*Emotion:* Kitty feels nervous.

Had Kitty's cognitive response focused on past public speaking triumphs, she might have made the judgment that the emotion she was experiencing was hope, not nervousness. In either case, Kitty is the one who makes the ultimate judgment about how she feels. Even if others expect Kitty to do well, if she perceives the situation as threatening, she will be nervous. Such differences in interpretation explain why two people may have very different emotional reactions to the same event. While Kitty feels nervous, another child in the group may be eager to read his or her report to the class. Such interpretations are neither right nor wrong, they simply define each child's current reality. Because emotions are tied to everything we do, people feel a whole range of emotions every single day.

## The Function of Emotions in Children's Lives

Young children experience many emotions throughout the early childhood years. They feel joy and affection; anger and frustration; sadness and shame; fear and anxiety; and trust, contentment, or pride. There are no right or wrong feelings, and *all* emotions play an essential role in children's development.

For example, *emotions help children to survive.* Jumping out of the way of a speeding tricycle or forming attachments between themselves and the important people in their lives are examples of situations that cannot be guided by intellect alone. In these cases, emotions propel children in certain directions without their having to "think" about what is happening (Ekman and Davidson, 1994). When they do have a chance to think, *emotions provide children with information about their well-being.* This often results in children taking some action to maintain or change their emotional state (Fox, 1994). Feelings like happiness and trust give children a sense of safety and security. They "tell" children that all is right with the world and cause children to repeat pleasurable experiences. Affection and pride signal children that they are loveable, valuable, and competent. Such feelings may cause them to be receptive rather than resistant and to seek out new experiences. On the other hand, some emotions signal discontent, misfortune, or danger. They alert children to the fact that something is wrong. Anger prompts children to try to overcome obstacles. Sadness brings a drop in energy, allowing children time to adjust to loss or disappointment. Fear prompts children to avoid, escape, or otherwise protect themselves from something (Goleman, 1995). In every case, emotions help children interpret what is happening to them and prompt them to adapt to changing circumstances. Finally, *emotions serve as a form of communication.* Emotional displays, such as smiling or crying, provide the first language with which infants and adults communicate before babies learn to talk. This communicative function continues over the lifespan as people use words and nonverbal cues to express what they are feeling and to better understand the feelings of others (Eisenberg, et al., 1994; Maccoby, 1992). Since emotions are such an important part of children's lives, the role of adults is to help children to:

Better understand their emotions.
Become more sensitive to the feelings of others.
Find effective ways to cope with the many different emotions they experience.

This process begins at birth and continues throughout the elementary years. To carry out this role effectively, adults must first understand the developmental aspects of children's emotions.

## ▼ CHILDREN'S EMOTIONAL DEVELOPMENT

Emotional development in childhood is characterized by four significant developmental sequences. These include the predictable phases through which:

- ▼ Children's emotions appear.
- ▼ Children understand their emotions.
- ▼ Children recognize the emotions of others.
- ▼ Children pursue the emotional tasks of childhood.

All of these developmental sequences are influenced by both maturation and experience. Understanding them enables professionals to respond to children with greater sensitivity and effectiveness.

### The Emergence of Emotions throughout Childhood

Children are not born with all the emotions they will ever have. In fact, some biologists say that at birth, beyond general contentment and distress, children do not exhibit true emotions at all (Berk, 1997). This is because newborns lack the necessary thought processes to interpret what they are experiencing physically. Thus, the first emotion-like displays we see, such as grimacing, are really reflexive reactions. For instance, when two-week-old Nadia is startled by a loud noise, she recoils, not out of actual fear, but simply as a reflex in response to an unexpected event (Jabs, 1985). However, within her first year, Nadia will experience real *joy* (at about six weeks), *anger* (at approximately four months), *sadness* (at about five to seven months), and *fear* (at approximately six to nine months). Joy, anger, sadness and fear, are the *core emotions* from which all other emotions emerge (Campos et al., 1983; Izard, 1991). For example, basic joy will gradually branch out to include contentment, pride, and affection for others.

Likewise, the core emotion of anger serves as a foundation for the eventual development of frustration, annoyance, jealousy, fury, and disgust. Combinations of these feelings produce more complex reactions, as when annoyance and disgust together lead to feelings of contempt. The four **core emotions** and their corresponding emotional clusters are listed in Table 5–1.

The appearance of the core emotions and the more differentiated feelings that follow, materialize according to a developmental sequence as predictable as those associated with language and physical development. For instance, joy almost always appears between six and eight weeks and is seen in the baby's first social smile. This is an unmistakable sign of infant pleasure, which is most often prompted by the face of the primary caregiver. By four months of age, infants express real anger when they become physically distressed (e.g., when wet or hungry) or when their goals are blocked (e.g., reaching for something they can't quite touch). Similarly, as creeping precedes walking, the expression of sadness always precedes that of guilt (Bukatko and Daehler, 1995).

Even as the later core emotions are surfacing, earlier ones are becoming more differentiated. Thus, by the end of the first year, a child's repertoire of emotions has moved beyond the basic four to include elation, frustration, surprise, shame, and wariness (Santrock, 1995). Further diversity and greater specificity of emotion is seen in the second year, with guilt, pride, affection, jealousy, and defiance being added to the list. By three years of age, children exhibit beginning signs of empathy and a difference between their affection for children and that for adults (Lewis, et al., 1989). Numbers of emotions and finer discriminations between emotions continue to increase with age (Bukatko and Daehler, 1995). The order in which emotions appear during the first three years of life is depicted in Figure 5–1.

### ▼ Table 5–1    Core Emotions and Corresponding Emotional Clusters

| JOY | ANGER | SADNESS | FEAR |
|-----|-------|---------|------|
| Happiness | Frustration | Dejection | Wariness |
| Delight | Jealousy | Unhappiness | Anxiety |
| Contentment | Disgust | Distress | Suspicion |
| Satisfaction | Annoyance | Grief | Dread |
| Pleasure | Fury | Discouragement | Dismay |
| Elation | Boredom | Shame | Anguish |
| Pride | Defiance | Guilt | Panic |

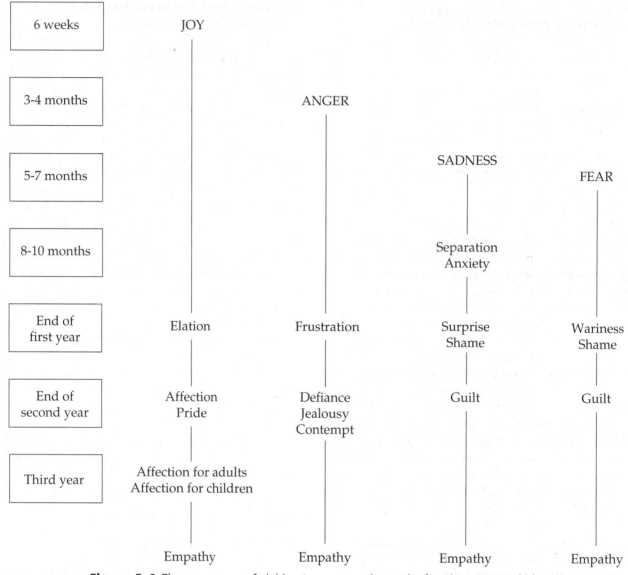

**Figure 5-1** The emergence of children's emotions during the first three years of life.

When they first arrive, core emotions are very intense. The dramatic outbursts so common among infants and toddlers underscore that intensity. However, as children's emotions become more differentiated, their reactions also become more varied and more subtle. Thus, as children mature, rather than relying on screaming to express every variation of anger, they may shout in fury, pout in disappointment, whimper in frustration, or express their upset feelings in words. This expanded repertoire of emotional expression is a result of several interacting factors—the presence of the core emotions, the context of each situation, and children's developing cognitive and language capacities. These elements also contribute to children's understanding of emotions in themselves and in others.

## Children's Understanding of Their Emotions

After her father scolded her, a two-year-old became angry and shouted back, "I'm mad at you Daddy. I'm going away. Good-bye."

A mother said, "It's hard to hear the baby cry." Her six-year-old child replied, "Well it's not as hard for me as it is for you. You like Johnny a lot better than I do! I like him a little, and you like him a lot, so I think it's harder for you to hear him cry."

(Bretherton, et al., 1986:536, 540)

These comments illustrate the dramatic change that occurs in children's understanding of their emotions during childhood. Over time, the simplistic declarations of the toddler give way to more complex reasoning and greater breadth of understanding. It all begins with children thinking that their emotions happen one at a time. When toddlers and preschoolers are angry, they are completely angry; when they are pleased, they are entirely pleased (Harter, 1977). These emotional responses alternate rapidly. One minute a child may scream, "No," yet the next minute crawl up in your lap for a hug. The quick changes children make from one emotional state to another are universally recognized as typical for children this age (Gonzalez-Mena and Eyer, 1997).

By ages five or six, youngsters begin to report that they can hold more than one feeling at a time as long as those feelings come from the same emotional cluster. Thus, a child would say that going to a birthday party might cause him or her to feel happy as well as excited (Wintre and Vallance, 1994). This same child, however, would not suggest that it is possible to be both happy and sad about the party. At this point in their development, children believe that opposing feelings can only be directed toward different things (Selman, 1981).

Sometime between the ages of eight and eleven, children come to understand that multiple and contrasting feelings toward the same event are feasible. With this new thinking in mind, a child might suggest that staying home alone prompts both scary feelings and proud ones (Wintre and Vallance, 1994). At first, children hypothesize that such feelings occur in succession, not all at the same time. One feeling replaces another rather than co-existing with it. This means children believe it is possible to be both happy and sad about the same event, but not at the same time.

By ages 10 to 12 years, children recognize that they can hold two or more very different feelings toward the same object or situation simultaneously. At this point children perceive that one feeling can blend into another. This blending of feeling sometimes results in a state of mixed emotions children label as "confusion." At other times, children describe their emotions as arguing over what to do or which one should predominate (Whitesell and Harter, 1989). These dilemmas most often occur when children experience two opposite emotions (e.g., happy versus sad, pleased versus angry, proud versus guilty) in which the negative emotion seems equal to or more intense than the positive one. For this reason, youngsters who feel both happy and sad about something often have difficulty sorting

their feelings out. When this happens, they may experience a general sense of anxiety over not having one clear-cut response.

The most mature thinking begins in late adolescence, when young people describe mixed feelings as producing new and different emotions. In this way, they may identify disappointment as a composite of anger, sadness, and regret. They now are able to analyze more accurately what all their emotions are. This analysis may occur internally or through conversations with others. The emotions of older children also last longer. As children mature, they do not shift emotional states as rapidly as toddlers and preschoolers. Older youngsters may even describe themselves as being in a good or bad mood, meaning they expect their general emotional state to remain relatively stable for some period of time. The developmental sequence described here is depicted in Figure 5–2.

## Children's Recognition of Emotions in Others

A two-year-old toddler notices another child crying and refusing to take a nap. Her comment is, "Mom, Annie cry. Annie sad."

A mother leaves her toddler in the pew with her six-year-old while she takes communion. The younger child begins to cry. Big brother says, "Aw, that's all right. She'll be right back. Don't be afraid. I'm here."

(Bretherton, et al., 1986: 536, 541)

As illustrated by these children's comments, in just a few short years, children shift from focusing on obvious physical cues to contextual ones as they interpret other people's emotions. In addition, older youngsters recognize shades of meaning and combinations of feelings that are not evident to infants and toddlers. This evolution occurs in a fairly stepwise fashion.

*Initially, children rely on facial expressions* to tell them how someone else is feeling (Hoffner and Badzinski, 1989). Between two and five years of age, they accurately identify other people's positive and negative emotions. However, such assessments are based more on how a person *looks* rather than on the context of the situation (Russell and Bullock, 1989). Relying on expressive cues, preschoolers are more likely to determine that a crying peer is sad based on the presence of tears than on knowing what happened. Likewise, they tell the difference between

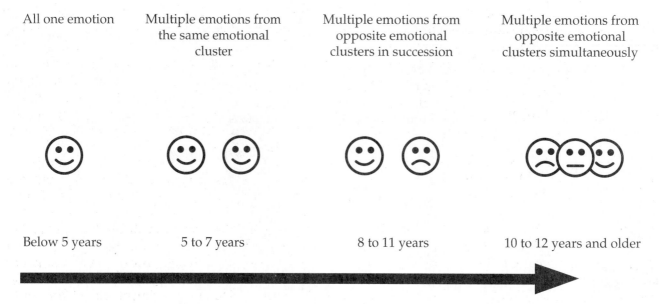

**Figure 5–2** Developmental sequence of children's understanding of emotion.

fury and irritation based more on the drama of a person's actions than on the context in which those actions are taking place. Not too surprisingly, at this age the core emotions are consistently easier for children to identify than are emotions characterized by more subtle cues (Michalson and Lewis, 1985). Younger children also focus on only one emotion at a time in others, just as they do in themselves. They are unaware of the complex blending of emotions that other people experience.

Children's accuracy in detecting other people's feelings increases with maturity (Gnepp and Klayman, 1992). *By middle childhood, youngsters take into account situational cues in addition to the expressive aspects of emotion* to determine how someone else is feeling. Thus, children recognize that a child may be sad because her toy is broken or because her dog is lost, not simply because she is crying. They also know that the same person could experience happiness if the toy were repaired or if the lost pet found its way home. Eventually, children move on to assessing a person's probable mental state. This means they understand that the source of feelings may be internal as well as physical and situational (Mussen, et al., 1990). For instance, they are aware that memories may produce feelings even though the original event is long past. When ten-year-old Janelle says, "Thom's sad. He's lonesome for his dog he used to have," she is demonstrating an increasingly mature concept of how and why emotions occur.

Predictably, the youngest children seldom suggest that a person might be feeling two emotions si-

multaneously (Harter, 1986). Over the years, children gradually become better able to imagine a succession of emotions that other people may feel. Finally children become more accurate at identifying potentially mixed emotions (Harter and Buddin, 1987; Wintre and Vallance, 1994).

Older children also become aware that the same events do not always lead to the same outcomes. Similar situational cues may prompt different responses in different people or different responses from the same person on separate occasions. For example, loud music may prompt happy feelings in Tricia while making Katrina feel overwhelmed. The same music may cause Janet to feel exuberant on Monday, but on edge Tuesday. Because of these variations, discriminating another person's emotions continues to be a challenge even for children in later childhood and adolescence.

At every age and in every situation, the perception children have of another person's feelings is influenced by more than just their intellectual capabilities. How well children know the person, how comfortable they feel with him or her, and how predictable that individual's behavior has been in the past all determine how well children recognize that person's emotional state at any given time. This is why children of all ages may recognize anger or pleasure more easily in a family member or close friend than in a companion they don't know well.

How adept children eventually become in understanding their emotions and the emotions of others has a direct impact on their social competence. Children who have greater emotional knowledge are better liked by peers and adults. As a result, they are more apt to experience success in their social interactions. Emotional awareness is associated with cooperative, friendly behavior and an increased ability to get along (Dunn, Brown, and Maguire, 1995; Garner, Jones, and Miner, 1994). This combination of knowledge and actions is popularly termed *emotional IQ* (Goleman, 1995). We have become increasingly aware that children who have strong emotional understandings (or a high emotional IQ) are more successful in life than children who do not. Therefore it is imperative that helping professionals do all they can to support children's emotional development and to enhance their skills. In addition to all the developmental changes described, children are faced with a series of emotional tasks that they must navigate successfully to lead happy, productive lives.

## The Emotional Tasks of Childhood

Currently, it is widely believed that people work through a series of emotional tasks over the course of their lives. The person who has most influenced our understanding of what these tasks are is Erik Erikson (1950, 1963). He has identified eight emotional stages through which people progress, four of which take place during the childhood years. Each stage is characterized by positive and negative emotions as well as a central emotional task. This task is to resolve the conflict that arises between the two emotional extremes. Although all children experience a ratio between both poles of a given stage, optimal emotional development occurs when the proportion is weighted toward the positive. These stages build on one another, each serving as the foundation for the next.

**Trust versus mistrust.** The first stage of emotional development takes place during infancy and was described in detail in Chapter 2. The emotional conflict during this stage is whether children will develop self-confidence and trust in the world or feelings of hopelessness, uncertainty, and suspicion. Children who develop positive feelings in this stage learn, "I am loveable and my world is safe and secure."

**Autonomy versus shame and doubt.** Sometime during their second year, toddlers who have developed a strong sense of trust begin to move away from the total dependency of infancy toward having a mind and will of their own. This begins a struggle between feelings of self-assertion and helplessness. What is at stake throughout this period is

whether the child will emerge with a sense of being an independent, self-directed human being, or one who has fundamental misgivings about self-worth. Autonomy begins with muscle control (holding on and letting go), then extends to the social life of the child. Autonomous children do what they can for themselves, whereas nonautonomous children do not act even when they and their caregiver believe that they should. Autonomous children also know that they can take advantage of help and guidance from others while still maintaining ideas of their own. Nonautonomous youngsters doubt their ability to control their world or themselves and so become overly dependent on other people. Children who develop a dominant sense of shame and doubt are those who have few opportunities to explore, to do for themselves, to experiment with objects, or to make decisions. Their attempts at exploration and independence usually are met with impatience, harsh criticism, ridicule, physical restraint, or resistance. In contrast, children who develop a healthy sense of autonomy are given numerous opportunities for mastery, are permitted to make choices, and are given clear, positive messages regarding limits to their behavior.

In order to promote a sense of autonomy many adults working in programs for young children emphasize giving them choices, ranging from which activity to pursue to where to sit at group time. Likewise, youngsters are encouraged to pour their own juice, to dress themselves as much as possible, and to become actively involved in cleaning up after play. Although any of these activities could be more efficiently and skillfully accomplished by adults, the point is to give children opportunities to practice and to let them experience the exhilaration of accomplishment. Autonomy issues also explain the heavy focus in early childhood education to encourage children to experiment with objects, to participate in "hands-on" activities, and to use their bodies to explore the environment. Opportunities for mastery are increased because activities are repeated numerous times and children have ample time to work with each material. Youngsters who successfully navigate this stage learn, "I can make decisions; I can do some things on my own."

**Initiative versus guilt.** During their fourth or fifth year, children develop a new sense of energy. The emotional conflict during this stage is whether this energy will be directed constructively and be valued by others, or whether it will be nonproductive and rejected. Throughout the preschool and early grade-school years, children have experiences with both initiative and guilt by:

Putting plans and ideas into action.
Attempting to master new skills and goals.
Striving to gain new information.
Exploring ideas through fantasy.
Experiencing the sensations of their bodies.
Figuring out ways to maintain their behavior within bounds considered appropriate by society.

Youngsters whose efforts fall short of their own expectations or adult expectations develop a sense of guilt. It is also typical for children to feel guilty for simply thinking "bad" thoughts because they equate thinking with doing. Adults compound this sense of guilt when they make children feel that their physical activity is bad, that their fantasy play is silly, that their exaggerations are lies, that their tendency to begin projects but not complete them is irresponsible, and that their exploration of body and language is so objectionable that they are no longer acceptable persons (Tribe, 1982).

On the other hand, children who develop a strong sense of initiative take pleasure in their increasing competence and find ways to use their energy constructively. They become better able to cooperate and to accept help from others. They also learn that they can work for the things they want without jeopardizing their developing sense of correct behavior.

It is this positive feeling of initiative that helping professionals in early childhood programs try to facilitate when they give children an opportunity to explore their skills in a variety of ways. This is why children are given real tools with which to work—magnifying glasses, tape recorders, kitchen utensils, woodworking tools. It is also why process rather than product is emphasized and why children are encouraged to create their own projects rather than duplicating models provided by adults. Planning activities in which a number of solutions are possible takes into account children's needs for experimentation, as does the introduction of dramatic-play materials.

Finally, when children's transgressions are handled reasonably and sensitively, too great a sense of guilt is avoided. The optimal outcome of this stage is a child who thinks, "I can do, and I can make."

**Industry versus inferiority.** The fourth stage of emotional development takes place throughout middle childhood (approximately six to twelve years of age). During this phase, children become preoccupied with producing things and with adult-like tasks. They also are more interested in joining with others to get things done and in contributing to the society as a whole. The central emotional issue is whether youngsters will come away feeling competent and able, or whether they will believe that their best efforts are inadequate. Although all children have times when they are incapable of mastering what they set out to accomplish, some experience a pervasive sense of failure. This happens when adult, peer, or school standards are clearly beyond their abilities or when they have an unrealistic view of what is possible to achieve. Strong feelings of inferiority also arise when children believe that mastery only counts in select areas in which they are not skilled.

Industriousness is fostered when adults recognize and praise children's success, when they encourage children to explore their skills in a variety of areas, when they help children set realistic goals, and when they set up tasks so children experience mastery. Providing guidance and support to children whose efforts fail eases the pain and gives children the confidence to try again. This is also an important time for adults to encourage children to work with one another in order to experience the satisfaction of working in a group as well as to learn the skills necessary to do so.

In the United States, this stage corresponds to the time when children are becoming deeply involved in formal learning. It also is a period when youngsters pursue extracurricular activities (4-H, Scouts, music lessons, athletics). Both types of experience give children opportunities to learn basic skills and knowledge that they will need to advance in society. However, if feelings of industry are to outweigh those of inferiority, supervising adults must employ the strategies discussed here. When this occurs, children emerge into adolescence thinking, "I can learn, I can contribute, I can work with others."

In this portion of the chapter we have considered four sequences that characterize children's emotional development: (1) how emotions evolve from the core emotions to their more varied forms, (2) how children come to understand what they are feeling, (3) how children recognize other people's emotions, and (4) the emotional tasks of early childhood. These sequences emphasized similarities in children's emotional development from one child to another. Now we will look at the ways in which children differ in their emotional development.

Three factors influence emotional variations: gender differences, cultural differences, and age-related differences.

## Gender Differences in Children's Emotional Expression

Conventional wisdom says that females are more emotionally expressive than males and that females are the more sensitive of the two genders to other people's feelings. Current research tends to support these popular beliefs. From their first year, girls smile more and cry more than boys do. Girls also tend to display more signs of anxious behavior while growing up (Orton, 1982). As they reach the end of their elementary years, girls continue to report feeling more comfortable than boys about openly displaying their emotions (Fuchs and Thelen, 1988). At the same time, girls, more so than boys, are able to figure out what other people are feeling. These tendencies continue throughout the teenage years (Matias and Cohn, 1993). Scientists believe that many of these gender differences are taught directly and modeled from the first days of life. Throughout the United States, parents use more expressive facial expressions with their infant daughters than with their infant sons. Also, they use feeling words more often in conversations with girls than with boys. While adults encourage little girls to express a wide range of emotions, they teach little boys to keep their emotions under control (Bukatko and Daehler, 1995). Although we cannot be sure of the exact role biology plays, these outcomes indicate that the social environment has a major impact on the differences girls and boys display in their expression of emotion. The same is true for children's ability to decode other people's emotional expressions. Another way in which socialization affects children's emotional development is through cultural variations.

## Cultural Variations in Children's Emotional Development

To become successfully integrated into society, children must learn their culture's unique set of *display rules* regarding emotional expression. These rules dictate how emotions are exhibited and which emotions are acceptable in certain situations and which are not. For example, many Chinese children learn to smile to show compliance when being scolded by an elder. Mexican-American children learn to look downcast to indicate respect. Traditionally, Japanese children are taught early in life to keep their emo-

tional impulses in check, and in particular to avoid crying (Harris, 1989). Likewise, many Navajo children come to recognize that they should lower their voices to express anger, unlike Euro-American children who learn to raise theirs in order to get the same message across (Opler, 1967). Children among the Kipsigis in Kenya learn that crying is a positive behavior in infancy, but that this form of emotional expression is viewed with increasing negativity as they grow older (Bukatko and Daehler, 1995). Variations in emotional expression like these are evident from one culture to another and from one family to the next. Children learn these things through observing and interacting with others (Goleman, 1995). Throughout childhood, adults play the central role in this form of socialization. They serve as models for children to imitate and provide relevant feedback and instruction in emotional situations. Obviously, younger children who have had fewer opportunities for such learning have a less sophisticated grasp of these concepts than do older and more experienced youngsters.

**Imitation.** At the lunch following her grandmother's funeral, three-year-old Meridith turns to see her mother grimace and begin to cry. The woman searches for her handkerchief, sobs, and blows her nose. Meridith runs to the buffet table. Grabbing a paper napkin, *she* begins to cry and blow her nose. In this case, Meridith was clearly imitating her mother's emotional expression to guide her own actions in a situation she had never encountered before. A similar, but more subtle form of social referencing occurs when Jorge falls down while running across the playground. He looks up to see how the nearby adult reacts to his fall. If the adult's face registers alarm, the child may determine that this is a worrisome event and begin to cry in response. If the adult's reaction is matter-of-fact, Jorge may register the idea that the fall is no big deal and simply pick himself up to continue his play. As children gain experience in the world, they use circumstances like these to experiment with various forms of emotional expression.

**Feedback.** Adults also provide feedback to children regarding the appropriateness of the ways they choose to express their emotions. Such feedback is offered through gestures and sounds. For instance, when a baby's smile is greeted with the excited voice of the caregiver, the adult's tone serves as a social reward. If this happens often, the baby will smile more frequently. If the infant's smile is consistently ignored, his or her smiling behavior will decrease. Likewise, when Carmen giggles out loud at a funny cartoon, her father laughs along with her. However, when she laughs at her brother who is struggling to play the violin, her father frowns slightly and shakes his head no, indicating that laughter is not an appropriate response in this circumstance. In both cases, Carmen was given feedback regarding her emotional reaction. Scenarios like these are repeated many times throughout childhood. Based on the feedback they receive, children gradually come to know better as to where, when, and how to express their emotions.

**Direct instruction.** In many situations, adults give children specific instructions about the standards of emotional expression. They do this when they point out appropriate and inappropriate reactions of others as well as when they tell children what is expected of them:

> "Look at Sarah—she's being such a baby. She's too old to be carrying on like that."
> "John did a good job of speaking up for himself at the meeting. He was angry, but he didn't lose his temper."
> "You shouldn't laugh at people in wheelchairs."
> "You just won first place. You should be smiling."

Rules such as these may be formal or informal and are enforced using a variety of social costs and rewards.

Taken altogether, imitation, feedback, and instruction contribute to children's ideas about which affective behaviors to retain and which to avoid. These lessons begin in the family and extend to society at large. For example, children who see adults express affection through hugs and kisses learn to use the same gestures to communicate their own caring. Youngsters who seldom witness such displays are less likely to use them. Similarly, when children observe people exhibiting, talking about, and responding to a wide range of feelings, they get the message that emotions are normal and can be shared. Children who witness people covering up their feelings, as well as ignoring the feelings of others, learn the opposite lesson. They also conclude that the way to deal with emotions is to keep them secret or to pretend that they don't exist. These variations in experience lead to variations in the way children express their emotions. Thus, not all children will express their emotions in exactly the same way.

## Variations in Children's Interpretation of Emotional Events

Just as children differ in the forms of emotional expression they exhibit, they also vary in their interpretation of the emotions they are experiencing. Some of these variations are age-related, whereas others are unique to each child.

Certain kinds of events signal certain clusters of emotion over the life span. Joy is a response to discovery, triumph, creative work, or the reduction of stress. Anger occurs when individuals are prevented from pursuing their goals or when they are offended, interrupted, taken advantage of, or forced to act against their desires. Pain or prolonged distress also contribute to angry feelings. Sadness comes about when people are separated from others or when they experience some other kind of loss. Isolation, rejection, and lack of caring all cause sadness. Fear is the emotional response to danger (Berk, 1997; Ekman and Davidson, 1994; Izard, 1977). Although the general events that trigger certain emotions remain constant, cognitive maturity and experience affect children's interpretation of what equates discovery or loss, what is offensive, and what is dangerous. These variations in how children interpret events result in their experiencing the same emotion based on different circumstances at different ages. To illustrates this concept, we examine children's changing notions of what is dangerous and, therefore, frightening.

### Developmental changes in children's fears

Yoko, age two, becomes frightened by the loud noise when her mom turns on the vacuum cleaner. She runs from the room crying.

Jason and Yuri, two sixth graders, one from Idaho the other from Russia, are penpals. In their most recent letters they have shared their anxiety over the final exams each must face at the end of the school year.

Both younger and older children experience fear, but they are not afraid of the same things. Yoko exhibited fear in the presence of loud sounds. Because of her immature thinking and limited experience, she interpreted this noisy, but harmless event as dangerous. In a similar situation, Jason and Yuri could reason that sounds cannot hurt them and remain unafraid. On the other hand, the two-year-old has no comprehension of the potential negative outcomes of a failed exam. As a result, she would be

| ▼ Table 5–2 | Childhood Fears from Birth through Adolescence |
|---|---|
| **AGE** | **SOURCE OF FEAR** |
| 0–6 Months | Loss of physical support, loud noises, flashes of light, sudden movements |
| 7–12 Months | Strangers; heights; sudden, unexpected, and looming objects |
| 1 Year | Separation from or loss of parent, toilet, strangers |
| 2 Years | Separation from or loss of parent, loud sounds, the dark, large objects or machines, unfamiliar peers, changes in familiar environments |
| 3 Years | Separation from or loss of parent, masks, clowns, the dark, animals |
| 4 Years | Separation from or loss of parent, animals, the dark, noises (especially noises at night), bad dreams |
| 5 Years | Separation from or loss of parent, animals, bodily injury, the dark, "bad" people, bad dreams |
| 6 Years | Separation from or loss of parent, the dark, ghosts, witches, bodily injury, thunder and lightning, sleeping or staying alone, bad dreams |
| 7–8 Years | Separation from or loss of parent, the dark, ghosts, witches, sleeping or staying alone, life-threatening situations |
| 9–12 Years | Separation from or loss of parent, the dark, life-threatening situations, death, thunder and lightning, tests or examinations, school performances (e.g., plays, concerts, sporting events), grades, social humiliation |
| Adolescence | Appearance, sexuality, social humiliation, violence (at home and in the street), war |

Sources: Data from Beardslee, W. R. "Youth and the Threat of Nuclear War." *The Lancet* (September 10, 1988): 618–620; Miller, L. C. "Fears and Anxiety in Children." In *Handbook of Clinical Child Psychology,* edited by C. E. Walker and M. C. Roberts. New York: John Wiley & Sons, 1983; Morris, R., and T. Kratochwill. *Treating Children's Fears and Phobias: A Behavioral Approach.* Elmsford, New York: Pergamon, 1983; Papalia, D. E., and S. W. Olds. *A Child's World: Infancy through Adolescence.* New York: McGraw Hill, 1996.

oblivious to the concerns that command Jason's and Yuri's attention.

Such developmental differences in what children fear are common all over the world (Yamamoto, et al., 1987). This is because certain fears typically appear as children reach differing stages of development (Brazelton, 1984). The emergence of these relatively predictable fears is outlined in Table 5–2.

As shown in the table, children's **imaginary fears** (e.g., fear of loud sounds or monsters under the bed; see Figure 5–3) gradually give way to more **realistic fears** (e.g., fear of physical danger or fear of social embarrassment). This progression parallels a developmental shift in children's thinking. That shift comes about from children's more mature understandings of cause and effect, their increasing ability to understand the difference between fantasy and reality, and the growing backlog of experiences they have to draw upon as they mature. In a recent study, 75 percent of the kindergartners, 50 percent of the second graders, and only 5 percent of the sixth graders ranked monsters as something to be afraid of (Papalia and Olds, 1996). In contrast, children's concerns about killing and war escalate with age

(Beardslee, 1988; Rohrer, 1996). War images in the media as well as military involvement by family and friends take on greater meaning as children develop the cognitive ability to understand the real danger of bullets and bombs.

**Learned fears.** The variations in children's fears described so far are mostly age-related. They evolve out of children's developing capabilities and understandings. As such, they are common to most youngsters. However, many children experience special fears that are unique to them and that are primarily learned (Papalia and Olds, 1996). As an example, take six-year-old Tessa's intense apprehension about visiting the dentist. Her fear may have arisen from actual experience (at an earlier visit, she had a tooth filled, and it hurt); she may have observed her mother becoming pale and anxious while settling into the dentist's chair and concluded that this was a frightening situation; or she may have been told directly, "If you're not good, the dentist will have to pull out all your teeth," a horrifying thought! Most likely, she experienced a combination of these influences and encountered them

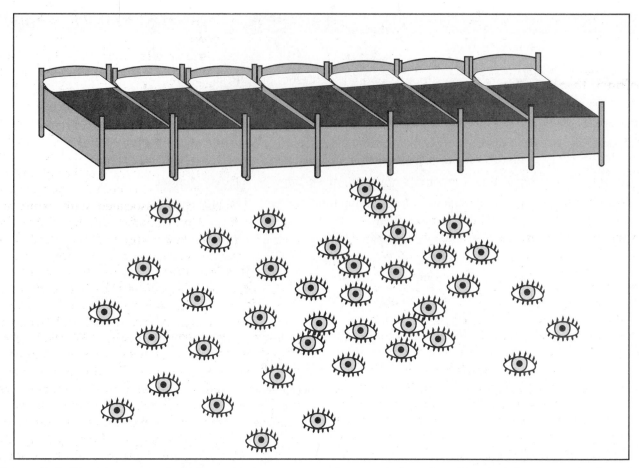

**Figure 5-3** "The Monsters Under Erik's Bed." A computer rendition made by Erik and his dad depicting Erik's fear of the dark at age 4.6 years.

on more than one occasion. In this way she learned to be frightened of going to the dentist. Another child in her place might have put together a different interpretation of these events as an outgrowth of his or her different experiential history. Age-related variations in children's interpretation of emotional events combine with what they have learned to produce certain emotional responses and interpretations. This underscores the fact that children will vary in how they respond to the emotional situations they encounter each day.

In this portion of the chapter, we have focused on many variables that affect children's emotional development. These have included predictable sequences of development as well as variations in how children express and interpret their emotions. The formulation of mature, emotional concepts evolves slowly and is still incomplete as children move into adolescence. As a result, children often experience understandable difficulty in dealing with emotions.

## ▼ Problems Children Encounter When Dealing with Emotions

Martin is so excited about going to the zoo that he keeps interrupting his father, who is trying to get directions for the trip.

Andrea has been waiting a long time to use the kite. Frustrated, she grabs it from Barbara, then dashes to the other side of the playground.

Marsha is jealous of Anita. She constantly "puts her down" to her friends.

Fred is worried about what will happen when his mother goes into the hospital. Rather than letting anybody know his fears, he pretends he doesn't care.

None of these children are handling their emotions particularly well. That is, none of them are dealing with their emotions in a way that will lead to greater personal satisfaction, resolution of a dilemma, or increased social competence.

## Difficulties Experienced by Children from Infancy through Age Seven

Children are not born knowing how to manage their emotions. As a result they sometimes rely on strategies that are not helpful to themselves or others. For instance, because of their lack of social skills and immature language capabilities, children often act out how they feel. They may pout when angry, huddle when frightened, or jump up and down when excited. In these situations, children expect others to interpret their emotions accurately and to respond in supportive ways. Unfortunately, nonverbal expressions of emotions may be misunderstood. For instance, an adult may assume that a crying child is tired, when fear is really the source of the child's distress. Putting the child to bed, which is a reasonable way to support tired children, is not the best strategy for helping children cope with fear. Miscommunication is even more likely when children express feelings like frustration, discouragement, wariness, anticipation, or curiosity. Such emotions often are expressed through subtle signals that do not stand out. As a result, children's less dramatic emotions may be ignored altogether.

Another problem for youngsters two to seven years of age is that they often choose inappropriate actions to show how they feel. Their poor choices may be due to poor modeling, lack of know-how, or their immature understandings of their own emotions. For instance, young children's tendency to recognize only one emotion at a time prompts them to feel each emotion intensely and totally. This is why they become angry with such a vengeance and affectionate with such a passion. Thus, the physical actions they choose to relay their feelings often are equally extreme. Such forceful behaviors frequently are viewed as socially unacceptable.

Finally, because children of this age have difficulty recognizing other people's feelings accurately, they may respond in ways that are inappropriate for the situation. This happens when Sam misinterprets Antonio's friendly teasing to be a purposeful insult. Sam may respond with an aggressive reaction that does not correspond to the other child's intent. If these kinds of misinterpretations become common for Sam, he will find it harder to have satisfying relationships with peers.

## Difficulties Experienced by Children Ages Seven to Twelve

Children in the later elementary years are more aware of their emotions and how to use words to communicate them. However, they are less likely to be open about their emotions than are younger children. Children ages seven to twelve often try to hide, minimize, or avoid their emotions altogether (Lewis, Wolman, and King, 1972). This happens because they are very aware of the social rules governing emotional behavior and because they wish to avoid the social costs associated with expressing certain feelings. Unfortunately, the discrepancy between their real emotions and what they think those emotions should be causes great emotional distress (Goleman, 1995). When children hide their emotions, they have no opportunity to discover that they have experiences in common with other people. This leads to feelings of isolation, self-doubt, and inferiority (Adler, 1923; Sullivan, 1957; Woll, 1990). Youngsters in these circumstances come to think of their emotions as unnatural and different from anyone else's or the established norm. The more intense this perception, the more damaging the outcome. A dramatic example of the harm that can come from trying to hide one's emotions is illustrated by Cathleen Brook's description of life in an alcoholic home:

> When I was growing up in an alcoholic home, one of the things that I was acutely aware of was that when I felt sad, or angry, or panicked, or hurt, there was no place—and no one—where I was safe enough to talk about how I felt.
>
> I also noticed something else: that when the adults in my life had the same feelings, they did something to try to make those feelings go away. They used a chemical, they used food, they used "busy-ness," they used control and management of themselves, others, and situations.
>
> I really believed that noise and upsetting and making people uncomfortable was what made things so bad in my house. So I spent my life trying never to make noise and always to be good, and never making anyone uncomfortable. And it didn't work.
>
> And I found alcohol, and it worked.
>
> It's amazing how well that stuff works. I spent 11 years of my life without it, and at 11 I put it in my body and I became who I had wanted to be. It was amazing. Alcohol was the only thing that made a great deal of sense to me. Had you been there to try to talk me out of using alcohol, I want to assure you that you would have been ignored and probably ridiculed.
>
> But had you been there to tell me you cared what I was feeling, you might have made all the difference.

Had you been there to tell me you might even know a little bit of what I was feeling, I might have believed that there was some human being in the world I could count on.

(Woll, 1990:1)

Not all children resort to drugs and alcohol to deal with their emotions. However, the fact that some do tells us that emotional development is not always an easy, healthy process.

## The Negative Effects of Adult Behavior

The difficulties children naturally experience in handling their emotions sometimes are compounded by inappropriate adult responses. Imagine what might happen to Paulo when he declares his pride in having won honorable mention in the cooking contest. If his teacher responds with a comment like, "Cool!" or "You're really excited," Paulo's pride is acknowledged and he receives the message that feeling proud is okay.

In contrast, if the teacher says, "That's nice, but when are you going to get that math assignment done?" Paulo may conclude that his feelings are unimportant and that he should not be talking about them. An even more blatant negative message is conveyed when the teacher says, "You should be more modest. No bragging!" Such comments teach Paulo that feelings of pride and accomplishment are inappropriate. Being told that his feelings are bad may cause the child to evaluate himself negatively for having experienced them. Since children naturally experience a wide range of emotions, if this trend continues, Paulo may come to view a natural part of himself as unacceptable.

When children arrive at such conclusions, they often choose maladaptive ways of coping. Paulo may become boastful as a way of bolstering his sagging confidence. He may reject compliments in an effort to adhere to an expected code of emotional conduct. Paulo may stop trying to excel as a way to avoid pride and achievement. He may develop a headache or stomachache in response to situations in which he might otherwise feel proud, or he may continually put himself down in an effort to look modest. All of these strategies take away from Paulo's future happiness.

There are four ways of responding to children's emotions that are ineffective or potentially harmful. These include ignoring children, lying to children, denying children's feelings, and shaming children (Fraiberg, 1968; Hendrick, 1996; Peake and Egli, 1982). All of these strategies not only cause damage

at the time they are used, but also eliminate the adult as a future source of emotional support on which children can rely.

**Ignoring children's emotions.** Sometimes adults assume that if they ignore children's emotions those emotions will simply go away. This does not happen. The emotions remain, but regrettably children have no better way of coping. To make matters worse, children are left with the impression that their feelings are unimportant. Neither outcome leads to greater social competence or positive self-esteem.

**Lying to children about emotional situations.** Sometimes, in an effort to "protect" children from difficult emotional experiences, adults fail to tell the truth. For example, Arnie is afraid about having blood drawn, and the technician attempts to soothe him by saying, "This won't hurt a bit." Similarly, Mary Ellen expresses concern to an adult about going to the church picnic because of another child who often picks on her. The adult, knowing that the bullying child will be attending, attempts to smooth over the situation by saying, "I heard he wasn't coming." Such lies fail to prepare children for the reality of the situations they are facing and damage the credibility of the adult. Bonds of trust, which take time to establish, are destroyed.

**Denying children's emotions.** There are many ways in which adults deny children's emotions. Sometimes, adults actually forbid children to have certain feelings. Phrases like "Stop worrying," "Don't be angry," or "You shouldn't be so scared" are examples of this approach. At other times, adults dismiss the importance of the emotion being expressed, as when Lucas cried, "Look, there's blood on my finger," and the adult responded: "It's just a little cut. You won't die." On other occasions, adults tell children they don't really have the emotion they claim to be experiencing: "You know you aren't really mad at each other," "Let's see you smile," "No more tears!"

When adults deny children's emotions, the message they are conveying is that these emotions are wrong and that children are bad for experiencing them. Neither of these messages is true nor helpful.

**Shaming children.** Making fun of children or attempting to shame them out of their emotions is a destructive practice. Adults demoralize children when they say things like: "What are you crying for? I can't believe you're such a baby about this," "All the other kids are having a good time. Why are you being so difficult?", or "Manny isn't afraid. What makes you such a scaredy-cat?" As with lying and denying, shaming makes children feel doubtful, inferior, and inadequate. It certainly does not cause them to respond positively or make them feel better. For this reason, it has no place in a helping professional's collection of skills.

Adults often resort to ignoring, lying, denying, and shaming when they are trying to avoid a scene or comfort children by minimizing the intensity of the moment. Such strategies have the opposite effect. They not only make matters worse but prevent children from learning more effective ways to handle emotional situations. In place of these destructive practices, adults can use alternative strategies to promote children's feelings of trust, competence, and worth and help them increase their interpersonal skills.

## ▼ APPROPRIATE WAYS OF RESPONDING TO CHILDREN'S EMOTIONS

To help youngsters cope more effectively with their emotions, adults must act in supportive ways. Rather than trying to eliminate or restrict children's feelings, adults should accept them, even as they attempt to change the behaviors children use in emotional situations. Such acceptance is synonymous with the idea of acceptance or unconditional positive regard described in Chapters 1 and 4. Adults are better able to take on this role when they keep in mind the following principles:

1. Children's emotions are real and legitimate to them.
2. There are no right or wrong emotions. All feelings stem from core emotions, which occur naturally.
3. Children cannot necessarily help how they feel, nor can they simply change their emotions on command.
4. All emotions serve useful functions in children's lives.

Words are a satisfying, more precise way to express emotions and frequently are an appropriate substitute for physical action. Thus, in working with either preschool or school-age children, one obvious solution to the difficulties children experience in handling emotions is to teach them to talk more openly about what they are feeling.

### Talking to Children About Their Emotions

The first step in encouraging children to talk about their emotions is to acquaint them with the vocabulary used to describe emotions (Peake and Egli, 1982). Because children learn best from first-hand experience, they benefit when their emotions are named and described to them when they occur. For instance, if Matt is angry and an adult identifies this emotion ("Matt, you look angry"), the child has a "hands-on" experience with the concept. Not only does he learn that his emotional state is describable, but he also has a relevant opportunity to take in both the internal and situational cues related to that emotion. This is a more relevant learning experience than simply having Matt identify emotions in hypothetical situations because it combines all three elements of mature emotional understanding—a situation, a body reaction, and an interpretation. The strategy adults can use to name and describe children's emotions is called an *affective reflection*.

### Affective Reflections

Affect refers to people's feelings or moods. **Affective reflections** are similar in form and intent to the behavior and paraphrase reflections presented in Chapter 4. They involve recognizing the emotions a child may be experiencing in a given situation and then using a reflection to name the emotions.

**Situation:** Barry has climbed to the top of the jungle gym. With a big smile on his face, he announces, "Hey, everybody, look at me!"

> *Adult:* You're *proud* you climbed so high. (Or, either of the following: It feels *good* to be at the top; You made it! That's *exciting*.)

**Situation:** Marlene complains that she had to clean up before her turn was over.

> *Adult:* You *wish* you didn't have to clean up just yet. (Or: You didn't get to finish your turn. That's *annoying*; It's *frustrating* to be interrupted.)

**Situation:** Earl is embarrassed about having to take a shower with the other boys after gym class.

> *Adult:* It makes you *uncomfortable* to take a shower in public. (Or: You *wish* you didn't have to take your clothes off in front of everybody; It really seems *unbelievable* to you that this is required.)

Affective reflections like these acknowledge and help to define children's emotions. In each situation, the adult's words and voice tone should match the emotional state being described, enhancing the completeness of the message.

**Benefits to children of using affective reflections.** Labeling children's emotions using affective reflections makes abstract, internal states more tangible; that is, naming something helps it to become more concrete (Berk and Winsler, 1995). In addition, known events are easier to comprehend than unknown ones. Labels allow sensations to become more familiar. Because emotions cannot be touched or held and have elements that are not directly observable, labeling them is a particularly important strategy.

Verbal labels also are the primary means by which people recognize and recall past events (DiVesta and Rickards, 1971; Mussen, et al., 1990; Vygotsky, 1978). An irritated child who has heard irritation described in the past is better able to identify her or his current emotional state. This recognition helps her or him draw from past experience to determine a possible course of action (Boneau, 1974).

Furthermore, language labels help to differentiate emotions that are perceptually similar but not entirely the same (Harris, 1989). On hearing the words annoyed, disgusted, and enraged, you think of slightly different emotional states. All of these are variations on anger, yet are distinctive in their own right. Hearing different affective reflections enables children to be more precise in understanding what they are feeling. Moreover, as youngsters hear alternate feeling words, they adopt many of them for their own use. The broader their vocabulary, the more satisfied youngsters are in using feeling words to express their emotions to others (Kostelnik, 1977). They also are likely to exhibit more varied emotional reactions. Annoyance, disgust, and rage, for instance, may cause a child to envision different behavioral responses. Support for this line of reasoning comes from language research that shows that as people learn new words, their understanding of experience and ability to categorize events is strongly influenced by speech (Berk and Winsler, 1995; Vygotsky, 1978; Waxman, 1989).

When adults acknowledge children's emotions using affective reflections, they exhibit sensitivity and caring in a way children can understand. This acknowledgement makes children feel heard and accepted (Ginott, 1972; Seligman, 1995). Not only do youngsters recognize that their emotions are respected by the adult, but as they hear their own and other people's emotions being described, they discover that their emotions are not so different from anyone else's (Bessell, 1970). This reduces the chances that they will view their own emotional experiences as abnormal. Affective reflections help children comprehend that all emotions, both pleasant and unpleasant, are an inevitable part of living.

The affective reflections just described are fundamental to enhancing children's emotional development. They can be used with children of all ages and in a wide array of circumstances. At times, the adult's purpose in using this skill is to focus more closely on the emotional aspects of an interaction. At other times, affective reflections are used to acknowledge the child's feelings while also dealing with other kinds of issues, such as making a rule or enforcing a consequence. Use of this skill also contributes to the construction of a positive verbal environment. Finally, as you progress through this book, you will see that affective reflections are a foundation on which many other skills are built.

## Helping Children Express Their Emotions to Others

In addition to helping children identify emotions through affective reflections, adults can also help children talk about their emotions and express them in acceptable ways. Children who are able to describe their emotions in words make it easier for others to know what they are feeling. Miscommunication is less likely, and the chances of gaining necessary support are better.

This type of emotional sharing is often referred to as *self-disclosure* and is considered a basic interpersonal skill. Interaction theories that stress open and honest communication all describe skills similar to, or synonymous with, this concept (Danish and Hauer, 1984; Gazda, 1995; Rogers, 1961). This is because there is strong evidence that the degree to which people are able to express their emotions to others influences their ability to maintain close personal ties (Salovey and Mayer, 1990). Also, when children learn to use words, they are less likely to resort to physical means to express negative feelings. Children who learn to say, "I'm angry" eventually realize that they don't have to shove or hit to make their point.

Children become better skilled at describing emotions when adults provide appropriate information about what people are feeling and why, rather than expecting children to know these things automatically (Hendrick, 1996). Younger children benefit from information related to expressive and situational cues (e.g., "Corine sure looks excited.

She is laughing and jumping," or "Rafe dropped the ball. He seems upset"). Older children profit from input related to people's internal affective states (e.g., "Esther is still upset about the score from yesterday," or "Boris, you enjoyed describing our picnic last year"). Additionally, children increase their social competence by learning actual phrases and scripts to use in emotional situations (Crary, 1993). For instance phrases such as, "I'm still working on this," or "You can have it when I'm finished" give children tools to express their needs when they don't want to give something up. Youngsters who have no such tools may resort to less acceptable physical actions or give way unnecessarily, leaving

them frustrated or upset. Likewise, scripts such as, "I want a turn," or "I'm next," make it easier for children to negotiate in highly charged situations such as deciding who gets the next turn on the tricycle or the computer.

Youngsters in difficult emotional circumstances become more adept at coping when, in addition to helping them acknowledge their own feelings, adults instruct them in how to make such situations more manageable. This can be accomplished either by teaching a child a specific skill or by remaining supportive to children who are working out these issues for themselves. The following section describes ways to implement such strategies.

## SKILLS FOR RESPONDING TO CHILDREN'S EMOTIONS

### Formulate Affective Reflections

**1. Observe children carefully before saying anything.** The context of a situation is important to its meaning. Pay close attention to children's facial expressions, voice tone, and posture as well as their actual words. If no words are spoken, you will have to rely on body cues alone. Because younger children tend to be more open about what they are feeling, the behaviors they display may be easier to interpret than those exhibited by older children. The emotions of grade-schoolers, who have been socialized to respond in certain ways, or who have learned to hide their emotions, may be more difficult to decipher. With these children, you must pay particular attention to nonverbal cues. A child who is talking "happy" but looking "distressed" most likely is distressed.

**2. Be sensitive to the wide range of emotions children exhibit.** Children manifest numerous emotions. Some are extreme, some are more moderate; some are positive, some are negative. All of their emotions are important. If you only take the time to notice intense emotions, or focus solely on the negative ones, children soon learn that these are the only emotions worth expressing. They get a broader perspective when all sorts of emotions are noticed and described.

**3. Make a nonjudgmental assessment of what the child is experiencing.** Form your impression of the child's feelings using only evidence about which you are certain. Avoid jumping to conclusions about why children feel the way they do. For instance, you may observe Jack entering the room crying. It is obvious that he is either sad or angry, but why he is so distressed may not be evident. Although you may assume that he is missing his mother, he might really be upset about having to wear his orange sweater to school. Because you cannot be sure what is bothering him, an appropriate affective reflection would be "You look sad," rather than "You're sad because you miss your mom." Opening the interaction with the first statement is potentially more accurate than using the latter.

**4. Make a brief statement to the child describing the emotion you observed.** Keep your reflection simple. Do not try to cram everything you have noticed about the child's emotional state into one response. Young children understand short sentences best. This also is true for youngsters for whom English is not their home language or those who are mentally impaired. Older children will appreciate longer sentences or combinations of phrases, but will resent being overwhelmed with too much adult talk.

*continued*

**SKILLS FOR RESPONDING TO CHILDREN'S EMOTIONS—continued**

**5. Use a variety of feeling words over time.** Employ many different words to describe children's emotions. This emphasis on diversity expands children's vocabulary of feeling words and makes your responses more interesting. Begin by using words to describe the core emotions (happy, mad, sad, afraid). Gradually, branch out to include related words that make finer distinctions (variations of happy, such as delighted, pleased, contented, overjoyed). Once you have reached the latter point, think in advance of two or three words you have not used recently and plan to employ them on a given day. Each time a situation arises for which one of your words is suited, use it. Repeat this process with different words on different days.

Finally, when you reflect using one of the more common feeling words in your vocabulary, follow it with a second reflection using a slightly different word ("You seem sad. It sounds like you're disappointed the model didn't fly").

**6. Acknowledge children's emotions even when you do not approve of them.** At times, children express emotions adults find unreasonable, unfathomable, or loathsome. For instance, Shavette comes to the recreation center, furious. Snarling through clenched teeth, she hisses, "I hate that teacher. All she knows how to do is give homework, and there's no time for anything else." At this point, it might be tempting to:

*Lecture.* "Shavette, I've told you never to say 'hate'. That's not a nice way to feel about anyone."
*Rationalize.* "Well, she really has to do that so you'll learn your math."
*Deny.* "You couldn't hate anybody, could you?"
*Ignore.* "Well, enough of that. Go pick out a board game to play."

Unfortunately, all of these responses communicate insensitivity to the situation from Shavette's perspective and make it unlikely that she will share her feelings with you in the future. Additionally, responses such as these cause her to react defensively or resort to more extreme measures to make her true emotions known. Her impression probably will not be

changed, and she has not learned constructive ways of handling her rage. A better response would be: "It doesn't seem fair to have to do so much homework," or "It sounds like you had a rotten day at school." Affective reflections like these are not only desirable but imperative. They force you to get beyond your own emotions and make you recognize a viewpoint very different from your own. This must be accomplished if children are to trust you and give you access to their private selves.

**7. Revise inaccurate reflections.** Affective reflections are tentative statements of your perceptions of the child's emotional state. If you reflect, "You seem worried," and the child says something like "No" or "I'm just thinking," accept the correction gracefully: "Oh, I misunderstood you," or "I'm sorry. I didn't mean to interrupt."

## Common Questions about Formulating Affective Reflections

The mechanics of formulating an affective reflection are not difficult. However, when adults begin to practice affective reflections, questions often come up regarding their implementation in real-life situations. We have identified the most common of these questions and have provided answers that should enhance your ability to use this skill more effectively.

**1. Do children really correct inaccurate affective reflections?** Expect that there will be times when your interpretation of a child's emotional state does not exactly match the child's perception. Initially, children may not know enough about their emotions to correct you. However, it is likely that there will be other times when your reflection is accurate. As children come to identify both the internal and situational cues that match the label you have applied, they will become more sensitive to your occasional inaccuracies. Once this happens, most children will not hesitate to correct a mislabeled emotion.

Correcting inaccurate reflections will come more easily to children once they become more familiar with your use of reflective responses and recognize that all reflections are tentative

## SKILLS FOR RESPONDING TO CHILDREN'S EMOTIONS—continued

statements. You reiterate this point when you say "You seem pleased" or "You look sad" rather than "You must be pleased" or "I know you are sad."

**2. How do I introduce feeling words that I'm not sure children already know?** One way to help children understand new feeling words is to use your body, face, and voice to illustrate the affective state to which you are referring. For example, if Annice seems to be frustrated, say, "You look very frustrated," and accompany the words with a serious tone, a frown, and a shrug of the shoulders.

A second approach is to tell Annice what it is about her behavior that leads you to believe she is frustrated: "You seem frustrated. Your body is very tense and you are frowning."

Another effective strategy is to use the unfamiliar word in a short reflection and then follow it with a second sentence defining the word you have used: "You seem frustrated. It can be discouraging to work and work and still the pieces don't fit," or "You're disappointed. You wish we didn't have to stay inside because of the rain."

**3. Why use an affective reflection, rather than just ask children about their feelings?** At times it may seem easier to simply inquire: "How are you feeling" or "Are you feeling sad?" or "Why are you so angry?" Well-meaning questions such as these sometimes are answered, but many times they are not. When you are involved in emotional situations, remember that children are not always sure what they are feeling or why. Also, they may not be ready to give you the answer you are seeking. In either case, children's discomfort may be increased by an inquiry directed at them. It is more supportive to first give children an indication that you are simply trying to recognize their emotional state. This is best communicated through an affective reflection, to which the child does not have to respond, and which is correctable. Children are more likely to answer questions after you have reflected first. Thus, it is appropriate to say: "You look sad. What happened?" In this situation, the child has the option of accepting your help or not. Regardless of which is chosen, the child knows you are available.

**4. What if, after I reflect, the child still doesn't want to talk to me?** Adults sometimes are nonplussed when they try to demonstrate their empathy through an affective reflection and the child remains unresponsive. For instance, you might reflect: "That looks like fun. You seem excited," or "You weren't expecting him to say that. You look upset," and the child does not acknowledge your comment. At times like these, it helps to remember that the purpose of any reflection is to indicate your interest in children without intruding on them. Once children come to understand this purpose, they frequently say nothing. Thus, lack of response may indicate that you are using the skill well. Moreover, if your reflection is accurate, there is no need for youngsters to confirm your interpretation. It is not likely that you will hear: "You noticed that I'm excited. Yes, I'm having a wonderful time!" or "You're right," or "Yes, I am." Children often do not talk because they are absorbed in what they are experiencing and prefer to focus on that, rather than on you. Yet, even in circumstances such as these, they have the opportunity to hear their feelings defined and to know that you are interested in what is happening to them. Both of these factors have a positive influence on children's emotional development. When children obviously are distressed but do not want to talk about it, it can be very effective to say: "You seem pretty angry. It looks like you don't want to talk about it right now. I'll be around if you want to talk later," or "I'll check back with you to see if you change your mind."

**5. Do I always have to reflect before I take action?** Some adults mistakenly presume that reflecting must always precede or take the place of action. They envision themselves having to have a long conversation with a child prior to intervening in a problem situation. This is an erroneous assumption. For instance, Billy comes in from the playground and says, "Teacher, teacher, Margo cut her knee!" The adult could easily respond to Billy, "You're worried about Margo's knee. Let's take a look," while hurrying over to the playground. Likewise, if two children are hitting each other, the adult should quickly grasp their hands while reflecting, "You two are very angry with each other." This

*continued*

## SKILLS FOR RESPONDING TO CHILDREN'S EMOTIONS—continued

affective reflection sets the stage for further action and explanations.

**6. What do I do if children use inappropriate behaviors to express their emotions?** Although children's behavior may be unacceptable, their feelings still must be acknowledged. Occasionally, this acknowledgment will be sufficient to satisfy the child's emotional needs. For instance, Mallory spits to demonstrate her anger. If the anger is recognized with an affective reflection, Mallory may no longer think it is necessary to spit to get her point across. The conditions are now set for the adult to assist the child in figuring out more acceptable ways to communicate anger. Even if Mallory were to continue spitting and the adult had to employ more extensive discipline strategies (many of which will be discussed later in this book), an affective reflection is the first step toward changing the child's behavior. What you must make clear to the child is that although all emotions are acceptable, all behaviors are not.

**7. What if I can't tell what the child is feeling?** Emotions that are not extreme sometimes are difficult to interpret. Additionally, some children are less expressive than others. Both of these circumstances may impede your ability to immediately recognize what a child is feeling. As you get to know individual children, you will become more adept at identifying the behaviors they use when they are experiencing certain emotions. Iris flexes her fingers rapidly when she is nervous; Phil makes long pauses between his words when confused; Justin becomes belligerent when frightened. If you do not know the child well, or there are no outward signs to guide you, use a behavior or paraphrase reflection as an entree to the interaction. Wait, and use an affective reflection after you have considered, via words and gestures, what the child may be feeling. If no such opportunity arises, ask children directly; they may or may not be willing or able to tell you. If none of these strategies have worked, continue to observe and remain supportive, but do not force children to pursue a conversation.

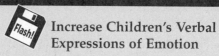

**Increase Children's Verbal Expressions of Emotion**

**1. Set an example for talking about emotions by bringing them up yourself.** Include emotions in your casual conversations. Talk about how everyday events affect you ("What a great day. I'm so happy to see the sun out," or "I hate it when this plumbing keeps backing up"). Discuss events in terms of how they will affect people's feelings ("It sounds like if we don't have macaroni for lunch, everyone will be disappointed," or "If we were to leave without telling Ms. Jones, she might be worried"). Ask children how they might feel about particular events as they arise ("Oh, it's raining. Who here likes rain? Who here doesn't like rain?" or "Today, we're going to hear a poem about trees. Everyone think of one way they feel when they look at a tree"). Discuss emotions experienced by people children know or people they have heard about in the news ("Mr. Sanchez, our principal, feels really good today. He became a grandfather," or "It was scary for the people along Spring Creek when the flood came"). Point out emotions experienced by characters in stories. Any kind of story can serve as a prompt for this type of discussion, not only "official" feeling stories ("Goldilocks was pretty frightened," or "Laura Ingalls felt excited about going to town with her pa").

**2. Help children recognize opportunities to describe their emotions to others.** Children often mistakenly believe that what they are feeling is obvious to everyone around them. Explain this is not always true ("You're disappointed that Melinda didn't help you like she'd promised. She doesn't know that's how you are feeling. Tell her so she'll know," or "You didn't want Claudia to take the hammer just yet. She didn't know that. Say that to her").

**3. Provide children with sample words to help them talk about their emotions.** Sometimes, children fail to express their emotions verbally because they lack the words or they are too emotionally involved to think of them. If this happens, do one of the following:

## SKILLS FOR RESPONDING TO CHILDREN'S EMOTIONS—continued

**a.** Suggest words to the child that fit the situation. This is, in essence, a verbal script (Kathy could be advised to say: "Claudia, I wasn't finished with the hammer," or "Claudia, I don't like it when you grab"). Younger or less experienced children benefit when given brief phrases to consider. Older or more experienced youngsters are better able to consider longer sentences and more than one alternate approach. Once children become more comfortable and adept at using the scripts you provide, help them think of some of their own ("You're upset with Claudia. Tell me words you could use to let her know that").

**b.** Ask children questions that prompt them to describe how they feel. Begin by using simple yes-no questions ("Marco took your pliers. Did you like it when he did that?") Over time, advance to more open-ended inquiries ("Marco took your pliers. How did that make you feel?").

**4. Help children figure out behavioral cues that tell how another person is feeling.** Children are not always aware of what other people are feeling, nor are they completely accurate in their interpretations. Point out specific signs of people's emotional expression to toddlers and less experienced preschoolers ("Pearl is crying. That means she is unhappy"). Prompt older, more experienced youngsters to notice these cues for themselves ("Look at Pearl. Tell me what she is doing and what she might be feeling"). If a relevant answer is not forthcoming, provide the appropriate information yourself.

**5. Draw children's attention to situational cues that contribute to people's emotions.** Tell toddlers and preschoolers what features of a situation triggered an emotion ("Julie and Chris both wanted the last banana cupcake. They decided to split it. They're pretty happy. People feel good when they can work things out," or "Garland, you had been waiting a long time to use the easel, and now it's all drippy. You look disappointed about that"). Ask older children to tell you what it was about a situation that they

thought prompted the emotional reaction. This strategy can be applied both to situations in which the child is an observer and to those in which the child is directly involved. In addition, point out similarities and differences in children's reactions to the same event ("You both saw the same movie, and it sounds like each of you enjoyed it," or "You both saw the same movie. Emma, it sounds like you really thought it was funny. Janice, you're not so sure").

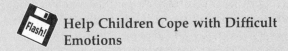 **Help Children Cope with Difficult Emotions**

**1. Acknowledge children's negative emotions and forbid destructive actions.** Do this using an affective reflection followed by a statement such as: "It's all right to be angry. It is *not* OK to hit." (More about this type of intervention will be presented in later chapters).

**2. Comfort children who are sad or afraid.** Offer physical and verbal consolation. In this way, you provide a safe, secure refuge for children in distress. It is from this secure base that they eventually may be able to face the cause of their feelings.

**3. Help children sort out mixed emotions.** Begin by listening to the child describe the situation. Acknowledge each of the emotions you hear or observe when multiple emotions are evident. Tell children that it is normal to have different feelings at the same time. Also, point out discrepancies between the child's words and what he or she might be expressing in nonverbal ways ("You're telling me everything is fine, but you look miserable").

**4. Provide children with information to enlarge their perception of an emotional event.** Point out to children facts about the situation they may have missed ("You thought Andrew was making fun of you, but he was laughing at a joke he just heard," or "You didn't notice that Melba wanted a turn too. She's been waiting a long time"). Help older children reconsider the meaning of negative situations. For instance, a

*continued*

## SKILLS FOR RESPONDING TO CHILDREN'S EMOTIONS—continued

disappointing outcome (e.g., not making the team or missing several words on a spelling test) could be viewed as failure or as a challenge for the future; an angry encounter with a friend could be interpreted as complete disaster or as a learning experience for next time. Begin with an affective reflection, followed by a brief information statement to refocus children's attention on the more positive interpretation ("You're disappointed with your score. That's understandable. A good thing that has come out of this is that now you have a pretty clear idea of what you have to work on," or "It feels bad to fight with such a good friend. One way to think about it is that now you know why Roger is mad. Maybe that will help you figure out what to do the next time you see him.") Keep your observation short and matter of fact. Do not insist that children agree with your reinterpretation of events. Simply provide additional information for them to think about.

When children are afraid, what they might imagine is often worse than reality. Again, information is useful. Tell children what to expect in new situations. Describe possible outcomes, both pleasant and unpleasant. Offer explanations for events as children experience them. ("When you hear the fire alarm it will make a loud sound. Some of you said you didn't like it being so noisy. It's loud like that so no matter where we are in the building, we can hear it. That alarm tells us we must leave. We will walk outside quickly and quietly all together. I'll be with you the whole time.")

### 5. Provide opportunities for children to observe how others cope in a situation they fear.
Encourage youngsters to watch peers who are unafraid in situations that are anxiety provoking for them. For instance, children who are afraid of the water often feel less fearful after watching other age-mates play safely at the water's edge. Likewise, children about to undergo their first dental visit have been found to benefit from observing a videotape of an older child demonstrating relaxed behavior and receiving verbal reinforcement during treatment (Murphy, 1985). Refrain from chastising fearful children if they do not immediately follow suit. In-

stead, allow them to observe, or even not observe, as long as they wish.

### 6. Allow children to approach a feared situation gradually.
Help children work their way to a point at which the fear becomes manageable. For example, a child who is afraid of dogs could benefit from going through the following steps:
a. Looking at pictures of dogs
b. Watching a video about a dog
c. Playing with a stuffed toy dog
d. Observing other children playing with dogs
e. Observing a puppy being held in the lap of an adult
f. Touching a puppy being held by an adult
g. Holding a sleeping puppy on his or her lap

There is no one right way to carry out such a process. Adults should be sensitive to the cues children exhibit and introduce a new, harder step only after a child has comfortably mastered the current one. Youngsters vary in how long the process takes and how elaborate it must be. Adult impatience only adds to their anxiety and negates the potential benefits that may be derived.

### 7. Teach children to use self-talk or self-encouragement ("I am a brave boy/girl"; "The water is a fun place to be").
Help children figure out the exact words they might say to themselves in difficult situations. Preschoolers benefit from hearing sample scripts, such as "I can do it." Older children appreciate developing sample words in collaboration with the adult. For example, you might say, "You're unsure of the _____. What could you tell yourself that will remind you it's not too bad?" Once the wording for a particular child has been mutually established, write it out on a 3 × 5 card for the child and make a copy for yourself. This will help each of you remember the phrasing should the occasion arise again.

### 8. Help children think of new strategies or learn new skills as a way to deal with difficult emotions.
Brainstorm a wide variety of ideas for how children can prepare themselves for

## SKILLS FOR RESPONDING TO CHILDREN'S EMOTIONS—continued

similar situations in the future or how they can respond to an ongoing problem. Here are ideas children have generated to master a personal crisis:

A child who was easily angered imagined his foe as having three funny heads.

A youngster who was frightened about going to a new school drew a map showing the way from the main office to her room.

A child who felt awkward at games decided to practice kicking the ball every day for 15 minutes.

If children cannot think of any ideas themselves, offer several suggestions of your own for them to consider. Accept their choice, even if it involves no choice being made.

 **Communicate with the Family**

**1. Provide information to family members about the emotions children experience during their time with you.** Focus on everyday affective happenings; do not wait for a crisis or for something extraordinary to prompt messages home from you ("Jamal built a city with all the blocks today. He was excited to have found a way to use every single block," or "Today, Jarad was very absorbed in writing in his journal about his time in New Jersey. Later he read his entry to the group. The other children asked him a lot of questions about his trip. He seemed pleased with their interest"). Such information can be shared in person, through short written notes, or through periodic calls home. Make it a goal to communicate with every family in your group at least once month in this regard. Keep an informal record of your communications to make sure you are not giving a lot of information to some families and very little to others.

**2. Elicit information from family members about children's emotional lives at home.** Stay attuned to changes in children's home lives. Day-to-day events such as a disrupted night's sleep, an anticipated trip to the store after school, or a friend coming over later in the afternoon prompt emotional reactions in children.

Likewise, more dramatic happenings such as an impending divorce, mom being away on a trip, dad's girlfriend moving in, or an upcoming family event influence how children feel during their time with you. Let families know that this kind of communication enables you to respond with greater understanding to the children.

Encourage family members to write short notes or to call you with bits of news, especially if daily personal contact is not possible. Talk about this kind of communication at orientation events. Make sure it is emphasized in written materials that go home. Establish "telephone hours," times when families know you are available to take calls, during the day or week. Such strategies confirm your desire to hear from family members.

Take advantage of informal opportunities to learn more about children's emotions. Make yourself available at the beginning and end of the day to chat as parents, grandparents, or siblings drop off or pick up younger children. Avoid being busy with housekeeping details or other program management–related activities during these family transition times. Make available a wipe-off board or a box labeled "daily communication center" for "walk-in" families to use to communicate with you. Attend family events (e.g., potlucks, science or book fairs, concerts, work parties, parent workshops) sponsored by your program to experience informal contact with children's families, even when these events are not particularly focused on your group. Becoming a familiar face in the program and bumping into family members at siblings' events are effective ways to increase your accessibility to families.

**3. Help family members better understand typical facets of children's emotional development.** Mr. Ramirez mentions that his seemingly happy three-year-old became hysterical at the sight of a clown giving out balloons at the mall. He wonders what might have prompted such a strong reaction. During a parent conference, a mother remarks that her fourth grade daughter is in a quandary about an upcoming dance recital. The parent says, "One minute she's excited; the next minute she's terrified. She seems

*continued*

## SKILLS FOR RESPONDING TO CHILDREN'S EMOTIONS—continued

so moody." Use what you have learned in this chapter to help parents recognize that such behaviors have their roots in child development. For instance, explain that it is normal for young children to become wary of masks and dramatic makeup during the preschool years. Likewise, having mixed emotions is a common circumstance during the elementary years and one that children often find confusing. Hearing that their child's behavior is developmentally based often gives parents welcome assurance. If the circumstances seem appropriate, convey to parents some strategies you have learned to deal with emotional situations like these.

**4. Pay attention to the emotions family members express.** The grown-ups in children's lives experience many emotions. These may be communicated through words and nonverbally. Watch for these cues and use affective reflections as appropriate. ("You look excited today," or "You seem upset"). Follow up with a question. ("Would you like to talk about it?" or "Is there something I can do to help?") Wait for the person to respond. Do not try to push parents or other family members into talking further. Respect their right of privacy. If a response is forthcoming, listen carefully and use the skills you have learned in Chapters 4 and 5 to convey interest, acceptance, and empathy.

**5. Accept parental emotions, even when those emotions make you uncomfortable.** There will be times when the emotions family members express are at odds with your own or with what you believe their reactions should be. For instance, when telling a mother about her son's excitement in using certain art materials, a kindergarten teacher was surprised that the mother reacted with irritation saying, "I don't want him wasting his time making pictures. I want him to concentrate on learning to read." A scout leader felt dismay when a parent announced with pride that his ten-year-old son had "thrashed a cousin good." An infant/toddler teacher became upset when a parent asked that the staff keep her fourteen-month-old child away from another toddler who experiences epileptic seizures. In cases such as these, your first task is to demonstrate understanding by

paraphrasing or acknowledging directly the feelings expressed. ("You'd rather Hyuk Jun not paint," or "It sounds like Raymond really stood up for himself," or "You're worried about Jessie having too much contact with LaRonda"). Acknowledging the parent's perspective in a matter-of-fact way requires you to put aside your own feelings for the moment and concentrate on the parent's point of view. This may be difficult, but it is crucial if parents are going to trust you and feel comfortable expressing themselves honestly in your presence. Information about how to follow up on your reflection and how to remain true to your values while demonstrating respect for parental positions is presented in Chapter 15.

**6. Put a check on defensive reactions when family members express anger aimed at you or the program.** A parent angrily confronts you in the hall: "I told you to keep Jessie away from LaRonda, but I just saw them playing together in the housekeeping area. Don't you people know how to listen?" You answer a furious telephone call from a grandmother: "This is the third time Teisha has come home with paint on her sleeves. She's ruining all her good clothes. I don't have money to keep buying new things. Why aren't you paying more attention to what happens in your program?" You receive a note from a parent: "This is not the first time Keil has come home missing buttons from his shirt. He says the kids are pulling them off on the playground. How can this be happening? I'm not paying tax dollars to have a bunch of bullies terrorize my child at school. Do something to resolve this situation immediately."

When family messages like these are received, you may feel attacked, and it is natural to feel defensive. This defensiveness is sometimes translated into dismissal of family concerns, immediate rationales and justifications, or counter-accusations. After all, you only have the children's best interests at heart. How could parents judge your intentions so poorly? How could they be so narrow-minded in their thinking? How can they expect you to be responsible for everything? When you begin to experience these kinds of reactions, take a moment to gather your thoughts and gain control of your response. Try

## SKILLS FOR RESPONDING TO CHILDREN'S EMOTIONS—continued

to reinterpret the situation from the family's point of view—the feelings behind such accusations often are ones aimed at protecting the child or furthering the child's opportunities. Considered in this light, angry feelings often are justified—a parent made a request, which she perceived as having been ignored; it does create a hardship when children come home with soiled or damaging clothing; parents do have beliefs they expect programs not to violate. In these situations, it is best to acknowledge the family member's sense of anger or injustice, then work to resolve the issue in ways that are mutually beneficial. Even when the source of familial anger is difficult to fathom or seems unreasonable, remember that family members are entitled to their emotions. Moreover, they cannot be expected to always express anger in ways that avoid hurting your feelings. On the other hand, as a professional it is expected that you will respond with respect and understanding despite the circumstances. This is a hard job, but it is part of the ethical code of conduct that separates professionals from lay persons.

The first step in any angry encounter is to move from an impulsive, quick reaction to a more measured one. If possible, take a moment to cool off before responding. Second, try to see things from the family's perspective. This is best accomplished if you treat the family member's remarks as a source of information about his or her point of view instead of as a cue to defend your behavior. Third, approach the problem by accepting family members' rights to have their own feelings. Finally, move into a problem-solving mode, as described in Chapter 15.

## ▼ PITFALLS TO AVOID

Regardless of whether you are responding to children's emotions individually or in groups, informally or in structured activities, there are certain pitfalls you should avoid. These pitfalls also apply to your communication with adults.

### Sounding "all knowing."

"You must be feeling sad."
"I know you're feeling sad."
"You're feeling sad, aren't you?"

All of these phrases make you sound all knowing. Their use makes it more difficult for children to correct a mistaken reflection. Because reflections are supposed to be tentative and correctable, phrases such as these should not be used.

**Accusing children.** Words like vicious, stubborn, uncooperative, nasty, greedy, manipulative, and belligerent are not feeling words, even when used in the form of an affective reflection. They are accusatory terms based on adult evaluations of child behavior rather than accurate interpretations of children's emotions, and so should not be used. For instance, a child who wants all of something may feel justified, wishful, or entitled, but certainly not greedy, which implies getting more than he or she deserves. Likewise, a youngster who remains fixed on doing something a certain way may feel determined, but would not identify his or her feelings as stubborn, meaning unreasonably obstinate. If you find yourself employing such a term, stop. Observe what the child is really trying to communicate, and then restate your reflection nonjudgmentally.

**Trying to diffuse children's emotions too quickly.** When children are involved in highly emotional situations, adults may feel compelled to dilute or modify what the children are feeling. They attempt to move children along to an affective state that is less intense or more comfortable for the adult. As a result, they may try to cajole children out of unhappiness, jolly them out of anger, or distract their attention from what they are feeling. Unfortunately, these tactics often do more harm than good. Children get the idea that they'd better "snap out of it" or risk the adult's disapproval. Also, they learn no constructive way to deal with their true emotions. A better approach is to make use of the strategies described in this chapter by acknowledging children's emotions and allowing them to talk about them. This may take place in one sitting or in several. Only after children have recognized what their feelings are is it appropriate to help them think of coping strategies.

**Coercing children into talking about their emotions.** In an effort to show concern, adults may probe into children's emotional states, ignoring signs that such inquiries are frustrating for the child or unwelcome. With preschoolers, repeated questions such as "Are you disappointed?" or "Why are you so upset?" may be beyond the child's ability to answer, thus creating pressure that children find stressful. Similarly, older children may find these probes intrusive, preferring to keep their reactions to themselves. The best way to avoid such negative circumstances is to remain alert to actions by children indicating they are not ready to talk. Turning away, pulling back, vague answers, mumbled replies, increased agitation, and verbal statements such as "I don't know" or "Leave me alone" should be respected.

**Forcing children to face frightening situations.** In the mistaken belief that children will overcome a fear by facing it directly, some adults force children into confrontations with what they fear most. Rarely does this alleviate the child's fear. Instead, the fear often is intensified and, in some cases, may last a lifetime. For instance, all of us know people who were forced to "sink or swim" as a child and who now hate the water. Coercing children also betrays their sense of trust. A better technique is to acknowledge children's fears and allow them to overcome them gradually.

## ▼ Summary

Emotions are an important part of children's lives. Positive emotions, such as joy and affection, feel good. They encourage children to reach out and to be receptive to people and experiences. Negative emotions, such as fear and anger, feel bad, inducing children to avoid, escape from, or surmount difficulties. Emotions are universal. They are triggered by particular events to which the body responds. People interpret what they are experiencing and take action based on their interpretation.

Emotions develop in a predictable sequence and arise from such core emotions as joy, anger, sadness, and fear. Clusters of related emotions and combinations of them emerge over time to form more complex emotional reactions. The events that prompt particular clusters of emotion are essentially similar over the life span. Cognitive maturity and experience affect an individual's interpretation of these stimulus events. How children experience fear as they grow up is an example of this developmental change.

People are thought to work through a series of emotional tasks over the course of their lives. Optimal growth occurs when the balance is toward the positive of the opposite poles in each stage. The developmental stages during which children work through emotional tasks are known as trust versus mistrust, autonomy versus shame and doubt, initiative versus guilt, and industry versus inferiority. In addition, changes in how children think about their emotions as they mature influence their emotional development. The youngest children believe that only one emotion can be experienced at a time; five- and six-year-olds begin to recognize that two emotions can be experienced simultaneously (but about different things); and ten- to twelve-year-olds begin to identify multiple reactions to the same event. Children's recognition of emotions in others follows a similar trend. However, even older children may not be accurate interpreters of others' emotions because similar behavioral cues may represent different feelings, and the same stimulus may prompt varying responses among different people or within the same individual at different times. Children's learning also affects their conceptualization of emotion. Adults are the most significant teachers of what emotions society values and appropriate emotional expression.

Children encounter difficulties dealing with their emotions. They often rely heavily on others recognizing their nonverbal cues, which may be overlooked or misinterpreted; they may choose inappropriate actions to show how they feel; and they may try to hide, minimize, or avoid their emotions. Inappropriate adult responses compound these problems. Adults sometimes resort to ignoring, lying, denying children's emotions, or shaming children. It is more supportive and helpful to talk to children about their emotions by using affective reflections. Affective reflections involve recognizing the emotions a child may be experiencing in a particular situation, then using a reflection to name them. Affective reflections make abstract, internal states more concrete. Verbally labeling emotions helps children recall past events, helps them to differentiate emotions that are similar but not identical, allows adults to demonstrate caring and understanding, and contributes to a positive verbal environment. Other ways to help children cope with their emotions are to use strategies that prompt them to talk with others about their emotions and to communicate with family members regarding the emotional aspects of children's lives.

## ▼ DISCUSSION QUESTIONS

1. Discuss the role of emotions in children's lives. Give examples based on your own childhood, or on your observation of young children, as to how this process actually works.
2. Malcom is three years old and his brother, William, is ten. Discuss how each of them probably thinks about his own emotions and to what extent he is likely to be aware of his brother's emotional reactions.
3. Describe each of the emotional tasks of childhood and identify children's behaviors that would be characteristic of each stage.
4. Describe the developmental and learned aspects of children's fears. Discuss these in relation to your own fearful childhood experiences or the experiences of children you know.
5. Describe at least three ways in which affective reflections benefit children's emotional development.
6. Discuss specific ways in which you could make your own affective reflections more effective.
7. In each of the following situations, describe:
   a. What emotions the children involved might be experiencing.
   b. How you would use the strategies presented in this chapter to help the children become more aware of their own feelings and the feelings of others, and how you would help them cope effectively with the situation.

   **SITUATION A:** Calvin and George are playing in the sandbox. Calvin wants George's pail, so he takes it. George begins to cry, but Calvin continues to play, unperturbed. George comes running to you, saying, "He took my pail!"

   **SITUATION B:** Sandy has been standing watching the others jump rope. It seems as if she'd like to join in, yet she makes no move to do so.

   **SITUATION C:** Curtis is in a quandary. He was just invited to a barbecue at Steven's house, but his best friend, Travis, has not been asked to come.

8. Describe typical problems children experience in dealing with their emotions. Identify corresponding strategies adults can employ to help youngsters cope more effectively.
9. Take five minutes to write down as many affective words and phrases as you can think of. Compare your list with one or two classmates'.
10. Read the following scenario. Refer to the NAEYC Code of Ethical Conduct presented in Appendix A. Find the sections of the code that provide insight into the ethics of the teacher's behavior in this situation.

    **SITUATION:** When Mrs. Huong, a parent, tells the teacher she is worried about her son sucking his thumb, the teacher offers her an article about thumb sucking to read. The teacher also refers her to another parent who had that same concern last year.

## ▼ FIELD ASSIGNMENTS

1. Keep a record of the affective reflections you use when working with children. When you have a chance, record at least four of your responses. Identify what the child was doing or what the child said and your response. Write at least two alternate reflections you could have said in that circumstance.
2. Describe one pitfall you have encountered using the skills presented in this chapter. Brainstorm ideas with classmates about how to deal with the problem in the future.
3. Describe a situation in which a child expressed his or her emotions. Discuss how you or another adult responded and the child's reaction. Critique the effectiveness of the adult's approach. If it was ineffective, what strategies might have been better?
4. Identify one family communication strategy you heard or observed related to children's emotions. Describe the circumstances in which it was used and the family member's reaction. Provide an assessment of the practitioner's effectiveness.

# ▼Chapter 6

## Supporting Children in Stressful Situations

## ▼ OBJECTIVES

*On completion of this chapter, you will be able to describe:*

▼ The nature of stress.

▼ Sources of children's stress.

▼ Children's physical, psychological, and behavioral reactions to stress.

▼ Strategies for helping children cope more effectively when they are under stress.

▼ Strategies for communicating with families of highly stressed children.

▼ Pitfalls to avoid in dealing with stressed children.

David is entering Hambly Middle School. He's never experienced a school as large as Hambly and is worried about remembering his locker combination, finding all of his classrooms, and undressing in front of everyone for gym. Lately, he feels dizzy and shaky and wonders if everyone else knows how he's feeling inside.

Three-year-old Karen has begun following her mother closely and crying inconsolably whenever they are separated. She often thinks of the violent fights her mother and father have been having and the fact that her father doesn't come home anymore. She wonders if her mother will go away, too.

Kevin, who is six, has come to dread going to school and especially fears reading time. He has a hard time doing what his teacher wants him to do—he would do the work if he could, but he can't. He wonders how other kids can make sense of the letters and words in the reader. His stomachaches are becoming frequent.

Although David, Karen, and Kevin differ with respect to gender, age, family situation, and many other characteristics, they do have one thing in common: childhood stress.

Many professionals are concerned that the task of growing up in today's world is getting tougher. Although not all children are experiencing difficulty, increasing numbers apparently have fewer sources of adult support, affirmation, and love than in the recent past, and many are being pressured to grow up faster (Elkind, 1981; Garbarino, 1995; Peterson, 1988). Childhood tensions cited range from the normative stresses of someone making fun of them and not being chosen for a role in the school play to the extremely painful and damaging stress experienced by children who are physically and sexually abused. It has also been suggested that children are viewed more frequently today as obstacles to adult fulfillment and careers; children also are seen as economic burdens (Packard, 1983).

In addition, the American Academy of Pediatricians has indicated concern about the growing numbers of chronically unhappy, hyperactive, or lethargic and unmotivated children now being seen by clinicians; these youngsters are inclined toward school failure, psychosomatic problems, and early involvement in delinquency and drugs (Elkind, 1981). Such children have been described as "unwilling, unintended victims of overwhelming stress . . . borne of rapid, bewildering social change and constantly rising expectations" (Elkind, 1981:3). When Swiss psychologist Jean Piaget first began lecturing in the United States, he was constantly asked about how to move children more quickly through the four stages of development he had identified. In response, he asked why Americans are always in such a hurry.

## ▼ THE NATURE OF STRESS

In young children, **stress** has been defined as "anything that imposes an extra demand on a child's ability to cope, often something that is new or different" (Furman, 1995:33). A child's *perception* of a stressor is extremely important, for it is only when individuals perceive that their resources to handle a situation fall short of what is demanded that they become "stressed." For example, a child who has been frequently abused by adults may perceive an adult's movement toward her or him as threatening when no threat is intended. Another child who has not experienced such abuse would perceive the event entirely differently. As a result, the event produces quite different physical, psychological, and behavioral responses in the children. The child who does not feel threatened simply assimilates the adult's movement into the general scheme of things; the child who feels threatened, however, is involuntarily moved to behave in some way, perhaps flinching, moving away, or shuddering.

A "piling up" of a number of seemingly mild stressors can result in some children feeling absolutely overwhelmed. In short, individuals quickly assess what meaning a particular, perceived stressor has for them. They match that with any previous understanding and react to avoid or modify the situation to protect themselves, restore equilibrium, or respond effectively to the presented challenge. Adults, with all of their experience to draw on, sometimes find demands are too great. Because childhood is looked on as a period of life that is less demanding, it is easy to forget that children can feel overwhelmed also. They are called on daily to make an extraordinary number of adaptations—at home, in the classroom or child-care setting, and in the peer group. Frequently, children must do so with severely limited resources and experience.

### Why Be Concerned?

There are two reasons to be concerned about childhood stress:

1. We have become more knowledgeable about both the short-term and long-term effects of stress. Evidence suggests that undischarged stress that is prolonged and/or especially intense leads ultimately to disease. There is also evidence that stress and trauma in children can trigger both behavioral disorders and increased psychological vulnerability (Trad, 1988).

2. It is believed that a child's stress-coping responses are learned early in life through watching how "significant others" (parents, siblings, extended-family members, teachers, and peers) cope when under pressure. These behaviors then become ingrained through habitual practice. When learned coping patterns are negative, they serve only to increase the demand in a child's life, making the child more vulnerable to stress.

Thus, a preventive approach must be twofold: (1) eliminating or modifying undue stress early in children's lives and (2) teaching children positive stress-management techniques before they learn negative coping patterns—and before the effects of stress have begun to take their physical and psychological tolls.

## ▼ SOURCES OF CHILDREN'S STRESS

Even very young children today are living in fairly complex ecosystems. Generally, as children's interactions broaden beyond the family, their world becomes potentially more stressful. Conversely, for children who live in chaotic family situations, expanding their contact with others outside the family system can open up additional resources. These better enable children to cope with stress.

### The Child's Own Personality in Generating Stress

Why some children "march to the left while almost everyone else seems to be moving to the right" is a question that puzzles many who interact on a regular basis with young children. These are the children who do not appear to be comfortable in any program, no matter how wide the range of offerings. They have noticeable trouble getting along with their parents peers, siblings, and people in general. As they grow older, they often continue to struggle with poorly developed social skills, difficult personal interactions, and low self-esteem. Whether such children are "just born that way" or whether their personalities develop as a result of poor socialization techniques on the part of the significant adults in their lives is receiving considerable attention from researchers in the field of personality development. Because children today are ingrained members of a "Hurry up, let's go!" society, those who cannot fit easily into tight schedules and a decidedly faster pace are children who are going to have trouble. (A further discussion of temperament may be found in Chapter 14.)

### Intrafamilial Stressors

Family life, which often serves as a buffer for children, also can be a source of stress for them. The ordinary aspects of family life may pile up to create demands for children that can range from mildly stressful to overwhelming. The birth of a sibling, the death of a pet, breaking a favorite toy, getting caught stealing or lying, carelessly spilling milk, losing a grandparent, or bringing home a bad report card all can be either opportunities for growth or highly negative experiences, depending on the responses of significant adults.

**Separation and divorce.** The divorce of their parents is one of the most confusing and disturbing events most children will ever experience (Everett and Everett, 1994:133). For some children, the rupture of family life caused by separation and divorce may be every bit as stressful as loss through death. Over 1 million children a year or almost half of all children experience the pain of seeing their parents divorce (Hetherington, Stanley-Hagan, and Anderson, 1996). It should be noted that predivorce family stress can go on for long periods before one or both adults finally make a decision to end the marriage (Clarke-Stewart, 1989). Because 70 percent of divorced spouses remarry within a three- to five-year period and 42 percent of them will again divorce, many children move in and out of a variety of family structures.

Accompanying these changes are all the problems associated with the breakdown, breakup, and restructuring of the relationships involved: loneliness; poor coping skills on the part of the adults; fractured ties with siblings, peers, neighbors, schools, churches, and extended-family members; and greater complexity in the maintenance of significant relationships (Soderman, 1985).

Two myths seem to persist about children's views of their parents' divorce: the first is that they probably are just as relieved to see the end of a bad marriage as are their parents; the second is that so many of their friends' parents are divorcing that the trauma probably has been reduced considerably. Neither of these ideas is true. Young children are unable to intellectualize divorce. Their focus tends to be on their own families, not on the record high numbers of families "out there" whose foundations are crumbling. Although seeing their parents argue is tremendously stressful for children, being separated from a parent ranks even higher as a stressor, particularly before the age of five.

Because attachments at early ages often are intense, fear of abandonment may cause a child to cling to the remaining parent. The child may throw an unexpected tantrum about going to school or to the child-care center and may begin tagging after the custodial parent, not wanting to allow him or her out of sight.

Much of this tension in children is caused by their uncertainty about what the separation or divorce means with respect to their own security. Will they get up in the morning and find the other parent gone, too? Does the separation mean that they will have to move to another neighborhood or go to a different school? Will the parent who left come back and take the dog? Did the parent leave because she or he is mad at the child? Parents add to children's stress when they fail to sit down with their children and explain, as much as possible, the changes that are in store for the family because of the change in the spousal relationship.

Also, because children's thinking at early stages tends to be egocentric and "magical" in nature, children younger than six years of age tend to feel somewhat guilty about certain events that happen in family life. Some children believe they may have caused their parents' separation or divorce by something *they* did—because of naughty behavior or wishing a parent away for one reason or another.

Children's problems are intensified when parents are unable to successfully restructure family life following divorce. Parents may continue to hurl insults at each other whenever possible, using their children as an audience. Ex-spouses who are unable to resolve their angry feelings may later use their only link with each other—their children—to vent their hostilities or to maintain some sort of control over each other. Children may be used as hostages to obtain child-support payments, as spies to find out what the ex-spouse is doing, or as messengers to carry information back and forth. Confusion may ride high for young children who are forced to adjust to the different life-styles and parenting approaches they encounter on the weekend as well as those they live with during the week with the custodial parent. Additional pressure is felt by both the parent and child who may want the visit to go perfectly. Neither may feel comfortable about "just hanging around" with each other, as ordinarily happens in intact families. A feeling often exists that, in order to maintain the relationship, the time spent must be "high quality" because there now is so little of it.

Tension also can be created by what "can't be talked about." Children wrestle with the dilemma of feeling disloyal to one parent if they appear loyal to the other. When a parent is openly hostile about the other parent, discusses the "sins" of that parent with the child in an attempt to vent some of his or her own feelings, or asks the child to keep certain information from the other parent, he or she induces additional stress as the child is forced to deal with the worry and guilt of handling adult-sized problems.

Even more stressful for some children, however, is the lack of opportunity to see the noncustodial parent or related grandparents because of continued hostility on the part of the custodial parent or severed affection by noncustodial family members. Adults who terminate relationships in an attempt to reduce their own pain can seriously add to a child's loss of self-esteem and support networks.

The transition time needed for most families to equilibrate following divorce is at least two years (Hetherington, 1979). A child's ability to handle tension depends greatly on the way parents are able to resolve their relationship problems. Many children, however, even those whose parents handle the transition well, manifest some signs of disequilibrium. For this reason, divorce has been targeted as the single largest cause of childhood depression. Boys tend to take the event harder than girls (Hetherington, 1990), and the most painful years for a child of divorcing parents range from fifteen months to fifteen years of age (Packard, 1983). Thus, not many children escape without some signs of distress.

Wallerstein and Kelly (1980) found that children's concerns, feelings, and behavioral responses to parental divorce regularly fell into categories by age and development. These are summarized in Table 6–1.

In subsequent studies, it was found that the emotional, economic, and psychological effects of divorce can be long-term and serious (Beal and Hochman, 1991; Wallerstein and Blakeslee, 1989). Children with divorced parents perceive themselves very differently than those who have intact families. They describe themselves as unsuccessful, more problem-filled, more anxious, more at risk of failure, robbed of childhood, more frequently depressed, and less satisfied in life; being less educated and holding less prestigious jobs; and experiencing poorer health, undermined sense of security, interrupted routines, loosened underpinnings of life, and skepticism (Children's Rights Council, 1996:9).

Not surprisingly, those children who adapted most successfully as they moved into young adulthood were:

▼ Children whose parents were able to cooperate positively with one another to ensure the child's proper development
▼ Children whose parents were able to restore their initially diminished capacity to parent, that is, to give time, to provide effective discipline, to be sensitive to their children's needs, and to separate the child's needs from their own
▼ Children whose mothers were in good mental health
▼ Children who were able to sustain a close and loving relationship with the noncustodial parent
▼ Children who had a positive father-child relationship
▼ Children who were not overburdened by responsibility for a parent's psychological welfare or required to serve as an instrument of parental rage
▼ Children who experienced good stepparent-child relationships when remarriage took place

**Single-parent families.** Currently, only seven out of ten children live with two parents, with 15.5 million children under eighteen living in a single-parent home. Most of these families are headed by women, and three out of five fall below the poverty line (U.S. Bureau of the Census, 1996). Subsequently, mother-only families are the most impoverished demographic group in the United States.

The stress a child encounters while living in a single-parent family has less to do with the marital status of the parent than with the resources available to the family. According to the National Center for Children in Poverty, child health outcomes are embedded in social and economic factors, such as "family income and structure, parental employment and education, child care, and housing and go beyond medical treatment and access to care" (1997:3). The world of the poor child is a "world of aching teeth without dentists to fill them, of untreated ear infections that result in permanent deafness. It is a world wherein a child easily learns to be ashamed of the way he or she lives" (Keniston, 1975:6). Dick Gregory's (1964) vivid account of his own experiences in growing up impoverished is especially poignant (Segal and Yahres, 1979:263):

The teacher thought I was stupid. Couldn't spell, couldn't read, couldn't do arithmetic. Just stupid. Teachers were never interested in finding out that you couldn't concentrate because you were hungry, be-

▼ **Table 6–1    Children's Reactions to Divorce**

**Three to Five Years of Age**
Marked silence during play
Fear of abandonment
Bewilderment and sadness
Worry about causing the divorce
Clinging behavior; reluctance to leave custodial parent
Anxious behavior, especially at bedtime
Regressive behavior

**Six to Eight Years of Age**
Better ability to grasp cause and effect of situation
Pervasive sadness
Crying (especially in boys)
Disorganized behavior
Unrealistic fantasies
Denial
Marked rise in or inhibition of aggressive behavior
Guilt
Hunger for affection and physical contact with adults
Increase in mastery play
Feelings of deprivation (seen in behaviors relating to food, toys, etc.)
Yearning for departed parent
Inhibition of anger at departed parent
Anger with custodial parent (mostly in boys)
Denial of feelings of responsibility in causing divorce
Fantasy about reconciliation of parents
Loyalty conflicts

**Nine to Twelve Years of Age**
Increased external show of poise, courage
Diffuse feelings of anxiety
Realistic perception of family disruption
Constant body motion
Shame over what is happening
Covering up of feelings
Mastery of feelings through activity and play
Anger at the parent who they blame for the divorce
Shaken sense of identity
Somatic symptoms (headaches, stomachaches, etc.)
Alignment with one parent

**Thirteen to Eighteen Years of Age**
Premature independence from parents; decreased participation in family
Worry about sex and marriage
Mourning (profound sense of loss)
Anger (at both parents, at parents' new partners)
Perceptions of parents as fallen idols or instant "saints"
Temporary or prolonged delay of entrance into adolescence
Pseudoadolescent behavior (sexual acting out)
Loyalty conflicts

cause you hadn't had any breakfast. All you could think about was noontime, would it ever come? Maybe you could sneak into the cloakroom and steal a bit of some kid's lunch out of a coat pocket. A bit of something. Paste. You can't really make a meal of paste or put it on bread for a sandwich, but sometimes I'd scoop a few spoonfuls of the paste jar in the back of the room. Pregnant people get strange tastes. I was pregnant with poverty. Pregnant with dirt and pregnant with smells that made people turn away, pregnant with cold and pregnant with shoes that were never bought for me, pregnant with five people in my bed and no Daddy in the next room, and pregnant with hunger. Paste doesn't taste too bad when you're hungry.

The strains commonly felt by almost all single parents—economic difficulty, role strain, loneliness, depression, and the need to rebuild self-esteem—also become strains for the children of these parents.

The care that is provided for children in single-parent families may be less than adequate because of financial strain. Some parents are forced to accept undesirable child-care arrangements for their children when working to keep food on the table, which must be a higher priority than providing for their child's emotional needs. As many as 100,000 children living in these families are homeless. They live in families that are typically plagued with higher levels of substance abuse, domestic abuse, and mental health problems. Not surprisingly, these children are more inclined to have developmental delays and behavioral and disciplinary problems than other children, even when the latter are also in poverty. In addition, homeless children share a "number of common physical and emotional problems, including malnutrition, poor physical development, aggressive and demanding behaviors, sleep disorders, abnormal social fears and speech difficulties. For children older than age five, more than half need psychiatric help." As expected, their school performance is consistently below average (DeAngelis, 1994:1, 38; Reganick, 1997).

Of the children who are living with single parents, some will suffer little stress. They are the children of parents who have the necessary resources to cope effectively with single parenthood—positive self-esteem, financial security, a supportive network of family and friends, parenting skills, and, in many cases, a workable relationship with their ex-spouse. Other children will feel the effects of living with parents who are struggling to do the best they can for their children. Sometimes, their best will not be enough.

**Blended families.**  Today, at least 20 percent of all children are living in a step family, and it is be-lieved that the blended or reconstituted (bi-nuclear) family quickly is becoming the most common family form in the United States (Visher and Visher, 1991). Often, because dependent children are involved, there may be fantasies that the new marriage will provide a normal and natural family life. Such expectations rarely are fully realized (Blau, 1993). Multiple problems that predictably beset such new families include those connected with weakened sexual taboos, biological ties that predate the new spousal ties, different life histories, difficulty in deciphering roles, competition between natural and stepparents and between step siblings, and matters of loyalty and affection.

These families often do not have the luxury of time to develop attachments between nonbiological parents and children. Occasionally, children can be blunt about seeing the stepparent as an intruder. Stepparents, on the other hand, often view stepchildren in much the same way—as driving a wedge into the marital relationship.

Major stressors that children encounter in a stepfamily situation have to do with feelings of insecurity and jealousy that crop up between them and other members of the newly formed family. The child who has formed an overly close relationship with a single parent may resent having to share that parent with a stepparent and/or step sibling. He or she may view the stepparent as having contributed to the breakup of their parents' marriage (which may or may not be the case). A child may constantly compare the stepparent with the biological parent who has been "lost" through death or divorce. Often, this parent is idealized to such a degree that only time and a reorganized perspective on the child's part can allow the child to accept anyone else.

Children may feel that their identity in a family is gone. For example, the oldest child may no longer be the oldest or the youngest child no longer the youngest. An "only child" may instantly have two or three siblings with whom he or she must now share the parent's attention (Visher and Visher, 1991). Resentment over a stepparent's efforts to discipline a child can be fierce, both by the child and the biological parent.

Stepparents can add pressure to the situation when their expectations of a stepchild are unrealistic or incompatible with previous expectations. Sometimes, expectations are based on experience with their own children's personalities and abilities; a stepchild's inability to be responsive may be viewed as insubordinate and uncooperative behavior when the child simply is at a loss about what the stepparent wants.

Barriers to open communication about natural parents can be highly damaging. For example, Roy, who had just returned from seeing his natural mother, innocently began telling his stepmother about the garage sale his mother was planning. He was startled at the fury in his stepmother's voice as she told him: "I'm sick and tired of hearing about your mother's financial problems. She probably told you that she has to have a garage sale in order to eat this week, didn't she? We don't want to hear *anything* about what she's doing. Just keep it to yourself!"

Life in a bi-nuclear family also brings with it the demand of maintaining a complex network of primary relationships for children. Keeping up with all of them can be overwhelming. For example, three-year-old Lissa wondered how the Easter Bunny could carry all those baskets! She had received one at home, another at her father and stepmother's, two others when she visited her maternal and paternal grandparents, and still another when she was introduced to her "new" grandmother and grandfather—her stepmother's parents.

**Death.** Generally, teachers of young children do a good job of helping children develop healthy understandings and attitudes related to gender differences, sexuality, and self identity. However, many of these same professionals actively avoid dealing with children's spontaneous questions about death (Riley, 1989). They may feel uncertain about how to comfort children who have experienced a significant loss of a pet, beloved grandparent, or parent. There are religious constraints on professionals as well, since the various beliefs of each family must be considered.

Death of a family member is recognized as a major stressor for both adults and children (Greenberg, 1996; Holmes and Rahe, 1967). Although all children older than seven months of age tend to show some distress when separated from a parent by death, the amount of trauma depends on the child's age, the child's understanding of the event, and how the loss affects the child personally, both now and in the future. Also important is the strength of the child's psychological attachment to the deceased person (Brenner, 1984).

Research currently available indicates that before age two, children understand very little about death (Jarratt, 1994). Beginning at about three years of age, however, there are three, overlapping developmental stages through which children proceed before achieving a realistic view of death. Although some disagreement exists about the age at which children move from one level of thinking to another, the consensus is that the factors that influence this process include children's egocentric thinking and the degree to which they grasp the concepts of time and cause and effect. Also, as the concepts in one stage become more fully understood, children may already have developed increased awareness, although not complete understanding, of concepts in the subsequent stage.

*Stage one (three to six years of age).* Children in this first stage of conceptualizing death do not believe that death is final. They think of it as temporary and reversible. They also believe that life and death are in a state of constant flux, that life as well as death comes and goes over a period of time (Safier, 1964). People who are dead can become alive again, just as someone who is sleeping can wake up or someone who is away on a trip can return. Some children think that death is a continuation of life on a restricted scale: people who are dead still eat, sleep, and walk around, although not very well (Kastenbaum, 1981). It also is common for them to equate death, which is unknown, with sleep or separation, which are familiar experiences.

Younger children may not react immediately to a loss or may not express grief in adult terms. They may not have the words to describe their memories of traumatic events, "but their memories are often disturbingly evident in their behavior and play" (Monahon, 1993:59). Because of this, adults frequently are misled in their judgments of the depth of children's misery. Young children can tolerate only short outbursts of grief, and because they are easily distracted, they may appear to be finished with mourning before they actually are (Brenner, 1984). There may be *little* crying, and the child may seem almost untouched by the event. This response also may occur when children are not able to grasp what the event truly means, that is, the *permanence* of the loss and the *extent* of the loss.

If a child is *very* young when the event occurs, full understanding may come even years later. When this happens, the stress may appear later, either physically or psychologically. Unfortunately, the later stress may be difficult to link to the earlier event, which may have long since been mourned and "taken care of" by adults. Because children are in the process of developing their cognitive structures, they may be temporarily thrown off balance psychologically when rethinking an earlier, critical life event. The possibility should always be considered that a seemingly unexplainable stressor for the child is not necessarily something that currently exists, but may be something that remains as "unfinished business" in the child's past experience.

The combination of what young children know and do not know about death leads to an active effort on their part to find out more. Hence, children demonstrate great curiosity about the concrete details of death: the funeral, the coffin, the burial, the wake. Their interest at this point focuses more on what happens once death has occurred than on what led to the death or how the death might have been prevented. This is a logical focus for children, based on their view that death is semipermanent. They are anxious to know how burial rites may affect the person's future state and his or her ability to return.

*Stage two (four to ten years of age).* A major advance in children's thinking occurs in the second stage as they become increasingly aware that all living things eventually die. As children work through this stage, they develop an initial understanding that death is final and irrevocable. Older children have a better grasp of this concept than do younger children. Although children begin to accept that other living things will die, at this stage they do not recognize their *own* mortality. Children in the second stage tend to attribute death to an outside agent (Safier, 1964). They believe that life is given and taken away by an external force whose role is to make life "go" and "stop." Within this interpretation, children may personify death in the form of a bogeyman, a skeleton, a ghost, or the angel of death. Although these personifications have humanlike characteristics, they also represent mystical power (Kastenbaum, 1981). Because death is a person, it can be eluded if one is careful and clever.

Children also typically confront their image of death by games in which killing plays a major role (Eddy and Alles, 1983). It is not uncommon for children to extend this confrontation to their dreams, which at times results in nightmares.

*Stage three (nine years of age and older).* The third stage represents the realistic notion that death is personal, universal, inevitable, and final. Those in this stage understand that all living things must die, including themselves. Rather than imagining life and death as being controlled by an external agent, children recognize the internal forces involved (Safier, 1964). As preadolescents come to accept the inevitability of death, they also become intrigued with the meaning of life. It is at this point that they develop philosophical views about both life and death.

For children who more fully understand the meaning of the death of someone they love, the stress may be intensified if they receive little support in working through the disequilibrium that will naturally result. These children are then at greater risk than others for later developing depression and other psychological impairment. When experiencing unexpected death, grief may be intense. Since children's experience with loss is so limited, they may feel that their overwhelming feelings of sadness and the urge to cry will never end. Adults need to help children realize that unhappy times have endings as well as beginnings (Balaban, 1985). Other intense feelings may include guilt, anger, and resentment, and children may be cut off from expressing these feelings if adults appear uncomfortable with or unaccepting of such expression. Children who realize that their visible hurt may be causing discomfort in adults may tend to hide their feelings. Children in these situations need caring and responsible adults; however, the adults should not become so overinvolved that they project their own issues or perspectives onto the child (Greenberg, 1996). Teachers need to acknowledge that something big has happened in the child's life, but not make a lot of assumptions about what the child may be experiencing.

**Working parents.** Whether children live in intact families, single-parent families, or blended families, an additional stressor today is the trend toward greater involvement in the work force by parents. Currently, 67 percent of married mothers work outside the home, compared with 37 percent in 1970 (U.S. Bureau of the Census, 1996). The fastest growing group of women entering the labor force are those with children under six years of age, 60 percent of these mothers are now in the labor force. Because these children have higher dependency needs and can be greatly stressed when those needs are not met effectively, demands are growing for early-childhood professionals, parents, and business and community leaders to work together to be responsive to and responsible about the needs of these children.

Frantic juggling of family and work responsibilities often leaves parents feeling exhausted, anxious, and guilty. The phrase "It isn't the quantity of time that parents spend with their children, but the quality, that counts" has become a tired cliche when one objectively considers the hurriedness of family life today.

Four-year-old Cameron and his nineteen-month-old sister, Amy, probably aren't articulate enough to express their feelings about the quality-versus-quantity issue. They have become somewhat accustomed to the rushed exits in the morning and the noise and confusion in the less than adequate child-care setting where, from infancy, they have spent their days separated for long periods from their parents and from each other. They endure, sometimes not very graciously, the equally rushed times when they are picked up at 6:00 p.m. to make the trip home, often with stops at the supermarket, drugstore, and cleaners. By 8:00, both children are in bed. Cameron and Amy's parents are genuinely concerned about the quality issue; in fact, it's one of the things that causes *them* a great deal of stress. Their commitment to quality, however, constantly is usurped by the need to take care of such routine daily demands as laundry, the report that has to be ready for a client the next day, a Tuesday-night meeting at their church, a retirement dinner for someone at work, a flooded basement, and cleaning the bathroom.

Next door to Cameron and Amy, another family wrestles with the dilemma of fitting family life into demanding work schedules. They have decided this year that, rather than contending with the hassle of finding someone to come in before and after school, they will experiment with leaving six-year-old Sammy by himself until they arrive home at 5:30. Sammy has found that he becomes afraid only occasionally in the morning after his parents leave and before he leaves for school; however, he has come to really dread the after-school period. Rather than tell his parents about his fears, he has begun a ritual of turning on all the lights and the television set as soon as he arrives home. He fantasizes about what he would do if a "burglar got in" and how he could escape.

It is difficult to evaluate the long-range effects of the stress children such as Sammy experience on a day-to-day basis. In many communities, efforts are expanding rapidly to offer all-day kindergartens and before- and after-school care for these children. Well-designed programs are tailored to the needs of the children and youth they serve, providing children with a comfortable environment and opportunities to move about and choose from a variety of games and activities. They have a safe place to learn new skills, interact with friends, read, do their homework, or just relax.

Where such resources are unavailable, or for children who prefer to go home after school, community and school professionals are providing information to children about self-help and safety procedures in case of emergency, hoping that such dialogue will minimize some of the strain children are feeling.

**Children in abusive or neglectful families.**
The personal transitions that many adults face to-day, when coupled with the strains of parenting, can have devastating effects on children. Garbarino and Gilliam (1980:3) describe such a situation:

> Joan Higgins is a 23-year-old mother of three children, ages 5, 3, and 1. Her life is a bleak procession of work and children, which she must face alone. She no longer lives with the children's father. She has few friends and none who are doing much better than she is coping with day-to-day life. Her money goes for rent, cigarettes, beer, and whatever food she buys for her family. Each of her children show signs of neglect. Often unattended, they have the dull eyes of children whose emotional and physical diet is inadequate. They do not see a doctor regularly and have little contact with anyone outside the family. Joan often feels like giving up, and she sometimes does. On one such occasion, a neighbor called the police when the three children were left alone overnight with no food in the house. Much of the time, she is lonely and apathetic. Sometimes she is angry. This is nothing new. Her life has been this way as long as she can remember.

The quality of care any child receives today is determined by a combination of social stress on the family and the adults' level of skill in caring for the child (Claussen and Crittenden, 1991). These two variables intermix to shape the transactions that occur. Effectiveness of skill in an adult depends on that person's previous opportunity to rehearse the role of caregiver (e.g., with a pet or younger sibling) and whether he or she had effective models of caregiving during his or her own development. Also important are having a realistic rather than idealistic understanding of children's development and being able to prioritize parenting responsibilities over self-gratification. When any of these abilities are absent, there is great potential for high stress in a caregiver.

Each year, millions of children "witness their mothers being emotionally abused, physically battered, even sexually assaulted in the home. They hear screams, see injuries, live in an atmosphere of terror and tension. And they learn that this is what home is like. That humiliation, disrespect, and beating are normal in a home. That violence is the appropriate way to solve a problem" (Berry, 1995:104). In multiproblem families, there are often concurring endemic problems such as substance abuse, poverty, lack of social support, emotional problems, a parental history of being maltreated as a child, and inadequate education (Murphy, et al., 1991). This, then, sets the climate for abuse or maltreatment of now well over 3 million children nationally, including excessive use of force, sexual abuse, emotional rejection, or inadequate provision of essential nurturance (Garbarino and Gilliam, 1980;

Murphy, et al., 1991). This problem is so far reaching, and the helping professional's role in dealing with it so critical, that much of Chapter 15 is devoted to it. What should be noted at this point is that abuse and neglect are a major source of stress for children. When psychological maltreatment is present, there can be serious developmental consequences affecting over 3 million children a year (Children's Defense Fund, 1996).

**Children in foster care.** Of the 500,000 children who move in and out of foster care, many will exhibit problem behaviors that result from short- or long-term family disruption and histories of neglect or abuse: picking fights with other children, an inability to form friendships with other children, attention-getting and disruptive classroom behavior, sadness, academic failure, school phobia, and truancy. In addition to a marked lack of appropriate social skills, they are overrepresented in children who require special services, but they often don't stay in one place long enough to receive the help they need.

Caregivers who hold reasonable expectations and focus heavily on teaching problem solving and building self-esteem will make the greatest strides with these children. Tasks these children are given to complete must be *developmentally* appropriate rather than *age* appropriate; that is, expectations must be closely matched with the abilities and the capabilities children have at that particular time. Professional caregivers can be a powerful force in the lives of many of these children by making sure children receive proper assessment to diagnose needs, as well as speedy referral and follow-up when necessary. Involvement with the child's foster family as a goal-seeking partner is critical. Professionals must keep the child's family status in mind when making arrangements involving family projects and be sensitive in selecting classroom materials, for example, books that represent children who live with others who are not biological relatives. When we look at children who are resilient and become successful adults despite tough childhood experiences, the one thing they share in common is a significant adult. Often, "that person was a teacher" (Noble, 1997:28).

## Extrafamilial Stressors

Obviously, not all the stressors children encounter today come from within the family. Although we have concentrated thus far on factors within families that contribute to tension in young children, most families are highly successful in doing what families do better than any other system—nurturing children.

As children move outward from the relative security of their family into the family's social networks (the neighborhood, the child-care center, and formal school systems), stressors naturally will increase. In addition to familial stressors, children will encounter additional demands in the form of rules, expectations, and interaction patterns that are significantly different from those in their own family. Other persons with whom children must interact frequently may not accept them as readily as their family does, resulting in decreased self-esteem and confidence. Infants and toddlers may react even more strongly to differences between the management techniques in their own family and those of a child-care provider by developing fear or anxiety. Subsequently, they may resist being dropped off by crying or clinging to a parent.

In moving between family and extrafamilial settings, children must adapt to differences between home and societal values, peer cultures, and the continuous pressure of exchanging the relative security of the family microsystem for the less secure realm of the outside world. And, there is evidence that children are having to make these adjustments at earlier and earlier ages.

**Poor quality child care.** Many studies have examined the stressful effects of maternal employment and child care on children (Belsky and Steinberg, 1978; Bronfenbrenner, 1977; Brooks, 1991; Burchinal, Lee, and Ramey, 1989; Kagan, 1977; Peters and Belsky, 1982; Rivara, et al., 1989). Researchers have looked at such issues as safety, attachment, delinquency, academic performance, responsibility, cognitive development, and parent-child relationships. To date, we have little evidence that there are significant differences between children whose parents work and those who have a full-time parent at home, if the care those children receive is developmentally sound. That is, the care they receive must fall into one of the following categories:

1. Comprehensive child-development programs that provide for all, or nearly all, the needs of growing children and their families—educational, nutritional, and health, as well as parenting instruction in child development and family counseling.
2. High-quality child care, which provides children with experiences that promote social and educational development.

These programs are staffed by trained professionals; learning resources, such as books and toys, are varied and in good condition; nutritional requirements are met; and medical care is offered. Moreover, a national child-care study indicated that children function best when interacting in small groups (no more than fourteen) and when adults are trained in early childhood education, special education, or developmental psychology (Doherty-Derkowski, 1995).

Many programs in the country fit the description of high-quality care. They are well-conceived programs that actively promote the general well being of children. When, however, the primary focus in a center is simply custodial child care, children may spend a great deal of their time in the care of untrained or poorly trained staff who promote activities such as television viewing for large parts of the day (Vandell and Corasaniti, 1990). Children from high-risk environments (that is, those characterized by family violence or instability) who are enrolled in such child-care arrangements prior to their first birthday experience negative effects (Peters and Belsky, 1982). What seems unclear is how much such children's emotional health has been affected by already weak attachments to parents and how much it is affected by the unstable child-care experience.

Most research on child care has been primarily restricted to high-quality, university-based programs rather than on a random sample of community programs. What must be examined further is what happens to the millions of children who are receiving less than adequate care: infants who have their needs met by any number of adults rather than a primary caregiver; children who become addicted to constant stimulation and rushing; children who spend 10 to 14 hours a day in crowded, noisy, and punitive environments—all potentially stressful situations. Also needing further attention are the stressful effects of limited family interaction: siblings growing up separated from one another and children and parents consistently spending little focused time with one another on a daily basis.

According to figures gathered by the Children's Defense Fund (1996), only thirty-one states and the District of Columbia meet the four-to-one infant-caregiver staffing requirements recommended by the National Association for the Education of Young Children.

There is no doubt that the United States must do a better job of taking care of its children. Despite gains made in providing quality child care, we continue to be the only highly developed country in the world without a national child-care policy.

Welfare reform efforts to move able adults into employment must be accompanied by national child-care and health-care policies that protect children in lower socioeconomic populations against mass warehousing while their parents work. It will take tax dollars to subsidize the caring environments needed for these children. However, if our society chooses not to meet that responsibility, those dollars will be spent later to mend the social problems that result when children's basic needs are ignored.

**Stress in formal school settings.** Once children begin their formal education, most will spend 6 hours per day, 180 days per year for 13 years in educational settings. This amounts to roughly 14,000 hours for the 71 percent who will finish school. Although a few children function poorly in school because of the stress they bring with them from home or because they have lower than average intelligence, many more simply are not ready developmentally for what is expected of them academically. Such youngsters experience high levels of stress because they lack the intellectual, physical, or emotional resources they need to perform the tasks given them in the classroom. All too often, this mismatch between a child's ability and curricular expectations is blamed on a deficiency in the child rather than in the system. Although both boys and girls are affected, the problem appears to be far more serious for boys, who later are overrepresented in resource rooms for nonreaders and the emotionally impaired (Soderman and Phillips, 1986).

Across the nation, a kindergarten "crisis" has developed. We have rushed to hurry children into activities (such as reading) that require interneuronal development between the two halves of the brain. Often, when children struggle or fail because their cognitive development is not advanced enough to allow them to meet these demands, we move to "remediation" with them. Because we experience success with some children who are on the advanced end of the normal cognitive continuum, we have come to believe that all children can achieve the same success if they can only learn to "crack the code." Instead, it is the children who have begun to crack under pressure.

Every fall, at least 10 percent of children entering school are not ready for what awaits them. Because physical and intellectual growth is more uneven in the early years than later, there are wider differences among children in the preprimary and primary years than will be found as this group of children moves into secondary schools. As children enter formal learning settings, these early differences may become more problematic when:

1. A child is significantly younger than the other children. Although chronological age by itself is not a reliable indicator of a child's school readiness, probably 80 percent of children experience similar patterns of development within a span of two years. Because boys are likely to be anywhere from 6 to 18 months behind girls developmentally in the early years and have less mature eye development, they are more likely to experience problems when entering school too early.

2. A child has not made the intellectual shifts (brain maturation) to reach new levels of learning that are required for formal schooling. This does not necessarily mean that a child will experience learning difficulties in the future. The child simply is not ready at this particular point in development and, as long as she or he is not pushed prematurely into a stressful learning experience, the child will catch up in the later years. Some even bypass their more ready peers in the future.

3. A child is emotionally unready for the pressure of moving into a large-group situation with unfamiliar adults and children. There may be too strong an attachment to a parent or fewer experiences than normal with people outside the family. The child may be experiencing unsettling family difficulties such as parental divorce or death. Any of these could temporarily undermine a child's emotional stability and security.

4. A child has some organic condition that will require special education for at least a period of time. Many of these conditions, including learning disabilities and other problems, and not discovered until a child enters a formal learning environment.

5. The kindergarten curriculum is so demanding that only the brightest and most mature kindergarteners achieve success.

The widespread movement in the United States and other countries in the past two decades toward developmentally appropriate practices holds the most promise of alleviating the stress that results from the mismatch between inappropriate educational expectations and children's ability to learn (Kostelnik, Soderman, and Whiren, in press; Burts, Hart, and Charlesworth, 1997).

Although young children may experience stress in adapting to the demands of formal education,

children entering middle school also experience their share of distress. They must move from the more protective environment of the elementary school to one that demands increased independence, responsibility, and competence on the child's part. When expectations by adults about what children should be able to do are inappropriate, stress will be increased for children who are not up to the task. More simply, children may have concerns about very basic needs such as locating classrooms and lockers. The child may harbor fears about the use of the rest rooms, being picked on by older students, keeping personal possessions safe, and undressing in front of others in physical-education classes. Belonging to a group, making at least one close friend, and learning to interact comfortably with the opposite sex become tremendously important as well as stressful (Soderman, 1984).

Children at this age benefit greatly from empathic parents and teachers who recognize the potential insecurities of venturing out further toward independence. Providing the child with specific information about new expectations, locations, rules, regulations, and schedules can help to reduce anxiety. Adults also can provide positive reassurance that transitions sometimes are hard but can be weathered pretty well, given some time and experience.

## Health-Related Assaults

Even more serious are the results we are seeing from maternal substance use and abuse during pregnancy, including all the problems related to low birth weight, infections, pneumonia, congenital malformations, and drug withdrawal (Anthony, 1992). Fetal alcohol syndrome is now the nation's leading known cause of mental retardation in children. The most severe cases leave children coping with physical malformation such as distinctive facial anomalies, short stature, and microcephaly. While facial characteristics associated with the syndrome become less distinctive as children approach adolescence and young adulthood, effects related to intellectual, academic, and adaptive functioning do not disappear. These include average IQ scores of 68, with only 6 percent of the children later able to function in regular classrooms without supplemental help. Average reading, spelling, and arithmetic grade levels average no higher than fourth grade, with arithmetic deficits most problematic. Socialization and communication skills and capabilities are notably deficient with "failure to consider consequences of action, lack of appropriate initiative, unresponsiveness to subtle social cues, and lack of reciprocal friendships" (Streissguth, et al., 1991).

Because of a marked increase in cocaine and crack use among childbearing adults, greater numbers of children are exposed in the prenatal period of their lives. There is decreased oxygen flow to the fetus and reduced fetal growth, head circumference, gestational age and birth weight (Hutchinson, 1991; Neuspiel and Hamel, 1991). Exposure effects at birth include irritability, tremulousness, vomiting, diarrhea, high blood pressure, and seizures—not a very good beginning. Because of low birth weight, a variety of disabling physical and cognitive symptoms may result. Crawling, standing, walking, and speech often take longer to develop than in nonexposed children. Motor and neurological problems may also include blanking out, staring spells, bizarre eye movement, fine motor dexterity difficulties, and gross motor clumsiness.

Further confounding the child's development are the interactional effects of the social environments in which these children are reared. Continued postnatal drug exposure may include passive inhalation, direct ingestion that is intentional or unintentional, or through breast feeding, resulting in a variety of neurobiological effects. Additional problems are related to family socioeconomic and education status, housing, foster care, nutrition, and environmental toxins.

Later, these children are described by professionals as being in constant motion, disorganized, impulsive and explosive, overly sensitive to stimuli, and generally less responsive to their environment. They have marked difficulty with transitions and are more inclined to test limits. Some refuse to comply and are less able to self-regulate or modulate their behavior. They have trouble making friends, since smiling at others and eye contact are noticeably absent. Problems related to temperament (low adaptability, low persistence, and arrhythmia) are prominent, and they have marked difficulty playing and working with others. Because they process information in very different ways than do nonexposed children, conflicts more often arise between them and caretaking adults or teachers, and academic performance in reading, mathematics, spelling, handwriting, and the arts is negatively affected (Delaphenha, 1993; Hutchinson, 1991). More research is needed to determine whether it is the prenatal drug exposure or the postnatal social and environmental factors that contribute most to the behavior and the developmental deficits seen in these children.

Equally tragic is the newest chronic illness of childhood, acquired immunodeficiency syndrome (AIDS). As of December 1995, 6,948 cases of AIDS had been reported in children under thirteen years of age (Centers for Disease Control, 1996). Because blood product recipients and hemophilia patients are no longer at risk for human immunodeficiency virus (HIV) infection as a result of the screening and inactivation of HIV antibodies in all donated blood products, primary infection in young children is now almost always from HIV-infected parents.

It has been estimated that the numbers of children infected with HIV may, in fact, be two to ten times greater and that we are very early on in what is certain to become an epidemic (Jason, 1991). If true, HIV-infected children, in terms of number, may outrank those with other chronic diseases such as cystic fibrosis, hemophilia, deafness, acute lymphocytic leukemia, chronic renal failure, or muscular dystrophy (Meyers and Weitzman, 1991:169).

Spin-off stressors for AIDS or HIV-infected children and their families include stigma and isolation from friends, neighbors, and the school setting; parental anxiety, depression, and death. Also included are catastrophic medical costs, painful fear of what the future may bring, and inevitable disease progression. Survival rates vary dramatically, with median survival approximately seventy-seven months and incubation periods ranging from four months to six years; some nine-year-olds diagnosed at birth have yet to experience symptoms (Neuspiel and Hamel, 1991).

When their infected parents are unable to care for them or precede them in death, many of these children become impossible to place in foster homes. Because these children often come from drug-abusing parents and frequently from minority populations enmeshed in poverty placement becomes an extremely difficult issue (Jason, 1991). Due to the HIV-infected preschooler's relatively immature immune system and increased vulnerability for infection, it is unwise to place them in situations where there are other young children who will be contracting natural childhood pathogens such as measles, mumps, and chicken pox. Neurological symptoms which impact negatively on their overall behavior and development further exacerbate the placement problem. As a result, increasing numbers of these children constitute the population known as "boarder babies" or those who remain in institutional settings that are not only costly but fail to meet the child's developmental needs (Taylor-Brown, 1991).

In line with Public Law 94-142, the American Academy of Pediatricians recommends regular program placement unless there are obvious lesions or biting behaviors. To date, no studies have disclosed a case of HIV transmitted through casual contact. Also, because of likely public hysteria, the child and family have the right to withhold diagnostic information from school personnel and parents of classmates. They are not obligated to inform the school that their child is HIV-antibody-seropositive (Waters, et al., 1988). However, it is recommended that *someone* in the school—a teacher, nurse, or principal—be informed in order to support the child's immuno-compromised condition (Meyers and Weitzman, 1991:180).

Our challenges in moderating the stressors faced by HIV-infected children include performing ethnically sensitive family-centered assessments and providing psychosocial support for foster families who are willing to tackle the formidable task of providing care. Also needed are coordination and development of needed services and revision of public policy to respond adequately to the needs of these children and families (Taylor-Brown, 1991).

The physical environments in which many children grow up can be significant health hazard. Increasingly, poor air quality, toxic chemicals, and other contaminants pose special risks to young children because their organs are still developing, they have less robust immune systems, and they "eat more food, drink more water and breathe more air in relation to their size than adults do" (Cushman, 1996:A-8). Between 1980 and 1993, asthma deaths among children and young people increased by 118 percent, according to the Centers for Disease Control and Prevention (1996).

During that period, it was also learned that children were being exposed to polychlorinated biphenyls (PCBs) prior to birth via their mother's consumption of contaminated fish or afterward through breast milk. Children with the highest levels of exposure are three times as likely to have below normal IQ scores and twice as likely to be behind in reading comprehension (Brody, 1996). Our growing understanding of the lifelong penalties to vulnerable children because of environmental contaminants have led to important legislation to structure protective measures and tougher regulations. In order to protect children, these regulations must be monitored and enforced.

**Natural disasters, war, terrorism, and violence.** A young child's world can suddenly be turned upside down through natural disasters such as earthquakes, floods, fires, tornadoes, or hurricanes, causing loss of possessions, their home, or loved ones. Because children are thrown most out of balance when predictability and stability in their world is threatened, high levels of stress and anxiety caused by fear and ambiguity can result.

Human-created social traumas, however, are much more frequent and increasingly affect more of our children. Some of these children live in communities that have been labeled war zones, where children become victims of or witness the use of weapons, rape, robbery, or assaults. These children have night terrors, become afraid to play outside, and come to believe early that life has little purpose and meaning or that they have no future. Anxiety, lack of impulse control, poor appetite, and poor concentration are characteristics of these children. School phobias and avoidance are also common (Barfield, Simpson, and Groves, 1992).

Even when they do not personally experience these events, the stark reality of what such events can mean for young children is brought directly into their lives through television. They see injured and dead children who are victims of violent acts such as the Oklahoma bombing, terrorist-related plane and train crashes, assassinations of political leaders, and the "scariness" of war in terms of homelessness, cold, hunger, disease, and the loss of limbs and eyes (see Figure 6–1). On milk cartons, they see pictures of children who have been abducted. They hear stories in the news about young children drowned by their own mothers and doctors who kill people.

In addition to the violence connected to events in the real world, children's TV programming adds immeasurably to their knowledge of alarming and violent possibilities. A recent release by the American Medical Association, *A Physician's Guide to Media Violence*, reports that the average American child watches about twenty-eight hours of TV per week and that each child's TV show contains about twenty-five violent acts each hour, adding up to a total of more than 200,000 acts of violence and 16,000 murders before a child turns eighteen

**Figure 6–1** Child's perception of war: "dangerous, not funny, and always scary."

(Gerbner and Signorielli, 1995). Up to 80 percent of the prime-time shows that children watch include beatings, shootings, and stabbings. *TV Guide* reports that during prime time, such incidents occur approximately every 6 minutes (Edelman, 1993). Child psychologists worry about a redefinition in children's minds about how we should treat others—that it's okay to "diss one another, push, shove, hit and kick" (Meriwether, 1996). In fact, the influence of this "normalization" of violence can be seen in-

creasingly in the violence that young children, especially boys, bring to their play and in the kinds of toys they request. Later, it is again enacted in the growing rate of violent crime among American youths, now the highest in the industrialized world (Levin, 1994, 1995). Table 6–2 depicts Levin's construction of a developmental framework for understanding the overall impact of this violence on younger children and how professionals can mediate the negative effects.

▼ Table 6–2    A Developmental Framework for Understanding How to Counteract the Negative
              Effects of Violence

| How Children Are Affected by Violence | How to Counteract the Negative Effects |
|---|---|
| • Sense of *trust and safety* is undermined as children see the world is dangerous and adults can't keep them safe. | • Create a *secure, predictable environment*, which teaches children how to keep themselves and others *safe*. |
| • Sense of *self* as a separate person who can have a positive, meaningful *effect* on the world without violence is undermined. | • Help children *take responsibility, feel powerful, positively affect their world*, and meet individual needs without fighting. |
| • Sense of *mutual respect and interdependence* is undermined—relying on others is a sign of vulnerability; violence is modeled as central in human interactions. | • Take advantage of many opportunities to *participate in a caring community* where people help and rely of each other and work out their problems in mutually agreeable ways. |
| • Increased *need to construct an understanding of violent experiences* in discussions, creative play, art, and storytelling. | • Provide wide-ranging *opportunities to develop meanings of violence* through art, stories, and play (with adult help as needed). |
| • *Endangered ability to work through violence* as mechanisms for doing so are undermined. | • *Actively facilitate play, art, and language* so children can safely and competently work through violent experiences. |
| • Overemphasis on *violent content as the organizer* of thoughts, feelings, and behavior. | • Provide deeply *meaningful content that offers appealing alternatives* to violence as organizers of experience. |

Source: Adapted with permission from *Teaching Young Children in Violent Times* by Diane E. Levin © 1994 Educators for Social Responsibility, Cambridge, MA.

## Other Assaults

Childhood historians believe we may be moving into a period in which children are less valued than in the past, and distinctions between adulthood and childhood are becoming dangerously blurred. They remind us that in bygone centuries, adults held naive, even cruel, views regarding children and tended to ignore their needs (Postman, 1982). Pearsall (1983:2) says that today we see children as "safe little Peter Pans [who are somehow immune from our] fast-paced, high-geared, McDonalized society." Evidence, of course, is to the contrary, and Garbarino (1995) goes as far as labeling these environments "socially toxic."

There are numerous assaults on children today, including the kinds of food we are feeding them, the amount of television to which they are exposed, the usurping of play by adult-directed extracurricular activities, and the continuous and ominous "forced blooming" that is taking place (Elkind, 1981). Many children today don't go to camp as a place to interact casually with their peers; they go to gain computer skills, athletic skills, or preprofessional skills. Additionally, they are encouraged to copy adults in dress and behavior, so many of the "markers" that indicated passage from childhood to adulthood are

missing. Elkind has remarked that we have not stolen away children's innocence; they are still innocent, but very confused and stressed innocents.

## ▼ CHILDREN'S REACTIONS TO STRESS

Carol Klein (1975), author of *The Myth of the Happy Child*, wrote that adults tend to sentimentalize childhood, concentrating on its playfulness, innocence, and freedom from responsibility. In reality, growing up also includes experiencing the *painful*, complex emotions that define us as human beings. In the process, we learn to cope with such feelings. Like adults who become overwhelmed when they are overloaded, understimulated, or faced with too much change, fear, or uncertainty, children exhibit individual responses when stressed. Personality characteristics, feelings of self-worth, learned coping skills, and the child's perception of how personally threatening any particular stressor is will affect each child's reaction when under pressure.

## Physical Reactions

Highly stressed children often *look* stressed. When compared with other children, they frequently exhibit slumped posture or a noticeably rigid body carriage. The child may appear to be "charged up" (one or more body parts in constant motion) or peculiarly passive. Breathing is concentrated predominantly in the upper chest rather than in the lower abdomen. The voice may have an explosive or shrill quality, and speech may be accelerated. In children who have experienced prolonged or intense stress, the hair often is dull, and there may be dark circles under the eyes (not usually seen in children). Frequency and/or urgency of urination may increase significantly, as do the numbers of somatic complaints such as headaches, stomachaches, and earaches (Pearsall, 1983). Appetite may increase or decrease dramatically, with accompanying gain or loss in weight. There may be vomiting, diarrhea, difficulty in swallowing, unexplained rashes on the face or other parts of the body, and frequent wheezing and/or coughing (Crow, 1978). The child may be particularly susceptible to colds, flu, and other viral infections.

## Psychological Reactions

When individuals are under prolonged or intense pressure, a common psychological reaction is lessened ability to attend to relevant stimuli. There also is a marked inability to internalize information available in the environment or to make the best use of that information. It becomes more difficult to make decisions. Those of us who have ever found ourselves in a group setting in which we felt upset, inferior, or unprepared can understand this. We probably found ourselves unable to attend to the activity going on around us, or tremendously anxious and tense. Most likely, we had little to offer that was relevant to what was going on because our psychic energy was directed toward our own equilibration. There is little reason to believe that young children feel any differently, although it often is difficult for them to articulate how they are feeling.

## How Children Cope with Stress

**The use of defense mechanisms.** Coping with disturbing amounts of stress calls into play two different coping strategies: facing the stressor and adapting to it, or avoiding it. The latter usually is an initial response to something that bothers us. In order to reduce the tension we feel, we employ **defense mechanisms,** strategies that allow us to temporarily regain a sense of balance. There often are both advantages and disadvantages in using any of them. Brenner (1984:5–6) describes four broad cate-

gories of evasive actions (flight responses) typically used by children:

**Denial.** When using denial, children act as though the stress does not exist. For example, a preschooler goes on playing with her toys while being told that her father has died. Denial serves to alleviate pain and thus can help children preserve their equilibrium. Youngsters may also deny by using fantasy to obliterate reality. They may conjure up imaginary friends to keep them company or rely on magical beliefs to protect themselves and their loved ones.

**Regression.** When children act younger than their years and engage in earlier behaviors, they are using regression. They become dependent and demanding. As a result, they may receive more physical comforting and affection than usual, thus easing the existing stress.

**Withdrawal.** In withdrawal, children take themselves physically or mentally out of the picture. They run from the stressful environment or become quiet and almost invisible. They concentrate their attention on pets and inanimate objects or lose themselves in daydreams to escape mentally when they cannot escape physically. Their efforts bring them respite from tension for the time being.

**Impulsive acting out.** Children act impulsively and often flamboyantly to avoid thinking either of the past or of the consequence of their current actions. They conceal their misery by making others angry at them. They seek quick and easy ways to stop their pain. In the process, they draw attention to themselves and find ways of momentarily easing their feelings of stress. However, in the long run, this coping strategy (and others, listed above) is almost guaranteed to be self-destructive.

**More serious responses.** When these strategies fail to reduce the psychological disequilibrium being experienced, a child may manifest other symptoms, such as panic, increased irritability, depression, agitation, dread, forgetfulness, distractibility, and sleep disturbances (including frequent nightmares). More serious symptoms of emotional distress may include children pulling out their hair, repeatedly inflicting pain on themselves or others (including animals), frequently annoying others to draw attention away from themselves, having severe temper tantrums, running away, defying authority often, stealing repeatedly, and expressing excessive or indiscriminate affection toward adults. Children in even more severe trouble may express the feeling that they are no good, hear voices or see things that are not there, often think people are trying to hurt them, have many

▼ **Table 6–3    Telltale Signs of Stress in Young Children**

Doesn't respond to friendly caregiver overtures

Daydreams frequently

Has grave, solemn face; rarely smiles or laughs (check first for iron deficiency)

Has frequent prolonged temper tantrums

Cries a great deal for months after entry into group care (even though caregivers have been gentle and responsive)

Acts sullen, defiant (says "I don't care" frequently when caregiver explains how misbehavior has hurt another)

Punishes self through slapping, head banging, or calling self bad names ("bad boy")

Is overly sensitive to mild criticism

Flinches if teacher or visiting adult approaches with caressing or reassuring gesture of outstretched arm

Reports proudly to teacher that he or she has hurt another child

Is overly vigilant about others' misdeeds, tattles, or jeers

Is highly demanding of adults although usually fairly self-sufficient

Bullies or scapegoats and may get other children to join in

Carries out repetitive, stereotyped play that may have destructive aspects

Clings to, shadows caregiver, although in group for months

Is unable to carry out sustained play with preschool peers

Has constant need to sleep although physically well

Is preoccupied with frightening images of monsters or other violent, threatening figures

Has dull, vacant expression, as if trying to ward off thinking about stressful trauma or tries to deny stressful feelings

Is hyperactive or restless, wanders around room, touches and disturbs toys and games, cannot settle into constructive play

Displays disturbed bodily functions; has trouble with feeding, constipation, or diarrhea, soils self frequently months after toilet training is completed

Has trembling of hands or facial twitches although apparently well

Talks compulsively about physical dangers and threats

Grinds teeth during naptime

Has rigid facial expressions from taut muscles

Displays loss of perceptual acuity

Displays reduced attentional capacity; even though caregiver is very clear in communicating, the child cannot focus well on activity or request

Stimulates self constantly (by prolonged thumb-sucking, masturbation, rocking body back and forth, or other such behaviors), which children normally do occasionally for self-comfort

Feels jittery

Stutters, uses dysfluent speech, or refuses to talk in group (older preschooler)

Is clumsy on easy manual tasks due to muscular tensions

Frequently acts aggressively against others, even adults

Has nightmares

Source: Reprinted by permission, A. S. Honig, "Research in Review: Stress and Coping in Children (Part 2) Interpersonal Family Relationships," *Young Children* (1986) 41(5):53.

unusual fears, or be preoccupied with death. They may refuse to respond when others talk to them and refuse to play with their peers (Crow, 1978).

Honig (1986) has developed a listing of common childhood stress signals (see Table 6–3). Kuczen (1982) has suggested that it is normal for children to demonstrate a few of these characteristics during childhood. These signs can be symptomatic of typical growing pains or of the process of wrestling with

a temporarily troublesome problem. However, multiple signals, lasting for a period of time and evident even when there is no apparent cause, may be a signal that undue stress is threatening the wellbeing of the child.

## Stress Coping as a Learned Behavior

People are not born with coping skills. Some of us were lucky enough to have had important adults around us—parents, teachers, or someone else we liked a lot—who modeled effective coping skills when they were under pressure. We watched what they did when things weren't going so well for them or when things were going *extremely* well for them, and we sorted out those behaviors that seemed to yield the best payoffs in certain situations.

Some children rarely see effective coping strategies being used. They are reared in authoritarian settings in which power and striking out pays off, at least in the short run. Others spend their days in laissez-faire settings in which no one really cares what they do so long as they are not bothering someone, or in overprotective environments in which they become extremely vulnerable to peer pressures or to the exploitive behaviors of others.

Children frequently are reared in confusing environments in which parents and/or teachers react to them according to the adult's mood at that particular moment. If things are going well, the children are treated permissively; if things aren't so rosy, the atmosphere becomes more threatening. These children try to become good at "reading" the given moment. They also have a tendency to become exploitive and lean toward a great deal of "testing-out" behavior when they aren't quite sure where they stand.

One of the most critical elements in child's ability to deal positively with strain and pressure is his or her self-concept. This develops in tandem with stress-coping abilities. The children who spend a great deal of their time with supportive and authoritative adults develop both high self-esteem and the best coping strategies. This is because they become aware that the way their life goes has a great deal to do with some of the choices *they* make and that there are consequences attached to those choices. They also learn that some consequences are more unpleasant than others and that those caring adults are a little cooler toward them when reasonable expectations have not been met. They discover that outcomes are not necessarily always in their control, but tend to be generally more positive when they have observed the limits set for them by others. They learn to see other people as predictable and are able to see strengths and weaknesses in both themselves and others.

These "styles of coping" do not happen randomly. They are the cumulative results of children's continuous observation, reflection, action, and interaction with other important people in their lives—people who ultimately have tremendous influence on how each child will approach life's

events (Soderman, 1985). We have become increasingly aware that not all children are traumatized in highly stressful situations; nor do effects become lifelong in some cases. E. James Anthony (1992), a well-known child psychiatrist, likened the most resilient children to dolls made of steel, which react with only a metallic ping to hammering. He contrasted these children with others who appeared to be "made of glass," shattering easily when struck, and still others who seemed to be made of plastic—those who definitely have battle scars but are not completely destroyed.

Why some children have lasting scars and others are quite resilient has been the focus of longitudinal research by Werner and Smith (1992), who report that approximately two thirds of the people they followed since 1955 were not able to overcome circumstances enough to be successful later in life; on the other hand, one third *were* able to skirt the learning and behavior problems, delinquency, mental health problems, and early pregnancies found in the others. Monahon (1993) and others indicate that protective factors may include:

▼ Easy-going response pattern to minor stresses
▼ Biological endowment of an easy temperament that allows adaptability
▼ Greater intelligence to reason and comprehend
▼ Generally more satisfying experiences in school
▼ Higher self-esteem and basic self-confidence
▼ Perception that a person can have an impact on the course of his or her life
▼ Tendency to master difficult situations with more ease
▼ Connections and greater support outside the family

There is evidence that the number of risk factors (e.g., poverty, large families, absent fathers, drug-infested neighborhoods) is an important factor in predicting whether or not there will be a "self-righting" of the individual or recovery in the long term. When there are eight or nine risk factors operating, *nobody* does well, according to Arnold Sameroff, a developmental psychologist (Gelman, 1997). The age of the child can also be a protective factor, depending on the nature of the threat. Younger children are more vulnerable whenever their caretaker is threatened but less vulnerable in situations they don't yet understand. Conversely, the older child often appears less stressed about potential separation from a caretaker; their stress seems to stem mostly from their ability to understand the long-range implications of an overwhelming event or crisis.

Caring adults need to recognize that today's bombardment of choices, temptations, and pressures are as distressing for children as for adults (Kuczen, 1982). Because of the increased incidence of stress-related disorders among children, it is important for helping professionals to both model and teach effective skills for withstanding undue stress.

## What Adults Can Do to Help Children Manage Stress

In order for adults to be effective in helping stressed children, they need a combination of knowledge, appreciation, skill, and self-awareness (Brenner, 1984). They must build a strong *knowledge base* about the variety of demands children face, their typical ways of responding, and the effects of particular stressors on children and families. Helping professionals also need to become familiar with the legal issues related to any action they might take on behalf of a child and/or family and the kinds of resources that are available in the community.

**Appreciation** involves respecting children's viewpoints as well as their coping modalities, including any negative strategies they currently employ in lieu of something more positive. This is where empathy becomes important, enabling the adult to see the stressor through the child's eyes. Moreover, a holistic look at the stressor in terms of what other demands the child and family are facing is necessary in order to avoid simplistic "solutions."

*Skill* in approaching children about the way they are responding to a stressor is of paramount importance in allowing both the adult and the child to progress toward stress reduction. This requires that adults respond to children in warm, nonthreatening, friendly, and helpful ways.

Caregivers must honestly examine their own *biases and belief systems* in regard to each kind of stressor and each kind of child and family. No matter how adept children become at coping with stress, it never is possible for them to be completely success-ful, to avoid all negative consequences, and to be able to take everything that comes. Children cannot cope with stress on a daily basis without help and support from at least one caring adult. For some children, a child-care center or school may be the only place where they can find such help.

The process of helping children begins when the helping professional "recognizes the child's 'loss of wholeness' or 'togetherness,' be it evidenced by fear and withdrawal, anxiety, inability to read or pay attention (or complete a task). It blossoms when the teacher is committed to furthering the overall goal of helping, which is to promote more useful behavior in children." The following questions may be useful in devising a strategy for intervention (Chandler, 1985:184):

1. Is it possible to reduce the child's stress through environmental manipulation?
2. Is it possible to reduce stress through changing the attitude and behavior of significant adults?
3. Is it possible to modify the child's extreme behavior so that it more closely approximates normal coping responses?
4. Is it possible to reduce stress by helping the child to adopt a more realistic perception of himself or herself and the life situation?

The process of helping children further unfolds when the teacher carefully and skillfully uses his or her attending and responding skills to promote increased self-exploration and self-understanding on the part of the child (Schultz and Heuchert, 1983:86). In addition, helpful caregivers also create a safe environment for children and actively develop stress-coping skills in the children with whom they are working. Working cooperatively with parents is another necessary element in the process of childhood stress reduction. The following are suggestions for supporting the development of positive stress-management strategies in children.

## SKILLS FOR HELPING CHILDREN COPE WITH STRESS

 **Develop General Stress-Reduction Skills**

*1. Recognize and respect the different coping styles of children.* Be alert for the withdrawn child as well as for the child who more openly displays negative feelings. Both may require tremendous patience on your part, since initial attempts to make them more comfortable may be met with resistance. The withdrawn child may become more intensely avoidant; the angry, aggressive child may refuse, at first, to work at controlling hostile behavior. Giving in to or ignoring such behaviors, rather than guiding these children toward more productive coping, only reinforces their feelings of insecurity.

*2.* **Use nonverbal attending skills.** Focus on the child's feelings as much as on what the child is saying in situations in which children obviously are experiencing difficulty. Carefully observe changes in posture, expression, tone of voice, and other paralinguistic characteristics, as these communicate affect. Use your own body language to demonstrate interest and concern. Keep your own emotions and behavior under control. Don't jump to conclusions or try for a "quick fix" when you don't fully understand the situation. Accept the fact that a child's stress can be very distressing for you as well as for the child. The child's greatest need, at first, is to know that someone understands and cares.

*3.* **Use effective responding skills.** Let the child know that you are earnestly involved in helping and also in guiding him or her toward more effective coping. Use reflections to encourage adequate self-disclosure. Verbalize your perceptions of the situations to check for accuracy. Communicate clearly and directly, using the skills learned in Chapters 4 and 5. Do not tell the child that he or she will "outgrow" the problem or that the problem is essentially insignificant. If it is stressful for the child, the problem is important from his or her perspective.

*4.* **Maintain ongoing surveillance of all children with respect to new or ongoing threats.** Solomon (1995:44) suggests that key elements of surveillance for caregivers include:

Having a good educational background with respect to child development

Eliciting parents' concerns about their child's development through open-ended questions, for example, "Do you have any concerns about your child's development recently?"

Having a "high index of suspicion" relative to possible abuse or neglect

Paying particular attention to gross motor milestones in the first year of life and language milestones in the second year of life

Using a developmental screening test (e.g., Denver II) periodically with all children in the program

 **Create a Safe, Growth-Enhancing Environment**

*1.* **Intervene immediately in aggressive encounters.** Make sure that children feel safe. At no time should they feel threatened with physical or emotional harm from other children or adults. Do not allow children to express tension by harming others. Use the skills outlined in Chapter 12. Develop rules that promote an esprit de corps or a sense of "we-ness" whenever possible by encouraging prosocial behavior. Praise children's efforts when they demonstrate respect for one another and when they behave empathically.

*2.* **Promote self-esteem in all children.** Take advantage of every opportunity to help children feel competent and worthwhile. Use appropriate nonverbal behaviors and reflective listening. Praise children who use prosocial behaviors. The following example illustrates the application of these skills in a stressful encounter. Juan had rebuffed his teacher's attempts to talk with him about his many conflicts with other children by holding his hands firmly over his ears. One morning, following a shouting match with another child, Juan was alone with his teacher. As she sat down next to him, she noted aloud that he still looked pretty angry. Although Juan sat sullenly with his arms locked tightly across his chest, for the first time he did not put his hands over his ears. His teacher was quiet for a

*continued*

moment and then added softly: "You're angry, Juan . . . but you're also listening. I appreciate that very, very much."

**3. Make every child the object of daily focused attention.** The younger the child, the more important it is to have a particular caregiver working consistently on a one-to-one basis with the child. Children never outgrow their need for individualized attention, however brief it may be. Keep a daily journal that you fill out after the children leave for the day. Briefly record your thoughts about the children with whom you recall having encounters. Reread the journal after multiple entries have been made. Evaluate your pattern of comments on children; determine if there are some children who rarely are mentioned. Make additional efforts to attend to those children; observe their behavior more closely. Another way to evaluate *your* performance is to go over a list of the children's names and mentally describe some aspect of their development such as motor skills or the ability to maintain peer relationships. If you cannot spontaneously recall information about a particular child, pay more consistent attention to that child.

**4. Give children opportunities to work out their feelings through play.** Accept the child's choice of a play theme. Do not try to direct play or determine how the details of play should be carried out. Play allows children to gain a sense of control when they are feeling fearful or uncertain. In the context of play, children can reduce their problems to manageable size and work at understanding them and themselves. For example, children commonly play "hospital" when they have just experienced hospitalization. Rarely are these children interested in being the patient. Instead, they prefer to play the role of doctor, making sure they are "in control" of the situation.

It also is common for children to play at death: falling down "dead," "zapping" a playmate, telling spooky stories, or pretending to be in a casket. Play is a safe and appropriate avenue through which death can be explored. Do not intervene when you see this kind of play even though you may feel it is morbid or un-

healthy. In fact, playing out difficult concepts and situations is the child's way of making them manageable.

**5. Eliminate unnecessary competition.** Protect preschool children, who are especially vulnerable to competitive activities. For example, "musical chairs," a game that may be highly enjoyed by eight-year-olds, creates distress for younger, egocentric children. Select cooperatively based group activities for grade-school children whenever possible. Focus on *group* achievement rather than on individual performance. In one instance, a fifth-grade music teacher held competitions for the spring performance. Although all the songs were to be chorus numbers, with a few speaking parts, she eliminated all but a few singers from the chorus. One child, who loved to sing and who was not chosen, cried nightly during the selection process and, according to his parents, would not sing on any occasion, including birthday parties, for the next three years! Prevent unnecessary stress whenever possible.

**6. Build relaxation breaks into the program.** Plan for periodic relaxation breaks in which everyone takes part in activities such as the stretching, tensing, and relaxing of muscle groups, aerobic exercise, or exercises designed to relax breathing. Children who participate in these activities are better able to concentrate and spend more time on assigned tasks. Take children on "fantasy vacations." Ask them to close their eyes and depart together on an imaginary journey. Use sensory vocabulary to encourage more elaborate imagery. Sometimes, ask children to pretend that they are going to attempt a challenging task, and ask them to pretend each step while breathing deeply. Help them to envision themselves as an actor, a doer, one who can face the challenge.

**7. Allow children to participate in decision making and conflict resolution.** Children should be included in the solving of real, genuine problems. This skill is developed fully in Chapter 9.

**8. Use teaching materials, strategies, and resources that promote divergent as well as con-**

## SKILLS FOR HELPING CHILDREN COPE WITH STRESS—continued

vergent thought. Promote the consideration of alternative solutions to problems by saying: "How else do you think we could use these materials?" or "If we use these another way, the end result may be very different. Let's try it!"

Choose textbooks or other curricular materials that depict males and females doing a variety of tasks. Select materials that depict variations in family structures and situation without implying that one family form or another is somehow deviant. A variety of cultural and racial groups should be depicted in positive terms.

**9. Plan how to modify individual differences that cause children problems in their interaction with others.** Although every effort should be made to respect individual differences, behaviors that are destructive to the child's own growth and/or destructive to others should be modified, if possible. Support the child while she or he is learning new behaviors. Say: "I know this is hard for you. I'll be right here to help." Acknowledge even the smallest effort at self-modification. Praise each modest success. If destructive behaviors are significantly difficult for you to change even after consistent effort, seek advice and/or assistance from other professionals who are more highly skilled.

 **Develop Preventive Stress-Coping Behaviors in Children**

Teach children how to cope with stress before they find themselves in a highly stressful situation. Behaviors that develop habits of exercise and good nutrition, when combined with self-understanding and good coping strategies, enhance children's abilities to deal with short-term and long-term stressors.

**1. Coach children on what to do in potentially frightening situations or emergencies.** Prepare children for these encounters through discussion and role play (Jarratt, 1994). For example, ask, "What would you do if you got separated from your parents in a department store?" or "What would you do if someone older and bigger than you tried to take your lunch money away?"

**2. Expand children's vocabulary to facilitate communication of troubling feelings and thoughts.** Read children's books that depict stressful situations for the characters, or suggest titles for independent readers. Use precise vocabulary when making affective reflections ("You're so enthusiastic today!" or "I sense that you're pretty disappointed"). Help children formulate descriptions of what they are feeling when under stress. Remember, stress can be produced by a very happy event, such as a party, as well as an unhappy event, such as the death of a pet.

**3. Increase children's sensitivity to their own body sensations when they feel angry, sad, tense, joyful, and so on.** Be specific in your reflections: "I can tell you're angry because your hands are in such tight fists." Provide information: "You're so excited that you seem just ready to jump. Every muscle seems ready to go."

**4. Allow children to experience the positive and negative consequences of their decisions unless doing so would endanger their safety or physical or emotional health.** Tell children that mistakes are one useful way to discover better ways of doing something. Ask them to generate other alternatives that might have led to different consequences. Do not intervene unless there is a clear risk to the child.

**5. Provide opportunities for vigorous daily exercise.** Teach children that regular exercise reduces the natural stress on the body and maintains health. Do not assume that children are getting enough exercise; this frequently is not true. Children and adults need at least 20 minutes of vigorous activity each day. Demonstrate the relationship of stress and activity: "I was feeling 'logy' because I've had such a hard day. Now that I've had a chance to do aerobics, I feel better! How do you feel?"

**6. Teach children specific relaxation techniques.** Encourage children to practice exercises such as deep muscle relaxation and relaxed breathing daily so they become habitual. Have children do some just before going home so they do not arrive there tense. One teacher asked chil-

*continued*

## SKILLS FOR HELPING CHILDREN COPE WITH STRESS—continued

dren to investigate their own bodies to find out where all their "hinges" were (neck, elbow, wrist, waist, pelvis, knees, ankles). She had the children practice "bending" these hinges, then "locking them up" to develop an awareness of how their bodies felt when tense and when loose. She taught them to "turn themselves into Raggedy Ann and Andy dolls" who become increasingly limp as they unlocked one hinge after another. This game, and others she developed, allowed children to contrast tense and relaxed feelings. One of the best breathing-and-relaxation exercises appears in *The Relaxation Response* (Benson, 1976). Practice these exercises yourself on a regular basis before using them with children.

**7. Teach children to practice positive self-talk in tense situations.** Teach children to tell themselves to take it easy or calm down and to sit quietly before responding to a situation. Young children may need to say these things out loud: "I am in control," "I can stay calm," "I'm scared, but I can handle this," "I can breathe in and out very slowly to help myself stay calm." In contrast, discourage children from saying how stupid, incompetent, or helpless they are when in the middle of a stressful situation.

Children cannot control their feelings, but they can learn to control their behavior. First, they must believe that they have control. Help them to develop **positive self-talk** that is appropriate to the particular problems that they experience: "I can get really mad, but I don't have to hit," "I can choose to yell instead of hitting," "I can tell them what they did that made me so angry." Self-talk contributes to self-control and decreases impulsiveness, which sometimes escalates a stressful event.

**8. Use encouraging responses to help children feel better about themselves.** When children have developed the habit of focusing verbally or mentally on the negative aspects of an experience ("I'm so dumb," "I knew everyone would laugh at me," "I can never remember anything!"), positive behavior changes can be facilitated by offering encouraging statements that verbalize positive aspects. These encouraging statements should not deny children's feelings ("You shouldn't feel that way," "It's not *that*

bad"). Rather, they should be used to point out the potential benefits or good in a situation. For instance, after missing the word "chaotic" in a spelling bee, Chris sits down, saying, "I'm not any good at spelling anyway." At this point, you could say: "You're disappointed that you missed a word. You lasted for five rounds. That's pretty good."

**9. Help children practice imagery.** Children who have very limited skills in a particular area or poor self-esteem often foresee themselves as performing poorly in a particular situation before they even begin. This tends to decrease their potential for performing at least adequately, if not well. Suggest that children pretend that they are going to perform very well the particular task that worries them. Tell them to begin the task in their minds and go through it step by step until it is successfully "completed." Have the children pretend with all their senses; for example, they might imagine themselves preparing for an oral presentation, reading, writing note cards, walking to the front of the group, and seeing classmates listening attentively. Encourage them to envision success and competence for this potentially threatening experience. Tell children to use this technique whenever they have to do something that worries or frightens them.

**10. Use ordinary experiences and daily activities to discuss feelings, thoughts, and behaviors that people can use when they are afraid, uncertain, faced with change, or overwhelmed by what is happening to them.** Discuss current events seen in newspapers, television shows that children watch, and experiences others share with the class. Highlight the coping techniques that were used. Explain to younger children how difficult the experience was for the person who went through it. For example, if a residence caught fire in the area, children will talk about it. Use this opportunity to discuss how frightening it was for the family and what they or their neighbors did to help. Stories also can be used as opportunities to play out some dramatic event. Do not deliberately try to frighten children; focus instead on positive steps they can take in similar situations.

## SKILLS FOR HELPING CHILDREN COPE WITH STRESS—continued

 **Provide Support for Children Coping with Loss**

**1. Use appropriate vocabulary when discussing death and dying.** Use the words "dead," "dying," and "died" when talking about death. Avoid analogies such as "dying is like going to sleep" or euphemisms like "passed on," "lost," or "gone away." Children are literal in their interpretation of language. Thus, words that are meant to soften the blow may actually make the situation more difficult for them to understand.

**2. Describe death in terms of familiar bodily functions.** In describing what it means to be dead, point out that normal body functioning stops: the heart stops beating; there is no more breathing, no more feeling, no more emotions, no more loving, no more thinking, no more sleeping, no more eating (Furman, 1978). Death is not like anything else. It is not like sleeping, resting, or lying still, and parallels to these activities should not be made. Children who overhear statements such as "She looks so peaceful, as if she were sleeping" may dread going to sleep themselves for fear that they will not wake up. This is particularly true for children in the first or second stages of conceptualizing death, who still think that death may be temporary and reversible.

**3. Explain why the death has occurred, giving children accurate information.** Eventually, children ask, "Why did he (or she) die?" When talking to a child about a person or an animal who died as a result of illness, explain that all living things get sick sometimes. Mostly, of course, they get better again. But there are times when they are so terribly sick that they die because their body cannot function anymore (Mellonie and Ingpen, 1983). When talking to children about a death that has occurred as a result of an accident or injury, help them differentiate between mortal injury and everyday cuts and scrapes from which we all recover.

**4. Explain death rituals as a means by which people provide comfort to the living.** Children often are confused by the mixed messages that funeral customs communicate. For instance,

children who have been told that a dead person feels nothing may find it disconcerting that soft, satin blankets and pillows have been provided. In their minds, these props are objects of comfort, and their presence reinforces the notion that death is like sleep. Adults can point out that articles such as these are for the aesthetic benefit of the mourners.

**5. Answer children's questions about death matter-of-factly.** Help children understand the details of death by responding calmly to queries about cemeteries, coffins, cremations, embalming, tombstones, skeletons, ghosts, and angels. Accept their questions nonjudgmentally. Answer simply and honestly. Sometimes, children's questions seem morbid, insensitive, or bizarre, such as "When are *you* going to die?" or "Do worms eat the eyeballs, too?" If you recoil in shock or admonish the questioner, you add to children's perception that death is a secret topic, not to be discussed or explored. Things that cannot be talked about can be frightening to children, adding to the stress of the situation. Remember, too, that children learn through repetition, so they may ask the same questions over and over again. Each time they hear the answer, they are adding a new fragment of information to their store of knowledge. Frequent questions do not necessarily indicate stress or fear, but rather, can reflect normal curiosity.

**6. Respect the family's prerogative for giving children religious explanations about death.** Avoid religious explanations. As a helping professional, you will work with children and families whose beliefs vary widely. It is your responsibility to respect those differences by allowing parents to tend to the spiritual needs of their own child. Be sensitive to the cultural mores of the families in your group. Insensitivity or ignorance can have disastrous results for children because your explanation may undermine what they have been told by a parent. The only exception to this rule is if you have been hired by a specific religious group to promote their philosophy. Then, because parents have chosen to send their child to you for religious teaching, it is appropriate for you to reiterate the philosophy of the institution. However, keep in

*continued*

## SKILLS FOR HELPING CHILDREN COPE WITH STRESS—continued

mind children's age and level of comprehension when giving explanations.

Sometimes, children will say that someone told them: "Baby brother is an angel" or "When people die, they can return in another life as something else." When this occurs, the best response is: "You're wondering if that is true. Many people believe that. Many people believe other things, too, and as you get older, you will learn about them and will understand them better" (Furman, 1979:189).

**7. Provide support for children who have chronic or potentially life threatening disease, such as AIDS or cancer, without overprotecting them.** Children who are in remission or well enough to attend school may need some privileges not accorded to other children related to the need for additional rest, medication, and nutritional limitations. Like other children, they need understanding, consistent limits on behavior, appropriate and reasonable academic expectations, and occasional help in forming classroom friendships. Teachers providing support for such children may find the experience both emotionally demanding and time consuming—but also deeply rewarding (McGee, 1982).

**8. Provide accurate information to other children who may be confused or frightened at having a health-impaired member of the group.** For example, a child recovering from chemotherapy may not have much hair. This condition is not catching, and when children understand the course of treatment better, they are more likely to accept the health-impaired child in their social activities. Parents or health professionals can provide the requisite information.

**9. Be alert for negative reactions to children who are siblings of a health-impaired child.** Some children may be reluctant to play or work with them for the same reasons they are reluctant to do so with the health-impaired child. Providing correct information will help them to be more sensitive to and supportive of children who have an ill brother or sister.

**10. For children experiencing their parents' divorce, explain that divorce is the result of** "grown-up problems." Tell children that adults get divorced because they can no longer find happiness in being together. Reassure youngsters that they are not responsible for the divorce, nor is it possible for them to bring their parents back together. Explain that although family members will be living in different households, they are still family, and the mother and father are still the child's parents.

**11. Acknowledge the pain that divorce inevitably brings to children.** Offer physical comfort; reflect children's emotions; remain available to children who wish to talk. Remember that the grieving process takes a long time, and children will vary in their reactions to it.

Lay a foundation for helping children cope with potential stressors such as death or divorce by using books dealing with such events even when they have not occurred in your classroom.

 **Mediate Children's Stress through Family Communication Strategies**

**1. Collaborate with parents to reduce childhood stress.** Once children move into a situation in which they receive a significant portion of their care from adults other than their parents, all of the adults then become linked in the delicate responsibility of guiding their socialization. For this link to be effective, the adults must be willing to share information that they believe the others need to know about a child in order to best support the child's needs. This calls for frank, open communication that is conducted in a nonthreatening, nonjudgmental manner, even when parents' behavior in a stressful situation has been less than optimal. Whenever one adult seeks to place blame or to unfairly criticize another adult's genuine attempts to be supportive, the thread that links them together is weakened significantly. Professionals can be most helpful to parents when they:

▼ Let them know when a child is manifesting signs of undue stress
▼ Remain alert for signs of parental stress
▼ Share information with parents about the effects of childhood and adult stress through seminars or newsletters

## SKILLS FOR HELPING CHILDREN COPE WITH STRESS—continued

▼ Listen empathically to parents when they speak of their own stress

▼ Let parents know they want to work cooperatively with them to support them and their child during stressful times

▼ Acknowledge parents' efforts to work cooperatively to reduce a child's level of distress

**2. Talk to separating or divorcing parents about the importance of explaining to children how divorce will affect their daily living.** Parents who are caught up in a divorce may not realize that children benefit from knowing such concrete details as where they will eat and sleep, with whom they will live, and how much they will be able to see the noncustodial parent. Draw parents' attention to these facts and help them think of ways to explain the issues to their children.

**3. Help parents whose young children are exhibiting stress when being dropped off.** Very young children sometimes have conflicting emotions about having their parents leave, particularly when they are first being introduced to a formal group setting, during periods when the family is going through a significant change (mother entering the work force, father leaving because of divorce), and often following holiday recesses. Children balk because they're feeling insecure about what may happen while they're in the program. Also, parents are the most significant persons in their lives and, quite frankly, children enjoy being around their parents more than anyone else. Children new to an educational setting do not know how much "fun" school can be, so it does little good for the parents or professional to plead that case. Children only know that they are in a place they would rather not be and that their "security person" is leaving them with unfamiliar people who cannot, at least at that moment, quite fill the void.

Parents who are introducing children to a new setting and new people should plan, if possible, on spending some time in the setting with the child to help her or him become more secure. Although not all parents can rearrange their work schedules, the possibility ought to be suggested at the parent orientation meeting held prior to the opening of the center or school.

Personality differences in children make it difficult to design foolproof guidelines for separating, but the following procedure provides useful information to share with parents:

▼ *Give parents ideas about how to help their children prepare for their participation in the program.* Suggest that they visit the building together, play on the playground, or drive or walk past the program site prior to the first day. Advise parents to tell the child that he or she will be attending the center or class and to describe in detail some of the things that will be going on each day. Encourage parents to bring the children to any orientation that might be offered.

▼ *Give parents specific guidelines for how to initiate the separation process once they arrive at the center or classroom.* The first step is for parents to find a material that looks interesting to them and to begin playing with it. This shows children that the setting is a fun, safe place to be. Have parents avoid asking, "Do you want to paint a picture?" or "Do you want to build with blocks?" Youngsters often perceive such questions as pressure to separate and therefore resist the invitation. After 5 or 10 minutes, if children have not become involved, parents can include them by saying something like: "I can't decide just where to put this block. What do you think?"

▼ *Encourage parents to gradually remove themselves from direct interaction with their child.* This step involves having the parent say something like: "You're having a really good time here. I have to write a letter (read this book, work on a paper). I will sit on that bench (near the door but inside the room). I'll be there if you need me." If the child follows the parent to the chosen spot, a compromise is possible. The parent might say: "I'll work here for 5 minutes. Then, I will join you." When the child becomes able to play comfortably for 20 minutes without checking on the parent, the parent can tell the child that he or she is going to the "secretary's office" for 5 minutes. It is important for the parent to

*continued*

## SKILLS FOR HELPING CHILDREN COPE WITH STRESS—continued

then leave, even if the child protests, emphasizing that he or she will return. The parent must then reappear at the appointed time. This lets even the unhappy child know that the parent will do what he or she has promised to do. Parents can then spend an increasingly lengthy time away from the room. Once children can participate for at least 30 minutes without crying the whole time, parents can plan to leave their children at the appointed hour and pick them up when the program is over. Tell parents to anticipate the need for additional time to work through any separation problems with their child. Adapt the preceding routine to the parents' time constraints as necessary. Some may not have the luxury of working through the process. Do not try to coerce parents into spending more time than they are able or make them feel guilty if they cannot stay as long as you might like.

▼ *Encourage parents to leave promptly once they have said goodbye.* Lingering departures or unexpected reappearances heighten children's anxiety by making the environment unpredictable. Escort parents to the door, if need be, and assure them that you will call them later in the day to explain how the child is getting along.

▼ *Physically intervene if necessary to help parents and children separate.* Frequently, parents wait for children to give them permission to leave. They try to obtain this permission with statements like: "Don't you want to stay here with all your friends?"; "You don't want me to lose my job, do you?"; or "You want me to be proud of you, don't you?" Children seldom cooperate in this effort. At this point, you should step in and say: "Carla, your mom is leaving now. I'll help you find something to do." Then, take the child to an activity. Assure the parent that this is part of your job and that you expect that eventually the child will become happily involved.

▼ *Caution parents to resist the temptation to sneak away as soon as the child becomes involved with an activity.* This damages the child's confidence in the parent and reinforces the idea that the school or center is not a place to be trusted. It can create a real sense of abandon-

ment and terror in a child and may later trigger a fresh and more intense outburst.

▼ *Alert parents to potentially harmful ways of dealing with separation.* Some of these include pressuring children, shaming them, or denying their feelings. Sometimes, parents admonish their children to "behave themselves," "be good," or "act nice." These cautions, although well intended, put pressure on children at a time when they least need additional worries. It is better for parents to say: "Have fun!", "Have a nice day," or "I love you. See you after outdoor time!"

In addition, children's anxiety increases when adults say: "Mommy will feel bad if you don't stop crying," "I feel sad when you don't like the school," or "Nobody likes to play with a crybaby." These tactics do nothing to relieve the child's despair. Children who are sad or angry about separation should not be burdened with the additional responsibility of making other people feel better.

Finally, phrases like "Don't worry" or "Don't cry" intensify rather than soothe children's feelings of distress. Such statements indicate that the child's feelings are wrong or unimportant, rather than helping him or her find a constructive way to cope. It is better to acknowledge a child's true feelings, no matter what they are.

▼ *Agree to telephone distraught parents to reassure them when their child has adjusted to the separation, if necessary.* Occasionally, the parent has more difficulty leaving the child than the child has in leaving the parent. The procedure outlined thus far may be accomplished in half an hour or one day, or it may take several weeks. Some children will enter a room confidently, wave goodbye to their parents, and immediately settle into an activity. When they don't, these guidelines can be activated.

▼ *Support the parent and the child as needed in other transitions.* Separating from children is not the only point at which parents experience problems with children in the program. Sometimes, the same kinds of behaviors are seen in children when parents participate in the setting (e.g., in a cooperative nursery) or return to take them home. When this hap-

## SKILLS FOR HELPING CHILDREN COPE WITH STRESS—continued

pens, the behavior probably springs from other causes. A child may show off or become aggressive or clinging when his or her parent is working for the day, simply not wanting to share the parent with other children. At pick-up times, the child may be involved in an activity and not want to be interrupted. The child may be cranky, tired, out of sorts, and even angry with the parent for leaving. At times like this, it is not helpful for professionals to make comments like: "I can't understand why Sammy is acting this way. He's an angel when you're not here" or "He's been so good all morning." These are "killer" statements that can make parents feel extremely upset. Parents may worry that they have less control over their children than do other parents or professionals or that the bond they have with their child is being weakened by their absence. Professionals should reassure parents that this behavior is normal in children. End-of-the-day transition procedures, such as caregivers alerting children that their parents are present and that they can get ready immediately or play for 5 more minutes, are helpful to parents. Some schools or centers even offer a lounge where parents can have a cup of coffee and relax a moment while the child and his or her belongings are readied for departure.

4. **Share tips with parents about moderating the influence of the media on their children.** The following are guidelines provided by the American Medical Association (AMA, 1996):

▼ Be alert to the shows your children see, particularly younger children who are more impressionable.

▼ Avoid using television, videos, or video-games as a baby-sitter. Simply turning the set off isn't nearly as effective as planning some other fun activity with the family.

▼ Limit the use of media. Television use should be limited to one or two quality hours per day, preferably with no television or video before school, during daytime hours, during meals, or before homework is done.

▼ Keep television off during mealtimes. Use this time to catch up with one another.

▼ Turn television on when there is something specifically worth watching. Don't turn it on "to see if there's something on."

▼ Don't make the television the focal point of the house. Don't place it in a prominent place in the home.

▼ Watch what your kids are watching. This will allow you to know what they're viewing and give you the opportunity to discuss it with them.

▼ Be especially careful of viewing just before bedtime. Emotion-invoking images may linger and intrude on sleep.

▼ Learn about movies playing and videos available for rental or purchase. Be explicit about your guidelines for which movies are inappropriate.

▼ Become media-literate. Learn how to evaluate media offerings. Learn about advertising and teach your children about its influences on the media they use.

▼ Limit your own television viewing. Set a good example of moderation and discrimination.

▼ Let your voice be heard. We all need to raise our voices and insist on better programming for children.

## ▼ PITFALLS TO AVOID

All children and all families experience stress. As has been pointed out, reactions to stressors will depend heavily on individual and familial assessment of resources to meet demands. Following are a few of the pitfalls experienced by caregivers in working with children and families under stress.

**Stereotyping of families.** Caregivers, who as individuals carry with them their own perceptions and, possibly, very different resources must be careful not to stereotype families based on composition, ethnicity, or financial resources. Much of a family's response in a stressful situation will depend on how they perceive a particular demand or crisis together with what they feel they can do to maintain their balance. It must be remembered that, although some individuals and families make what seem to be terribly poor decisions, they are doing the best they can given their current perceptions of their options and resources. In other words, people do not purposely or consciously "mess up" their lives. Mentally healthy individuals are always striving towards equilibrium.

**Skewed and inappropriate responses.** Because withdrawn children cause us fewer problems in the classroom, there often is a tendency for helping professionals to see the aggressive or overly dependent child as the one who most needs help. In these cases, we probably are responding as much to our own needs as to the needs we see in the children. Their behavior increases our own stress levels, prompting us to do something about it. What we model to children when they put us under pressure is far more important than what we say or "teach" about stress management. It helps to keep in mind that children who are at their worst often are those who have the poorest coping skills and are most in need of our understanding and help. The children who suffer quietly may be particularly vulnerable, and we need to be alert for the subtle cues they present. These children need help in dealing with overwhelming thoughts and feelings; they will need particular help in learning to communicate what is bothering them and in learning to cope with these stressors rather than run away from them.

Problems in the educational setting occur when we see only the irritating behavior in a child, not the child's distress. When we find ourselves getting angry about a child's negativism, we need to remember that this is the child's strategy for coping with a particular situation. Although we will want to guide the child toward finding a more positive strategy, we must remember that effective behavior changes do not occur overnight. They require patience, consistency, and firmness on the adult's part and the development of trust on the child's part. A sensitive approach to troubled children need not be seen as a "soft" approach. Children do feel safer with a strong adult; what they don't need, however, is a punitive adult who strips them of their faulty defense mechanisms without providing anything more effective. This only makes an already vulnerable child feel more bankrupt and out of control.

**Dictating "appropriate" responses.** Although everyone experiences the same range of feelings, re-

actions to particular situations vary among individuals. Situations arise in which you expect a certain reaction, such as remorse, sadness, or tension. When the person does not respond in the expected manner, the reaction may be perceived as "inappropriate." Remember, there are no right or wrong feelings. Your role is not to tell children or members of their family how to feel, but rather to help them learn constructive ways of making their feelings known to others.

If a child or family rejects your offer for help, you may feel annoyed and unappreciated. Keep in the back of your mind that in most cases, an individual's response is based on his or her reaction at the moment and has nothing to do with you.

**Pushing children to talk when they are not ready.** The skills you have learned thus far emphasize verbal communication. Children, however, often show their distress through their behavior rather than through words. Although talking can help a troubled child, it must take place when the child is ready. Children vary in the time it takes them to reach this point. Thus, adults can let children know they are available, but should not pressure them into talking or make them feel obligated to talk in order to obtain the adult's approval. You can say things like "If you want to talk, I'll be around." or "Sometimes people feel better when they talk about their feelings." If a child seems hesitant or expresses a desire to be left alone, respect his or her need for privacy by following up with a statement like "I'll still be here if you want to talk later; and, if you don't, that's all right, too."

**Making a perfunctory diagnosis of a child's behavior.** When helping professionals know that a child and his or her family are going through a stressful time, they may erroneously assume that all of the child's inappropriate behavior is a direct result of a particular stressor. For example, adults often are quick to say: "He's biting because his mother went back to work," "She has trouble making friends because her parents are divorced," or "She's complaining about an upset stomach—it must be because of jealousy over the new baby." Although the stressful situation at home may be contributing to these behaviors, there is the chance that other factors are involved. Adults must carefully consider the range of possibilities. For instance, the child who is biting may not know an alternative way of getting what he wants; the friendless child may not recognize other children's attempts to make contact, or may lack basic conversational skills; and the child with the stomachache may, in fact, be simply reacting to something she ate.

**Looking for a "quick fix" or a superficial solution.** When adults feel they don't have the time, the energy, or a ready solution to a particular problem, they sometimes fall into the trap of trying to get the situation over with as quickly as possible. This can be difficult for children because the adult's notion of a solution may not match the child's real need. For example, all of us, at one time or another, have seen adults trying to cajole or shame a crying child into being quiet. When this strategy fails, it is not unusual to hear the adult say coercively, "Either you stop crying, or I'll give you something to cry about!" At other times, adults may force children to prematurely confront a situation in the mistaken belief that this will make the child "get over" feelings of fear, revulsion, or unhappiness. Statements like "There's nothing to be afraid of," "Just get in there and do it," and "You'll get over it" are typical of this approach. In any case, the child's real feelings are neglected, and the adult is focusing on his or her own convenience. Helping professionals must recognize that helping is not always convenient and that emotional assistance takes time and energy. In addition, solutions do not necessarily come about within one encounter and may require repeated effort.

**Failing to recognize your own limitations.** As a helping professional, it is not always within your power to eliminate the source of a child's distress. Although you perform an important function when you provide emotional support, it may not be possible to alter the child's environment or to change the behaviors of others in the child's environment who are negatively affecting the child. It also is important for professionals to know where their sphere of influence ends and when it is time to link families with other helping professionals (see Chapter 15).

**Forgetting that parents have other roles that require their time and energy.** The reaction of young children who run into their teachers at the supermarket or elsewhere in the community is often amusing to adults. The children seem absolutely amazed that the teacher can be anywhere but in the classroom and in the role of teacher. Ironically, professionals and parents hold like perspectives, unless they happen to travel in similar social circles that allow them to meet one another frequently outside the educational setting. Parents and professionals tend to think of one another narrowly and only in terms of the role each plays in their interactions. Thus, when parents think of helping professionals, they may forget that these people also are parents, spouses, adult children, voters, and home owners. Similarly, helping professionals can forget that although parents may play the parenting role 24 hours a day, other roles can and do become more dominant in their lives during that 24-hour period. They, too, experience the pressure of meeting job demands, maintaining a home, nurturing intimate relationships with persons other than their children, furthering their education or training, responding to their own parents' needs, and performing a wide variety of community obligations.

**Being inflexible and/or insensitive to the needs of financially troubled parents, working parents, single parents, teenage parents, divorced parents, stepparents, parents of handicapped children, and bilingual or migrant families.** Professionals sometimes are seen as distant and unfeeling about the pressures many parents face in their everyday lives. Notices arrive home regularly reminding parents to put their children to bed early; to provide a quiet place to study, and to be sure that children eat a balanced diet. Parents whose homes are small and crowded, those who are unemployed, and those who are going through painful marital transitions or other unexpected crises must experience additional distress when receiving these reminders.

In order to be sensitive to the total ecosystem, or context, in which children are developing, it becomes imperative to learn about the families we are serving. When we are insensitive to or ignore the stresses and hardships they are experiencing, we deprive these families of the understanding, flexibility, and insightfulness that can ease their burdens.

**Overreacting to negative parents.** The less confident we are of our own position regarding a controversial issue, the more we will tend to become defensive when our views are challenged. As experience and continuing education allow us to integrate what we know about children and families with what others know, we will become more relaxed and open when others present a different, even hostile viewpoint. When we overreact to a critical and negative parent, we exhibit our fear of being proven wrong, our uncertainty, and our confusion.

A parent can make an important point, one that is based on very good intentions and might truly be helpful; however, she or he may deliver it in such a negative manner (blaming, sarcastic, derisive) that we fail to really listen. A message delivered in such a way that it puts the receiver in a highly charged emotional state often fails to be heard. Professionals need to work hard to stay calm in such a situation, to actively listen and to perhaps reflect to the parent: "You're really angry. I think we need to talk about that, but I *am* hearing what you're saying about the need for a better information-delivery system, and I believe you're right." Occasionally, hostile remarks and behavior by a parent may have little to do with the professional or with what is really going on in the program. The parent may be feeling overwhelmed or out of control in other important areas and may see no other outlet for expressing his or her frustrations. Some careful probing, combined with understanding responses, sometimes can help such a person to understand what is happening and reevaluate his or her behavior.

## ▼ SUMMARY

There is growing concern by early childhood professionals and pediatricians about increasing levels of childhood stress. Two reasons for that concern are that we now believe that undischarged stress and prolonged periods of stress lead ultimately to disease and that stress-coping styles are learned in childhood. As described in this chapter, childhood stressors range from mild to severe. However, even a number of seemingly mild stressors can be cumulative enough to cause a child extreme discomfort. Moreover, what may seem insignificant to an older child or adult with more experience can be perceived by a younger child as insurmountable and highly stressful.

Sources of childhood stress include the child's own personality as well as familial stressors such as death of a family member, marital transitions, intense work-force involvement of all adults in the family, and abuse. Also significant are extrafamilial stressors such as negative child-care experiences, stress experienced in the formal educational arena, and stress experienced in natural disasters and other traumatic and violent events, including what is learned from the media. Some professionals believe that children may be less valued in today's society, causing adults to hurry children prematurely into adultlike status.

Children react to stress physically, psychologically, and behaviorally. They learn positive or negative coping styles by watching significant adults in their environment. Strategies caregivers can use to help children cope more effectively with stress include using attending and responding skills, creating a supportive environment for children, developing children's active coping skills, and working with families to reduce children's stress. What is important in gauging the potency of children's stress is to remember that one child's reaction may be very different than another's. Reactions in individual children will result differentially, depending on how threatening or demanding the child perceives the stressor to be, the personal resilience of the child, the types of support or resources available for modifying the stressor, and the coping skills that have been internalized by the child in previous experiences.

Stress is inevitable. As our world grows more and more complex, our ability to adapt positively to both negative and positive stimuli also must grow more sophisticated. Childhood is the period during which much of that critical learning will take place—or not take place. Because today's children spend much of their time in daycare and educational settings, the influence of helping professionals working in those settings will be enormous. Although we cannot always improve a child's environment, we can provide every child with more effective tools for mastering that environment.

## ▼ DISCUSSION QUESTIONS

1. With three or four of your classmates, compare one another's most common physical, emotional, and behavioral reactions when under pressure. How are your reactions similar? How are they dissimilar?
2. A parents' group requests that you bring a speaker to discuss childhood stress. What aspects of the topic do you believe ought to be covered if the speaker has only an hour?
3. In your own childhood years, were there any significant stressors that you can remember, such as the death of a pet, parental divorce, or loss of a friendship? Discuss your own reaction or the type of support you received from significant others around you.

4. Discuss: (a.) As many aspects of poverty as possible that you believe can contribute, either directly or indirectly, to increased stress in children's lives and (b.) Aspects of middle-class children's lives that differ from the experience of poverty that also may create stress.

5. A co-worker tells you: "All this stuff you read about children's stress is tiresome. We had stress growing up, too. Why make so much of it?" Share what you know about the importance of coping more effectively with stress.

6. You are eating lunch with several professional colleagues. One of them begins discussing the older brother of a child you have in your classroom, inserting negative remarks about the child's family. She asks you if you've had similar experiences with the parents and younger child. Refer to the NAEYC Code of Ethical Conduct in Appendix A and cite the section that is relevant in forming a response to her question.

7. Often, professionals focus on children of divorced families as children who may be distressed. Discuss the kinds of significant stressors that may exist in families that are intact but troubled—stressors that may be somewhat hidden.

8. Brainstorm with another person about the different kinds of helping agencies and professionals in your community that can provide support to distressed families and children. What are some factors that could limit a family's ability to get help from these resources?

9. Talk about aspects of a preprimary or primary program with which you are familiar that you believe are stress producing or stress relieving for the children in that program.

10. You have a child who is not adjusting very well to his mother leaving him each morning. The child is at a table, putting together a puzzle but keeping a wary eye on his mother. She says to you, "Is it all right if I leave now?" What do you say?

## ▼ FIELD ASSIGNMENTS

1. Having books available or reading to children about difficult situations that others have experienced is a highly positive way to enhance their understanding of such crises, whether or not they have personally experienced them. Using a nearby library that features a children's reading section, identify a book (title, author, publisher, date of publication) at the preschool, early elementary, and later elementary levels for the following: children's fears; parents' separation, divorce, or remarriage; death; handicaps/illness.

2. The behavior of distressed children can be stressful to adults, particularly if the adult does not feel in control of the situation. Observe closely five separate situations where adults are handling distressed children. Evaluate whether the adult's responses toward the child have a calming or a stress-heightening effect and why.

3. When children respond inappropriately under stress, they are coping in the best way they know. When we want to eliminate such behavior, we must replace the child's present coping strategy with a more effective and appropriate one. This calls for observation of the behavior to see how often it happens and under what conditions, identification of a reasonable alternative, and effective communication with the child about substituting the new skill. It also calls for follow-up to see whether or not the child is able to adopt the alternative behavior successfully. Choose a child who needs supportive intervention for altering behavior and implement the procedure just outlined. Keep a journal of sequential steps and outcomes until the child successfully adapts with more appropriate responses.

4. Professionals need to have ready a list of other helping professionals to link needy or stressed families with community resources. Identify a helping agency that would be supportive to a parent if:
   a. The family is struggling with resources for food, shelter, or heat because of unemployment.
   b. Someone in the family has a chemical abuse problem.
   c. A family member is being physically or sexually abusive.
   d. Someone in the family is suffering from emotional anxiety or depression.
   e. A parent is considering separation or divorce.
   Include the name of the helping agency, address, telephone number, services provided, fees charged, and name of a contact person.

# ▼Chapter 7

## Enhancing Children's Play

## ▼ OBJECTIVES

*On completion of this chapter, you will be able to describe:*

▼ The function of play.

▼ Various types of play.

▼ Developmental trends in various types of play.

▼ The role of the adult in facilitating children's play.

▼ Communications with parents about children's play.

▼ Pitfalls to avoid in facilitating children's play.

**SITUATION:** Two children are playing family roles of husband and wife.

*Anne:* (Looking at rocking horse) Gotta go.

*Phillip:* Go?

*Anne:* Gotta go to work.

*Phillip:* No, you cook.

*Anne:* Can't cook, gotta go to work. (Climbs on the horse and begins to rock)

*Phillip:* No, you cook and stuff. I'll go to work. (Holds the reigns of the rocking horse)

*Anne:* Gonna be late for work. You stay and cook.

*Phillip:* Don't you know? *You* cook and *I* go to work.

*Anne:* (Trying unsuccessfully to rock) Drop you off on my way to work.

*Phillip:* (Mounts the horse behind her)

The play of these two children nearly floundered for lack of a shared meaning for the roles that they were playing. Fortunately, they were able to agree on the notion of both riding the horse to work even though they did not fully realize the difficulty of their differing perceptions of the roles of wives. Anne's mother had been employed throughout Anne's four years of life, and Phillip's mother was a full-time homemaker.

Adults who work with young children frequently observe play that demands conceptual shifts of the participants. Play is both common and complex. Frequently, adults take it for granted, referring to this exciting activity of childhood as "just play." Although play is a predominant social activity of early childhood, it continues to provide common ground for informal social exchange as children mature. Therefore, adults who guide the social development of children need to understand the nature and function of play.

## ▼ THE NATURE OF PLAY

Any definition of play must take into account the gleeful game of chase a toddler plays while running from his mother, the intense dramatization of an irate father played out in the nursery school, the boisterous and rough horsing about of young boys on the playground, the concentrated practice of a ten-year-old as she shoots basket after basket in the gym, the chanting cadence of the jump-rope rhyme, and the patience and strategy of the school-age child accumulating wealth in a Monopoly game.

*Play,* although not easily defined, has certain definitive characteristics (Frost, 1992). Play is essentially pleasurable or enjoyable; although players may not be actively laughing, play still is highly valued. Play is intrinsically motivated; there are no extrinsic goals. It is essentially an unproductive activity in which the process is more important than the ends. Play is voluntary; to be play, the activity must be freely chosen by the child. Play also involves activity; the player is actively engaged in the process. In addition to these universal characteristics, play has certain systematic relationships to other aspects of development: cognition, language, knowledge about the world, perceptual and motor development, and social and emotional development.

Adults sometimes contrast play with other concepts. The opposite of play is reality, or seriousness, rather than work. People can play at their work, enjoying it thoroughly, and may work hard at developing play skills necessary for a sport. Six- and seven-year-old children readily distinguish between work and play yet describe "in between" characteristics of play that are more worklike and work that is fun (Wing, 1995). Therefore, work and play are not necessarily opposites.

Play is determined as play by the players. This means that the player may begin, end, or alter the activity in progress without consulting anyone but the other players. Play is fun, or at least pleasurable. Adults do not order children about in play. Such behavior would make the episode unplayful.

Helping professionals may be asked why they allow children to play and what benefits play provides for the child. Therefore, the relationship of "play" to "nonplay" aspects of development are briefly described. These relationships are graphically illustrated in Figure 7–1.

## Genetic Foundations

Play is a species behavior (Ellis, 1973; Fagen, 1981; Mc Donald, 1995). This means that all humans play. However, as with other behaviors, there may be individual differences. The characteristics of adaptability and behavioral flexibility have had great survival value for humans and are practiced and enhanced throughout play. Other species also play. The most familiar forms of animal play are *play fighting* and *play chasing*, which are the nonthreatening chasing, wrestling, and hitting seen in the friendly tussles of puppies and kittens (Fagen, 1981). Overall, individual animals of many species that play a lot appear to be more socially adjusted to their group and in better physical condition (Mc Donald, 1995). This play in animals has its own distinct communication signals and social conventions. Similar play-fighting and play-chasing behaviors are common among children as well (Blurton-Jones, 1976).

## Cognition

The relationship of play to cognitive development has been the focus of many scholars (Levenstein, 1976; Nourot and Van Hoorn, 1991; Saltz and Brodie, 1982). Children tend to play in ways that are consistent with their cognitive development. Toddlers delight in sensory activity and toys that make noise or move as a result of their activity. Three- to seven-year-olds test their understanding of the social world through pretend play. Older youngsters pursue a variety of games having complex rules.

Play with objects also seems to enable preschool children to solve problems and to achieve flexible, innovative solutions that they replicate on other occasions (Frost, 1991; Sylva, Bruner, and Genova, 1976). Their problem-solving abilities become increasingly efficient. For example, when children explore various shapes and sizes of containers in a water play table, they learn something about fluids and about containers that they can then transfer to tasks such as pouring juice or watering plants.

Probably one of the greatest achievements of early childhood is understanding that an object and the word representing it are distinct. This ability to distinguish an object from its name is demonstrated when a child names an object something else, such as calling a stick a spoon in play (El' Konin, 1971). Of course, this achievement is an indicator of abstract thought and requires mental flexibility.

## Language

Language is used systematically in play and can be the subject of play. Almost all levels of organization of language are potential play material (Garvey, 1977). Children play with sounds and make up words, imitate adults or other children in amusing voices, and repeat their own statements with rhythm and rhyme. Certain occurrences, such as a group of four-year-olds chanting "Delicious, nutritious, delectable juice" with great glee and accenting the syllables by pounding the table with cups or hands when faced with the detested apricot nectar, are a playful variation of the adult's words. Older

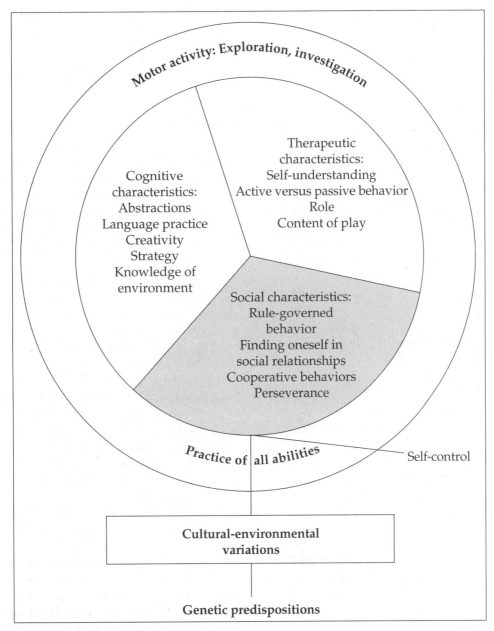

**Figure 7–1** The integrative function of play.

children base jokes on the multiple meaning of words, and use all aspects of speech such as noises, intonation, and pauses as they play.

Children tend to play with language early in the process of acquisition of a skill, practicing and varying their own performance in solitary play and modifying their language play in social contexts.

The language used in play is far more complex than that used in regular conversations. Children use more adjectives and adverbs, and the utterances are longer (Cathrine Hutt, as quoted by Chance, 1979). In fact, the general level of cognitive functioning in self-directed play may be far above the level expected of the same children in academic subjects in school (Chance, 1979).

### New Information Skills

Play and learning have a complex relationship, with new learnings being used and practiced in play. Play may not be an activity in which concepts are acquired, but it surely is where they are reinforced, where parameters are explored, and where competence is acquired. Children practice what they learn, and when they are more skilled they try to vary the play. For example, once Maddy learned to jump rope, she learned to cross the rope and jump, and to jump backwards on her own. She then learned to jump with Amelia, who delighted in the complex jumping rhymes that require many patterns and other children. As children become more competent, the complexity of their play alters, creating a play-learning spiral. For example, young children do not understand the principles that determine which materials will float and which will sink. However, with opportunities for water play and a variety of materials to play with, children will begin to predict which things are best for constructing boats: the flat-bottomed plastic butter tub is selected over the glass bowl, the flat leaf over a crumpled one with holes. Experience in making play boats provides the opportunity to determine which characteristics of materials are likely to provide better results. As children continue to construct boats and float them, they become increasingly proficient in selecting materials and estimating the weight a particular boat will be able to carry without sinking.

## Perceptual-Motor Development

The relationship of play to physical development usually is the most obvious to adults. Skill in movement and coordination comes as a result of maturation and experience. Grasping rattles, building block towers, making mud pies, playing tug-of-war, running races, and other vigorous play contribute to the organization of motor behavior and perceptual development.

## Emotional Development

Since the days of Freud, the relationships of play to wish fulfillment and to the mastery of experiences have been explored. Life among adults, who are powerful, is filled with frustrations, and children are too powerless to rebel. They can, however, suspend the rules and alter the outcomes through fantasy play (Peller, 1971). The child who received immunizations at ten o'clock in the morning can be the physician or nurse who gives the shots later in the day through pretend play. Children's role selections display their concerns with the nurturer/provider relationships, with the aggressor/victim dichotomy, with good and evil, romance, and for older children, with their fearful fantasies (Curry and Arnaud,

1982; Gould, 1972). Through play the small and helpless child may become strong and powerful; the timid child can be very brave; and the most compliant child might pretend to be the monster. Children explore emotionally laden issues while attaining some degree of distance from the self. Young preschool children may not be able to sustain appropriate distance in pretend and may frighten themselves and their playmates with their energetic portrayal of animals or monsters.

Children who enjoy playing, and who play more, seem to be happier than those who play less. They are fun to be with and are the preferred playmates or are more popular than less skillful players (Chance, 1979). Fantasy play allows for the personal integration of temperament, experience, and concepts that help the child understand the all-important question, "Who am I?" and thereby become a mentally healthy person. When Dr. Brian Sutton-Smith was asked by a mother whether her young son would be likely to have mental health problems if he continued in his extensive fantasy play, he responded that the child was in greater danger of being an outstanding artist or scientist, as research showed that these people engaged in a lot of play, including fantasy play, when young (Chance, 1979). When children pretend, they manipulate objects, events, and actions, which gives them a sense of competence, an important ingredient in mental health. Through play, children also learn that their actions have an effect on others and on objects. The direct feedback from playthings or playmates provides for the sense of competence, or of being an actor or doer, that is so important in the development of self-concept.

## Social Development

One of the concepts developed earlier in this book is that children learn many things indirectly through experiencing the consequences of their actions. For example, in one study, preschool children who played school made an easier adjustment to kindergarten than did other children (Sarah Smilansky, as quoted by Chance, 1979). These children had acquired a notion of the rules prior to entry. Their play served to focus attention on the salient behaviors that would be expected of them and to demonstrate that they could affect events somewhat themselves.

The ability to make eye contact is learned partly through play. Another skill learned in play is the ability to empathize, or to be sensitive to others' emotions. This skill is demonstrated when children portray a variety of emotions in pretend play. Turn taking is learned in toddlerhood with simple games like peekaboo or rolling a ball back and forth. This is, of course, a primitive form of cooperation, which becomes elaborated as children share, engage in pretend play, and participate in team play. Children also may learn about competition, struggling toward arbitrary goals, rules, and aggression as they play.

**Sex roles.** Sometimes, new information is acquired as children try out roles that will be helpful as they gain experience in the larger society. The episode at the beginning of the chapter illustrated the differing ways a familiar role like "wife" can be played. Recently, studies of *sex-role* development have focused on early play behavior for insight into the different outcomes for girls and boys.

Boys and girls differ in their play, which may be accounted for by parents' differential treatment (Caldera, Huston, and O'Brien, 1989). In fact, even for toddlers, toys and furnishings are differentiated by sex (O'Brien and Huston, 1985; Rheingold and Cook, 1975). Parents and peers often reward sex-appropriate play and punish cross-sex play (Fagot, 1977, 1978), although they may find it more acceptable for girls to play with materials traditionally thought of as "boyish" than for boys to play with "feminine" toys. This may account for the tendency of girls to participate more frequently in housekeeping settings and boys to engage in pretend play in garage, spaceship, or work-related settings (Howe, et al., 1993). Preschool children have no difficulty in discriminating sex-stereotyped toys for boys and girls, even though they may not choose to restrict themselves to the toys intended for their gender (Eisenberg, 1983); however, boys' toy preferences are more sterotypic than girls (Carter and Levy, 1988). Children's knowledge of sex stereotypes and awareness of gender constancy become uniform during the elementary school years. Increasingly children have more detailed information about the specific characteristics of their appropriate sex role and how to act accordingly (Bem, 1985).

In general, girls' play activities generate rule learning, imitation, task persistence, bids for recognition, compliance, remaining close to adults, and help-seeking behaviors, whereas boys' play activities force them into creative problem-solving behaviors, exploration, and the restructuring of prior learning (Block, 1979). These behaviors usually are considered by society to be typical for the sex role of children.

**Categories of social participation.** Social participation is important if children are to practice in-teracting with other children. Interacting with other children is more difficult than interacting with a parent or another adult. Clearly, watching others play is easier than coordinating one's behavior with one or more other players. The types of social participation described in the following list once were thought to represent increasing degrees of ability, but it is now recognized that, although acquired in sequence, each type of participation has independent important characteristics (Parten, 1932; Smith, 1978):

1. **Unoccupied behavior.** The child is not engaged in any task or social participation. She or he spends most of the time looking around or wandering around, but is occupied with no specific task.
2. **Onlooker.** The child watches other children and sometimes talks with them. The child is actively engaged in observing specific activities.
3. **Solitary play.** The child plays with toys alone and independently, without interacting with others.
4. **Parallel activity.** The child plays independently, but the chosen activity brings him or her among other children who are engaged in the same activity. Two children putting puzzles together on the same table is typical of this type of play.
5. **Associative play.** The child plays with other children and interacts with them around a similar, but not identical activity. For example, Niki rides his truck back and forth near a block construction where Dennis and Mark are working together. Occasionally, he stops to comment and then continues his "deliveries."
6. **Cooperative or organized supplementary play.** The child plays in a group that is organized to make some material product or to strive for some common goal. A simple game of ring-around-a-rosy is cooperative play, as is the previously mentioned play of Dennis and Mark, who are engaged in building.

Solitary play and group play are not hierarchical categories for children between two and five years of age (Moore, Everton, and Brophy, 1974; Rubin, Maconi, and Hornung, 1976; Smith, 1978): Certain levels of maturity are required for each type of play, and most preschool children participate in both types, depending on the situation. Solitary play is not necessarily an immature form of play. In fact, it has been suggested that solitary play fosters the formation of novel behavior patterns and exercises creativity, whereas social play serves to enhance the bonds between individuals (Dolgin, 1981).

Solitary play is the most common form of play for toddlers, partly because they lack experience in interacting with peers and partly because there is a point in their development at which toddlers switch from treating peers as objects to treating them as people. Obviously, it is more complex to interact with an unpredictable peer than to roll a ball. Midway through the second year, toddlers are capable of mutual involvement, turn taking, and repetition in playful activities between two children (Hay, Ross, and Goldman, 1979).

Overall, the adult may see various forms of social participation in play. For example, the onlooker, although not socially involved, may be acquiring the knowledge that later will enable him or her to participate more directly. Some children may need time to wander through the play setting to see what their choices are before making a decision. Therefore, each kind of social participation has something to contribute to the child's development.

**Social status.** When children play together, they invariably learn about status in the group, dominance roles, and other power relationships. Their play provides a safe way to explore their own position in the group and also to indirectly comment on the existence of power relationships (Swartzman, 1979). Children also may resort to applying specific classroom rules in situations where their wishes might be thwarted by another player. For example, a child might call forth the rule of "no guns" when another child has constructed a weapon and playmates are intrigued. Such assertions as "Only four can play," "Take care of what you get out," and "First come, first served" may be recalled and applied by four- and five-year-old children only when they serve the purposes of the child calling on the rule (Jordan, Cowan, and Roberts, 1995). Other less overt strategies are equally effective. For example, Toby, who faces Jeanette and announces, "Let's play house," is communicating her desire to play but also is excluding Marie, on whom she has turned her back. This message is equally clear to all concerned. Toby has established her role of leader by initiating the play activity and may continue by defining the ongoing play.

Like Toby, children who have a high status in the group tend to direct their messages to specific players. Often they do this with more than one playmate, each in turn. Preferred players, though, must also be contingently responsive to other children and act so as to maintain the play. Even when rejecting a play idea, the high status child may offer an explanation, or an alternative rather that an outright rejection, thus continuing the interaction (Hazen and Black, 1989).

Competent school-age children behave in ways that are relevant to the ongoing activity and are responsive and appropriate to the social initiations by their peers, moving gradually toward developing friendships. Less effective children are less attentive to social cues, much more likely to engage their peers in aggressive or coercive cycles, and are frequently rejected or isolated by their playmates. These lower status youngsters appear to be less connected to the group and unable to "read" the social situations in order to coordinate their activities with others (Pettit and Harrist, 1993).

## ▼ TYPES OF PLAY

### Exploratory Behavior

The manipulation and examination of objects often has been lumped into the category of play, although in some ways it differs from true play. Children engaging in exploratory behavior are scanning the environment, scrutinizing, feeling, smelling, mouthing, shaking, hefting, moving, operating, probing, or otherwise investigating the nature of the object at hand. The questions being addressed are: What can this do? How does it work? What is the nature of this object or situation? Exploratory behavior of novel objects precedes true play behavior (Hutt, 1971). Investigative exploration also is the first step in learning about objects and in solving problems.

Adults who take into account the tendency of children to explore objects and materials in the environment allow time for this behavior, even such problem-solving activities as using a microscope to look at a drop of water. Children who have the opportunity to examine the changes in focus, the use of the various lenses, and the glass slides before beginning the planned experiment will have a clearer understanding of the microscope and its uses than children who move from microscope to microscope glancing at each prepared view.

The need for exploratory behavior in the very young child is related to the behavior of infants and toddlers described earlier in this book. Every object is new; every event is novel; independent movement is a new event to be explored. This is why young children seem so busy, getting into one thing after another, and why safety is such a concern, as very young children are as likely to mouth or bite an electrical cord as they are a new food.

As children mature, more objects become familiar, or similar to familiar objects, and may take less time to explore. The toddler may notice that cubes used to make a pattern on a card are similar to the blocks he or she played with as a baby, differing only in color and size. Exploration time still is needed, but it may be less than a minute or two.

During the preschool years, children explore paste by tasting, smelling, and smearing before using it to adhere pieces of paper. Water and sand are poured, patted, tasted, and smelled. Paper is crumpled, torn, cut, and chewed. All of these are simple exploratory behaviors. Exploration becomes play when the child shifts from the question, "What does this object do?" to a slightly different question, "What can I do with this object?" The object itself ceases to be the major focus of concern as the child incorporates the object into play in which meanings and goals are assigned by the player.

Children shift from exploration to play repeatedly during a single episode of using an object (Hutt, 1971). For example, Renzell, age four, picked up a stethoscope, blew into the bell, looked at the earpieces, put the earpieces in his ears, tapped the bell, then walked over to a doll and announced that he was a doctor. He played out this role with several dolls, listening to their bodies all over. When Michael walked into the area, Renzell said, "I think you are sick," and began to listen to Michael's arm. Michael told him, "Listen right here," pointing to his chest. Renzell listened to Michael's chest and said the thing didn't work. He then listened to Michael's chest in different places, asking, "Can you hear that?" every now and then. He also listened to the radiator, to the hamster, and to other children, momentarily forgetting his doctor role.

## Play with Objects

Children use a variety of toys, materials, and other objects in their play. The *novelty* of an object attracts attention and stimulates exploration. However, the *complexity* of an object is more important in sustaining interest. This is true of all objects for all ages (Weilbacher, 1981). Children will play with anything: real things (utensils, furnishings, leaves and sticks, animals); reconstruction materials or instructional materials (memory games, puzzles, stacking toys); construction materials (blocks, paints, clay, cardboard); fluid materials (water, sand, snow); or

toys (cars, dolls, and other miniature replicas). Play behavior can occur anywhere: in the car, yard, playground, nursery school, living room, classroom, or hallway. The play context including space, materials, time, and other people influences the selection of play. The experiences of all the children engaged in the play as well as the terrain, plants, or other objects in the physical space suggest content and type of play (Reifel and Yeatman, 1993). In addition, the quality of the play context is highly associated with children's social problem solving in child care and other settings (Goelman, 1994). Therefore, the space, playthings, and other elements of the context may be constructed to promote the safety of children and desirable social behaviors and to minimize undesirable behaviors.

**Aspects of toys.**   Some assumptions about toys have been made by researchers investigating other areas of development (McBride, 1981). The first assumption is that toys are *attractive:* they will lure children into exploration and independent behavior or engender a sense of security because of familiarity. The second assumption is that toys are *stimulating:* they heighten sensory-perceptual arousal and provide feedback and information. It is also assumed that the stimulating quality of toys will strengthen motor responses and elicit language production and cognitive and social behavior. The third assumptions is that toys are *symbolic:* they represent family relationships, provide cues for appropriate sex role behavior, symbolically represent the child's own personality or self-concept, and transmit cultural values (Sutton-Smith, 1986). For example, toys from around the world may be provided so that children learn early that there are many countries where children like themselves play with toys (Swiniarski, 1991). Adults who support children's play should keep these assumptions in mind and select toys that are likely to meet one or more of them. Of the alternatives available in the marketplace, some toys won't meet any of the assumptions, and others are likely to meet several. A doll might be both attractive and symbolic, and a brightly colored puzzle, stimulating.

**Complexity.**   Another aspect of objects is the number of ways in which they can be used. This may be influenced by the responsiveness of the material or object itself. For example, play dough or clay is more responsive than plaster of Paris, which hardens rapidly. The level of complexity may increase if the pieces come apart and can be combined in a variety of ways.

Perhaps one of the most complex toys of all is the computer game. Essentially children must use a broad range of physical skills, coordination of eye and hand, and strategy, as well as having good luck to beat the machine. In fact, the computer game incorporates all of the characteristics of a good game: chance, skill, and strategy (Sutton-Smith, 1986). Some games are designed so that players compete against each other as well as the machine. Older children trade games, discuss them, and when they play frequently, they watch television less (Sutton-Smith, 1986).

The presence of more equipment on playgrounds seems to encourage individual behavior and more movement, and less equipment tends to encourage more social contacts and more aggression. On the other hand, movable equipment tends to elicit a greater variety of pretend play than would the same pieces if immobile. Children use the immobile equipment with a greater variety of movements and are more likely to initiate group games unrelated to the equipment (Weilbacher, 1981).

**Spatial arrangements.** In an indoor setting, activities in which there are materials or space for only one player are more likely to elicit antisocial behavior than are activities in which materials and space are designed for more than one. In multiple-niche play spaces, such as when playing with a large set of blocks, children socialize more and engage in more helping and sharing behavior than they do in single-niche play spaces, such as when playing with a single box of Lincoln Logs (Doyle, 1981).

**Design.** Some playthings are realistic, and others are more abstract. Toddlers need realistic materials to pursue a play theme. They simply do not have enough experience or knowledge of what to do with abstract pieces. However, school-age children will play longer and engage in more complex play with abstract toys (Trawick-Smith, 1990). Children between two and six years of age play with less structured materials like sand, water, blocks, and dough for substantial periods of time, but they seem to need more realistic props for complicated dramatic play.

There are basically two aspects of play with objects. The first involves characteristics of the objects that are likely to influence the quality of play. Complexity, degree of structure, attractiveness, sensory-perceptual qualities, and symbolic value have been

briefly discussed. However, characteristics of the child determine the nature of the actions that can be brought into play with objects. Children are limited by their motor competence, cognitive functioning, and social skills. Once some of the basic competencies of early childhood have been achieved, play becomes more refined, more challenging, and more elaborate.

## Developmental Changes in the Use of Objects

Object play in infancy shifts from repeated motor behavior, such as banging the top of the table with the hand, to repetitious action on objects, such as dropping the spoon to the floor over and over. In the last quarter of the first year, babies begin to explore objects and, by the end of the first year, to use them functionally. For example, drinking motions are used with a cup. This is followed by exploring longer and beginning to combine objects and actions, such as putting the cup on a saucer or pretending to stir in it with a spoon. By the end of the second year, toddlers use longer sequences of action related to the functions of the objects, such as stirring in a cup with a spoon, feeding a doll, combing its hair, and putting it to bed. By the time the child reaches the third year, he or she can assign to the doll the role of actor. In other words, the doll is made to "pick up the spoon" and "eat" (Lowe, 1975).

The shift from simple manipulation of objects to dramatic play is made during the second year. Children learn to make this shift from the literal use of objects to pretend play as a result of their interactions with adults (Eiferman, 1971; Smilansky, 1968). In subsistence cultures, and in cultural groups in which people work more with objects than with abstractions, the shift to pretend play may occur in middle childhood or may not occur at all (Swartzman, 1978).

What general sequences occur? The following list is a sequential summary of the play behaviors that occur as the very young child develops play with objects.

1. Repetitive motor behavior, mouthing.
2. Systematic exploration of objects.
3. Actions begin to be appropriate for objects.
4. Objects that have functional relationships are combined.
5. Action patterns are combined to form larger sequences (stirring in, pouring from, and washing a bowl).
6. Action patterns are applied to self (may be simple pretending; e.g., eating or sleeping).

7. Action patterns are applied to others or to replicas (doll "eats").

8. The ability to act is attributed to replicas (doll "feeds" teddy bear).

9. Objects that are not present but are needed to complete a logical sequence are "invented" (pretends a spoon to stir with).

10. Objects are transformed for use in sequences (uses pencil for spoon).

The term **transform** means to substitute one object for another. For example, a three-year-old might use a pencil, a stick, a tongue depressor, or a screwdriver in the absence of a spoon to stir a drink or to feed a doll.

The first six behavior patterns are sometimes combined and practiced in order to gain mastery over an object. Mastery play or practice play is repetitious, but may have slight variations until the properties of the object and what it can do have been thoroughly mastered. One two-year-old manipulated a set of seven nesting cubes in thirty different ways. Each cube was combined with one, two, and three other cubes, in addition to the full set. She also tried stacking the cubes. Mastery play, as well as exploratory behavior, is common when people of any age encounter objects that are novel and complex. Older children engage in similar play with newly introduced technologies.

**Individual differences.** Some children respond to the symbolic potential of objects more readily than others. Their play style has been called the **dramatist style.** However, other children respond to other attributes of objects; they are more interested in the color, texture, shape, form, and other physical characteristics of the materials. They are the **patterners.** The dramatist approaches materials with the question, "What story can I tell with these things?" The patterner approaches the materials with the question, "How can I arrange these things so that they are beautiful?" Patterners differ in their approach to materials in that between the ages of two and three, these children communicate meaning by the spatial location of objects. For example, Gieshala poked holes into a wad of tissue paper to represent eyes for her snowman, who needed to see. The dramatist simply would have pretended the eyes. By three years of age, patterners tend to communicate meaning mostly by spatial location. They also are concerned with design elements and the functions of the structures or arrangements that

they make. A child who is a patterner may use all the trucks and arrange them by size, color, function, or other criteria. Adults who do not recognize this style of play sometimes expect the child to give up some of the trucks to other players, who could be satisfied with using one in the dramatic style. However, the removal of several units of the design would totally disrupt the purpose of the play. For the patterner, the objects themselves are the significant elements of the play. Children's play style appears to develop early and to carry on as a preferred mode of play throughout childhood (Shotwell, Wolf, and Gardner, 1979).

Between two and three years of age, both patterners and dramatists will build with blocks in horizontal and vertical axes. The dramatist, however, builds more simply, just enough to construct the house or store where the people live and shop. The patterner of the same age combines blocks in larger, more complex, more elaborate structures, experimenting with line and balance.

### Dramatic Play

**Dramatic play,** or *pretend play*, probably is one of the most apparent forms of play seen in young children. In middle-class families, dramatic play begins at about one year of age, and the amount of time spent at it peaks between the ages of five and six (Smilansky, 1968). With experience and an opportunity to play with others, young children engage in pretend play with others or **sociodramatic play,** in which they share goals, a theme, and materials. Older children also participate in pretend play, but school and group games take more of their time. Children from less advantaged circumstances may develop pretend play skills later, engage in shorter bouts of sociodramatic play (Weinberger and Starkey, 1994), and participate in pretend play more about the age of ten (Eiferman, 1971). Youngsters' play may not flourish if the setting is not culturally similar or sensitive (Nourot and Van Hoorn, 1991). Pretend play is learned from adults who coach children in using symbols with words, actions, situations, and objects. Many families tend to do this without thinking about it, and others tend not to think of doing it at all.

**Object substitution.** Children need to develop several skills before they can easily pretend play with other children. First, they need to be able to substitute one object for another, or transform one object into another. The closer the substituted object resembles the object needed for the dramatization, the more likely the child will be to use it. A shell can be substituted for a cup, but not for a bat. Between two and three years of age, children can substitute one object in their play, but not two. For example, an abstract wooden object might be used for a horse and a cup for a drinking trough, but the play breaks down if the child is given the abstract wooden object and a shell. In the third year, children will substitute a cup for any container: potty-chair, bowl, hat, or dish. Adults know the child is substituting because the object is renamed or because the action with the object is clearly an action appropriate for the object being substituted for. However, four-year-olds tend to use objects more realistically (Trawick-Smith, 1990). They are more likely to engage in group pretend play, or sociodramatic play, in which all the players must agree on the meaning of each pretend object. There are obvious complications in having many substituted objects in group play.

**Object invention.** Next, children need to be able to invent an object—to imitate its use through actions even when no object is at hand. This **object invention** is simple pantomime, and in its simplest form, only one pretend object at a time is used. A child may use a stirring action above a bowl to invent a spoon, or twirl an arm above the head to symbolize a rope. Younger children find it very difficult to mime without a placeholder object (a real object that takes the place of another real object, such as a stone used as a car). Between three and four years of age, they pretend with nothing to hold onto. School-age children do it readily.

Children who have not learned how to pretend may approach toys in an exploratory mode and then respond to them as if they were real. In one preschool room, Emily entered the housekeeping area and examined the model stove, turning the knobs, gingerly touching the burners, and opening the oven to peer inside. Then, she pulled the stove from the wall and examined the back. Putting her hands on her hips in great disgust, she addressed the teacher, "This damned stove won't work!" She was upset when the adult responded that the toy stove was not supposed to work like a real stove.

**Changes of time and place.** Children also learn to transform time and settings. They might substitute a climber for a spaceship in flight or pretend that the sandbox is a beach during the period when prehistoric animals lived. Players are very

aware of this convention and tend to play consistently with it. For example, Mia, the "baby," climbed out of her bed to iron on the ironing board. Her "mother" admonished her that babies can't iron or they'll get burned. Mia climbed back into her bed, said: "Grow, grow, grow. I'm the big sister now," and returned to the ironing board, condensing many years into a few seconds. Time and place have no restrictions except in the information of the players. In addition, children who have no knowledge or experience of objects such as buses and airplanes are quite unable to initiate play situations involving them.

**Role playing.** The young player must learn to take on a role. The simplest kind of role is the **functional role** or *behavioral role* (Watson and Fisher, 1980): the child becomes a person who is driving a truck. This role does not contain a permanent identity or personality but is defined by the person in the present situation. A child taking on a **character role,** however, engages in many behavioral sequences appropriate for the part. Character roles include family roles (mother, father, sister), occupational roles (fire fighter, doctor), and fictional roles (superhero, witch). Family roles are played with much more detail than the others. Younger children tend to limit themselves to roles with which they have had direct experience (baby, parent), but older preschoolers are more likely to act out roles that they have observed (husband, wife) and try more occupational roles. Lastly, preschool children are able to portray multiple roles. One thirty-month-old girl was observed playing "mother" to "baby" and "wife" to "husband" while coaching "husband" in how to perform the role of "father" (Miller and Garvey, 1984). Older children and adults are capable of assuming a broad variety of character roles. Role and action representations initially are affected by the availability of realistic props.

**Cultural and experiential differences in children.** Children bring to the play experience their cultural background and life-style as sources of information. Considerable variety can be expected. For example, one child tried to bounce an orange. He had never eaten an orange, but had played with balls. Because of the orange's roundness, he treated it as a ball. This is not a situation for a reprimand, but for information.

Some children play out life experiences that are completely foreign to their teachers, such as being evicted, gang fighting, family violence, and burglaries, as well as explicitly sexual activities. Privacy in some households is limited, and children may have observed adult behavior that is kept more private in other households. On one hand, adults may not want this play in the group, but on the other, children may need to play out their experiences. Children may be redirected into other aspects of role behavior such as going to work or cleaning house. They should not be scolded or shamed about theme or role depiction.

Acceptance in play of all the cultural elements that might be expected in a group of children is basic to accepting the children. Race, ethnicity, religion, age, gender, family composition, life-style, economic circumstances, presence of disabling conditions, sexual preferences of familiar adults, as well as specifics related to the local community may appear in children's play content. One eleven-year-old sought information about what to call the grandchildren of her father's second wife by her first husband and whether or not they should be invited to the wedding that she was enacting with adult figures. Adult responses of surprise, shock, or confusion can usually be reduced when they seek to understand the cultural milieu of all the children.

Play behavior is built on variations of nonplay behavior, then repeated, combined in a number of ways, reduced to unimportance through humor, or magnified through play ritual. Children, of course, must use what they know, regardless of content. As in all other behavior, experience is important in determining how children play with objects and participate in dramatic play.

**Peer communication about play.** The term *metacommunication* means a communication about communication (Bateson, 1971). Metacommunications about play may indicate what is "play" and what is "not play." Four-year-olds can understand the meaning of the paradox in "Let's pretend this fire is real!" Metacommunications may be nonverbal, such as beginning to "shovel snow" in the middle of summer, or they may be verbal. These messages *frame* play so that it is socially defined as play and is not, therefore, "for real." To maintain play, some messages must be said "out of frame" in order to share information so that the play can continue.

The **play frame** encompasses the scope of the play event. Included in the play frame are all the ob-jects and people relevant to the play scenario. Players within the frame are linked by communication and by their shared goals. For example, if a child is involved in an episode where he or she must leave the "restaurant" to get some more "food" from across the room, the child is still in the frame. If a photograph were taken of a pretend play episode described at the beginning of the chapter, the photographer would automatically move back to include the children and the rocking horse. This would be so even though other persons might be in either the foreground or background of the photo. Persons and objects nearby, but not linked by communication and common goals that further the play, are out of the play frame.

Metacommunications begin and end play, but also are used in planning and negotiating the content and direction of play and in coordinating role enactment. Helping professionals support and promote skill development when they demonstrate or suggest typical metacommunication devices to children who are less skillful (Table 7–1).

Some statements are procedural, such as "Do you want to play house?" or "It's my turn." Other statements that serve to initiate play are statements about role, objects, or setting, or about planning the theme (Garvey, 1977; Garvey and Berndt, 1977). Children mention another's role ("You can be the daddy"), their own role ("I'll be the nurse"), or a joint role ("We can be neighbors").

Children mention objects, transforming them into something else ("This is the car," while arranging four chairs in a square) or inventing an object ("Here is the menu. What do you want?" while handing a pretend menu to a patron).

Children transform settings ("This here [pointing to some blocks] is the boat on the ocean") and also invent settings ("We are lost kids in the forest," while standing in the middle of the play yard).

Children make plans about the behavior or feelings of another character ("Pretend you are lost and scared"), about their own actions ("I gotta go shopping and I'm in a hurry"), or about joint plans ("We better build a big house so the monster won't get us").

Some statements terminate the play. These statements can be about the role ("I'm not the daddy anymore"), about actions ("I'm not chasing you"), about props ("This isn't a boat anymore"), or about settings ("We are not in the forest").

**Influencing the direction of the play.** Preschool children tend not to expose their pretend il-

▼ Table 7–1   Purpose of Metacommunications about Play with Verbal and Nonverbal Examples

| CHILD'S PURPOSE | VERBAL COMMUNICATION | NONVERBAL COMMUNICATION |
|---|---|---|
| Initiating the play | "Wanna play?" <br> "Let's run." | Enters a play setting and engages in behaviors that start the play such as "cooking" or "offering" blocks to another child. |
| Establishing a theme | "Let's pretend we are in space and we get lost." <br> "This baby is sick and I need a doctor." | Uses props that suggest a theme such as a menu for a restaurant or a cash register for a store. |
| Transforming settings or inventing them | "It's night, and dark here." <br> "This can be my house and over there is your house." <br> "Mission control is at the table." | Engages in actions that suggest a setting, such as making water-flow noises while aiming a hose. |
| Establishing a role | "I'm the mom." <br> "I'll get this ship working. <br> "This will be the biggest building I ever did!" | "Comforts" a doll. <br> Carries the "tool box" over to the ship. <br> Builds with blocks. |
| Establishing another's role | "You better watch where you are going" (to the driver). <br> "You be the daddy." | Hands another child the objects to be used, such as the flowers in a "flower shop." |
| Establishing joint roles | "We are just kids and we are running away." <br> "You get to be the monster, then I do." | (Used only with children who play together frequently) <br> Child acts as though experiencing great pain and falls to the ground in front of another player. |
| Transforming objects or inventing them | "Take this ship to Mars" (while sitting in a nest of large blocks). <br> "Here is the money" (while the child gestures only). | Uses a teacup to feed or water model animals in the "farm" constructed of blocks. |
| Making plans about the feelings or the behavior of another | "Let's say you are really mean." | |
| Making plans about his or her own feelings or behavior | "This place is really scary so I better hide." | |
| Establishing their joint feelings or behavior | "We can put this fire out really fast. Get another hose." | |
| Terminating play with communication about theme, role, props, or settings | "I don't want you to chase me anymore." <br> "Let's play . . ." <br> "Put the stuff in the box and let's have a snack." | Walks away. <br> Looks away, attends to something else. <br> Shakes head or uses other gestures to indicate disengagement. |

lusion unnecessarily. If possible, they keep their communications "within frame," but metacommunications lie on a continuum from deeply within frame to completely out of frame (Griffin, 1984). As suggested by Griffin (1984), there are several ways in which the content of the play can be redirected.

Children use **ulterior conversations,** which might appear to be role enactment but do alter the

▼ **Table 7–2    Summary of Strategies Children Use to Redirect Play within the Play Frame**

| STRATEGIES | DESCRIPTION | EXAMPLE |
|---|---|---|
| Ulterior conversations | Statements that are a part of pretend play and also suggest what the other players should do next | "These children are really very hungry." |
| Underscoring | Statements made by one player to inform the others about what they are doing. These are usually used when nonverbal enactments may not work. | "I will go to work, then I will come home again." |
| Storytelling | Statements that elaborate the theme or those that set up a problem that must be solved within the theme. | "Smoke! Smoke! The house is on fire and we gotta get out of here fast!" |
| Prompting | One player informs another on what to do or say. This is often in a stage whisper, but may be mimed, or through gestures. | (Whispered) "That's the bride hat. If you want a hat put on this one for the groom." |
| Formal pretend proposals | One player suggests a major shift in the play to the other players. The intent is to remain in the play sequence with all the players but change the theme. | (During house play) "What do you say that this family goes on a vacation to the beach?" |

course of the play. The query "Is it nighttime?" from the "baby" effectively initiates a caregiving sequence from the "mother."

**Underscoring** provides information to other players (for example, "I'll get the dinner now," spoken in character voice). Underscoring also is used to "magic" something: "Grow, grow, grow. Now I am big." Another common example is "Wash, wash, wash" for dishes or laundry. This making of "magic" is done in a rhythmic, sing-song voice.

**Storytelling** frequently is couched in the past tense and often is spoken in cadence. It allows for the development of more elaborate plots: "Let's say this spaceship went up, way up . . . and the computer went out . . . and the moon wasn't there."

**Prompting** is a technique in which one player instructs another on how to act or what to say, often in a stage whisper or a softer voice: "I'm ready for breakfast now; . . . (whispering) no, you have to cook the eggs first before I eat."

**Formal pretend proposals** sometimes are embedded into ongoing play, as in "Let's pretend the family goes to the beach." The suggestion for play variation usually is used when the play scenario is becoming repetitive or falling apart. Usually, the more indirect methods are preferred once a

play sequence is begun. These are summarized in Table 7–2.

When children pretend using small figures and blocks or a doll house, nearly all of the story line is provided by narrative rather than by action of the dolls. When children themselves are the actors, however, they are more able to use nonverbal communicators as well to supply the content of the play.

**Role selection.** The social relationships in a group of children are reflected in their play (Swartzman, 1978). High-status children can join ongoing play by imperiously adopting a role or defining an activity ("I'll be the aunt, coming to visit"). Lower status children must ask permission to join the play ("Can I be the sister?") and may be restricted to particular roles. Often, higher status children will assign lower status children to the roles they may play ("You can be Grandma, who's sick"). The roles assigned may reflect actual status in the group. Play leaders also use rejection statements ("You can't play here" and counter-defining statements ("We aren't in a forest—we're in a jungle").

The role play of children is very complex. They must participate as writer-directors of their make-believe play from outside the play frame and enact make-believe roles and events within the play frame.

Children tend to resist certain kinds of make-believe. They are much more willing to change generations than to change gender. Boys prefer male roles, whether they are baby or grandparent roles, and will not readily take mother roles.

High-status children tend to resist taking a lower status in the make-believe play, preferring to be the parent rather than the baby, the captain rather than the seaman, and so on. When one player refuses to play an unsatisfactory role, she or he usually is incorporated into the more desirable role. For example, a child unwilling to be the victim becomes one of two monsters, and the victim is invented.

Children resist interrupting pretend play with reality. For example, if a child trips and falls down, he or she is likely to pretend a hospital-doctor sequence rather than interrupt the flow of the play to seek help from an adult. The child simply incorporates the event into the play if at all possible.

**Combining the pretend play skills.** Once children have become skillful players, they modify and extend their pretend play. Children first use the pretend skills in short sequences then combine them into more complex sequences. These *play schemes* are named by topic such as "cooking," "playing babies," or "driving the car." Generally, these schemes combine pretend with action or object and role play into action-based portrayals of real life situations (Roskos, 1990). As children gain in maturity and skill, they join a group of related play schemes and transform the play into a more elaborate *episode* that is socially organized and has a specific problem to solve inherent to the plot. It could be a family going on vacation with no suitcases. Episodes are tied together through the topic and rely on language to integrate and hold the play sequence together.

An episode is played out in stages. First, the children ready the play area by handling the materials and moving the props around (even if they are familiar with them). Second, children share directing the course of play when the roles are determined, the ground rules are established, the problem is stated or implied, and the story is narrated (Roskos, 1990). Both schemes and episodes are commonly called sociodramatic play or thematic play and may portray a variety of topics. However, in the episode, there will be a problem to resolve. They will be problems like relatives coming to visit (but there are not enough beds),

playing store (where no one comes to buy), or playing post office (where there are insufficient numbers of stamps). Favorite schemes such as "comforting the baby" could appear in all of these, and often do, as children signal each other to repeat a preferred sequence. Episodes tend to have a story-like structure with a clear beginning, development of the problem, resolution of the problem, and an end.

School-age children play more elaborately, with more characters, and with more detail when they are in an environment that allows them to pretend (Curry and Bergen, 1987). They also select more dramatic problems such as capture and rescue. Seven- to twelve-year-olds are able to increase the layers of pretend such as when their episode is that of writers and actors performing in the theater. The pretend play of rehearsal and script writing may take much longer than "the play" they are producing. They may also engage in improvisational contests or act out storybook or television themes.

## Construction Play

Children play with objects for the purposes of pretend, but they also play with them for the purposes of manipulating them based on their physical properties alone. Some aspects of this have previously been described as children's handling of objects as dramatists or as patterners.

**Young children.** During the second half of the first year of life, children can bang on objects and twist, turn, push, pull, open, and shut them. Between one and two years of age, children acquire the abilities to empty and fill objects, to hammer a peg into a peg board, and to separate play dough. Real construction begins during the second year when the child learns to connect objects together (such as threading beads or attaching the pieces of a train) and develops the corresponding ability to disjoin objects (such as snap beads). Children also learn to stack and knock down blocks and to build both vertically and horizontally with them.

Between two and three years of age, children make constructions and name them "houses" and may combine various construction materials, such as mixing blocks with cars or toys. This often is done for the purpose of initiating pretend play. Given the guidance of supporting adults, they also will learn the use of tools, such as knives and rollers for clay, cookie cutters, scissors, and hammers and nails. At this age, children's constructions are very simple; they are more interested in the process than the product.

By the time children are four, their constructions become more detailed and elaborate. They might construct a house of blankets and boxes and blocks, or a toy world with miniature dolls, trucks, and soldiers. They also make music in time, particularly with percussion instruments. They begin to show interest in their paintings as products and to cut paper designs.

Between five and seven years of age, children have sufficient small-muscle control to plan and make a variety of things. They can do simple sewing and weaving; they can use pot holders and cook simple dishes. At this time, they also begin to make costumes or other supplementary props for their pretend play.

**Older children.** Children in elementary school may be interested in model construction, handicrafts, weaving, woodworking, metalworking, bookbinding, basketry, carving, and a variety of other projects. They also construct some of their own games and do creative writing. Skillful pretend players also build sets, make costumes, and put on their own plays; the planning of script, actors, action, props, and sets may take hours, days, or weeks, whereas the production itself may be less than 10 minutes long. This also is the period of collecting and hobbies (Sutton-Smith and Sutton-Smith, 1974).

## Play with Movement

Adults are familiar with the joyous running, jumping, and laughing of children coming outside for recess. Physical educators have extensively studied the motor development of older children and described the development of the fundamental motor skills of early childhood: walking, running, jumping, hopping, skipping, and striking (Seefeldt and Haubenstricker, 1982).

Most physical games are composed of these skills in combinations that improve strength, endurance, balance, and coordination. Youngsters also acquire these attributes through informal play over time as they mature. For example, maintaining balance and just hanging on is the first stage of swinging. Children then try to imitate peers through the trial-and-error process, but their movements are not synchronized, and they have limited success, usually "stomaching" the swing. Eventually, they adapt their strategies to suit their own abilities and limitations, frequently kicking the ground to increase

their swing. Then the timing improves so the swing may be pumped, with unskillful jumping from the moving swing attempted. With practice, they delight in demonstrating their prowess to their peers, sometimes competing, even though optimum amplitude is not achieved. Refinement and efficiency of movement occurs as youngsters eventually attain security in their own skills and become capable of experimenting with "bumping" or other possibilities with the motion or the swing itself (Fox and Tipps, 1995). In a safe setting, with opportunities to observe more skilled players, practice, and time, children attain skills in many movement activities.

Babies express pleasure in motion itself. Piaget (1962) noticed that babies repeated a movement sequence over and over, getting more enjoyment out of the experience each time and paying decreasing attention to the outcome. The fun was in the movement. Babies are soothed by walking and laugh when they are held high or experience vertigo with a trusted adult. Once in motion, they are intrepid travelers, enjoying mightily the movement itself as well as the new experiences it brings.

The feeling of sheer splendor experienced by a preschooler racing down a hill, feet thudding on turf, wind blowing through the hair and on the skin; the careful placement of each step as a timid child threads a way up to the top of the climber; the amazingly empty feeling in the stomach of a child on a zooming sled: these all involve play with motion itself. The children may or may not laugh, but they are exquisitely satisfied and pleased with their performance.

Play with movement begins in infancy and continues throughout adulthood, as is evidenced in the popularity of swimming pools, ski resorts, and bowling alleys. Helping professionals, themselves players, usually are sensitive to the more mature forms of play with movement. Four aspects of movement play will be addressed that will illuminate the safe supervision of children's play: practice play, challenge, risk taking, and rough-and-tumble play.

**Respecting repetitious activity.** *Practice play* begins in infancy and continues throughout childhood (Eiferman, 1971). Quite simply, it is a behavior repeated over and over. For example, Esther, age five, wanted to try the high slide in the park. An adult went with her and offered to catch her the first time. Hesitant and timid at first, Esther went up the slide and down with growing satisfaction and pleasure. She took twenty-one turns on the slide without ever repeating exactly her previous performance. She varied the placement of hands and feet; went down on belly, bottom, and back; climbed up the slide forward and backward; went down feet first and head first. The adult observed her, commented on her performance, and stood close to the slide when concerned for Esther's safety. This child, who began hesitantly, left the experience with satisfaction and greater confidence in her ability.

From infancy to adolescence, what the child practices varies but the process remains much the same. In the second year, toddlers walk, run, march, throw, climb, and dance. Between two and three years of age, they jump from low heights, hop on one foot, balance on a beam, and hang by their arms. Between the ages of three and four, they begin to catch balls, climb jungle gyms, and ride tricycles. Between four and five years of age, they roller-skate, swim, ride scooters and other vehicles, dance to music, bounce balls, and play catch. Between five and seven years of age, they can use stilts, swing and pump the swing, and jump rope. Older children are likely to practice for specific sports.

**Maintaining interest in movement play.** The selection of a play activity usually is based on its potential *challenge* for the child. The challenges undertaken are those that require slightly greater skill than the child already possesses. Usually, the child observes the action, tests his or her ability to do it, seeks instruction or help if necessary, and then practices the skill until it has been mastered. Children who are obese, clumsy, or disabled find the natural movements of much younger children challenging and need additional support and encouragement to attempt even those simpler skills (Javernik, 1988). Because play is not "for real," children are free to drop a task that is too difficult for them without loss of self-respect. Sometimes, this is verbalized as "just playing around."

Interest in the action remains high until mastery is completed. If a mastered skill, such as dribbling a ball, can be varied and incorporated into other skills, such as evading and running, interest may remain with the activity for long periods of time. In this sense, challenge comes from within the players and is a test of their own skills. This self-challenge should not be confused with a challenge from another player, such as "I can run faster than you," which then turns the movement play into a game. At its best, challenging play helps children to understand themselves and their competencies and to

recognize their own accomplishments against the background of previous behavior.

**Understanding risk.** There frequently is some *risk* in play with motion. Skiing is definitely more risky than running. Some youngsters seem like monkeys, climbing high into trees; others of the same age are frightened of simple climbing frames with padded mats beneath. Temperament and previous experience influence the willingness of children to take risks in play. Toddlers have little sense of potentially dangerous situations and must be protected by adults. Preschool children, however, should be provided many opportunities to try out appropriate developmental skills in supervised play so that they can learn just how competent they are.

By the age of seven, most children can judge for themselves the risk involved in any activity and are unlikely to go beyond their limits unless urged by peers and adults to do so. For example, Gwendolyn was well coordinated for a seven-year-old, was an excellent swimmer, and could ride a two-wheel bike. Jeff, only two weeks younger, moved easily enough but couldn't swim or do gymnastics. He spent more of his time at indoor activities. When the children were playing together outside, Gwendolyn climbed a tree and invited Jeff up. After being urged and called a scaredy-cat, Jeff attempted the climb. He fell three times because he couldn't catch the branch with his hands and pull himself up by his arms as Gwendolyn could. Bruised and shaken, he clung to the trunk once Gwendolyn had pulled him up. Apparently realizing that the tree was too risky for Jeff, Gwendolyn swung down and procured a ladder to help him in his descent. Children frequently assume that an activity that is easy for them will be easy for an age-mate and may need guidance in recognizing the difference between being supportive to peers and challenging them to potentially dangerous activities. Children rarely attempt feats that are beyond their abilities unless pressured to do so.

**Supporting social and physical testing.** Many children participate in rough motor play, which increases both the challenge and the risk. At a high pitch of activity, children run, hop, jump, fall over, chase, flee, wrestle, hit at, laugh, and make faces. Usually played in a group, **rough-and-tumble play** differs from aggression, which includes such behaviors as pushing, taking things, grabbing, frowning, and staring down another (Blurton-Jones, 1972, 1976).

Play fighting is similar to rough-and-tumble play in that the participants know it's not real (Aldis, 1975). Play fighting is carried out in interrupted sequences or in incomplete actions. For example, a child will say "Bam!" while striking at another but without following through with physical contact. Play fighting has clear metacommunication signals to let the participants know that it is play and not aggression. For example, one third-grade child passed a note to another girl, making her intentions quite clear (see Figure 7–2).

All preschool children engage in rough-and-tumble play, although boys do so more often than girls. Boys tend to play in this way in larger groups at the perimeter of the play yard and girls are more likely to carry out rough-and-tumble play near equipment and in a more restricted area. This play nearly always is accompanied by shrieks, shouting, howling, and laughter. Rough-and-tumble play at this age frequently is combined with character roles of superheroes (Kostelnik, Whiren, and Stein, 1986). Usually, young children spend more time watching this kind of play than participating in it.

School-age children usually play with children of the same sex, unless the play specifically requires a member of the opposite sex. One game, called "kiss or kill," requires one player to chase another of the opposite sex, get him or her down, say, "Kiss or kill?" and proceed with the kiss or the "strike" as the downed player prefers. Rough-and-tumble play is most likely to occur after the children have been engaged in set tasks or when they are just coming outdoors for recess. When older children participate in rough-and-tumble play, it most frequently flows into games with rules, not aggression (Pellegrini, 1991). Tag often follows rough-and-tumble chasing. Interestingly, rough-and-tumble play is closely associated with social competence and high status in older boys. Unpopular boys, on the other hand, don't seem to be able to discriminate between aggression and rough-and-tumble play. Apparently they have not learned to distinguish the appropriate cues and respond to playful acts with aggressive ones (Pellegrini, 1991).

Both children and helping professionals must be able to discriminate between real aggression and rough-and-tumble play or play fighting. The differences often are apparent only in facial expression, such as a smile, a silly face, or a frown. Laughter and noisemaking (such as "monster sounds") often

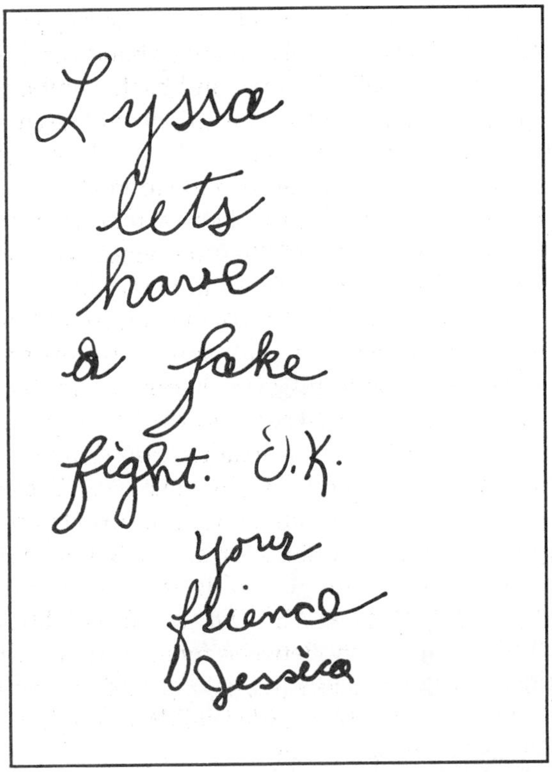

**Figure 7–2** A written play signal for rough-and-tumble play that was passed between two nine-year-olds in school.

signify that an activity is playful. Other play signals also are used to indicate the intent to play rough-and-tumble, such as "Let's play chase!" The adult's task is to help children indicate to peers whether or not they want to play ("Don't chase me—I'm not the dragon anymore," or "I'm not playing"). Often, safety zones must be established to avoid inadvertent involvement of unwilling players.

Adults usually want to squelch rough-and-tumble play, perceiving it as aggression. It is, however, a form of play typical of many species (Aldis, 1975; Fagen, 1981) and may well serve the overall development of children in other ways not yet understood. Experienced helping professionals note that children not allowed rough-and-tumble play in one setting (school yards, recreational settings) do so in others (bus, neighborhood, backyards). It is better to supervise this play to minimize the risks to children's safety.

**Violent combinations of dramatic and rough-and-tumble play.** Not all children's play is pleasant, cooperative, or peaceful. Adults are frequently concerned about the violent content of play. Violent content comes from several sources. First of all, children imitate violent adult behavior that they observe in the home, neighborhood, and school. Secondly, violence is portrayed in all news media as a result of natural events such as storms, volcanic eruptions, and earthquakes, as well as other catastrophes such as car accidents, firestorms, war, and crime. The third source of violence is related to children's inner needs to cope with their feelings of aggression and helplessness. Even children whose contact and knowledge of violence and unpleasantness from the surrounding community is controlled or limited are likely to respond to these inner pressures. Fourth, children frequently enact scripts that they see on television. Literary sources for children's play themes have a long history including pulp novels at the turn of the century, radio, comic books, movies, videos, and television (French, 1987). Lastly, there is masked play in which the child plays for the purpose of behaving aggressively against others without having to be responsible for the consequences of the serious aggressive act.

Professionals are responsible for guiding children's play into channels that lead to social competence and to positive mental health. Adults supervising preschool children may observe enactments of physical abuse as a part of the role of spouse, parent, or sibling. Simple redirection or discussing alternative ways to get people to cooperate are frequently sufficient for most play of this sort. Older children are less likely to be so specific in portraying private family concerns. Prolonged, repetitive, detailed enactments of violence on another may be an indicator that the child is living in an unwholesome environment that requires additional attention.

Children who have lived through a natural disaster, who have observed a serious accident or a violent crime, or whose home or school is unstable, experience fear and helplessness. Rough-and-tumble and pretend play are vehicles for expressing strong feelings and attaining mastery over situations beyond their control. Youngsters are able to work out a variety of solutions to terrifying situations in play, thus developing some control of their feelings (Kostelnik, Whiren, and Stein, 1986). The roles of rescuer, superhero, or soldier are all powerful ones that enable the child to explore many facets of the fearful situation. A "superhero" may be selected by a young child as a protector and used in new or potentially threatening situations. Adults help most when they provide accurate information about real incidents and when they provide reassurance to the

players that they are safe and the environment is stable. Often other children will portray roles of nurturer, comforter, or offer reassurance.

Television has increased in the number of violent programs and in the intensity of the violence within the programs since deregulation (Carlsson-Paige and Levin, 1988). Many programs are sponsored by toy companies that produce the materials with which to enact the episodes so the probability that children imitate the action sequences seen on television is unsurprising. Often this play is purely imitative with little elaboration based on the child's imagination, cooperation among players, or the use of problem solving and verbalization (Ritchie and Johnson, 1988). Such play appears to be of the "hit and flit" presentation that does not emerge as more advanced forms of sociodramatic or rough-and-tumble play. Characters may be stereotypic, racist (usually toward beings of strange colors or mutants), and sexist (Guddemi, 1986; Ritchie and Johnson, 1988). Young children also do not appear to comprehend the "moral lesson" usually delivered at the end of the program and tend not to perceive that the fantasy heros are particularly helpful, kind, or gentle (French, 1987). Adults are legitimately concerned about low-level play that appears to be aggressive and that does not appear to have redeeming characteristics of advanced sociodramatic play. Helpful strategies in organized programs for children are restricting access to television, guiding and redirecting play into more productive forms, and limiting the time and place for superhero play. Also helpful are eliminating superhero toys and weapons, providing other sociodramatic play opportunities and information for alternatives, and assessing the individual needs of children that make superhero play so attractive (Kostelnik, Whiren, and Stein, 1986; Ritchie and Johnson, 1988).

Sometimes children announce that a real act of aggression was "just play." When the victim is not playing rough-and-tumble, or when the attack appears to be a surprise, then the adult should treat the behavior as aggression. Older children particularly may use this strategy to avoid the consequences of their inappropriate behavior.

### Games

Games involve other players, have rules, and are eminently social. Games develop gradually as children's social skills mature, from the simple turn taking of toddlers to the complex games of older children. Older preschool children can play hide and seek or any number of games with a central person, like follow the leader or "duck, duck, goose." They are able to take turns if the wait isn't too long. With more experience, they become able to change roles, playing various versions of hide and seek such as kick the can, or hide and seek combined with tag. Between five and seven years of age, children play games of acceptance and rejection, such as "farmer in the dell," and of attack and defense, such as snowball fighting. Seven- to nine-year-olds add games of dominance and submission such as "Mother may I," card and board games, and sand-lot sports such as modified forms of softball and kick ball. Older children, more concerned with outcomes, enjoy intellectual games such as charades or trivia and are more likely to participate in organized teams. The roles older children take in games are likely to depend on special skills they may have, such as playing guard in a basketball game.

Games may be based on *chance* (most dice games), *skill* (baseball), or *strategy* (checkers). Most American children have experience with all three types of games. Games of skill are most directly linked to movement play. Many games of skill have become sports in which the play is administered and directed by adults, such as Little League coaches, rather than by the children. In this book, we will focus on the informal games in which children can follow, make, or change the rules themselves.

Adults who guide the social development of children should understand that young children do not approach a game in the same way that adults and older children might. Young preschool children play games in much the same fashion that they participate in movement play. They observe a particular way to move and imitate it. They are, in fact, frequently confused. In the game of tag, for example, a young child will run to avoid getting caught but is likely to have difficulties if tagged and declared to be "it." At this point, a very young child may refuse to play or may just stand there. If older players are willing, they may allow the little one to tag them so the game can go on.

Older preschool children frequently perceive rules as an interesting example of how to play rather than a required behavior. When playing together, they sometimes have difficulties regulating sequential turn taking. Nor are they concerned with what other players do; they simply are interested in their own actions. Each player is on his or her own. This is not the same as cheating, although adults observing young children playing a simple board game might interpret it as such.

Seven- and eight-year-olds begin to be concerned with problems of mutual control, winning, and losing. They are likely to discuss the rules before play but may have conflicting notions on what the "real" rules are. Conflicts may break out; these can be handled as discussed in Chapter 8. Children of this age often regard rules as sacred and untouchable, emanating from adults and lasting forever (Piaget, 1976; Sutton-Smith and Sutton-Smith, 1974).

Rules may vary for some games, especially those that are passed on verbally by children themselves. Adults should observe the play and ask older or more skillful players about the rules before arbitrating the play. Children develop skill in negotiation as they decide among themselves what the rules are to be.

Games are varied and are combined with many other forms of play. There are singing and dancing games, games using a variety of objects, movement games, games associated with dramatics (Dungeons and Dragons or charades), language games (Scrabble), and games that involve construction (Bug). Fortunately, most public libraries have good collections of books on games suitable for children to play in groups or individually.

## Humor

Adults usually do not find the humor of young children very amusing, if they even recognize that the child is trying to joke. Children's humor is limited by their experience and their cognitive development, so what they perceive as funny is altogether too obvious for the adult. Children are not likely to find adult humor funny, either, especially if they do not get the point of the joke. Understanding the development of children's use of incongruity for humor will help adults appreciate attempts at humor by the very young (McGhee, 1979).

**Incongruity in children's humor.** When an arrangement of ideas, social expectations, or objects is incompatible with the normal or expected pattern of events, it is *incongruous*. Although incongruity is not the only ingredient in humor, it may be the most common element in children's humor. Incongruity does not always elicit amusement, however. Children may react with interest, curiosity, anxiety, fear, or amusement. Humor, like other play forms, is framed by clear play signals. The younger the child, the clearer the play signals need to be—laughter or a traditional joke opening such as "knock, knock"—if the incongruous statement is to be treated as humor. Otherwise, the child will ignore it or treat it with curiosity. Something too outrageous might be frightening; Halloween costumes sometimes have this effect on three-year-olds.

Laughter and smiling have many causes. They denote pleasure in infancy, but not humor. Humor is dependent on the ability of the child to pretend and to have a playful orientation toward the situation in which humor occurs (Singer, 1973). If children do not have a playful orientation, they may enjoy the incongruity but not find it funny.

Humor also is social. Children laugh longer in a group than when alone. They also try to share their jokes with people with whom they already have a close bond. Playful attitudes or moods are more easily maintained in a social group than when alone, as well. Parents often are the ones selected to hear a joke, as Chukovsky (1976:601) reports:

> One day in the twenty-third month of her existence, my daughter came to me, looking mischievous and embarrassed at the same time—as if she were up to some intrigue. . . . She cried to me even when she was still at some distance from where I sat: "Daddy, oggie-miaow". . . . And she burst out into somewhat encouraging, somewhat artificial laughter, inviting me too laugh at this invention.

**Developmental trends in children's humor.**
Incongruity humor, like other aspects of development, proceeds sequentially (McGhee, 1979). The child first experiences humor while engaged in object play during the second year. The child simply uses an object in a way known to be inappropriate. For example, picking up a parent's shoe and using it as a telephone might lead to laughter if the child is in a playful frame of mind. The fantasy is known to be at odds with reality.

The second stage of the development of children's humor frequently overlaps with the first as language is used to create the incongruity with an object or event. Children simply give names to objects or events that they know to be incorrect. For example, young children delight in calling a cat a dog or an eye a foot. In initiating this type of humor, however, adults should remember that the confidence of very young children in the naming of objects is not great; if a joke is made without clear play signals, a two-year-old may think that new information is being presented.

In the third stage, between the ages of three and four, children delight in conceptual incon-

gruity. For example, drawings of a cat with no ears, or a dog with such long ears that they trail on the ground, are seen as funny. The distortion must be clear, but enough normal elements must be present for the child to recognize the familiar object. Another form of humor typical of this stage is to call someone by the wrong name. Older preschoolers who have mastered gender-related concepts may find it funny to call a girl a boy. However, this is threatening to some children and may be taken as an insult.

Preschoolers are perceptually oriented. A drawing of a bicycle with square wheels or stories of a "backwards day" or an elephant sitting on a nest all are perceived as funny. In the same way, young children are likely to laugh at people with disproportionate facial features, disfigurements, or noticeable handicapping conditions. They also laugh when someone falls in a funny way. Because of their cognitive limitations, very young children are unable to empathize, and although their amusement may appear cruel, it is not intended to be. Children who are very active and have short attention spans tend to initiate behavioral humor or slapstick whereas general language competence is more predictive of language humor (Carson, et al., 1986).

This period also is the beginning of producing nonsense words from regular words: "Doggie, loggie, moggie," "Lyssa, missa, rissa," "Hamburger, samburger, ramburger." Inventing new nonsense words also is amusing at this age. For example, children might set out to capture a "torkel" with great glee.

The fourth stage in the development of humor, when children understand multiple meanings of words, starts at about age seven. This is the beginning of humor that is most similar to adult humor. Puns or simple play with the meaning of words begins, such as: "Why are ghosts like newspapers?" "Because they appear in sheets." Incongruous actions also are incorporated into the question-format joke: "What goes 'Zzub! Zzub!'?" "A bee flying backwards." Jokes dealing with "what is it" questions and "knock, knock" jokes also appear:

*What's black and white and red all over?*
*A sunburned zebra. (older children)*
*A newspaper. (younger children)*

| | |
|---|---|
| *Knock, knock.* | *Knock, knock.* |
| *Who's there?* | *Who's there?* |
| *Ether.* | *Stella.* |
| *Ether who?* | *Stella who?* |
| *Ether Bunny.* | *Stella 'nother Ether Bunny.* |

Older school-age children, having well-developed cognitive abilities, are able to enjoy humor based on illogical behavior, such as a person buying a cat when they don't like cats so they can use up the cat shampoo that they got on sale.

Younger children imitate older ones in attempts to generate humor. However, they frequently forget the punch line or substitute a logical answer to the question, thereby "destroying" the joke.

Humor also may be used as a means for gratifying sexual aggression, or inappropriate desires. For example, young children often use words related to bowel or bladder functions shortly after control has been established. Helping professionals usually have witnessed young children saying, "Pooh, pooh," "Pee," or "Doo, doo," to the merriment of their peers.

**Valuing children's humor.** Children's humor can be encouraged by adults who understand the developing child's attempts at humor, listen attentively, and at least smile at the jokes. Admonishing children to stop being silly or quit fooling around inhibits the development of humor. In addition, children imitate humor from adults and older children.

Humor is a social experience for children. It can be used to help define the child as a member of a group, enhance the member's position in the group, or increase morale. As an aspect of play, humor also is supported by those adult behaviors that support play in general.

By knowing how humor develops, adults can recognize and support children's development of a sense of humor. In the early phases, children's humor isn't recognizable to many adults, who may then ignore, suppress, or even reprimand children for attempts at humor. Although the content of humor changes as the individual matures, the skill and confidence that children develop in this area enables them to participate successfully in a variety of social situations.

Even though each type of play has its own sequence of development in childhood, all require the support and guidance of caring adults if the quality of the play is to become optimal for each child.

## SKILLS FOR SUPPORTING, ENHANCING, AND EXPANDING CHILDREN'S PLAY

 **Set the Stage for Children's Play**

**1. Establish the necessary conditions for play.** Plan for play when children are not excessively tired or hungry. Provide snacks during play and comfortable nooks where children can rest or sleep. Quality play, in which the players use their full array of skills, rarely occurs when children are experiencing stress. If children are experiencing physical pain, fear, or extreme anger, follow the guidelines in Chapter 5 for responding to children's emotions. Quality play is not possible until these more pressing concerns are addressed.

**2. Say to yourself, "It's OK to play, to laugh, to have fun."** Accept the playfulness in yourself and in the children.

**3. Stand or sit near children at play.** Keep children in view from a little distance—from 1 to 6 feet away from the play space for younger children. Be outside the play area, but adjacent to it for children of all ages. Hovering over children stifles their play. However, do not stand at one end of the play yard while children are dispersed 30 feet or more from you. This great distance communicates lack of interest and may not provide adequate supervision of children's activities.

**4. Pay attention to what the children are playing and what they say and do.** Observe carefully; concentrate. Listen, and begin to remember the play preferences and styles of individuals within the group. Begin enjoying their play behavior.

**5. Schedule playtime in segments that are long enough for play concepts to be developed.** For example, in a preschool program, an hour or more usually is devoted to activities in which children can choose either to play or to engage in other experiences. If time is segmented for the group in 10- to 15-minute intervals, children spend most of their time waiting or in transition and cannot develop a play theme. On the other hand, elementary-school children can engage in movement play during a 15-minute recess, although well-developed fantasy play or extended group games take much longer. Older elementary-school children may work in interrupted shifts preparing a drama that they have created themselves. The preparation time (including related play) may be spread over several days and may amount to an hour or two for the final 10-minute production. The amount of time needed depends on the age, experience, skill, and interests of the group of children. Children of all ages need time to develop high-quality play.

**6. Provide adequate space for the number of children playing.** Match the number of children and the quantity of play materials to the given area. A board game for four players requires enough space for the children to play without interruption or congestion. In addition, a sense of privacy is essential if children are to develop quality dramatic play. Block play usually requires a large play area.

**7. Provide quality playthings for all types of play.** Children will play with anything, and some of the most interesting playthings, such as sand, water, and mud are not toys. Provide materials for construction, such as bristle blocks, unit blocks, paints of various types, paper, musical instruments, clay, and dough. Children of all ages love to take on roles; make available props that promote pretend play for occupations such as community helpers, for family roles, and for fictional characters. Give young children realistic props; offer older children less realistic materials. Movement-and-skill play may require jump ropes, balls of various sizes, and other appropriate materials such as tricycles, ice skates, or basketball hoops. See that these are at hand. Provide different types of games: those that require cooperation (lifting one child in a parachute); those that encourage competition; some that are played in small groups indoors, such as checkers; and others that are played in larger groups outdoors, such as volleyball.

**8. Encourage exploration of materials.** Delay any demonstration of material use until children ask for assistance. Refrain from setting limits until children actually misuse the materials.

## SKILLS FOR SUPPORTING, ENHANCING, AND EXPANDING CHILDREN'S PLAY—continued

Point out new or interesting uses of materials by other children when appropriate. Use nonverbal strategies such as smiling, watching, and offering or accepting materials. Assume that children may do anything with the materials that is not expressly prohibited by the setting, unless the well-being of others is at stake or property could be damaged.

9. **Provide the props, materials, and the necessary information for children to create a variety of sociodramatic play scenarios.** Many play themes revolve around family activities (camping, gardening, traveling) community activities (postal services, hospital, veterinarian clinics) and literary characters (Three Pigs, Goldilocks, or Madeline). Children need the information and the story lines that will allow them to enact pretend play characters based on familiar experience or literary foundations. Read and reread good children's literature and information books that provide the background for play. Tape favorite stories so that children can listen independently. Provide specific props critical to the stories. Children who have a rich source of play materials will not be so dependent on television as a source of stimulation for their play episodes.

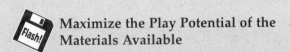 **Maximize the Play Potential of the Materials Available**

1. **Mix unrelated toys together.** Put water or play dough in the housekeeping area. Place the furnishings of the dollhouse in a box in the block area. Fasten butcher paper onto the wall of the building outdoors where children usually ride tricycles, and provide paints. Put Lego blocks and other small construction toys into a pretend play area set up as an office or hospital. Don't be limited by these suggestions: think of all the possible, then the not-so-possible recombinations of materials. Materials need not have any obvious relationship. The point is to stimulate the creative potential of the children.

2. **Introduce novel toys and materials slowly.** Avoid putting out all the new things at the same time. The stimulus value of each one competes with the others, and all become stale too soon. One teacher made the mistake of thinking that new toys would engage the children so well that they would be engrossed during playtime for the entire week. Much to her surprise, the children dashed from toy to toy, attempting to get at everything and really playing with nothing. They explored, but did not develop their play. Because of their high mobility level, they also experienced many more conflicts. A different approach was used by Miss Davison, who set up a housekeeping area for a group of four-year-olds in a daycare center. It had dishes, pots and pans, stove, refrigerator, table and chairs, and sink. On the second day, she added dolls, a doll bed, and a rocking chair. On the third day, she put a bowl of uncooked macaroni on the table. On the fourth day, she put out a small clothes rack containing shirts and dresses on hangers. On the fifth day, she put hats for men and women in a box nearby and adult shoes under the rack. The following week, she did nothing for two days, but then removed the macaroni and put a pail of water near the sink.

3. **Rotate playthings.** Remove some play materials. When brought out again, they will generate increased interest. For example, a first-grade teacher had both Candy Land and Raggedy Ann board games. The games required about the same skills. She would leave one game out in the children's play area and put the other in the cupboard for a month or two, then switch them.

Similar to simple rotation is the practice of having a special set of toys that are used only in the late afternoon in child care. The "new" materials, although similar to those used in the morning, generate much better play than would the same materials played with earlier.

4. **Arrange the materials to encourage interaction between children.** Set out two sets of Lego blocks instead of one. Place several puzzles on a large table rather than one on a small table. Have enough dress-up clothes for several children to play. When too many children want to play in the housekeeping area, suggest that some of them construct a home next door so that they can play neighbors. Other children are by far the most novel, interesting, and complex

*continued*

## SKILLS FOR SUPPORTING, ENHANCING, AND EXPANDING CHILDREN'S PLAY—continued

resources for play; children should be encouraged to play with one another.

Older children enjoy many of the new games that emphasize cooperation and working together. As children mature, they are able to play in larger groups, and materials such as cards and board games can be played with as many as six players. Make materials for such activities available and arrange them so that several children can play at once.

**5. Suggest new uses for materials or ask other children to do so.** Help children identify problems with their play and to seek information or help from peers. "It seems your car does not roll very far on the carpet. Ask Soo-Jin what she thinks might be used to make it go further." Soo-Jin might suggest a cardboard runway, boards, or movement of the car to a harder surface or the adult might do this. Let the children try things out, even if they try something like a scarf, which you already know won't work. A general request for ideas is also appropriate: "Angelo needs some money. Does anyone have an idea of what to use?"

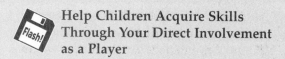 **Help Children Acquire Skills Through Your Direct Involvement as a Player**

**1. Play with materials.** Children love to see adults smear the finger paint, work with a paintbrush on an easel with drippy paint, or build in the sandbox. Comment on your play, saying things like: "I'm smearing my paint all over," or "I'm glad the sand is wet so my house stays up." Then, wait for children to comment on what they are doing. When modeling, respect your own play. Bring your play to some closure: flatten the sand castle, finish the painting, or announce that you are through. Children should not expect you to give way to them automatically when they want to play or when they just grab your materials. Simply tell them, "I'm nearly finished, and then you can have this place," as you complete whatever you are doing.

**2. Use verbal or nonverbal prompts from outside the play frame.** Mime the action that might be appropriate to the child once you have

caught his or her eye. This is especially useful for children who are about to move to another level of play on their own or to those who really do not want adults to interfere. Such actions are "batting" or "throwing" in movement play, big smiles in a humorous situation, or a physical enactment in pretend play. Using a stage whisper for giving direction or prompting also is helpful for some children.

**3. Take a role to encourage pretend play.** Select either a behavioral role, such as saying "Varoom, varoom" as you "drive" a truck down a block highway, or a character role, such as becoming the parent, the baby, or the spaceship captain. Use a variety of techniques to influence the direction of the play, such as engaging in ulterior conversations or storytelling. Respond to the role cues of other children, and remain in character while in the play frame. Remember that you can't get out of the play frame to give directions without some clear signal that you are not playing any more. Gradually take a less active part until you can exit the play frame altogether.

**4. Demonstrate movements as necessary.** If you should see a two-year-old attempting to jump down a step but walking it instead, the most playful thing to do is to jump youself, with feet together, landing with knees slightly bent and using your arms for balance. A simple demonstration of jumping, hopping on one foot, or striking with a bat or hockey stick provides information, and if briefly and playfully done, it can be a part of the ongoing play. Prompting, such as saying "Bend your knees when you land," then resuming the game or movement play, also is acceptable.

**5. Participate fully in the game.** Play by the rules as you understand them and participate fully, taking turns, running, or whatever is required. Children learn some games, especially games of strategy, only by observing a better player. Chinese checkers is like this, as are Risk, chess, and Monopoly. Discuss the play as other players do, pointing out what you did and why, if appropriate. Be careful not to become so engrossed in your play that you forget that your goal is to support the play of the children.

## SKILLS FOR SUPPORTING, ENHANCING, AND EXPANDING CHILDREN'S PLAY—continued

 **Help Individual Children Change the Level of Social Participation in Play**

**1. Observe the child at play; note patterns of play alone and with others.** Solitary play is valuable. Children explore objects and often engage in imaginary scenarios using figures, blocks, trucks, or other materials. In some cultures, individual play is highly valued. Appropriateness of the level of play is influenced by age, experience, and culture. For example, if a child between twenty-four and thirty months spent most of the time watching older children play, this level of play is very appropriate. Children learn from each other, especially through observation and imitation. Watching others play is also very appropriate for youngsters who are new to the group and for those who have had minimal opportunities to play with others. Friendly observation of a child at play is encouraging to the child and communicates the interest of the adult.

Sometimes, talented and bright children play alone, not because they cannot play with others, but because they do not have any real peers in the group. Shifting them into more social experiences requires identifying an aspect of development that is most like that of other children in the group. For example, a child with outstanding musical ability might best pursue that area independently and be matched with another player with similar motor abilities for movement play.

**2. Observe the child for cues that the present level of participation is inadequate.** Cues indicating that children may need help in increasing their level of participation might be: prolonged observation of a group at play (more than 10 minutes); following more skillful players from one activity to another; forceful crossing of the play boundaries, or disruption of others' group play; crying, complaining, or stating that they want to play too.

Children who appear to be satisfied with their level of participation should be allowed to continue to function at a comfortable level. They usually appear to be relaxed, happy, and fully involved in what they are doing.

**3. Match the activity to the child's level of skill.** Observe children carefully so you know what level of skill is typical for them. Allow children to practice playing alone or in parallel play until they are comfortable with this level. Notice when individuals shift from parallel play to short episodes of greater social interaction. Usually, parallel play is unstable and will shift into more direct interaction or solitary play (Bakeman and Brownlee, 1980). Again, select a potential playmate based on similar levels of competence in a particular area.

**4. Play with the child yourself.** Less skilled players perform more easily with a predictable, responsive adult than with other children. Give clear play signals and use a variety of metacommunications.

**5. Invite the child and a second, less skilled player to play with you, then ease yourself out of the situation.** Do not try to match the best player or the most popular child with the least skilled player. The disparities in skill may be too great for the play to continue. Remember that children are sensitive to social status in developing their play role.

 **Escalate the Level of Play Gradually by Varying Your Play Performance or by Giving Cues Through Play Signals or Metacommunications**

**1. Extend object play by imitating what the child is doing, then vary the activity a little.** Incorporate the child's ideas into your modeling. This may be accomplished by using the same object in a slightly different way, such as tapping a maraca with your hand instead of shaking it, or talking to a doll in an emotionally expressive tone of voice instead of a normal tone or monotone.

**2. Suggest that children use specific play signals to initiate or sustain play.** Tell the least skillful player what to say to indicate the play: "Tell James, 'I'll be a policeman.'" This active approach is more likely to lead to success than the more general question, "Do you want to play?"

Select the type of play signal that is commonly used by other players in the group. Con-

*continued*

## SKILLS FOR SUPPORTING, ENHANCING, AND EXPANDING CHILDREN'S PLAY—continued

sider ulterior conversations, underscoring, storytelling, prompting, or formal pretend proposals. The less skillful player will then have your prompting as well as opportunities to observe other children as a means of improving his or her skills. For example, when one player seems exasperated with the inability of another to play a role correctly, lean over the props and stage-whisper directions: "Whisper to the mail carrier that she is supposed to give the letters to other people, not read them herself." Or perhaps if the play theme seems to be floundering, note the materials of interest and suggest the storytelling approach to one of the players: "Think what would happen if there were an earthquake and the city had to be rebuilt. Tell the story."

Demonstrate how to use nonverbal play signals when they would facilitate the play, especially if they will enable less skilled players to enhance their skills. For instance, show a child how to "fall ill" just outside the pretend hospital by making moans and holding a part of the body as if in pain. Show a child how to portray being a sad "baby" outside the housekeeping area as a way to get a response from other players. Some children may need much more support and direction than others, but play skills can be learned and enhanced.

**3. Withdraw from the play and resume the role of observer once the play is well under way.** Think of a way to exit the game gracefully. ("Let's pretend that I am a teacher and I have to go to work now") or step out of the play and state clearly that you aren't playing anymore. If you have a central role, such as pitcher in a softball game, you might just say that your turn is up, and ask who would like to pitch.

 **Coach Children Occasionally from Outside the Play Frame**

**1. Suggest a related theme.** If children are playing house and the play is disintegrating, extend the theme by suggesting that they go on a picnic, move, go on vacation, or engage in some other family-related activity.

**2. Add a necessary prop.** Children "going on a vacation" need a suitcase, and the play may break down without it. When you observe this occurring, go to the storage area, get the suitcase, and place it near the play area. Obviously, you should not leave children unsupervised for long periods of time while you search for materials, but when possible, make such impromptu additions to enhance their play.

**3. Introduce new players from outside the play frame.** One way to introduce a new player is to indicate that she or he would like to join the ongoing activity. Say something simple and direct, like "Mary has been watching you play and would like to play, too." The children participating in the play may or may not accept Mary. It's their choice. Should they not want Mary to play at this time, help Mary find another place to play, providing several alternatives. Small group games and pretend play are much more difficult to enter than are activities such as artwork or block construction, because the children in play with an ongoing theme have already established roles and relationships. Don't force acceptance of another player; the play may completely disintegrate if established roles, themes, and relationships are disrupted. Play, by definition, is child directed and voluntary.

A second approach is to offer a new character role for a player joining the group ("Here is the grandmother, coming to visit"). Additions of mail carriers, meter readers, relatives, guests to a party, and so on, can be incorporated into the ongoing play. Do not give the entering child a role that overshadows the other players, such as a space person landing in the yard. The new player is likely to be "killed off" or rejected.

**4. Teach players to use a clear signal when leaving the play frame.** Clear communication probably is most important when children are engaged in rough-and-tumble play. Say: "Tell Sarah you don't want to be the monster anymore," or "John doesn't know you don't want to chase him. Tell him that." Such suggestions will allow children to exit the play and will reduce the likelihood of the nonplaying child responding to rough-and-tumble play with aggression.

**5. Make suggestions to further the goals of children, such as pointing out a problem or re-**

## SKILLS FOR SUPPORTING, ENHANCING, AND EXPANDING CHILDREN'S PLAY—continued

**stating game rules.** Offer specific help when it is needed to keep a game going. For example, if a child's block construction is wobbling, point out the area where the problem is occurring if the child does not see it. If children are confused about how a game should proceed, restate the relevant rules. When children are involved in superhero play, suggest that they think about the problem and talk about the characteristics of the true hero. Identify ways other than physical might to solve problems, or remind them to identify children who are and are not playing.

**6. Talk about play events that disintegrate for older children who are rejected playmates or isolated by their peers. Assist them in identifying the social cues that they misinterpreted and suggest alternative behaviors.** Ask them to tell you what they think happened. Probe for details. Correct misinterpretations and point out the behaviors that would lead to more acceptable responses and the maintenance of play. Initiating the social interactions, entering an ongoing play frame, and participating during rough-and-tumble play are particularly difficult for many youngsters.

**7. *Teach children games when necessary.*** Children between the ages of three and seven may not have had the opportunity to learn games from the older children and so must be taught by an adult. Have all materials set up, and know the rules yourself. Invite the children to participate. Then, give brief directions, one at a time. For example, in the game of "duck, duck, goose," say, "Take hands" (to form a circle). You may have to help by giving more specific directions, such as, "Jacob, hold Susan's hand." When the children are in a shoulder-to-shoulder circle, ask them to sit down. Once they are all seated, stand up and announce that you will be "it" the first time. Walk around the circle, tapping heads and saying "Duck, duck, duck, *goose!*" When the word "goose" is said, direct the child to chase you, then run around the circle, sitting in the child's empty space. Then, direct the standing child to be "it." With very young children, go with the child who is "it" for the first time as he or she taps heads and says, "Duck, duck, . . . , goose," and then run with the child to the empty space of the new person who

is "it." Give directions and demonstrate in alternating patterns. With young children, don't give all the directions at once.

Allow the children to play until all have had a turn or their interest diminishes. Repeat the directions as necessary each time you play the game until the children can play it by themselves.

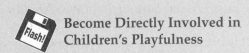 **Become Directly Involved in Children's Playfulness**

**1. Demonstrate a nonliteral approach to resources.** Playfully respond to the environment and to commonplace situations. For example, Mr. Phipps used to sing little songs or make up verses about ordinary things as they occurred during the day: the rain on the windowsill, blocks falling down, parents going to work, or children not wanting naps. He did this quite unconsciously to amuse the children. No one noticed until parents commented that their children could make up songs and poetry by themselves and wondered what the school was doing to promote such creativity.

Another way to do this is to propose impossible conditions: "I wonder what if . . . ?" What would happen if so much snow fell that the houses were covered? What would happen if all the girls grew wings and could fly? Encourage children to be expansive and to try to imagine all the possibilities. This often generates a lot of laughter. Show your interest in each child's contribution regardless of how silly it is.

**2. Be accepting of young children's humor.** Smile and show interest even if you do not have the least idea of what the joke is. When group glee strikes, with every child laughing uproariously, laugh along with them. They will quiet themselves down eventually. It is not at all unusual for the children not to know what they are laughing at either.

**3. Explain that a child was only joking when someone misinterprets the meaning of what was said or did not recognize a play signal.** It is especially important that play signals be recognized when some members of the group are older or more mature than other members. For

*continued*

## SKILLS FOR SUPPORTING, ENHANCING, AND EXPANDING CHILDREN'S PLAY—continued

example, to call a boy a girl is a serious insult, except in a joke, which would be common for older preschool or kindergarten children. Nonsense names or other names used to address people may be very distressing to children not in on the joke or too young to understand it.

**4. Use affective reflections when preschool children laugh at disfigurement, falls, or handicapping conditions; then, provide brief but accurate information.** Preschool children are not mature enough to take another's perspective and do not intend to hurt another person's feelings with their laughter, although this is often the result. Say, for example: "You thought Mr. North walked very funny. He cannot help that because one leg is shorter than the other. People who cannot help the way they walk feel sad when other people laugh at them."

### Guide Children's Rough-and-Tumble Play

*1.* **Decide whether rough-and-tumble play is to be allowed, and if so, when, where, and under what conditions such play will be permitted.** Expectations of adults must be clear. Decisions should be made so that all adults in a program are consistent. Some people limit rough-and-tumble play to outdoors in early childhood programs or to recess and do not allow it in the classrooms. Limiting such play to a specific area or space is another choice. In other situations, children may engage in rough-and-tumble play, but only during specified periods of the day or in specific spaces, such as a gym or large motor playroom. Once clear limits as to time and place for rough-and-tumble play are made, adults can use the following guides to direct the children toward more pleasant experiences.

**2. Caregivers may choose to decrease the violence in play instead of trying to eliminate rough-and-tumble play.** Do not display or provide any weapons. Toys that suggest violence suggest themes that lead to violence in the enactment of play. When children "make"

weapons of blocks, sticks, wads of paper, or anything else, remind them that they may not "kill" anyone or shoot, stab, or use a weapon.

Use videos that are information rich and avoid cartoons and television programs that are violent. Encourage parents to monitor children's program viewing. This is discussed in Chapter 12.

**3. Ask children to use specific, verbal play cues to initiate rough-and-tumble play.** All children must agree to be players in order to minimize being frightened or feeling that they are being attacked. Individuals have a right to say "no" to this type of play.

**4. Coach children in how to say "no" to play.** Give scripts to children who do not care to engage in rough-and-tumble play. "No," "I don't want you to chase me," or "I want to play something else," are all statements that children can be taught to use in order to decline play.

**5. Provide for a "safety zone" so that when a child enters the zone, rough-and-tumble play stops.** This is similar to tag games where some object becomes a "safe" place. Children who are playing rough and tumble sometimes frighten themselves, and they need an easy way to stop playing.

**6. Provide information about heros.** Frequently, superhero play focuses on the most violent aspects of fantasy character dramas. Children miss the protection of the victim, the plot, and the array of nonviolent characters in the media portrayal. Helping, protecting, and honorable motives are central to superheros, but these aspects are often omitted by young children. If children portray real superheros, their play resembles pretend play with bouts of chasing.

Providing information about real heros and the obstacles that they have overcome can provide for similar play that may meet the needs of the children for power and control.

**7. Suggest that the villain or victim be imaginary.** This way all of the children can be runners and no one needs to be chased.

## SKILLS FOR SUPPORTING, ENHANCING, AND EXPANDING CHILDREN'S PLAY—continued

**8. Remain in close physical proximity to children engaging in rough-and-tumble play.** If adults see three or four youngsters running in a pack, distant from themselves and the play equipment, this is probably the beginning of a rough-and-tumble play sequence, and the adult should move toward the action. The episode is more likely to remain playful than degenerate into overt aggression when an adult is close by.

**9. If the rough-and-tumble play ceases to be fun, and someone is hurt or frightened, adults should stop the behavior.** It is no longer play. Playing must be fun and voluntary for everyone. When it is not, adults must move to protect the children from hurting others or being hurt themselves. Strategies for doing this are discussed in Chapters 4, 5, 10, and 11.

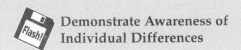 **Demonstrate Awareness of Individual Differences**

**1. Accept the young child's approach to games with rules.** Little children are not cheating or committing a moral error if they don't play precisely by the rules. Simply restate the rule in question and go on with the game. Children learn to play games with rules by playing with better players who know the rules.

**2. Match the play activity to the skills of the players.** Children from less advantaged circumstances may not be as skilled in taking roles as are much younger children from middle-class families. Therefore, they will need the opportunity to participate in pretend play well into the grade-school years. They also will need to have more adult interventions so that their skills will improve. Play skills are developed by experience. All children should begin with simple games, roles, and constructions and move on toward more challenging activities as their skills develop. Use the developmental information provided in this chapter to help you match the level of play to the skills of the players.

**3. Accept the child's play style preferences.** Both patterners and dramatists engage in high-quality play. It is hoped that all children will experience both construction and role-taking play, but if children have a clear style, let them develop in their preferred mode.

**4. Provide support for younger boys when girls outperform them in movement play.** Girls' motor skills often develop faster than do boys' until the later elementary grades, when the trend is reversed. Boys may be vulnerable to feelings of failure when the girls run faster, jump farther, and ride bikes earlier. Reassure them that they too will be able to do all of these things soon.

**5. Support children in their choice of play activities; do not limit play to sex-stereotyped choices.** Boys frequently are teased if they choose to play jacks or jump rope because these are "girl games." Such teasing should be treated as you would any other form of verbal aggression. Sometimes, girls are called "tomboys," or parents become concerned with their rough-and-tumble play, which they perceive as inappropriate for girls but acceptable for boys. Allow young boys to take nurturing roles as well. Children need opportunities to try out all kinds of activities, and they benefit from the varied experience. Play, after all, is not serious, and it allows children the opportunity to develop other perspectives.

Older children frequently exclude the opposite sex in their free play. Choices of playmates should be respected whenever possible as both boys and girls develop sex role–related skills in their play. However, when you organize games, avoid assigning children to teams based on gender. Pitting the boys against girls is not fair. It would be better to count out the teams so that they are evenly balanced.

**6. Respect cultural and experiential differences in children.** Allow children to explore play themes that might be unfamiliar to you. Encourage children to freely express their ideas and emotions in their play. Refrain from responses that automatically reject or diminish others' cultural experience.

*continued*

## SKILLS FOR SUPPORTING, ENHANCING, AND EXPANDING CHILDREN'S PLAY—continued

 **Share Information with Parents about Children's Play**

**1. Respond with information about the value of play to children's overall development when parents ask, "Why do they spend time playing?"** Part of the cultural ethic in the United States is that play is not worthwhile. If it is fun, it has no educational value. It's a frill, and valuable lessons learned of any sort are generally more worklike than playlike. The belief is similar in quality to the notion that medicine must taste very nasty if it is to do any good. Once you have identified this attitude in a parent, respond with information ("It seems you feel that when the children are playing, they are not profitably engaged in school") and then follow it up with details relevant to the child's development in your program.

**2. Write notes about children's success in a play episode informally throughout the time the child is in the program.** Label paintings with the child's narrative. Share photos of children's constructions with a few comments about the developmental significance of the event. Write glad notes when a child finally participates successfully in a game with others. Let parents know where budding friendships might be encouraged through discussion at home. De-

scribe a play event that illuminates the child's comprehension of ideas.

**3. Provide information about suitable play materials for the age group with whom you are working.** Written resources are available from your state cooperative extension service through the county extension agent, as well as from the Association for Childhood Education International and the National Association for the Education of Young Children. In addition, many good articles are published in family magazines in November of each year.

**4. Encourage families to participate in community-wide events that support children's play informally for all age groups.** Send information about events in the community home during breaks or holidays. When other agencies or groups participate in park cleanup days, attend yourself and ask families to join you.

**5. Ask parents about the child's play at home and in other settings, as well as what the child mentions about play in your setting.** Parents know a lot about their own children. Their observations are likely to be very useful to you and may help in the planning and supervision of each child at play.

## ▼ PITFALLS TO AVOID

Sometimes, when people are trying to use the skills described here, certain attitudes and behaviors may interfere with their ability to carry them out in a truly playful spirit.

**Believing that children learn only what they are taught.** Learning is something that children do for themselves. Adults may structure the learning, but the information learned by direct instruction is limited compared with the information children acquire from the environment, from their families and friends, and at play. Adults can facilitate children's learning to play; but they should not require children to perform to specification. Facilitation requires that the adult truly believes that the children have the capacity to learn, to perform, and to be competent within themselves.

**Organizing play to meet academic ends.** Children learn from all of their play experiences. Adults should not try to limit the songs they sing to number songs and alphabet ditties. These activities are designed by well-intentioned adults who use children's play interests to meet other ends. Play is only play when it belongs to the children, is voluntary, and is fun. If children choose to put together an alphabet puzzle, fine; however, a clown puzzle is just as good from a playful perspective.

**Watching for mistakes.** Play is not serious, so mistakes in play simply do not count. By all means, assist a child when asked to do so, but never point out mistakes to a playing child. Let the child discover the error independently. Many interesting products were invented out of mistakes that someone played with.

**Making demands for specific responses.** Children do need to learn specific information about their world, and these tasks are organized into lessons. Lessons about materials, for example, should not be substituted for play with materials. For example, adults may present a lesson on the effects of mixing paint colors and ask the child to predict the color to be produced. The scientific approach to light and color has its place. However, it should be separated from the creative activity of painting a picture, in which some colors might become mixed. Answer questions if asked, otherwise, leave the child alone to manage the situation without giving instruction. The distinction between curious investigation from a scientific perspective and playful exploration often is not clear. The best criterion to help distinguish between the two is to determine who has control of the situation. If the child does, and the adult only responds to inquiries, then the adult is behaving appropriately. However, if the child is passive and the adult is talking quite a bit, requiring answers from the child, or giving a series of directions, then this is a lesson, not play.

**Setting too many restrictions.** Children cannot play if they are expected to maintain silence, not move, create no disorder, never touch one another, remain clean and tidy, and never create a mess. Play requires action. Action inevitably leads to disorder, messes, noise, joy, conversation, and, usually, jostling about. When adults set unreasonable restrictions on play, they simply are typing to prohibit play altogether. Of course, even the youngest player can be expected to clean up after the play, but that is a task in social responsibility, not play itself.

**Squelching the creative use of materials.** Consider whether there actually are reasons of safety or economics that restrict the use of a particular material. For example, poker chips make better money to carry in purses than do puzzle pieces, and most children would rather use them; and puzzles are ruined if pieces are missing. However, the same thing does not apply to macaroni, strings, Lego blocks, or other small items that might be used in role play. The challenge is in planning to manage the proper return of the items once play is finished for the day. One teacher maintained a pail for small items, and children deposited them there whenever they were found. Later, they were returned to the appropriate storage area.

**Having no constraints at all.** Play is planned disorder, or organized, rule-governed interactions that do not fit adult predetermined conceptions. Play simply does not flourish when there are no rules or means of controlling its scope or parameters. Rules regarding safety, rights and feelings of others, and other necessities of group living are essential prerequisites of quality play. Children who do not have limits spend most of their time in social testing to see just where the boundaries of acceptable behavior are rather than in productive play. You will learn about setting limits in Chapters 10, 11, and 12.

**Ignoring play.** Given the right conditions, play probably will develop without adult prodding. However, quality play, that which stretches the imagination and the social and cognitive abilities of the player, does not develop in a vacuum. Writing lesson plans, cleaning cupboards, planning menus, or chatting with other adults unrelated to the ongoing activity while the youngsters are engaged in play is inappropriate. Save these activities until the session is over or for when the children are asleep.

**Amusing yourself with materials without responding to children's play.** Adults who do not focus on what children are doing sometimes play with materials in a fashion that is disconnected to the children's activities. To expand play, the adult's behavior must be based on observed child behavior and varied in some way.

**Encouraging premature competition.** Children under eight years of age do not understand games with rules well enough to engage in competitive games in which winning and losing is stressed. They may want to bat balls thrown to them or catch and toss balls, all of which is movement play. Most sandlot games do not have the two-team, win-and-lose systems; turns usually are rotated so that each player plays for the fun of the process. Sometimes, adults misinterpret this play as competitive sport and take over, making it competitive.

**Directing play or games too soon.** Children learn from the process of deciding on rules or setting up a fantasy play situation. It may take longer to do these tasks than adults think is necessary. Unfortunately, adults often move in too soon and usurp the planning and organizational functions. Unless children ask for help, or unless conflict erupts that the children are unable to resolve themselves, adults should show interest but remain uninvolved.

**Asking children to explain their humor.** Asking for an explanation quickly kills all the fun of a joke. If one does not "get it," using a social smile, social laughter, or a simple pleasurable expression is an appropriate response.

**Admonishing children to be quiet or to quit being silly when engaged in humor.** Sometimes, adults are annoyed by children's laughter, especially if it occurs in the wrong time and place. In such cases, let children know you understand their merriment ("You kids are having a great time telling jokes"), then explain why their humor is inappropriate ("I'm concerned that I won't be able to drive safely in this traffic with all the distraction"). Don't just set limits on children's humor in a general, disapproving way.

**Becoming too involved in the play.** You may find yourself having so much fun playing that you forget that the purpose of participation is to stimulate children's high-quality play. Play should go on nicely once you have ceased to be so active. If it does not, you might have been dominating the play, the activity might have been above the children's level, or the role you had chosen might have been so central to the theme that the play cannot continue without it. Facilitate rather than dominate.

## ▼ SUMMARY

Play is a normal part of childhood, allowing children to practice skills in motor coordination, language, reasoning, social behavior, and in learning to cope with emotionally challenging problems. It is pleasurable, voluntary, and valued for the process of play from the players' perspective rather than for any useful product.

There are several types of play: play with movement and objects, construction play, and fantasy play. Within each play form, sequences of development were suggested through which children pass before they become skillful players. Most of these sequences occur in early childhood, with older children using early skills in new combinations for more complex forms of play.

The role of the adult is to facilitate play. This means that the adult must establish an atmosphere conductive to play, provide appropriate materials and facilities, and guide the skill development of the children toward increasing levels of performance. Responsiveness to children's observed behaviors is essential to this role as is communication with children's parents.

Several pitfalls were identified so that you can avoid them as you begin to support children's play.

## ▼ DISCUSSION QUESTIONS

1. Why is it unlikely that play can ever be eliminated as a human behavior?
2. What is the function of play in the overall development of children?
3. Describe the characteristics of play and give examples of playful and nonplayful behavior.
4. Why aren't the concepts of work and play opposites? Why is it more accurate to contrast play with seriousness than with work? Use your own life experience to elaborate on this.
5. List the skills needed for children to participate in dramatic play. Give examples of each one.
6. What does metacommunication mean? Describe play signals that are nonverbal and those that are spoken.
7. When a young child starts to tell a joke but forgets the punch line and then laughs, how should you respond?
8. When a group of school-age children of mixed ages are playing softball and are not following the Little League rules on their own, how should you respond?
9. When older children are fully involved in play and everything is running smoothly, what should you do?
10. Referring to Appendix A, NAEYC Code of Ethical Conduct, determine if these situations pose an ethical dilemma. Identify the section that influences your answer.
    a. A teacher leaves the children unattended on the playground with the intent of watching them from a window and assumes that if there is an emergency, one of the children will come to get her.
    b. Three children are having a noisy confrontation while engaged in dramatic play. The teacher does nothing.
    c. One teacher complains to a colleague that Ms. Gace (another colleague) runs a room that is just too structured and the children don't get any real play time.

    **d.** A little girl is playing house and another child comes in and wants to be the mother. The children agree to have two mothers playing in one house. The adult intervenes and insists that families have one father and one mother in each house.

## ▼ FIELD ASSIGNMENTS

1. Using simple, direct statements that you would use with the children, write out the directions to a game. Indicate where you would demonstrate what to do or play along with the players in order for them to get the idea of the game. Then try out the game with a group of children. How well were they able to follow your directions? What would you do differently?

2. Observe a group of young children over several days. Record whether or not you have observed the following behaviors for each child:

    **a.** Substitutes an object for another during pretend

    **b.** Invents objects and uses gestures or movements to indicate existence

    **c.** Transforms time or age of player(s) or self

    **d.** Transforms place

    **e.** Takes on a behavioral or functional role

    **f.** Takes on a family or fantasy character role

    Now arrange to play with these children and devise strategies to encourage the development of these skills. What materials will you need? How will you coach them? If they can perform the basic skills, what should your role be?

3. Collect materials that would be useful to parents in making toy selections for specific age groups.

# ▼Chapter 8

## Supporting Children's Friendships

## ▼ OBJECTIVES

*On completion of this chapter, you will be able to describe:*

▼ Why peer relationships are important to children.

▼ How children's ideas about friendship change over time.

▼ Variables that influence children's friendship choices.

▼ Skills necessary for making contact, maintaining positive interactions, and negotiating conflicts.

▼ Behaviors that differentiate children who make friends easily from those who have difficulty making friends.

▼ Adult strategies to increase children's friendship skills.

▼ How to help family members understand and facilitate children's friendships.

▼ Pitfalls to avoid in supporting children's friendships.

---

Randy, eight years old, is the pariah of the school playground. He regularly pushes, hits, and trips his classmates. During group games, he runs to the center of the circle, grabs a ball, and dares the other youngsters to catch him. His loud, aggressive behavior has earned him a reputation as a bully, and most children avoid him whenever they can.

Four-year-old Alisha is reserved and very quiet around her peers. She often can be seen standing on the fringe of an activity, simply watching. Even when invited to join the play, she usually shakes her head "no." After several such refusals, children have stopped asking and now generally ignore her.

---

To the casual observer, Randy and Alisha seem worlds apart. Yet, both are typical examples of children who have difficulty making friends. Helping professionals observing children having these prob-

lems may feel sorry for them, but assume there is little they, as adults, can do to improve the situation. We now know that adults can support children as they try to establish friendly relations with peers and help them increase their chances for success (Asher, Oden, and Gottmann, 1977; Combs and Slaby, 1978).

### Why Friends Are Important

Children become increasingly interested in having friends as they grow older. By first grade, many report that it is almost intolerable to be without a friend (Hendrick, 1996). Why is this so?

One reason is that people need satisfying relationships with others for stimulation, guidance and assistance, companionship, physical and ego support, social comparison, and for intimacy and affection (Parker and Gottman, 1989). Through friendship, children interact with familiar partners and playmates who spend time and share activities, provide information, fun, and assistance, as well as encouragement and feedback about how the child is seen by others. In addition, friends offer close, trusting relationships, thus providing a safe haven for self-disclosure (Santrock, 1996). Children derive these benefits from both adults and peers, but in different ways.

Society has defined certain expectations for each party in the adult-child relationship. Interactions between adults and children are characterized by a difference in status. Adults' refined skills, accumulated knowledge, and greater experience make them authority figures to children. Whether the relationship involves parent and child, teacher and pupil, or coach and player, adults are supposed to function as leaders and experts, and children are expected to respond as followers and novices. Although these relationships can be marked by love and respect, they are basically unequal. That is, children must respond to adult initiatives (Youniss, 1980). These roles are clearly defined, and children have few chances to change them.

Peer interactions occupy an increasing amount of children's time and energy during childhood (Hartup, 1991). Peers are children of about the same age or maturity level and are to be distinguished from friends, a specially chosen group of playmates (Santrock, 1996). Friends offer unique opportunities for children to learn among equals. Hence, with friends, a child can be expert in one circumstance and learner in another. Each child has chances to lead, to follow, to contribute ideas, to respond to suggestions, to negotiate, and to compromise.

Because society has few formal guidelines for children's interactions with friends, they can take risks with one another they would not attempt with elders. They can more easily speak up, disagree, exert their will, ignore a request, or bargain for power. They can afford to experiment with different behaviors, to seek new friends if they are rejected, or to develop new interests (Rubin, 1980). Thus, it is with friends that children learn the give and take that will influence their future relationships as adults (Hartup, 1991; Hartup and Moore, 1990).

Such relations also help children understand and value their own traits, attitudes, and skills by providing natural comparisons with age-mates: Am I tall? Am I a good singer? Will people listen to my ideas? Are there things I can do that others cannot? Am I the only one who has trouble with spelling? Does anyone else feel scared in the dark? Through their observations and interactions with peers, chil-

dren check the validity of what they believe and feel about themselves (Asher, 1978).

Peer relationships provide an opportunity for children to learn new skills and refine current ones. Children know what is relevant to other children and so offer support and guidance in arenas overlooked or disdained by adults. The ability to spit between the teeth, jump double Dutch, balance on a skateboard, and clear the screen in Nintendo are examples of accomplishments children may value. Age-mates can teach these things to one another unself-consciously and without the total disparity in status that marks the adult-child relationship. Additionally, only other youngsters can truly appreciate the satisfaction and status that accomplishing such milestones represents.

Finally, it is in the peer group that children achieve a sense of belonging. They feel valued and important to people beyond their own family. Because friends offer support and affection by choice, they assure the child that he or she is a lovable, desirable companion.

For all of these reasons, children want and need friends. It is no surprise that much of their time and energy is devoted to answering the question "Who will be my friend?"

## What Happens When Children Cannot Find a Friend

Because all relationships have their ups and downs, children eventually experience the woe of rejection by someone they wish would be their friend. Even children's peers described as popular are rebuffed about 30 percent of the time (Gottman and Parkhurst, 1979). This is a natural and normal part of growing up (Damon, 1988). When rejection occurs, children's reactions vary greatly from matter-of-fact acceptance to real anguish: one child will become depressed; another will do anything he or she can to regain the lost friendship; a third will immediately begin looking for a replacement (Rubin, 1980). Regardless of the response, the impact of this loss on the child should not be underestimated. Upset feelings should not be dismissed lightly, nor should children be chastised or ridiculed when friendships do not work out. It is usual for most children to recover in a reasonable time and engage in other productive relationships.

There are some children, however, who are consistently rejected by their peers or who themselves reject all possible friendship choices. Researchers have separated these children into two distinct groups, neglected children and rejected children (Coie, 1993; Parker and Asher, 1987). Children who are neglected lack friends as a result of poor friendship-making skills, but are not actively avoided, as are rejected children. Rejected youngsters exhibit behaviors and characteristics other children find repulsive such as disruptive and aggressive behavior. Regardless of which is the case, this can be a problem for both the child and society because there is evidence that the quality of peer relationships in childhood has a major effect on adjustment in later life. Friendless children are unhappy children and have more than their share of difficulties as they grow older (Hartup and Moore, 1990; Kupersmidt, Coie, and Dodge, 1992; Kupersmidt and Patterson, 1993; Parker and Asher, 1987). For instance, they are more likely than their more popular counterparts to:

Become juvenile delinquents.
Drop out of school.
Receive a dishonorable discharge from the military.
Experience psychiatric problems.
Commit suicide.

No one knows for sure whether friendlessness causes these serious problems or whether the behavior traits that lead to delinquency and emotional instability also lead to peer rejection. In either case, there is a strong relationship between children's ability to form close friendships, later feelings of self-satisfaction, and the capacity to get along with others. In fact, one study found that one third of a group of children who were rejected in third grade maintained that status in the first year of middle school (Coie and Dodge, 1983).

Although completely friendless children are rare, many youngsters grow up wishing they had more friends. For instance, one national study showed that 18 percent of the third-, fourth-, fifth-, and sixth-graders interviewed reported having no friends or only one friend (Gronlund, 1959). More recently, when grade-school children were asked to name three children they would choose for a friend, 10 percent of the youngsters were chosen by no one. An even larger percentage reported feeling lonely.

For many children, the critical factor is not how many friends they have, but the quality of the peer relationships they establish (Stocking, Arezzo, and Leavitt, 1980). Some children want many friends, and others are happy with only a few. Clearly, all children think having friends is important, and many wish they had more satisfying relationships with others.

## ▼ CHILDREN'S CHANGING IDEAS ABOUT FRIENDSHIP

Three-year-old Ella:
    Why is Yihua your friend?
    *Because I like her.*
    Why do you like her?
    *Because she's my friend.*
    Why else do you like her?
    *Because she rides in my carpool.*

Six-year-old DeWayne:
    Why is Jared your friend?
    *Because he sits next to me and gives me candy.*
    Why else is he your friend?
    *Because he comes to my house and I go to his.*

Eight-year-old Chrystal:
    Why is Kayla your friend?
    *Because we both love to play horses.*
    Are there other reasons?
    *She helps me do arithmetic problems.*

Twelve-year-old Jaclyn:
    Why is Jennifer your friend?
    *Because I can tell her anything and she won't tell.*
    Why else is she your friend?
    *Because she'll always be my friend.*

What exactly is a friend in the eyes of a child? Do children see their friends in the same way adults view theirs? What many adults may not know is that children's concept of friendship—their notion of how it works, their expectations, and the rules that govern their actions toward friends—changes over time.

Harvard researchers Robert and Anne Selman (1980) theorize that all children pass through a sequence of five overlapping stages. Each stage is characterized by its own distinct logic, which becomes increasingly complex as children mature.

In the beginning stages, children are preoccupied with their *own* emotions, with the physical characteristics of their companions, and with what is happening here and now. In the later stages, children are more sensitive to the desires and concerns of others, they appreciate psychological traits such as humor and trustworthiness, and they think about the future of their relationships as well as the present. Children progress from the first stage to the last as a result of age; increasing intellectual, physical, and language abilities; and accumulated experience.

Many children have temporary difficulties when their ideas about friendship lag behind or move far beyond those of their peers. These problems are reduced once children and their age-mates catch up to one another. In the meantime, children may choose to associate with younger or older peers who are in the same stage of thinking. Adults cannot necessarily accelerate children's progress through the sequence, but they can attempt to understand children's behavior by knowing more about their philosophy of friendship at each stage.

## Stage Zero: Momentary Playmates (Three to Seven Years of Age)

Young children call "friend" those peers with whom they play most often or who engage in similar, activities at a given time. In this way, children define their friends by proximity ("He's my friend; he lives next door"). In addition, friends are valued for their possessions ("She's my friend. She has a Barbie doll") or because they demonstrate visible physical skills ("He's my friend because he runs fast").

Because children of this age are egocentric, they think only about their own side of the relationship. Consequently, they focus on what they want the other child to do for them. They have no thought of their own duties to the relationship and so do not consider how to match their behaviors to the other child's needs. Moreover, it is common for youngsters to assume that friends think just the way they do. If this proves false, they become very upset.

Stage zero youngsters are better at initiating an interaction than they are at responding to others' overtures. Hence, they may inadvertently ignore or actively reject other children's attempts to join their play. This can happen even when the nay-sayer has expressed interest in finding a friend. We have observed that this phenomenon happens most often once the play has been established. By that time, a solitary player or group of children has centered on carrying out the play episode in a particular way, which includes only those currently involved. It then becomes difficult for them to expand their thinking to envision how the newcomer could be included. Their refusal to allow another child access to their play is a cognitive dilemma, not a deliberate act of cruelty.

## Stage One: One-Way Assistance (Four to Nine Years of Age)

In stage one, children identify those age-mates as friends whose behavior pleases them. For some children, good feelings are engendered by a play-mate who will give them a turn, share gum, offer them rides on the new two-wheeler, pick them for the team, or save them a seat on the bus. For others, pleasure comes from having another child accept the turn, the gum, the ride, inclusion on the team, or the seat. Because each friend is concerned about whether his or her wants are being satisfied, neither necessarily considers what to do to bring pleasure to the other. If by chance, their individual wants and behaviors are compatible, the friendship lasts. If not, the partners change in short order.

Another characteristic of stage one is that children try out different social roles: leader, follower, negotiator, instigator, comic, collaborater, appeaser, comforter. As part of this process, they experiment with a variety of behaviors that may or may not match their usual manner. Thus, it is normal for children who are practicing their roles to manifest extreme examples of them. That is, a child who wants to be more assertive may become bossy and overbearing; a child who discovers the benefits of comedy may become silly or outrageous.

By the time youngsters reach this stage, their desire to have a friend is so strong that many prefer to play with an uncongenial companion rather than play alone. They will try almost anything to initiate a relationship and may attempt to bribe or coerce another child to like them by saying: "If you'll be my friend, I'll invite you to my party," or "If you don't let me have a turn, I won't be your friend." Children who resort to such tactics are not malicious, but are merely experimenting with what works and what does not.

Stage one also is notable for the fact that boys play with boys and girls play with girls. This occurs because children continue to focus on outward similarities, and gender is an obvious way of determining likeness.

Although youngsters concentrate much of their energy on the friendship process, they have difficulty maintaining more than one close relationship at a time. An outgrowth of their struggle to identify friends is that they become preoccupied with discussing who is their friend and who is not. This is when children can be overheard to say, "You can't be my friend: Mary's my friend." Pairs often change from day to day and frequently are determined by who gets together first, by what people are wearing or by a newfound common interest. However, some friendship pairs remain relatively stable over time, as long as the two children see each other frequently (Park and Waters, 1989). There is also evidence that some friendships begun in the preschool may last throughout kindergarten and even beyond and that these stable friendships predict future success for both children in their peer relationships (Howes, 1988; Ladd, 1990).

## Stage Two: Two-Way, Fair-Weather Cooperation (Six to Twelve Years of Age)

The thinking of children at stage two has matured to the point at which they are able to consider both points of view in the friendship. This leads to a notion of justice that dictates how the relationship should proceed.

Children expect friends to be "nice" to each other and often trade favors as a way of helping each other satisfy their separate interests: "You helped me yesterday; I'll help you today"; "We're playing my game first and then your game." They recognize that each person should benefit from the relationship and that the friendship will break up if this does not occur: "If you call me names again, I won't be your friend"; "That's not fair! I waited for you yesterday." Friends are concerned about what each thinks of the other and evaluate their own actions as they feel the other might evaluate them: "Steve will like me if I learn to catch better"; "Nobody will like me with this fuzzy permanent."

It is in this stage that conformity in dress, language, and behavior reaches a peak as children try to find ways to fit in with the group. As a result, it becomes very important for children to carry a lunch box decorated with the latest movie cartoon character, wear their hair in special ways, or take swimming lessons. Why? Because "all the other kids have one (or do it)." As can be seen from these examples, the emphasis throughout this period is similarity. Forming clubs is a natural outgrowth of this. Clubs, although short lived, have elaborate rules, and the major activity involves planning who will be included and who will be excluded. To further confirm their unity, friends share secrets, plans, and agreements.

Friendships tend to develop in pairs. In particular, groups of girlfriends are loose networks of best-friend partnerships; male friendship groups are characterized by broader interaction patterns and fewer best-friend relationships (Hartup, 1991). Within both male and female groups, friends are very possessive of each other, and jealousy over who is "friends" with whom is quite pronounced.

## Stage Three: Intimate, Mutually Shared Relationships (Nine to Twelve Years of Age)

Stage three marks the first time that children view friendship as an ongoing relationship with shared goals. Now, children are collaborative rather than simply cooperative. This means they are not concerned with the tit-for-tat reciprocity that marked the previous stage; rather, they become involved in each other's personal lives and have a stake in each other's happiness. They gain satisfaction from the emotional support they enjoy within the relationship. On this basis, friends share feelings and help each other solve personal conflicts and problems. They reveal thoughts and emotions to each other that they keep from everyone else. Friendship has now become intimate and the best-friend relationship a crucial one. Because this is such an intense learning experience, children often only focus on one best friend at a time. It is natural for them to become totally absorbed in each other. Such friendships are both exclusive and possessive. In other words, friends are not supposed to have another close friend, and they are expected to include each other in everything. Friends do share approved acquaintances but are not allowed to pursue a relationship with someone one of them does not like. The greatest betrayal comes when someone breaks these rules. Only after children have developed friendship to this point are they able to branch out and have close ties with more than one peer at a time.

## Stage Four: Mature Friendships (Twelve Years of Age and Older)

For persons at the mature-friendship stage, emotional and psychological benefits are the most valued qualities of friendship. Friends are not as possessive of each other as they were in previous stages; they can have some dissimilar interests and can pursue activities separately. Children in this stage are able to allow their friends to develop other close relationships as well. Thus, they can have more than one friend at a time and can have friends who are not friends with each other. In this way, friendship becomes a bond that involves trust and support. These elements sometimes are attained by coming together and sometimes by letting go. As a result, friends now are able to remain close over long distances, over long periods of time, and in spite of long separations.

## Choosing Friends

*Eric and Sandy are like peas in a pod; they dress alike; they talk alike; they act alike. They are the best of friends.*

*Sasha and Tabitha are as different as night and day. One is short, one is tall; one is boisterous, one is* quiet; one likes cats, one likes dogs. Still, they are inseparable.

---

Adults often wonder why children choose the friends they do. Name, physical appearance, race, gender, age, ability, and attitudes all are cues children consider in selecting a potential friend (Hartup, 1991). For instance, names go through cycles of popularity. Children who have names other youngsters like often are viewed as the most desirable playmates, and those who possess unpopular names are not as sought after (McDavid and Harari, 1966). The popularity of a particular name varies according to culture and geographic region. It should not be too surprising that the names children prefer are those that occur most frequently in the population (Lansky, 1984). One possible explanation is that such names are familiar ones, and children may feel more comfortable approaching a child whose name is not entirely new to them. Although it is not preordained that children with unusual names will be friendless, they may have to work harder at making advances to their peers rather than waiting to be approached first.

**Physical appearance and likeness.** Another factor that contributes to children's friendship selection is personal appearance. Children who are overweight, mentally impaired, disabled, slovenly, or physically unattractive are less likely to be chosen as friends than are youngsters who fit children's concept of beauty (Hartup, 1991; Langlois, 1985). Interestingly, the same standard of beauty is held by children of all ages and cultures and fits many of the stereotypes promoted through the popular media (Cross and Cross, 1971). Long hair, fine features, and wide eyes set far apart are some of the attributes many children find appealing. Children attribute the positive qualities of friendliness, intelligence, and social competence to those they consider attractive. Likewise, they associate negative attributes with peers they think of as unattractive (Dion and Berscheid, 1974; Lerner and Lerner, 1977).

Children also pick their friends based on race and are most likely to choose friends from their own racial group (Shaw, 1973). However, parental attitudes do influence how children feel about making friends with someone of another race or culture. If children perceive their parents as accepting of racial differences, they are more likely to include children of different racial or ethnic backgrounds among their friends.

Gender and age also are dominant considerations in who is "friends" with whom. Children prefer same-sex, same-age playmates throughout childhood and even at a very early age tend to exclude opposite sex and non–age-mates from their play (Hartup, 1982; Singleton, 1974). Although friendships between males and females do occur, same-sex friendships tend to be more lasting and stable over time. This is due in no small measure to the reinforcement children receive from adults and peers for choosing friends of their own gender (Fagot, 1977; Serbin, Tonick, and Sternglanz, 1977). When friendships develop between children of different ages, it usually is because the participants are developmentally similar in some ways. For instance, shy children who have less confidence in their interaction skills may seek out younger friends with whom they feel more comfortable socially (Zimbardo and Radl, 1982).

Friends also may resemble one another in terms of achievement, physical or cognitive skill, and degree of sociability (Bukowski, Sippola, and Boivin, 1995). Consequently, it is not unusual to see children choose as friends peers who share their love of sports, reading, chess, or stamp collecting. Nor is it uncommon for bright, agile, impulsive, or outgoing children to seek friends much like themselves. In addition to searching for likenesses, youngsters often choose as friends those peers whose characteristics complement their own personality and capacities (Rubin, 1980). This often involves attributes that they themselves lack and for which the other child can serve as a model. Thus, loud children and quiet children, active children and passive children, serious children and cut-ups may choose one another as friends. Yet, even when this occurs, one must remember that these youngsters have found enough common ground that they see more similarities than differences in each other.

Concurrently, when children who are dissimilar in some fashion discover that they share like attitudes, they feel more positive about one another. This awareness facilitates friendly relations between children who initially perceive themselves as totally different. Such knowledge has been found to promote increased friendships among children of differing races and between nondisabled and disabled youngsters (Bukowski, Sippola, and Boivin, 1995; Byrne and Griffit, 1966; Insko and Robinson, 1967).

Children look for obvious external clues to determine whom they will choose for a friend. This means that adults will see children select friends who are most like them: boys will pick boys; girls will pick girls; Euro-American children will stay together and so will many Asian-American children. This explains the cliquishness that develops in groups. Adults who want children to experience the rewards of friendships with children of the opposite sex, of another race, or whose abilities do not match their own must provide opportunities for the children to recognize more subtle similarities. Specific strategies for achieving this aim are presented in the skills section of this chapter.

**Problematic friendships.** Adults sometimes express concern about children's friendship choices when they observe what seems to be an unequal relationship between two youngsters. For instance, five-year-olds Lily and Carmen play together every day. Carmen appears to dominate. She chooses where they will play, what they will play with, and who else is allowed to play with them. Carmen is often perceived as bossy and Lily is viewed as helpless and compliant. From the children's point of view, however, the situation appears to be quite different. Lily may choose to play with Carmen because Carmen has lots of ideas and takes responsibility for directing the play. Lily is happy because she can play without having to think about what to do next. Carmen also is satisfied because there is no question as to who is in charge. Over time, as Lily has a chance to observe how Carmen asserts her will, she, too, may venture to test her own assertiveness. In the meantime, Carmen may grow tired of such a passive playmate. If the girls do not respond to each other's changing needs, chances are that each will select a new companion. While they are in the process of working out their relationship, adults can help each child express her changing desires to the other, as well as aiding them in exploring new potential friendships. Usually, it should be left up to the children, not the adults, to judge the best time to change the nature of their association or to move on.

Another issue of concern to adults is what is sometimes referred to as "peer pressure." This influence occurs most frequently by middle and later childhood. During those years, children's expanding social horizons cause them to be aware of the opinions of friends and other youngsters in their peer group to an even greater degree than was true of early childhood. In addition, children spend more of their free time in less closely supervised play situations, such as the school playground or their home neighborhood. Children are also developing a more mature notion of friendship and these relationships tend to be more consistent and long-lasting than previously. Peer conformity becomes an increasingly important manner of behavior as children strive for peer acceptance (Berndt, 1979). Thus, children in groups are likely to yield to the norms that the group has established. When this occurs, adults fear that those group norms may run counter to the standards they have for children's behavior. Professionals who work with children at this phase of development must recognize that they cannot eliminate peer pressure. However, they can influence the values that children bring to their social interactions with age-mates, as well as helping children sort out their beliefs with respect to particular behaviors, such as honesty. Furthermore, adults can be valuable resources in offering support and suggesting alternative responses that children can use when confronted by pressures from peers that are incompatible with those beliefs. In addition, helping professionals can help groups of children to establish and maintain a positive group image. Finally, it is important to note that while the peer group has a greater effect on children's behavior in middle childhood than in early childhood, parents and teachers continue to be powerful and important socializing influences as well (Santrock, 1996).

## ▼ MAKING FRIENDS

There is a body of research that supports the premise that children's own behavior greatly influences how they are accepted by peers (Ladd and Coleman, 1993). Their interaction patterns, for the most part, are a primary factor in determining whether they will be perceived by others as desirable or undesirable as companions. Positive actions generally beget positive reactions; whereas negative behaviors, such as aggressiveness, induce negative responses from others. Therefore, while the complexity of making friends begins with an initial attraction, based on such external attributes as name, physical appearance, race, gender, and age, once this has begun, the child must successfully navigate the following pathways to friendship: making contact, maintaining positive relationships, and negotiating conflicts.

### Making Contact

Before a friendship can "get off the ground," one person must make an approach and another must respond. How this contact is carried out influences each child's perception of the other. Children make good impressions when they engage in the following actions (Coie, Dodge, and Kupersmidt, 1990; Shapiro, 1997; Stocking, Arezzo, and Leavitt, 1980):

| | |
|---|---|
| Smile and speak pleasantly or offer greetings. | "Hi" or "Hey! What's up?" |
| Ask for information. | "What's your name?" or "Where's the cafeteria?" |
| Respond to others' greetings and inquiries. | "I'm new, too" or "Come with me. I'll show you." |
| Offer information. | "My name's Rosalie. This is my first day at Central." |
| Invite participation. | "Wanna play catch?" or "You can be on our team." |

By these signals, children are able to let others know that they want to be friends. Another behavior widely interpreted as a friendly overture is imitation. Children enjoy being imitated and are apt to be friendly toward peers who copy their actions (Guralnick, 1976; Hartup, 1978; Widerstrom, 1982). Thus, children can slowly move into a game or activity by matching their behavior to that of the other players.

From this discussion, it can be seen that youngsters who are cordial elicit positive reactions and are better accepted by their age-mates (Goleman, 1995; Hazen and Black, 1989). This is true whether the child is the initiator or the respondent. Yet, although the logic of acting pleasantly in order to gain friends may seem obvious and the related strategies self-evident, many youngsters fail to make the connection. These are children whose timing is off or who have the right idea but an inappropriate way of showing it. They may be truly unaware of the importance of such strategies or may fail to recognize how or why their behavior affects others as it does. Whatever the explanation, such children often attempt to make contact by grabbing, pushing, barging in, whining, threatening, ignoring, begging, criticizing, or being bossy (Shapiro, 1997; Stocking, Arezzo, and Leavitt, 1980). Children who rely on these approaches are rejected frequently. As their lack of success becomes more habitual, they tend to withdraw or become hostile. Both reactions exacerbate their difficulties (Asher and Renshaw, 1981). Over time, they develop a reputation of being unfriendly or undesirable as a playmate. As a result, not only are their own attempts at contact rebuffed, but the other children stop initiating contacts with them as well. This causes the offensive youngsters to be further isolated and have fewer opportunities for positive interactions. Hence, it becomes increasingly difficult for such children to break out of this maladaptive pattern of behavior on their own. In cases such as these, adults can help children learn to make more positive contacts and hence improve their chances of finding a friend.

## Maintaining Positive Relationships

The positive behaviors that characterize successful beginnings continue to be important as the relationship grows. Popular children of all ages are described by peers as sensitive, kind, flexible, and fun to be with (Hartup, 1970; Roff, Sells, and Golden, 1972; Shapiro, 1997). In particular, how well youngsters communicate influences their likeableness. So, children who speak directly, are attentive to everyone involved in specific situations, respond interestedly to and acknowledge the play signals of others, and who offer many alternatives are sought after as playmates (Hazen and Black, 1989). The following techniques characterize their interactions with others:

| | |
|---|---|
| Expressing interest | Smiles, nods, establishes eye contact, asks related questions. |
| Cooperating | Takes turns, agrees to share something, agrees to work together. |
| Expressing acceptance | Listens to another child's ideas, adopts another child's approach to a play situation. |
| Expressing affection | Hugs, holds hands, or says: "I like you" or "Let's be friends." |
| Expressing empathy | "That's a neat picture you made," "You look sad; want me to sit with you while you wait?" |
| Offering help and suggestions | "Maybe we could try it this way." "I'll hold the box while you tie it." |
| Praising playmates | "That was a great hit." "Neat idea! I think it'll work." "You're pretty." |

Children who use these tactics actively demonstrate respect and affection for others. This has the happy outcome of making them desirable companions because people seek out friends who are enjoyable (Stocking, Arezzo, and Leavitt, 1980). Thus, it is true that positive behaviors elicit positive responses, which in turn reinforce children's efforts and prompt them to continue their successful actions.

In the same way that positive cycles are established, so, too, are negative ones. Children who are aggressive or uncooperative or who act silly, show off, or display immature behavior irritate, frustrate, and offend their peers. They tend to further isolate themselves by daydreaming or escalating their negative behavior (Asher and Renshaw, 1981; Gottman, Gonso, and Rasmussen, 1975).

Similar problems arise when children try to act appropriately but misjudge how to do it. They may rely on insincere flattery, express their affection too roughly (giving bear hugs), or communicate their appreciation too effusively. Others miss the mark by constantly correcting rather than suggesting or taking over instead of merely helping. In any case, these behavior patterns sabotage children's efforts to maintain friendships over time.

## Negotiating Conflict

Perhaps the most severe test of a relationship occurs when the friends disagree. How the conflict is managed on both sides determines to a large extent whether the friendship will continue or be abandoned. Children who use constructive ways of resolving differences, while still meeting their own needs, are most successful in pursuing lasting relationships (Goleman, 1995). This is because they are able to preserve their dignity and at the same time take into account another person's perspectives. Children who are so passive that they never stand up for themselves lose self-respect and, eventually, the respect of peers. Those who respond aggressively also are rejected. Neither extreme is conducive to eliciting positive reactions.

There is a strong correlation between children's effective use of **negotiation skills** and their ability to communicate accurately (Holden, 1997). Successful conflict negotiation depends on all parties having a common idea of the source of the problem and being able to express to others their ideas for a solution. Children who use threats, shame, or coercion to force a solution violate these fundamental requirements. Consequently, other children begin to avoid them or retaliate in kind. Successful negotiators are children who implement the following strategies (Stocking, Arezzo, and Leavitt, 1980):

| | |
|---|---|
| Express personal rights, needs, or feelings. | "I want a chance to pick the movie this time." |
| Listen to and acknowledge others' rights and feelings. | "Yeah, you *have* been waiting a long time to see that movie." |
| Suggest nonviolent solutions to conflicts. | "Let's flip for it." |
| Explain the reasoning behind a proposed solution. | "This way, we each get a chance." |
| Stand up against unreasonable demands. | "No, you got to pick the last time. Now, it's my turn." |
| Accept reasonable disagreement. | "Okay, I hadn't thought of that." |
| Compromise on solutions. | "Let's see both, or go swimming instead." |

## Improving Children's Friendship-Making Skills

Because the distinction is so clear between successful friendship-making strategies and those that are not, you may wonder why any child would choose techniques doomed to fail. Children are not born automatically knowing the best ways to make friends. They must learn by observing others, by practicing, by experimenting with a variety of social behaviors, and by experiencing the consequences of their actions (Dodge, 1983). Children who are better observers and more accurate evaluators of what is effective and what is not acquire friends more easily than those who make poor observations and assessments or those who have poor role models at home or among peers. This does not mean the children who experience difficulty have no chance for improvement. On the contrary, there is encouraging evidence that children can learn how to make productive contacts, maintain positive relationships, and manage conflicts constructively (Asher and Renshaw, 1981; Holden, 1997; Kostelnik and Stein, 1986). Several recent studies point to the improved **friendship-making skills** of some neglected and even rejected children who underwent a specific course of study designed to increase their awareness, teach them particular behaviors, and to decrease their aggressive responses (Coie and Koeppl, 1990; Murphy and Schneider, 1994).

The behaviors designated as successful for each phase of the friendship-making process are, in fact, skills that children can learn and then adopt for their own use. Three methods adults can use to teach children these skills are to model them for children via friendship skits, to assist youngsters in role-playing friendship skills themselves, and to train children to use friendship skills by way of friendship coaching.

**Friendship skits.** Research has shown that children improve in their ability to assimilate friendship skills when they have a chance to watch enactments of them while a narrator points out instances of their use (Evers and Schwarz, 1973; O'Connor, 1972). Such skits frequently are presented to children using puppets, dolls, or small figures. A majority of the studies conducted thus far have involved filmed demonstrations; however, these are not easily available to most practitioners. Fortunately, research has shown that live demonstrations with props are a good substitute (Kostelnik and Stein, 1986).

**Role-playing friendship skills.** A variation on skits with props is to have children role-play each character's part and then report their feelings and reactions to each role (Cummings and Haggerty, 1997; Spivack and Shure, 1974). Onlookers and participants then discuss what transpired and sug-

gest alternate courses of action. Through role-playing, children try out various roles and experience the consequences associated with them in a risk-free, "pretend" situation. They also obtain concrete examples of social behavior that are easier to recognize than those offered through discussion alone.

**Friendship coaching.** For some children, the methods just described are not enough to help them assimilate the social skills that lead to peer acceptance. These are youngsters who, over time, demonstrate an inability to pick up and act on cues they receive from age-mates. In some cases, they are totally unaware of how to endear themselves to peers. In other circumstances, they can describe relevant social behaviors but do not demonstrate them in their own interactions. Such children have shown to benefit from direct, individual instruction or **coaching** (Feshbach, 1978; Holden, 1997; Sharp, 1988). A variety of coaching methods have been developed. All include the same basic steps: discussion, demonstration, practice, and evaluation.

---

## SKILLS FOR SUPPORTING CHILDREN'S FRIENDSHIPS

 **Encourage and Facilitate Friendships**

Children vary in the degree to which they will find adult support necessary and beneficial. However, all children profit when adults create an environment in which their friendships are respected and encouraged. The following guidelines will help you create such an environment for the children with whom you work.

*1.* **Provide opportunities for children to be with their friends informally—to talk, to play, and to enjoy one another's company.** In group settings, develop a daily routine that includes planned times when children can respond to one another freely. Don't fill every minute with adult-oriented tasks and enforced silence. Also, these planned times should not consist solely of transitions between activities or structured talking times like "circle time" or "show and tell." Unstructured time spent with peers is neither wasted nor uneducational. Rather, it provides rich opportunities for children to practice social skills and to learn more about themselves.

*2.* **Plan ways to pair children in order to facilitate interactions.** Pairing children gives them a chance to practice their friendship-making skills in a relatively risk-free situation. Assign children to do jobs together or have them carry out a joint project as a way to create common interests. Children feel closer when they see themselves working toward a collaborative goal. Finally, encourage parents to carpool or to invite age-mates home for a visit as another way to provide contact and opportunities for discovery of common interests. When you first team two children, point out some similarities you have observed or give them an opportunity to discover some for themselves. This is particularly true when pairing children who outwardly seem much different. Remember that it is the perceived similarities that cement a friendship.

*3.* **Pair a shy child with a younger playmate who is less sophisticated socially.** Begin by pairing him or her with a younger child of the same gender. Gradually, include age-mates of the same and opposite sex. This arrangement

## SKILLS FOR SUPPORTING CHILDREN'S FRIENDSHIPS—continued

enables the shy child to practice social skills with a nonthreatening, often openly approving younger admirer (Zimbardo and Radl, 1982).

**4. Take children's friendships seriously.** Listen when children talk about their friends. Reflect their involvement and concerns. Ask questions to show your interest. Never minimize the importance of children's friendships by ignoring, dismissing, teasing, shaming, or denying children's emotions.

**5. Carry out group discussions that focus on children's self-discovered similarities.** First, set the scene by having children discuss their reaction to an adult-posed condition, for instance, "Things I like best." Then, invite each child to answer a question such as "Paul and I both like . . . or "I like the Mets and so does . . . " This tactic helps children recognize peers with whom they share similar attitudes, interests, and concerns.

**6. Help children learn each other's names.** Because names are a basic form of recognition, children feel most comfortable making contact with peers whose names they know. Less common names can become familiar if you refer to each child by name. Make sure you know how to pronounce every child's name correctly and that you do not avoid using names that are unfamiliar or unattractive to you. Use children's names when you praise them as a way to create a positive image of each child to the group.

**7. Give children on-the-spot information to help them recognize the friendly overtures of others.** Children often overlook or misinterpret the friendly advances of other youngsters because they are so involved in what they are doing that they are unable to recognize the positive nature of the approach. Instead, they may interpret the newcomer as a potential competitor for space or materials and thus feel threatened rather than pleased. Be alert for such occurrences. Step in if you see a child rebuff another without giving a reason. Paraphrase the newcomer's positive aim. Then, let the child decide for himself or herself whether the contact is welcome. Do not force a youngster to accept the

attentions of another if the idea continues to be repugnant.

Frequently, however, children will be more receptive to another's overtures once the friendly intentions are made clear. For example, Matt was an active four-year-old who longed for a friend. He frequently talked with teachers about who his friends might be. Yet, his actions often contradicted his words. One day, he had the entire block area to himself. He worked for a long time building a bus. As he was busily "driving to Chicago," Courtney arrived on the scene and asked if she could go, too (the perfect opportunity for a friendly contact!). Matt scowled and said, "No." Courtney repeated her request and was again rebuffed. This time she said: "Well, I'll just stand here on the corner until someone gets off. Then, I'll get on." Matt looked confused. At this point, an adult approached and said: "Matt, you're having fun driving to Chicago. Courtney is telling you she would like to play. She wants to be a passenger on your bus. That way, she can be your friend." Matt looked pleased and relieved. He had not recognized the cues Courtney was using to signify her interest in his game. Information provided by the adult put a whole new light on the situation, and the two children played "bus" for most of the morning.

**8. Help children recognize how their behavior affects their ability to make friends.** Frequently, children are unaware of the link between what they do and how other people react. Offer information to make this association more clear. For instance, Steven pushed Daisy to get her attention. She stalked off. He became angry when she rejected him. The adult noted his surprise, took him aside, and said: "It seems as if you want to be friends with Daisy. Pushing hurts. When you push her, it makes her so angry that she doesn't want to play with you. Friends don't hurt each other. Next time, you could say her name and tell her what you want." The adult gave Steven important information that he had not picked up very well on his own. This information would have to be repeated several times and in several different circumstances before Steven could really follow the advice. If the negative pattern persisted, Steven would be a likely candidate for

*continued*

## SKILLS FOR SUPPORTING CHILDREN'S FRIENDSHIPS—continued

the coaching strategies discussed later in this chapter.

Information need to be confined to corrections. Tell children about the positive skills they exhibit so they can repeat them another time. For instance, if you notice children sharing, taking turns, smiling at each other, or coming to a compromise, point out the positive effects these actions have on their relations with one another: "You two figured out a way that you could both wash the blackboards. That was a friendly way to settle your disagreement."

**9. Get children involved at the beginning of a play episode so they will not be viewed as interlopers.** Children who hang back before attempting to join a group often are penalized because once the group has been established, it is difficult for its members to imagine any other configuration. If you notice that certain children are hesitant to become involved and subsequently are shut out, try one of the following approaches.

First, plan ahead with the child and help her or him identify an activity to choose as soon as play groups begin to form. In this way, the child will not have to cross any social barriers but instead will be an initial participant. If this is too difficult for the child, an alternative is to help her or him move into the group with you. To do this, you might choose a potential role and approach the activity within the role. For instance, if several children are pretending to fly to the moon, you could walk toward them, saying: "Carol and I will be Mission Control. We'll talk to you up in the spacecraft." As Carol becomes more comfortable and the group more accepting, gradually back out of the play. Do not be surprised if at first Carol walks out when you do. With your continued support, she eventually will feel more relaxed and be able to maintain her membership in the group on her own.

A second tactic is to advise a hesitant child to play near the desired group and at the same type of activity. Gradually, the group may allow that child to join them and become their friend. An alternative to this approach is to help the child build a new group by inviting other children to draw, build, compute, or cook with her or him.

**10. Help children endure the sorrows of friendship.** When a potential friend rejects them, an old friend snubs them, or a good friend moves away, children have a real sense of loss. Their feelings range from misery to frustration to fury—all of which are normal reactions. As an adult, you cannot assuage the child's feelings, no matter how much you would like him or her to be spared. You can accept the child's emotions, reflect them, and talk about them, if the child so desires. You also can offer your condolences: "I'm sorry you and Tricia weren't able to patch up your differences. It's really sad to lose a friend." Another important way to provide support is to not push children into new relationships before they are ready.

The strategies just described are simple ones that build on skills you have learned in previous chapters: reflecting, giving information, and supporting children's play. The conflict-negotiation skills you have recently learned also facilitate friendly relations among children. These approaches are relatively informal and are easily integrated into day-to-day interactions. Later, we will explore two additional techniques that are more formal and require advanced planning: presenting friendship activities to children and friendship coaching.

**11. Assist children in developing conversation skills.** Children who are successful at making friends are likely to use conversation or information exchange in their interactions with others (Ladd and Coleman, 1993). Two- to six-year-old children are just learning how to talk comfortably with one another. To hold a successful conversation and keep it going, children must identify a topic of mutual interest, stay on the same subject, and share information (Sharp, 1988). It helps if they look at each other and take turns talking. The more children practice this skill, the better they get. Your role in this process is to act as a link between children, providing support so they can participate in the dialogue. Do this by referring children's questions and comments to one another. For example, if Jeremy approaches the block area where other children are working and says to you, "Can I build?," refer his question to one of the builders. "Jeremy, you want to build. Tell Russell." Pro-

## SKILLS FOR SUPPORTING CHILDREN'S FRIENDSHIPS—continued

vide a script if necessary. "Say, 'I'm ready to help you.'" If Russell fails to respond, offer information to one child or the other to help the interaction along. "Jeremy, Russell didn't hear you. Get closer to him and tell him again." Or "Russell, Jeremy is trying to tell you something. Stop, look at him, listen to his words." If children become engaged in a conversation, avoid interrupting, but stay nearby to help as needed. Intervene when the conversation falters. If, for example, children lose track of the topic and no longer seem to be connecting, help them refocus. "Jeremy and Russell, you were talking about how to get the arch to balance. Russell, tell Jeremy what you discovered."

Sometimes, children who are not yet conversant benefit from having their rudimentary language interpreted by the teacher to the other children. Thus, when Melissa asks Jane, "Do you want orange juice?" and Jane responds, "Ju." Melissa may not understand. Pause to see if she has or not. If Melissa seems confused, paraphrase Jane's words, "She said, 'juice.'" On the other hand, if Melissa addresses a question to Jane, "How about some juice?" and Jane does not answer, again, act as an interpreter. "Jane, did you hear Melissa's words? Look at her and she'll ask you again." Once children begin talking to one another, bow out of the conversation, lest you become the focus of their attention.

Older children, ages six to twelve, may need guidance in initiating a conversation topic or in attending while another child is speaking. To help a reticent child, suggest that he or she comment on the object or event with which a potential playmate is engaged. The comment may be an observation or question. Well informed, talkative children may need help attending to what another child wants to say. Coach such children to listen attentively with comments such as, "Try to remember the details of what Hessa is saying" or, "Watch Lydia's face and hands while she is talking so you can tell how she's feeling." Later, ask the child whether he or she was able to implement these strategies successfully. Discuss together other strategies that might fit similar situations in the future.

**12. Carry out group discussions that highlight friendship-related terms, facts, and principles.**

Refer to Table 8–1 for examples of friendship terms, facts, and principles appropriate for children aged two through twelve. Introduce one or two items at a time for children to explore. You may stimulate their thinking by reading a book, telling a story, or showing them pictures that relate to the ideas you have chosen. Prompt discussion through the use of open-ended questions such as "How does it feel when a good friend moves away?", "What can you do when a friend hurts your feelings?", or "How can you let someone know you want to be friends?" Listen carefully. Reflect children's answers. Offer relevant information as openings in the conversation occur. Do not be concerned with obtaining a "correct" answer or reaching consensus. Instead, focus on allowing children to explore each idea in their own way. Provide every youngster with an opportunity to contribute, but avoid pressuring children into talking if they prefer not to. Summarize key points of the discussion, either aloud or on paper, for the children to refer to later.

**13. Help neglected or rejected children develop satisfying relationships.** Observe children carefully to determine whether they are neglected or rejected children. If you decide a child is neglected, concentrate on helping the other youngsters discover that individual, using the strategies outlined in the chapter. When dealing with a rejected child, focus first on direct intervention with that child, using the on-the-spot coaching techniques outlined later.

 **Design Skits that Demonstrate Friendship Skills**

Children as young as two and a half years of age have shown interest in watching short dramatizations. Children of that age benefit most when professionals simply act out a scene and then explain it. Older preschoolers and grade-school children benefit from additional group discussion as well.

**1. Choose a friendship skill to teach.** It usually is best to focus on only one skill at a time. This way, children can more easily identify the exact behavior being demonstrated.

*continued*

▼ **Table 8–1    A Partial Listing of Friendship Terms, Facts, and Principles**

**Friends Defined**

1. Friends are people who like you and whom you like.
2. Some friends are members of your family; some are outside your family.
3. Friends may be like you in many ways and different from you in others.
4. Friends often spend time together doing the same or similar things.
5. Friends share ideas, play, work, and share secrets and feelings with each other.
6. People experience a variety of feelings about each other, some positive and some negative.
7. Sometimes friends hurt each other's feelings.
8. Sometimes friends can forgive each other, and sometimes they cannot.
9. Sometimes friendships end.
10. Having a friend:
    a. Makes people feel good.
    b. Gives people someone with whom to share ideas, play, and work.
    c. Gives people someone with whom to share secrets.
    d. Gives people someone with whom to share feelings.
11. It can be sad or confusing when someone no longer wants to be your friend.
12. People can make new friends.

**Making and Keeping Friends**

13. People's behavior affects their ability to make and keep friends.
14. People use their bodies to express friendly emotions such as smiling, playing near someone, and looking at them when they speak.
15. People use words to express friendly emotions, such as conversing, listening to their ideas, inviting them to play, and exchanging thoughts and feelings.
16. People feel friendly toward those who act positively toward them.

## SKILLS FOR SUPPORTING CHILDREN'S FRIENDSHIPS—continued

**2. Choose the medium through which the skill will be demonstrated.** Dolls, pictures, and puppets all are good choices. Children learn best from concrete example that include props they can point to, handle, and discuss.

**3. Outline a script that, consists of five parts.** The script should include:

a. Demonstration of the skill
b. Demonstration of lack of the skill
c. An explanation by the adult
d. Discussion by the children
e. An opportunity for children to use the props to make up their own version of the skit. The best skits are only a few lines long.

**4. Write out the statements and questions you will use to stimulate discussion in the group.** Discussion will revolve around which character was demonstrating the skill and which was not, how viewers arrived at their conclusions, and what skill they would suggest the characters use the next time.

**5. Rehearse the skit in advance.** Gather your props. Practice the skit, privately or with friends. Revise the skit until you can do it from memory and feel comfortable about carrying it out.

**6. Present your skit to children either in a group situation or in a one-to-one interaction.** Speak clearly and with expression. Elicit group discussion. Listen carefully and accept children's answers nonjudgmentally. If children are way off track, give them information that will clarify the situation and make a mental note to revise your skit to make the point more clear next time. Praise children as they watch and again as they discuss what they have seen.

**7. Later in the day, evaluate how well your skit got your point across.** If it seemed that children

## SKILLS FOR SUPPORTING CHILDREN'S FRIENDSHIPS—continued

were interested and were able to generate relevant conversation about the selected topic, plan to repeat the same skit using different props and dialogues the next time. Over time, gradually introduce new information for youngsters to consider. If children were uninterested, determine whether they were distracted by things in the environment or whether your activity was unappealing. Observe children carefully or ask their opinions as a way to find out. Children will not be attentive if the skit is too advanced or too babyish, if you fumble or seem tense, or if you press too hard for one "right" answer.

A sample of a type of skit that can be effective with young children is outlined in Table 8–2. It illustrates a scenario designed to teach friendship-initiation skills. Such vignettes could be adapted to illustrate any of the friendship skills discussed in this chapter.

**8. Encourage older children to make up skits of their own that dramatize a problem with friends.** Sometimes, children between ten and twelve years of age will be willing to enact their skits for peers or for younger children. The same procedures just discussed apply, regardless of the age of the skit planner.

 Teach Children to Role-Play

Most children aged four through twelve enjoy **role-playing.** However, it cannot be assumed that they automatically know how to do it. Rather, helping professionals must teach youngsters how to take on a role prior to expecting them to glean factual information or insights from enacting a vignette or from watching one carried out by others. This can be accomplished using the following strategies.

*1.* **Explain what role-playing is.** Define it as a particular way of pretending in order to present a lesson. Describe roles as parts children play in a scene. Tell youngsters they may now act out how they would feel in a given situation or how they think another person might feel under those circumstances. Point out to the children that for each role-play episode, some youngsters will be taking on roles while others watch,

and everyone will have a chance to discuss the results. Show them the boundaries of the physical area in which the enactment will take place as well as any props available to the actors.

**2. Set the scene.** Present a theme, script, or problem for the role-players to act out. You may also suggest certain emotions for them to portray. Give each child a specific role to play and a few hints about related actions or words that might characterize their role.

**3. Help the role-players get into character.** Allow youngsters to select a prop or costume item as a way to further establish their roles. This step is critical for children younger than seven years of age who otherwise might have difficulty enacting and sustaining a role. Young children may need to hang a picture or symbol around their neck if the role is abstract or a good prop is not available.

**4. Watch the role-players attentively.** Applaud their efforts.

**5. Discuss what occurred during the role-play episode.** Elicit comments both from the participants and the observers. Refer to the friendship facts presented in Table 8–1 as a way to support and extend the discussion.

**6. Ask children to develop alternate scenarios.** Have youngsters act these out, then discuss the varying outcomes.

**7. Summarize the key points of the children's discussion.** Identify similarities in their thinking as well as differences. Highlight the one or two major points that seemed most important to the group.

 Carry Out Friendship Coaching

Coaching begins when you have determined that a child has fallen into a destructive pattern of interactions or is unhappy with his or her inability to make friends and seems at a loss for what to do next. Coaching consists of short, regularly scheduled sessions with the child in

**▼ Table 8–2    Sample Skit for Teaching a Friendship Skill**

**General Instructions**

Seat children in a semicircle facing you. Make sure everyone can see your face and hands and the space directly in front of you. If you are sitting on the floor, it is useful to kneel so you are more easily visible to the children. If you are sitting in a chair, a low bench or table can be used to display the props. As the script unfolds, manipulate the dolls in corresponding actions. Be expressive with your face and your voice. Use dialogue for the characters that seems appropriate for the situation; use different voices for each character.

**Materials**

Two dolls (or puppets); several small, colored blocks.

**Procedure**

*Adult:*  Today, we are going to talk about friends. Here are two dolls. We are going to pretend that these dolls are real children just like you. Their names are Max and Gus. They are four years old and go to a school just like ours. Watch carefully and see what happens when Gus and Max try to be friends. (Set up one doll [Gus] as if "playing" with several blocks. Place second doll [Max] facing Gus but at least a foot away.)

*Adult:*  Here is Gus. He is playing alone with the blocks and is having a good time. Max sees Gus and would really like to play with him, so he watches Gus very carefully. Gus keeps playing; he doesn't look up. Max feels sad. He thinks Gus doesn't want to be friends.

Question for discussion:
1. Tell me what Gus was doing.
2. Tell me what Max wanted to do.
3. Did Gus know Max wanted to play? How do you know?
4. What else could Max do to let Gus know he wanted to play?

As children answer these questions, provide information to help in their deliberations; "Gus was so busy playing, he didn't look up. That means he never even saw Max standing there. He didn't know Max wanted to play. Watch again and see what Max does differently this time."

*Adult:*  Here is Gus. He is playing alone with the blocks and is having a good time. Max sees Gus and really would like to play with him. So, he watches Gus very carefully. Gus keeps playing. He doesn't look up. Max walks over to Gus and says: "Hi. I like your building. I'll help you get some more blocks."

Questions for discussion:
1. What was Gus doing?
2. What did Max want to do?
3. Did Gus know Max wanted to play?
4. How could he tell?
5. What will Gus do next?
6. Let's think of some other ways Max could let Gus know he wants to play.

As children suggest ideas, paraphrase them and write them down where all the children can see them. Accept all ideas regardless of originality, correctness, or feasibility. If children have difficulty thinking of ideas, prompt them by providing information: "Sometimes, when people want to play, they can say: "Hi. I want to play," or they can ask a question like, "What are you building?" This lets the other person know they want to be friends. What do you think Max could do?" Once children have suggested their ideas, replay the scene using each suggestion, one at a time. Ask the children to predict how Gus will react in each case. Play out the scene as they suggest. Provide further information as appropriate: "John, you said Max could help Gus build. Let's try that." (Maneuver the dolls and provide appropriate dialogue.) "Tell me what you think Gus will do now."

## SKILLS FOR SUPPORTING CHILDREN'S FRIENDSHIPS—continued

which you work on particular friendship skills together. Your approach is very similar to that suggested for use with children in groups. The difference is that you are working with one child at a time and giving that child specific, on-the-spot feedback about his or her performance. Some children may need considerable help with several skills, and others may progress rapidly with more limited intervention. In addition, you may use children as friendship coaches (Matson and Ollendick, 1988). Select child trainers on a volunteer basis and have them practice what they will say to a targeted child and how they will give feedback on the child's response. Follow the procedure as outlined below, whether it is you or a child who is acting as the coach.

**1. Select a skill to work on.** Identify a friendship skill that will address the child's particular difficulty. It can be challenging to narrow your choice to one skill if you see a child who seems to be doing "everything" wrong: ignoring peers, rejecting them, grabbing, pushing, interrupting, taking over, teasing. It is tempting to plan a complete make-over. However, trying to do too much all at once usually ends in frustration and failure. A better approach is to work on one problem area at a time. In this way, both the child and you experience success each step of the way. This encourages continued efforts and may ease the way for learning in related areas.

**2. Initiate coaching.** Experts emphasize the importance of selecting a neutral time to begin coaching rather than immediately following a disagreeable encounter. Otherwise, the targeted child may feel singled out and react defensively (Stocking, Arezzo, and Leavitt, 1980). Your goal is to have children perceive these sessions as enjoyable activities, not as the negative consequence of their behavior. Initiate the coaching session by taking the child aside at some dispassionate time and saying: "Robert, today you and I are going to have a special time together. Come with me and I'll tell you all about it."

**3. Describe the skill to the child.** Introduce the skill you are going to focus on, such as expressing acceptance, by describing it in observable terms rather than generalizations.

*Appropriate:* "When you want someone to be your friend, it is important to listen to his (her) ideas. That means looking at him (her) and not talking while he (she) is trying to tell you something."

*Inappropriate:* "When you want someone to be your friend, you should act more interested."

**4. Demonstrate the skill.** Model the behavior or point it out in other children who are playing so the child can actually see what you are talking about: "Here, I'll show you. Tell me one way we could play with these puppets and I will listen to your idea" or "Look at Jeremy—he's listening very carefully to what Sondra is saying."

**5. Provide a rationale for the skill.** Give the child a reason for why the new behavior is important: "When you listen to people's ideas, it makes them feel good. That helps them to like you better."

**6. Tell the child to practice the skill.** Have the child rehearse the skill with you. It usually is helpful if the child can first differentiate between examples of good and poor skill usage. Again, you can demonstrate or use puppets and dolls: "Here are two puppets, Rollo and Gertrude. Rollo is telling Gertrude an idea. Watch and listen. Tell me how well Gertrude shows Rollo she wants to be friends." After several demonstrations, Robert can then rehearse the new behavior by role-playing with you or another child or by manipulating the dolls and puppets himself. This opportunity to practice helps children feel more comfortable with their new skills. They can more directly experience what it is like to be both the recipient and the initiator of varying social behaviors. As a result of this phase, children may suggest their own ideas about other ways to demonstrate the skill. They also have a chance to ask questions and discuss their emotions and reactions.

**7. Evaluate the child's use of the skill.** Praise children's efforts and improved performance throughout the practice session. Point out instances of the child's appropriate use of the

*continued*

## SKILLS FOR SUPPORTING CHILDREN'S FRIENDSHIPS—continued

skill. Commend the child for trying. Provide physical support through smiles and hugs.

In addition, offer corrective feedback aimed at improving the child's use of the skill. Focus on behaviors: "You listened to some of my ideas. You didn't hear them all. Let's try again."

*8.* **Repeat the coaching procedure several times.** Change the props and the hypothetical circumstances more than once. Remember that children vary in the rate at which they learn new behaviors. Some will progress quickly; others will move at a much slower pace. As you see each child increase his or her use of the targeted skill in day-to-day interactions, you should praise their efforts and offer some on-the-spot information that will help them polish their performance. As improvement becomes evident, plan to introduce a new skill for the child to work on or, if that is not necessary, gradually fade out the coaching sessions. Coaching should not be ended abruptly at the first signs of progress. Children need the continued feedback and reinforcement such sessions offer in order to maintain their use of each skill. As they experience more and more success with peers, the natural environment will become rewarding enough that the coaching sessions are no longer the child's primary source of reinforcement.

Children who need coaching are those who have not acted on the subtle cues present in the everyday environment; therefore, the adult must make those cues more explicit and focus the child's attention on them. The professional's role goes beyond discussing and pointing out appropriate skills to include the elements of practice and evaluation. These latter steps are critical, both in the session and outside of it.

 **Communicate with the Family**

Help family members understand and support children's friendships. Facilitate family communication using the following strategies.

*1.* **Make yourself available to discuss friendship-related issues with families.** Talk with parents and guardians about the normal course of children's friendships. Listen carefully to

what they have to say and reflect their thoughts and emotions. Provide information to them by explaining the characteristics of the particular friendship stage their child is experiencing. This enables adults to view their children's behavior in the context of expected development. Simply knowing that most children find making and maintaining friendships a rocky road may give family members comfort and assurance. When children say such things as, "You can't be my friend," or "I'll be your friend if you invite me to your birthday party," parents and other adults are frequently appalled at the child's insensitivity. Offer some of the strategies cited earlier in this chapter so parents can better understand where children's attempts are coming from and can deal more effectively with unacceptable behaviors in positive and supportive ways. Explore other issues with family members as they arise, such as having "best friends," or the disappointment of failed friendships. Offer suggestions in terms of the ideas presented in this book. For instance, children may not need advice, so much as they would benefit from active listening; give parents a brief "script" in which you outline this technique. Older children's parents are frequently concerned about the groups their children are participating in and the pressure for conformity within those groups. If this or other issues arise repeatedly in your discussions with parents, think of ways to initiate a parent workshop on the subject.

*2.* **Help families facilitate children's friendships beyond school time.** As children mature, the frequency of requests for "someone to come over to play" increases markedly. Such opportunities provide an important link between the family and the peer social system. Interestingly, the extent to which parents engage in this form of peer management may vary, with the families of more popular children taking less initiative than do families of less popular or shy children (Ladd, Profilet, and Hart, 1992). Mutual home visiting is easy to arrange within a small and close neighborhood, where families tend to know one another and are familiar with each other's parenting styles. Visiting can be somewhat more involved when the children are friends at school, but their families don't espe-

## SKILLS FOR SUPPORTING CHILDREN'S FRIENDSHIPS—continued

cially know one another. Several situations that families encounter in the process of finding and keeping friends may arise:

a. Sometimes adult family members are looking for a new friend for their youngster. Suggest to them the names of other children in the group who you believe might be potential friends. Use the criteria suggested in the beginning of this chapter in determining which children might be suitable friends for a particular individual. The children's age, gender, proximity, relationship in the program, interests, and stage of friendship are all attributes for you to consider.

b. Parents appreciate help in figuring out ways to make visits between children go more smoothly. They wonder whose "rules" should govern a "guest's" behavior, whether or not their child should have to share everything, or what to do when host and visiting children get into an argument. Work with families to establish "helpful hints" for parents, so that daytime and, in the future perhaps, overnight visits will be fun for children and livable for adults. A group of parents, teachers, and students at the Brushwood Elementary School generated the following set of ideas.

  (1) *Arranging the visit:*
  (a) Make sure the arrangements for the visit are clear to both families. Such plans should include: time of visit, duration, who is to pick up and deliver the child (if necessary), which meals or snacks (if any) may be expected to be served, and a contact phone number.
  (b) Plan how and under what circumstances visits are to be ended. Discuss and decide what will be done if children get into prolonged squabbles or if the visit seems not to be working out for either or both of the children.
  (c) Exchange information about which adult(s) will be at the home to supervise the children.

  (2) *When children's friends are visiting your home:*
  (a) Establish indoor and, if appropriate, outdoor places where children may play safely that are within view and/or hearing.
  (b) Involve the host child in decisions regarding which items are to be shared with the friend and which are to be put away for the duration of the visit.
  (c) Make provision for siblings of the host child to either be admitted to the play scene or to play elsewhere. Sibling involvement has the potential to become problematic, especially when that child is viewed as the "third wheel," or, in the case of older siblings, when that sibling is perceived as "stealing" the friend.
  (d) Clearly articulate household policies to the visiting child, such as which areas are within or off limits, how snacks are to be obtained, and any other practices that may be unique to your specific family. Be sure to show the child the bathroom.

  (3) *When your child is a guest:*
  (a) Talk with your child about how to be a good "guest." This means listening to and obeying the host's parents, being polite, and following the household rules and procedures, even when they differ from your own. This latter point may require specific explanation from you, if you know the information in advance. Tell your child to ask questions if he or she is unsure about what is expected.
  (b) Urge your child to try new foods, or at least, to decline politely food that he or she doesn't like. Phrases such as, "No, thank you," and "Yes, please," are appropriate in any setting.
  *Additional tips for overnight visitors, include:*
  (i) Begin with a daytime visit. Gradually increase the amount of time children are together before planning a nighttime stay.
  (ii) Talk in advance about specific routines or rules and any differ-

*continued*

ences there may be from one household to the next. For instance, a visiting child may not be required in his or her home to clear the dishes, whereas the host child is accustomed to doing so. The host child may be the communicator of this policy.

(iii) Suggest that the visitor bring favorite bedtime objects, such as his or her pillow and/or cuddly toy.

Offer other assistance, as requested, and help families assess the success of the visits.

**3. Institute classroom policies that enhance children's friendship development.** For example, a kindergarten classroom had a policy that unless all children in the group were to be asked, invitations to parties were to be offered by mail or phone, so as not to hurt other children's feelings and to avoid the confusion of a message getting into the wrong child's hands. A situation that required communicating with families after the fact was when Mr. Swick's fourth-grade children began to bring candy or other treats to school and shared them with only a select few children during the day. Mr. Swick sent a note home to the children's families describing the problem and relating the children's actions to their level of friendship development. He then asked for parental input in formulating some rules. The resulting guideline stated that children were permitted to share treats with their special friends during lunchtime only and that the logical consequence of bringing out the candy at other times was for the children to temporarily give it up until lunch period.

**4. Initiate classroom events that enable families to get to know one another.** Parents and guardians may be understandably hesitant to invite a child to their home or to allow their child to visit a family with whom they are unfamiliar. This deprives children of an important aspect of friendship development, that of shared activities outside the program. One solution is to invite family members to a sing-along or potluck dessert function. This kind of experience offers families the opportunity to "break the ice," as the children can introduce their families to each other. Casual conversation helps people feel more comfortable and may result in "play dates" for the children. This strategy is especially helpful if the program draws families from an area wider than the few blocks around the program site.

**5. Talk to adult family members about their neglected or rejected children.** Sometimes children experience more than the usual pains of friendship. When parents describe their children in ways that lead you to believe that their lack of friends is the result of serious dysfunction, or when you have made similar observations, speak openly and compassionately with the adults in a private setting. Listening carefully to what they say is an essential part of your determination and will guide you in offering helpful advice. Respond to their anguish or uncertainty using affective reflections. Inquire about the child's friendships beyond the school setting and within the family (siblings, cousins, etc.). Be aware that some children have strong friendships out of school; they do not feel the desire to have a special school friend. Keep this in mind in your conversations with parents. Document examples of the child's unsuccessful attempts at friendship making or his or her rebuff of the overtures of others. Try all the strategies suggested in the text. If, over a sufficient period of time (weeks or months) the child fails to move forward, take the issue seriously and recommend intervention. Use the guidelines in Chapter 15 to help you recognize and deal with this aspect of extreme behavior. Help families seek community resources, such as counselors, social workers, or psychologists, who might be available to give assistance. Sometimes group therapy in a protected setting with a skilled facilitator can provide the youngster with the appropriate feedback from peers. Actions such as these may head off grave consequences.

## ▼ PITFALLS TO AVOID

Regardless of whether you are supporting children's friendships individually or in groups, informally or in structured activities, there are certain pitfalls you should avoid.

**Barging in too quickly.** When adults see children struggling over friendship issues, such as who will play with whom, or when adults see children using hurtful or inappropriate means of making their friendship preferences known, it is tempting to step in as a mediating figure immediately.

No one likes to see children hurting each other's feelings. On the other hand, children benefit when they have an opportunity to try out strategies and solutions on their own. Unless there is some physical danger that should be dealt with quickly, it is important to take a moment to observe the situation and to thoughtfully determine what form of intervention is best. At times, simply moving physically closer to the situation defuses it. In other instances, direct use of the strategies described in this chapter is more appropriate. Regardless of which course you follow, remember that the more children practice friendship skills with the least help from you, the more quickly they will learn how to be successful in their interactions with peers.

**Missing opportunities to promote friendly interactions among children.** Adults sometimes become so centered on interacting with the children themselves that they fail to recognize opportunities to help children increase their friendship skills with peers. For example, an adult who is carrying on a conversation with one child may view the arrival of a second child as an interruption or may carry on two separate conversations simultaneously. A better approach would be to use reflections or provide information that would help the children talk to each other as well as to the adult:

*Juan:* We went to the store last night.

*Anita:* We had pizza for dinner.

*Adult:* You both did interesting things last night. Juan, tell Anita what you saw at the store.

**Insisting that everyone be "friends."** Although it is natural for adults to want children to like each other, it does not always turn out that way. Instead, children in groups tend to form close relationships with only a few children at a time. Liking someone is not something that can be dictated; insisting that everyone like each other not only is unrealistic but denies children's real emotions. In every group, there are people who rub each other the wrong way. Part of what children can learn is how to interact constructively with the people they like best *and* the people they like least. Adults must show children alternative acceptable ways of making their preferences known.

**Requiring everyone to be together all the time.** It is a mistake to think that friendship is built on constant companionship. Although familiarity does breed common interests, forcing children to play together when they do not really want to detracts from, rather than enhances, their relationships. With this in mind, adults are cautioned to allow children opportunities to engage in solitary activity and to help each child to constructively explain his or her desire for privacy to curious or well-meaning peers. In addition, adults should aid the child who is rebuffed by a peer who would rather be alone. This can be accomplished by explaining the nay-sayer's desire for privacy and by helping the youngster who is turned away to find an alternate activity or companion.

**Breaking up children's friendships.** At any time in the preschool and early elementary years, a child will develop a best-friend relationship. During this time, the two children involved become inseparable. Adults often worry that this closeness is interfering with the children's ability to develop other friendships. As a result, adults frequently decide to intervene by limiting the children's time together. This is a mistake. As children begin to develop "special relationships," it is natural for them to center on the object of their admiration.

It must be remembered that when children first become interested in making friends, their main goal is simply to be included in group activities. However, once this has been accomplished, children begin to want to have an influence on their relationships. In other words, they want others to listen to their ideas, accept their suggestions, and involve them in decision making. From the children's viewpoint, this is a relatively risky process. So, they seek the security of a one-to-one relationship within which to test their skills. In friendship pairs, risks are reduced because the two children involved come to know each other well and therefore are more accurate in predicting another's reaction. In addition, they build up a history of good times, which helps them weather the bad times that are sure to occur. It takes a long time for children to work through these needs. When adults interrupt the process, they deprive children of important opportunities to learn the true meaning of friendship. Adults should allow children to experience this important phase of relationship building.

**Failing to recognize children's friendship cues.** Children may use inappropriate behaviors in their efforts to make friends. For instance, children may taunt to initiate an interaction, physically force other children out of an area to have exclusive access to a favored peer, or try to coerce a friend into rejecting another as a way of confirming their own friendship bond. On the surface, these may appear to be straightforward limit-setting situations. However, an observant adult will recognize that the issue relates to friendship and will seize the opportunity to help the erring child learn more constructive friendship skills such as better ways of making contact or expressing affection.

## ▼ SUMMARY

Friendships with peers are important events in the lives of children and offer them unique opportunities to develop socially, emotionally, and intellectually. Some children make friends easily; others do not. The repercussions of not having a friend or of being dissatisfied with the relationships one does have represent severe difficulties in childhood, which can last through maturity. Completely friendless children are rare; however, evidence does indicate that many children wish they had more or better friends.

Adults may wonder whether children really understand what friendship means. Although children's ideas about what constitutes friendship are different from adults' and change as children mature, it is clear that even very young children are interested in having friends who are like them in age and experience and who share their intellectual and physical abilities. Increased facility in communicating also has an impact on children's relationships. Children progress from an egocentric view of relationships to one of mutual support and caring.

When first choosing a friend, children focus on obvious attributes such as name, physical appearance, race, gender, age, ability, and attitudes. In general, it can be said that children seek out friends whom they perceive as being similar to themselves. At times, these likenesses are apparent only to the children involved.

The social skills children display also have a major impact on their ability to make and keep friends. Making friends is not an automatic or magical process. Children who "win friends and influence people" know how to make contact, maintain positive relationships, and negotiate the inevitable conflicts that arise. These are skills that some children learn on their own but with which many children need help.

Adults can play a vital role in increasing children's friendly behavior. This can be accomplished through informal, day-to-day techniques, planned activities, or structured coaching sessions. Family members may also be involved in promoting children's friendships both in and out of the formal group setting. Professionals can be of great help in supporting them in their efforts.

## ▼ DISCUSSION QUESTIONS

1. A Chinese proverb states, "One can do without people, but one has need for a friend." React to this statement, discussing the reasons why people need friends.
2. Think about a childhood friend. Describe what attributes made that person important to you.
3. Describe how children's ideas of friendship change over time. Describe children you know who fit into each stage and explain your conclusions.
4. Describe two children you know—one who seems to have many friends and one who seems to have no friends. Discuss what variables might be influencing each child's situation.
5. As a group, develop a friendship skit aimed at teaching children how to make contact with a potential friend. In addition, generate at least five discussion questions.
6. Pretend you have been invited to a parent meeting to describe friendship coaching. Outline what you might say to parents regarding the rationale for this technique as well as its component parts.
7. Referring to Appendix A, NAEYC Code of Ethical Conduct, judge the ethics of the following situation: You and your best friend work in the same program. One evening your friend tells you that sometimes when the children are happy she goes outside for a cigarette, leaving the children unattended.

8. Identify a child you know who might benefit from friendship coaching. Describe the area in which coaching would be most useful and explain how you would implement the coaching procedure.

9. Pretend that a child's parent has spoken with you about concerns regarding his or her child's peer relationships. What information would you require in order to give an appropriate response? What suggestions could you make to the parent to help foster this child's friendships outside of school?

10. Identify the pitfall in this chapter to which you think adults are most susceptible and describe ways to avoid it.

## ▼ FIELD ASSIGNMENTS

1. Discuss three situations in which you supported children's friendships. Describe what the children were doing. Next, talk about what you did, making specific reference to the skills you have learned in this chapter. Explain how the children reacted to your approach. Conclude by evaluating your skill usage and describing any changes you might make in future situations that are similar.

2. Choose a friendship skill. Design an activity through which you will teach the skill to children. Write down your plan in detail. Also, include a description of how you expect children to react to the activity. *Carry out the activity with a small group of children.* Evaluate in writing your presentation, state any unexpected outcomes, and describe any changes you would make if you were to repeat this activity in the future.

# ▼Chapter 9

## Influencing Children's Social Development by Structuring the Physical Environment

## ▼ OBJECTIVES

*On completion of this chapter, you will be able to describe:*

▼ Decision-making processes in caregivers and children.

▼ The adult's role in structuring the physical environment.

▼ The influence of the daily schedule on children's behavior.

▼ The influence of room arrangement on children's behavior.

▼ How to select and organize materials to promote social development.

▼ How to change the daily schedule or room arrangement with minimal disruption.

▼ How to help children become decision makers and managers of their own environment.

▼ How to communicate with parents about structuring to support children's social development.

▼ Pitfalls to avoid in structuring the physical environment.

---

Jerry, aged three-and-a-half years, sits quietly on the rug placing blocks carefully on a tower when his friend walks past carrying a sign saying "CLEAN UP 5 minutes" and ringing a small hand bell. Jerry surveys his structure and then carefully removes the blocks, replacing them on open shelves that are marked with the silhouette of each shape.

Mitsy, age five, hurries to her cubby, removes her one-piece snowsuit, spreading it out on the floor where she promptly sits in the middle. With quick efficiency she puts on her clothing and prepares to go outside announcing, "The snow will pack today!" Her kindergarten classmates move with equal efficiency and independence and soon leave the cubby area and emerge into the thick, damp snow.

Edward, age seven, scans his long pictograph to be sure that he has completed all of the starred activities for the week. Now that it is Thursday, he smiles as all of the required activities have been attended to and he can do whatever he chooses. He watches other children for several minutes, then moves into the science area where one of his friends is looking through a microscope at something. He marks the science pictograph with a crayon to record his participation and begins to examine the materials placed in the center.

---

Each of these children is functioning independently in an environment that has been designed to foster autonomy. The open storage for blocks with the shelves clearly marked enabled Jerry to put away his materials. Convenient coat storage and instruction in putting on outer wraps enabled Mitsy and her classmates to move efficiently from one environment to another. The use of a pictograph facilitated record keeping for Edward and provided the necessary information he needed to plan his day at school. The functioning of each of these children is influenced indirectly by the adult's management of the resources of the programs. Such management is deliberate and is the result of careful planning for which the ultimate goal is to facilitate harmony among the children and warm, positive relationships between children and adults.

In addition to functioning independently, specific social goals that may be supported by managing the physical environment are as follows:

▼ Respecting the rights of others
▼ Promoting friendships
▼ Supporting and promoting play
▼ Promoting prosocial behavior
▼ Reducing interpersonal stress
▼ Minimizing and/or resolving conflict
▼ Maintaining safety for all
▼ Protecting property

**Structuring** is the term given to the management of time, space, and materials to promote children's social development. Adults rely on this process to convey messages indirectly to children about what is appropriate and inappropriate behavior. Sometimes this is called **indirect guidance.** In addition, children must learn to manage resources appropriate for their own development. With adult assistance, they learn to make decisions, plan, act, and evaluate for themselves. The process is the same for the children who are learning and for the adult who is structuring the environment to facilitate the process.

## ▼ THE BASIC PROCESS OF STRUCTURING

Structuring is a skill that is goal directed and can be learned. It requires thoughtful consideration of all its component parts: making decisions, setting goals, planning, implementing the chosen plan, and assessing the outcome.

### Motivations for Structuring

Adults structure the environment to meet the *needs* of children (Maslow, 1954). **Physiological needs,** such as an adequate diet, enough sleep, and appropriate room temperature, must be satisfied in order for children to survive and to function. **Safety needs,** such as freedom from physical danger and fear, can be met by the judicious use of resources. **Social needs** include the child's need for acceptance and a sense of belonging, and **esteem needs** include

self-respect, recognition, and status. Something as simple as a pair of mittens may meet the physiological need for warmth, the safety need to prevent frostbite, social needs in that the child can play outside with other children, and esteem needs in that by joining in the outdoor play, the child is perceived as a contributing group member.

Adults also structure in order to meet *demands* from external sources such as fire safety, tornado or fire drills, and sanitary handling of food. Adults also structure the environment in order to satisfy *values* that are all-inclusive, deeply internalized personal qualities and beliefs that direct action (Berns, 1996). Because values are so pervasive and important in professional decision making, much of Chapter 15 is devoted to this topic. Values such as human dignity, equity, justice, and sociability are repeatedly emphasized in this book.

A *concern* is the affective side of a value and is often voiced in personal messages. When an adult says, "I'm concerned that you will fall if you run downhill on the gravel path," he or she is expressing a concern related to the value of health and the need for safety. Other concerns are expressed nonverbally by organizing space, materials, and other resources to promote children's social development by controlling the physical setting. A summary of the motivations for structuring is presented in Table 9–1.

### Establishing Goals

A *goal* is an end that can be accomplished. Some goals can be readily achieved in a short time; others are long-term endeavors that require years to accomplish.

A *standard* is a measure of quality, quantity, or method of goal attainment. Standards are a means for determining if the goal has been accomplished, or if something is "good enough." For example, to achieve the goal of sharing the standards for a one-year-old, a four-year-old, and a seven-year-old are different. Usually toddlers perceive all objects as "mine" and cannot understand sharing. Four-year-olds may fight over objects but may be able to negotiate with each other with help. Seven-year-old children probably understand the concept well and often can share without adult support. Older children who do not meet the standard require the support and assistance typical of younger children.

### Decision Making

Decision making permeates the entire structuring process and includes the following:

1. Identifying the problem; recognizing the need for a decision

▼ Table 9–1    Examples of Related Motivations for Structuring

| MOTIVE | DEFINITION | EXAMPLE |
|--------|-----------|---------|
| Need | Essential for function or survival | Acceptance by others |
| Demand | Required by law or by individual programs | Regulations to protect children |
| Value | Desired quality | Respect for all people |
| Concern | Affective component of a value | Worry about a child frequently fighting and hurting others |
| Goal | An outcome that can be accomplished | Promoting prosocial behavior |
| Standard | Degree of goal attainment | Child is included in the play of others |

2. Obtaining information and formulating alternatives
3. Considering consequences; projecting possible outcomes
4. Choosing a course of action

Most problems that arise in working with children require high-speed responses. Many of these decisions have been presented in earlier chapters and taught as skills. Other high-speed decisions can be made by using decision rules.

**Decision rules.**  General practices that can be applied in many instances and that often shorten the time involved in determining a course of action are called **decision rules.** Some sample decision rules that have been used by early-childhood teachers are as follows:

1. Safety first!
2. The job at hand is less important than the child doing it.
3. Minimize the need for limit setting by organizing the environment.
4. Never do for children what children can do for themselves.

### Giving Children Choices

Children also practice decision making from toddlerhood on. When adults offer them choices, children feel good about themselves and have an opportunity to practice decision-making skills: generating alternatives, seeking information, considering consequences, and, eventually, accepting responsibility for the outcome (Hendrick, 1996; Maccoby, 1980).

Collaborating with children requires enlisting them in the decision-making process from the beginning. Setting goals, planning, determining standards, and deciding how and by whom the activity should be supervised all are part of the total process. Young children may participate in only a small part of the process, such as choosing between two acceptable alternatives; older children can engage in all aspects of management. The role of the adult is to demonstrate, explain, and guide the process. Children learn to manage by doing and are more likely to "own" the decisions they themselves make. Involved children are less likely to resent the consequences of decisions that turn out to be less desirable than anticipated when they have made them themselves.

Group decision making takes more time than individual decision making, and supporting the process with a group of children takes even longer. When adults decide to let the children choose as a group, they also have committed a substantial time resource to the process. Extensive communication is required in order to arrive at a decision. However, the time is well spent because children are more committed to a course of action if they have participated in determining it. Some decisions that groups of children might make are which song to sing, which game to play, whether to participate in a fund-raising activity, or how a holiday should be celebrated. Some groups of children are allowed to participate in choosing displays to make, rearranging furniture, and organizing storage.

Most decisions that involve structuring of the physical environment, time, and energy can be made in the absence of children and is discussed in the next part of this chapter. The goals of providing a safe, healthy environment in which children can learn to live and work together cooperatively are assumed, as these are common to most programs for children.

### Developing a Plan

Once a specific goal is chosen, a plan of action is needed to implement it. The planning may be done by an individual or by a small group and must take into account the resources that will be needed, the people that will implement the plan, the time frame in which it will be implemented, and some criteria or standard for evaluating it.

Some plans are comprehensive and complex. The daily program schedule, adults' work schedules, or equipment purchase plans are of this type. Other plans are quite simple and may become routines or habits for the children and adults. An example of a simple plan is a diapering schedule that merely indicates which adult checks the diapers of which infant and at what time.

How a plan of either variety can be initiated, carried out, and evaluated is illustrated in the following scenario. Mrs. Rouge's goal was for the three-year-olds in her daycare center to independently wash their hands clean. She noted that the children did not have very clean hands when they sat down to lunch even though the rule had been made clear. Implementing the consequence of sending them back to wash again did not help, so she observed the children washing to determine where the difficulty lay. She noticed that the shorter children had difficulty reaching the water, as their armpits just reached the edge of the sink; the taller children could reach the water, but had difficulty handling the soap, which frequently shot from their hands onto the floor. Based on this observation, she realized that the children were unable, rather than unwilling, to comply with the rule.

Mrs. Rouge decided that the best way to address the problem was not to set more limits, but to change the environment. Her method of altering the environment was to put something under the sink for the children to stand on so they all could reach it better. She also chose to modify the soap by drilling a hole through each bar and attaching it to the faucet with a string. She reasoned that even if the soap were to slip from their hands, the children would be able to retrieve it easily.

Next, she listed the steps for changing the current procedure and implementing the new one:

1. Discuss the new procedures with the staff.
2. Ask for volunteers to set up the platform and prepare the soap.
3. Assemble the materials needed to do the tasks.
4. Begin implementing the procedure by telling the children about it.
5. Assign staff to the bathroom to encourage children to follow the procedure. Ask staff to demonstrate the procedure as necessary.

In this instance, planning included an analysis of the problem and depended on Mrs. Rouge being able to break down the task into its component parts. The plan addresses the substance of the problem and includes a means for carrying out the solution. Effective communication with both the staff and children were necessary to put the plan into effect. In evaluating the effects of changing the hand washing routine, Mrs. Rouge noted a sharp decline in adults' reprimands before meals and children's more relaxed and confident behavior. Materials, equipment, skill, time, and knowledge are the resources being used in this management task.

A plan may be used over an extended period of time or it may be designed for a single instance, such as a plan for creating a new facility or school. The planning process involves many decisions, as each step has numerous feasible alternatives.

## Implementing and Evaluating the Plan

Direct action is necessary to implement the plan. The most complex or interesting plans are a waste of time if they are not carried out to completion. In child-care programs and other settings where adults cooperate in providing a learning environment for children, groups of adults work together to achieve the desired outcome. The roles of the adults may vary, but someone must function as leader when two or more adults are involved. Willingness to try new approaches is essential from all team members. Communication and control of the process are required at this stage. Some generally accepted ideas about the nature of control are as follows (Smith, 1980):

1. Develop a plan with clearly defined limits.
2. Consider acceptable variations of the plan.
3. Develop a procedure to check the current status in relation to the planned status.
4. Adjust supervisory behavior if the plan is not being implemented as anticipated.

The whole point of control is to keep children's and adult's behavior in line with the goals of the plan. This requires **organization**—structuring the materials and the people's roles in such a way that the plan can be implemented. Second, implementing requires **facilitating** the process—initiating and sustaining the action, and finally, it requires *coordinating* the activities of all involved.

**Supervision.** In child-centered programs most of the tasks that adults supervise have goals related to the children accomplishing some skill (building a campfire or reading a story). They also have goals for them to work toward independently (clean up their own tent or write a letter) and for them to develop leadership skills (plan and initiate play, or be a discussion leader). Therefore, the selection of strategies adults use to supervise tasks is important for the potential effect on children's social skills. This selection is also significant for the efficiency and effectiveness of getting the job done or the child performing the skill at the desired standard.

**Supervising** children or adults in implementing a plan requires that clear directions be given before the task is begun. Also, someone must carefully observe the task being carried out so that errors can quickly be detected and corrected and those being supervised can proceed with confidence. Supervising includes giving people **feedback.** This may be as simple as remaining in the area to answer questions or as demanding as observing and commenting on the step-by-step process in detail. For example, an adult may give feedback nonverbally by pointing to the paper towel dispenser when a child starts to leave with dripping hands. Feedback may also be given by additional directions when a child appears to need the information. "Alex, step up on the block so you can reach the sink." It can be supplied by providing behavioral reflections, "Rachel, you were able to get all the fingerpaint off your hand by yourself." One adult might also give feedback to another who is in a leadership role with the children such as, "The hand washing routine seems to be working," or "The children do not seem to be able to get these puzzles put together without a lot of help." Feedback should always focus on the behaviors of the people being supervised and lead them toward success.

Two approaches to supervision have been identified: **guiding,** which utilizes the facilitation dimension, and **directing,** which utilizes the action dimension. Usually guiding is the preferred approach with children. The adult focus is on the child rather than the task, and the overall intent is to let the child learn the process gradually while building both skill and confidence. Directing is most appropriate when issues of health and safety are involved. The adult who controls by directing tells children what to do and how to do it; the adult who controls by guiding makes suggestions, generates alternatives, and helps children to determine the standards. For example, a camp counselor might encourage children to plan and implement the setup of tents and the arrangement of equipment using guiding techniques. He or she could then shift to a direction mode when it comes time to make a campfire. **Checking** is required in either mode of supervision as responsible adults cannot assume that the activity will be carried forward just because they have

given clear directions on how to do so. **Adjusting** requires changes in the original plan so that the end goals are more likely reached. For example, the camp counselor might notice that the children have arranged their tents too close to the fire pit or with one tent placed in a very low spot when checking their layout of tents. He or she could then point out the potential problems so that the campers can make appropriate adjustments. Three categories of adjustment are possible: making little or no change; rearranging procedures according to a predetermined goal, plan, or standard; or shifting the underlying goal (Gross, Crandall, and Knoll, 1980).

**Evaluation.**  Evaluating plans cannot be left to chance. Did the plan work? Are children functioning more effectively or more independently? Are adults satisfied with the outcome? Is there less friction between adults and children?

Questions relating to overall satisfaction with the plan's outcome must be considered. Evaluating the implementation and outcome of a plan may help in establishing new goals to work toward, but equally important, it will provide adults and children an opportunity to recognize success.

The process of setting goals and objectives, making decisions, developing plans, implementing the plans, and evaluating them are applicable to most activities for children. Opportunities to manage materials and events appropriate to the child's age help children feel they are competent and that they have some control over their immediate environment (Marshall, 1989). These feelings of autonomy and confidence contribute to positive self-esteem and eventually to greater social capability. As youngsters learn how to manage for themselves by learning to use the management process from supportive adults who use similar techniques, they build leadership skills as well as fundamental social skills. Adults use the same skills to structure time, space, materials, and other aspects of the physical environment so as to influence children's behavior. This form of management is frequently called indirect guidance (Hildebrand, 1994).

## ▼ STRUCTURING TIME

Time is a concept that has individual, physical, and cultural interpretations. It cannot be saved or stored but is only perceived in relation to change. Time is the one resource that is equally distributed to all people. Infants function first in biological time; the markers are changes in behavioral state, hunger, or comfort. Adults value time as a resource and are concerned with helping children to function within the cultural definitions of time that adults use. One way adults help children to use time efficiently is by teaching them a sequence of behaviors, or a habit, for activities that are repetitious and are used regularly. Sometimes, adults become angry with children when they are slow to develop a desired habit. At such times, the child either may not know an appropriate sequence of behaviors, or the sequence is so new that he or she must concentrate closely on each action in the sequence.

A typical example of not knowing an appropriate sequence is when a kindergarten child puts on her or his boots before the snow pants, or when the first garment put on by the child is the mittens. The helping professional may not realize that the parents may have dressed the child every day and that the mittens are the only garment the child has ever put on independently. Adults can become irritated when such incidents make the group wait, mostly because they do not realize that the situation requires teaching rather than demanding and limit setting.

Another way adults help children learn the cultural meaning of time is by organizing events into predictable sequences or routines.

## The Daily Schedule

**Schedules** are organized time segments related to the program. In a summer camp, for instance, blocks of time will be set aside for maintenance of the environment, meals, rest, group sports, swimming, and crafts. These blocks of time are arranged in a certain order, with children moving from one activity to another in a predictable pattern.

Even the youngest infant establishes a rhythmic pattern of sleeping, eating, playing, and quietly observing the surroundings. This regular pattern of behavior varies among children within a family and varies more among different families. Some schedules are more flexible than others. When a child first enters a formal group setting, the familiar patterns developed within the family often must be altered to fit the new situation. This change results in distress and confusion and often is referred to as the initial adjustment to the program. The problems of adjustment are ameliorated as children and families incorporate the new pattern into their behavior.

The daily schedule or routine supports the child's ability to act autonomously. Events can be predicted; expectations for behavior are clear. The need for constant guidance in what to do and how to do it is minimized, so the child's dependence on adults is decreased.

Routines, however, must be learned. Adults first must adapt to the toddler's schedule, then gradually teach the child to function within a group schedule. Young children take longer to learn routines than older ones. They simply have more difficulty remembering. Children under six years of age may take as long as a month to adapt to a new daily schedule. Children in the elementary grades often adjust in two weeks or less; at this age, a pictorial chart or written schedule may help them to adjust more quickly.

Routines may be flexible, allowing a little more time to finish an activity if the change is compatible with the requirements of other program segments. Sometimes, however, as when large groups of children must use the same resources, schedules must be quite rigid. The use of the swimming area in a summer camp requires that all children must arrive, enter, and leave the water in an orderly fashion if standards of safety are to be maintained; every group must operate on clock time if all groups are to be able to swim each day. In contrast, in an after-school family daycare center where the pool is part of the family home, children may swim whenever adult supervision is available; a rigid clock-time schedule is unnecessary.

The predictability of a routine offers emotional security to young children. After a distressing encounter with another child, Cara, age four, chanted the daily schedule several times: "First we play, then we wash, then we have a snack, then we hear a story, then we go outside, and *then* my mama comes to take me home." After each repetition, she appeared more cheerful and ultimately was able to participate comfortably for the rest of the day. Young children also will comprehend the sequence of the daily routine before understanding the concept of time. Ross, three and a half years old, was distressed when his mother left him at the daycare center. He played for about 45 minutes, then asked if the children could go outside. This was a drastic change of schedule—usually, outside play was the last activity of the day—but the teacher allowed Ross and two other boys to go outside with an assistant. Ross played happily for a few minutes, then informed the adult that his mother would be there soon to pick him up! He had erroneously inferred that playing outside caused his mother to arrive because of the contiguity of the events.

A good schedule is continuous, fluid, and goal directed. It has blocks of time that allow children to finish tasks and provides for individual differences in speed. Waiting is minimal, and the transitions in which the whole group must participate are as few as possible. A **transition** occurs when one time block is finished and another begins. Transitions usually occur when children move from one room to another or when there is a complete change of materials. In Cara's verbalization of her routine, she located all the transitions by saying "then." In public schools, transitions occur before and after recess and lunch and also may occur between activities, such as between math and social studies.

Generally, there is a marked increase in the number of interaction problems between children and between adults and children during transitions. Children may be confused about how to behave after one activity is over and before another begins. Older school-age children use this time for conversation and play, with a resulting increase in noise. Therefore, decreasing the number of transitions results in less probability of interaction difficulties.

Short attention spans and differences in working speed can be managed by grouping a variety of activities together in a larger time period and allowing children to change activities individually. For example, in a second-grade room, a teacher combined reading groups, workbook activities, and selected games involving one or two children into one block of time. In programs for very young children, a large variety of materials usually is available at any one time. In general, the schedule should be adapted to the length of time children need to complete tasks rather than to rigid periods, with particular attention to the age of children and time of year. Youngsters tend to focus on their tasks longer as they mature, and from fall to spring (Gareau and Kennedy, 1991). In any case, the goal is to meet the individual needs of children; strategies and standards for doing so differ according to program demands.

When multiple adults are involved, the schedule should be supplemented with a flowchart that assigns adults to tasks, areas, or other responsibilities that will facilitate the supervision of children. A sample flowchart and schedule for a 2½ hour preschool program is illustrated in Table 9–2. Such a plan should be posted so that all adults know when they are supposed to be in a given area as well as what activity should come next. As can be seen, the divisions of time for adults are more frequent than the transitions for the group of children.

In addition, adults are stationed in areas before children enter, and they leave with the last child. The children in this group will experience an even

flow of events without a lot of confusion. The nature of the schedule varies with the type of program, the ages of the children, and the number of adults involved. Sometimes, more complex schedules are developed to incorporate weekly events.

The schedule in Table 9–2 was carefully planned so that children would have the maximum opportunity to interact with one another and make small decisions and so that adults would be able to help and support children in their activities as they supervise the classroom. The head teacher will check to see that the plan is implemented and will communicate any adjustments to other staff members should the need arise.

## Rate and Intensity of Programs

The *speed, rate,* or *pace* of a program may be described by the number of transitions per unit of time. For example, some children may experience three or more transitions in 1 hour. This is a fast pace with a rapid rate of change, providing only 15 to 20 minutes for each segment. A moderate pace would have at least one activity period of 45 to 60 minutes and others of varying length of time. A low-pace program would have few group transitions and two long periods in a half-day program. Typically, in a preschool program these long periods would be indoor free play and outdoor free play, each having a selection of activities. Children move from one activity to another at their own rate of speed.

The pace of the program generally depends on the age of the children, the length of the program day, and the purpose the program is to serve. For example, a preschool child-care program open for 10 hours a day typically is operated at a moderate to slow pace. Some traditional elementary classrooms may be very high paced. A toddler program that is only 1 hour long might be very fast paced because children return to home settings, which are usually slow in pace.

The **intensity** of the program generally refers to the amount of change within a time segment and the degree to which children must attend to an adult. High-intensity programs have three to five novel experiences per week with fewer opportunities to repeat or practice skills. The adult-child interaction is high and the number of adult-initiated activities greater. In low-intensity programs, children have one or two novel activities per week and many opportunities to repeat and vary familiar activities; the role of the adult is that of observer and facilitator.

The dimensions of pace and intensity are important when considering social interactions because the adult may choose to change these char-

▼ Table 9–2    Schedule and Flowchart for a 2½-Hour Program

| SCHEDULE | | CARL | JOHN | EVELYN |
|---|---|---|---|---|
| Arrival | 9:00 | Greet children | Help children with coats | Set up art activity |
| Free play | 9:15 | General supervision; blocks | Supervise dramatic play | Supervise art and bathroom areas |
| | 9:30 | | | Clean up art; general supervision |
| | 9:45 | Introduce new Lotto game | | |
| | 10:00 | Supervise picking up of table toys | Supervise cleanup of dramatic-play area | Support cleanup where needed |
| Snack | 10:15 | Assist in bathroom | Prepare snack; set out juice | Encourage children to wash up |
| | 10:25 | All adults sit with children for snack | | |
| Large group | 10:40 | Call children to story time | Clear snack | Supervise settling for story |
| | 11:00 | Announce outdoor time | Assist in locker area | Dress for outside; go outdoors to receive children |
| | 11:10 | Help last child prepare art to go home | Go outside; supervise tricycles | Supervise swings and slides |
| | 11:15 | General supervision outdoors | | |
| Depart | 11:30 | Greet parents | | Go indoors to clean up room |
| | 11:40 | | Go indoors; help Evelyn | |
| | 11:45 | All children have left; discuss day together | | |
| | 12:00 | Lunch for adults | | |

acteristics if the social interaction patterns of the children are not optimal. Children may be overstimulated, rushing from one thing to another, or they may be bored with a very low-intensity program. In either extreme, children find it difficult to have congenial, easygoing interactions with their peers.

The pace and intensity of programs affect children's interactions because these dimensions also affect *fatigue*. The phrase "tired and cranky" reflects the common knowledge that fatigue influences children's ability to cope with social interactions. A child who is able to solve interpersonal problems when rested may simply cry or become distraught if required to face the same situation when tired.

The following are possible explanations for fatigue (Gross, Crandall, and Knoll, 1980):

1. Bodily changes resulting in *impairment* that might be the result of "running hard" for a long time.
2. *Frustration* with one's inability to cope with a situation.
3. *Boredom* with the activity.
4. The normal wear and tear of life due to *stress*.

Individual children will respond differently to the same program. It is quite possible to have some children in a program frustrated, others bored, and still others exhausted from the stress of working under pressure to keep up. Factors that influence the rate at which children can function are motivation, health, knowledge, skill, practice, age, stamina, habit, and the number of people involved in an activity (Berns, 1993). The skillful swimmer is more efficient than the less skillful one and is not as tired at the end of thirty laps as the less skillful swimmer is at the end of five. Crowded conditions are more tiring than those in which the density is lower. Interacting continuously with someone is more tiring than sporadic contact during the day. Interruptions lead to frustration and to fatigue.

**Synchronization.**   In most programs where children spend the majority of their day, there are many different adults involved in supervising the children. In a public school a principal, a group of classroom teachers, resource teachers, and often specialty teachers must work together to provide a program for children. When their work is well organized, one daily routine for each classroom may be maintained throughout the week, with youngsters participating in a variety of experiences. However, when the efforts of the group are not synchronized, children may experience specialty events as interruptions. In addition, their schedules may not be regular one day to the next, or even one week to the next. With the increasing transitions, children experience more frustration, fatigue, and social disruptions. In child-care settings, camps, and other group environments, similar constraints of facilities and human resources may be disruptive if the structuring is not carefully done; however, if the adults coordinate their efforts in organizing time and physical resources, the children can have a positive experience.

The facility and the management of space and materials are within the limited control of the helping professional and therefore will be examined next.

## ▼ STRUCTURING SPACE AND MATERIALS

Buildings, furnishings, materials, and elements of the natural environment are concrete, visible resources that can be managed to facilitate the social development of children. The physical environment in which children play and learn has much to do with the presence or absence of disruptive behavior (Mehrabian, 1976). Many "discipline problems" in classrooms can be traced directly to the arrangement and selection of furnishings and materials (Olds, 1977). On the other hand, self-control develops in a well-designed and well-arranged physical

space. The general consensus of researchers and theorists is that a well-designed environment creates a positive, supportive setting for the group using it (Ard, 1990).

### Facilities

Usually, such things as location, buildings, parking lots, and plumbing are taken for granted by the new professional. Rarely are beginning professionals required to develop plans for construction or renovation; yet, attributes of the facilities themselves influence the daily program and the frequency of limit setting. Factors such as construction materials, lighting, ventilation, temperature control, safety from environmental hazards, environmental noise, and actual layout and dimensions of the space influence children's behavior.

**Safety.**   To protect children, states define standards for environmental safety for private-sector programs. Daycare centers, camps, and other settings in which children spend prolonged time away from their parents must be licensed. Minimum standards typically are set for fire safety, sanitation, water, and food preparation. Most states also have standards that prohibit overcrowding and ensure adequate supervision by establishing maximum acceptable adult-to-child ratios.

The temperature of the environment should be comfortable for the level of activity. Ideal room temperatures are determined by the age of the children and the type of activity in which they are engaged.

Professionals who work with groups of children should be familiar with the standards and procedures for ensuring their safety and should support the maintenance of the standards. For example, an exit should not be blocked by trash waiting to be carried out while children are in the building; rooms should be clean, and children should be taught sanitary practices when the group is doing cooking projects; fences and climbing equipment should be regularly checked for necessary repairs. Adults who work directly with children are likely to be the first to see areas that need improvement and can initiate the structuring process by reporting concerns to individuals responsible for planning. Regular safety checks are necessary. Failure to use ordinary caution and to maintain established standards is considered negligence.

**Interior design.**   The general principles of quality design apply to environments for young children. Unfortunately, many schools and hospitals have been constructed using "hard" architecture (Sommer, 1974). The spatial arrangements are similar to those of a factory, with ease of maintenance enjoying the highest priority. Frequently, the spaces are unattractive, make people feel closed in, allow limited movement, and reverberate with sound. Fortunately, modifications can be made.

*Walls.* Light colors with bright accents are a big improvement over dark hues or large spaces with bright primary colors. As most people know, color hue and intensity influence distance perception and the general atmosphere of a room. Wall surfaces that are covered with easily washed paint or with wallboard that has a hard, cleanable, fire-retardant surface work well. Children invariably leave fingerprints on surfaces and often can clean up after themselves if the wall texture is appropriate.

*Sound control.* Noise is absorbed by soft materials like carpet, draperies, ceiling and wall tile, stuffed furniture, and pillows. A certain level of noise is to be expected as children talk and move about. However, reverberating noise and yelling and screaming adults and children are not normal. If adults need to raise their voices to be heard when children are behaving appropriately, some modification of the environment must be made.

Variation in texture usually influences the sound level and tends to humanize the environment. Hard surfaces on floors are useful in art areas, kitchens, bathrooms, and entrances and where children play in sand or water. Carpets are easier to sit on and are softer to land on if a child falls from an indoor climber. In the block corner, a firm-surfaced carpet reduces noise without reducing the stability of blocks. One enterprising teacher hung three tumbling mats on a cement wall. This solved the problem of storing the mats when they were not in use, decreased the reverberation of noise in the basement room, and added color and texture to the wall. Public schools and other formal settings for children often have carpeted and hard-surfaced floors, and most administrators will allow staff to bring additional rugs into such settings.

*Lighting.* Adequate lighting is necessary for children to perform detailed tasks, but it also can be boring and monotonous to be in a brightly lit space all the time. Lower lighting, and lighting dispersed around the room, are most conducive to social interaction (Meers, 1985). Although artificial lighting has not been found to affect performance, nearly everyone prefers sunlight to artificial light (Meers, 1985). The use of dimmer switches rather than off-on switches gives the adult greater control, especially if switches are available for various areas of the room (Marion, 1995). The use of dimmer switches in schools is rare, but they are inexpensive and easy to install.

*Vertical and horizontal space.* Varying a room's height by building a platform in a corner can increase the total available floor space and add interest to less usable space. Wells can be constructed in the floors of buildings, as can low platforms, both of which clearly separate visual space as well as adding visual interest. These dimensions are more difficult for the helping professional to change, but they should be explored if any major renovation to facilities is being considered because vertical relationships between people do influence interactions. Higher position in space represents greater power, and children get much satisfaction from looking down from greater heights to the people below. This concept was explored more fully in Chapter 3.

Though individual caregivers do not generally plan and implement facility decisions, they can act to modify the effects of some of those decisions as they supervise children's programs. Examples of such adjustments are illustrated in Table 9–3.

## Arranging Furnishings and Equipment

A supportively built environment allows children to control their surroundings when appropriate and permits and encourages movement so that children can interact freely with objects and people (Marion, 1995). Because safety always is of highest priority, adults should plan environments to minimize risk for children.

A supportive environment is arranged into **learning centers,** or areas that provide for individual, small-group, or large-group activities (Crosser, 1992). When these are organized, physical limits are clear and regulate the use of materials and the behavior of children. Conflict between children is reduced, and conditions for high-quality learning or play are established. The number and kinds of areas needed are determined by the age of the children and the size of the group. If an **activity space** is defined as that occupied by a child using a material, then the number of activity spaces for a block area may be four or six because that number of children could reasonably use the blocks at one time. To prevent waiting, it is recommended that there be roughly one-third more activity spaces than there are children (Marion, 1996). For a group of twenty children, areas that could accommodate a minimum

▼ Table 9–3    Adjusting Aspects of the Facility to Influence Children's Behavior

| DIMENSION | CONDITION OBSERVED | ADJUSTMENT | IMPACT ON CHILDREN |
|---|---|---|---|
| Safety (Temperature) | Hot and stuffy room | Open windows and doorways | Children experience less stress and greater comfort |
| | Drafty or unusually cool room | Press towels or diapers on window sills until permanent insulators are installed | |
| (Cleanliness) | Water droplets on bathroom floor | Wipe up water | Prevents adults and children from slipping |
| (Equipment) | The latch on the play yard gate leading to the playground is broken | Tie a rope around the gatepost and keep the gate closed and/or stand at the gate to let children and adults through until repairs are made | Prevents children from dashing into areas where moving cars might injure them |
| Interior design (Walls) | Walls are clean, plain dull yellow | Mount children's paintings in a single color and cover one area of the wall | Children are proud to have their artwork displayed, especially if it's adding to the aesthetics of their classroom |
| | Children don't play in the manipulative toy area | Cover the room divider with a bright hue (cherry or orange) construction paper using two-way tape so the "papering" is temporary | Children are attracted to bright colors and will more likely move into the area |
| Sound control | Children are hammering on the "Pound a Peg" toy that is resting on a table | Place a folded section of newspaper under the toy | The child who is pounding can continue to enjoy the activity without distracting others |
| Lighting | Bright sunny day | Turn off electric lights and use lighting from windows alone, or | Dimmer lighting tends to encourage quiet interpersonal interactions |
| | | adjust blinds or drapes to prevent glare in the eyes of people | Glare increases eye fatigue and children are not able to do close visual work in these conditions |

of twenty-seven children would be needed. Realistic estimation based on the physical space and the children's age is necessary to attain the desired outcome. Generally speaking, preschool children play more successfully in groups of two to four and school-age children may organize some of their play in slightly larger groupings. When individual materials are involved, such as a puzzle or watercolor materials, then the number estimated should match exactly the number of materials. Do not count sharing except when the supply of materials is large, such as with blocks. Most manipulative sets of construction materials are suitable for one or possibly two children, so multiple sets are needed if you in-

tend for more children to play. Activity spaces can be estimated as follows:

| | |
|---|---|
| Pretend play | Four |
| Blocks | Four to six |
| Six puzzles | Six |
| Board game | Two to four |
| Listening center with six headphones | Six |
| Writing center | One to four |
| Reading area | Two to four |
| Watercolor painting | Two to four |

**Private space.** A **private space** is an area designed for one child, or maybe two, to which the child can retreat from social interaction. In one second-grade classroom, the teacher had painted an old bathtub red and filled it with pillows. A child in that area, usually reading or simply watching others, always was left undisturbed. A private area of this type is not to be used for punishment or time-out but to provide a sense of relaxation, comfort, and privacy in the midst of a public environment. The use of private space may reduce stress and eventually help a child attain higher levels of self-control.

**Small-group space.** A **small-group space** is designed for fewer than eight children. In most programs for young children, four to six children may be playing together (housekeeping, blocks, water play) or engaged in studying (insect, collections, number lotto, weighing cubes). A small-group work area should have spaces for sitting and a surface for working. Primary-school teachers generally conduct reading groups in a small-group area with the children sitting in a circle or around a table. Some areas of this type, such as an art area, are specialized so that materials may be stored on adjacent shelves. Areas are more flexible when their use is not predetermined and materials may be brought into or removed from the area. Opportunities for social interaction abound in small-group settings.

**Large-group space.** Most settings have a **large-group space** of that can accommodate all of the children at one time. This type of indoor space usually is used for a variety of activities: language arts, creative dance, group discussion, games, and music. Participation in large-group activities helps children to see themselves as a part of the larger social network.

**Boundaries.** Clear, physical boundaries tend to inhibit running, provide cues to where the child is supposed to participate, curb intrusions and interruptions, and designate appropriate pathways for children to move throughout the room. Usually, furnishings and low room dividers are used to mark separations in areas. Less clear boundaries, such as those formed by floor tape, are more difficult for children to recognize, and boundaries described verbally are readily forgotten by most youngsters under age eight. Each learning center may be further defined by distinctive materials, such as books and cushions in one area and child-sized tables and chairs with board games in another.

The large-group area may have different types of learning centers at different times, with block play one day and a climber on another if there is not suf-

ficient space to have them both. In addition, two learning centers may be side by side, and deliberately left permeable to encourage small groups of children to interact (Schickedanz, et al., 1997).

Areas also should be arranged within the room so that activities do not conflict with one another or offer distractions. Quiet activities should be separated from more vigorous ones. For example, it is better to locate a study carrel near a work area or the independent reading area than near the block or game area to avoid setting limits for children who unintentionally intrude. The number, type, and arrangement of activity areas are within the control of the helping professional. Activity areas can be added, removed, or relocated to facilitate the achievement of program goals.

Activity areas are as useful outdoors as indoors. Usually, boundaries are established outdoors by varying the surface. Asphalt may be used on a ball court or a tricycle path, grass on the playing or running field, and sand or wood chips or other resilient materials under climbing equipment. Resilient surfaces promote safety, decreasing the frequency of adult cautions and limit setting. Constructed boundaries, like fences and pathways, are clear to children and provide them with clues to appropriate behaviors, as well as providing greater safety. Within well-defined areas, adults can influence social interaction by the use of mobile equipment and materials, such as the addition of water or shovels and pails to a digging area.

**Pathways.** Activity areas also must be arranged so that movement between areas is easily accomplished without interfering with the activities in progress. Such pathways need to be sufficiently wide to allow children to pass one another without physical contact. Usually, 30 to 36 inches is adequate indoors; outdoors, wider pathways are necessary to avoid collisions when children run. In some rooms, the area designated as the large-group area also serves as a means of access to other activity areas. Sometimes, the pathway is like a hallway without walls, with the large-group area at one end and small-group and private spaces arranged on either side of a central pathway. This arrangement may encourage running by toddlers but may be more efficient for older children. Effective storage supports children's independent behavior and promotes appropriate handling of materials and equipment.

**Storage.** Storage is essential to all programs. Stored items should be sorted, placed at the point of first use, and arranged so that they are easy to see, reach, and grasp and easy to replace by those who use them most often (Berns, 1993). Storage units should be planned to fit the items to be stored. Mobile storage units equipped with casters can be used to set boundaries. Materials that are used regularly should be readily accessible from pathways or activity areas. Storage of equipment and materials used outdoors should be suitable in size and accessible from the playground areas. Adult storage space that is inaccessible to children also is desirable for safety. Cleaning compounds, medicines, power tools, and other potentially harmful substances and equipment should be stored where children cannot get to them. Less frequently used materials and equipment also may be stored well away from the program area.

## Controllable Dimensions

The physical setting is composed of a number of dimensions involving the facility, the furnishings, and the materials used by children: soft-hard, open-closed, simple-complex, intrusion-seclusion, high mobility-low mobility (Jones, 1981). The particular combination of these dimensions varies according to the type of program (hospital, playroom, YMCA recreation area) as well as the goals of the program and the philosophy of the adults. These dimensions determine the overall comfort and atmosphere communicated by the physical environment.

**Softness.** The **soft-hard dimension** describes the responsiveness of the texture to the touch. A wooden desk chair is hard, and an upholstered chair is soft; asphalt is softer than cement, but turf is more responsive than either. Malleable materials such as sand, water, and play dough are softer than rigid materials such as blocks, books, or tricycles. Hardness usually is associated with efficiency and formality, and softness is associated with relaxation and comfort.

**Openness.** The **open-closed dimension** describes the degree to which the material itself restricts its use. When a material is closed, there is only one way to use it. For example, puzzles, form boards, and tracing patterns are closed. These materials also have been described as "reconstruction materials," indicating a predetermined end product (Whiren, 1977). Relatively open materials, or basic construction materials such as large blocks or a toy stove, allow greater alternatives in outcome. When a material is open, such as clay or mud, neither the alternatives nor the outcomes are limited. In furnishings, a storage cabinet would be closed if it were too high or if visibility of its contents were impeded. A relatively open cabinet would be low but with unlocked doors or glass doors. An open cabinet is low, visible, and available for use. More open settings encourage curiosity, exploration, and social interaction, and completely closed settings prohibit such behavior altogether.

**Complexity.** The **simple-complex dimension** describes the material in terms of the number of alternatives that can be generated. A simple unit has only one obvious alternative (a ladder), but when it is combined with other materials or parts to increase its complexity, children are able to use it imaginatively (two ladders hinged at the top, or a ladder and a large box). The complex material may be used in a variety of ways (a unit block). A "super unit" has three or more parts (ladder and two climbing triangles, or a water table with a water wheel and containers). Children tend to play cooperatively with complex and super units more frequently than with simple units, which often elicit solitary or parallel play activity. For older children, an Erector Set with wheels and motors is a semiopen, complex unit that will keep a small group solving problems for hours. Complexity encourages deep exploration, and variety encourages broad exploration. Formal group settings need some of each so that children will focus on an activity for an extended period of time, which is more likely with complex activities, but also can move to other alternatives for a change of pace.

**Seclusion.** The **intrusion-seclusion dimension** describes the permeability of two types of boundaries: the boundaries between the program and the things and people outside it and the boundaries between people and things inside the program. A hospital-based child-care center, for example, ordinarily has a lot of people coming into its classrooms as would a teaching hospital with a pediatric play program. People do not just look; they usually come inside and do something. These programs have much more intrusion than most others. A city classroom in a warm climate may have the windows open for ventilation, permitting traffic noise and factory fumes to enter. This is another kind of intrusion. Many classrooms have no seclusion within them. Children who are overcome by the stress of continuous interaction in a large group act up, cry, or daydream to escape for short periods. Private areas, as described earlier, are spaces in which children would have a degree of seclusion.

Small-group spaces are partially secluded. A reading or listening center may be secluded, as well as an area under a loft.

**Mobility.**   The dimension of **high or low mobility** is simply the degree of opportunity for the children to physically move their bodies in a learning center or with a material. A learning center in a gym where children throw a ball at a target is very high in mobility. A learning center where children are using headphones to listen to a story is very low in mobility. A child on a large climber is using large muscles; another, coloring with a crayon, is mostly sedentary but does have the opportunity for limited movement of the hands and arms. Children who have the opportunity to choose some sedentary activities and some active pursuits usually choose both in the course of the day. Prolonged sedentary activity causes children to wriggle to ease their muscles and to become bored and restless regardless of the interest or importance of the activity. They frequently engage in inappropriate behavior, irritating peers and adults and necessitating limit setting. To prevent this, daily schedules should provide for a balance between vigorous movement, moderate activity, and more quiet pursuits. When children's need for mobility is taken into account, the selection of equipment and the use of space usually are changed.

Each of the dimensions varies by degrees and may vary over the course of a year or within a single day. Each dimension affects the social relationships of children in the setting. An open, moderately secluded, soft environment with low-to-moderate mobility is a conversation area, much like a living room, in which children can relax and interact informally.

## Structuring for Goals

The environment should suit the goals of the program and the objectives set by the helping professional. If the leader of a toddler-parent learning group wanted to have the children move to music in a group, a moderately soft (adult lap on carpet) and closed (nothing on open shelves; toys in closed cupboards) large-group area is most appropriate. Such an activity, although simple for preschool children, is complex for toddlers who may be interacting with other adults and children for the first time in addition to getting guidance from someone other than parents. Mobility is high, so sufficient space is needed to avoid collision. Seclusion is provided by the availability of the parent's lap if the activity be-

comes overwhelming. Changing one dimension would affect the patterns of social interaction. For example, if the toys were out on open shelves, adults would spend most of the interaction in setting limits and redirecting the children. Children would have little opportunity to observe other toddlers and would have less pleasant experiences with other adults.

Adult behavior also is influenced by the physical environment. The organization of the space and the availability and number of materials accessible to the children directly influence the behavior of the adult (Polloway, 1974). If materials are scarce and sharing is mandatory, adults spend more time monitoring the materials. If space is limited, and few or no boundaries are clear, children tend to intrude into others' space, increasing the need to limit setting (Polloway, 1974).

In a third-grade classroom, children who had desks arranged in small clusters screened by dividers, a conversation area, and a private space where children could be alone had longer attention spans, were less distractable, and answered more problems correctly than did the comparison group. The seclusion in this classroom was substantially higher than in a less successful room. The teacher, however, was much more mobile, spending one-fifth as much time at her desk as her counterpart and using considerably fewer behavior restrictions (Zifferblatt, 1972). The amount of space also influences the amount of verbal and nonverbal controlling behavior used by adults. When the density of children increases, so does the frequency of limit setting (Phyfe-Perkins, 1982). Adults who can decrease controlling behavior have more opportunities to engage in satisfying social interactions with children and are better able to meet program goals as well.

**Learning centers.**   A particular application of goals to the learning environment is in the planning and implementing of classroom learning centers.

The selection of centers in Table 9–4 is based on general goals of having children manage their own behavior for at least a portion of their day. Also, it is based on them having positive feelings about themselves and others, and that they learn through the active engagement with materials within their environment and from their peers. Adults must periodically check to see that children are achieving success in their learning and social interactions and adjust the activity if they are failing to do so.

The specific selection of centers, the number of them, and the length of time that they are used in a

▼ Table 9–4    Sample Learning Centers by Age

| THREE-YEAR-OLDS | FIVE-YEAR-OLDS | SEVEN-YEAR-OLDS |
| --- | --- | --- |
| Art center | Art center | Art center |
| Large hollow blocks | Large hollow blocks | |
| Unit blocks | Unit blocks | Unit blocks |
| Library | Library | Reading center |
| | Writing center | Writing center |
| | Listening center | Listening center |
| Messy play (sand, water) | Messy play | |
| Manipulative toys | Manipulative toys | Math center |
| Science, living things | Science center | Science center |
| Housekeeping | Housekeeping/thematic play | Housekeeping/thematic play |
| | Story reenactment | Story reenactment |
| | | Computer |

daily program is variable in an age group as well as across age groups. The needs of specific children within the group must also be taken into account. Children vary in their ability to manage their own behavior, their skills at decision making, their experience in settings outside the home, and in personal experience. For example, Harry has been told never to do anything unless he has had previous permission. He is likely to need a different level of support and supervision than Anthony, who expects that he can do everything that is not expressly forbidden to him. Yet, in all cases, when adults arrange the physical space according to the principles described, both of these children are more likely to be successful in a well-organized environment.

The furnishings, room arrangement, and general quality of the physical environment are important components of the setting. In addition, the materials used by children and the way they are managed influences interpersonal relations between children and between adults and children. The word *materials* includes everything that children use in the program: textbooks, pencils, art supplies, tennis rackets, tableware, or toys.

## Choosing Appropriate Materials

Adults can promote competent and independent behavior in children by providing a moderately rich assortment of exploratory materials (Dodge, Dombro, and Koralek, 1991). It also is desirable to structure the environment and organize the materials to enhance all aspects of the child's social development as well as to meet basic needs (Ard and Pitts, 1990). However, materials also may be a prime cause of many disruptive behaviors.

**Developmentally appropriate materials.** Materials should reflect the goals of the program and the various levels of competence of children. Adults would think it strange if someone gave a chemistry set to a five-year-old. Not only would the child be at risk of swallowing some of the chemicals, but in all probability, the set would quickly be destroyed and the child frustrated with failure. However, the same set given to a twelve-year-old could provide hours of pleasure and instruction. Frequently, materials intended, for older children create potential risks and failure for younger ones. In addition, when older children use equipment and materials designed for young children, they lose interest because there is no challenge, and they find new, often destructive ways to use them.

**Structurally safe materials.** Materials should be examined for potential safety hazards. Sturdiness, durability, craftsmanship, and appropriate construction materials all contribute to safe products. For example, a metal climbing frame may be a sensible, safe purchase for three- to five-year-olds, but a wooden one would be much safer for toddlers and young preschoolers in cold climates. Young children, tend to put their tongues on the metal in winter and can become stuck to it and badly injured. Tricycles available in local stores are not as sturdily constructed as those designed specifically for use by groups of children.

Maintenance of equipment is necessary to ensure continued safety. Eventually, even the most sturdy toys break down. Maintenance in terms of cleanliness is especially important for young children, who are likely to put things in their mouths. Care also should be taken to see that materials aren't likely to cause choking. If an object is small enough to get into a toddler's mouth and has a diameter between that of a dime and a quarter, it might get stuck in the throat.

**Materials that work.** Children become frustrated when equipment and materials do not operate, which sometimes leads to disruptive behavior. The wheels of trucks should turn; scissors should cut; finger paint should be thick, and the paper heavy enough or glossy so that it doesn't fall apart. It is nearly impossible to trace accurately through standard typing paper; tracing paper and paper clips make the job much easier. Children cannot use basketballs, kick balls, or volleyballs that are underinflated. Seeing that all materials are usable is the responsibility of the adult.

**Complete materials that are ready to use.** Puzzles should have all their pieces. If one gets lost, it can be replaced by molding in some plastic wood to fit the hole. One ten-year-old was extremely upset when, after working on a hooked pillow cover for weeks, she discovered that there was insufficient yarn in the kit to complete it. Incomplete materials lead to unnecessary feelings of failure and frustration and loss self-esteem.

In addition, when materials need to be brought out by an adult for a demonstration or for children's use, they should be assembled in advance so that children don't have to wait while the adult rummages around in a cupboard or drawer for a pair of scissors or a bit of wire. Waiting children usually lose interest or become disruptive. Complete preparation by the adult includes some plan for cleaning up, so having a damp sponge in a pan would be appropriate preparation for a messy activity. In this way, the adult never needs to leave the group of children and can offer continuous guidance.

**Organizing materials.** Storage should be where the material is most frequently used or where it is first used and located in logical areas. If children know where something is located, they can go and get it themselves to complete a project. This is especially important for common items like paper, crayons, scissors, and the like.

Materials also should be stored so that children can take care of them. For example, taping shapes of unit blocks on the back of a cupboard so that children know where to put each size and shape encourages independence. Materials that have many pieces, like beads, small math cubes, or Cuisenaire rods, should be placed in sturdy containers such as

plastic shoe boxes or tiny laundry baskets because the cardboard boxes soon wear out. In this way, children can keep all materials that go together in one place.

**Attractively displayed materials.** Neatness and orderliness are aspects of attractiveness. Materials are easier to find and more inviting if they are not crammed into a crowded area. Young children simply have difficulty in selecting materials on crowded shelves.

Materials that are displayed in a moderately empty space on the shelf are most likely to be used. Some materials should be available to children and displayed on low, open shelves. Puzzles in a puzzle rack or laid out on a table ready for use are more appealing than a large, heavy stack of them (Whiren, 1977).

**Appropriate size of equipment and materials.** Tables, chairs, desks, or other equipment add to the comfort and decrease the fatigue of children if they are sized correctly. Adults also should have at least one chair that fits them to sit on occasionally.

Fewer problems would be encountered at mealtime if preschool children were offered six-inch plates, salad forks, and four- or five-ounce glasses to use. Serving dishes (soup bowls) with teaspoon servers would enable children to serve themselves amounts of food that they can reasonably consume. Using small, unbreakable pitchers for milk and juice encourages independence as well. When children determine portion size for themselves there is less wasted. Children who are entering the growth spurt around the ages of eleven or twelve might reasonably use large, divided trays that can hold substantial servings.

Young children spend much time in adult-sized environments. Therefore, in programs designed for them, the environment and all the materials should be appropriate for their sizes. Long mirrors in a toddler, room should be mounted horizontally, slightly above the molding on the wall; for preschoolers, mirrors can be set vertically, but again, low. The height of sinks, toilets, and drinking fountains can be adjusted by building platforms around adult-sized facilities, or child-sized fixtures can be installed. If materials, equipment, and furnishings are appropriate in size, children can act more independently and develop good habits.

**Quantities appropriate to the number of children.** If there are enough materials for a particular activity, children can work without conflict. If there is an insufficient supply, either the number of materials should be increased or the number of children using them decreased. For example, if a third-grade teacher has twelve books and fourteen children, she can either hold two consecutive sessions of seven children and use the books on hand or get two more books. Either solution is better than having children rush to the reading area in order to get a book for themselves. Toddlers do not comprehend sharing. In addition, a toy being played with by another child is more appealing than one on a shelf. Duplicate toys allow the desires of the toddler to be met without conflict.

The number of materials that should be made available during free play in an early-childhood program also is related to the number of children. Usually, the total number of play units should be two-and-a-half times the number of children (Whiren, 1970). A *play unit* is an object or set of objects needed by a child to use the material effectively. A book is one play unit; a small set of Tinker Toys or a small set of Lego blocks is one unit; a doll with its clothes and blanket is one unit. Having an adequate number of play units allows the child to use a variety of materials in one play space. In a complex, open area such as a housekeeping area, there may be four spaces for children and ten or more play units, enabling children to engage in cooperative sociodramatic play for an extended period of time without conflict. With fewer play units, the children either would compete for the materials or would discontinue the activity sooner.

Adequate supplies of materials are necessary for any program regardless of the children's age if children are to be reasonably successful. If hospitalized children paint ceramics, each child needs a figurine or plaque to paint on and paint within reach. Sharing paints between beds is not practical because of the distance involved and lack of mobility of children in traction or receiving intravenous feeding.

**Adjusting space and materials.** Choosing materials appropriately and organizing and displaying them carefully are strategies used to *prevent* frustration, interpersonal conflict, loss of property, and physical risk. These strategies are the result of advanced planning with ultimate goals of supporting positive social interactions and appropriate behavior. Administrators are responsible for purchasing, as well as organizing the overall program. Teachers or program leaders are responsible for arranging the space and materials for the children to use on a

daily basis (Kostelnik, Soderman, and Whiren, in press). In addition, supervising adults must make adjustments based on individual or group needs as children interact within the space, use equipment, and engage in the activities with materials in meaningful ways.

The most common adjustments that adults make to the environment are to *add materials, take them away, or childproof the environment.*

**Adding to the environment.** There are many ways adults add to the environment. A picture related to the concepts that are being taught might be hung and discussed with the children. An artifact, or an article of clothing representative of the cultural heritage of one of the children might be brought in to share. Fresh flowers or living plants and animals might be added temporarily in the setting to enhance the science learning of the children.

**Taking away from the environment.** Taking away a misplaced container of water from the library area and putting it back in the watertable where it belongs would be appropriate. Taking away inedibles from the guinea pig cage such as splinters of wood, or removing a frog from someone's pocket into a terrarium until it can be returned to a more suitable place, would protect the lives of these animals. Sometimes the removal is temporary, but necessary, such as moving all the chairs away from a table so children can cook, or putting materials out of sight so they don't distract children from group times.

**Childproofing the environment.** Lastly, adding materials, taking them away, or altering them are necessary for childproofing the environment. Childproofing means providing the necessary adjustments to ensure the safety of the children. It is usually done before children enter the environment but may occur when safety risks are first detected. Several examples of this are illustrated in Table 9–5.

The amount of space necessary may have been incorrectly estimated for an activity. For example, Mr. Bongard placed an indoor climber about 18 inches from an open, screened window one hot summer day because he thought that the vigorous activity would benefit from the potential air circulation. However, as he was watching Brad and Doug climb to the top between the window and the climber, they attempted to stand on the nearby window sill. He hastily lifted Brad down and asked Doug to climb down before he moved the climber at least 3 feet away from the window. The quick adjustment to increase safety was essential. Sometimes space should be limited instead of increased. Miss Adkins took her kindergarten children to the gym to run simple relay races. At first, she set the activity up so that children would run the length of the gym. She noticed that they were quickly tired and restless as they had to wait so long for a turn. She then shifted to running a second group of relay races across the width of the gym, which still gave ample room to run but cut down the waiting time. Adjustments by moving equipment or by increasing or decreasing space most appropriate for an activity are fairly typical of most child-centered programs.

Sometimes adjustments are made in the ways in which directions are given. At the beginning of this chapter, Edward used a pictograph so that he could assess whether or not he was free to choose completely on his own what he should do. Using sequence photographs or drawings for routine activities such as washing hands, tying shoes, taking off wraps, or doing chores on the campsites are easy structuring strategies that support directions already given to children on how to do the task. In addition, individual children may not understand the directions on the use of equipment or materials so that additional explanations and demonstrations are necessary for each person to be successful. For example, having a classroom computer with a variety of programs as one of the learning centers is not useful if the children do not know how to operate

the machine. One demonstration to the group is generally inadequate. Mr. Rock discovered that children were hesitant to attempt independent use. He therefore adjusted his strategy of encouragement to one of training a few of the children in the kindergarten to use the machine readily and then asked those children to give demonstrations to their peers. This, each one teach one, adjustment also supported social interaction and contributed to the prosocial goal of helpfulness.

Occasionally, a center is adjusted by simply closing it. Mrs. Perry closed the thematic play center "Seed Store" when children were just throwing the seeds around instead of engaging in productive play. Upon close appraisal, she decided that the children didn't have the necessary understandings about seeds, their use, or how they were bought and sold to engage in the play. Once the necessary instruction had been given the center was reopened successfully several days later.

Most frequently, adjustments are very simple behaviors that make the children more likely to be successful.

---

Miss Peabody noticed that the four children at the table were pushing each others' materials around and arguing as they tried to place large pieces of paper on the table. A basket with lots of scissors was in the middle, so Miss Peabody removed enough scissors for

### ▼ Table 9–5    Examples of Adjusting Materials to Increase Safety

| OBSERVATION WHEN CHECKING | ACTION TAKEN |
| --- | --- |
| A toddler has put some toys in the toilet and is happily playing. | Take away the toys, put them in hot soapy water with disinfectant, and close the bathroom door. |
| A three-year-old has put on the hot water at full force to wash her hands. | Adjust the water temperature and flow. |
| A group of seven-year-olds are filling balloons with water and throwing them in the hall. | Stop the balloon throwing. Give children a mop and pail and show them how to clean up the mess. |
| The cord to the coffee pot is hanging over the edge of a table in the teachers' area, but in sight of youngsters. | Fold the cord loosely and fasten it with a wire twist or rubber band. |
| Pointed, adult scissors are left on the activity table in the kindergarten. | Take away the scissors out of children's reach. |
| A rung of the wooden ladder is broken. | Take away the ladder. |
| A mother gave the child a sack with medications and directions for administering them and sent her into the primary classroom. | Take the medicine from the child and place it in a safe spot. |

each child from the basket, placed them on the table, and put the basket on a nearby shelf, where it was still accessible; this adjustment left enough space for each child and eliminated the cause of conflicts.

Mr. Turkus responded to the frustrated cry of three-year-old George, who slapped his painting with the paint-brush and exclaimed, "Is not red." The red drippings on the outside of the jar did not match the muddy, purplish red color of the paint inside. Mr. Turkus showed George how to rinse the brushes and jars, and provided a small amount of the three primary colors. He then demonstrated how to keep the red paint red by using a separate brush for each color. George continued to paint happily.

Ms. Polzin noticed Nicholas riding his truck through the block area and ramming into block structures that Claire and Raphael were building. When they moved to hit him, he seemed oblivious to the cause of their anger. Once a settlement between the children was complete, Ms. Polzin used masking tape to mark off a road for the truck where block structures could not be built.

Mr. Stetson wanted to increase the cooperation skills of his boy scouts so he asked them to reorganize the camp storage shed. They discussed the problem together and then implemented their plan. When some of the equipment was too bulky for one child, Mr. Stetson suggested that he ask others to help.

Miss Clark attended to a child who got a sliver in his hand from the edge of the climber. She then sanded the rough place to make it safer.

In each of these instances, the adults added, took away, or substituted materials or childproofed the environment to enhance the success of the children in their care. Each adjustment was made as a result of the adults' checking on children's activities and assessing the nature of the problem to be solved by the presence, absence, or condition of the appropriate materials or equipment. Additional examples of structuring the physical environment for a preschool are provided in Table 9–6.

| ▼ Table 9–6 | Sample Structuring Strategies in a Preschool Setting | |
|---|---|---|
| **AREA** | **SITUATION** | **ACTION TAKEN** |
| Open floor near manipulative toy area | Children are walking through the play space, dislocating pieces of the small construction materials. | Move the construction materials out of the way. Add a hula hoop on the floor to define separate space for building. |
| Manipulative toy table | Children are tracing the pieces of the holiday puzzle using a large crayon that is coming off on the puzzle. | Add some large pencils and avoid restricting the tracing activity. |
| | Colored 1-inch cubes are on the table. Children do not appear to be showing any interest. | Play with the cubes. Using 1-inch graph paper and crayons, make a simple pattern and offer it to expand the play. Offer crayons and paper for the children to record the patterns they make with the cubes. |
| Pathway near the manipulative toy table | Clutter is on the floor from small blocks and Duplos. Children cannot pass easily. | Offer the storage containers and assist children in cleaning up the clutter during the free play period. |
| Manipulative toy storage | Puzzles are on top of other materials. Some puzzles are taken apart but put on the stack during free play. | Bring a puzzle rack to the manipulative display/storage area. Help children complete puzzles and place them in the rack. Remove puzzles that children systematically leave uncompleted. |
| Easel | The paint brushes are very full of paint and the paint appears crusty on the top. | Remove the brushes, wash them out, and then return them. Add water to the paint to thin it a little. |
| | Paint is dripping on the floor as children paint. | Add a damp sponge and demonstrate how to wipe up the floor, rinse, and wipe again. |

*continued*

▼ **Table 9–6—continued**    **Sample Structuring Strategies in a Preschool Setting**

| AREA | SITUATION | ACTION TAKEN |
|---|---|---|
| Art area | Collage materials fall off a child's art construction. | Add paste or glue showing the child how to do it. (If the child is not present, you may consider pasting it yourself.) |
| | Child is gluing wood blocks, which are slipping. | Add paste to the glue, about half and half. |
| Book corner | Child has a crayon poised for writing in a book. | Remove crayons from the area. Put them away. |
| | A child turns a page that simply falls out. | Assist the child with looking at the book and then remove it from the collection for repair. |
| Pathway near book corner | Books are scattered on the floor and children are walking on them. | Offer a choice of which book to remove from the pathway. |
| Large group area | A child takes a small figure out of his pocket and plays with it, showing others and not letting people touch it during the story. | Remove the toy. Offer to put it in his bag or locker. |
| | A child walks to the piano and begins to strike the keys vigorously during cleanup time. | Close the piano. Tell the child she may play during free play. |
| Snack table | Two small pitchers are on the table where children are waiting impatiently and telling those with the juice to hurry up. | Fill a third juice pitcher. |
| | Children are touching several crackers in the basket. | Offer a choice between a Ritz and a graham cracker. Then remove the basket. |
| | Child's job is to set the table but is just looking at it. | Repeat the standard directions one step at a time. |
| Woodworking bench | Child is having difficulty pounding two pieces of wood together. | Offer a bottle cap or a soft, thin piece of wood for nailing. |
| Water table | Children are splashing a lot in the water table, trying to get one another wet. | Offer containers to fill and suggest a play sequence. |
| Dramatic play area | The dress-up clothes are on the floor and the dishes are scattered. No children are present. | Adjust by cleaning up the area and organizing it. Put materials in logical places. If too many clothes are available, remove some. |
| Cubbies | Child is not removing his wraps. | Offer a choice of which item to remove first or offer a choice between now and in 5 minutes. |
| Music center | Homemade shakers are coming apart, losing contents. | Repair or replace them. |
| Outdoors | An adult is facing away from the group, but toward two children digging. | Move to the other side of the diggers so that you can see them as well as most of the group. |
| Bathroom | Children are not flushing the toilet. | Point to the pictograph and help children remember the routine. |

## SKILLS FOR INFLUENCING CHILDREN'S SOCIAL DEVELOPMENT BY STRUCTURING THE PHYSICAL ENVIRONMENT

Structuring is a process in which some change occurs. Good management means changing in order to meet short- and long-range goals. You will be able to apply this process to many problems in professional practice. In this section, we will discuss how to formulate and change a daily schedule, how to teach a habit, how to arrange and alter activity areas, and how to influence behavior by adding objects to or removing them from the environment.

### Establish and Support a Daily Schedule to Enhance Social Development

**1. Know the daily schedule of the program.** Follow the basic daily schedule of the program and the flowchart so that you are able to coordinate your activities with others. Find out about any events that might change the routine. Know the schedules for other groups (playground use, special teachers, etc.), if appropriate, so your activities are coordinated.

**2. Plan the schedule in detail and write it down.** Write a time sequence in 15-minute intervals starting 30 minutes before children arrive and ending 30 minutes after they leave. Include all events that are predetermined, such as meals, naps, recess, or special activities. Estimate the time needed for these activities and mark it off on the paper. Estimate the time needed to get the children to and from each of these events and mark it off. Now, you have large sections of time that can be used for other program goals.

List activities that are appropriate to your program. Cluster together those activities that children can do during the same time period. Consider factors such as noise, mobility of children, and individual differences in pace. Allow sufficient time for the slowest child to complete an activity and enough variety so that children who finish sooner can do something other than wait. Estimate the time needed for each cluster or each activity period. Most groups of children need at least 1 hour of uninterrupted time so

they are able to complete a task satisfactorily every day. These activity periods may involve total group participation or may include small-group and individual activities. Maintain a balance of whole-group and small-group or individual activities. Both self-started and adult-selected activities should be planned. Enter these estimates into the plan. (A complete schedule was presented in Table 9–2.)

If there are multiple adults, discuss the plan and determine which adult will supervise which activities. Determine the timing of movements of adults. In general, adults should precede children or move with them from one place to another. Write this into the plan. Determine who will make the decisions as to implementing the schedule with the children.

Identify the advance preparation that needs to be done before the children arrive and the cleanup after they leave. Assign tasks to adults, or fit some cleanup tasks into the activities themselves. Write these into the schedule as well.

Write out a schedule with the details appropriate for your role until the schedule is learned.

**3. Describe the daily schedule to children.** Tell children the sequence of events before they occur. Communicate with parents of toddlers about the schedule prior to the children's entry into the program. Older preschool children may simply be told the broad schedule; grade-school children should be told the schedule, or the schedule should be posted in writing when they arrive. In all cases, the basic sequence of events should be clear. Remind children of the next event during the program to help them judge time and to complete activities when appropriate.

**4. Walk children through the schedule on their first day or assign another child to escort them when moving between unfamiliar places.** A new child in camp or in a hospital setting will not automatically know where specific facilities are, regardless of the child's age.

*continued*

## SKILLS FOR INFLUENCING CHILDREN'S SOCIAL DEVELOPMENT BY STRUCTURING THE PHYSICAL ENVIRONMENT—continued

Reassure the children and tell them in advance of changes or unusual events.

**5. Tell children and adults clearly what they are expected to do.** Use phrases such as "You may go to the playroom and paint" instead of "You don't need to stay in this room all the time."

Communicate with other adults if slight changes in the schedule are necessary so that children do not get confusing messages. Say: "Mrs. Carter, I will be delayed in getting to the playroom for about 5 minutes. Will you keep the children here or send someone with them?" rather than just arriving late.

**6. Check that program activities are prepared in advance of the children's arrival or provide time for the older children to prepare their own materials.** For children to use materials well and to take care of property, provide for easy access of what is needed. Survey the area, remove unnecessary clutter, and ensure that there are enough materials available for the number of children who are likely to participate.

**7. Begin activities when the first child arrives.** Do not delay. Patient waiting is extremely difficult for all children and many adults. Repeat directions if necessary for children who join the activity a little later than others.

**8. Evaluate the effectiveness of the schedule at regular intervals.** Make the first assessment at the end of the first three or four weeks of implementation. Continue to assess the schedule every three to four months after that. Frequently, a change of season results in a change of schedule. Switching outdoor and indoor activities according to seasonal variations is typical.

Observe children for signs of boredom and stress and share this information with others so that adjustments to the schedule, the space, the pace, or the intensity of the program may be made. Aimless behavior, wandering, or flitting from one thing to another may indicate that there are not enough interesting activities available.

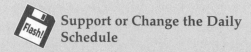 **Support or Change the Daily Schedule**

**1. Establish clear goals before altering the schedule.** Know why the alteration is taking place.

**2. Communicate the revised plan to the staff.** Make necessary alterations in staff assignments. If whole clusters of activities are being reorganized, a written plan will be necessary, but if you are switching one cluster with another, this may not be needed. Clarify any alterations in your duties and write down the new schedule to carry with you during the first few days until the new schedule becomes routine.

**3. Tell the children about the new schedule in advance.** Encourage children to ask questions. Discuss any new signals that you will use to indicate transitions. Remind individuals if they become confused.

**4. Carry out the new schedule and allow a substantial period of time before evaluating it according to the new goals.** Expect children to be confused, disorganized, and possibly stressed when major schedule changes are made. Young children may take as long as three weeks to fully adjust to a major change in schedule, older children are likely to take several days. This transition period is a time for review of program materials, not a time to introduce novelty, especially for younger children.

**5. Monitor the results over time and make minor adjustments as necessary.** Observe and report on behavior of the children under your supervision. Reassure children. Check to see if social interactions improve using the new schedule.

**6. Evaluate the new schedule in terms of long- and short-term goals for the children as well as**

## SKILLS FOR INFLUENCING CHILDREN'S SOCIAL DEVELOPMENT BY STRUCTURING THE PHYSICAL ENVIRONMENT—continued

**in terms of the new objectives.** Was the outcome worth the time, effort, and confusion involved? Are children helping, sharing, and cooperating? Are there fewer instances of limit setting in the new time frame?

### Facilitate Children's Transitions

**1. Tell children in advance that a transition will occur.** Simple statements such as, "It will be time to put your things away in 5 minutes" allow children an opportunity to finish their projects or organize their materials.

Give clear signals that a transition has begun. A nonverbal signal such as an open palm raised high may indicate to children to assemble at that place. Playing a song or a chord on an instrument also may indicate a transition. Straightforward directions also can be used, such as "Push your chair under the table and walk outdoors."

**2. Send the children to a place or an activity rather than simply away from one.** Children should never wonder what they are supposed to do. Give clear directions to children so that they move to the place and do the action required: "Hang up your coat, then sit on the rug to look at a book." This may also occur during option times with individual transitions: "When you have completed the painting, wash your hands before going on to another activity." Clear, specific directions are essential when the entire group is moving from one place to another: "We are going outdoors. Mr. Gibbs will go first. Put your hands at your sides as you go through the hall."

**3. Ask children to tell you what they plan to do next when they have a choice, as they leave one activity for another.** Simply inquire, "What are you planning to do next?" If a child cannot seem to decide, suggest alternatives. Once a child voices a choice, he or she is less likely to wander and engage in aimless behavior that is sometimes seen in preschool programs and open primary classrooms.

**4. Dismiss children from a larger group individually or in sets of three to five.** When twenty or more children are moving at the same time, they inevitably make noise, jostle one another, and sometimes engage in rough-and-tumble play episodes. Smaller groups and individuals move more quickly and with less stress. Social conversation is more common than defensive behaviors.

**5. Be sure that an adult always precedes younger children.** Lead the line as children are moving through a hallway together, such as going to the gym or outdoors during a fire drill. With preschool children, one adult should lead and one should end the group. Sit in the large-group area and begin an activity from when the first child arrives until all children are present. Finger plays and songs are typically successful. With multiple adults available, direct them to the activity areas before the first child leaves the group.

More experienced children (ages six to twelve) may lead the group when the transitions are part of the familiar routine.

**6. Count the children before you leave and after you arrive in a new area in a whole-group transition.** Be sure that no child has been left behind or has gone to the toilet just as the group is leaving. This separation is both dangerous and frightening to the child.

**7. Establish clear expectations for appropriate behavior for transitions and teach these to young children.** Tell them what to do and how to do it. Walk them through the process, giving directions one step at a time. Children entering new programs typically do not know what to do during transitions. They may not know how to perform self-help skills such as removing wraps or boots. This is best handled as an instructional opportunity. Transitions that are really difficult for young school-age children are getting on and off a bus, entering and leaving the school, leaving the classroom, and going to the school cafeteria or even out to recess. Simplify transitions by telling children how to behave and then

*continued*

## SKILLS FOR INFLUENCING CHILDREN'S SOCIAL DEVELOPMENT BY STRUCTURING THE PHYSICAL ENVIRONMENT—continued

practicing with them until they can perform acceptably. Take them to the places where they will have to go when few other children are present. An actual orientation to the space may diminish their fears and confusion.

Preschool children may have difficulty participating in fire and tornado drills, cleaning up the classroom, and moving from one space to another as a group in a building. Again, discussing expectations and practicing appropriate behaviors with trusted adults help children be more successful.

**8. As quickly as possible, help children to handle transitions as routine events.** Use the same pattern such as a song, verse, hand clap, or sentence to indicate a transition at the same time each day. This will help the children to predict what comes next and to know what they are to do. Change your pattern for handling a transition only when it is clearly ineffective. Adults and children have difficulty with change, thereby experiencing moments of stress, bewilderment, confusion, and sometimes anger. To minimize these less desirable feelings, try to make transitions quick and efficient.

**9. Minimize waiting time.** With adequate planning and structuring of the physical environment, much of the time that children spend waiting can be diminished. Some suggestions to do this are as follows:

▼ Provide a sheet of paper for children to sign up for activities that everyone can do. Children as young as three appreciate having their name recorded or making marks to represent their names.

▼ For older children, write a weekly assignment so that they know what must be done during learning center time. They can then use a pictograph strip or a chart to indicate when they have completed the tasks and are ready for the teacher's feedback.

▼ Unless conditions are unsafe, let children get a drink, go to the toilet, or eat their snack whenever they need to. If the source is too far

away, use a buddy system that requires two children to go together.

 **Teach Routines**

Planned routines usually are taught to young children and usually relate to some aspect of daily life that is repeated regularly, such as self-help skills like eating, dressing, and storing daily supplies. Once learned, children can act independently and the need for limit setting is diminished.

**1. Determine the need for the habit.** A routine is appropriate for an activity that is repetitive and time consuming but basically motoric in nature.

**2. Seek information about how to do the task efficiently.** Experienced professionals are a good source of information. Maria Montessori wrote out various skills of daily living, such as hand washing and table cleaning and setting, in detail over her career. Observe an efficient adult doing the task and write down each step in sequence. Note the placement of objects before and after use.

**3. Write out the steps in sequence.** Include all steps that a child would have to do to carry out the task.

**4. Try out the sequence on an adult or older child.** Give directions according to the sequence and ask the person not to do anything until told. Identify omissions and unclear directions, then revise the sequence.

**5. Discuss the sequence with other staff members to identify potential problems.** Post the sequence in the area in which children are most likely to need to use the habit. Know the details of the established routines, write them out on a card to carry with you in the beginning, clarify any questions that you have with experienced adults in the situation, and then implement the routine.

## SKILLS FOR INFLUENCING CHILDREN'S SOCIAL DEVELOPMENT BY STRUCTURING THE PHYSICAL ENVIRONMENT—continued

**6. Give direct instructions to children using clear, simple "do it" statements.** These statements generally consist of a verb and a phrase. A sequence for putting on a coat for a preschool child follows:

> *Find* your coat.
> *Take* it out of the cubby.
> *Put* it on the floor (with opening up).
> *Find* the collar of your coat. (Point to it if necessary.)
> *Stand* with your toes near the collar.
> *Put* both arms in the arm holes. (Point.)
> *Lift* your arms over your head (with arms in the coat).
> *Bring* your arms down behind your back, and push your hands out of the sleeves.

Ordinarily, this sequence would continue until the child's coat was buttoned or zipped and the child was ready to go outside.

**7. Check on the children's daily progress.** Remind children of the next step in the sequence when they get partway through it and need help. Praise their successes.

**8. Adjust the time spent on the task.** Newly introduced tasks will take more time for children to complete than ones that have become habitual. Allow more time for unfamiliar tasks; shorten the time allocated as children become more proficient.

**9. Evaluate the procedure.** Determine whether the process is efficient and is helping you to reach your goals for children's social development. If it is, continue the practice; if it is not, adjust the plan. Once a habit is established, alter it only if absolutely necessary.

### Arrange the Room to Support Social Development

Classrooms, playrooms, gymnasiums, and other spaces are used for children's activities. Following are some general guidelines for initially setting up a room. However, the nature of the program and the nature of the space will greatly influence the specifics.

**1. Survey the space.** Note the placement of potential hazards such as electrical outlets, probable pathways such as doorways, water sources, and windows.

**2. Imagine how children might move within this space and try to predict the problems they might encounter that are likely to require setting limits.** For example, children do not usually carry water well and are likely to spill it. Spilling or dripping paint is not unusual. Extension cords are a trip hazard for children and adults. Even older youngsters have poked things into electrical outlets. Surfaces next to areas where children form lines are usually touched, leaving dirty fingerprints. Younger children trip and fall quite frequently. Youngsters frequently run and mill about during arrival and dismissal as well as other schedule transitions.

**3. Arrange the furnishings in the room so that the need to set limits is minimized and children are safe, comfortable, and as independent as possible.** Consider all of the dimensions of the space so that children are most likely to interact together appropriately, play together, and are less likely to interrupt each other or come into conflict. Some specific suggestions are as follows:

▼ Place quiet activities, such as looking at books, away from the more active areas of the room.
▼ Place cubbies or lockers near doorways, electrical equipment near outlets, paints near a water source.
▼ Place messy activities on hard surface floors and potentially noisy activities (blocks, workbench) on carpets.
▼ Attach fabric to the open shelf units with Velcro fasteners so that the shelves may be closed off during group time.
▼ Interrupt long pathways that invite running by placing interesting activities partway

*continued*

## SKILLS FOR INFLUENCING CHILDREN'S SOCIAL DEVELOPMENT BY STRUCTURING THE PHYSICAL ENVIRONMENT—continued

down them that would require children to turn right or left.

▼ Use shelving that allows storage and display of materials such as paper, glue, pencils, crayons, and scissors to be readily accessible and near where they would be used; this prevents children from having to cross areas of the room repeatedly. If necessary, for older children have writing supplies in all centers.

**4. Evaluate the placement of furnishings in terms of social development goals.** If peer conflict regularly occurs in the same place, consider reorganizing the space. Are children able to move through the space with confidence and ease without interrupting someone else? Where do most of the limit-setting instances occur? Use the answers to these questions to help you restructure the area.

a. *Place activities that use water near a source of water if possible.* These activities might be water play, art, or food-preparation activities. Place related equipment and storage nearby. If water is not available in the room, place this center in a low-traffic area and bring water in pails.

b. *Place the cloaking area near the entrance to the room or in a hallway outside the room.* Provide for the storage of boots, mittens, clothing, and personal belongings with open shelving, cubbies, or lockers. A bench or seat for putting on boots also is needed here.

c. *Select an appropriate spot for large-group activities to take place.* Pick a section of the room where an electrical outlet is available so that audiovisual equipment can be used conveniently. Put a carpet in this area to define the space and to deaden noise.

d. *Use storage units, seating, variation in flooring, and small dividers to form boundaries.* This reduces interruptions.

e. *Place high-mobility activities in one section of the room and low-mobility activities in another section to minimize interference.*

f. *Allow space for moving from one activity to another without going through the middle of an activity area.*

g. *Place materials and equipment in areas where they are most frequently used.*

h. *Put seating in areas according to the number of children who are to use the area.* The size of the private area should be very small, with room for just one. The number of chairs at a table in a work area will be determined by the number that can work at a particular activity. Remove extra chairs. Sketch out a plan to use the space first, then move the furniture. When in doubt as to sizes or fit of major furnishings, measure them and the space before moving them.

**5. Adapt the room arrangement as needed to meet the needs of children experiencing physical or mental challenges.** Children in wheelchairs must have more space in pathways than children who are independently mobile. Children with broken limbs who are temporarily experiencing limitations in mobility may also require space adjustments so they may do what they can for themselves. Children with sensory or mental impairments may require greater attention to maintaining clear walkways, background noise control, or opportunities for seclusion from time to time. Parents and specialists usually can provide suggestions for meeting the special needs of individuals. In principle, adults structure the environment to enable the successful participation of all the children within it.

 **Change the Qualities of the Room**

Given the inflexible nature of objects and rooms, there are basically two kinds of things you can do. You may *add* something, or you may *take away* something. Sometimes things can be repaired. These options apply to the controllable dimensions discussed earlier, to furnishings, and to materials.

**1. Observe how the children use the space.** Pay attention to noise, mobility, comfort, traffic patterns, ability to concentrate, frequency of interruptions, intrusions, level of wander-

**SKILLS FOR INFLUENCING CHILDREN'S SOCIAL DEVELOPMENT BY STRUCTURING THE PHYSICAL ENVIRONMENT—continued**

ing, or engagement in activities. Share observations with other adults working in the environment.

**2. Determine whether or not the physical environment supports your goals for the children.** Consider such factors as softness, openness, complexity, mobility, and seclusion.

**3. Add or subtract objects in the physical environment to achieve specific goals related to children's social development.**

**a.** To increase the softness of the room, add draperies, rugs, pillows, upholstered furniture, stuffed animals, and activities using pliable materials such as papier-mâché, water, sand, and play dough. To add hardness, remove these things.

**b.** To increase the openness of the environment, add open shelves, remove the doors of cupboards, or place materials within the reach of children. Add construction materials such as blocks, art supplies, and the soft materials mentioned earlier.

**c.** To decrease the openness, shut cupboard doors or cover open shelving with a sheet. Provide materials that require one correct response, such as puzzles or workbooks.

**d.** To increase complexity, add related elements to a unit. For example, a teacher of ten-year-olds had twelve activity cards to do in sequence related to fairy tales that children could complete in an individual activity area. Books, paper, pens, paints, and a variety of other materials were available to use. For little children, hats or dress-up clothing may be added to the housekeeping area or dinosaurs to the sand-play area.

**e.** To promote simplicity, remove all materials except those absolutely necessary for the task. The simplest room is an empty one, which would be ideal for playing games; complexity is provided by the number of children involved.

**f.** To increase seclusion, make the boundaries clearer and stronger. Add dividers to the table so that children can't see one another;

add small room dividers between activity areas.

**g.** To increase intrusion, remove the items just mentioned. Improve the access to outdoors, if possible, by allowing children to move in and out. Minimize the barriers between rooms of the building. Invite community members to the program; borrow materials from businesses for displays; use audiovisual materials that bring into the classroom experiences from distant places or times.

**h.** To increase mobility, remove objects such as tables and chairs to unclutter the space. Add activity areas to the room. Increase the number of materials that can be used at the same time and the number of simple activities.

**i.** To decrease mobility, add complexity and softness to the environment. Another alternative is to add seclusion to the environment. When programs have too much space and children are running around, boundaries that decrease the space being used, such as a row of chairs across a gym floor, work well.

**j.** To decrease noise, add softness and seclusion.

 **Maximize Safety**

The safety of children is every adult's responsibility, regardless of role. Usually, the adults in charge of a program will check the environment and childproof it so it is safe. Occasionally, however, people overlook less obvious risks or forget to follow through in making the adjustments. Therefore, all adults must make it a habitual part of daily practice to apply the principles of childproofing the environment. Taking simple precautions is much better than telling children to be careful or scolding them for playing near something hazardous. You always have the option of inquiring about a situation you think is unsafe.

*1.* **Scan the environment inside and out for potential safety hazards when supervising children.** Look at the spaces you habitually use so that hazards can be removed. People may throw

*continued*

## SKILLS FOR INFLUENCING CHILDREN'S SOCIAL DEVELOPMENT BY STRUCTURING THE PHYSICAL ENVIRONMENT—continued

beer bottles or cans into children's play spaces. Sometimes, when space is used by other people during other time periods, materials and equipment are left out that may pose a danger to the children. Remove these promptly.

**2. Keep safety in mind when supervising activities.** Some materials are potentially hazardous if used improperly but otherwise are safe. A stapler used properly is safe, but little fingers can get under the staple. Large blocks usually are safe, but a tall construction may require an adjustment of a lower block to ensure balance of the whole structure.

**3. Act promptly when a safety hazard is noticed.** Do not delay if you perceive a hazard to children. Act conservatively and if your judgment is at fault, it is better to be more protective than less protective in an ongoing program for children. For example, if some eight-year-olds are tasting the fruit of a bush near the play yard with which you are unfamiliar, remove the fruit and the children from the area and contact the local poison control center according to program procedures. If the plant turns out to be harmless, consider it a fortunate event rather than an embarrassment. If three preschool children are at the top of a slide all trying to come down at once, climb the slide, help one child to go down at a time and monitor the number that are able to get to the top to take a turn. Hesitancy to act may increase the risk to children.

**4. Review any actions during the program day with other adults so adjustments that can be implemented before the children arrive may be completed.** For example, plants not known to be safe can be removed from the environment or these areas can be protected by additional fencing. Adults who are not with the children for the full time they are in session also need information so that the same hazardous situation does not reoccur.

**5. Know the local and state legal guidelines and periodically check that they are being maintained.**

### Manage Materials

Problems with cleanup done by children can be minimized by organizing according to the following guidelines.

**1. Store materials to be used by children in durable containers near the point of first use and so that they are easy to reach, grasp, and use.** Help children place materials in the correct storage container, if necessary.

**2. Establish a specific location for materials so that children will know where to put them.** Maintain the storage area in an orderly fashion so that children will know what it is supposed to look like. Mark storage areas with words, symbols, or pictures as needed to identify materials that should be located there.

**3. Check equipment and materials to be sure they are complete, safe, and usable.** Prevent the frustrating experience of trying to do something that simply is not possible. Repair materials and equipment promptly or remove them from use.

**4. Demonstrate the proper care of materials.** If necessary, tell the children exactly what to do while doing the task yourself, then take the materials out again so that the children can imitate the behavior. A camp leader may need to demonstrate the cleaning and folding of a tent several times before children learn to do it correctly.

**5. Give reasons for the standards that you set.** For example, say: "Put the pieces in the puzzle box before putting it in the rack. That way, the pieces won't get lost." You might ask older children to read the numbers on the spine of a book and replace it exactly so that another reader can find it.

**6. Supervise the process of putting materials away, giving reminders as necessary; praise children who are achieving the standard and those who are helping others to do so.** Allow children to choose between two or three tasks. If they are unwilling to choose which task to do,

## SKILLS FOR INFLUENCING CHILDREN'S SOCIAL DEVELOPMENT BY STRUCTURING THE PHYSICAL ENVIRONMENT—continued

assign a task and support the child through the process. (These skills are discussed in Chapters 10 and 11.)

### Minimize Conflict Between Children and Adults

*1. Provide only enough chairs for the maximum number of children that can participate in an activity.* Children become confused if there are five chairs at a table, but only three children may participate in the activity. To avoid this problem, remove extra chairs.

**2. Arrange space and materials so there are clues to appropriate behavior.** Use signs, labels, or pictographs that can be placed so children understand what is expected. For example, put one colored cube in a plastic bag and tape it to the exterior of the opaque bin that holds the cubes. Place a label on the container as well. Then draw a cube, color it, and label the shelf where the bin is stored. Children will know how and where to place the cubes when pick-up time occurs.

Use more floor area for larger groups and less space for smaller groups. For example, the computer, table, and two chairs can be placed in a small area near the library comfortably. However, the thematic play space should be three to four times larger as more children are likely to play there. Usually children move through large open space or bring materials into the space to use.

**3. Make all activities appear to be appealing and attractive.** In center-based activities, and during child-selected activities, children may cluster at one or two areas instead of dispersing across many different activity sites. Such clustering results in crowdedness, congestion, and inadequate amounts of materials available in the most desired areas. This generally leads to conflicts between adults and children or between children. Adding color may attract children such as placing blue construction paper under a puzzle, much like a placemat. Beginning to engage in an activity also may attract

children, such as painting at the easel. Opening a few books with lovely illustrations and arranging them so that children can see them from afar might draw children into the library area. Wherever excessive clustering occurs, sit on the floor or in a small chair and really look to see if all of the activity areas are equally appealing.

**4. Encourage children to personalize their space by letting them make room decorations, use the bulletin boards, or have a display area.** Allowing children to help decorate the room minimizes graffiti and writing on the walls. Keep written messages, pictures, and photographs at children's eye level.

**5. Provide for appropriate activities for a private space.** Plan activities that children may do alone. This allows the child who needs some seclusion an opportunity to behave appropriately while withdrawing from the main flow of action.

**6. Provide materials that are developmentally appropriate.** Know the typical kinds of materials that children of the age you work with enjoy. Make these available. Avoid offering activities that are too simple or too difficult. Modify the planned activity if necessary for children to participate. Use information available from other professionals and from the literature if you are uncertain about the appropriateness of an activity.

**7. Provide furnishings of appropriate size.** Chairs that are either too high or too low are uncomfortable and induce unnecessary fatigue. Children have excessive difficulty in safely using equipment that is not sized correctly, such as scissors that are too long or a climbing structure designed for much younger children.

**8. Have all the materials ready and all the equipment and furnishings in place when the program begins.** This allows you to supervise the children continuously rather than leaving to get supplies. Survey the areas you are supervising, check the materials for usability, quantity,

*continued*

and safety, and confer with the leader, if necessary, to ensure the smooth functioning of activities. Then you are free to interact with the children.

**9. Organize materials so that physical work is minimized both for children and for yourself.** Observe children and other adults for ways to eliminate or simplify unnecessary work. For instance, use a tray to carry several items instead of making many trips.

**10. Send children to an activity or an area rather than away from one.** Give children a clear notion of what alternatives they may pursue. This can be done by giving a direction, such as "Put away your books and come to the large-group area," or by asking the child what he or she plans to do next. Avoid ending a statement by saying things like "You should finish up" or "You're all done." Neither statement helps the child decide what activities are open for him or her next.

### Minimize Potential Conflict Between Children

**1. Provide materials in an appropriate number for the task and situation.** In an open classroom, use the ratio of two-and-a-half activity or play units per child. Check the number of spaces and the amount of materials available when mobility is excessive or when child-to-child conflict is frequent. Either too many or too few activities can produce this effect. Either add or remove activity areas and play units, based on your assessment.

**2. For young children, especially toddlers, provide duplicate or near-duplicate play materials.** When conflict over an item arises, substitute a duplicate or similar object for the one under contention.

**3. Arrange the space so children can get materials and take care of them without interfering with other children.** Place furnishings so children can move to and from storage without bumping into other people or asking them to move their activity.

 **Help Children Make Decisions and Manage Independently**

**1. Offer many different choices to children each day.** Anticipate situations in which choices could be offered, and plan what those choices will be. For instance, if you know you will be reading a story to the group, consider giving children a choice about where to sit, whether they would like to follow up the story by writing a poem or drawing a picture, or what character they would like to portray in a re-enactment of the tale.

**2. Take advantage of naturally occurring situations in which to offer choices.** As you pass out plates, even if they all look the same, give children a choice of which one to use, or ask children which side of the table they would like to sit on or whether they would like to pass out the napkins or the spoons.

**3. Offer choices using positive statements.** Give children acceptable alternatives rather than telling them what they cannot choose. It would be better to say "You can use the blocks to make something like a road, a house, or a rocket" than to say "You can make anything except a gun." The former statement helps children to recognize what alternatives are available; the latter directs children's attention to the very thing you do not want them to consider.

**4. Offer choices for which you are willing to accept either alternative the child selects.** Pick alternatives with which you are equally comfortable. If you say "You can either water the plants or feed the fish," you should be satisfied with either choice the child makes. If what you want is for the child to water the plants, do not make plant watering optional. Instead, offer a choice within the task, such as watering the plants in the morning or just after lunch. These choices are presented as either-or statements or

## SKILLS FOR INFLUENCING CHILDREN'S SOCIAL DEVELOPMENT BY STRUCTURING THE PHYSICAL ENVIRONMENT—continued

"you choose" statements. For example, "You can water either the big plants or the little plants first" or "You choose: big plants or little plants first?"

**5. Allow children ample time to make their decisions.** When making choices, children often vacillate between options. Allow them time to do this rather than rushing them. Give youngsters a time frame within which to think: "I'll check back with you in a few minutes to see what you've decided," "While you're finishing your painting, you can decide which area to clean up," or "I'll ask Suzy what she wants to do, and then I'll get back to you."

**6. Allow children to change their minds if the follow-through on the decision has not yet begun.** If Camille is trying to decide between the blue cup and the red cup and initially chooses the blue one, she should be allowed to switch to the red cup as long as her milk has not already been poured into the blue one or the red cup has not been given to someone else.

**7. Assist children in accepting responsibility for the choices they make.** Once children have made a decision and it is in process, help them stay with and follow through on their choice. For example, Kent decided he wanted to water the plants after lunch; a gentle reminder on his return that afternoon may help him to act on his decision if it seems that he has forgotten. Use a neutral tone and noninflammatory language; say: "Kent, earlier you decided to water the plants after lunch. It's about time to do that now" rather than "Kent, how are you ever going to learn to be responsible if you don't follow through on your decisions?" Similarly, if you had already poured the milk into the cup Camille had chosen but she wanted to switch at that point, your role would be to help her live with the consequences of the decision. Reflect: "You changed your mind" or "You're disappointed that the red cup is gone." Talk about how the child may choose differently another time: "Today, you chose the blue cup. Tomorrow,

you'll have another chance to choose. If you still want the red cup, you can choose it then." Comfort children who are unhappy about the results of their decision.

**8. Encourage children to make specific plans to implement their decisions (Casey and Lippman, 1991).** Ask leading questions such as: "How will you accomplish this?" or "What materials will you need?" or "Are there other ways to accomplish the same thing?" or "What steps will you need to take to be able to do this?"

**9. Provide opportunities for children to set goals, make decisions, and implement them commensurate with their experience.** Engage children in a series of simple tasks that they cannot plan independently successfully. A three-year-old might be able to select the invitation for a birthday party and identify guests, but would be unable to plan the event. Children under six usually plan for very specific activities, such as the decoration of a refrigerator box being transformed into a house. Older children may make more elaborate and complex plans such as building a tree house. Relate each new, more challenging task with one they already know they can do.

**10. Allow children to carry out and complete tasks by themselves.** If a child appears to flounder, help him or her to do it another way by giving step-by-step instructions, or by demonstrating the particular step that is causing the difficulty. Doing the task for the child implies the child is not competent.

**11. Teach strategies to accomplish the task.** Break tasks down into smaller steps. If one strategy does not work, show the child another. For example, in putting on rubber boots over shoes, the child may just try to cram the shoe into the boot. If it is a tight fit, slip the shoe into a plastic bag first and it will go on easier. Often when a child says, "I can't," he/she means, "I don't know how." This is also true of older children, but they may not verbalize their difficulty. In a

*continued*

**SKILLS FOR INFLUENCING CHILDREN'S SOCIAL DEVELOPMENT BY STRUCTURING THE PHYSICAL ENVIRONMENT—continued**

camping situation, one eleven-year-old just walked away when it was his turn to do the dishes. When asked why the task wasn't done, he replied that his mother was at home. He had no idea of where to begin the task; especially since he had no garbage disposal, no sink, and no automatic dishwasher that he had observed his mother use at home. Fortunately, the counselor demonstrated each step and verbalized what to do and why, so that all the boys in the group would be more independent in accomplishing this task.

**12. Help children learn to evaluate their own accomplishments.** Focus on what has been accomplished compared to what was intended. "Did this picture turn out the way you planned?" You may also point out that the child could do something, given the effort, "You tried twice to get those boots on, but you did it in the end." Sometimes children need to have feedback on how to assess if they have accomplished the task. Ask them in advance questions such as, "How will you know if the dishes are really clean?" Ultimately, children will learn to provide feedback to themselves, but this takes much practice and experience. Avoid comparisons between children.

**13. Help children to use the evaluation of their activities to develop new plans for themselves.** On selected activities, help children to identify the skills they have and the ones they are ready to attempt. The three-year-old who participated in planning parts of one birthday party, may be ready to help plan other parts when turning four. A child who successfully uses one computer program may be ready to attempt a new, more challenging one. Statements such as, "You have completed all the games on this program successfully. Are you ready for a new program or would you like to have additional practice with this one?" Let the child make the choice of when to move. Sometimes, children who can do the task still lack confidence and need more feedback from their own successful practice.

**14. Allow older children to collaborate with you on major management problems, such as storage of materials, proposed rearrangement of space, or planning of a holiday party.** Involve children in the entire process: "It's nearly Halloween; would you like to celebrate it? . . . What do we need to plan for?" List all the options and discuss the time and work necessary to carry out the activity. If children obviously have forgotten an important part, point it out. "Have you considered how long the games will take? Will we be finished in time to clean up the room before dismissal?" Older children can serve in supervisory capacities such as team leader for the cleanup squad or chairperson of the refreshment committee. You still will need to check on all of the plans and implementation and provide gentle reminders when needed.

### Supervise Children

**1. Observe carefully the children and other adults in the group.** Watch for children having difficulties with materials or other children. Note the needs of other adults as they are engaged in interactions so that you may supply materials or give assistance as needed. Try to avoid daydreaming or other intruding ideas when supervising children as needs arise quickly and need your attention.

**2. Situate your body so that you can view the whole space and all of the children.** Scan the room intermittently. Watch children in front of you, nearby or across the yard or room. Survey for the location of other adults as well. Know what is going on around you! Usually have your back to a wall, a corner, or a boundary. If seated in an area where visibility is limited, stand up occasionally.

**3. Take action if necessary to protect children.** Adjust the blocks if they appear to be unstable. Retrieve a toddler if the child has managed to open a gate and go through. Ask unfamiliar adults if you can help them if they remain in the vicinity of the playground for awhile. (The per-

## SKILLS FOR INFLUENCING CHILDREN'S SOCIAL DEVELOPMENT BY STRUCTURING THE PHYSICAL ENVIRONMENT—continued

son may or may not be a threat to the children.) *If safety is the issue always act without delay.* If another adult is closer and is moving into the situation, return to your place, scan the whole area, and continue your activity. If an accident should occur, reassure the other children and continue with the program.

**4. Regularly check the children under your direct supervision and all of the children in the room.** Scan the space regularly. Are all the children engaged in meaningful activity? Count the children regularly especially when outdoors, on field trips, or moving between rooms in a building. If a child appears to be missing, notify the group leader and count again before searching.

Check children under your immediate care. Are they able to work independently or do they need assistance? Assess what they need and think how you will give help without directing everything they do. Take advantage of opportunities to promote prosocial behavior.

**5. Guide children in accomplishing the tasks they attempt.** Let them do as much as they can by themselves. Demonstrate techniques such as showing a child how to control the amount of paint on a brush if the child is not figuring this out independently after several attempts. Give information to children so the step can be accomplished and wait until help is needed again. Avoid taking over the activity or directing all of the steps yourself. Help only as needed to support the child, even when they ask. For example, a kindergarten child might ask you to zip up the coat and you reply, "Let me see you try. I see that you are having difficulty getting started. I will put the two parts of the zipper together and you can do the rest yourself. Watch how I do it. Put this slide into this slot."

**6. Adjust materials, space, and equipment as needed.** Add or remove materials so that children can proceed with their activities without distractions but with all the resources they need to do the task. Adjust space to promote proso-

cial behavior, comfort, or safety if needed. Reorient the activity if it appears to be beyond the ability of the children to one that they can accomplish. For example, many first-grade children wanted a turn in constructing the "bus" from a refrigerator box and were clustered around the children who were trying to make windows of cellophane. The student teacher redirected some of these children by providing the materials to make the driver's side panel in the bus that shows the speed and gas gauges. She also added pictures from books and magazines so the youngsters would have an idea of what they might represent on the panel. In another situation, the school librarian pulled a number of books from the shelves and placed them on the table so the children could easily choose. When Patrick could not make up his mind, she removed three of the books from one table and suggested that he make his selection from the remaining three. Both of these adults made adjustments to facilitate the interest and success of the children in their charge.

Simplify the activity so that children who have special needs or who are less mature may participate. Add complexity or extend the activity in some way for children who are very adept and confident. Encourage children to assist others who are less skillful but probably capable of engaging in the activity. Constantly scan for health and safety concerns.

**7. Evaluate the actions that you have taken and those you did not undertake.** Were your behaviors consistent with the long-range goals of the program? Did you support children's own decision making and their development of social skills or did you take over their activity? Did you choose not to intervene when, in retrospect, it would have been in the best interest of the children if you had done so? What cues in the situation did you misinterpret? Were the adjustments you made useful to the children? How do you know? In supervising children, all adults make decisions to act or not to act with great frequency. Skill in making these decisions is acquired when adults reflect on what they

*continued*

## SKILLS FOR INFLUENCING CHILDREN'S SOCIAL DEVELOPMENT BY STRUCTURING THE PHYSICAL ENVIRONMENT—continued

have done and why, so that if similar situations occur, they might make best choices.

 **Share Ideas about Structuring the Physical Environment with Parents**

**1. Apply structuring strategies to behavioral problems that parents bring to your attention.** Structuring the environment to promote appropriate behaviors is applicable to many situations that parents encounter during the childrearing years. Strategies that are used for children in groups may be modified and applied to family situations. Below are some fairly typical experiences with some structuring possibilities that might make family life more pleasant.

▼ *Toileting accidents.* Can the child easily walk to the toilet, remove clothing, and get on and off the toilet easily and independently? Do these accidents generally occur at the same time of day or in the same conditions, such as when they are outside? Modifying clothing, adding a small stool, or monitoring the reminders parents give their children are examples of structuring.

▼ *Rough-house-play in the car.* Add something for them to do.

▼ *Sibling fighting or older children hitting younger ones.* This usually occurs when the younger child intrudes on the older child's space or possessions. Parents can clarify which things are personal possessions, which belong to both, and where each is stored. They also can provide opportunities where either child is free from intrusion.

▼ *Cleaning up play space.* Principles related to storage and schedules apply here. Children need a warning that play is finished at home as well as school and are able to learn a standard that is acceptable for the home. Young children should help, and eventually they will learn how to do this if they can see where things are to be placed. Open shelves and plastic containers at home work well.

▼ *Stress in travel or moving.* Involving even the youngest child in planning and packing may help the child feel more comfortable. Early personalizing with toys or favorite objects also facilitates the child's adjustment.

**2. Communicate with parents about any major changes in the child's group membership, room arrangements, daily schedule, or major changes in equipment and furnishings.** When parents know about changes in advance, they are able to reassure the child. They are also less likely to experience distress than if they discover the changes all on their own. In child-care settings, older toddlers move from the comfortable room they know into a new group of preschool children. Both the children and the parents should be part of this transition. Adding a loft to a kindergarten in the middle of a semester is stressful, although usually it is seen very positively. Usually changes that involve the group are communicated in a newsletter, and changes that involve an individual are communicated in person or on the phone.

**3. Tell parents how structuring is used to support the child's appropriate behavior in the group setting.** After listening to your ideas parents can adapt them at home. They also know that the adults in the program are taking some responsibility to promote acceptable behavior. For example, friendship is often supported by seating in a classroom. Noting this effect of physical closeness, parents might consider inviting children who live nearby to come to their homes for play. Separating materials for older and younger children is another easily transferable idea.

**4. Structure parents arrival, observation or participation, and dismissal so that they and their children have a successful experience.** Some mothers breast-feed their infants in workplace child-care programs; therefore a secluded area and a chair with armrests are most comfortable. New parents may wish to observe their children, whereas others may want to visit the

## SKILLS FOR INFLUENCING CHILDREN'S SOCIAL DEVELOPMENT BY STRUCTURING THE PHYSICAL ENVIRONMENT—continued

program for short periods and leave again. Parents who volunteer in grade school may want to observe their child during a session. Regardless of parental needs, professionals should structure these events so that parents, children, and staff are all comfortable with the plan.

Transitions between home and programs are often rushed, hectic, and full of opportunities for adult/child stress or conflict. The physical facility, adjacent parking, traffic problems, and the timing of when children arrive and leave influence how the process should be structured. With plenty of parking, parents may bring children into a building, but with very limited parking or when children leave at the same time, adults may deliver the children to their parent's cars. Each program should follow principles of structuring to minimize the stress and increase the comfort of everyone involved.

### Engage Parents in Structuring the Physical Environment

**1. Invite parents to participate in events that contribute to the maintenance and beauty of the facility.** Periodic yard cleanup days or paint-and-fix days (held for 3 or 4 hours, two to four times a year) contribute to the quality of the program at a lower cost than if carried out by contractors or employees. These events are usually done by nonprofit organizations but may also be implemented by public schools or public parks. If carefully structured, adults enjoy themselves and feel very positive about contributing to their child's program. Structure the event as follows:

▼ Set reasonable goals. Estimate how many hours per person are required for each task. Don't try to do everything and then finish nothing. For example, you might be able to do a yard cleanup or paint a hallway with the number of volunteers available, but not both. Choose one.
▼ List all materials or tools necessary for each task. Either supply them or ask parents who will be working on the task to bring supplies

with them. Try not to have one parent using another's tools if at all possible.
▼ Give clear, specific directions. If you know that one of the parents is knowledgeable and others are not, talk to them as a group and ask the more skilled parent to answer ongoing questions as needed.
▼ Monitor the work, giving lots of feedback. Let people know you appreciate their efforts. If corrective suggestions are in order, make them positive: "A smooth paint job is best for spaces with young children. The youngsters tend to pick at the drips and mar the paint."
▼ Provide for snacks and rest periods. Help workers to find additional small tasks if they finish early or reassign them to a bigger job.
▼ Ask adults to help throughout the cleanup process, including putting tools away.
▼ Thank everyone for their support and work.

**2. Ask parents to contribute materials or equipment to the program.** Paper rolls, fabric scraps, wood scraps, plastic food trays, baby food jars, film canisters, wrapping paper, holiday cards, and many other materials that some people discard can be used by programs for young children. Dress-up clothing, computers, toys in good repair, or surplus household items that might be sold may also be willingly contributed. If you are soliciting contributions, write a very specific request to parents using the following guidelines:

▼ Tell parents exactly what you want. For example, old shirts in boy's size 10–12 are better for dress-up or paint shirts than are men's sizes for preschool youngsters. If you are looking for a computer in good working condition with a hard disc drive not more than five years old, say so. People feel better about giving if the gifts are used and may be upset if their contribution was not incorporated into the classroom.
▼ Be specific about when and where to deliver the materials and how much is needed. You may have many more paper rolls than you can use or store if the request is unclear. Moving a computer or other equipment is

*continued*

**SKILLS FOR INFLUENCING CHILDREN'S SOCIAL DEVELOPMENT BY STRUCTURING THE PHYSICAL ENVIRONMENT—continued**

more difficult and time consuming, so include a phone number for discussing this equipment. Sometimes programs participate in recycling winter coats, food drives, or other charitable events sponsored by other community groups. Providing information on the items sought and the time(s) and date(s) for drop-off is essential in managing these events.

▼ State clearly the acceptable conditions such as "a doll carriage in good working order," "clean baby food jars with the labels removed," or "clean, squeaky baby toys in good condition."

▼ Accept all contributions with thanks, gracefully and individually. Avoid making an issue of contributions for children whose families were unable to participate.

▼ Provide a written thank-you for the contribution of items that might be sold so that parents may use the contribution in their income taxes. You do not have to state the dollar value of the gift.

## ▼ PITFALLS TO AVOID

In structuring the physical environment to enhance children's social development, there are certain pitfalls you should avoid.

**Making too many changes at once.** Children need security and predictability. Even though you can think of several major alterations to make, such as altering the daily schedule and rearranging the room, do them gradually. Younger children are more upset than older children by major changes.

**Evaluating too soon.** Sometimes, when new materials are added, rooms changed, or schedules altered, you will anticipate an immediate positive result. Young children usually are very active as they refamiliarize themselves with the area. Increased noise and confusion can be expected immediately, with improvements more discernible after three weeks.

**Failing to supervise.** Never leave children unattended by an adult. Children may misuse materials usually considered safe. Even if you are just gone for a minute, a situation that could endanger a child may occur at that time. In addition, children may lose interest and behave inappropriately.

**Planning inadequately.** Don't initiate major adjustments in the daily schedule or room arrangement on the spur of the moment. Of course, you can add materials, such as a plant, books, or toys. But impulsive major changes upset children, especially younger ones. Follow the guidelines.

Sketch major furnishings on a floor plan before moving heavy items. If they don't fit, you will have to move them again, thereby increasing your fatigue and frustration.

**Adhering rigidly to the plan.** When you have evaluated the situation and it is clear that the plan won't work, either adjust the plan, modify it, or give it up. Sometimes, the very best plans don't work out as anticipated and must be adjusted.

**Directing rather than guiding when supervising children.** Occasionally adults are more focused on the product than on the children doing the activity. Therefore, they tend to make all the decisions, establish the standards of what is good enough, and tell children what to do and how to do it at all points. Directing is *only the best choice when an issue of health or safety is involved*. If adults direct too much, they diminish children's autonomy, confidence, and feelings of competence.

**Assuming that a child knows how to do a routine.** Learn to distinguish whether a child does not know how to do something or is refusing to do it. Children do not automatically know how to dress, undress, wash, put away materials, or clean cupboards. If you are supervising a child, teach the child how to do a task correctly rather than criticizing the child's best effort. Comments such as "Didn't your mother teach you anything?", "If you can't do it right, don't do it at all," or "Can't you even wipe a table? I'll do it myself" are all inappropriate. Instead, use comments like "You are having a hard time with that. I'll show you how and you can finish it."

**Assuming that the observations of support staff are not important.**  Support staff are usually working near the children and can see how they are functioning in an area and with the materials. It is their responsibility to share this information with the group leader who then can work toward more effective planning. If you are the head teacher, encourage support staff to share what they observe and find ways to make this a regular part of the program. If you are in a support role, be observant and share your observations with your head teacher or others in charge.

**Assuming that nothing can be done.**  Sometimes, you may go into a room and assume that the present arrangements can't be improved. You may not be able to do much, but most spaces can at least be made attractive and can be personalized. When you don't know whether the materials, furnishings, or decorations can be changed, ask someone in authority. Usually, an extra pillow or small table is no major problem. Such things may be available.

**Failing to communicate your plans to other adults and to children.**   When engaging in any aspect of the management process, change is involved. This requires communication to all parties. Everything will run more smoothly if adequate preparation of children and adults has been accomplished.

**Allowing children complete freedom to choose.**   No one can do whatever they want. There are limits to all things. Children need to collaborate and be involved in decisions, but giving them complete freedom places a burden on them that they are not yet prepared to carry. Children who are given the opportunity to "do anything" may not even be able to generate choices. This complete freedom of choice is stressful for children, and they will become confused and distressed. This distress usually is accompanied by noise and disorder as all the children try to determine if you really mean that they can do *anything.*

**Assuming that parents understand the principles of decision making and know how to structure for their children.**  Though professionals learn specifics about decision making and can teach this to children, parents may not even think of providing their smallest children with simple choices such as which sock to put on first. Sharing such strategies supports the continuity between home and school.

## ▼ SUMMARY

The process of structuring to achieve the goals of the program was discussed. Motivations for establishing goals and standards are the needs of the children and adults in the programs as well as the external demands of the community. Decision making permeates the structuring process and can be taught to even the youngest children. Planning and implementing change that is goal-directed may be time consuming but leads to satisfaction and to new management strategies.

General structuring processes were applied specifically to time management in programs for children. Special consideration was given to the importance of predictability and routine for children's sense of security and emotional adjustment to the environment.

The structuring also was applied to the selection, storage, and use of materials and to the arrangement of space. The quality of the environment influences social interaction among children and adults and can be manipulated to meet program goals.

Skills were described for establishing and changing schedules and room arrangements, supervising children, and for promoting efficient use of materials. Techniques were presented for adding to or subtracting from the environment as a means to facilitate social interaction. Finally, skills were described for helping children to become responsible decision makers and participants in the management process. Suggestions were made to help parents use structuring to support their child-rearing practice and to organize opportunities for parents to donate time and materials to the program.

## ▼ DISCUSSION QUESTIONS

1. Describe the structuring process as simply as you can so that someone who does not know the vocabulary would understand.
2. Why do the principles of structuring seem to be so familiar and easy to grasp while adults obviously have difficulty in making everyday decisions?
3. Why might the standards of order and efficiency differ among similar kinds of programs in different settings?
4. Describe how the decision-making process is applied to each step of the structuring process in a program for young children.
5. Why do adults involved children in the decision-making process? How does it influence their social development?
6. Explain the role of communication between adults who work with children, various strategies by which it can be facilitated, and situations in which it might be problematic.
7. Why would a decision rule such as "The job at hand is less important than the child doing it" become widely accepted among professionals and be frequently repeated to professionals in training?
8. Explain how the management of time and of the daily schedule is related to children's social and emotional development. Is it important throughout childhood? Why?
9. Explain the importance of having a private space in programs for groups of children.
10. Select any activity for children and identify all the opportunities for children to make choices in carrying out the activity. Identify alternatives that are unacceptable to you, and state your reasons.
11. Think back over your own childhood and recall instances in which you were denied opportunities to make choices. How did you feel? How did you behave? Did the adults make explanations to you? How did they behave?
12. Write a letter that could be sent to a group of parents asking for materials for the program or asking them to participate in a volunteer workday. Make the letter friendly and inviting, as well as very specific. Exchange your letter with a classmate and discuss the differences and reasons for those differences.
13. Referring to Appendix A, NAEYC Code of Ethical Conduct, determine which of the situations listed here would constitute an ethical problem and identify the principles and ideals that influence your thinking.
    a. Showing up 20 minutes after you were expected without calling in advance in a program with young children.
    b. Failing to mention that the gate to the fenced playground is broken.
    c. Letting a preschool child carry a pot of very hot water.
    d. Scooping the pieces of many sets of materials together and dumping them in one container to make cleanup faster.
    e. Failing to have images of adults and children of all racial groups and some handicapping conditions available to children.
    f. Moving a toddler from the infant toddler room to a preschool room without informing the parent or preparing the child.
    g. Placing the cooking project on a table that is across the pathway where children walk and using an extension cord to connect the hot plate.

## ▼ FIELD ASSIGNMENTS

1. Observe a professional working with children. Describe incidents in which children were offered a choice. Write down how this was worded or how it was implemented. Describe incidents of children who are managing their own activity. What aspects of the situation or setting enable the children to act on their own with minimal support? Write out any errors you think the adult made and what corrections might be possible.
2. Supervise a group of children doing a simple activity. Later, write out a description of how you checked, adjusted the environment, and guided the children. Evaluate your own performance.

3. Observe any program for children and note the daily schedule as posted. Compare it to what actually happened. What adjustments were made and why? Did you note instances where children could be taught a routine or habit so that they would do a simple task more efficiently? Write out the sequence of this routine as you think it could work in that setting.

4. Make a visit to an early childhood program. Draw a detailed floor plan of one of the rooms. List the strengths and weaknesses of the room arrangement in relation to children's social development. Suggest improvements in the physical layout.

# ▼Chapter 10

## Fostering Self-Discipline in Children: Expressing Appropriate Expectations for Their Behavior

### ▼ OBJECTIVES

*On completion of this chapter, you will be able to describe:*

▼ Emotional, developmental, and experiential factors that contribute to the development of self-discipline in children.

▼ Variations in the degree to which people display self-regulated behavior.

▼ How different adult guidance styles affect children's behavior and personality.

▼ What a personal message is and when to use it.

▼ How using a personal message enhances the development of self-discipline in children.

▼ Guidelines for formulating each part of the personal message.

▼ Strategies for communicating with families regarding behavioral expectations.

▼ Pitfalls to avoid in formulating and using personal messages.

---

Cross at the light.

Cover your mouth when you sneeze.

Pet the puppy gently.

Wait your turn.

---

These are typical expectations that children encounter growing up. Although no one standard of behavior is universal, all societies have behavior codes to keep people safe and to help them get along (Shaffer, 1994). Adults have the primary role in transmitting societal expectations to the next generation. They often refer to this responsibility as teaching children to behave. *Socialization* is another term used to describe the process. It involves guiding children to function in ways that are acceptable to the community in which they live. Adults socialize children to carry out desirable actions like sharing, answering politely, and telling the truth. They also socialize children to avoid inappropriate behaviors such as shoving, tattling, spitting on the sidewalk, or taking all the chocolate-covered cherries for themselves. How well children learn these lessons influences their ability to function successfully in a variety of microsystems and in the community at large.

Initially, adults enforce societal expectations through their direct presence—they remind children of what is expected and show them how to comply. They reward children for behaving in acceptable ways and punish children for misconduct. However, they hope that eventually children will assume responsibility for monitoring their own behavior rather than relying on others to regulate it for them. Thus, the ultimate goal of socialization is for children to become self-disciplined.

## ▼ WHAT IS SELF-DISCIPLINE?

When we say children are **self-disciplined** we mean they can judge for themselves what is right and what is wrong and then behave appropriately. In such cases, children use their personal values and the feelings or needs of others to determine what to do and what not to do (Newman and Newman, 1997). People who lack self-discipline often act appropriately only when someone else is available to tell them how to behave or to make sure that they do it. Self-disciplined people rely on internal behavior controls; those who are less self-disciplined rely on others to control their behavior for them. When such external controls are absent, they may act improperly. These differences are illustrated by Casey and William, two third-graders rushing to get to a T-ball game in the park. On the way, they come across a huge expanse of ground that has been freshly seeded and covered with straw. A large sign announces, "PLEASE STAY OFF THE GRASS." Casey looks around. He will abide by the rule if park personnel are nearby; however, seeing no one else in sight, he quickly cuts across the newly seeded area. William also notices that no one is around, but reasons that stepping on the grassy shoots could damage them. Although he is tempted to take the shortcut across the new seed, he suppresses that impulse in order to preserve the grass. He walks around the space, even though it takes a little more time. In this situation, William is demonstrating a greater degree of self-discipline than Casey. William made his decision to go around the grass based on his personal sense of what was right, not because his actions were being monitored by anyone else.

Self-discipline is made up of several behaviors, all of which require individuals to initiate or inhibit certain actions without being made to do so. For instance, self-disciplined people initiate positive social interactions as well as make and carry out constructive social plans (Knopczyk and Rodes, 1996). They also refrain from certain acts that might harm themselves or others. Resisting temptation, curbing negative impulses, and delaying gratification are important inhibiting behaviors (Bukatko and Daehler, 1995; Fabes, 1984; Mischel, 1978). The five behaviors that display self-discipline are presented in Table 10–1.

## ▼ VARIATIONS IN CONDUCT AND MOTIVATION

The self-discipline–related actions listed in Table 10–1 require children to know when and how to differentiate acceptable behaviors from inappropriate ones and then act accordingly. As children mature, they vary in how well they do this. Generally, younger children are less self-disciplined than older youngsters. However, there is no guarantee that all human beings will exhibit the same degree of self-discipline simply because they reach a certain age. Numerous theorists have tried to explain these variations in human development (Gilligan, 1992; Hoffman, 1970; Kohlberg, 1976). Although there are differences among their points of view, they generally agree that people do not achieve self-discipline immediately or all at once. Self-discipline emerges gradually throughout childhood. Children progress through a series of categories of self-discipline that differ according to what motivates them to behave in socially acceptable ways. In this book, these categories are labeled amoral, adherence, identification, and internalization (Kelman, 1958).

### Amoral

Children are not born with a concept of right or wrong; they are **amoral.** That is, they are not able to make ethical judgments about their actions. Thus, when baby LeRoy reaches for his mother's glasses as they sparkle close by, he cannot think about the potential pain he might inflict or damage he may cause if he is successful in pulling them off. Nor can he stop his investigation merely because his mother frowns or scolds him. LeRoy has not yet learned to interpret these parental behaviors or to interrupt his own activity as a consequence. It is the adult who must exercise control of his movements, either by removing the glasses or by handing him a substitute. Either way, the adult, not the child, manages LeRoy's behavior. Over time, through maturity and experience, this complete lack of self-monitoring begins to change. Most young children learn to respond to external cues to guide their actions. The most basic way this occurs is adherence.

### Adherence

**Adherence** is the most superficial level of self-discipline and occurs when people follow a rule or ex-

| ▼ Table 10–1 | Signs of Self-Discipline |
| --- | --- |
| **BEHAVIOR** | **EXAMPLES** |
| Children initiate positive social interactions. | Walter comforts Latosha who is sad over missing her mom.<br>Michael shares his headphones with a newcomer to the listening center. |
| Children make and carry out constructive social plans | Marcus wants a turn with the watercolors. He figures out a strategy for getting some, such as trading chalk for paint, and then tries bargaining with another child to achieve his goal.<br>Courtney recognizes that Graham is struggling to carry a dozen hula hoops down to the gym. She helps Graham by taking several hoops from his arms and walking with him downstairs. |
| Children resist temptation. | Woo-Jin walks all the way over to the trash can to dispose of her sandwich wrapper, although she is tempted simply to drop the crumpled paper on the ground.<br>Juan turns in a change purse he found in the hallway, even though he is tempted to keep it for himself. |
| Children curb negative impulses. | Ruben suppresses the urge to strike out in anger when Heather accidentally knocks him over during a soccer game.<br>LaRonda refrains from teasing Richard about the "awful" haircut he got over the weekend. |
| Children delay gratification. | Carla waits for Tricia to finish talking to the scout leader before announcing that she is going to Disney World.<br>Lionel postpones taking another Popsicle until everyone gets one. |

pectation solely to gain a reward or to avoid a punishment (Hoffman, 1979; Kohlberg, 1976). For instance, a child demonstrating adherence will share, but only as a way to gain praise or to escape a reprimand. This behavior is entirely self-serving and shows little regard for other people's welfare. Children whose thinking falls in the adherence category have little understanding of *why* sharing is good; they simply know it is expected. As a result, children perform the required behaviors under direct supervision only (Bukatko and Daehler, 1995). In the absence of a punishing or rewarding adult, they have no rationale for following the rule on their own and may resort to hitting or grabbing to get what they want whenever the adult is out of sight. While children remain at this level of compliance, adults must continually monitor their activities rather than relying on them to exercise self-control. The longer children depend on adults to reward or punish their actions, the more they become conditioned to expect this control. Consequently, children develop few other strategies for determining right or wrong and have no way to figure out how to conduct themselves appropriately in unfamiliar situations (Stengel, 1982). Also, children may behave in the presence of certain authority figures, but fail to obey other adults, to respect the rights of their peers, or to comply with rules if the threat of a punishment or the promise of a reward is not apparent.

## Identification

A more advanced degree of self-discipline occurs when children follow rules so they can be like someone they admire. This happens when children imitate the conduct, attitudes, and values of the important people in their lives (Hoffman, 1970; Papalia and Olds, 1993). Children's compliance with certain rules may also be a strategy for establishing or preserving satisfying relationships with those persons (Erikson, 1950; Freud, 1938). This phenomenon is called **identification** and it happens for several reasons (Kagan, 1971). First, children want to be like the people they revere. For instance, Fiona admires her swimming coach and wants to follow in her footsteps. Second, children assume they are like the model. Fiona believes that she and her swimming coach share many traits in common—a drive to win, a sense of fair play, and sensitivity to others. Other people affirm this identification with comments such as, "I can tell you're one of Coach Zimmer's girls. You know how to give it your all." Third, children experience emotions similar to those they observe in the model. In this case, when the coach expresses sadness over the death of her dog, Fiona shares the coach's grief, not for a pet she didn't know, but because the coach's sadness makes her feel sad too. Finally, children act like the people they admire. They adopt their mannerisms, their words, and their ways of behaving. Typically children identify with parents or other family members. Helping professionals in the formal group setting are also sources of identification. In every case, the persons with whom youngsters identify are nurturing, powerful people—usually adults or older children (Bandura, 1977; Mussen, et al., 1990). They are individuals with whom children have strong affectionate ties, not people with whom children have negative or neutral relationships.

Identification is important in children's lives. It moves them beyond the simple formula of rewards and punishments and provides them with many of the ideas and standards they carry with them into adulthood. Children who share an item as a result of identification use sharing as a way to further their own aims—confirming their similarity to an admired person who advocates sharing or pleasing that person through their actions. They do not recognize the inherent fairness in sharing or the real needs of the person to whom they lend something for awhile. Sharing is maintained as long as the relationship lasts but may give way if the ties become less intense. Moreover, children who are governed by identification rely on second-guessing how someone else might behave in a given situation. If they have never seen the model in a similar circumstance, children may not know what to do and lack the tools to figure it out for themselves.

## Internalization

**Internalization** is the most advanced category of self-discipline. When people treat certain rules as a logical extension of their own beliefs and personal values, we say they have internalized those rules (Hoffman, 1970; Shaffer, 1995). It is this internal code that guides their actions from one circumstance to another. The course of action they choose in each situation is aimed at avoiding self-condemnation rather than acquiring external rewards or gaining approval from others. People whose behaviors fall within the internalization category understand the reasons behind certain behavior standards and feel a moral commitment to act in accordance with those standards. They also recognize how specific actions fit into larger concepts like justice, honesty, and equity. Individuals who reason according to internalized beliefs take into account the impact their following a rule will have on others. For instance, Mariah, who has internalized the value of sharing, will offer to give another child some of her crayons, not because the teacher said so or because anyone else is watching, but because sharing seems the appropriate thing to do. Engaging in this positive action makes Mariah feel good. She enjoys knowing another child will have a chance to draw too.

Once children have internalized a rule, they have a guide for how to behave appropriately in all kinds of circumstances, even unfamiliar ones. Attaching reasons to rules gives children the ability to weigh the pros and cons of alternate actions and to choose behaviors that match their ideals. This eliminates the need for constant supervision. Children can be depended on to regulate their own behavior. Most importantly, internalized behaviors are long lasting. Children who adopt beliefs in justice, honesty, or fairness as their own will abide by those ideals long after their contacts with certain adults are over and in spite of temptation or the opportunity to break the rule without being discovered (Newman and Newman, 1997; Thomas, 1995).

Table 10–2 provides a summary of the amoral, adherence, identification, and internalization categories of self-discipline just described.

**Are children capable of internalization?** There is strong evidence that the behavior of preschoolers and children in the early elementary years is almost completely controlled by external factors (adults; rewards and punishments) (Bandura, 1986; Walker, deVries, and Trevarthen, 1989). The transfer of this control to internal mechanisms is only gradually achieved and takes many years to accomplish. Eventually, however, most people do internalize some rules. This means early and middle childhood are times when children develop the fundamental skills and understandings that lead to the higher-order reasoning characteristic of internalization. Also, during these years children accumulate a backlog of experiences from which they continually derive clues about what constitutes appropriate conduct, what comprises inappropriate behavior, and what distinguishes the two.

In addition, children do not move from an amoral orientation to higher levels of conduct strictly according to age. Research supports the notion of a developmental progression but also indicates that children achieve greater self-discipline at rates and

| ▼ Table 10–2 | Four Categories of Self-Discipline | |
| --- | --- | --- |
| CATEGORY | DEFINITION | SOURCE OF BEHAVIOR CONTROL |
| Amoral | Children have no sense of right or wrong. | External to the child |
| Adherence | Children respond to rewards and punishments; they often anticipate these and behave accordingly. | Shared between others and the child—primary responsibility remains with the adult |
| Identification | Children attempt to adopt behavioral codes of admired others; they second-guess how that person might behave in varying situations and act likewise. | Shared between others and the child—child assumes greater responsibility than was true at adherence |
| Internalization | Children govern their behavior using an internal code of ethics created from their own values and judgments. Their actions take into account the needs and feelings of others. | Internal to the child |

in degrees that vary from child to child (Bukatko and Daehler, 1995). For instance, one child may require several experiences to learn to take only so many crackers at snack time, whereas another child grasps this notion much sooner. Furthermore, the same child at different times may be motivated by adherence or identification or internalization. The reasons why children follow rules at one level or another are often situation bound (Burton, 1984). For example, Julia may keep away from the iron to avoid a scolding. She may adopt a similar attitude toward picking up litter as an admired teacher, and she may stop herself from teasing a peer because it would not feel right to bring her friend to tears. In the behavior of young children, these patterns typically vacillate a great deal.

**Do all people internalize everything?**  The answer to this question is no. In fact, a very small number of people never advance beyond the amoral level of compliance (Magid and McKelvey, 1987). We describe such individuals as having character disorders and sometimes read or hear about their lack of conscience as the result of some horrific crime. The exact number of people this involves is not known. Estimates range from 0.05 to 15 percent of the total adult population (Rosenthal, 1970). More information about early warning signs of this disorder and what might be done for the child is offered in Chapter 15, Making Judgments. The good news is that most people exhibit internalized behaviors for some things; common sense tells us no one functions according to an internalized code of ethics in every instance. In fact, as people reach ma-

turity, they still at one time or another exhibit behaviors related to adherence, identification, and internalization (Cairns, 1979). The same individual will halt at a stop sign to avoid getting a ticket, will wear clothes in the same style as a good friend, and will avoid cheating to uphold an internal sense of fairness. However, as children move into adolescence, one category of self-discipline starts to dominate their behavior. By adulthood some people maintain a mostly external orientation to rules based on rewards and punishments or the opinions of others. Other people are more self-regulated (Shaffer, 1994). Because self-discipline is such a desired goal, it is important to ask why these different outcomes occur. There are developmental as well as experiential factors that provide the answer.

## ▼ DEVELOPMENTAL PROCESSES THAT INFLUENCE SELF-DISCIPLINE

Children's capacity for self-discipline increases with maturity. Although preschoolers learn to follow certain familiar rules, they are not capable of the same degree of self-discipline as children in the upper elementary grades. There are many naturally occurring developmental processes that help explain why this is so. The most notable of these are changes in children's emotional development, cognitive development, language development, and memory skills.

### Emotional Development

Two emotions that strongly contribute to self-discipline are guilt and empathy (Eisenberg, 1986;

Erikson, 1963; Hoffman, 1984). **Guilt** feelings warn children that a current or planned action is undesirable. Guilt prompts regret for past misdeeds. **Empathy,** or feeling a little of what another person feels, conveys the opposite message. Empathy causes children to initiate positive actions in response to emotional situations. Children as young as two years old are capable of both guilt and empathy (Emde, et al. 1991; Zigler and Finn-Stevenson, 1987). However, these emotions are aroused by different events for young children than those to which older children respond.

**Guilt.** The situations that arouse guilt evolve from simple, concrete incidents in toddlerhood to abstract, complex situations in later adolescence (Emde, 1991; Williams and Bybee, 1994). Initially, children feel guilty over their *transgressions*—actions that violate known rules and the expectations of others. Spilling their milk, damaging a toy while using it, or stealing something from a classmate are examples of the actions children might feel guilty about during the early childhood period. In the later elementary years, children report feeling guilty when their lack of action leads to distress for others. Thus, Thomas, a fifth grader, might feel guilty when classmates tease a child on the playground and he does nothing to stop it. By middle school an increasing number of children report feeling guilty over neglecting responsibilities, such as forgetting to let the dog out before leaving for school or failing to attain ideals they have set for themselves like making the track team or achieving a certain grade-point average. Students in high school add inconsiderate behaviors, lying, and inequity to their lists of things that they feel guilty about (Hoffman, 1990). By this time, the main things that make people feel guilty are related to personal standards, rather than failing to satisfy other people's expectations. This gradual shift in focus contributes to the inner control needed for self-regulation.

**Empathy.** The beginnings of empathy are also present early in life (Lamb, 1994). Empathic feelings occur when children identify with another person's emotions and feel those emotions themselves. Infants express empathy to other children by simply mimicking their distress. For instance, many babies cry upon hearing or seeing the cries of other babies. Between one and two years of age, the infant's global reaction grows into more genuine feelings of concern for a particular person. Such youngsters also recognize that some action is required as part of

their response. This is demonstrated when one toddler pats another who is crying as a result of falling down. In the later preschool and early elementary years, children make more objective assessments of other people's distress and needs (Miller, et al., 1995). They begin to recognize emotional reactions different from their own, and they become more adept at responding in a variety of ways to provide comfort and support. By the time children reach the age of ten to twelve years, they demonstrate empathy for people with whom they do not interact directly—the homeless, the disabled, the victims of a disaster. This increased sensitivity to the plight of others is a contributing factor in children's development of self-discipline–related behaviors.

## Cognitive Development

Children's ability to distinguish between appropriate and inappropriate behaviors evolves in conjunction with changes in their cognitive powers (Kohlberg, 1964; Tisak and Block, 1990). In general, it can be said that as children's cognitive capacities expand so does their ability to regulate their behavior internally. These evolving capabilities are influenced by changing notions of right and wrong, the degree to which children comprehend the perspective of other persons, the extent to which children make connections among events, and the cognitive characteristics of centration, cause and effect, and irreversibility.

**Children's notions of right and wrong become more objective over time.** Toddlers and preschoolers use rewards and punishments as their main criteria for making judgments about right and wrong. Children interpret actions that result in social rewards as desirable and those that incur social costs as undesirable. This is true even if the behavior is viewed differently by society. For instance, children may conclude that putting materials away neatly is good because teachers praise them or that writing in picture books is bad because they are corrected for this behavior. On the other hand, children who observe a classmate gain attention by taunting others may interpret teasing as "good" because it is reinforced. Likewise, they may conclude that defending a peer is "bad" if it results in rejection from other children in the group (Kostelnik, Soderman, and Whiren, in press).

As children move into the elementary grades, they also decide that actions are "bad" if they result in physical harm to people or property or if they violate people's rights (Tisak and Block, 1990). Those that do, such as hitting or breaking things, or calling names, are readily identified by them as unacceptable. However, behaviors that disrupt the social order of the group, such as not putting toys away, and those that violate interpersonal trust, like telling a secret, are not construed as inappropriate until later childhood.

Older children (ages eight and up) use more sophisticated reasoning in thinking about rules. Not only do they think more abstractly about right and wrong, but they are able to consider people's intentions and the eventual aftermath of their actions. For this reason, children become aware that a person's thoughtless words may unintentionally hurt someone else's feelings. Also, they see beyond immediate results and project long-term outcomes. Thus, fourth graders might conclude that although whining could result in attainment of a short-term goal such as attention, the potential for rejection by their peers in the long-run is too great to risk. By this time too, children value interpersonal trust and recognize the need for maintaining some form of social order to protect the rights of individuals and the group.

**Children's perspective-taking abilities become more accurate with maturity.** To interact effectively with others and to make accurate judgments about what actions would be right or wrong in particular situations, children must understand what other people think, feel, or know. Called **perspective taking,** this capacity is not fully developed in young children. Youngsters, five years of age and younger, often have difficulty putting themselves in another person's shoes. That dilemma is a result of being unable, rather than unwilling, to comprehend or predict other people's thoughts (Vasta, Haith, and Miller, 1992). Thus, children have trouble recognizing other peoples' viewpoints, especially when those views conflict with their own. They erroneously assume that their interpretation of events is universal. Frequently, such differences must be brought to children's attention before they begin to recognize that their perspective is not shared.

Youngsters between six and eight years of age begin to recognize that someone else's interpretation of a situation may be different from their own. However, they cannot always recognize what the differences are. Often they assume that the differences they become aware of occurred simply because each person had received different information or were actually in different situations. As a

result, these youngsters may go to great lengths trying to convince others of the validity of their view. The seemingly endless arguments and rationales they generate are an outgrowth of their immature reasoning, not tactics deliberately aimed at frustrating the persons whom they are trying to persuade.

Nine- and ten-year-olds recognize that their own thoughts and the thoughts of another person are different and may even be contradictory. They understand that two people can react to the same data in opposite ways or that the same person can have a mixed reaction (Forbes, 1978). However, they are only able to think about their own view and another person's view alternately.

Eleven- and twelve-year-olds are able to differentiate their own perspective from that of other people and are able to consider the two perspectives simultaneously (Selman, 1976; Shantz, 1975). They also can speculate about what other people currently are thinking or what they might think in the future. These abilities help children determine how to behave in an increasingly varied number of situations.

**Making connections.** Children ages two through six think of social incidents as totally separate events and do not easily make connections among them. For instance, they often fail to recognize underlying principles that make it possible to categorize certain behaviors as acceptable or not acceptable. This explains three-year-old Chad's lack of understanding in the following incident.

---

Chad and his mother were in the car going to the store. Chad's mother had a headache. She asked Chad to stop clicking the ashtray because it bothered her. Chad said, "Okay" and left the ashtray alone. Within a few minutes he began tapping his feet against the seat. He was startled when his mother expressed irritation at his "disobedience." He thought he had complied. He did not see a connection between clicking the ashtray and tapping his feet.

---

Had Chad's mother pointed out that clicking and tapping both produced noise and it was the noise that was the real problem, Chad might have had a better chance of understanding why clicking and tapping were similar events. Without that kind of verbal explanation, the two actions bore little resemblance to one another in his mind. This kind of thing happens often to children because adults assume they recognize links from one incident to another, which are not really evident to the child. Older children become better able to mentally group similar actions or happenings and to identify interrelationships that might exist. Thus, a preschooler may see no connection between the act of hitting and the act of pinching, whereas a grade schooler would recognize both as hurtful actions. Similarly, younger children do not necessarily distinguish "home" behavior, "restaurant" behavior, and "church or temple" behavior. They tend to treat all these locales as the same. With maturity and experience, children recognize that each setting requires a particular array of behaviors, some of which are not expected across all settings. Children come to these realizations as their categorization skills increase and as they hear explanations about the links other people think are important. These mental processes continue to form during the teenage years, and it is not until then that children can be expected to make accurate connections entirely on their own.

**Centration.** Throughout the early childhood period, children tend to direct their attention to only one attribute of a situation, ignoring all others (Peterson and Felton-Collins, 1991). This phenomenon, known as **centration,** restricts children's ability to see the big picture and to generate alternate solutions to problems they encounter. Thus, young children have a limited rather than comprehensive perception of events. Centration causes them to overlook important details relevant to their actions and the behavior of others and to persist in using a singular approach to achieve their aims. This explains why youngsters may try the same unsuccessful strategy repeatedly and why they have difficulty shifting their attention from one facet of an interaction ("She knocked over my blocks" or "He has all the gold glitter paint") to another ("She was trying to help me stack the blocks higher" or "There are several other colors of glitter from which to choose"). Even when youngsters recognize that actions such as grabbing or striking are inappropriate, they may be unable to generate suitable alternate behaviors at the moment such thinking is needed. The younger the child, the more this is so. Likewise, the more emotional the situation is for the child, the more difficult it is for him or her to think about other approaches. Decentering occurs only gradually, as children are confronted with multiple perceptions and methods of resolution. Adults enhance the process when they point out options to children and when they help youngsters brainstorm suitable

alternatives as relevant circumstances arise (Kostelnik, Soderman and Whiren, in press). However, centration continues to influence children's thinking well into adolescence. Even as adults, all of us experience times when we center on a particular part of an issue or one certain approach and have a difficult time "seeing" more or generating alternate strategies. Clearly it is an easier task for individuals to decenter in later childhood than it is for younger children to do so.

**Cause and effect.** Children must be able to predict the probable outcomes of a vast array of social behaviors in order to make judgments about which actions to take and which to avoid. For instance, a child tempted to sneak a forbidden cookie could end up with a flavorful snack. However, the outcome could also be a reprimand or losing the opportunity to have such treats in the future. Whether children are dealing with rules at the levels of adherence, identification, or internalization, they must understand such causal relationships to thoughtfully choose their course of action.

Initially, young children are not very accurate reasoners about what makes some things happen. Preschoolers often attribute outcomes to magical, personal, or otherwise erroneous factors (Clarke-Stewart, 1983; Fitch, 1995). Consequently, a four-year-old might not recognize that by spending all of his tokens in the first few minutes of a playmate's party at a local game center, he won't have any to spend later. When he runs out of tokens, the child may assume he didn't get enough or as many as other children who still have tokens to spend. It is not likely he will understand that his behavior contributed to an outcome that he perceives as negative. As their cognitive abilities increase and they gain additional experience, youngsters become more accurate at recognizing the link between particular actions and their corresponding outcomes. For instance, running inside a crowded classroom may cause a child to fall against something and get hurt; teasing a classmate may cause that person or others in the group to reject the child as a potential friend; and slamming the computer keys may cause the machine to break. Eventually, children use their understanding of these cause-and-effect relationships as a tool for self-regulation. However, it is not until adolescence that such ideas are fully realized. In the meantime, it is up to adults to point out cause-and-effect relationships to children and to help children recognize the results of the various actions in which they engage.

**Irreversibility.** Toddlers and preschoolers do not routinely mentally reverse actions they initiate physically (Fitch, 1995; Flavell, 1977). In other words, their thinking is **irreversible.** This means they are not proficient at readily thinking of an opposite action for something they are actually doing. If they are pushing, it is hard for them to quickly pull instead; if they are reaching for something, it's a challenge to draw back. Young children also have difficulty spontaneously interrupting an ongoing behavior. For example, if a child is in the act of hitting, she might complete the hitting action before reversing it either by taking her hand away or dropping it to her side.

---

Jennifer, a three-year-old, was busy gluing dry macaroni to her collage. In her effort to get to the bottom of the glue bottle, she tipped it upside down, and the glue ran all over. The caregiver said, "Don't tip the bottle." Jennifer continued gluing and the glue kept on dripping.

---

When the adult called out her warning, she assumed Jennifer knew how to reverse tipping the bottle. To the adult, it was obvious that returning the jar to an upright position was the reverse of holding it upside down. However, she should not have anticipated that Jennifer would know this. Young children have not had enough experience to picture in their minds how to transpose a physical action. For this reason adults must help preschoolers reverse an inappropriate act by showing them or telling them how to do it. The same holds true for older children in unfamiliar situations. Although children who have moved beyond the preoperational stage of thinking are better able to halt or slow down if an adult says, "Don't run in the hall," they are less likely to respond successfully in a situation that is new to them or that takes place in unfamiliar surroundings.

## Language and Memory Development

Not only is the capacity for self-discipline affected by children's emotional development and cognitive capabilities, but language and memory play a role in the process too.

**Language.** The phenomenal rate of language acquisition during the childhood years plays a major role in children's development of internal behavior controls. This is because language contributes to children's understanding of why rules are made and gives them more tools for attaining their goals in socially acceptable ways. By the time they are three years old most children have command of a well-developed receptive vocabulary and the ability to express their basic needs. However, they are not always successful at responding to verbal directions or at telling others what they want. As a result, it is not unusual for preschoolers to resort to physical actions to communicate. They may grab, jerk away, fail to respond, push, or hit rather than use words to express themselves. Gradually, children learn to use language more effectively. They become more successful at telling others what they want and better equipped to understand and respond to the verbal instructions, requests, explanations, and reasoning used by others as guides for behavior (Maccoby, 1984; Marion, 1995). Consequently, they find words a more satisfactory and precise way to communicate. When this occurs, their physical demonstrations become less frequent and intense.

**Private speech.** Children also use **private speech** as a means for self-regulation (Berk and Winsler, 1995; Vygotsky, 1978). That is, they talk out loud to themselves as a way to reduce frustration, postpone rewards, or remind themselves of rules. While putting on her shoes and socks, Molly says to herself in a sing-song voice, "One shoe, one sock, one foot." Olga sits down in the writing center and says to no one in particular, "Hmmm, what do I need? I know, paper, pens, and tape." When Abdul begins losing patience putting a model together, he quietly repeats to himself, "Slow down, take your time. You'll get it." This kind of talk is common in early and middle childhood, accounting for 20 to 60 percent of what children say (Papalia and Olds, 1993). The normal developmental progression is for toddlers and three-year-olds to repeat audible rhythmic sounds. Children of ages four to seven or eight years "think out loud" in conjunction with their actions. They generate whole phrases to plan strategies and monitor their actions. Children in the later elementary years mutter single words in barely discernable tones (Frauenglass and Diaz, 1985). Studies of children's behavior in problem-solving situations indicate that they rely on private speech most when a task is difficult. Moreover, children's performance typically improves following the self-instruction they provide themselves (Bivens and Berk, 1990). In adolescence, audible private speech becomes the silent, inner speech that people use throughout their lives to organize and regulate day-to-day activities. Although private speech is a naturally occurring phenomenon, it appears that children also can be taught to use such "self-talk" as a deliberate means for self-regulation.

**Memory skills.** Memory is another variable that influences self-discipline. Although scientists have not yet determined whether memory actually increases from one year to the next, it does seem that as children grow older, they become better able to use the information they have stored in their memory as a resource for determining future behavior (Maccoby, 1984). Consequently, they become less dependent on others to show or tell them how to respond to each new situation. Instead, they use remembered information to guide their actions. (Boneau, 1974). This means helping professionals working with children in formal group settings should expect that children will periodically "forget" the rules. Also, youngsters may be unsure of how to respond in unfamiliar circumstances. From toddlerhood through eight to nine years of age, children often need frequent reminders about rules and procedures and clear explanations about what to expect when routines change or new activities are introduced. Older children benefit from periodic reviews of the rules, but are better able to remember them without continual adult support.

## ▼ HOW EXPERIENCE INFLUENCES SELF-DISCIPLINE

Because most young people experience the developmental changes just discussed and thus acquire some of the basics for internalization, the reasons for variation in their compliance with rules can best be attributed to differences in experiences. Children learn the rules of society from others through direct instruction, observation, reinforcement, punishment, and attribution (Berreth and Berman, 1997). Infants and preschoolers are chiefly responsive to parents and other adults with whom they have a positive relationship; grade-school children are also influenced by peers (Smith, 1982).

### Direct Instruction

Throughout childhood, adults regulate children's behavior using physical and verbal controls. These are forms of **direct instruction**. At first, they rely mainly on bodily intervention to keep youngsters safe and help them get along. Adults separate squabbling siblings, remove dangerous objects from reach, extract forbidden items from children's grasp, and restrain them from dashing across busy streets. These actions usually are accompanied by brief verbal commands such as "Stop," "No," "Give me that," or "Wait for me." Gradually, physical intervention gives way to greater reliance on verbal directions and warnings, to which children become increasingly responsive (Lytton, 1979; Maccoby, 1984).

Typical adult instructions usually fall into the categories outlined in Table 10–3.

Verbal instructions are the quickest way to let children know what the appropriate, inappropriate, and alternate behaviors are. They are particularly effective when combined with another technique known as modeling.

### Modeling

Adults **model** a code of conduct through their own actions (Bandura, 1989). Returning library books on time, helping an injured animal, or resisting the urge to eat a candy bar before supper all convey messages to children about desirable behaviors.

Setting a good example is an important way of teaching children right from wrong. However, although it is true that children imitate much of what they see, modeling is most effective when the model's behavior is obvious to children. This means youngsters are best able to imitate a model with whom they can interact (Serbin, 1981) or whose behavior is pointed out to them (Meichenbaum, 1977). This helps children to recognize important details that they might otherwise not notice. Thus if the object is to demonstrate gentle handling of animals, it is best to work directly with the child and demonstrate the task. It is also useful to say, "See, I'm picking up the chicks very gently so I don't hurt them or crush their feathers. Look at how loosely I'm bending my fingers." Simply showing children the proper procedure without direct explanation may not cause them to imitate the appropriate behavior themselves at a later time.

Verbal descriptions of modeled behaviors are especially valuable when the adult hopes children will recognize that a person they are watching is resisting temptation or delaying gratification (Toner, Parke, and Yussen, 1978). Children may not recognize what the person is doing unless told. Statements such as the following assist children in recognizing someone's efforts to delay gratification: "Raymond really wants to use the unabridged dictionary, even though the college dictionary is available now. He has decided to wait until Karen has finished with it so he can use it next." Children also benefit when an adult model clearly states a rule he or she is following and

▼ Table 10–3     Modes of Adult Instruction

**Telling Children What Is Right and What Is Wrong**
"It isn't nice to pull the cat's tail."
"Share your toys."
"Stealing is bad."

**Informing Children of Expected Standards**
"Pet the cat gently."
"Put your toys away."
"Give Grandma a kiss."

**Restricting Certain Behaviors**
"Five more minutes on the swing."
"No painting until you put on a smock."
"Use this tissue, not your sleeve."

**Advising Children about How to Meet the Standards They Set**
"You could stack all the big plates on one side and the little plates on the other, like this."
"You could use the ball together or you could take turns."
"If you think about something else, that will make the waiting go faster."

**Redirecting Children's Behavior**
"Go outdoors. Don't bounce that ball inside."
"That spoon is too big. Try this one."
"You can tell him you're angry. Don't bite."

**Providing Children with Information about How Their Actions Affect Themselves and Others**
"He hit you because you hit him."
"Every time you tease her, she cries."
"Mr. Martin really appreciated your helping him rake the leaves."

**Giving Children Information about How Their Behavior Looks to Others**
"Comb your hair. People will think I don't take good care of you."
"When you don't say 'Hi' back, he thinks you don't like him."
"When you forget to say 'Thank you,' people don't know you appreciated what they did."

the rationale for not committing a certain act (Grusec, et al., 1979). For example, explaining that the guinea pigs are eating and that it is important to let them finish before picking them up illustrates this technique. Children who watch a model delay action and understand what they are seeing are better able to postpone gratification in subsequent situations themselves (Bandura and Mischel, 1965).

Unfortunately, modeling not only accentuates positive actions; children also learn from the negative models they observe. Youngsters who see others act aggressively with no negative consequences learn powerful lessons. These actions frequently are duplicated in their own behavior (Bandura and Walters, 1963; Mussen, et al., 1990).

## Reinforcement and Punishment

In addition to instructing children about how to act and modeling particular behaviors themselves, adults reinforce desirable deeds and punish those they consider unacceptable. **Reinforcement** involves providing some consequence to a behavior that increases the likelihood the child will repeat that behavior in similar situations. **Punishments** are consequences that reduce the probability of a particular behavior being repeated. Although the principles of reinforcement and punishment are relatively straightforward, appropriate enactment is complex. For this reason, Chapter 11 is devoted entirely to this subject. For now, it is important merely to recognize that children experience both rewards and penalties as a result of their behavior and that these play a major role in their acquisition of self-discipline.

## Character Attribution

Another means of influencing children's behavior is **character attribution.** Attribution is a verbal strategy adults use to affect how children think of themselves and thus their behavior (Moore, 1986). When adults assign particular characteristics to children by telling them, "You are patient," there is evidence that children's behavior changes in response; namely, that they become even more patient (Grusec and Mills, 1982; Grusec and Redler, 1980). On the other hand, when adults tell children that they are sloppy or irresponsible, children adopt these characteristics to an even greater extent. In this way, children view themselves in much the same terms ascribed to them by adults and take on the corresponding behaviors (Dreikurs and Soltz, 1964). Thus adult attitudes and verbalizations have a profound impact on children's self-image and eventually influence the extent to which children believe they are capable of demonstrating socially acceptable, self-controlled behavior.

## Integrating Development and Experience

The individual interactions children experience each day help them create a unique internalized map of the social environment (Boneau, 1974). That is, children mentally chart their experiences and make note of which behaviors make them feel guilty, which make them feel good, which are rewarded, and which are not, and under what circumstances those conditions apply. Gradually, this map grows in breadth and complexity. Over time, children catalogue a growing number of experiences and make finer discriminations among events. They draw on information gleaned from these episodes to fit their behavior to situational demands rather than depending on other people to direct them at that moment. In addition, their increased developmental competence enables them to interpret more accurately the cues they receive and to envision more varied responses to those cues. As a result, they become progressively more successful in monitoring their own behavior.

Gradually, other children also contribute data to children's understanding of what constitutes desirable and undesirable behavior. The combined experiences with adults and age-mates lead to greater self-discipline. Interactions with adults teach children about obligations, responsibility, and respect, and peer relations give children firsthand experience with cooperation and justice (Youniss, 1980). This difference in perspective is a result of children's general interpretation that positive behavior with adults means obedience, and positive behavior with peers involves reciprocal actions such as sharing or taking turns. This chapter and the next concentrate on the adult's role in helping children achieve self-discipline. Chapter 8, Supporting Children's Friendships, describes how peers influence this process as well.

## ▼ How Adult Behavior Affects Children's Behavior

All adults rely on instruction, modeling, rewards, punishments, and character attribution to teach children how to behave. However, the combination of techniques they use and the way in which they apply them differ. Such variations have been the subject of research for the past twenty-five years. It has been found that the blend of socialization strategies parents and helping professionals adopt has a major influence on children's personality development and whether children follow rules because of adherence, identification, or internalization. Both short-term and long-range effects have been noted (Franz, McClelland, and Weinberger, 1991; Hoffman, 1970, 1983). Although most research has focused on the parent-child relationship, other adult-child interactions, including ones between children and helping professionals, have been examined. All of these studies yield similar results.

In a series of landmark, longitudinal studies, Diana Baumrind identified three common adult discipline styles—authoritarian, permissive, and authoritative (Baumrind, 1967, 1973, 1977). These three discipline styles continue to be the standard for comparison today (Bukatko and Daehler, 1995; Marion, 1995; Santrock, 1996). Each is characterized by particular adult attitudes and practices related to the dimensions of control, maturity demands, communication, and nurturance.

**Control** refers to the manner and degree to which adults enforce compliance with their expectations. **Maturity demands** involve the level at which expectations are set. The amount of information offered to children regarding behavior practices constitutes the **communication** component. **Nurturance** refers to the extent to which adults express caring and concern for children.

Differences among the three styles of discipline are reflected in differing combinations of these dimensions and are depicted in Figure 10–1. Authoritarian adults are high in control, high in maturity de-

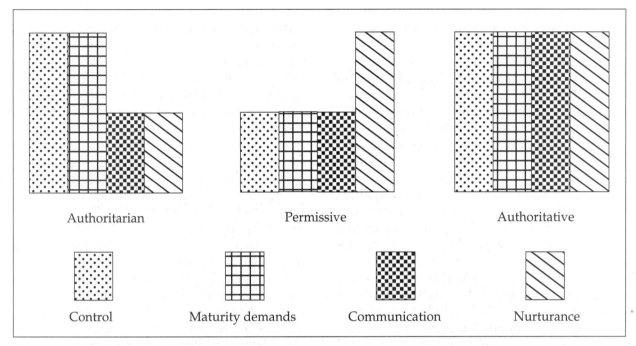

**Figure 10-1** Differences in attitudes and practices among authoritarian, permissive, and authoritative discipline styles.

mands, low in clarity of communication, and low in nurturance. Permissive adults are low in control, low in maturity demands, low in communication clarity, and high in nurturance. Adults high in all four dimensions are described as "authoritative." Although no adult uses only the few strategies representative of a particular category, their behaviors do tend to cluster according to one pattern or another.

Understanding the characteristics of each discipline style and their impact on children is important knowledge for helping professionals to have. It enables them to assess their use of discipline in the formal group setting and provides insights as to why children respond as they do.

### The Authoritarian Discipline Style

**Authoritarian** adults put all of their energy into the action dimension of the socialization process. They spare little time for facilitation. To achieve the high standards they have for children's behavior, they are vigilant rule enforcers who value children's unquestioning obedience above all else. Theirs is the philosophy of "Do what I tell you," and "Do it because I said so!" Explanations and reasoning do not fit into their view of themselves as the ultimate authority. Broken rules are dealt with swiftly and forcefully, most often through ridicule, shame, or physical punishment. Not too surprising, authori-

tarian adults have cold, distant relationships with the children in their charge. Youngsters view them as harsh taskmasters who focus more on finding mistakes than on recognizing their attempts to comply (Shaffer, 1994). This approach, sometimes referred to as power-assertive discipline, keeps children dependent on adults to dictate right from wrong (Newman and Newman, 1997). Youngsters follow rules out of fear or blind obedience, not out of empathy or concern for others. This hampers their ability to develop the reasoning skills and emotional sensitivity necessary for internalization. Under authoritarian conditions, children follow rules at the adherence level. Children whose primary experiences are with authoritarian adults generally become unfriendly, suspicious, resentful, and unhappy. They tend to be underachievers, to avoid their peers, and to exhibit increased incidents of misconduct, as well as more extreme acting-out behaviors (Baumrind, 1991; Maccoby and Martin, 1983; Weiss, et al., 1992).

### The Permissive Discipline Style

At the other extreme is the permissive discipline style. **Permissive** adults emphasize facilitation at the expense of the action dimension of the helping relationship. In formal group settings supervised by permissive adults, children are treated with warmth and affection. Such adults sees themselves as resources to children but not as active agents responsible for shaping children's present or future behavior. They accept a wide range of children's actions based either on the conviction that external controls thwart children's development or out of uncertainty about how to achieve compliance. Consequently, permissive adults provide little instruction to children about how to behave. They ignore children's transgressions, make few demands, and seldom give children opportunities to assume responsibility. At those infrequent times when they feel compelled to administer a penalty for gross misconduct, the favored technique is temporary love withdrawal ("I don't like children who hurt people") (Baumrind, 1978; Shaffer, 1994).

Unfortunately, children subjected to this approach show few signs of internalization. Since they receive almost no cues about which behaviors are socially appropriate and which are not, they fail to develop mental guidelines or strategies to draw on in their day-to-day social encounters. Moreover, they have little chance to develop feelings of empathy for others because cause-effect relationships are not explained. Their unrestrained behavior is often viewed as immature, inconsiderate, and unacceptable by peers and adults. The general negative reception that such behaviors receive contributes to children's feelings of anxiety and low self-esteem. As a rule, children whose world is dominated by permissive adults tend to be withdrawn, unproductive, and unhappy. In adolescence, this style is frequently associated with delinquency and poor academic performance (Patterson and Stouthamer-Loeber, 1984; Pulkkinen, 1982). Such children exhibit the lowest levels of independence and self-regulation of all three discipline styles summarized here (Baumrind, 1967, 1995).

### The Authoritative Discipline Style

**Authoritative** adults combine the positive attributes of the authoritative and permissive discipline styles, while avoiding the negative ones. They respond to children's needs with warmth and nurturance; they have high standards and establish clear behavioral expectations (Bukatko and Daehler, 1995). Authoritative adults also rely on additional strategies that permissive and authoritarian adults fail to use altogether. In this way they address both the facilitation and the action dimensions of the helping relationship. Thus, helping professionals who exemplify an authoritative style are friendly

and affectionate toward children. These adults make children feel important by allowing them to assume appropriate responsibility and acknowledging their accomplishments. They also teach children relevant social skills to help them meet their needs in socially acceptable ways. Simultaneously, authoritative adults establish high standards for children's behavior, but gear their expectations to match children's changing needs and abilities. Although quick to respond to children's misbehavior, they use explanations, demonstrations, suggestions, and other types of reasoning as their primary socialization strategies (LeFrancois, 1992). These adults use discipline encounters as opportunities for discussions related to guilt and empathy and as a means for teaching lessons about which behaviors to choose, which to avoid, and which to try instead. This nonpunitive form of behavior regulation is sometimes called inductive discipline because adults induce children to regulate their behavior based on the impact their actions will have on themselves and others.

The authoritative discipline style is the one most strongly associated with the development of self-discipline in children (Franz, et al., 1991; Vasta, Haith, and Miller, 1992). Children know what is expected of them and how to comply. Moreover, they become sensitive to the needs of others, happy, cooperative, resistant to temptation, and socially responsible. They are also better able to initiate and maintain tasks on their own (Baumrind, 1991). Their behavior is the most socially competent of the three patterns described in this chapter. For these reasons, young children benefit when the adults in their lives display an authoritative discipline style.

Refer to Table 10–4 for a summary of all three discipline styles and the corresponding patterns of child behavior with which they are associated. Recent evidence not only supports the relationships depicted but also indicates that such outcomes tend to endure from early childhood into later maturity (Baumrind, 1988, 1995; Dornbusch, et al., 1987).

### Implications

As evidenced by the behavioral outcomes associated with the three dominant patterns of adult supervision, each has a profound impact on children's immediate and long-term development. Heavy-handed discipline produces children who are compliant, afraid, dependent, and angry (Weiss, et al., 1992). Coercive tactics, such as physical force,

▼ Table 10–4    Discipline Styles and Associated Patterns of Child Behavior

| DISCIPLINE STYLE | BEHAVIORAL PROFILE |
|---|---|
| Authoritarian | Aggressive<br>Fearful, apprehensive<br>Moody, unhappy<br>Suspicious<br>Withdrawn<br>Hostile<br>Unfriendly<br>Aimless<br>Low self-reliance and self-control |
| Permissive | Rebellious<br>Withdrawn<br>Unhappy<br>Impulsive<br>Aggressive<br>Domineering<br>Low achiever<br>Immature<br>Aimless<br>Low self-reliance and self-control |
| Authoritative | Cooperative<br>Friendly<br>Happy<br>Empathic<br>Socially responsible<br>Curious<br>High achiever<br>Goal oriented<br>High self-reliance and self-control |

Sources: Adapted from Baumrind, D. "Current Patterns of Parental Authority." *Developmental Psychology Monographs* 4, no. 1, pt. 2 (1971); and Shaffer, D. R. *Developmental Psychology: Childhood and Adolescence.* Pacific Grove, Calif.: Brooks/Cole Publishing Co., 1995.

shame, and dictatorial demands cause youngsters to act out of fear or blind obedience, not out of empathy or concern for others (Raffini, 1980). This interferes with their ability to develop the reasoning and caring that is necessary for internalization (Hoffman, 1967). Thus, control exerted without explanation or affection does not help children become self-disciplined. Instead, they maintain an external orientation and remain at adherence.

Likewise, internalization does not occur when adults are affectionate but fail to provide children with direction or predictable expectations. In these situations, children have few opportunities to receive accurate feedback about how other people perceive them and how their behavior affects others. With so few cues about what is socially appropriate, they are unable to create a realistic foundation of experience to serve as a guide for future behavior. For them, the world often is unfriendly because other adults and peers who do not share the same permissive standards find their unrestrained behavior unacceptable. The resulting rejection contributes to feelings of anxiety and low self-esteem. Unfortunately, such children also are less likely to develop feelings of empathy for others (Damon, 1978; Hoffman, 1983). These omissions add up to a dismal prognosis for youngsters who are the product of a permissive discipline style.

Obviously, the adult behavior pattern that is most likely to lead to internalization is the authoritative style. Authoritative adults effectively address all three factors contributing to self-discipline: emotions, cognition, and experience.

When adults are able to convey acceptance to children while at the same time making it clear that they have expectations for their conduct, children feel secure knowing that they are cared about and that they have a resource for determining how to behave. Discipline encounters provide an opportunity for discussions about guilt and empathy, two emotions not easily acknowledged by a child who is defensive or hostile as a result of power assertion or concerned over love withdrawal (Hoffman, 1970).

Reasoning with children also contributes to their cognitive development because they are exposed to moral judgments that are beyond their own. This strategy has been shown to be an important element in developing higher levels of thinking about what is right and what is wrong. In addition, children acquire precise information about which behaviors to choose again, which to avoid, and which alternatives to select. This increases the breadth and depth of their cognitive map of the social environment. Such youngsters are most likely to maximize the potential successes available to them because they have learned to satisfy their needs within guidelines established by adults.

**From a child's point of view.** If children were to rate the various discipline styles just described, how might they judge each one? That was the question posed, using simple scenarios, to children ages four through eighteen (Siegal and Cowen, 1984). Inductive methods were the disciplinary strategies most preferred by children of all ages. Children overwhelmingly rated as "right" or "very right" situations depicting rational disciplinarians, regardless of the discipline styles they experienced at home. Physical punishment came in as the second best approach with love withdrawal being favored by no one. Moreover, outright permissiveness was categorized as "wrong" or "very wrong" by all groups studied. Lack of supervision and limits were of particular concern to children aged nine years and below. From these results, it is apparent that young children see a need for adults to intervene and stop children's socially unacceptable behavior. A further implication is that if most children view induction as the "right" disciplinary technique, they may be more accepting of behavioral intervention from an adult whose style reflects that approach (Shaffer, 1995).

**A cross-cultural perspective.** Some people wonder whether the authoritative approach to discipline represents the needs and best interests of people of varying ethnic/cultural and socioeconomic backgrounds. To date, research with white children, children of color, middle-class children, and children from poorer backgrounds indicates that the principles of combining warm, affectionate relationships with high standards and clear expectations are associated with children's development of positive self-esteem and self-discipline regardless of background (Baumrind, 1995). However, readers are reminded that each child lives in an ecological niche unique to that child. The details of how relationships are established and how compliance is achieved vary. Alternative life conditions may call for techniques that differ in form but correspond in concept to those associated with an authoritative perspective. For instance, the Green family lives in a housing project riddled with drugs and violence. Mrs. Green is faced with having to keep her son safe in a hostile environment. She may demand quicker compliance and more absolute obedience in that environment than she would if she lived elsewhere. Moreover, what children and the significant adults in their lives interpret as warm and supportive depends on past experiences and current interpretations. This means one child may interpret teasing from adults as a positive relationship-building strategy, whereas another views teasing as a strategy of rejection. Likewise, sarcasm may be understandable to some children as a gentle admonition to be taken seriously ("Go ahead, make me tell you a second

time"), whereas other children would miss the message entirely. Children's comprehension is tied to the customs of speech with which they are familiar. For this reason, helping professionals must be cautious not to judge other adults' socialization styles too narrowly, and they must seek ways to adapt their skills to meet the needs of children and families whose backgrounds vary widely. The skills provided later in this chapter fit these criteria.

### Becoming Authoritative

Once it was thought adults were instinctively authoritarian, permissive, or authoritative. We now know that although some people's personality or temperament seem more aligned with one style or another, through training and practice any adult can learn to be more authoritative (Peters and Kostelnik, 1981). Adults must pay attention to how they establish relationships with children and to how they make children aware of their expectations (Greenspan, 1985). Skills presented in previous chapters have focused on relationship enhancement. Thus, you have already learned one major component of the authoritative approach. The skills presented in this chapter will focus on making children aware of adult's standards and expectations.

## ▼ STATING BEHAVIORAL EXPECTATIONS

Adults can best express their behavioral expectations for children through a personal message. A **personal message** consists of three parts. The first is a reflection in which the child's point of view is acknowledged. In the second portion, the adult articulates his or her emotions about the child's behavior, names which specific action prompted those feelings, and explains why. The third segment, used only in situations in which behavior change is desired, involves describing an alternate behavior for the child to pursue. This last step is, in fact, a statement of a rule that the child is expected to follow for that situation.

The ultimate aim of using personal messages is to give children the information they need for both current and future reference. Personal messages help children better understand how their actions affect others and provide them with cues about desirable and undesirable behaviors.

In favorable circumstances, personal messages tell children what they are doing right so they can repeat the behavior in subsequent interactions. For instance, an adult who values cooperation may acknowledge two children's efforts to share by saying: "You're working together. It makes me feel happy to see you sharing. Sharing is a good way of cooperating."

In problem situations, personal messages set the stage either for children to comply on their own or for the adult to impose consequences when children fail to obey. For example, adults who want to redirect a child's anger away from hitting and toward talking could say: "You're angry. It upsets me when you hit. Hitting hurts. Tell Stuart what he did that made you so mad." For now, we will turn our attention to personal messages aimed at changing problem behaviors, later, we will consider how to use them in positive situations.

## Knowing When Behavior Change Is Necessary

Every day, adults are faced with situations in which they must decide whether or not a child's behavior is appropriate. If a behavior is not acceptable, they must also determine what conduct would be more suitable. In order to make these decisions, the following questions must be asked:

1. Is the child's behavior unsafe either for self or others?
2. Is the child's behavior destructive?
3. Does the child's behavior infringe on the rights of someone else?

If the answer to any of these questions is yes, it is a clear sign that the adult should intervene (Galambos-Stone, 1994; Hildebrand, 1994). If the response is no, then demands for behavior change are unnecessary.

For example, concern about *safety* is the reason why children are stopped from running with scissors, prevented from dashing across a busy street, or kept from playing with matches. Similarly, the sanctions adults impose on writing graffiti or writing in library books are aimed at *protecting property*. When children are rebuked for copying from someone else's paper or for bullying a timid classmate, adults are making an effort to teach children *respect for others*. In all of these situations, there are legitimate grounds for trying to alter children's behavior.

On the other hand, adults are not justified when they insist that children behave in certain ways simply because it is traditional or more convenient. Hence, requiring children to take their seats on the bus in alphabetical order rather than sitting with their friends is an example of unnecessary and inappropriate adult intervention.

Finally, adults also must decide whether a problem behavior is important enough to warrant persistent attention (Gootman, 1988). This can be described as the *principle of importance*. In other words, is the behavior serious enough to deal with each and every time it happens? When a behavior meets these criteria, a personal message is in order. For example, when Mr. Smith sees children throwing rocks on the playground, he takes action to stop it regardless of when he sees it or how tired or preoccupied he is. Because rock throwing is so dangerous, preventing it is a top priority for Mr. Smith. In this case, a personal message that forbids rock throwing is appropriate.

On the other hand, it annoys Mr. Smith when children scuff the toes of their shoes on the cement. Sometimes, he tries hard to get them to lift their feet when they walk. However, if he has a headache or has put in a long day and a child scuffs her shoes, Mr. Smith pretends not to see it rather than dealing with the problem. The intermittent nature of Mr. Smith's attention to this behavior is a sign that the standard is not important enough, at least for now, to warrant a personal message.

The standards of safety, property, and people's rights are simple and all encompassing. They provide basic guidelines by which to judge children's behavior. However, it should be noted that because adults differ, their interpretations vary as to what constitutes a dangerous situation or a potential threat to another's self-esteem. People's personal standards are uniquely influenced by past experience, family, community, and culture. This means that no two adults' standards match exactly. However, when adults relate the standards they set to at least one of the principles just described, they minimize major variations, which are confusing to children.

An assessment regarding all of these criteria must be made prior to making your standards known. With so many factors to consider, adults may wonder if prompt action can ever be taken. Experienced professionals consider all these points quickly and intervene in a timely fashion. It may take the novice slightly longer to decide if a personal message is appropriate.

## Part One of the Personal Message

In order to successfully teach children how to achieve their aims appropriately, adults must first understand what children are trying to accomplish.

Once this has been established, it is easier to determine an acceptable alternate behavior that will satisfy both the adult and the child. Based on this rationale, the first step of the personal message is to recognize and acknowledge the child's perspective using a behavior, paraphrase, or affective reflection.

There are several reasons why a personal message begins with a reflection. First, in problem situations, adults and children often have very different points of view. For example, when four-year-old Allison lifts her dress up over her head in the supermarket to show off her new panties, she feels proud, but her mother is mortified. At times like these, adults wish children would act differently, so it is common for them to center on this desire and forget that children's emotions are legitimate, although contrary to their own. Reflecting helps adults avoid this pitfall. It compels them to remember that each child has a unique perception that must be considered prior to subsequent action.

Another advantage of reflecting first is that it serves as a clear signal to the child that the adult is actively attempting to understand his or her position. Children are more willing to listen to adult messages when they think their own messages have been heard. Even when children have chosen a physical means to express their desires, knowledge of adult awareness reduces their need to escalate the behavior in order to make their feelings known. For instance, if Sam is angry, he may be ready to fling a book across the room to make his point. When the adult reflects, "Something happened that really upset you," Sam may not feel so compelled to throw the book to show his anger because someone has already acknowledged it.

A third value of reflecting first is that it is a way to mentally count to ten before committing yourself to a particular line of action. If offers a moment in which adults can sort out their emotions, organize their thoughts, or readjust their approach. It reduces the risk of overreacting or responding thoughtlessly. For instance, from across the room, Ms. Romano notices Danny painting a picture with tempera dripping all over the floor. Her first reaction is one of annoyance. She hurries to the easel, a reprimand on her lips. However, as she approaches, she becomes aware of Danny's obvious pride in his work and his total absorption in his painting. By reflecting, "You're really excited about your painting," she is able to put a check on her initial response. Instead of blurting out, "How many times have we talked about keeping the paint on the paper," she is able calmly to provide him with important information.

"Some paint dripped on the floor. I'm worried someone might slip and get hurt. Get a sponge and we'll clean it up." In this way, the reflection served as a reasoned entry into what could have been an emotionally charged situation.

Finally, reflecting is a way for adults to show their respect and caring for children. This demonstration of positive regard must continue, particularly when disciplinary action is in order. When used in conjunction with the other portions of the personal message, reflecting unites the two components of the authoritative style: affection and clear behavioral expectations.

To summarize, in problem situations, the child has one perspective, the adult another. In order for a resolution to take place, each must accurately and correctly take into account the other's attitudes. This mutual understanding forms the basis for a shared response that will join the two separate lines of thought. The reflection represents the adult's effort to assess the child's attitude; the second portion of the personal message is aimed at helping the child recognize that of the adult.

## Part Two of the Personal Message

The second portion of the personal message describes the adult's emotions, identifies the child's behavior that led to those feelings, and gives a reason for why this is so:

> "I feel annoyed when you hit. Hitting hurts."
> "It upsets me when you interrupt. I keep losing my place."

### Why adults should talk about their emotions.

Helping professionals often have an emotional reaction to children's behavior. They feel pleased when children cooperate, distressed when they fight, annoyed when they procrastinate. Emotions are just as natural for adults as they are for children.

Experienced practitioners learn to use their own emotions as a guide to interacting more effectively with children. They do this by talking about the emotions as they arise. When adults disclose their emotions to children, they illustrate the universality of feelings. They demonstrate that at different times, everyone feels unhappy, pleased, frustrated, worried, proud, satisfied, or angry. This helps children realize that all human beings experience emotions and, as a result, makes them more willing to accept feelings in themselves and to recognize them in others (Hendrick, 1996). Talking about emotions also aids children in learning that people have different reactions to the same situation. They find out that what makes them happy may prompt sadness in others, or that an event that causes them anxiety is welcomed by someone else. Children do not automatically know this and, instead, often assume that their current feelings are shared by everyone else. As they hear more about other people's emotions, they gradually become aware that this is not always the case. Another advantage is that adults serve as a model for using words to express emotional states. Children discover that people can have a variety of reactions and still be capable of verbalizing how they feel. Eventually, children find that emotions can be put into words and that words offer a satisfying way to communicate with other people.

Adults who wish to maintain positive relationships with children also should keep in mind that sharing their feelings with children promotes closer ties. People who are able to talk honestly about their emotions are considered more trustworthy and helpful by the persons with whom they interact than are those who avoid such conversations (McCarthy and Betz, 1978). When adults risk revealing something personal about themselves, it is seen by children as a demonstration of the regard in which they are held (Raffini, 1980). In addition, when such revelations are the norm, children find it less threatening to reveal their own emotions. This leads to mutual understanding and respect.

Finally, children are interested in how the significant adults in their lives react to what they say and do. They care about how adults feel and are responsive to their emotions. In fact, adults who describe their own disappointment or disapproval regarding a particular child's behavior place that child in an optimal state of arousal for receiving the rest of the information contained in their message (Hoffman, 1983). Without this type of sanction, children will not be induced to seriously consider the adult's reasoning. On the other hand, adults who depend on power assertion or love withdrawal as a way to communicate their concern provoke such strong reactions in children that they are unable to attend to the specific content of the message. Thus, when children refrain from hitting because it would upset their teacher, or when they share materials because the caregiver has advocated cooperation, they are demonstrating identification. It is from this base that they eventually will begin to internalize some of the behavioral expectations adults think are important.

**Focusing on children's behavior.** Once adults have described their emotions, it is important that they tell the child which behavior has caused them

to react. Children often don't know which of their behaviors is prompting the adult's reaction. This means identifying by name the undesirable behavior that the child is displaying. This helps children pinpoint actions to avoid (Newman and Newman, 1997). For example, a personal message that includes the statement "It bothers me when you keep jumping out of your seat" tells the child what behavior prompted the adult's irritation and describes an issue that can be resolved. On the other hand, remarks such as "It annoys me that you're showing off" or "I get upset when you're such a slob" are accusations that attack a child's personality and do not further mutual respect and understanding (Chernow and Chernow, 1981).

Behaviors are actions you can see. Taking turns, hitting, kicking, handing over, and coming on time are all visible. Using specific behavior names is an objective rather than a subjective way of describing how people act. On the other hand, descriptors such as lazy, uncooperative, hyperactive, vindictive, greedy, hostile, nasty, and surly are all subjective and accusatory labels. They make children feel defensive without giving them clear cues as to which specific actions are being discussed. Youngsters who are under attack are not likely to be receptive to adult desires for compliance. Instead, they may become hostile or think that satisfying the adult is beyond their capability. In either case, effective behavior change is more difficult to achieve. To avoid such adverse reactions, use objective behavior names rather than subjective labels.

**The importance of giving children reasons.** Children are better able to understand and respond to adult expectations when these expectations are accompanied by reasons (Baumrind, 1972; Marion, 1995; Miller, 1996). This is why the second portion of the personal message also includes giving children an explanation for the adult's reaction.

Why are adults upset when children hit? Because hitting hurts. Why are they frustrated when children dawdle? Because they may be late for something important. Why do they become annoyed when children interrupt a story over and over again? Because interrupting interferes with their train of thought, or it makes it difficult for others to concentrate. Although such conclusions may be perfectly clear to adults, they are not so obvious to many children.

When adults give children reasons for their expectations, they help them to recognize that behavior standards have a rational rather than an arbitrary base. Reasons also help children see the logic of expectations that they might not discover on their own. In addition, reasons offer children information about the effect their behavior has on others. This increases their understanding of interpersonal cause and effect, that is, the relationship between their own acts and the physical and psychological well-being of another person (Damon, 1978).

Reasons make the connections among actions clearer. Although adults easily identify common attributes among those actions they consider undesirable as well as among positive ones, children may not automatically perceive the same linkages. For instance, a child who has learned that hitting is not allowed because it is hurtful may not conclude that scratching and biting are equally inappropriate until an adult explains their negative effects as well. When such explanations are offered over and over again, children eventually use them as guidelines for making their own judgments about what is right and what is wrong (Shaffer, 1994). A child who says to himself, "I shouldn't eat a candy bar before supper because it will spoil my appetite," is relying on reasons he has heard previously as a way to control current behavior.

Reasoning is the hallmark of the authoritative adult. It has been shown to be more important than any other single factor related to helping children achieve self-control (Parke, 1977; Toner, 1986). Youngsters who see adults model reasoning as a way to resolve problem situations demonstrate more self-discipline and less aggression than do children for whom such models are not available (Baumrind, 1995). Children can only internalize standards that make sense to them and that help them to predict the possible aftermath of the things they do or say. Thus, reasoning leads to the establishment of long-term behavioral controls.

### Matching reasons to children's understanding.

A child's current developmental level has an impact on what types of reasons will make the most sense to him or her. For instance, preschoolers are most responsive to demonstrable, object-oriented rationales, such as "Be careful with the magnifying glass. It's fragile and it might break" (Parke, 1974, 1977). They also understand reasons that emphasize the direct physical effects of their actions: "If you keep pushing him, he'll fall down and cry" (Hoffman, 1983). Young children are less able to comprehend explanations that focus on ownership or the rights of others, such as "Don't touch the magnifying glass, because it belongs to Timmy."

On the other hand, children six years of age and older are more receptive to reasoning that focuses on the rights, privileges, and emotions of other people. The most effective reasons at this age emphasize the psychological effects of children's actions ("He feels sad because he was proud of his tower and you knocked it down") as well as explanations that focus on the fairness of the child's actions in terms of someone else's motives ("Wait before you holler—he was only trying to help") (Hoffman, 1983).

**Variations in part two of the personal message.** As discussed, the second portion of the personal message consists of a statement of the adult's emotion, a reference to the child's behavior, and a reason for this reaction. These three components can be arranged in any sequence after the reflection. Adults should always reflect first and then proceed with the second part in a way that seems most comfortable for them. There is no one correct order. For example, in the case of Allison, who was lifting her dress over her head in a proud display of her underwear, more than one response is appropriate:

1. "Allison, you're proud of your new panties. Underwear is very personal clothing. It's not meant for everyone to see. It upsets me when you lift your dress so high."
2. "Allison, you're proud of your new panties. It upsets me when you lift your dress over your head. Underwear is very personal clothing and is not meant for everyone to see."

How adults decide to articulate the second part of the personal message will depend on what they think of first and on their own individual style. What matters is that all the components are accounted for.

In addition, individuals are not all alike in their reactions. Some adults may have felt amused at Allison's performance, some would be indignant, and others might be embarrassed. Personal messages are ideally suited to account for these variations. They enable adults to respond to each situation individually based on their own impressions, without having to second-guess how someone else might respond in their place. Instead, the adult's emotions serve as a guide for how they will proceed. In the situation just discussed, if the adult is amused, she or he may do nothing but smile; if the adult is indignant or embarrassed, she or he probably will tell Allison to put her dress down. In the latter case, depending on which emotion is involved, explanations for why the child is required to assume a more modest demeanor will differ somewhat, thus enabling each adult to express personal views.

Finally, if the adult uses a behavior reflection as an introduction to the personal message, the behavior does not have to be mentioned again in the second portion. For instance: "Allison, you're lifting your dress up over your head. That upsets me. Underwear is very personal clothing, it is not something everyone should see." In this case, the reflection specified the behavior in question, making it unnecessary to repeat.

## Part Three of the Personal Message

Telling children an appropriate course of action for a particular circumstance is the function of the third portion of the personal message. Due to children's relative lack of experience and the influence of centration and irreversible thinking, it is not enough to tell them which behaviors are unacceptable. They must also be told what to try instead (Mendler and Curwin, 1988). This appropriate substitute behavior serves as a rule for children to follow. Thus, the "rule" portion of the personal message is a guide for behavior—it tells children what to do (Miller, 1996). Some examples are:

"Walk, don't run."
"Keep your dress down."
"Turn your homework in as soon as you get to school."
"Share the jump ropes."
"Talk quietly in the lunchroom."

Rules make the world more predictable because they help children recognize what they can and cannot do. This knowledge enables them to be more successful in interacting with both peers and adults (Gordon, 1992; Hendrick, 1996). When children are not sure what the rules are, they are less likely to know how to get what they want in ways that enhance rather than interfere with their relationships with others (Moore and Olson, 1969). In addition, if the rules they must follow are arbitrary, unreasonable, or inappropriate for their developmental level, youngsters may be unable or unwilling to comply (Krasner and Krasner, 1972; Raffini, 1980). Thus, how rules are set has much to do with how well children are able to follow them (Gnagey, 1975; Reynolds, 1996). Therefore, it pays for adults to learn the specific attributes that characterize good rules.

**Rules must be reasonable.** Reasonable rules are rules children are capable of following. Being capable means having both the ability and the knowledge necessary to carry out the desired behavior. To create reasonable rules, adults must take into account children's development, their past experiences, their current abilities, and the type of task required (Brophy and Putnam, 1979; Kostelnik, Soderman, and Whiren, in press). For example, if a child is expected to put the Cuisenaire rods back in the box according to shape and color, it must first be determined whether he or she has the skills necessary to perform the task. In this case, a child would have to be able to manipulate the rods, distinguish color, know that like pieces go together, and also know that all of the rods should lie flat and in the same direction. If the child lacked know-how in any of these areas, the expectation would have to be revised to correspond to what the child could do. This might mean telling the child to simply gather the rods, or to pile them into the box randomly, or to work with another person to collect the materials.

In addition, rules must have long-term positive effects that benefit the child, not just the adult (Katz, 1989). Hence, adults must decide whether a rule enhances a child's development or hinders it. Development is enhanced when expectations promote significant increases in children's interpersonal, academic, or life skills (Clarizio, 1980; Kostelnik and Kurtz, 1986). Development is hindered when adults fail to take into account children's individual needs and abilities or when they prohibit children from engaging in constructive activities. Such instances occur when adults set standards capriciously or solely for their own convenience. Thus, forbidding all the children in a mixed-age group from climbing on the high jungle gym because the youngest ones are afraid, preventing a crying child from clutching a blanket for comfort because the adult thinks it is high time she grew up, forbidding a boy from using a loom because the leader sees weaving as too feminine, or demanding that children be silent during lunchtime because the principal wants to make sure they don't yell across the table are all growth-inhibiting measures. They deprive children of potentially beneficial experiences.

Adults avoid such problems when they recognize that each child is an individual and that although some standards are appropriate for a group (such as walking rather than running inside), others are best applied on a child-by-child basis. For instance, because physical mastery is important for everyone, younger children could be encouraged to tackle a low climber, while older youngsters could attempt a more challenging apparatus. Moreover, adults should examine their own attitudes for biases that curtail children's exposure to a wide range of opportunities. Intolerance and sexism, as illustrated in the preceding blanket and loom incidents, are examples of these. Additionally, in an effort to deal with definite problem behaviors, such as shouting during lunch, adults must be careful not to exact a standard that is unnecessarily extreme. Because children benefit from peer interaction, they should be encouraged to talk informally with classmates. Teaching youngsters to monitor the volume of their voices is a better approach to the problem of too much noise than eliminating conversation altogether.

Finally, adults must continually re-examine their rules in an effort to keep them up to date. A rule that is appropriate for a child of four may be inhibiting at age six.

**Rules must be definable.** Rules are definable when both the adult and the child have the same understanding of what the rule means (Miller, 1996). Good rules specify the *exact* behavior that adults value and find acceptable. It is confusing to children when adults use language that is open to many interpretations or that requires abstract reasoning (Jackson, Robinson, and Dale, 1977). This is exemplified when adults tell children to "behave," "act nice," "be good," or "act like a lady." Such phrases mean different things to different people. The child may construe these generalizations in one way, the adult in another. Youngsters who make genuine attempts to carry out the instructions become frustrated when their efforts fall short of the expected standard. For example, the teacher's notion of "nice" might mean sitting quietly with hands in lap, while the fidgeting child thought that he was complying by refraining from spitting at a teasing classmate.

Problems also arise when adults devise and rely on pat phrases to tell youngsters how to behave. Unfortunately the meaning of such phrases often is ambiguous to children and does not give them a clear idea of what the adult expects. Some examples of ambiguous phrases appear in Table 10–5.

Often, the difficulty is compounded when adults assume that because they use the same phrases over and over, children *must* know what they mean. For instance, a teacher tried to stop two children from fighting. She said: "You're angry. I get upset when you fight. Someone could get hurt. Use your words." Following her directions, one child said to the other, "Okay. You @–$@!" The adult did a quick double take . . . she certainly didn't mean *those* words! Adults who want children to use words to express their emotions, who want children to cooperate, or who want children to stop acting up must tell them a specific way to accomplish these things.

| ▼ Table 10–5     Undefined Adult Phrases | |
|---|---|
| **WHAT ADULTS SAY** | **WHAT ADULTS MEAN** |
| Use your inside voice. | Talk quietly. |
| Act your age. | Stop making fun of him. |
| Use your words. | Say "I'm angry" rather than hitting. |

**Rules must be positive.** Children are most successful at following rules that tell them what to do rather than what not to do or what to stop doing (Hoffman, 1970; Marion, 1995; Parke, 1972). In other words, it is easier for children to respond appropriately when they are told "Put your hands in your pockets" rather than "Stop pushing"; "Walk" rather than "Don't run"; and "Eat your food" rather than "Don't play with your food."

One reason why preschoolers are slow to respond to inhibiting commands is that they don't pay much attention to the words "don't" and "stop." Rather, they focus on the verb in each directive as a guide for what to do (Luria, 1961). Thus, the child who is told, "Don't play with your food," hears "Play with your food." This problem is intensified when the adult speaks forcefully because children respond to the tone or physical energy of the message and actually are stimulated to continue. Also, although school-age children are more aware of the importance of listening to all the words of an instruction, it is not unusual for them to miss the "don't" or the "stop" in unfamiliar or highly emotional situations (Ginott, 1972; Gordon, 1992).

Finally, adults are reminded that the irreversible aspects of children's thinking also make negative commands difficult for them to comprehend. Children are much more successful in following rules that help them redirect an action, rather than reversing or interrupting ongoing behaviors.

The steps that make up a complete personal message are summarized in Figure 10–2. A shorthand method for remembering all the necessary components is to think of each personal message as containing three parts and four R's: part one—reflect, part two—react and give a reason, and part three—state the rule.

Part One—**R**eflect
    Use a behavior, paraphrase,
    or affective reflection.

Part Two—**R**eact
    Describe your emotion and
    the child's behavior.

**R**eason
    Give a reason for your message.

Part Three—**R**ule
    Tell children what to do
    versus what not to do.

**Figure 10–2** Creating a complete personal message.

## Articulating the Entire Personal Message

The following situations illustrate the integration of all three parts of the personal message:

**SITUATION 1:** A child is poking Mr. Kee in order to get him to listen to her story.

*Adult:* You're anxious to tell me something. I don't like it when you poke me to get my attention. Call my name or tap my shoulder lightly.

**SITUATION 2:** Several youngsters have left their gym towels scattered about the locker room.

*Adult:* You're in a hurry to get back to class. It bothers me when you leave your dirty towels all over the locker room because then I have to pick them up. Put them in the laundry basket before you leave.

**SITUATION 3:** It is a hot, humid day. The class is restless and children are beginning to fidget and whisper while a classmate is reporting on the life of Sojourner Truth.

*Adult:* You're hot and uncomfortable. It's distracting to Karl when you whisper while he's giving his report. I'm concerned his feelings will be hurt. He worked hard to find this information. Sit quietly until he is finished.

Messages such as these can be given to individual children or to groups. In addition to being used to correct children's behavior, personal messages should also be implemented as a way to reinforce appropriate actions.

### Positive Personal Messages

A positive personal message contains only parts one and two of the format just described and therefore is a variation on the basic skill. Previous emphasis on problems should not be taken to mean that you can expect primarily negative behavior from children. In reality, the evidence is to the contrary. Children often strive to comply with adult expectations and, in fact, frequently initiate constructive actions on their own (Green, Forehand, and MacMahon, 1979; Lytton, 1979). As a result, not all of the emotions prompted by children's behavior are ones of anger or concern. For this reason, personal messages should be used to identify adults' positive reactions as well. Adults must "catch" children being "good"—displaying behaviors that are socially desirable—and tell children what those behaviors are: "You made a rule to take turns in the rocketship. I'm pleased you all talked it over and figured out a way to give everyone a chance" or "You waited until I came back to start the tape. Thank you. I wanted to hear it, too" or "You cleaned up all the art scraps without anybody reminding you. I'm delighted. Now, this table is ready for making popcorn."

A message used in this way is a special kind of praise. Adults go beyond telling children that they have done a "good job" or "great work." Instead, they are saying that the child's specific behavior had special meaning for them. Research has shown that this type of response is very effective because it describes the impact a particular behavior has had on the person offering the praise (Chernow and Chernow, 1981). General terms such as "good," "nice," or "pretty" soon lose their meaning for both children and adults if they are used over and over again or applied indiscriminately. Moreover, children interpret effusive remarks that glorify them . . . rather than their behavior . . . as insincere or "too gushy." Thus, it is more effective to say: "You worked hard on your essay. I really liked it. It made me want to know more about "Harriet Tubman" than to say, "You are a born writer." In the same vein, children learn more about their behavior from a statement such as "You're trying to comfort Andrew. It makes me feel good that you noticed he was so sad. He needs a friend right now" than from a comment like "You're a terrific kid."

When adults identify behavior they are pleased to see children display and tell them why, they encourage youngsters to repeat those actions another time. All too often, adults take children's proactive behaviors or compliance for granted; they simply expect children to do as they are told or to automatically behave in an appropriate fashion. When this happens, adults have failed to recognize that it takes effort for children to achieve these productive outcomes.

Readers will note that positive personal messages share many of the characteristics cited earlier regarding effective praise. Both are useful tools for helping children recognize the positive behaviors they demonstrate. The difference between the two is in who evaluates the child's behavior, the child or the adult. Effective praise prompts self-evaluation by the child, since the adult acknowledges the effort or accomplishment solely from the child's viewpoint, without offering any opinions about it. Positive personal messages, on the other hand, offer a more direct way for adults to tell children what they think about children's appropriate behavior. These are most useful when children are first learning how to behave in a particular circumstance and are looking to adults for specific cues in this regard. As children become more adept at complying with rules on their own, most positive personal messages should give way to effective praise statements. This allows children to judge for themselves the extent to which their conduct is in keeping with the internalized codes they are beginning to develop. However, it is always appropriate for grown-ups to let children know when their behavior has affected the adult personally and positively. Children appreciate hearing statements such as, "You helped me shelve a lot of books. I appreciate it. That saved me hours of work" or "You remembered I had a hoarse voice and were very quiet while I read the story. I'm glad. That made it easier for me to talk."

**Formulating positive personal messages.** Positive personal messages begin with a reflection. This step clarifies the situation from the child's point of view and alerts children that the adult has noticed what they are doing. Next, the adult identifies a personal emotion regarding the child's action and gives a reason for it. In addition, the specific behavior that prompted the adult's emotional reaction is described. This may seem like a lot of words when a simple "Thank you" or "Good" would do. However, the purpose of a positive personal message is to teach children which behaviors they should retain for future use. Thus, the positive personal message is a teaching tool aimed at helping children internalize the constructive behaviors they display. Again, the emphasis is on helping children move from adherence to higher levels of social conduct. Children need reasons why they should behave in certain ways as much as they need to know why they should not engage in particular actions. They also need to know that the adults with whom they identify are sources of approval as well as correction.

At this point, you have learned about parts one, two, and three of the personal message. Rationales for each component have been offered and suggestions made for how to use personal messages in both positive and negative situations. Following are specific guidelines for how to carry out effective personal messages.

## SKILLS FOR EXPRESSING EXPECTATIONS FOR CHILDREN'S BEHAVIOR

 **Reflect in Problem Situations**

**1. Observe children carefully before reflecting.** Enter a problem situation by first considering what the child may be trying to achieve and why.

**2. Formulate reflections that accurately describe the child's perspective.** Maintain a nonjudgmental stance. This means avoiding thinly veiled accusations, such as "You just don't want to cooperate today" or "You thought you could pull a fast one." These statements represent adult bias and are not real reflections.

**3. Remind yourself to describe the child's point of view before your own.** At times, because of haste, indignation over a child's behavior, or surprise, you may launch immediately into an expression of your own feelings. One way to avoid this self-centered reaction is to develop the habit of taking a deep breath prior to speaking. That breath can serve as a cue that the reflection comes first. If you catch yourself skipping the reflection, stop and begin again. Later, think of alternate reflections you might use should the situation arise another time. This type of mental practice will help you in future encounters.

**4. Pay attention to children's age when deciding which type of reflection to use.** Affective reflections generally are most effective in satisfying children under eight. For instance, if two first-graders have come to blows over who will get the next turn at bat, it would be accurate to say, "You're hitting," and then proceed with the rest of the personal message. However, it would be nearer the mark to reflect: "You're really angry. You each thought it was your turn next." This acknowledges what the children consider to be the real problem (the dispute over turns) and provides a more helpful introduction to the subsequent message.

On the other hand, older children may resent the adult's interpretation of their feelings in front of others. It seems too personal an approach. In such a case, the more neutral behavior reflection or paraphrase reflection would be more appropriate.

**5. Avoid using "but" as a way to connect the reflection to the rest of the personal message.** The word "but" means "on the contrary." When it is used to connect two phrases, the second phrase contradicts the first. For example, if a friend were to meet you on the street and say, "You look wonderful, but . . . " you would know that the initial praise was a perfunctory introduction to what the person thought was really important. The same is true when it comes to the personal message. Adults who say, "You wish the story would end, but I want to finish it" are telling children that their feelings do not count. This betrays the true spirit of the reflection.

**Express Your Emotion(s) to Children**

**1. Identify the emotions you experience.** State your emotions clearly to the child. Do not rely on nonverbal cues alone. Adults sometimes tap their fingers to show irritation, wrinkle their nose to convey disgust, or sigh to indicate exasperation. Children often misinterpret these signs or miss them altogether. They do not automatically know how you feel and, in fact, are often surprised to find that your feelings may be quite different from their own. Subtle hints will not get your message across. Children benefit from the explicit communication that words provide. Words are specific and to the point. They help children know how you feel and why you feel that way:

> "I feel pleased . . . "
> "It makes me angry . . . "
> "I'm annoyed . . . "
> "It's important to me . . . "
> "I wish . . . "

**2. Become sensitive to your own array of internal cues that signal a particular emotional state.** Perhaps your cheeks get hot when you start to feel angry, your stomach gets jumpy when you are anxious, or your head seems heavy when you are overwhelmed. At first, it will be the more extreme emotions, like anger, fear, or excitement that will be the easiest to discern and express. Eventually, you will become better able to recognize and talk about more moderate emotions such as contentment, irritation, discomfort, or confusion.

*continued*

## SKILLS FOR EXPRESSING EXPECTATIONS FOR CHILDREN'S BEHAVIOR—continued

**3. Use a wide range of feeling words of differing intensities.** Purposely select an assortment of feeling words. The greater the vocabulary at your disposal, the more likely you are to be attuned to the range of emotions these words represent. If you find yourself using the same few words over and over, look up or discuss possible variations to use in the future.

### Pinpoint Behaviors

**1. Name the behavior that is affecting you.** Be specific. Describe actions you can see or hear. Avoid generalities that clump several behaviors together or that are open to misinterpretation. Rather than saying, "I get upset when you are mean," say: "I get upset when you (hit me; throw things; tease Jacque; punch Frank)." Both you and the child must know exactly what you find acceptable or unacceptable.

**2. Describe the behavior, not the child.** It is inappropriate to tell children that they are not nice, bad, nasty, a hard case, "hyper," incorrigible, that they should be ashamed, or that they should know better. All of these descriptions malign children as persons and should not be used.

### Formulate Reasons

**1. Give children specific reasons for why you approve or disapprove of their behavior.** This means providing children with information that helps them see what will happen if they carry out the behavior in question, either for their own safety and happiness or to protect the rights and safety of others. Rationales such as "Because I said so," "Because I want you to," "Because it's important," "Because it's not nice," "Because that's the rule," or "Because that's how we do things around here" are not real reasons. They do not clearly relate to any of the criteria for deciding when behavior change is appropriate. Phrases like these often are employed when adults cannot think of anything else to say or when they are demanding unquestioning obedience rather than rational compliance. If you cannot think of a legitimate

reason for your reaction, reexamine the situation to determine whether your expectations really are appropriate.

**2. Phrase reasons in terms children understand.** Use familiar language and short, simple sentences. Focus on one main point rather than offering an explanation that incorporates several ideas.

**3. Give a reason every time you attempt to change a child's behavior.** Do not assume that because you gave an explanation yesterday for why running is prohibited, the children will remember today. Children often forget the rationale or may not realize that the reason still is legitimate after a lengthy time lapse. They must hear the same explanations repeatedly before they are able to generalize from one situation to another.

### Formulate Rules

**1. Study child-development norms.** Learn what behaviors and understandings might realistically be expected for children of a particular age. Become familiar with the knowledge and skills of children younger and older than those with whom you are working so you will have an understanding of the wide range of children's abilities that are apt to be represented in the group. This also will help you realize what sequence of skills and concepts children must master to move from one point to the next. Identify actions and concepts that are clearly beyond the capability of most of your children.

**2. Get to know the children in your group as individuals.** Recognize differences in interaction style, reactions to new situations, mood, level of involvement, tolerance for frustration, and attention span. Identify specific abilities exhibited by each child as well as those concepts and skills they have yet to master.

**3. Think about what combination of knowledge and action children must carry out to successfully follow a given rule.** Analyze your rules and determine exactly what they entail.

## SKILLS FOR EXPRESSING EXPECTATIONS FOR CHILDREN'S BEHAVIOR—continued

**4. Only implement legitimate rules.** Use the criteria of safety, protection of property, and respect for others and the principle of importance in determining whether a rule must be set. If the child's behavior cannot be linked to any of these, reconsider the validity of the rule.

**5. Tell children what the rules are.** Rules should be explicit rather than implicit. Do not assume that children know a rule just because you know it, or that they remember it from past experience. Remind children of what the rules are at a time when the rules are not an issue. Calm, rational discussions of why certain rules are enforced help children understand the value of and reasons for specific expectations. Also, remind children of the rules in situations in which those rules apply. For instance, it is more effective to say, "Remember to walk in the classroom," when a child is caught running than to say, "How many times have I told you about running indoors?" This last generalization assumes that the child knows that the actual rule is "walk." Although the child may recognize that running is not allowed, there is no guarantee that he or she remembers the rule that specifies what to do instead.

**6. Reward children's approximations of the rule.** Do not expect children to comply perfectly with all rules every time. Recognize behaviors that show that children are attempting to follow the rule, although they may not be totally successful. For instance, if the rule is that children must raise their hands and wait to be called on in order to talk in a group, you should not expect perfect silence as you survey the waving hands before you. That would be too much for children to accomplish all at once. At first, it is likely that raised hands would be accompanied by excited vocalization as children attempt to gain your attention. Rather than focusing on the infraction of talking, it would be better to praise them for remembering to raise their hands. Gradually, with time and many reminders, fewer children will call out when they raise their hands to speak.

**7. Use positive personal messages thoughtfully.** When children follow a rule or act in other appropriate ways, draw their attention to their desirable acts with a personal message. Point out to them the favorable effect their behavior had in terms of safety or preserving people's rights or property. These on-the-spot observations are memorable to children and make it more likely that they will remember the rule in the future. As children demonstrate increasing skill at following rules independently, shift to more frequent use of effective praise.

**8. Use positive attribution to promote children's favorable self-impressions and to increase their repertoire of socially acceptable behaviors.** Look for situations in which children demonstrate delay of gratification, impulse control, resistance to temptation, or the ability to carry out prosocial plans. Identify these instances for them.

> "You're waiting patiently."
> "You wanted that extra cupcake, but you let Carol have it instead. That was hard to do and you did it."
> "You put a check on yourself when you were going to hit Anthony. That took a lot of control."
> "You remembered the guinea pigs had no water. It was very responsible of you to come back over lunchtime to fill their waterbottle."

**9. Revise unreasonable rules.** If you become aware that a child is not able to follow a rule as you have formulated it, do not press on in the mistaken notion that rules must be absolute. It is better to revamp the rule at a level at which the child is able to comply. For example, this would mean changing a rule from "Everyone must raise his or her hand and wait quietly to be called on before speaking" to "Everyone must raise his or her hand in order to be called on." The "wait quietly" portion of the rule should be added only after most children have demonstrated the ability to raise their hand.

**10. Use language that is clear and to the point.** Identify a specific behavior that you wish the child to enact. *Avoid generalizations*, such as "be nice," "don't be mean," "don't act up," "act

*continued*

## SKILLS FOR EXPRESSING EXPECTATIONS FOR CHILDREN'S BEHAVIOR—continued

your age," "make me proud of you," "behave yourself," "be good at school," "don't make me ashamed of you," or "mind your manners."

**11. Ascertain whether children have the same understanding of the rule that you do.** Ask children to repeat the rule in their own words, or get them to demonstrate their comprehension in some manner. At other times, you will depend on more subjective evaluations, such as considering children's facial expressions or the "look in their eyes."

**12. When in doubt, assume that children have not understood, rather than concluding that they are deliberately breaking the rule.** If children have not understood your rule, you will have to do something to make your rule more clear. Some things you can try are:
a. Repeating your words more slowly and articulating more clearly.
b. Rephrasing your message in simpler, more familiar language and emphasizing key words.
c. Restating your message using a combination of gestures and words.
d. Taking the child to an area where there is less interference from noise and other distractions.
e. Emphasizing your message using physical prompts such as pictures or objects in combination with gestures.
f. Demonstrating what you want by doing it yourself.

**13. Practice thinking about what you want to children to do as well as what you wish they would refrain from doing.** Anticipate potential problem situations and the positive actions children could take to avoid or remedy them.

**14. Catch yourself saying "No" or "Stop."** Rephrase your negative instruction as a positive statement. This may mean interrupting yourself in the middle of a sentence. Also, couple negative instructions with positive ones, such as saying: "Don't run. Walk."

**15. Tell younger and less experienced children what the alternatives are. Let older or**

**more experienced children generate alternatives for themselves.** If a young child is pushing to get out the door, you could say: "You're anxious to get outside. I'm worried that when you push, someone will get hurt. Take a giant step back away from the door and we'll try again." The message to an older child might be: "You're anxious to get outside. I'm worried that when you push, someone will get hurt. Let's think of a way everyone can get outside safely."

Selection of one response or the other will be determined by the adult's estimation of children's previous experience and their potential readiness to negotiate. Two-year-olds, a fifth-grade class that has come together for the first time, or a group of youngsters frenzied with excitement probably will have neither the skill, the patience, nor the trust necessary to work out a compromise. However, youngsters who have had lots of practice generating ideas and alternatives and who are calm usually will rise to the challenge.

**16. Talk and act simultaneously.** Immediately stop children's actions that may be harmful to themselves or others. Use physical intervention if necessary. For example, if two children are fighting, stop the hitting by grasping their hands or separating them. If a child is about to jump off a too-high step, move quickly to restrain him or her. If children are using the saw inappropriately, gain control of it. Once the dangerous situation has been neutralized, youngsters are better able to hear what you have to say. It is at this point that personal messages have their greatest impact.

**17. Invite children to participate in the rule-making process.** Gather the children in a group and ask them to help create rules for the group or a particular activity. Record their ideas on paper and post them for all to see. Refer back to the children's rules as the year goes by. Periodically discuss whether or not revisions are necessary. Participating in the self-governance of the group increases children's understanding of rules and promotes their feelings of internal control. They receive clear evidence that their

## SKILLS FOR EXPRESSING EXPECTATIONS FOR CHILDREN'S BEHAVIOR—continued

ideas are worthwhile and that they can influence events in the classroom.

 **Communicate with Families**

**1. Become familiar with overall program rules related to child and family participation.** All early childhood programs have guidelines or expectations for family behavior relative to their involvement in the program. These often are communicated to families through written program policies. Know what these policies are. For instance, there may be guidelines for when children are too ill to attend, requirements that families sign permission slips for field trips, restrictions on the kind of toys children may bring from home, or requirements that children have an emergency card on file in order to remain in the program. Your awareness of these expectations will support program functioning and keep families from receiving mixed-messages, which would happen if staff members varied in their application of such rules.

**2. Help to maintain overall program rules as necessary.** Sometimes family members are unaware of program rules, forget them, or hope that "just this once" the rule will be waived. When this happens your role is to gently remind family members of the rule. Depending on the circumstance, either state your expectation that the rule be followed or refer them to a person in authority to whom they may make their case. For instance, a typical program policy is that staff members will not accept children's tuition payments when families are dropping off their children at the beginning of the program day. Such payments should be mailed or delivered by a family member directly to the program office. This is to ensure that payments are not lost and that families receive a receipt immediately upon payment. However, a parent in a hurry may ask you to take his or her payment to the office "just this one time." In this instance, it is best to politely decline the request, remind the parent of the rule, and direct him or her to the office to make the payment: "I'm sorry. I am not allowed to deal with tuition payments. You will have to deliver your payment to the office or mail it in." On another occasion you may discover that a child has arrived with a fever and a nose seeping green mucus. For many programs, these are conditions that warrant children remaining at home or receiving care in a "sick child" program. If a family member is present, you might say, "It looks like Sammy isn't feeling well. I'm concerned he may be too sick to stay here today. Let me get Ms. Carlson (your supervisor) so you may talk with her about this." If no family member is present, alert your supervisor right away or if you are in a position of authority, call the family to take the child home.

**3. Find out what expectations families have for their children's behavior.** Every family has certain ways in which they expect their children to act at home and away from home. Knowing what these expectations are helps early childhood professionals to better understand individual families and to support families in their child-rearing role. Obtain such information through individual and group discussions held during the year, ask families to complete a brief written form on which they identify some of the "home rules" they have for their children, and talk with families informally as related circumstances arise. Remain open and accepting. Avoid making judgments regarding the merit of certain family rules.

**4. Provide examples and explanations to families regarding your expectations for children's behavior in the formal group setting.** Convey to families typical classroom rules and the reasons behind them. Do this in writing and in person. Here is an example provided by a teacher of four-year-olds to the families of children in her classroom. This brief written notice appeared in her first newsletter.

> One thing many families want to know is how children are supposed to behave at the center. Here are some basic expectations I have for the children in our class. All of them are aimed at keeping children safe, at protecting the rights of everyone in the group, and at safeguarding be-

*continued*

## SKILLS FOR EXPRESSING EXPECTATIONS FOR CHILDREN'S BEHAVIOR—continued

longings. We will talk about these in more detail at the family orientation next week. In the meantime, I'd be happy to answer any questions you have and to hear your comments about our classroom rules.

Children will walk in the classroom.
Children will use materials in a safe manner.
Children will refrain from hurting other children and will express how they feel in words.
Children will climb only on appropriate objects, not on furniture or windowsills.
Children will participate in cleanup according to a job they have chosen.
Children may only knock down their own block structures and may only dispose of their own artwork and not someone else's, unless they have been given permission to do so.
Children pour their own juice at snack time.
Children will dress and undress themselves as much as possible.

Throughout the year, the children and I will discuss these rules and others that the children think are important. As the year progresses, we will spend a lot of time working on ways to make our classroom a safe, happy, caring place to live and learn.

Many practitioners provide such information in the introductory materials they send home, during parent orientations and conferences, and in workshops revolving around discipline-related topics. This gives family members a sense of your priorities, a chance to ask questions, and an opportunity to offer relevant feedback. Such exchanges set the stage for furthering understanding between family members and program personnel, as well as for developing mutual expectations between the main settings in which children function.

**5. When talking to family members whose discipline style differs from the authoritative one you are learning, emphasize similarities rather than concentrating on differences in philosophy.** Professionals sometimes believe they have little in common with family members who hold nonauthoritative attitudes toward discipline. Likewise, family members who espouse more authoritarian or permissive philosophies may question the authoritative techniques you use. Under these circumstances, the most effective approach is to emphasize the common ground between these approaches, not the discrepancies (Bolin, 1989). With this in mind, remember that authoritarian and authoritative styles both advocate firm control and high standards; permissive and authoritative styles promote warm, accepting relationships between children and adults. Discussing authoritative strategies in terms of how they support these overarching principles provides some common ground between them. For instance, family members with more authoritarian attitudes may believe that reasoning is unnecessary or undesirable because youngsters should simply do as they are told. To help such persons feel more comfortable with your giving reasons to children, point out that you will establish boundaries on the child's behavior by stating a rule and that you are prepared to enforce that rule as necessary. The reason is a tool that helps the child make sense of the rule and to which the child may refer in the future. This explanation combines an authoritative value (helping children think through a problem) with an authoritarian one (achieving compliance) and builds a bridge between the two.

## ▼ PITFALLS TO AVOID

Regardless of whether you are fostering children's self-discipline individually or in groups, informally or in structured activities, there are certain pitfalls you should avoid.

**Talking in paragraphs.** Effective personal messages are brief and to the point. However, beginners who are struggling to include all of the parts may inadvertently add extra words or sentences. An awkward example would be: "You seem really unhappy about not getting a turn. I'm sorry you didn't get a turn but you are hitting Tanya with a stick. When you hit her with a stick, I'm afraid she could get hurt. I'd like you to hand the stick to me." This mouthful of words probably will have a discouraging outcome for several reasons. First, children cannot distinguish the main point, and may have forgotten what was stated in the beginning. Laborious personal messages are those children are most likely to ignore. They get tired of listening and tune out.

When first learning this skill, talking too much is better than forgetting an important element. If adults find themselves delivering a particularly long personal message, they should think afterward of a more concise way of expressing it. For instance, the preceding example could have been condensed to: "You're upset. It worries me that if you hit Tanya with a stick, you could hurt her. Hand the stick to me."

**Failing to use the personal message for fear of making a mistake.** Adults may become tongue-tied at moments when a personal message would be appropriate. They dread stumbling over the words, getting the order wrong, or forgetting parts. Unfortunately, the more adults remain quiet, the less practice they get, and so improvement and comfort with the skill does not develop. The only remedy is to make fledgling attempts whenever the opportunity arises. It often is easier to begin with positive personal messages because there is less risk involved. Once these flow smoothly, corrective messages seem less difficult.

**Talking about personal feelings only in problem situations.** Some adults have a tendency to focus primarily on children's mistakes. They are quick to express their dissatisfaction, and tend to see their role as one of admonishing children who fall short of their expectations. This outlook fails to recognize that behavior change is not solely a product of telling children what they are doing wrong but is also a function of strengthening those positive behaviors children already display. Thus, in order for children to keep certain behaviors in their repertoire, they must hear that adults feel pleased, excited, amused, appreciative, comforted, or supported by their actions.

**Giving up midway.** Children do not always wait patiently to hear an entire corrective personal message. They may turn their heads or simply walk away. Sometimes when this happens, adults become flustered and give up. A better approach is to use the nonverbal strategies presented in Chapter 3. Adults should lightly hold onto an uninterested child or pursue youngsters who dash off in an attempt to avoid confrontation. This does not mean

jerking children around or forcing them to establish eye contact. It does mean trying to gain the child's attention for the entire duration of the message. It also is important for children to be told that adults become annoyed when children do not listen: "You don't want to hear what I'm telling you. It upsets me when you walk away while I'm talking. Stand still and listen."

**Focusing on short-term rather than long-term goals.** In problem situations, adults sometimes find it easier to simply say "No" or "We don't do that here." Occasionally, these shortcuts have the desired effect: children stop what they are doing. Unfortunately, such success usually is temporary because it does not prompt children's internalization of the rule. Instead, adults have to repeat their admonitions over and over again. Moreover, children may not comply without direct supervision. Personal messages are worth the time they take because they contribute to increased self-discipline.

**Making expectations known from a distance.** When adults see children in threatening situations, their first impulse is to shout a warning: "Look out! You'll drop the fish tank" or "Watch it! The floor is slippery." In cases such as these, children frequently ignore the message because they do not realize it is directed at them. The adult's loud voice may cause alarm or stimulate children to become louder or more active themselves. In either case, the adult's message is not received adequately. A better approach is to move quickly over to the child and state expectations in a face-to-face interaction. The benefits of such a direct approach outweigh the seconds lost to achieve it.

**Waiting too long to express emotions.** In an effort to avoid committing themselves to a line of action, some adults refrain from expressing less intense emotions and allow their emotions to build up over time. When they do react, it is often when they have reached the limit of their endurance. Then, their irritation explodes into fury, concern blossoms into real anxiety, or confusion escalates into panic. None of these are constructive responses because they are so intense that rational action becomes difficult. In addition, children usually are shocked at such extreme reactions and are genuinely uncertain as to what led to the eruption. Adults who rely on this approach also model that only extreme emotions are worth expressing. They should not be surprised when children copy their example. This pitfall can be forestalled by discussing your emotions when first aware of them.

**Attempting to disguise expectations.** Adults who feel nervous about telling children what to do often disguise their rules. They do this in any number of ways. The most common tactic is to phrase the rule as a question. Instead of saying, "It's time to clean up," they cajole: "Don't you want to clean up, now?"; "Clean up, okay?"; "You wouldn't want us to have a messy room would you?"; or "We want a clean room, right?"

In every case, adults are hoping children will see things their way. Yet, children usually interpret these messages not as rules, which they are obligated to follow, but as questions, which are optional and that can be answered with either "Yes" or "No." Adults who are unwilling to hear "No" eliminate ambiguity when they phrase their rules as statements: "Start cleaning up"; "It's time to clean up."

Another way adults camouflage rules is to tell children that they "need to" or that the adult "needs them to" do something rather than saying children "have to" or adults "want them to." This confuses children because "needs" relate to basic physical and psychological necessities, such as food, sleep, love, and shelter (Maslow, 1954). Sitting down together does not fall into this category. The adult does not "need" the child to sit down; the adult *wants* the child to sit down, and for very good reasons: so others can see, so the child can get information, so the teacher is not distracted. Children as young as two years of age talk about what they want and have an understanding of this concept. They also understand the notion of "have to" ("I have to go to the bathroom," "Mommy has to go to the store," "We have to eat supper now"). The concept of "need" is much more nebulous and less precise. It is more accurate to use the words "want" and "have to."

A final error that obscures a behavioral requirements is for adults to include themselves in the rule when they have no real intention of following it. For instance, adults say, "Let's wipe our bottom until it is clean," when what they mean is, "Wipe your bottom," or they say, "Let's brush our teeth," rather than "Brush your teeth." Adults who do this imply that children should look to them as a model of the behavior in question. When this does not mirror reality, the statement is confusing.

Adults who use disguising tactics limit children's chances to be successful. They do a disservice to youngsters who are trying to discover what the real rules are and how to obey them. Thus, rules should be phrased as statements rather than questions, using words with precise, rather than ambiguous, meanings, and in a way that leaves no doubt as to who is expected to follow them.

# ▼ SUMMARY

All children must learn to behave in accordance with the expectations of their culture if they are to be accepted by society. Adults are responsible for teaching children what those expectations are, and they spend much of their time engaged in this role. Their ultimate aim is not only to teach children specific standards but to help them develop the ability to regulate their own behavior.

Self-discipline is composed of several capabilities: curbing initial impulses that might be damaging to self or others; resisting temptation; postponing gratification; implementing plans of action; and initiating appropriate social behaviors. How children feel about their behavior, how they think about it, and their previous experiences affect children's ability to achieve self-discipline. Guilt and empathy are emotional factors influencing this capacity. The development of moral reasoning, role-taking abilities, impulse control, desire for independence, language, memory, and understanding of how events are associated are cognitive processes that influence children's achievement of self-control.

It is generally agreed that children become more self-disciplined as they grow older; however, even in adulthood, people exhibit a wide range of behavior ranging from no self-control to much self-discipline. Amoral, adherence, identification, and internalization are terms used to describe these variations. Adherence is the most primitive form of compliance; internalization is the most sophisticated. Individuals' behaviors generally fall into one or another of these categories, although it should be noted that everyone at different times and in different circumstances may display any of them.

Because most people experience the developmental and emotional changes previously described, thus acquiring some basis for internalization, the reasons for variation can best be attributed to individuals' experiences. Children learn the values of society through direct instruction, observation, reward and punishment, and attribution. Adults tell and show children what is expected of them—explicitly in words and implicitly by their own behavior. Different discipline styles, authoritarian, permissive, and authoritative, have been linked to emotional and behavioral outcomes in children. The authoritative mode produces children who feel good about themselves and are most likely to internalize standards of behavior. Therefore, it is the style of interaction most desirable for adults to adopt.

Authoritative adults can express their expectations through a personal message. This consists of a reflection acknowledging the child's point of view, a statement to the child that describes the adult's response to a specific behavior of the child and the reason for the reaction, and, finally, an alternative, desirable behavior in which the child is to engage. This last step is used only in situations focusing on behavior change and serves as a rule that governs the child's behavior for that situation. Circum-

stances under which rules are appropriate deal with safety, protection of property, and the rights of others. The rule portion of the personal message must be reasonable, definable, and positive. Personal messages also should be used to reinforce existing constructive behavior. Difficulties students encounter when first learning how to formulate personal messages can be overcome by paying close attention to the rationale for this particular skill.

Finally, it is important to communicate with families regarding program-related approaches to discipline. Elicit information from families and provide information to them as appropriate. Strive to develop a working partnership with family members aimed at enhancing children's development of self-discipline as well as family involvement in the formal group setting.

## ▼ DISCUSSION QUESTIONS

1. Define self-discipline and describe its component parts.
2. Jamal is a preschooler. His older brother Ahmed is ten. Discuss how guilt and empathy would figure into each child's thinking.
3. It has been shown that children become more capable of self-discipline as they mature. Explain the developmental changes that contribute to this increased capacity.
4. Define amoral, adherence, identification, and internalization. Then, discuss which behavioral cues tell you when a person is operating at any one of these levels.
5. Name three rules you had to follow as a child. Talk about whether your compliance with each rule was at the adherence, identification, or internalization level.
6. Describe all of the things you could do in relation to instruction and modeling to teach a child how to handle guinea pigs safely. Make sure you take into account children's varying levels of maturity.
7. Think about a teacher you had while growing up. Describe that person's behavior to someone else, keeping in mind the three discipline styles discussed in this chapter. See if the listener can categorize the teacher's behavior based on your description. Then, discuss the effect that style had on your learning.
8. Describe what changes you might have to make in your own interaction style to make it more authoritative.
9. With classmates, identify the three parts of the personal message and provide no less than three reasons per part why each is included.
10. Refer to the NAEYC Code of Ethical Conduct presented in Appendix A. Find sections that address the following situations related to rules.
   a. The Brown family and the Smith family both have children in your class. Mrs. Brown approaches you, saying that she doesn't want her child to interact with the Smith child. She expects you to enforce this rule.
   b. One of the families in your group is from another country. The father approaches you, saying he wants his four-year-old daughter to learn to act in the ways of her culture. This means she must be very deferential in her interactions with adults. He is disturbed that she calls out at group time, seems bossy in her play, and makes decisions such as where to play. In all of these cases, he believes that she should be more submissive. He wants you to support his family's expectations.

## ▼ FIELD ASSIGNMENTS

1. Keep a record of the personal messages you use in your field placement. When you have a chance, record at least three of your responses. Begin by describing what the child(ren) said or did to prompt your re-

marks. Next, write down the exact words you used. Critique your effectiveness and correct any inaccurate personal messages. Finally, record two alternate personal messages you could have tried in each situation. Make sure to identify both personal messages used to change children's behavior and ones used to reinforce positive actions.

2. Describe a situation in which your use of a personal message was effective, both from your point of view and the child's. Next, describe a situation in which your use of a personal message was ineffective. Analyze what went wrong and how your response could be improved in the future.

3. Identify a situation involving the children with whom you work, in which it may be necessary for you to establish a rule. Write out your rule. Record how well it fits the criteria for an effective rule, as described in this chapter. If necessary, change your rule to make it more appropriate. Next, talk about what you will do and say to remind children of the rule and to enforce it as necessary. Later, discuss whether or not you had to use the rule you made. Describe any changes you enacted in carrying out the rule and why. Conclude by describing the children's reactions to your rule.

4. Read program materials designed to acquaint families with program policies regarding their participation and that of the child (e.g., enrollment materials, program handbook, introductory newsletter). List at least five rules, policies, or expectations for families and describe the reasoning behind these. If the reasoning is not obvious to you, talk to someone in the program to find out more about them.

# ▼Chapter 11

## Fostering Self-Discipline in Children: Implementing Consequences

## ▼ OBJECTIVES

*On completion of this chapter, you will be able to describe:*

▼ Typical reasons why children exhibit inappropriate behavior.

▼ Ways adults can change their behavior to make children's compliance more likely.

▼ Four different kinds of consequences.

▼ The difference between consequences and punishment.

▼ Effective ways of implementing consequences.

▼ How to combine personal messages and consequences to enforce limits on children's behavior.

▼ Time-out.

▼ Family communication strategies related to supplementary consequences with children.

▼ Pitfalls to avoid in implementing consequences.

In the previous chapter, you learned about personal messages. This skill provided a mechanism for establishing rules in formal group settings. Now, we turn our attention to enforcing such rules through the use of consequences.

Adult: You're enjoying the easel. It's time to clean up. I'd like some help because there is a lot to put away. Please cap the paints or tag the projects that are already dry.

Child 1: No.

Child 2: You can't make me.

Child 3: I don't want to.

Child 4: I cleaned up last time. It's someone else's turn today.

As everyone knows, there are times when children do not listen, when they misbehave, and when they disobey. In fact, it is no secret that problems with enforcing rules are a major concern to helping professionals and parents (Charles, 1996).

When children act inappropriately, some adults attribute their behavior to family, cultural, social, or economic conditions. They conclude that there is little that helping professionals can do to change their behavior. Others believe that youngsters just want to misbehave. Both assumptions are faulty. First, although a variety of ecological factors do influence how children behave away from home, helping professionals *can* teach children how to conduct themselves more appropriately in the formal group setting. Moreover, there is strong evidence that most children want to comply with adult expectations (Berk, 1997; Green, Forehand, and MacMahon, 1979).

Yet at one time or another, all children engage in unacceptable behavior. When this happens, it could be for any one of several reasons:

1. They cannot identify appropriate alternate behaviors to substitute for unacceptable actions.
2. They are unaware of the rule or are uncertain about what behaviors are demanded.
3. They are not capable of meeting the standards set.
4. They do not know how to control impulsive behavior.
5. They have developed faulty perceptions about how to gain acceptance.
6. They have been taught by other significant adults, siblings, or peers to use behaviors that differ from those desired by the helping professional.
7. They have concluded that the rule is unwarranted.
8. They have learned that certain behaviors labeled unacceptable actually are rewarded, or that the rule makes no difference in what happens to them.
9. They are trying to determine the boundaries of the situation and whether the adult will maintain them over time.

Any one or a combination of these reasons may be why children act inappropriately in most instances. Such problems may improve when adults make changes in their own behavior.

## Behavior Problems and Their Solutions

**PROBLEM 1:** Children's inability to determine appropriate actions to replace inappropriate ones.

**PROBLEM 2:** Children's uncertainty about what the rules are and which behaviors are required to satisfy them.

**PROBLEM 3:** Inappropriate adult expectations for children's behavior.    The first three reasons cited for children's misbehavior are a result of the inappropriate ways adults sometimes make rules (Flavell, 1977; Reynolds, 1996). In each case, unacceptable actions come about because children are incapable of following the rule rather than unwilling to do so. In essence, the way the adults structure the rule predetermines failure. If this experience is repeated frequently, children may cease trying to comply, convinced that their efforts are hopeless. What began as a problem related to inappropriate rule setting may escalate into one of children disobeying because they assume that is the best they can do.

**Solution.**    As described in Chapter 10 adults must tell children what alternative behaviors to substitute for the inappropriate ones in which they are engaged. They do this by stating explicit rules that are reasonable, definable, and positive. When adults follow these guidelines, children are less likely to misbehave.

**PROBLEM 4: Acting on impulse.**    At times, children act without thinking: an idea or desire pops into their heads, and they are in motion; they see something they want and grab for it; they think something and blurt it out (Calkins, 1994). Impulsivity decreases with age, and by six years of age most children can inhibit their impulses relatively well. However, there are youngsters who remain impulsive because that is their cognitive style. These children continue to act immediately on their desires, in contrast to their more reflective age-mates, whose cognitive approach is to respond more thoughtfully (Harrison and Nadelman, 1972; Reed, 1991).

**Solution.**    Children as young as three years of age, as well as older youngsters described as impulsive, can be taught specific tactics to help them learn to wait and respond more carefully (Ritchie and Toner, 1985). For example, children who hear themselves described as patient eventually become more so and become better able to delay gratification. This happens because when adults tell children they are patient, children incorporate a notion of self-control into their self-concept and try to live up to that image.

In addition, young people can be taught self-instructional strategies as a way to inhibit impulses and resist temptation (Mischel and Patterson, 1976; Toner, 1986). For instance, children who are taught to say to themselves "It is good if I wait" will find it easier to hold back than youngsters who do not have such training. The same is true when adults tell children to repeat pertinent rules to themselves, such as "I shouldn't touch the stove" (Mischel and Patterson, 1976). Moreover, children are less impulsive when they talk to themselves about the task in which they are involved rather than focus on a possible reward for their behavior (Fabes, 1984). Thus, it is more effective to teach them to say "I am putting away the books" rather than "When I'm through, I'll get to go outside."

**PROBLEM 5: Children's faulty perceptions.**    Some children engage in unacceptable behavior because they have an erroneous perception of how to achieve group status. There are three common perceptual errors. Certain children mistakenly believe that the only time they are valued is when they are the center of attention. Others are sure they must have power over peers and adults in order to be important. Still others conclude that they never will be special to anyone and so devote much of their energy convincing people that they are as unlikeable or as helpless as they imagine themselves to be (Dreikurs and Soltz, 1964; Greenspan, 1995). These children can be described in turn as attention seekers, power seekers, and hopeless children. Regardless of which perception prompts their behavior, such youngsters are unable to consider the needs of those with whom they interact and are incapable of recognizing the destructive impact of their actions. As a result, they tend to perpetuate negative interaction patterns that support their erroneous conclusions.

For instance, *attention seekers* demand constant, undue notice by playing the clown, bragging, badgering, engaging in games of one-upmanship, demanding continual praise, and deliberately breaking known rules in order to elicit a reaction. Adults inadvertently encourage these problem behaviors by responding to inappropriate demands for attention and/or by failing to recognize appropriate behaviors.

*Power seekers* exert their power blatantly, using brute force, or more subtly by resisting other's requests. This often results in power struggles in which the child's goal is to outwit the adult. Children who have no legitimate power over their lives are those most likely to succumb to this maladaptive pattern.

*Hopeless children* are those who have given up all prospects of gaining attention or power. They may feel so completely rejected that their only gratification comes from hurting others, thereby eliciting a response (Dreikurs, 1972). Children in this state of mind sometimes are violent or vengeful. They make it their business to discover the vulnerability of the people with whom they come in contact and take advantage of this knowledge. This counterproductive approach gains them the notoriety they seek.

Not all hopeless children resort to hurtful behavior, however. Some act completely helpless in an effort to discourage anyone from expecting too much of them (Garber and Seligman, 1980). They avoid any situation in which there is a chance for failure. Their perception of absolute inadequacy is reinforced when adults focus primarily on their mistakes or take over rather than allowing them to do things for themselves.

**Solution.** Changing children's perceptions is no easy matter; yet, in situations such as these, it is the key to making permanent improvements in their behavior. Adults must first recognize and acknowledge misconceptions, then make a conscious effort to help children learn alternative ways of establishing their self-worth (Seligman, 1995).

*Attention seekers.* The positive behaviors of the attention seekers should be rewarded by personal messages and praise. When the child engages in inappropriate actions, the adult can choose either of two options. The first is to ignore minor eruptions and wait for the child to choose a more appropriate action before giving attention. The second option better suited to more severe bids for notice, involves reflecting the child's desire for attention, explaining that it will not be given until he or she demonstrates more desirable behavior, then following through with this plan (Greenspan, 1995).

*Power seekers.* Power-seeking youngsters should have an opportunity to experience legitimate power. Giving children choices, allowing them to make decisions, and requesting their participation in planning are effective and appropriate ways to achieve this. When power struggles occur, the key to defusing them is to remain calm, to refrain from fighting, and to refuse to give in (Dreikurs and Cassel, 1972). The exact ways in which adults can get themselves out of these entanglements will be described later in this chapter.

*Hopeless children.* When children feel hopeless, it is critical for adults to recognize that this is the basis of their antisocial or apathetic behavior. Such youngsters are the ones who most need to experience nurturing relationships with adults to boost their self-esteem. It is particularly important that adults not demonstrate agreement with children's dismal assessments of their capacities by becoming punitive or detached. Instead, they must see through children's defenses and show the children that there are some things about them that are likable and worthy. It often takes imagination and effort to identify such qualities, but it is obvious that if adults cannot see them, children never will.

**PROBLEM 6: Contradictory rules.** It is not at all unusual for the influential people in children's lives to have differing ideas about how children should behave. As a result, they may actively support conflicting codes of conduct (Morrow, 1989). For instance, school personnel may tell children to settle disagreements peacefully, but family members may encourage them to "fight it out." In this situation, the school's main focus is on teaching children harmonious group living, and parents are interested in teaching them self-defense skills. Both goals have merit, but are different. This puts children in a dilemma. In an effort to obey one set of expectations, they may have to violate another.

**Solution.** Helping professionals must remember that their expectations are not the only appropriate ones, nor are they the only ones with which children are expected to comply. Consequently, they must work with the other members of children's mesosystems to minimize the dilemmas youngsters face. How this can best be accomplished is described in Chapter 15, Making Judgments.

Furthermore, when adults use personal messages, they help children realize that adults have differing reactions to their behavior. This enables helping professionals to stress that certain standards may be situation specific: "You're upset. At home you don't have to pick up. It bothers me when the puzzles are all over the floor. We could lose the pieces. Here at school everybody helps. There is a puzzle for you to put away."

**PROBLEM 7: Controversial rules.** Children often reject rules that seem silly or unwarranted (Rich, 1984). Although most youngsters see the value of moral guidelines (such as those advocating honesty and justice), they are less inclined to treat social conventions (such as answering politely or eating with a certain fork) in the same way (Damon, 1978; Turiel, 1978). Hence, they may conclude that a rule is "stupid" and feel no inclination to comply.

**Solution.** Adults minimize children's rejection of rules when they explain why the rules have been set. Moreover, children are most willing to adopt a code of behavior in which they have some say (Rich, 1984). Children as young as three years of age can participate in discussions about why rules are important to groups of people living and working together and what rules should be observed (Glasser, 1985; Hendrick, 1996; Kostelnik and Stein, 1986). When children have opportunities to make up some of the rules that govern their lives, they come to recognize those rules as social agreements of which they are a part.

**PROBLEM 8: Mixed messages.** Even when a rule is appropriately stated to children, adult actions may undermine it. This happens when adults fail to reward compliance, ignore broken rules, or give in to noncompliance (Miller, 1996; Parke and Slaby, 1983). Such acts create an unpredictable environment in which children cannot be sure what the real expectations are. For example, at Roosevelt Elemen-

tary School, the rule is that children should eat their lunch at a moderate pace. Youngsters are understandably confused when, on the days they eat slowly, no one notices. Additionally, on some days they are scolded for gobbling their food, but on other days, they are urged to eat faster (adults are running late), and on still other days they are ignored when they wolf down their sandwiches (adults are too tired to cope). Adult actions have made enforcement of the rule arbitrary. Over time, youngsters will conclude that the rule has no real meaning and so will not feel obliged to uphold it.

**PROBLEM 9: Testing the limits.** Children constantly try to determine what constitutes in-bounds and out-of-bounds behavior. The only way they can discover these differences is to test them out by repeated trial and error. Moreover, because adults vary in their willingness to obtain compliance, children test each adult with whom they come in contact to discover that person's limits. Both forms of testing frequently result in children engaging in inappropriate behavior.

**Solution.** The way to resolve behavior problems related to mixed messages and limit testing is to enforce rules consistently through the use of consequences. The following portion of this chapter will focus on this important skill.

## ▼ CONSEQUENCES

Consequences are events that make a particular behavior more or less likely to happen in the future. Positive consequences increase the chances that behaviors will be repeated, and inhibiting consequences reduce them.

### Positive Consequences

**Positive consequences** are those that **reward children for maintaining a rule.** One of the most common, and most effective, is to reinforce children with a positive personal message (Gordon, 1978; Reynolds, 1996). When adults affirm children's compliance using this skill, children are likely to comply again in the future. This is because a positive personal message reminds children of the rule and its rationale at a time when they have demonstrable proof that they are able to follow it. For instance, the adult who says: "Leroy, you remembered to raise your hand before talking. I'm pleased. That gave me a chance to finish what I was saying" is highlighting the child's appropriate behavior in a way that will make an impression on him. In addition, it acknowledges that following the rule took effort. This type of confirmation is beneficial to children of all ages.

Another positive consequence with which readers already are familiar is effective praise. This nonevaluative acknowledgment of children's rule-related behavior further underscores their growing ability to act in socially acceptable ways. An example is when the adult points out, "You're walking. You remembered that was the safest way to get down the hall" or "You've been trying hard to help yourself remember not to hit. You haven't hit anyone all morning."

Similarly, when adults acknowledge the accumulated benefits of following a rule over time, they promote children's feelings of self-satisfaction and pride in their own performance. For instance, if the rule were "practice the piano every day," the adult might say: "You were a big hit at the recital. All of your practicing really paid off."

Positive consequences also can take the form of earned privileges. For instance, if the rule is "handle library books carefully," children might be told that when they demonstrate this skill they can use the books without adult assistance. This type of reward actually formalizes the natural aftermath of their positive behavior. It also emphasizes the positive outcomes that accrue from their actions. When this information is articulated, the linkages between behavior and outcome become more evident.

### Inhibiting Consequences

Behavioral scientists commonly refer to all **inhibiting consequences** as punishments (Baumrind, 1977; Parke, 1974). However, data show that some uses of punishment are effective in promoting self-discipline, and others are not. In order to clearly distinguish between the two, we will label strategies that enhance self-control as **negative consequences** and strategies that detract from self-control as **punishments.** There are significant differences between the two. These are summarized in Table 11–1.

**Punishments.** Punishments are harsh, unreasonable actions taken against children whose conduct is disapproved. They depend on the use of power or force to change behavior and often occur when adults lose self-control. As a result, adults re-spond in haste, in anger, or without thinking (Fields and Boesser, 1994; Sheppard and Willoughby, 1975). As described in Table 11–1, punishments are a form of retribution, the goal of which is to make perpetrators pay for their misbehavior (Mendler and Curwin, 1988). Adults who resort to punishments assume that children have little capacity to reason; they believe youngsters respond only to conditioning. Based on this premise, they think children will avoid misbehaving for fear of being punished. In reality, youngsters learn to avoid the punishing agent and spend much of their time figuring out how to escape being caught (Newman and Newman, 1997; Parke, 1977). In addition, although punishments serve to satisfy the adult, they often promote fear and hostility in the child or leave children feeling demeaned (Belsky, Lerner, and Spanier, 1984; Hoffman, 1983). None of these emotions enhances the probability of future cooperation.

Another characteristic of punishments is that although they serve as sanctions against certain behaviors, they do not emphasize the desirable alternatives. Thus, children may come to learn that particular actions are disapproved, but gain no information on how to correct them. Moreover, because punishments are so intensely negative, children become so emotionally involved that they are incapable of carrying out the cognitive reasoning necessary to correct their behavior on their own (Hoffman, 1983).

Finally, adults who rely on punishments fail to model calm, rational approaches to problem situations (Caldwell, 1977; Miller, 1996). Instead, they display the very actions they may be trying to curb in children. This type of behavior keeps children at an adherence level because it gives them none of the tools necessary for internalization.

**Negative consequences.** Negative consequences are constructive actions aimed at helping children recognize the impact their behavior has on themselves and others. They are founded on the idea that reason is the basis for behavior change, and they are implemented with the long-term goal of teaching children self-discipline. Negative consequences help children learn acceptable conduct from the experience of being corrected (Mendler and Curwin, 1988). They enable children to approximate the desired acts. These serve as practice for the future and make it more likely that children will succeed in repeating the behaviors (Fields and Boesser, 1994; Wolff, Levin, and Longobardi, 1972).

## ▼ Table 11–1   Differences Between Negative Consequences and Punishments

| NEGATIVE CONSEQUENCES | PUNISHMENTS |
|---|---|
| Suggest that the children are accepted, although their behavior is not | Imply that children themselves have been rejected |
| Are instructive—they teach children how to correct problem behaviors by having them approximate acceptable behaviors or restore the situation to a more positive condition | Are not instructive—they merely inform children that an infraction has occurred, but do not teach them how to correct it |
| Have a clear and easily discernible relationship to the unacceptable behavior based on content or timing | Have no relationship to the behavior to be changed |
| Are thoughtfully imposed | Are arbitrary and demeaning |
| Communicate that children have the power to correct their own behavior | Communicate the personal power of the adult |
| Enable children eventually to change their own behavior | Force adults to assume the entire responsibility for behavior change |
| Focus on prevention of future infractions | Focus on retaliation for current infractions |
| Are applied matter-of-factly | Are applied with obvious resentment |
| Imply that misbehavior is a product of the situation | Imply that misbehavior is due to the "badness" of the child |
| Are applied in direct proportion to the magnitude of the transgression | Are severe and exceed the magnitude of the infraction |
| Require adults and children to reason together and correct problem situations | Require adults to use coercion to correct problem behaviors |

Sources: Data from Dreikurs, R., and P. Cassel. *Discipline Without Tears.* New York: Hawthorn Books, 1972; Mendler, A. N., and R. L. Curwin. *Taking Charge in the Classroom.* Reston, Virginia: Reston Publishing Co., 1988; and Gartrell, D. *A Guidance Approach to Discipline.* Albany, N.Y.: Delmar Publishers, 1994.

When properly applied, negative consequences also encourage children to think about characteristics of problem situations, which may be useful to them in future encounters. For example, what prompted the episode, how and why did people react to the child's behavior, and what acceptable alternatives were suggested? This self-analysis is possible because negative consequences do not elicit intense feelings of fear or shame, which interfere with children's ability to reason.

Another attribute of such consequences is that they make the children's world more predictable; they know exactly what will happen when a rule is broken. Infractions are dealt with matter-of-factly and consistently, no matter who the perpetrators are or how often they have broken the rule before. In this way, negative consequences serve as the logical outcome of particular actions. They

have nothing to do with personality, favoritism, or vengeance.

## Types of Negative Consequences

Negative consequences come in three varieties: natural, logical, and unrelated.

**Natural consequences.** Natural consequences happen without intervention (Fields and Boesser, 1994; Reynolds, 1996). They show children that their actions are significant and do influence what happens to them. For instance, children who come late for lunch may suffer the natural consequence of eating cold food or eating alone because everyone else is finished. Children who talk while the homework is being assigned may miss the page numbers. Children who fail to put their sneakers in the locker may lose them. These repercussions all are a direct result of circumstance rather than of adult manipulation of the environment. Hence, there are times when adults do not have to create a consequence because the outcome follows directly from the child's action. Children will learn to come on time for lunch if they dislike eating cold food or eating by themselves; they will learn to listen when directions are being given if they value their grades; and they will remember to put their shoes away if they expect to find them quickly.

Natural consequences are very effective in teaching children what to do and what not to do and are well suited for many situations. However, they cannot be relied on when children's safety is jeopardized. For instance, the natural consequences of letting a child run in the street or drink cleaning fluid would result in serious injury, an outcome no adult would permit. In these types of situations, logical consequences are more appropriate.

**Logical consequences.** Logical consequences are directly related to the rule. This means there is an obvious connection between the child's behavior and the resulting disciplinary action (Dinkmeyer and McKay, 1988; Dreikurs and Grey, 1990). Penalties of this type help children either approximate the desired behavior or correct problem situations. For example, if Rudy is running down the corridor, the logical consequence would be to have him go back and walk. The act of walking serves as a more vivid reminder of the rule than would simply scolding him or making him sit out for several minutes. Walking actually enables Rudy to "rehearse" the appropriate behavior he is expected to use in the future. Having children practice rules to be remembered increases their chances for future success (Wolff, Levin, and Longobardi, 1972).

At times, such rehearsals are less feasible, and so restitution is more appropriate. For instance, if children throw food on the floor, it would be logical to insist that they clean it up prior to getting anything else to eat. This type of action restores the situation to a more acceptable state and shows children that the unacceptable act of throwing food will not be tolerated.

Forbidding children to play outside for a week is not a logical consequence for fighting with peers over the ball. Although this approach temporarily halts the dispute, it does not teach children how to deal with the issue more effectively in the future. A better solution would be to tell children they must

take turns if they wish to continue to play, and then help them carry out this plan if they are unable to do so on their own. This proposal teaches children that sharing can be a viable solution. The same is true if Maranda spills the paint seemingly on purpose. It would be more logical to have her wipe it up than to send her out of the room or to relegate her to a desk in the corner for some portion of the day.

Another benefit of using logical consequences is that they teach children behaviors that are incompatible with the noncompliant behaviors (Gootman, 1988). As these incompatible responses are strengthened through practice and positive consequences, the less desirable behaviors that they replace are weakened. For instance, children who must go back and walk each time they run down the hospital corridor are rehearsing walking in the specific situation in which it is called for. This rehearsal makes it more likely that they will remember to walk on their own once in a while. If such instances are noted and praised, eventually youngsters learn to replace the disallowed behavior (running) with the more desired behavior (walking).

**Unrelated consequences.** The third type of negative consequence is the **unrelated consequence.** As the name implies, these consequences are not the natural outgrowth of a child's behavior, nor do they enable children to approximate desired behaviors or rectify less desirable ones. Instead, they are outcomes manufactured by the adult in response to children's misbehavior. Examples might include forbidding Lisa to watch television until she brushes her teeth or to choose a work station until she hangs up her coat. Brushing teeth has nothing to do with watching television, so denial of television neither teaches Lisa how to brush her teeth nor corrects her unclean mouth. However, if Lisa really values her time in front of the set, she will quickly learn that watching television is contingent on tooth brushing. The same is true regarding the coat. Forbidding Lisa to choose a work station neither approximates hanging up her coat nor rectifies neglecting it. What it does do is create an aversive situation that the child can make more positive by doing what is required.

Most unrelated consequences involve loss of a privilege or introduction of a penalty. Because they have such little relation to the broken rule, adults must take particular care to enforce these in the true spirit of consequences, not punishments. Furthermore, the most beneficial unrelated consequences are those that, although dissimilar in content, are linked in time to the infraction. It is more effective to withhold the next event in a sequence than one far in the future. Therefore, it is better to deprive Lisa of participating in some portion of the free-choice period for forgetting to hang up her coat than to keep her in from recess several hours later.

## Deciding Which Negative Consequences to Use

Negative consequences are important instructional tools that have the power to teach children to discern right from wrong, to help them distinguish appropriate from inappropriate behavior, and to demonstrate to them the potential impact of their behavior on themselves and on others. With so many valuable lessons to offer, they cannot be carelessly applied. Rather, adults must thoughtfully formulate the consequences they use. The three types of negative consequences should be considered in order, from natural to logical to unrelated.

**Step one.** It is best to consider first what natural consequences pertain to the situation and to determine if it is acceptable to let them happen. It should be noted that acceptability is an idea that varies from adult to adult. What might be permissible to one adult might be unthinkable to another. As mentioned earlier, the natural consequence for children who arrive late for a meal is to have cold food or eat alone. Some caregivers might view these outcomes as reasonable; others could not bring themselves to maintain them. Instead, they would find themselves reheating the meal or keeping the child company. If the latter is true, and adults can predict that they will be unable to sustain a hands-off policy, the natural consequence is not the consequence of choice; in fact, no negative consequence would occur for the child. In this case, a logical or unrelated consequence would be more suitable. The decision to use one of these instead of a natural consequence also is mandated in situations in which nonintervention obviously would lead to injury or property damage.

**Step two.** If the adult has contemplated the natural consequences and found them unacceptable or difficult to maintain, logical consequences should be considered next. These can be tailored to fit any situation. Adults should think about ways in which

the rule could be reenacted (such as repeating an action correctly or carrying out the behavior with adult help) or ways in which a problem situation might be redressed. Although logical consequences take more imagination than stock favorites such as sitting in a chair in the corner, going to detention, or being sent to the principal's office, they are much more effective in helping children learn appropriate alternate behaviors (Dreikurs and Grey, 1990).

**Step three.** As a last resort, unrelated consequences should be implemented. Although they are effective, they must be used sparingly because their primary value is in curtailing behavior for the moment (Clarizio, 1980). For long-term change to occur, children must learn acceptable substitutes for which logical consequences are preferable. Unrelated consequences should be implemented only when no logical consequence is available.

## Implementing Negative Consequences

When children are engaged in potential problem situations, adults should first remind them of the rule in a serious, firm tone (Charles, 1983; Kostelnik Soderman, and Whiren, in press). Within the sequence of skills presented in this book, the rule portion of the personal message serves as this reminder. Often, such prompting is all that is needed for children to comply. If at this point, children obey, they should be praised. However, if they continue to disregard the rule, the adult must implement an appropriate negative consequence.

The consequence is first stated to the child in the form of a warning (Hendrick, 1996; Mendler and Curwin, 1988). The **warning** is phrased as an either-or statement that *repeats the rule and then tells the child what will happen if he or she does not follow it.* For example, if the rule is "wait your turn to get a drink," the warning could be "Either wait your turn, or you will have to go back to the end of the line." If the rule is "share the watercolors," a warning might be "Either find a way to share the watercolors on your own, or I will help you find a way."

In each case, the warning gives children an opportunity and an incentive to change their behavior in accordance with adult expectations. It also notifies children that this is the last chance for them to control the situation prior to the adult taking over.

The warning is not intended to be frightening, abusive, or retaliatory. Rather, it is a plain statement of fact. This means adults must warn children calmly. They should not scream at children, shake them, wave a fist in their face, or incorporate threats such as "Just you wait" or "I'll show you" as part of their statement.

Once the warning has been given, the adult pauses to give children an opportunity to comply. Children's reaction times are somewhat slower than adults sometimes wish. Adults have to take care not to jump in before the child has had time to respond. For instance, when Alex is told to wait his turn or go to the end of the line, he may take several seconds deciding what to do. His delay poses no real threat to those around him, and so it can be tolerated. On the other hand, there are times when safety is jeopardized. These circumstances call for immediate physical intervention, even as the warning is being stated. For example, if Amy is about to throw a stone, the adult should quickly catch her hand while saying, "You can either put the stone down yourself, or I will take it from you." Even here, a moment's pause is necessary to give Amy a chance to drop the rock herself. The adult should maintain a grasp on Amy's hand and try to sense her intention, based on whether she remains tense or begins to relax, as well as by what she might be saying. If Amy were capable of releasing the stone herself, she would be displaying a modicum of self-control. If she were not, the adult would exert the maximum external control by taking the stone away from her. This last step is a follow-through on the stated consequence and is very important.

## Following Through on Negative Consequences

It is not enough simply to tell youngsters what the negative consequences will be. Adults must enforce them if children do not comply (Canter and Canter, 1983; Newman and Newman, 1997). This is called **following through.** The follow-through is a critical part of the discipline process because it involves the enactment of the negative consequence. Because appropriate negative consequences are instructional in nature, this step provides children with valuable information about how to redirect inappropriate behavior. It also demonstrates quite clearly that adults mean what they say and that there is a limit to the amount of out-of-bounds behavior they will tolerate. It is from discipline encounters such as these that children begin to build an accurate picture of their effect on the world and its reaction to them (Hoffman, 1983).

When adults find themselves in situations that demand a follow-through, there are certain things

they must say so that the reasoning behind their actions is made clear to the child. It is important for children to recognize that negative consequences are a result of their own behavior; they are not arbitrary or vengeful actions on the part of the adult.

The follow-through begins with a brief reflection that summarizes the situation from the child's point of view. Next is a sentence that restates the warning. This often is prefaced by the words "Remember, I told you. . . . " Then, the adult repeats the consequence as a statement of what will happen next as a result of the child's behavior. This statement often begins with the word "now." Thus, a typical follow-through would sound like this: "You're still anxious to get ahead in line. Remember, I told you, either wait your turn or go to the back. Now, go to the back." While this is being said, the adult might have to escort the child to the back of the line as a way to physically affirm what was stated.

## When to Implement Negative Consequences

Two key factors influence how well children learn from the consequences they experience: consistency and timing. *Consistency* involves how often the rule is enforced. *Timing* refers to the period between when the rule is broken and enforcement is initiated.

Rule enforcement must be consistent (Canter and Canter, 1983; Reynolds, 1996). Every time the rule is broken, the adult must be prepared to enact appropriate negative consequences to ensure compliance. Rules that are administered one day and neglected the next are ineffective. Because children cannot be sure whether or not the rule is in operation, they are not likely to follow it. As a result, youngsters who experience erratic rule enforcement tend to demonstrate more incidents of deviant behavior than do children whose experience has been more regular. Because consistency is so important, adults are cautioned to insist on only a few rules at a time. It is better to unwaveringly enforce one or two important rules than to half-heartedly attempt many rules.

In addition to being consistent, rule enforcement must be immediate. Long delays between the moment when the child breaks the rule and the moment when the follow-through takes place weaken the impact of the consequence (Marion, 1983; O'Leary, 1995). Thus, statements such as "Wait 'til your father comes home" or "I'll have the head teacher deal with you when she gets back" are nonproductive. Children must have an opportunity to associate their inappropriate behavior with the resulting consequence. The further removed the consequence is in time from the act itself, the more difficult it is for children to make a connection. For the same reasons, consistency and immediacy are important to the implementation of positive consequences as well.

## ▼ COMBINING THE WARNING AND FOLLOW-THROUGH WITH THE PERSONAL MESSAGE

Up to this point, we have focused on the appropriate use of both positive and negative consequences. Yet, consequences do not stand alone. Rather, the follow-through stage of rule enforcement represents the final step in a sequence of skills aimed at enhancing children's development of self-control. This sequence consists of a personal message succeeded by a warning and then, if necessary, a follow-through. The sequence is illustrated in the following situation:

SITUATION: Mr. Howard, a student teacher, enters the bathroom to find Allen stuffing several paper towels down the toilet. Water and towels are all over the floor. The child does not see the adult come in.

*Personal message.* Mr. Howard quickly approaches Alan and stands close to him. He catches Alan's hand just as the child reaches for another towel. Mr. Howard says, "Alan, you're having fun. I'm worried that with this water all over the floor, someone will slip and get hurt. Start cleaning up this mess." Mr. Howard pauses a moment and waits for Alan to comply. Instead, Alan tries to edge toward the door. Mr. Howard stops him.

*Warning.* You'd rather not clean up. Either you figure out where to start cleaning, or I'll tell you where to start.

Again, Mr. Howard waits a few seconds in the hope that Alan will begin. The child just stands there. Mr. Howard calmly hands Alan a bucket and a sponge.

*Follow-through.* "You didn't make a choice. Remember, I said either you choose, or I'd choose. You can start in this corner." Mr. Howard places the sponge in Alan's hand and bodily edges him toward the puddle.

### Skill-Sequence Rationale

By combining a personal message with a warning and follow-through, Mr. Howard was using a step-by-step sequence designed, in the short run, to change Alan's unacceptable behavior. Its long-range objective is to provide a structure through which Alan eventually learns to regulate his own behavior.

**Short-term benefits.** The immediate advantages to both Mr. Howard and Alan of the sequential use of a personal message, warning, and follow-through are outlined in Table 11–2.

**Long-term benefits.** The skill just described offers short-term advantages to adults and children, but it also provides long-term benefits as well. Combining a personal message, a warning, and a follow-through helps adults deal with children's problem behaviors consistently, both for the same child over time and among different children. This consistency enables helping professionals to establish an authoritative pattern of interaction with youngsters in the formal group setting. In addition, the time adults initially invest in using the sequence with children pays off later in fewer future incidents (Reynolds, 1996; Stein and Kostelnik, 1984).

Children also profit when their confrontations with adults are eventually reduced. They feel more successful and better able to satisfy their needs in ways that result in social rewards rather than social costs. The resulting positive self-appraisal enhances their feelings of self-esteem. Moreover, as children experience this sequence on a variety of occasions, they gradually shift from complete dependence on external, adult control, as embodied in the follow-through, to greater internal control, as prompted by the personal message and warning.

When the sequence is first introduced, most youngsters will test the adult's predictability and resolve by proceeding all the way to the follow-through. As children become more familiar with both the adult and the sequence of steps described here, they often respond to the warning without having to experience the follow-through directly. This happens because they have learned that the adult means what he or she says and that a warning indicates that a follow-through is forthcoming unless the behavior is changed. Behavior change at this point shows that children are beginning to exercise some self-regulation. They are at the adherence level, in order to avoid a consequence or gain the benefits of compliance.

Eventually, children reach a point at which a personal message is all that is needed to guide their actions. In this way, they begin to exert greater control

▼ **Table 11–2**     **Short-Term Benefits of the Sequential Use of a Personal Message, Warning, and Follow-Through**

| | **SHORT-TERM BENEFITS FOR MR. HOWARD** | **SHORT-TERM BENEFITS FOR ALAN** |
|---|---|---|
| Step 1a: Personal message | Has a way to enter the situation calmly and rationally | Is treated with respect and acceptance |
| | Has a means of communicating respect and acceptance of the child, but disapproval of the behavior | Is alerted that his behavior is inappropriate and is told why |
| | Has a blueprint for what kinds of information to provide the child initially | Is informed via the rule of what to do instead (clean up the mess) |
| Step 1b: Pause | Has a chance to see if Alan can comply before he exerts further external control | Is given a chance to change the inappropriate behavior on his own, thereby exercising internal control |
| | Has a moment to think of an appropriate consequence to use if necessary | |
| Step 2a: Warning | Has a constructive way to exert increased external control over Alan's behavior | Is reminded of the rule |
| | Establishes a legitimate foundation for carrying out the follow-through if necessary | Gains a clear understanding of what will happen if he does not comply |
| Step 2b: Pause | Has a chance to see if Alan can comply before he exerts further external control | Is given a chance to change the inappropriate behavior on his own thereby exercising internal control |
| Step 3: Follow-through | Has an authoritative way to resolve the situation without becoming abusive or giving in | Is able to rehearse an acceptable behavior he was not able to carry out on his own |
| | Has been able to stop the negative behavior as well as remedy the problem situation | Has evidence that the adult means what he says and is predictable in his actions |
| | Has had an opportunity to demonstrate that he means what he says, increasing his predictability in the eyes of the child | |

over their behavior, while the adult exerts less. Initially, this change occurs because children respond to the emotions of the adult with whom they identify. Gradually, however, they take into account the reasoning behind the expectation and, as a result, consider the effects their actions have on those around them. Such reasoning ultimately leads to internalization. As this occurs, it is the child who assumes the greatest responsibility for his or her conduct, not the adult. Thus, the adult's use of the skill sequence in any given situation will match the child's ability to exercise inner control. If the child is able to comply based on the reasoning of the personal message, further intervention is unnecessary. However, should a youngster need more support, it is provided.

The relationship between children's degree of self-discipline and the skill sequence is depicted in Table 11–3.

## Successive Use of the Skill Sequence

It is not unusual for children to resist complying by attempting to divert the adult's attention from the issue at hand. Shouting, protesting, escalating the problem behavior, or running away are common strategies. All of these tactics are aimed at getting the adult to forget about enforcement, allowing the child to escape consequences. Unfortunately, if adults throw up their hands and say, "I can't do anything with this child," they are teaching him or her that these tactics work. As a result, children begin to rely on inappropriate strategies more and

▼ Table 11–3    Four Types of Compliance

| TYPE OF COMPLIANCE | DEFINITION | SOURCE OF BEHAVIOR CONTROL | STAGE OF THE SKILL SEQUENCE THAT APPLIES |
|---|---|---|---|
| Amoral | Children have no sense of right or wrong | External to child | Child requires a follow-through |
| Adherence | Children respond to rewards and punishments; they often anticipate these and behave accordingly | Shared between others and the child—primary responsibility remains with adult | Child responds to warning |
| Identification | Children attempt to adopt behavioral codes of admired others; they "second-guess" how that person might behave in varying situations and act likewise | Shared between others and the child—child assumes greater share of responsibility | Child responds to personal message |
| Internalization | Children govern their behavior using an internal code of ethics created from their own values and judgments | Internal to child | Child monitors self |

more frequently. This dilemma must be avoided at all costs because the more ingrained an inappropriate behavior becomes, the more difficult it is to change. The best way to deal with such situations is to defuse them right at the start. This means always following through once a warning has been stated and the child has failed to demonstrate compliance. For example, if the warning is "Either walk, or I will help you," that is exactly what must happen. If Ginger runs away, she must be retrieved; if Camille flails her arms, they must be grasped; if Vince curses, it is best to ignore his words; if Saul becomes stiff or goes limp, his feet should be shuffled along. Even a few steps is enough to make the point.

In addition, there are times when one problem behavior will lead to another. For instance, four-year-old Linda climbs to the top of the bookcase as part of her Super Hero play. The helping professional approaches and goes through the sequence to the warning, which is "Either come down by yourself, or I will take you down." Linda laughs and shouts, "You can't get me!" Grasping the child's foot, the adult begins to follow through. As she takes the child into her arms, Linda starts to kick. Kicking represents a new problem behavior and is treated as such. The adult initiates the sequence again. This time, the warning is "Either stop kicking, or I will hold your feet until you do." The adult then follows through until Linda becomes less agitated. In this way, the adult has demonstrated that

he or she will follow through over and over again until no negative behaviors are evident. When adults enforce their rules as illustrated here, they create a predictable, stable environment for children and leave no doubt in children's minds as to what will happen when rules are followed or broken. This type of consistency is absolutely necessary if children are to learn that there is no ultimate behavior they can display to which the adult is unable to respond rationally and firmly.

## ▼ TIME-OUT: THE ULTIMATE CONSEQUENCE

### Temper Tantrums

Most people know a **temper tantrum** when they see one. There is no mistaking the physical signs: red face, flailing arms and legs, screaming, and crying. Although such behavior can be disconcerting to adults, it is important to remember that a temper tantrum is such an intense emotional and physical response that children's normal thought processes are no longer available to them. This means that the impassioned child cannot hear or respond to adult directions or efforts to comfort; cannot think out a logical, more socially appropriate sequence of actions; and can no longer gauge the effect his or her behavior has on self or others. Any child, at any time, may become involved in a tantrum, and although such behavior is most common in toddlers, older preschoolers as well as school-age children may, on occasion, resort to these volcanic outbursts.

Children have tantrums for several reasons. Tantrums initially appear when urgent wants are not immediately gratified. Later, tantrums may occur because adults have previously given in to children's tantrums, because children are fatigued, because they receive little attention for positive behavior, because they are continually subjected to unrealistic adult demands, or because rule enforcement is unpredictable (Brooks, 1996).

The best way to avoid temper tantrums is to acknowledge children's feelings before they become intense, to teach children alternative ways to express their desires, to respond positively when children behave in appropriate ways, and to make reasonable rules and enforce them consistently. Yet, children occasionally will resort to temper tantrums in spite of all these precautions. When this happens, the goal is to help them regain their self-control. In the case of toddlers, whose outbursts are extreme but short lived, the best way to restore calm is to ignore their outrageous behavior and let them quiet down in their own way and time. Older children, whose emotional states are longer lasting, benefit from the logical consequence: time-out.

## Habituated Antisocial Behavior

At times, all children engage in some antisocial behaviors, such as kicking, hitting, or biting. These occasional bouts of misbehavior are best dealt with using personal messages and the consequences described earlier. For some children, however, reliance on harmful actions becomes **habitual**—they engage in these negative behaviors again and again because they have learned that punching, pushing, or pinching gets them the attention they want, intimidates others to give in, or enhances their prestige with some members of the group by allowing them to gain power over others. When adults recognize that children have established a pattern of antisocial behavior, they must work at stopping the problem behavior as well as interrupting the pattern of positive reinforcement that has allowed it to continue. Here again time-out is an appropriate consequence to consider.

## The Purpose of Time-Out

**Time-out** provides out-of-control children with a cooling-off period during which they can regain their composure privately (Gartrell, 1994). When children are engaged in habitual antisocial behavior,

time-out interrupts the sequence of events that has reinforced children's negative behavior and eliminates the further possibility of such rewards (Crary, 1993). In both cases, the goal of time-out is to help children develop coping skills while discouraging inappropriate behavior. In this way, time-out becomes a logical consequence enabling children to rehearse the skills they need to function more effectively in the classroom. Whenever it is used, children should leave time-out feeling better about themselves, not worse.

## The Time-Out Place

There is disagreement in the literature as to whether a specific time-out place should be designated somewhere in the classroom. Some authors believe that identifying such a spot institutionalizes time-out as a form of punishment (Clewett, 1988; Gartrell, 1994). This most often happens when children are sent off by themselves to sit in a "time-out chair." Such arrangements are similar to banishing children to the corner. Under these circumstances, adult support is unavailable and children are often on public view, adding to their distress. Other authors advocate having children participate in deciding where the time-out place will be. They believe that children who know exactly where time-out will take place are more comfortable going there when necessary. They also suggest that designating a part of the room as the time-out area helps children understand that this is a space where they go to feel better again. Predesignation also gives adults and children a chance to consider issues of safety and privacy in advance (Duffy, 1996). Whichever approach you choose, the main criteria for an appropriate time-out place is that it be a quiet, unused part of the room in which children will feel safe. An alcove or screened off area increases privacy and makes it easier for the adult to focus on helping the child rather than being distracted by whatever else is going on.

## Preparing the Group for Time-Out

Children benefit when they have an opportunity to talk about time-out in advance and participate in planning for it (Duffy, 1996). This reinforces the notion that time-out is a helpful procedure and that the time-out place is a spot where children go to eventually feel better. Talking about time-out with a group should take place at a calm time after you have begun to develop a relationship with the children. The conversation could be an outgrowth of talking about emotions and how people express them in different ways. Adults can say things like:

> There are times when people become so angry, or so excited, or so sad that they use their whole body to let other people know what their feelings are. Sometimes, when people use their bodies in this way, there is a danger that they will hurt themselves or someone else. If this happens in our group and I am worried that someone could be hurt, I will have a time-out with the child who is upset. Time-out means time away from the group in a safe, quiet place. It is a chance for the person who is very upset to calm down. If you need a time-out, I will be with you in the time-out area to make sure you are safe. I will not be talking to you, because that may make it harder for you to think about what's on your mind. Once you feel more relaxed and comfortable, you can return to the group. Then we can talk, if you would like.

Depending on the circumstances, the adult could also say: "If I have a time-out with a child the other children can continue to play until we are finished," or "Ms. Lindstrom will stay with the other children until the time-out is over." Once time-out has been described, children can identify areas where time-out should take place.

Throughout the discussion, adults are reminded to use the words "time-out" in their description. It is important that children learn that time-out is a particular consequence with specific steps and goals that are implemented in response to out-of-control or dangerous behaviors.

### Preparing an Individual Child for Time-Out

Time-out for children whose antisocial behavior has become habituated is very similar to the procedure described for temper tantrums. The major difference is that adults must first establish that the problem behavior is habitual. That is, there must be a pattern to the child's actions that the helping professional has documented over time. For example, five-year-old Lila seems to be involved in several pinching incidents. Her teacher begins making a record of these. What she discovers is that the child pinches many times in a day and usually without any obvious provocation. When asked, Lila can't say why she pinches. Adults try keeping an extra close eye on Lila, but even so, the pinching continues. Their attempts at logical consequences involving rehearsal and restitution do not decrease the behavior. Other children are afraid of Lila, and she is becoming an isolate in the classroom. This is a case in which time-out could be considered. Once such a decision is made, the behavior is identified

privately to the child during a time when the misconduct is not actually present. At this point, the use of time-out as a consequence for future misbehavior also is described: "Lila, there are many times during the day when you pinch. Pinching hurts. You must stop. Every time you pinch, you will have time-out for 3 minutes. Time-out means time away from the group in a quiet place. There is no talking and no playing in time-out." Note that when time-out is used to correct this type of behavior, the adult states in advance under what conditions time-out will occur and how long it will last. Implementation should take place every time the problem behavior happens.

### Implementing Time-Out

A specific sequence of steps must be followed in order to implement time-out correctly:

1. The child is warned, and if the behavior continues, he or she is removed to a suitable time-out area.
   a. When a child is in the midst of a tantrum, the adult first warns him or her of the consequences of such behavior: "You're very upset. I can't talk to you when you're screaming (kicking or biting) like this. Please stop. Either calm down here or we will have a time-out." If the child continues the tantrum, the adult follows through by saying, "Now, we will have a time-out," and then leads the child to the time-out place. This often is easier said than done. The adult may have to bodily remove the child by using a firm grasp and possibly lifting the child and carrying him or her. Children should never be jerked, pulled, or shoved as the adult attempts to move them along. One effective method of physically handling a struggling child is for the adult to position himself or herself behind the child, crossing the child's arms across the body and holding on. Simultaneously, the adult spreads his or her legs so that the child's kicks will not be harmful. In this position, the adult then sidles out of the room. This is a safe approach regardless of the child's size or physical movement.
   b. In the case of a child who demonstrates habitual antisocial behavior, the adult already has warned the child that time-out will take place if the behavior is repeated. If it is, time-out is immediately initiated by saying: "Lila, you pinched. Time-out." The child then is led

to the time-out area. If the child resists, proceed as in step 1a.

2. Once in the time-out area, the adult reflects the child's feelings and provides basic information so that he or she will know what to expect: "You're still very angry. When you're more quiet we can talk about what's bothering you," or "You pinched. You will have time-out for 3 minutes."

3. The adult holds to the stated limit before allowing the child to leave the time-out area. One to two minutes of quiet usually is appropriate for children between the ages of three and six; five minutes is satisfactory for older school-age youngsters. This means a prescribed period of calm. Any time the child spends screaming is not included.

4. The adult remains with the child in the time-out area. Children should never be left alone. If the child tries to leave the area before calming down, he or she should be returned to it.

5. Throughout the time-out process, the adult must remain silent. This is not the time for a lecture. Talking only aggravates the situation. First, it may prolong the time-out because the child may not yet be at a point at which she or he is able to focus on what is being said. Second, talking teaches the child that one way to get undivided adult attention is to engage in unacceptable behavior.

6. Any attempts to harm the adult or self must be stopped immediately. Hurting an adult can lead to later feelings of guilt and fear that the child may find hard to overcome. In addition, adults will find it extremely difficult to react rationally and calmly if they have been injured. Also, a child cannot be allowed to inflict self-harm. One way to prevent injury is to *physically restrain* the child. Physical restraint involves holding the child in a passive "bear hug" to keep the child from harming himself or herself or anyone else (Gartrell, 1994). Wrapping your arms around the child's arms and your legs around the child's legs is the easiest way to accomplish this. Some adults prefer to sit with the child on a chair, others sit in a "pretzel" position on the floor. In either case it is best to have the child facing away from you to reduce stimulation. Restraint calms some children and further incites others. Unfortunately, you do not always know in advance how a child will react. If you learn that holding a child will add to his or her distress, physical restraint should be avoided, if possible. If the situation seems potentially unsafe, it helps to say: "You don't want me to hold you. I will only hold you if it looks like you could get hurt. If not, I will stand here, but I won't touch you."

7. If peers seem curious about what is going on, an adult should reflect their concerns and remind them about time-out. It should be emphasized that the child went into time-out to feel better again. Assure children that the child is unharmed and that he or she will be returning to the group when he or she is ready.

8. Children who have had a tantrum should leave time-out when they are ready to rejoin the group. Children who have gone to time-out because of habitual antisocial behavior must satisfy the stated conditions (e.g., 3 minutes). Children should never remain in time-out beyond these time periods.

9. Following time-out, children should have an opportunity to discuss the incident and to make decisions or plans about future behavior. This discussion should not take place in the time-out area; in this way, the child will learn that problems can be solved in the regular group setting rather than only in a special place. Some children will not want to discuss the incident at this time. If that is the case, the child should be allowed to resume his or her place in the group without being forced into conversation.

10. A child who has completed time-out as the result of a tantrum should be praised for the hard work he or she put into calming down.

11. Later in the day, the adult who implemented time-out should have a pleasant contact with the child to reassure him or her of the adult's continuing affection. When adults maintain a nurturing relationship with the child, she or he becomes better able to exercise control in subsequent situations.

### After the Child Leaves Time-Out

One question often asked is whether children who have just been through time-out should be required to comply with the adult demand that may have triggered it. In other words, should Cecily have to put away the materials she didn't want to put away earlier, or should Harley be made to finish all the problems on page 2? For children who have resorted to a tantrum, it must be remembered that time-out was implemented as a consequence for out-of-control behavior, not as a consequence for failing to clean up or for not finishing an assignment. Self-control is a prerequisite to achieving the other desired behaviors. If self-control has been regained, the child has learned a big lesson. It is up to the adult to decide whether the child will benefit from attention to the secondary goals at this point. However, adults should never become so enmeshed in their own immediate desires (cleanup rules, completed assignments) that they lose sight of their long-term goals for children.

When youngsters have gone through a time-out for habituated antisocial behavior, a good follow-up is to have them perform an act of kindness for their victim sometime during the day. This does not mean making the child apologize; rather, it involves some positive behavior, such as helping the victim do something (Schickedanz, Schickedanz, and Forsyth, 1982). Restitution reduces the chances of the victim feeling a need to retaliate, and helps teach the erring child a substitute form of interaction.

## Variations on Time-Out

Time-out can be implemented as described here with both preschool and school-age children. So far we have described a procedure carried out by an adult in response to children's actions. However, there are times when *children initiate time-out themselves* because they are on the verge of losing control. When this happens, helping professionals should be sure to use positive personal messages and effective praise to underscore children's efforts to control their own behavior. At other times, it is not the child who needs a time-out from the tensions of the formal group setting, but the adult. All of us have experienced the rising feelings of anxiety that occur when the pace of the day seems too frantic or we think we can't possibly cope with one more disaster. At times like these it can be hard to maintain composure. If that begins to happen, it is best to *take a time-out yourself* for a few minutes to calm down. Something as simple as taking a deep breath, getting a drink of water, or moving to another part of the room for a few minutes may be all it takes to reduce the tension. Asking another adult to help you in a particularly difficult situation or to take your place for a little while as you walk outside or sit alone for a few moments are other examples of adult versions of time-out.

## Time-Out Versus Sitting Apart

In closing this discussion of time-out, it is worth noting that the procedure outlined for time-out is not the same as simply having children sit apart from the group for a while (Reynolds, 1996). **Sitting apart** involves temporarily removing a child from an activity or group time because he or she is caus-

ing harm or disruption, but is not having a temper tantrum or engaging in habitual antisocial behavior. The following scenario illustrates sitting apart.

> During circletime, Elka is enjoying tapping Brandon's back with her feet. She has been told to scoot back and keep her feet still. She refuses. Her kicking is becoming more vigorous and Brandon is becoming more unhappy. In this case, the adult might say, "Either keep your feet still or you'll have to sit away from the group so you can't kick Brandon any more." Elka continues her kicking game. The adult follows through. Elka is moved a little ways from the circle to a spot where she can still see the story but where she has no physical contact with the others in the group. She is told she may return when she can sit without kicking.

Elka will remain there until she signals that she is ready to return or the story is over, whichever comes first. Thus, she is able to practice the desired behavior in a setting in which she will have success. Sitting apart used in this manner is a way to rehearse sitting without kicking people, making it a logical consequence.

Besides the differences in behavior that prompt the two different consequences, sitting apart differs from time-out in the following ways. First, children are usually kept in the same area as the rest of the group and are permitted to return as soon as they are ready or when a new activity begins. In addition, children may initiate the procedure themselves, sitting apart for awhile (e.g., in their cubby or in the story corner) as a way to collect their thoughts or reduce stimulation for a brief time. It is expected that sitting apart will be used much more often than will time-out since time-out is reserved for only the most extreme behaviors.

## The Misuse of Time-Out

Unfortunately, what is basically a sound practice, giving children an opportunity to gain control of their own behavior, is frequently misused in many formal group settings. Such misuse may not only be ineffective but may be damaging to children (NAEYC, 1996). This has caused child-development experts to warn against the inappropriate use of time-out (Clewett, 1988; Duffy, 1996; Miller, 1984).

▼ **It is not appropriate to use time-out for every infraction of classroom rules.**

EXAMPLE: Ms. Hannah uses time-out a lot. When children push in line, the consequence is time-out; when children refuse to put on their coats to go outdoors, the consequence is time-out; when children are involved in a squabble over a toy truck, the consequence is time-out.

BETTER PRACTICE: Each of these circumstances would be better addressed using natural, logical, or appropriate unrelated consequences. When time-out is overused, it loses its effectiveness and violates the understanding that *time-out should only be implemented when children have a temper tantrum or engage in habituated antisocial behavior.*

▼ **It is not appropriate to use time-out as a threat.**
EXAMPLE: "Roberto, are you itching for a time-out? One more remark like that, young man, and you go into time-out." The teacher's threatening words clearly imply that if Roberto doesn't "shape-up" he will be banished from the room. The focus here is on coercing the child to obey rather than on teaching him how to do so.
BETTER PRACTICE: Threats undermine trust between adults and children. They damage children's feelings of worth and are incompatible with an authoritative approach to discipline. *Time-out is only effective when it is treated as a coping mechanism, not as a form of punishment.*

▼ **It is not appropriate to use time-out to humiliate children.**
EXAMPLE: When Margie, a third grader, acts silly in class, she is sent for time-out to the kindergarten room. The teacher says, "If you want to act like a kindergartner then you can go and sit with the kindergartners until you're ready to act your age."
BETTER PRACTICE: In this situation, time-out became a punishment, not a logical consequence. As a result it encompasses all the negative features of punishment outlined in Table 11–1. *Time-out should help children to feel better about themselves.*

▼ **It is not appropriate to use time-out in lieu of helping children learn better alternatives to problem behaviors.**
EXAMPLE: Jamal and Wally are arguing over who will get the next turn on the computer. They have had several disagreements already today. The teacher marches over and tells the children, "Take a time-out!"
BETTER PRACTICE: Although it can be frustrating to adults, children need many opportunities to practice appropriate social skills. Each disagreement the boys have is an opportunity to teach them alternate ways of getting what they want. Coaching the boys through their dispute or using a logical consequence such as having them plan together a way to share the computer would teach them more of what they need to know than does time-out. *Time-out should only be implemented when no other appropriate strategies are available.*

▼ **It is not appropriate for time-out to last longer than the time it takes for children to calm down.**
EXAMPLE: Roger had a time-out when he became hysterical over the fact that his boots wouldn't go on easily. The classroom aide was keeping an eye on him but gradually became caught up in what was happening in the classroom. The next time she thought about Roger, he had been in time-out for half-an-hour, even though he had quieted down 15 minutes ago.
BETTER PRACTICE: Time-out is not simply a means for getting "problem children" out of the way. It takes time for children to calm down. However, once that has happened, the purpose of time-out has been accomplished, and children should return to the mainstream of classroom activity. *Time-out should be used as cool-down time only. It should end when children are ready to return to the group.*

▼ **It is not appropriate to place children in time-out simply for adult relief.**
EXAMPLE: Amidst gales of laughter, Morgan and Sheldon have been purposely passing gas for the last several minutes. The after-school provider has talked to them twice about their behavior. Nursing a bad headache, she feels frustrated and out of sorts. Walking over to the children she announces, "Okay, you two, time-out!"
BETTER PRACTICE: There are times when adults feel like they can't put up with children's misbehavior for even 1 minute more. It may be tempting on these occasions to put children into time-out simply to get them "out of your hair" for awhile. This violates the purpose of time-out. *A better solution is for adults to take time-out themselves to regain their composure.*

It is clear from these examples that time-out can be mishandled and even abused. In order to avoid such misuse, some professionals avoid using time-out altogether. Unfortunately, that deprives some children of a potentially beneficial consequence for the extreme situations in which they sometimes find themselves. Although we believe all other avenues should be explored before instituting time-out, we also think that time-out can prove helpful for children who are out of control or who have well-established patterns of antisocial behavior. Having said this, we caution that *time-out is only effective when it is used sparingly, compassionately, and correctly.*

## SKILLS FOR IMPLEMENTING CONSEQUENCES

### Create Appropriate Consequences

*1.* **Anticipate consequences that fit the rules you make.** Generate in advance some possible consequences for common rules you expect to make. For example, if you are working with preschoolers, think about consequences you will use to enforce rules about sharing, sitting through group time, independence in dressing, and keeping quiet at nap time. If the children in your group are older, decide on consequences for resolving playground conflicts with peers and to enforce rules for paying attention, turning assignments in on time, and doing one's own work. These are all typical situations in which rule enforcement may be necessary. Think first of the natural consequences you might use. Then, plan out possible logical consequences. Consider unrelated consequences as a last resort. Generate ideas for positive consequences as well; consider forms of praise as well as earned privileges.

*2.* **Give children opportunities to generate their own ideas for consequences.** Just as children benefit from formulating some of the rules that govern their lives; so, too, do they learn from helping to generate potential consequences. This approach can be utilized with children as young as four years of age and continues to be effective throughout childhood (Hendrick, 1996). Introduce potential problem situations at a time when an infraction is not an issue, and help children consider open-ended questions such as "What should we do when people knock down others' blocks?" or "What should we do when people keep wandering around the room and interrupting those who are working?" or "What should we do when people push ahead in line without waiting their turn?" When youngsters weigh out the value of the rule and what action might lead to better compliance, they are directly experiencing the causal relationship between behavior and outcome. They also have an opportunity to explore why the rule is important and to discuss the role of consequences. It is not unusual for such talks to begin with children suggesting lurid, cruel, or totally unfeasible penalties. Do not reject these outright, but include them for analysis along with the other suggestions. Experience has shown that once the novelty of such outrageous notions has dissipated, children settle down to serious discussion.

*3.* **State consequences in the form of a warning.** Link the rule and the consequence in an either-or statement to the child: "Either choose your own place in the circle, or I will help you choose one," "Either put that puzzle together, or you won't be allowed to get another off the shelf," "Either stop whispering, or I'll have to separate you."

*4.* **Give warnings privately.** Children who are preoccupied with saving face as a result of public humiliation are not inclined to comply with rules. When giving warnings, move close to the child. Use a firm, quiet voice in explaining what will happen should the misbehavior continue. Remember to use the child's name.

*5.* **Point out the natural consequences of children's actions.** Provide information to children about the natural consequences of their behavior in a matter-of-fact, nonjudgmental tone. Children benefit from factual information such as, "When you shared the paste with Tim, he was willing to share the glitter with you" or "When you forgot to feed the fish, it meant they went hungry all day." Children tune out when they catch a hint of "I told you so" in your words or demeanor. Resist the temptation to tell children how smart you were all along. They will learn more from supportive explanations of the facts. Thus, instead of saying: "See. Those were never intended to go every which way in the box," say, "You've discovered that when the pieces go every which way, they don't fit in the box."

*6.* **Use the personal message, warning, and follow-through in order.** Do not vary this sequence or skip parts of it. To do so invalidates both the short-term and long-term benefits described earlier in this chapter.

*7.* **Allow children enough time to respond to each step of the sequence.** Approach discipline encounters with the idea of spending at least a

## SKILLS FOR IMPLEMENTING CONSEQUENCES—continued

few minutes. At each phase of the sequence, wait at least several seconds so children have time to comply if they are able. In situations you consider dangerous, stop the action physically and watch for signs that the youngster will obey. In less pressured circumstances, a time lapse of a few minutes between personal message and warning, then warning and follow-through may not be too long. For instance, Mr. Gomez, the social worker, has decided it is time for LouEllen to choose a work station rather than flitting in and out, disrupting everyone. He says: "LouEllen, you haven't found an activity that really interests you yet. It bothers me when you wander around because it is distracting. Pick one spot where you would like to work. I'll check on you in a minute or two to see which you decide on." Three minutes later, Mr. Gomez checks and finds that LouEllen still is unoccupied. Approaching her, he says: "LouEllen, you're still looking for something to do. You can either select a station, now, or I'll pick one for you." He stands by the child for 30 seconds or so. She does not move. At this point, Mr. Gomez enforces the rule by stating: "You still can't decide. Remember, I said you choose, or I'd choose. Now, we'll try bird calls." Mr. Gomez takes LouEllen by the hand and heads in the direction of the bird-call station.

Notice that in the prolonged interaction, a reflection prefaced each portion of the sequence. Reflecting helped to reclarify the situation each time and provided continuity from one step to the next.

Helping professionals who work in a team should be alert to fellow team members who are caught up in a limit-setting situation. When this occurs, other adults should provide supervision to the group until the follow-through has been completed. Professionals who work alone may have to follow through while simultaneously maintaining a global view of the room throughout the procedure. In addition, they should be prepared to tell other children in the group what to do until the situation is resolved. ("Dolores and I have to work this out. Review Chapter 4 until we are through").

**8. Finish the follow-through once you begin it.** Although it is important to give children enough

time to respond, it also is critical to enforce rules once you progress to the follow-through phase of the sequence. If you have begun to say, "Remember, I told you . . . " and the child vows never to do it again or says, "Okay, okay, I'll do it," continue to implement the consequence calmly and firmly. Do not get sidetracked at this phase by other issues. Reflect the child's concern or promise, thereby acknowledging it, and then point out that the consequence is for current behavior, not future actions.

**9. Communicate with other adults regarding rule enforcement.** Sometimes, children push the limits with one adult and then move on to someone else when a follow-through is forthcoming. In this way, the same child may engage in problem behavior all over the room with no real enforcement. Prevent this from happening by alerting other adults about the warning you have given a certain child. Do this within the child's hearing so that she or he is aware that the warning remains in effect even though the location has changed. Be receptive when other adults advise you of their warnings. Follow through on their warning if necessary. For example, if Kathleen has been warned that if she pushes another child on the playground one more time, she will have to sit on the side for 5 minutes, tell other adults that this is the case. Thus, anyone seeing Kathleen push again can enforce the consequence. This creates a much more predictable environment for Kathleen in which she will learn that pushing is unacceptable.

**10. Avoid power struggles.**

*Adult:* Yes, you will.

*Child:* No, I won't.

*Adult:* Yes, you will.

*Child:* No, I won't.

This is the common language of a power struggle. It typically occurs when adults try to implement consequences and children refuse to comply (Dreikurs and Cassel, 1972; Mendler and Curwin, 1988). The situation escalates when both become more adamant about their positions. Power struggles usually involve a verbal

*continued*

## SKILLS FOR IMPLEMENTING CONSEQUENCES—continued

battle and often happen in front of an audience. Unfortunately, there are no winners—both parties stand to lose something. The adult may gain temporary adherence, but may well have lost the respect of the child. On the other hand, if the child gains superiority for the moment by having the adult back down, he or she likely will suffer future repercussions from an adult who feels thwarted or ridiculed. There are a number of strategies you can use to circumvent this quandary:

a. Avoid making unnecessary rules.

b. Do not embarrass children in public—keep all communication between you and the child private.

c. Remain calm.

d. Avoid contradicting children's assertions. For instance, if the warning is "Either take a drink without snorting, or I will take your straw" and the child snorts, reach for the straw. If the child says, "But I didn't mean it," do not debate the purposefulness of the act. Instead, acknowledge the child's contention with the words, "That may be. . . ," and continue to implement the consequences: "You didn't snort on purpose. That may be. Remember, I told you, any more animal sounds and I would take the straw away. Now, I'm taking the straw."

e. Stick to the main issue. Do not allow yourself to become involved in an argument over extraneous details.

f. Discuss the power struggle privately with the child. This strategy is particularly effective with older children who have learned some attributes of compromise. Tell the child directly that a power struggle seems to be developing and that you would like to work out the issue in another way.

g. Avoid entrapment. When children begin to argue, refuse to become involved. You can do this either by quietly repeating the rule and the consequences and then resuming your normal activity, or by telling the child that you would be willing to discuss it later when you both are more calm.

**11. Help children understand legitimate differences between home rules and your expectations for their behavior in the program.**

Sometimes, there are real differences in expectations for what children are to do at home and what is required in the formal group setting. When this occurs, acknowledge the child's confusion or distress and point out that certain standards may be situation specific. "You're upset. At home you don't have to put things back on the shelf when you're through. That may be. It bothers me when there are puzzles all over the floor. Pieces could get lost. Here at the center everybody is expected to help clean up. Now please find a puzzle to put away."

*12.* **Teach children self-instructional strategies.** Help impulsive children exert greater self-control by teaching them to tell themselves "I can wait," "I am patient," "I am picking up the books, one at a time." Support youngsters' attempts at self-regulation with reflections of your own: "You waited very patiently," "You're picking up the books, one at a time."

*13.* **Acknowledge children's compliance with rules.** Use positive personal messages, effective praise, and earned privileges to help children recognize and repeat socially acceptable conduct. Do this for all children in the group, especially those who frequently misbehave. These latter youngsters need confirmation that they are indeed capable of achieving success in this regard.

*14.* **Actively attempt to alter children's faulty perceptions.** Give attention seekers appropriate attention. Provide power seekers with legitimate power. Confer on hopeless children your affirmation of their worth. Refer to the earlier portions of this chapter for ideas on how to accomplish these goals.

*15.* **Prepare in advance to use time-out.** Review the steps for time-out presented in this chapter so that when you have to use this consequence, you will know what to do. If you are working in a team, discuss time-out with your colleagues and come to some agreement about how the procedure will be conducted and how the classroom will function when a time-out is in progress.

*16.* **Use time-out only with children who are having a temper tantrum or who exhibit ha-**

## SKILLS FOR IMPLEMENTING CONSEQUENCES—continued

bituated **antisocial behavior.** Remember that time-out is a consequence of last resort. Avoid implementing it indiscriminately. Do not use it when another, logical consequence could better teach the child how to follow the rule. For instance, if Benny forgets to raise his hand before blurting out an answer, it would be better to tell him that he won't be called on until he does raise his hand than to send him into the hall for time-out.

 **Communicate with the Family**

**1. Listen empathically to family members who express frustration about their children's misbehavior.** There are times when parents and guardians need a chance to talk about their children's negative behavior without feeling guilty or embarrassed. At other times, they benefit from the opportunity to explore their concerns and to determine the relative seriousness of certain behavior problems they are encountering. In all of these circumstances, your role is to listen. Use the skills you learned associated with the facilitation dimension to provide support and convey your interest and concern. Refrain from giving advice. Sometimes, parents just need to talk things through. Refer really troubled family members to program personnel whose job responsibilities include such counseling.

**2. Help family members recognize signs that their children are achieving greater self-control.** Provide information to parents and guardians illustrating children's increasing abilities to delay gratification, resist temptation, curb their impulses, and carry out positive plans. Short notes home or brief verbal comments are ideal ways to convey such messages. "Today, An Sook offered her turn at the easel to a child who was anxious to paint before time ran out. She decided this all on her own. I thought you'd enjoy hearing about her growing awareness of the needs of others," or "Perry was very angry that our field trip was canceled. He wrote about this in his journal and suggested that our class develop a back-up plan for next time. I was impressed that he used such constructive strategies to deal with his frustra-

tion and just wanted you to be aware that he is making great progress in this regard."

**3. Clarify who will enforce rules when both family members and staff members are present.** Family members and professionals often feel uncertain about who should step in when both witness an incident in which the family member's child engages in disruptive behavior, such as refusing to get out of the car at drop-off time, resisting coming out of the bedroom during a home visit, or hitting another child in frustration. To avoid such confusion it helps to have preestablished guidelines for what to do when these things happen. Many families and professionals have found the following guidelines both fair and useful.

**a.** Parents are in charge of the "home front." In other words, when a professional is making a home visit or meets a parent and child in a public setting such as a store or at a concert, parents are in charge of their own children and should take action as necessary.

**b.** Program staff are in charge during program hours in program-related environments, including field trip sites.

**c.** Parents who are acting as volunteers or aides in the program take responsibility primarily for children other than their own and leave the handling of their own children to another volunteer or the professional. If this is an accepted procedure in the program, adults should be quick to attend to problems involving another volunteer's child. For example, if Mrs. Sanchez is attempting to read a story to a group of children and her own child continually interrupts, the professional or another volunteer should move swiftly to deal with the situation.

Be aware of the policies for your program and follow them. If no such policies exist, discuss this topic with fellow staff members and generate ideas about how to handle such incidents before the need arises.

When confronted with a situation in which you must intervene with a family member's child in that person's presence, act matter-of-factly and use the skills you have learned in this chapter. Say something to alert the person to your intentions if the conditions seem appropri-

*continued*

ate for such a remark. For instance, if Jeremiah refuses to get out of the car at drop-off time, you might say to his mom, "I'll get Jeremiah out of his car seat." Give Jeremiah a personal message and a warning. If you must proceed to the follow-through, calmly unbuckle the seat and lift the child out of the car, even if he is crying hard. Thank the parent for waiting for you and assure her that you will let her know how Jeremiah is doing later in the day.

**4. Communicate your discipline approach to families.** Families have a right to know how you plan to carry out discipline in the formal group setting. This includes the kinds of rules you will enforce with children and how that enforcement will take place. Such information may be shared with families at an introductory orientation, in a parent handbook, in newsletters sent home, at conference time, or in informal conversations with family members.

**5. Answer family members' questions about program-related discipline strategies honestly and openly.** Sometimes family members wonder, "How can you expect children to listen to all that talk," or "Why don't you make children apologize every time they hurt someone?" Answer such queries directly rather than trying to ignore them or responding in a defensive manner. One way to convey acceptance is to say something like, "That's a good question," or "A lot of parents wonder about that, especially at first," or "That's a common thing people want to know." Then proceed with your response. Refer to scientific evidence as well as personal philosophy. This helps people recognize there is an expert knowledge base to the profession and that we use it to guide our actions in the field. Thus, you might answer a parent's query regarding too much talk in the following manner. "That's a good question. All of the adults in our classroom are trying to help children develop self-control. Our goal is for children to learn to obey rules without constant adult monitoring. It's quicker to just say, "no" and sometimes children even listen, for the moment. Unfortunately, such success is usually short-lived. We have pretty good scientific evidence that shows that children learn self-control best when adults reason with them. That means we have to talk

about emotions, give reasons for rules, and point out what *to do* instead of focusing on what not to do. That is a lot of talk. But based on our understanding of child development and from results we've seen with children here in the center, we know it works. As the year goes on, let me know how you think it's going."

Recognize that family members may or may not agree with your response. However, they will have a better idea of why you do what you do and that your actions are based on more than personal opinion. In addition, you have kept the door open for further conversation in the future.

**6. Discuss with family members mutual ways to help children achieve self-control.** Interact with family members to identify strategies for use both at home and in the formal group setting to promote children's positive behaviors and to address problematic ones. One way to do this is to ask if such behaviors occur at home and what family members do about them. Make note of these strategies and whenever possible use them in creating a plan for working on the behavior in the formal group setting. If the behavior is not evident at home, talk with family members about what is happening in the program, describe current strategies, and ask for feedback and/or additional recommendations. Similarly, listen attentively when family members describe behaviors they observe in their offspring. Talk about the extent to which such actions manifest themselves away from home and what people in the program may be doing about them. Agree on one or two common strategies that family members and program professionals will use. Discuss a time table for checking in with one another to determine progress and alterations. If you are the professional in charge, carry out your plan, confirming the results with family members and making adjustments as necessary. If you are a student participant and a family member mentions such an instance to you, acknowledge the person's concern and say that you will bring the matter to the attention of the head teacher or some other appropriate person in the program. Follow through on your conversation. Later, get back to the family member, letting him or her know that you informed the appropriate person as promised.

## ▼ PITFALLS TO AVOID

Regardless of whether you are fostering children's self-discipline individually or in groups, informally or in structured activities, there are certain pitfalls you should avoid.

---

### Reluctance to follow through

Jonathan, you're having a good time up there. I'm worried you might fall. Climb down, please.

Jonathan, I mean it: climb down.

Jonathan, I really mean it this time.

Jonathan, how many times do I have to tell you to climb down?

Jonathan, am I going to have to get angry?

Jonathan, I'm getting mad.

OK Jonathan, I'm really mad now—climb down.

Jonathan, that's it! I'm going to carry you down.

---

This scenario illustrates a common problem for many adults: their reluctance to follow through on the limits they set. In an effort to avoid a confrontation, they may find themselves repeating a warning or some variation of it numerous times. They do this out of a mistaken desire to give children another chance to comply. In reality, adults undermine the predictability of the children's world when they vacillate in this way, giving them no way of knowing at what point the adult will no longer be willing to wait for compliance. In this situation, will that point be reached after the third warning, the fifth, or the sixth? Perhaps yesterday, the adult waited until the fifth warning; tomorrow, he or she may stop at the second. Children are not mind readers and can only predict an adult reaction by testing it out. The one way to avoid this situation is always to follow through after you give the first warning. In this way, children learn that the description of the consequence is a cue for them either to change their behavior or to expect the consequence.

**Relying on convenient or familiar consequences rather than finding one best suited to the situation.** It is natural for adults to feel frustrated or unsure when first implementing consequences. In an effort to ease this discomfort, they may utilize the same consequence over and over.

Frequently, they choose an unrelated consequence, such as removing children from a situation or having them lose a particular privilege. Although such consequences may stop the behavior for the moment, they do not teach an appropriate alternative for children to use in future situations. Over time, children may learn to anticipate the consequence and may decide that certain misbehaviors are worth it. This problem can be avoided by varying consequences to fit the situation at hand.

**Ignoring natural consequences.** Sometimes adults fail to recognize that a natural consequence has taken place and so institute additional, unnecessary consequences. For instance, Peggy accidentally stepped on her guinea pig. She was terribly distressed over the possible injury and attempted to soothe the animal. Her distress was the natural consequence of her error. The 4-H leader completely missed the importance of the natural consequence and proceeded to scold Peggy for being so careless, then told her she was not to hold the guinea pig for the next hour, even though the child already had recognized the negative results of her actions. Because the purpose of a consequence is to make children aware of the impact of their behavior, no further penalty was called for. Instead, the adult could have talked with Peggy about ways to avoid future injuries. Unfortunately, many adults do not think the natural aftermath of a child's mistake is enough. They cannot resist the desire to drive the point home by lecturing, moralizing, or instituting more drastic consequences (Mead, 1976). However, children who feel victimized are less able to change their behavior. Adults who ignore natural consequences by intervening either prematurely or unnecessarily fail to provide children with opportunities to learn from their own actions. The best way to avoid this pitfall is to survey the situation carefully and note any natural consequences that may have occurred. If these are evident, no further consequences should be imposed.

**Demanding cheerful compliance.** When adults follow through with a consequence, they should not expect children to comply cheerfully. This means that a child may pout, complain, mutter, or stomp as he or she adheres to the rule. Adults must keep in mind that the aim of the follow-through is to enforce the consequence. It is too much to insist that a child also put a smile on his or her face when doing something he or she really does not want to do. Adults create unnecessary confrontations when they insist that youngsters obey with pleasure. Although it may be annoying when children show their obvious distaste for the rule, attitude is not something over which adults have control, and it should not become a major issue in adult-child interactions.

**Harboring grudges.** After imposing a consequence, the adult's motto should be "forgive and forget." It is counterproductive to allow feelings of anger, resentment, or hostility for past actions to color present interactions. Once a consequence has been imposed, that is the end of it. Treat each new day as a fresh start. Furthermore, if on a particular day, one adult has had continual confrontations with the same child or is feeling frustrated or overwhelmed, she or he should take a break, or, in a team-teaching situation, ask someone else to deal with the child for a while.

**Insisting that children apologize.** Frequently, adults think that if they can just get children to say they are sorry, the problem is solved. With this in mind, they may force children to say "sorry" even when they don't really mean it. Unfortunately, this causes children to conclude that apologizing takes care of everything. They figure they can engage in any behavior they like as long as they are prepared to express their regret at the end. They also learn that insincerity is okay. Sorrow and remorse are emotions. We *cannot* make children experience these emotions on demand. Children *can*, however, be taught to make restitution for a wrong they have committed. This may involve having the child soothe the victim, get a wet cloth to wash the victim's bruised knee, or repair a broken object. Research has shown that children definitely grasp the concept of restitution prior to understanding the true significance of an apology (Hendrick, 1996; Irwin and Moore, 1971). As a result, concrete reparations have the most meaning for children. Only when children feel genuine remorse should they be encouraged to express their regret using the words, "I'm sorry."

**Avoiding time-out to save time.** In an effort to shorten the time-out period, adults may try to avoid enforcing a time-out when it is obviously necessary or may try to coax an out-of-control child into calmer behavior. Such approaches rarely help the child regain control. Instead, the youngster usually has recurrent difficulties throughout the day. Ulti-

mately, adults who had hoped to save valuable minutes spend more time in repeated confrontations with the child than they would have spent in working out the problem in the first place. A subsequent disadvantage is that children who have numerous negative interactions each day begin to lose self-esteem. This frequently leads to further misbehavior because children who feel bad about themselves are not likely to behave in positive ways.

**Talking too much in time-out.** Adults sometimes forget that the real purpose of time-out is to help children regain control or to interrupt a negative chain of rewarding circumstances. In a mistaken effort to hurry children along, they attempt to engage them in conversation. Conversation in the time-out area nullifies its neutrality. Remarks aimed at distracting, cajoling, or bribing children into being quiet are perceived by them as rewards: they have the adult's undivided attention for an unlimited period of time. Children should be rewarded for returning to the group, not for being separated from it. Talk during time-out should focus on explaining to children why they are in time-out and what they must do for time-out to be over. Other conversation is unnecessary and detracts from this process.

**Misjudging the length of time-out.** Children vary in how long it takes them to regain their composure sufficiently to return to the group. A child who is still sobbing and hiccuping, grinding his or her teeth, or clenching and unclenching his or her fists is not ready to leave time-out. Wait until the child seems more relaxed or says calmly that he or she is ready. Time-out should not be terminated prematurely, nor should it be prolonged beyond the period that it is useful for the child to remain in the area. This means that once children have regained their composure, they should be permitted to re-enter the mainstream of activity.

**Using time-out for inappropriate reasons.** Time-out is not simply a convenient way of eliminating unruly children from the group. Furthermore, adults who put children into time-out and then forget they are there, or who force children to stay in time-out after it has ceased to be beneficial, are misusing the technique. It also is inappropriate to implement time-out as a consequence for behavior that is not extreme. Time-out should only be used when a logical consequence or a less severe, unrelated consequence is impossible.

**Expecting too much, too soon.** Adults sometimes are nonplussed when they begin to implement consequences and children react by sassing, ridiculing their new way of talking, registering indifference to their feelings, or looking incredulous at what they are hearing. It is not unusual for children to say:

"So what?"
"I don't care how you feel."
"You talk funny."
"Don't try that stuff on me."

Such reactions are common among older children who may suspect helping professionals' motives; from children with whom adults have been working a long time and who become wary of the changes they perceive in the adult's manner; and from youngsters with whom such reasoning has seldom been used before. With children who are unfamiliar with the adult or who are inexperienced with this type of reasoning, the best tactic is to continue trying to build rapport and to keep using the skills so they become more commonplace. For children who are dubious about a changed style, it often is beneficial to tell them what you are trying to accomplish. Such youngsters become more tolerant when better informed: "I'm trying to find a better way to communicate and work with you. I'm still new at this and hope to improve so that I don't sound so stiff or funny." In any case, children's derision should not prompt you to abandon the technique prematurely. Continue the sequence to the follow-through, regardless of its reception. This shows children that adults mean what they say and that they will not be thwarted in their efforts to elicit appropriate behavior change. As adults become more adept, children will become more cooperative.

## ▼ SUMMARY

There are times when children do not follow the rules set by adults. They may misbehave because they lack the capability or the understanding to follow the rules, because adults have given mixed or unclear messages as to which behaviors are desired, or because they believe the rule to be unwarranted. On other occasions, youngsters misbehave because they are impulsive or because they have developed faulty self-perceptions. Adults can avoid or counteract these problems by making rules that take into account children's development, by clarifying or rephrasing their expectations, and by helping children develop positive, appropriate alternative behaviors. In addition, adults can monitor their own behavior so that their words are congruent with their actions, offer explanations for rules, and provide opportunities for children to become part of the rule-making process.

Adults enforce rules through the use of positive or negative consequences, which are aimed at helping children recognize the impact of their behavior on self and others. Positive consequences are instructive, have a clear relationship to the undesirable behavior, are based on a rational approach by both child and adult, and are humanely and matter-of-factly administered. Negative consequences for rule infractions are categorized as natural, logical, or unrelated. Natural consequences happen without adult intervention, logical consequences are directly related to the rule, and unrelated consequences (to be used only when the others are not possible) are manufactured by adults. The latter should be linked, at least in time, to the rule infraction. Adults must carefully weigh many factors in deciding which consequences to use in particular situations.

Adults implement negative consequences by reminding children of the rule, and then, if compliance is not forthcoming, repeating the rule and articulating a warning as an either-or statement. Adults pause long enough to give children an opportunity to correct their behavior on their own. If they do not, adults follow through with the consequence. All consequences should be implemented consistently and immediately.

Personal messages combined with the warning and follow-through allow adults to help children to learn to regulate their own behavior. As children become more accustomed to this process, they learn to respond to earlier phases, decreasing the necessity for adults to go through the entire sequence. At times, when one problem behavior leads to another, adults must exercise patience and implement appropriate consequences for each problem behavior.

The ultimate logical consequence, time-out, is used for children who are out of control or who exhibit habituated antisocial behavior. In this technique, the child is removed from the environment in which the behavior is occurring to a predetermined, secluded spot. There are special considerations to take into account when choosing a time-out area, when preparing children for time-out, and when carrying out this procedure. In addition to working directly with the children to foster self-discipline, it is important to join with parents as partners in the process.

## ▼ Discussion Questions

1. Describe six reasons why children misbehave and their corresponding solutions.
2. Discuss the faulty perceptions that may prompt children's misbehavior. Describe (without naming) a child you have observed whose behavior might indicate that such a perception was in operation. Explore strategies that might be employed to alter the child's perception.
3. Discuss the similarities and differences between positive consequences, negative consequences, and punishments.
4. Generate ideas for positive consequences and for natural, logical, and unrelated consequences for the following rules:
   a. Walk, don't run, down the hall.
   b. Throw the ball, don't kick it.
   c. Only use your own gym towel.
   d. Handle the computer keyboard gently.
   e. Walk on the sidewalk, not in the flower bed.
   f. Tell someone when you need help.
   g. Call people by their real names, rather than mocking their names.
5. Discuss the importance of following through on consequences as well as the results of not doing so.
6. Referring to the NAEYC Code of Ethical Conduct in Appendix A, identify the principles or ideals that will help you determine an ethical course of action in the following situations:
   a. A parent is walking with her child to the car. Suddenly the child dashes away from her into the busy parking lot. The parent, obviously frightened, grabs the child and smacks her three times saying, "You scared the life out of me. Never do that again." You are getting out of your car nearby when this happens and witness the interaction.
   b. You notice a colleague in the hallway arguing with her own child (four years old) who is enrolled in the program. The child is screaming and trying to pull away as the adult escorts him toward the door. Suddenly the adult turns the child around and gives him two swats on the bottom. You and several children from your class see the incident.
   c. A large group of third graders are playing T-ball on the playground. Another adult comes to you and says, "I have to go in now. I told Jeff he couldn't play T-ball any more today because of his fighting. Please make sure he doesn't play T-ball." The adult goes inside. There are 20 minutes left to play. A few minutes later Jeff, who has been watching from the sidelines, is called into the game by his friends. He looks to you and says, "I've learned my lesson. Can't I play?"
7. How would you respond to another helping professional who said: "The sequence takes too long. Besides, children can't respond to so much talking. Just tell them what's not allowed and be done with it"?
8. Identify any difficulties you have had in implementing the skill sequence described in this chapter. With classmates, brainstorm ways to improve.
9. Describe a time-out you have observed. Discuss why it was done, how it was done, and what its effect was.
10. Pretend you have been assigned to describe your center's use of time-out to a group of parents. Give a 5-minute presentation to a group of your classmates. Then, generate a list of questions parents might ask and discuss how you would respond.

## ▼ Field Assignments

1. Briefly describe a situation in which you will be working with children in the coming week. Identify any potential behavior problems that could arise within that circumstance. Using the entire skill sequence discussed in this chapter, write out the step-by-step process you would go through should such a problem actually occur. Later, record whether or not the issue came up. If it did, discuss how you handled it. Talk about any changes that were made in your original script and why they were made. Identify ways you will improve your performance the next time.
2. Write down three situations in which, as you worked with children, you did or could have used the entire sequence of skills from personal message to warning to follow-through. Begin by describing what the

child(ren) said or did to prompt your response. Then, record your exact remarks (regardless of their correctness). Briefly discuss the child's reaction. Next, discuss the strengths and weaknesses of your approach. Conclude by describing an alternate strategy that might fit the situation or another way you could have phrased your message.

3. Observe another adult in your field placement handle a child's inappropriate behavior. Describe the situation and how it was addressed. Describe the adult's approach and discuss how it compared with the strategies you have been learning about in this book.

4. Discuss your use (or that of a supervisor or colleague) of one of the family communication strategies listed in this chapter. Describe what you (or he or she) did, the role of the family member, and the outcome of the situation. Critique how the skill was used. Suggest how you would handle the same situation if it were to happen again.

# ▼Chapter 12

## Handling Children's Aggressive Behavior

## ▼ OBJECTIVES

*On completion of this chapter, you will be able to describe:*

▼ The four types of aggression.

▼ Differences between assertiveness and aggression.

▼ Factors that contribute to aggressive behavior.

▼ Adult actions that increase children's aggressive behaviors.

▼ Techniques that reduce children's aggression.

▼ A model for conflict mediation.

▼ Strategies for communicating to families about childhood aggression.

▼ Pitfalls to avoid in mediating children's conflicts.

---

Frog face.

Wart nose.

Take that back!

No, I won't. You take it back!

Slam! Bang! Hit! Kick! . . .

Mrs. Phillips comes running across the playground. Leroy and Robert are at it again, fists flying. She wades into the fray.

---

Inevitably, anyone working with children will be faced with such a scene. At these moments, helping professionals wonder why children act so aggressively, whether aggression is a natural part of growing up, and why some children are more aggressive than others. Most of all, they want to know what can be done about children's violent behavior.

## ▼ WHAT AGGRESSION IS

Aggression is any behavior that results in physical or emotional injury to a person or animal, or one that leads to property damage or destruction. It can be either verbal or physical (Bandura, 1973; Newman and Newman, 1997). Slapping, grabbing, pinching, kicking, spitting, biting, threatening, degrading, shaming, gossiping, attacking, reviling, teasing, breaking, and demolishing are all examples of aggressive actions. Although each of these behaviors has hurtful results, children engage in them for different reasons.

### Types of Aggression

In this book we will discuss four distinct types of aggression: accidental, expressive, instrumental, and hostile. Effective strategies for responding to each type vary. Thus, knowing their similarities and differences will enhance your ability to respond effectively when children are aggressive.

**Accidental aggression.** Often, without thinking, children hurt others in the process of their play. When this occurs, it is called **accidental aggression.** Stepping on someone's fingers while climbing the monkey bars, tagging a friend too hard in a game of hide and seek, telling a joke that unexpectedly hurts someone's feelings, or crushing a butterfly in an effort to keep it from flying away are all circumstances in which there is no conflict and the aggression happens by chance.

**Expressive aggression.** Expressive aggression is a pleasurable sensory experience for the aggressor. It occurs when a child derives enjoyment from a physical action that inadvertently hurts someone or interferes with their rights (Orlick, 1978). The aggressor's goal is not to get a reaction from the victim or to destroy something; instead, he or she is preoccupied with the enjoyable physical sensation of the experience. For instance, when Roger knocks down Sammy's building, he feels satisfaction in a well-placed karate chop; when Elizabeth laughingly bites Tulana, it is because it feels good; when Marvin rams his bike into the back of Jack's wagon, it is because he likes the sudden jolt he receives. Expressive aggression is marked by the absence of angry, frustrated, or hostile emotions. It is a playful or exploratory act that causes unintentional unhappiness in someone else.

**Instrumental aggression.** Instrumental aggression results when children engage in physical disputes over objects, territory, or rights and someone is hurt in the process. As children try to get what they want or defend what they believe to be theirs, they do not intend to harm anyone, but that is what happens. For instance, when Marsha and Celeste struggle over a rolling pin, their pushing and shoving leads to Marsha being smacked in the eye and Celeste having her fingers smashed. The result is two unhappy children, both of whom have been injured. Neither child started out trying to hurt the other; each simply wanted the rolling pin for herself. However, from lack of knowledge and skill, they eventually resorted to force to pursue their aims. In this case, the resulting aggression was a by-product of the girls' interaction, not its main purpose. Similar results happen when children resort to shouting, hitting, grabbing, or pushing to establish who has the next turn or who sits next to a favorite peer at circle time. Lack of premeditation and lack of deliberate intent to do harm are the two factors that distinguish instrumental aggression from more purposeful attempts to hurt people or reduce their

self-esteem (Berk, 1997; Hartup, 1974). The following list provides examples.

▼ *Instrumental aggression often occurs over objects:* Jessica and LaTesha both run to the swing at the same time. Each wants it for herself. They become involved in a heated argument over who can have it. Soon they are shoving and pushing. The goal of the children's actions is to gain possession of the swing. In the process of struggling toward that objective, aggression occurs.

▼ *Instrumental aggression often occurs over territory:* Raymond has taken over a large part of the block area to build his airport. He becomes upset when other childrens' block-roads cross into the space he has reserved for his building. In the subsequent dispute over who can build where, children start hitting. The goal of the children's actions is to establish control over territory in the block area. Unfortunately, the means they use to pursue that goal are hurtful.

▼ *Instrumental aggression often occurs over rights:* An argument breaks out as several children rush to the door all at once. Each wants to be the "line leader." In this situation, the children's main goal is to establish who will have the right to be first in line. The aggression that results is an unfortunate by-product of their efforts to achieve that goal.

**Hostile aggression.** Children who display **hostile aggression** experience satisfaction based solely on someone else's physical or psychological pain (Caldwell, 1977; Shaffer, 1994). Their hurtful actions are purposeful attacks that serve as retaliation for prior insults or injuries or as a way to get a victim to do what they want. Due to its deliberate nature, hostile aggression is different from all other types of aggression.

Children use hostile aggression to make themselves feel more powerful when they are threatened with loss of face or security or when they think someone is purposely trying to sabotage what they are doing.

**EXAMPLE:** Several fourth-graders are rushing to get to their lockers before the bell rings. In her effort to get in and out on time, Jean inadvertently knocks Claudia down. Before anyone can respond, Claudia, red faced, jumps up and runs into the classroom. Later, as the children line up at the water fountain, Claudia shoves Jean and says, "There, see how *you* like it."

Initially, Jean's behavior was an example of accidental aggression. However, Claudia interpreted it as a deliberate blow to her ego, which required her to pay Jean back at the fountain later in the day. By pushing Jean, Claudia felt they were "even," and her honor was restored. In this case, the act of pushing Jean is a premeditated, deliberate attempt to hurt her. Therefore, it is an example of hostile aggression. Unfortunately, this may begin a cycle of hostile retaliation between the two girls that could escalate over time.

## Assertiveness Versus Aggression

A socially acceptable alternative to aggression is **assertiveness.** Children display assertiveness when they engage in purposeful actions to express themselves or protect their rights while respecting the rights and feelings of others (Hegland and Rix, 1990; Slaby, et al., 1995). Assertive children behave in the following ways (Slaby, et al., 1995; Stocking, Arezzo, and Leavitt, 1980):

▼ Resist unreasonable demands: "No, I won't give you the eraser. I still need it."
▼ Refuse to tolerate aggressive acts: "Stop calling me names" or "No pushing."
▼ Stand up against unfair treatment: "You forgot my turn" or "Cutting in line is not allowed."
▼ Accept logical disagreements: "Okay, I see what you mean."
▼ Suggest solutions to conflict: "You can have it in a minute" or "I'll use it again when you're through."

Assertiveness is related to children's emerging sense of autonomy. You will remember from earlier discussions that children develop positive feelings about their own abilities when they can express themselves and when they can exert some control and influence over others. They also benefit from having opportunities to make some of their own decisions without always conforming to other's wishes. Toddlers are expressing their need to assert their will when they say "Me," "Mine," and "No." It is not by chance that these words are among the first that children learn and use.

Preschoolers also try out many strategies to expand their influence. Their widening circle of contacts gives them more frequent social opportunities that include both cooperation and confrontation. Because young children have not mastered all the social skills necessary to get along, their efforts to be assertive may take the form of aggression. Through observation, instruction, feedback, and practice, children learn the more constructive, socially acceptable behaviors that are associated with positive assertiveness. The early years therefore mark a crit-

ical period for children to learn to be assertive rather than aggressive (Slaby, et al., 1995).

Youngsters in grade school who fail to shift from aggression to assertiveness tend to be rejected by their peers and disliked by adults (Dodge, 1985; Rubin, 1980). Such reactions contribute to a reduction of self-esteem in aggressors. Aggressive reactions also limit their opportunities to practice other, more acceptable approaches. This increases the likelihood of hostile, angry feelings, which lead to further aggression. When such a pattern develops, it is difficult to break.

Obviously, it is important for children to learn to substitute assertiveness for aggression right from the start. How this can best be accomplished is more easily understood if you first know why and how aggression develops.

## ▼ WHY CHILDREN ARE AGGRESSIVE

In explaining the roots of aggression, scientists do not agree on how much can be attributed to biology and how much is a result of learning (Lorenz, 1966; Patterson, 1982). However, there is general agreement that, from infancy onward, children's aggressive behavior is shaped by both factors. There is no single cause of aggression.

### Biology

Some scientists believe that aggression is an instinctive component of human nature (Lorenz, 1966). According to this hypothesis, children are genetically programmed to be aggressive, particularly when safety or other basic needs are threatened. In addition, the presence of high levels of androgen and testosterone (male sex hormones) have been linked to aggressive impulses (Nottleman, et al., 1987; Olweus, 1980). This may explain, in part, why boys generally are more aggressive than girls and why boys who have higher concentrations of these hormones generally are more aggressive than boys with lower levels.

Temperament may also play a role in children's aggressive tendencies. For instance, infants who have irritable and nonadaptable temperaments are more likely to be aggressive in early childhood than babies who are more relaxed and flexible (Bates, 1982; Thomas, Chess, and Birch, 1968). Preschoolers who are temperamentally noisy, active, and distractible and who have difficulty adjusting to changes in routine, more often resort to aggression than children whose temperaments are more mellow. Such children tend to interact physically by hitting, touching, and grabbing objects from peers, whereas their quieter classmates stay more physically distant, avoiding interactions that may lead to aggressive outcomes (Berk, 1997; Soderman, 1985). From findings like these we know that biology contributes to childhood aggression, but it is not the only factor involved.

## The Frustration-Aggression Hypothesis

For some time, it was widely believed that frustration was the source of all aggression (Dollard, 1939). Today we still believe that a frustrated child is more likely to be aggressive than one who is contented, but we also know that other variables such as biology and learning prompt aggressive impulses as well (Shaffer, 1994). Alternately, a person can respond to frustration in ways that are nonaggressive. For instance, children may react to frustrating experiences by trying harder, requesting help, simplifying the task, giving up, or taking a break. Thus, frustration does not guarantee an aggressive response.

## The Cue-Distortion Hypothesis

Aggression sometimes results when children misinterpret neutral social interactions as hostile ones. For instance, when Trevor is hit from behind by a ball as he walks across the play yard, he may assume that someone did it on purpose even though the action was really the result of a wild throw. As explained earlier, any child could react to accidental aggression in this way. However, some children are more prone than others to respond as though others' actions are purposeful. Such youngsters are generally poor social observers. They find it difficult to interpret accurately other children's affective cues, such as facial expressions or words that would help them to understand no hostility was intended. As a result, they develop a history of not getting along with peers. Their interactions are marked by bickering, physical fighting, and false accusations. Gradually, they develop the self-perception that other children do not like them. This in turn causes them to expect hostility from age-mates (Dodge, 1986; Holden, 1997). When something bad happens they automatically attribute hostile motivations to others. Thus, even when the other children appear apologetic for the wild throw, Trevor feels obligated to retaliate. Trevor's aggressive response may then trigger counteraggression from the other children. This reinforces his impression that peers are hostile toward him. A vicious cycle becomes established, increasing the antagonism that exists between Trevor and the youngsters with whom he must in-

teract each day. Additionally, as Trevor's reputation for aggression becomes more firmly established, classmates may become less patient in dealing with him and be quicker to resort to physical force than they would with a less aggressive friend (Dodge and Frame, 1982; Shantz, 1986). All of these circumstances promote increased aggression among all the children involved.

## Direct Instruction

In many cases, adults actually tell children to use aggression to resolve a problem situation. This instruction has a powerful effect on children's behavior. For example, in an experiment involving children six to sixteen years of age, 75 percent of the children carried out an aggressive action in order to comply with adult expectations (Shanab and Yahya, 1977; Staub, 1971). "Hit her back," "Stick up for yourself," "Don't be a sissy," and "Prove you're a man" are common examples of such commands.

## Reinforcement

There are many ways in which children are rewarded for aggressive behaviors. One involves the reinforcement they receive when they hit, bite, scratch, taunt, or threaten in order to assert their will, and other children give way by withdrawing from the conflict, crying, or yielding to their wishes (Patterson, Littman, and Bucker, 1967). Success in one situation prompts the aggressor to repeat the behavior toward the same victim in the future. For instance, if Mary Jane teases Viola to the point that Viola gives up her place in line, it is likely that Mary Jane will try the same tactic the next time she wants something from Viola. As her rate of success increases, Mary Jane may generalize this approach to other children as well.

In addition, many aggressive children have low self-esteem and feel they are incapable of eliciting positive reactions from others. Their interactions with adults and peers are characterized by rejection, disapproval, humiliation, lack of affection, isolation, and retaliation (Feshbach and Feshbach, 1976). Such children fall back on the one sure way to get attention—aggression. The problem is made worse when adults generally pay attention to children only when they are aggressive (Clarke-Stewart and Koch, 1983). Since negative attention is better than no attention at all, children quickly learn to use aggression to get adults to notice them.

Another instance of reinforcement occurs when a child's aggression prompts reciprocal aggression from someone else. Over time, the aggressor comes to anticipate this predictable response and tries to elicit it on purpose. In this way, an aggressive pattern is established (Mussen, et al., 1990). For instance, ten-year-old Shavette knows how to get a rise out of her younger brother, Chad. All she has to do is chant "Chad is a baby, Chad is a baby" over and over. Before long, Chad will cry and rush at her in an effort to bowl her over. Laughing, Shavette can hold him at arm's length as he kicks helplessly. This chain of events bolsters her feelings of power and prompts her to repeat her actions in the future.

Additionally, aggression may be one of the few strategies available to children for creating a little excitement in an otherwise boring environment (Roedell, Slaby, and Robinson, 1976). Children are rewarded by the stir that comes from their actions. For instance, during a story he had already heard twenty times, Carl began poking his neighbor as a way to liven up the afternoon. This simple beginning set the stage for retaliation and an escalation of the negative behavior. As such, it became an exciting way to relieve the boredom.

Our discussion so far has focused on the reinforcement children may receive for aggression within the microsystem of home, school, or neighborhood. However, there is increasing evidence that macrosystem influences also are powerful reinforcers. Cross-cultural studies consistently indicate that some societies (or subcultures) reinforce aggression to a greater degree than do others, with predictable results. The United States is one such society. Violence permeates many facets of our lives. For example, Americans generally are permissive in their attitudes toward physical punishment (Belsky, 1980; Bukatko and Daehler, 1995). Weapons are easily available within the population and power assertion is a common means people use to address their grievances. Every day 135,000 children take a gun to school. Firearm violence—whether homicide, suicide, or accidental—is the third leading cause of death among children ages five to fourteen years (Children's Defense Fund, 1997). On a percentage basis, the incidence of rape, assault, robbery, and homicide is higher in the United States than in any other stable democracy (Shaffer, 1994). Yet, groups such as the Amish, who live within the boundaries of the United States but form their own communities within the society, strongly discourage aggression among their members. The result is few incidents of aggression at home or in the community. Thus we must realize that

a person's tendency toward aggression depends in part on the extent to which violent actions are supported by both micro- and macrosystem forces.

## Modeling

Another explanation for why children behave aggressively is that they learn how to be aggressive by watching others (Bandura, 1973; Patterson, 1982). The models they observe may be adults or peers in their family, at the center, at school, or in the community. Such models may be live or on film. For instance, children see television programs in which disputes are settled by violence; they observe Aunt Martha shake Tony in order to make her point; they watch peers and siblings use physical power as a successful means to get what they want. Children experience aggression directly when they are smacked, pulled along, or shoved as punishments for misbehavior.

All of these examples illustrate to children that aggression is an effective way to assert one's will. They also break down any inhibitions children may have regarding the use of force (Bandura, Ross, and Ross, 1963; Garbarino, 1995). It makes little difference that adults frequently admonish youngsters not to resort to violence or advise them to "act nice." Instead, for children, seeing is believing, so adults must realize that the old maxim "Do as I say and not as I do" is totally ineffective. Moreover, children are most likely to imitate notable or outstanding behaviors in others. Due to its violent nature, aggression stands out, generally overshadowing neutral or less dramatic prosocial behaviors. Unfortunately, the problem is further compounded because children exposed to aggressive models retain the effects long after a particular incident is over. They remember what they see and hear and are able to imitate it months later (Hicks, 1965). All of these factors contribute to the enormous influence aggressive modeling has on children's lives.

**Television and aggressive modeling.** Children witness aggressive models every day. One of the most pervasive sources of such modeling is what they see on television. Children watch a lot of TV, on the average, 21 hours per week (NAEYC, 1990). They watch programs designed for them as well as many aimed at adult viewers. (See Chapter 6, Supporting Children in Stressful Situations, for further information about the amount of television children watch and the violent content of the programs they see.)

The effects of televised violence on those who watch it have been studied more extensively than

▼ Table 12–1    The Television-Aggression Link: What Is the Connection?

**Children Develop a Sense of the World as a Threatening, Fearful Place**
The mean and dangerous world depicted on television heightens children's sense of insecurity, vulnerability, and mistrust. Such messages are conveyed through fictional programs as well as ones depicting real events.

**Children Acquire Distorted Views of the Effects of Violence on People and Animals**
Children conclude that hurting someone isn't serious but rather a source of amusement, since it is sometimes portrayed as funny.
Children believe that no one really gets hurt by aggressive actions, since the effects of violence on individuals and families is seldom presented accurately or completely.

**The Nature of Children's Play Changes**
Children tend to imitate the aggressive acts they have seen rather than creatively constructing their own play themes and episodes.
Children use program-related toys in imitative rather than imaginative ways, rehearsing characterizations and program scripts instead of making up their own.

**Children's Values Are Negatively Influenced**
Children conclude that violence is a normal and acceptable response to stress or uncomfortable emotions.
Children conclude that violence is an acceptable way to get what they want, since the characters they watch are reinforced for using those means.
Children come to believe that aggression is the best way to solve problems, since the only difference between the hero and villain is that the hero is stronger.
Children become less sensitive to the suffering of others in the real world.
Children more willingly accept violence perpetrated against others.

**Children's Behavior Becomes More Aggressive and Less Prosocial**
Verbal hostility, negative play interactions, violence on the playground, and the intensity of children's aggressive responses increase.
Sharing behaviors, enthusiasm for school, imaginative play, and helping behaviors decrease.

any other aspect of the media. The evidence accumulated from a wide variety of sources indicates that television violence has a harmful effect on child development and learning. In Table 12–1, we have summarized ways in which television violence contributes to childhood aggression (Frost, 1992; ICAVE, 1985; Liebert and Sprafkin, 1988; NAEYC, 1990).

### Lack of Knowledge and Skills

Children sometimes resort to aggression because they don't know what else to do when their goals are blocked or when they come under attack by another child. Thus, children may resort to physical violence after they run through their entire repertoire of social skills and still fail to get what they want or protect something important to them (Goleman, 1995). Immaturity contributes to this problem, but so does lack of experience. Children who have few

opportunities to practice nonviolent strategies or to learn the skills associated with assertiveness are most likely to be aggressive (Carlsson-Paige and Levin, 1992).

## ▼ THE EMERGENCE OF AGGRESSION

The causes of aggression are varied and complex. Any combination of the factors just described may result in antisocial behaviors. The particular form in which aggression is manifested also depends on differing personal variables such as maturity, experience, and gender.

### Maturity and Experience

How children express aggression changes with their cognitive maturation and experience. It is about age two that aggressive actions (other than accidental incidents) begin to emerge (Hay and

Ross, 1982). Most aggression exhibited by children aged two through six is instrumental, with the majority of violent outbursts happening in disputes over materials and toys (Humphreys and Smith, 1987). The aggression of older children is more likely to be hostile (Hartup, 1974). These variations occur for several reasons.

**Aggression in early childhood.** Toddlers and preschoolers are impulsive. When they want something, they go after it immediately. They don't stop to think about what is right or what is wrong. Children this age also have limited language skills and know only a few strategies for getting what they want. If asking or saying "please" does not achieve their aims, they often resort to physical force because they don't have any other constructive strategies to rely on. In addition, when toddlers and preschoolers are asked to share, their egocentric view of the world makes it hard for them to give up objects. All of these developmental characteristics increase the likelihood that young children may hit, grab, kick, or bite to get what they need or to defend whatever they believe is theirs.

Interestingly, although preschoolers' arguments are often highly emotional, their less developed memory skills keep them from holding a grudge. For them, once a dispute has been resolved, the episode is over. They tend to resume their play almost as if nothing had happened. They do not see conflict as a challenge to their honor, so no retaliation is necessary. Thus, conflicts among very young children, although very intense, tend to blow over quickly (Smith, 1982).

Instrumental aggression reaches its peak during the preschool years. Disagreements of this sort are so common that they comprise the largest number of aggressive encounters a child will experience during his or her entire lifetime (Hartup, 1974).

**Aggression throughout the elementary years.** The greater cognitive and language skills of school-age children lead to a reduction in instrumental aggression. Yet, these same, more advanced abilities contribute to an increase in hostile aggression. This is because grade-school children more clearly recognize the negative motives others may have toward them and have memory skills that are well-developed enough that they can remember angry encounters long after they are over (Flavell, 1963). Because these children are more aware of the reciprocal nature of relationships, they also are more likely to

value "getting even." This is particularly true of six-, seven-, and eight-year-olds, who, when aggression is aimed at them, have great difficulty differentiating accidental from intentional acts. Consequently, they respond to any hurtful behavior as if it were purposeful, regardless of whether or not it actually was (Coie, et al., 1991; Dodge, Murphy and Buchsbaum, 1984). During the later elementary years, youngsters begin to make these distinctions and respond less aggressively if it is clear to them that a hurtful incident was not deliberate. Another reason why instrumental aggression becomes less frequent as children mature is that youngsters eventually figure out that negotiation is a relatively painless and more effective way to achieve the goals they previously addressed through forceful means (Shantz, 1987). For them, getting into a physical fight over an object or right is not worth the bother or the social costs it might incur.

Due to their past experience, older children also shift from physical to verbal strategies. Their increased facility with language makes the verbal taunt a satisfying weapon that leaves no visible traces. Also, the probability for hostile aggression intensifies as rivalry among peers increases. Children between the ages of six and twelve spend much of their time comparing themselves with agemates. Consequently, it becomes more common for them to feel threatened by the accomplishments of peers and to try to build themselves up by tearing others down. As a result, physical fighting lessens during the elementary-school years, but verbal disputes increase. Minor disagreements or misunderstandings can quickly escalate to expressions of hostile aggression through insults, baiting, and rejection (Goleman, 1995).

Finally, there is evidence that aggression becomes a somewhat stable attribute over time. The amount of aggressiveness children display as preschoolers tends to carry through into grade school (Olweus, 1987). Similarly, a child's characteristic level of aggressiveness at about age eight is a reasonably good predictor of his or her tendency toward aggression in adulthood (Tremblay, 1994). Thus, the aggressive patterns children establish early in life have a powerful, continuing influence on their development.

## Gender Differences in Aggression

One question often asked is whether there are differences in aggressive behaviors between boys and girls. A number of studies have shown that boys are more aggressive than girls and that these differences are apparent in children as young as two years of age (Hyde, 1984). Males instigate aggression—both verbal and physical—more often than females do and are more likely to strike back when aggression is aimed at them. Boys also find themselves the targets of aggressive behavior on more occasions than do girls (Darville and Cheyne, 1981; Maccoby and Jacklin, 1980). Sex differences in aggressive actions are found in all social classes and all cultures (Parke and Slaby, 1983).

Some researchers suggest that the male's greater concentration of androgen and testosterone, as well as his greater physical strength and more vigorous motor impulses, are the biological reasons for this difference (Jacklin, 1989). Others point out that learning also is a factor because aggressive behavior is more approved and reinforced for boys than it is for girls (Berk, 1997; Bukowski, 1990). Girls who rely on physical aggression tend to be rejected by peers and disliked by adults (Fagot and Hagan, 1982). It is more socially acceptable for girls to scold, gossip, resist, reject, and argue than it is for them to punch and kick. In addition, although both boys and girls frequently are reprimanded for physical aggression, boys tend to be more successful than girls in achieving reinforcement for physical violence. When little boys hit, adults say "Boys will be boys"; when little girls hit, they are scolded for acting inappropriately. On the other hand, boys who engage in verbal aggression may be treated with scorn and labeled as sissies; girls who practice the same techniques are tolerated. In this way, the stereotypes of the "tough guy" and the "shrewish female" are perpetuated.

As the previous discussion illustrates, most children will at times exhibit aggressive behavior—some more, some less. Although aggression may seem inevitable, it is possible and desirable to reduce the amount of hurtful behaviors children display. How well children learn alternatives to aggression depends a great deal on adult intervention. Most adults agree that this is an important responsibility for them to assume, but often are at a loss about what to do. As a result, they may unwittingly choose strategies that stimulate or prompt aggression rather than diminish it. Thus, helping professionals must learn not only which strategies are useful, but which ones to consciously avoid. Fortunately, there are substantial research data that clearly differentiate effective techniques from those

that are detrimental. We will explore each of these, beginning with those that should be discarded.

## ▼ INEFFECTIVE STRATEGIES ADULTS TRY TO REDUCE CHILDREN'S AGGRESSIVE BEHAVIOR

### Physical Punishment

Many adults adhere to the old adage "Spare the rod and spoil the child." Their response to children's misbehavior, including those instances when youngsters exhibit aggression, is to resort to aggression themselves by using physical punishment. The assumption that guides their actions is that children will learn to adapt their behavior to adult standards in order to avoid the pain of a spanking (Dobson, 1987). However, these ideas are not borne out by the research.

A wealth of evidence shows that physical punishment actually increases, rather than limits, children's use of aggression (Eron and Huesmann, 1984; Feshbach, 1980). There also is documentation that such effects are long lasting. The more frequently and the more severely children experience physical punishment when they are young, the more aggressive they are as adolescents (Farrington, 1993). Several factors contribute to these outcomes.

First, when adults rely on spanking, slapping, shoving, pinching, shaking, or pulling children roughly, they stand out as aggressive models for youngsters to imitate. Their actions demonstrate the power of aggression as a means of asserting one's will. From such episodes, children quickly discover that "might makes right" and that aggressive solutions are effective ones (Riak, 1994).

**SITUATION:** Miss Chang had tried everything to get four-year-old Rose to stop pinching when she became angry. She had talked to Rose, made her sit out, scolded her, and warned her that other children would not want to play with her, but Rose continued to pinch. Miss Chang felt stymied. Finally, in exasperation, she said: "Rose, you don't seem to understand how much pinching hurts. . . . There" (pinching Rose). "Now, you see what I mean."

Miss Chang hoped that by pinching Rose, the child would learn her lesson. Although Rose did learn a lesson, it was not the one Miss Chang intended. Rose found out that being pinched was painful, but she also noted that Miss Chang used pinching to make her point. Rose concluded that to get away with pinching she simply had to be bigger, stronger, or older than the victim. She resolved to limit her pinching to younger, smaller children in the future.

A second problem with Miss Chang's approach to Rose was that even if the child recognized that pinching was inappropriate, she had no idea of what to do instead. Miss Chang failed to model a nonaggressive alternative to pinching. Children who are subjected to physical punishment for their aggression see aggressive solutions to problems, not nonaggressive ones. Consequently, they have a hard time picturing a substitute for their own aggressive actions. This makes it less likely that their aggression will decrease.

A third negative outcome of physical punishment is that children view it as a form of retaliation. They assume that adults use hurtful actions to get even with children for doing things they don't like. Thus, Rose may conclude that Miss Chang pinched her in revenge for making her angry. Many youngsters quickly adopt this same retaliatory behavior with their peers (Riak, 1994). If a classmate does something that displeases them, they strike back aggressively as a form of punishment. When children think and act in this way, hostile aggression increases.

Finally, when children are punished physically, they focus primarily on their own discomfort, not on the impact their misbehavior may have had on another person. Thus, Rose, who is pinched for pinching others, concentrates on her own pain, not on the pain of her victims. This egocentric focus adds to the difficulty of dealing with the child's hostile aggression because hostility can be reduced only when children begin to feel empathy or concern for others.

Although a sharp pinch interrupts Rose's negative behaviors for the time being, her compliance is at the adherence level. Continual surveillance by the adult will be required if Rose's obedience is to be maintained. Miss Chang's action did not help Rose internalize values that are inconsistent with aggression. If children are to move beyond the adherence level, adults must implement consequences that contribute to children's abilities to reason and to understand how their behavior affects others.

The undesirable effects just cited make a strong case against the practice of physical punishment. Unfortu-

nately, even though few helping professionals advocate striking children in anger, adult aggression is practiced and even mandated in many formal group settings under the rubric "corporal punishment."

**Corporal punishment in the United States.** Physical punishment has been banned in prisons, in the military, and in mental hospitals, but it is still practiced in elementary, middle, and high schools throughout this country. This makes schools the only institutions in the United States in which striking another person is legally sanctioned. Paddling children in schools has been declared constitutional by the United States Supreme Court (*Baker v. Owen*, 1975; *Ingraham v. Wright*, 1977), and 23 out of the 50 states still permit school personnel to use "reasonable force" against children as a way to maintain discipline (Yorker, 1994). The majority of reported incidents involve children in the elementary grades, children with learning and mental disabilities, children of color, children from low-income families, and youngsters of small physical stature attending middle school (Ball, 1989; Zirpoli, 1990). In 1995, more than 1 million such cases were recorded. The majority of schools that permit spanking require written permission from a child's parents prior to corporal punishment being used with that child. Interestingly, a significant number of parents provide this consent. With so much support from government, schools, and parents, you might conclude that corporal punishment must be an effective strategy for controlling children's behavior in formal group settings. Nothing could be further from the truth.

**The case against corporal punishment.** The consensus of medical, psychological, and educational researchers is that **corporal punishment** yields *no* positive outcomes. It is neither necessary nor useful and is, in fact, counterproductive to children achieving self-control (Cryan, 1987: NCACPS, 1994). For instance, the National Center for the Study of Corporal Punishment and Alternatives in Schools reports that children subjected to corporal punishment in school become more aggressive, coercive, and destructive over time (Hyman, 1990). Increased incidents of vandalism, attacks against teachers, and more disruptive student behavior in the classroom, in the halls and lunchrooms, and on the playground have been reported (Ball, 1989). Possible explanations for such trends include the obvious fact that, regardless of how the situation is structured, the person administering corporal punishment is modeling aggressive behavior as a way to deal with another human being. This has several potential outcomes:

1. Children whose behavior already is out of bounds will not learn alternatives to aggression from methods so closely resembling their own approach to a problem situation: physical force.
2. Youngsters can become so accustomed to physical pain that such pain is no longer important to them, becoming useless as a deterrent to future violence. In addition, habitual offenders may interpret their ability to withstand the paddling without flinching as a badge of honor. This increases their status with peers, causing offenders to repeat their provocative behavior.
3. The use of corporal punishment often serves as a stimulus for counterattacks by the child in the future.
4. The availability of corporal punishment discourages teachers from seeking more effective, alternate means of discipline.

Thus, corporal punishment benefits neither its recipients nor the adults who carry it out. Furthermore, paddling has undesirable long-term side effects for children. Why, then, is corporal punishment still common practice? The answer involves a complex amalgamation of politics, societal beliefs regarding the value of so-called old-fashioned discipline, and lack of awareness of how else to control children's behaviors (Hyman, 1990). Exasperated and at their wit's end, some teachers and administrators use spanking by default because they are at a loss for what else to do to maintain order in the classroom (Gootman, 1988).

The latter issue is of particular significance because people can learn nonviolent alternatives. There *are* school districts, even in states in which corporal punishment is legal, that prohibit its use. It has been found that teachers and children are able to function effectively in such settings regardless of whether they are in rural, suburban, or urban areas (Dunne, 1990; Hyman, 1990). Although each of these schools has its own approach to positive discipline, there are certain tenets to which they all subscribe. First, school personnel make the basic assumption that each child has the capacity to solve problems. Consequently, they believe that children can learn appropriate behaviors if they know what to expect and if rules and consequences are enacted

in an authoritative rather than authoritarian manner. A second principle is that the best way to improve school discipline is to improve school climate. Taking a preventive rather than a remedial stance to discipline is a third point of agreement. Some of the specific ways in which these principles have been implemented across the country include the following (Clarizio, 1981; Coletta 1994; Gootman, 1988; Hyman and D'Alessandro, 1984):

> Providing a clear orientation to pupils and parents about school programs, school rules, grading systems, and special services.
> Developing school rules that are reasonable rather than arbitrary.
> Including staff, children, and parents in developing a school-wide discipline plan.
> Welcoming parents at the school or center and encouraging them to become involved in program activities.
> Enforcing rules firmly, fairly, and matter-of-factly.
> Training teachers and administrators in authoritative classroom management techniques.
> Making the curriculum relevant to pupils.
> Providing feedback to students about their behavior.
> Teaching children how to express emotions appropriately.
> Creating a positive verbal environment.
> Effectively implementing rewards and consequences.
> Using democratic procedures for solving classroom problems.
> Using therapeutic approaches for some behavioral problems.

Other effective techniques that preclude paddling involve the development of well-planned alternative-school programs, in-school suspension, the appropriate use of time-out, and peer and cross-age counseling.

From this discussion, it can be seen that there are many alternatives to corporal punishment. The pursuit of these is critical because not only does spanking have the potential for hurting young children, but it does not promote development of self-respect or teach children substitute behaviors—two primary building blocks of self-control. Finally, corporal punishment violates the NAEYC Code of Ethical Conduct (see Appendix A, Section 1). This code states that " . . . we shall not harm children. We shall not participate in practices that are disrespectful, degrading, dangerous, exploitative, intimidating, psychologically damaging, or physically harmful to children." Given the damaging outcomes of corporal punishment and the viable alternatives available, the authors believe there is no justifiable reason for helping professionals to slap, spank, or otherwise inflict pain on children in an effort to control their behavior in the formal group setting.

## Ignoring Aggression

Sometimes, adults ignore children's aggressive acts in the hope that these behaviors eventually will go away. This is a mistake. Numerous studies have shown that when adults ignored children's aggressive behavior, aggression increased (Lefkowitz, 1977; Patterson and Stouthamer-Loeber, 1984). Children assumed that adults who could stop the aggression but did not were, in fact, condoning it. Inaction by an adult encourages an aggressor to persist and prompts victims to yield (Smith and Green, 1975). This creates a permissive atmosphere in which both the aggressor and victim learn that aggression has its rewards (Slaby et al., 1995). Aggressive children continue unabated, and children who cannot depend on a protective adult eventually begin to counterattack. As children's counterattacks become more successful and they are less frequently victimized, they begin to initiate aggressive acts toward others (Patterson, Littman, and Bucker, 1967). In this way, unchecked aggression in a group setting not only perpetuates itself, but escalates.

## Catharsis

Some people believe that every now and then, children (who are not feeling particularly aggressive at the time) should be given opportunities to engage in controlled aggression. The aim is to help children "drain off" aggressive tendencies, thereby averting future aggressive incidents. With this in mind, adults give children toy weapons or violence-oriented action figures, in the hope that children who express aggression in their play will not resort to aggression in real-life interactions. This process is called **catharsis.** It assumes that aggression results from internal urges that build over time to dangerous levels, and which require venting. This is analogous to thinking of the child as a tea kettle, who must periodically let off steam or risk exploding. Unfortunately the analogy does not hold true. As we have discussed, aggression is not simply hor-

monal, it involves learning as well. As a result, research evidence shows that acting out aggression, or experiencing it vicariously by watching others commit antisocial acts, encourages rather than discourages aggressive behaviors (Berkowitz, 1993). For instance, children exhibited a significant increase in verbal and physical attacks after playing with aggressive toys such as guns. However, aggression did not rise when children played with neutral materials (Feshbach, 1970; Turner and Goldsmith, 1976). Moreover, children who saw violence demonstrated on film imitated the violence in their play (Bandura, Ross, and Ross, 1963; Murray, 1980). These youngsters also were less likely to consider violence inappropriate (Comstock, 1980). It has been hypothesized that this occurred because the play actually served to instruct children in how to be aggressive and that the aggression felt good, providing reinforcement (Yarrow, 1983). In either case, it is clear that children who play at aggression tend to be more aggressive than children who do not.

## Displacement

There are those who think that the way to deal with children who are angry and aggressive is to have them displace their emotions from the original source of anger to some unrelated target. For instance, they would encourage a youngster who was frustrated with a playmate to leave that situation and pound some clay, punch a pillow, or smack a Bobo doll as a way to express his or her feelings. Once these actions were carried out, the adult would assume that the child's anger was resolved and that his or her need to express that anger had been satisfied. The evidence is to the contrary.

Children who are taught that **displacement** is the ultimate means of handling angry feelings continue to believe that aggression is an effective response to problems (Berkowitz, 1993). They do not learn how to deal with the real source of their emotions (such as lack of cooperation from a peer) and fail to develop strategies for confronting problems constructively or for preventing problems in the future. It is not surprising that such children eventually become frustrated at never having an opportunity for direct resolution and so become increasingly hostile.

Additionally, as children mature, they may shift the "safe target" chosen by an adult to one of their own choosing, such as a child down the street, a family pet, or a younger sibling. Although displacement of angry feelings from a person or animal to an inanimate object is an appropriate first step in teaching some children how to cope with their emotions, it is not an adequate solution in and of itself (Slaby, et al., 1995).

### Inconsistency

A fifth ineffective means of dealing with children's aggressive behavior is to be inconsistent. Adults who are haphazard in their approach promote increased aggression (Hom and Hom, 1980; Parke and Slaby, 1983). "Coming down hard" on one child while avoiding confrontation with another, or sticking with the rules today and ignoring them tomorrow, leads to confusion and frustration for children (Stein and Kostelnik, 1984). In addition, this sets up a pattern of intermittent reinforcement for the aggression. Intermittent reinforcement means that rewards (when a victim yields, when the child gets a predictable rise out of an adult, or when adults overlook violent transgressions) do not follow a predictable pattern, and so children never know whether or not a reward is forthcoming. The only way to find out is to try it. Even if punishment is the result now, there still is no guarantee that such will be the case later. Children therefore persist in seeking undesirable rewards. This, then, is a potent pattern of reinforcement, which leads to continued aggression.

It is obvious that physical punishment, permissiveness, catharsis, displacement, and inconsistency all contribute to, rather than reduce, aggressive behavior in children. These methods fail because they allow the aggression to continue and/or because they fail to provide children the opportunity to learn acceptable alternatives for future use.

## ▼ EFFECTIVE STRATEGIES ADULTS USE TO REDUCE CHILDREN'S AGGRESSIVE BEHAVIOR

Strategies found to be effective in decreasing children's aggression are those that teach children how to exert their will nonaggressively as well as how to respond assertively to the aggression of others. Just as children learn to be aggressive through modeling, reinforcement, and instruction, they can learn to be nonaggressive through these same channels. Such learning takes place whether a child is in the role of aggressor, bystander, or victim. In all cases, the key to reducing children's aggressive behavior is to help them internalize values and methods of

interacting that are incompatible with violence (Slaby, et al., 1995).

### Modeling

There are two ways adults can influence what behaviors children imitate. First, they can model nonaggression through their own behavior. For instance, when children see adults talking about problems, reasoning with others, and making compromises, they are likely to view these approaches as desirable alternatives to aggression (Bandura, 1989). Moreover, when adults treat children calmly and rationally regardless of the situation, youngsters gain firsthand experience by watching someone adopt a nonaggressive solution to a problem. In both cases, adult modeling provides a standard of peaceful conduct for children to emulate.

Besides serving as appropriate models themselves, adults can screen out some of the aggressive models and materials to which children are exposed. Toys, games, films, books, pictures, television programs, and live demonstrations that depict aggression are powerful, pervasive teachers. It has been shown that when these aggressive models and materials are reduced, children's aggressive acts become fewer (Bandura, 1989; Potts, Huston and Wright, 1986; Yarrow, 1983). Although helping professionals cannot eliminate all of the aggressive influences in children's lives, they can limit aggressive models within the formal group setting and help children find satisfaction in nonaggressive play. Thus, ray guns, light sabers, plastic bazookas, punching bags, and slingshots have no place in child-care centers or schools, nor do posters, books, or films that portray violence as a way to solve problems.

### Reinforcement

As with any other behavior, children are more likely to repeat nonaggressive strategies for making their desires known when those strategies are rewarded. One type of reinforcement adults can use is to acknowledge children's efforts with positive personal messages or other forms of effective praise. Positive personal messages are especially helpful because they identify specific behaviors and give children a reason for why such behaviors are desirable. Adult praise gives youngsters the important information that their peaceful behavior is both appropriate and appreciated. Another way children find such behavior rewarding is when it helps them to successfully reach their goals. Hence, Pablo, who asks for a turn with the kite rather than grabbing it, and who ultimately gets a chance to use it, is likely to incorporate asking into his future repertoire of social behaviors. Even though he occasionally is turned down, if, over time, his requests are honored more often than not, he will learn that asking is a useful approach.

### Direct Instruction

The following are a number of instructional techniques adults can use to minimize children's aggressive behavior.

**Reducing the frustration in children's lives.** Because frustration makes aggression more likely to occur, its reduction leads to fewer aggressive incidents. Appropriate structuring of the physical environment is an excellent way to reduce potential frustration. For example, children are less aggressive when there are sufficient materials for them to use and when the physical environment allows freedom of movement without overcrowding or interference among activities. Routines that eliminate excessive waiting and sitting lessen frustration too. Children are less likely to experience frustration when adults keep rules to a minimum as well as warn them in advance about changes in the daily routine. Frustration also is reduced in classrooms where cooperation is emphasized over competition. Finally, children are less likely to resort to physical force when adults provide sufficient support during free-choice times or in activity areas where aggression is liable to occur, such as on the playground or in the block area (Hendrick, 1996; Slaby, et al., 1995).

**Helping children feel more competent.** Children who feel they have some control over their lives are less likely to resort to aggression as a way to establish power. When adults give children choices, help them to develop their skills, and avoid insisting on perfection, they influence children to be less aggressive (Hendrick, 1998; May, 1972).

**Fostering empathy among children.** Aggressive children are often unconcerned about or unaware of the harmful effects their behaviors have on others (Bryant, 1982). However, such youngsters can be taught to recognize people's emotions, to imagine how victims feel, and to identify the negative consequences of their aggressive actions. When this happens children are less likely to hurt one another or to gain pleasure from the discomfort of a victim (Feshbach and Feshbach, 1982). The strategies identified in Chapter 5, Responding to Children's Emotions, are effective measures to achieve these aims.

**Teaching children prosocial behaviors.** Kindness, helpfulness, and cooperation are incompatible with aggression. When adults actively teach children these behaviors, aggression diminishes (Caldwell, 1977; Marion, 1995). Because this is such a powerful strategy, all of Chapter 13 is devoted to it.

**Helping children recognize instances of accidental aggression.** Frequently, victims of accidental aggression react as though the aggression were intentional. Providing accurate information changes the child's view of the purposefulness of the act and reduces the necessity for retaliation (Dodge, Murphy, and Buchsbaum, 1984; Holden, 1997). Adults defuse the situation when they identify the victim's feelings and clarify the accidental nature of the incident ("You were surprised to get hit. It hurt. He wasn't trying to hurt you; he was trying to keep the ball from going out of bounds" or "You look upset. She didn't mean to snap at you. She isn't feeling well today").

This kind of information does not excuse the aggression but rather attempts to explain its unintentional nature. Added benefits occur when adults point out to the aggressor the impact that the action had on the victim, and, when possible, enlist the aggressor's aid in repairing the damage: "When you jumped for the ball, you knocked Jesse over. His knee is scraped. Come with us and we'll fix it up together" (Schickedanz, Schickedanz, and Forsyth, 1982). Using this approach helps both victim and aggressor better understand the context of the incident and gives them a constructive way to resolve it.

**Rechanneling children's expressive aggression.** When carried out safely, kicking, pounding, throwing, and knocking down are appropriate physical activities for children. Youngsters derive satisfaction from mastering the environment and their bodies by kicking or throwing a ball as hard as they can, from pounding at the workbench, or from crashing down something they've built.

Problems arise when children go beyond these safe situations to gain pleasure from ones that are potentially damaging to people or property. Thus, Rodney may become so engrossed in his play that he fails to notice that the ball he is throwing is interfering with other children's games or that the blocks he is pushing over are someone else's prized construction. Likewise, when he chases Joel, he may assume that Joel, in spite of his protests, is experiencing the same thrill that he is. Because of their potentially destructive outcomes, these circumstances represent expressive aggression and require adult intervention. The focus of that intervention should be on allowing the child to continue the pleasurable physical movement while structuring the situation so it becomes harmless. This is accomplished through substitution. *Substitution* consists of replacing the unacceptable target of the child's expressive aggression with one that is more suitable (Parke and Slaby, 1983). Rodney could be redirected to throw the ball away from the group, to tumble only his own block tower, or to chase a more willing playmate. Rodney is still allowed to throw the ball or crash the blocks, but in an acceptable way. Thus, the alternative offered by the adult continues to support the child's activity but redirects his actions more suitably.

At this point, you may notice some similarities between substitution and the ineffective strategy of displacement discussed earlier in this chapter. Both attempt to redirect children's inappropriate behavior. However, there is an important difference between the two. Substitution is used *only* with children engaged in expressive aggression. Such children are happy, not frustrated or angry. Their actions are acceptable, but the target of their actions is not. The redirection that takes place teaches them what they need to know in the situation. For instance, children learn that knocking down blocks is okay, but they must be your own blocks; throwing something is allowable, but what you throw must be considered carefully. Displacement strategies, on the other hand, do not teach children what they need to learn in difficult situations: how to deal with the source of their anger or frustration. A child who is redirected from expressing his angry feelings toward someone does not learn a better way to confront that person. Pounding clay or painting an angry picture are unrelated activities that fail to teach children appropriate assertiveness skills. For instance, if Rodney were chasing Joel because Joel had done something to upset him, the displacement technique of telling Rodney to "work out" his anger by pounding the clay would be ignoring his need to confront Joel directly.

**Helping children de-escalate potentially aggressive play.** Frequently, play episodes that begin as positive social interactions escalate at a rate and in a manner children do not intend or expect (Caldwell, 1977). This may lead to accidental aggression, which, in turn, may develop into an angry confrontation. Adults can head off the development of purposeful aggression by keeping an eye on children as they play and by watching for early signs of difficulty. When youngsters stop laughing, when their voices become upset or complaining, when their facial expressions show fear, anger, or distress, and when words move out of the realm of pretend into real-life menace, aggression is likely (Kostelnik, Whiren, and Stein, 1986). If such signs become apparent, adults should intervene immediately by redirecting the play or by becoming involved in the play themselves. For example, in a game of chase, if a child shows signs of angrily turning on her pursuers, the helping professional could defuse potential problems by laughingly becoming the object of the chase.

Similarly, there are times when children's solitary play escalates into aggression due to frustration. Children become angry when a toy does not work, when they are unable to produce the picture they envision, or when something interferes with the accomplishment of a goal they have in mind. At times like these, children often lash out, throw something, or explode in fury. Alert adults can de-escalate aggression by helping children to cope directly with the source of their frustration rather than simply criticizing them for acting inappropriately: "You're upset! That model keeps falling apart. The glue you're using works better on paper than it does on plastic. Let's look for a different kind of glue."

Such intervention may involve giving children information, offering assistance, helping them reevaluate their goals, breaking the task into more manageable steps, or offering a means by which they can take a break before resuming the project.

**Making it clear that aggression is unacceptable.** When physical or verbal aggression occurs, adults must intervene before children experience the satisfaction of getting what they want through negative means (Hendrick, 1996; Sherman and

Bushell, 1975). Interrupting aggression takes away the reward of such behavior and provides a perfect opportunity for adults to help children identify and carry out appropriate alternative actions to achieve their aims.

When helping professionals establish that aggressive behavior will not be tolerated and when they reason with children and point out the harmful effects of aggression, violence diminishes, even when the adults are not immediately present (Baumrind, 1966; Berkowitz, 1973).

**Teaching children alternatives to gunplay.** Evidence shows that when children play with toy guns or any facsimile of a gun their play becomes more violent over time (Slife, 1982; Turner and Goldsmith, 1976). These effects are long lasting, with children continuing to engage in aggressive behavior even after the guns are put away (Yarrow, 1983). Additionally, gun-like objects are potentially dangerous. Someone could easily get poked, cut, or punctured in the course of an excited interchange. What's more, in the United States real guns are highly visible and widespread. There are almost 200 million guns in public hands and approximately half of all households in the country contain at least one firearm (National Rifle Association, 1988). Thus, many children live in or visit homes containing a gun. Unfortunately youngsters cannot be counted on to differentiate pretend guns from real ones or to know how to handle real weapons safely. The tragedy that results from children's mistakes is evident from the accidental shootings that often make the headlines (National Safety Council, 1989). Consequently, both gun rights advocates and gun control supporters agree that children should be taught to treat all guns as potentially real and therefore dangerous. (Center to Control Handgun Violence, 1991; National Rifle Association, 1988). For all these reasons, it is best to discourage children from bringing toy guns to the program and to tell those who do bring such items from home to "check" them at the door until the session is over. During the session, children who use other objects such as sticks or fingers as gun substitutes, should be redirected into less violent play themes or into discussions of alternate means for resolving their make-believe differences. In each case, it is important for adults to explain to children that guns are serious business and are not to be treated as toys. Moreover, even pretending to kill people or animals is not in keeping with the nonaggressive goals of a developmentally appropriate classroom (Kuykendall, 1995).

**Teaching children to generate potential responses to the aggression of others.** Many children become frustrated because they do not know what to do when someone teases them, hurts them, or calls them names. They may either yield to the aggressor or counterattack. Neither strategy is desirable because both lead to further aggression. Adults who take children's complaints of aggression seriously and intervene directly or model appropriate ways of handling problem situations, contribute to a reduction in the aggressive behavior of younger children. For instance, Mr. Monroe notices Callie calling Georgio "Georgio-porgio." She is laughing, enjoying the sound of the words. Scowling, Georgio rushes at her to make her stop. The adult intervenes quickly and says, "Georgio, you're upset that Callie is calling your names. I'm worried if you knock her down she'll get hurt. *Tell* her how you feel." Mr. Monroe remains with the children, helping Georgio figure out the words he will use to express his displeasure to Callie. The child eventually says, "I don't think you're very funny. My name is Georgio." This kind of coaching helps victims learn skills they need to handle such situations more effectively in the future. It also reduces the likelihood that they will use aggressive means to resolve the problem.

With older children, direct intervention may lead to later reprisals by the aggressor. Indirect approaches, such as discussing possible motives behind the aggressor's behavior or brainstorming with children about the potential advantages and disadvantages of various responses, are more effective (Smith, 1982). Some children also appreciate having an opportunity to rehearse what they are going to say or do before actually trying it out.

It also is useful to help identify other children with whom a victim of continued aggression could establish a relationship. Perpetual victims tend to feel isolated and so are likely to tolerate continued aggression directed at them, thus reinforcing it. It is especially common for young children not to recognize alternate playmates but instead to center on maintaining their interaction with the aggressor. Helping them to recognize others as potential choices breaks this nonproductive cycle. Finally, the comfort and information offered by a caring adult goes a long way toward helping children feel that they do indeed have some power within the situation.

**Teaching alternatives to aggression through planned activities.** One major source of aggressive behavior is children's inability to generate alternate solutions to conflict situations (Schickedanz, Schickedanz, and Forsyth, 1982). Children who depend on only a few ways to get their point across tend to think that the fastest, surest approach is through some kind of attack (Smith, 1982). On the other hand, children who can envision a wide range of possibilities are less apt to resort to violence (Spivack, Platt, and Shure, 1976). Fortunately, there is growing evidence that even very young children can increase their repertoire of appropriate options through planned activities (Crary, 1993; Wittmer and Honig, 1994). One approach is to have group discussions with children. These can center around effects of aggression, nonviolent ways to get what they want, how to resolve problem situations, and how to respond to the aggression of others. Another strategy involves teaching children specific skills related to assertiveness and negotiation (Slaby, et al., 1995). Adults can use puppets, stories, flannel boards, skits, or open-ended vignettes to illustrate the skills and stimulate debate.

Helping professionals who use these techniques on a regular basis report that children improve in their ability to identify, describe, and suggest socially appropriate alternatives to aggression (Mize and Ladd, 1990; Ridley and Vaughn, 1984). This indicates that planned activities serve as an appropriate introduction for teaching children how to substitute positive behaviors for aggressive ones.

**Teaching alternatives to aggression through conflict mediation.** Even when youngsters are able to talk about sharing and taking turns in planned activities, they sometimes forget and resort to instrumental aggression in the heat of real-life confrontations (Crary, 1993). At times like these, adults may be tempted to simply separate the children or remove the disputed object. Although such tactics halt the aggression, they do not teach children better ways to handle conflict. A more effective strategy is to use such occasions to help children practice nonviolent approaches to conflict resolution. The helping professional's role becomes that of supporting children as they attempt to resolve their differences. Sometimes children are able to work

out solutions without direct adult intervention. Keeping this in mind, adults should allow children to argue as long as their actions do not turn to violence. If a resolution comes about, positive personal messages can be used to identify children's appropriate behaviors and bring them to their attention. However, if aggression occurs or children seem at a loss for what to do next, the adult can become directly involved as a conflict mediator.

**Conflict-mediation** involves walking children through a series of steps beginning with problem identification and ending with a mutually satisfactory solution (Greenberg, 1992). The adult provides more or less direction as necessary until some conclusion is reached. The aim of the process is not for adults to dictate how children should solve their problem, but to help them figure out a solution of their own. Children experience several benefits from working through their differences in this way (deVogue, 1996). Conflict mediation:

▼ Contributes to more peaceful program environments
▼ Builds trust among children and between children and adults
▼ Teaches constructive ways of dealing with highly emotional situations
▼ Teaches children problem-solving strategies
▼ Encourages positive actions instead of fighting
▼ Promotes friendliness among children
▼ Promotes feelings of competence and worth among children

During conflict mediation children learn the skills necessary to reach peaceful resolutions. These skills involve communication, compromise, the ability to see how different aspects of a dispute are related, and the ability to consider their own perspective as well as that of another person (Carlsson-Paige and Levin, 1992). At first, children need a great deal of support to proceed all the way to a negotiated settlement. The mediator provides this support, serving as a model and as an instructor. As children learn problem-solving procedures and words, they become increasingly capable of solving problems for themselves. There is also evidence that these childhood learnings are maintained throughout the adult years (Goleman, 1995).

Like any other social skill, children require numerous opportunities to practice conflict resolution under the guidance of a more experienced person (Anziano, et al., 1995). In most cases, this is an adult.

However, over the past decade ten-, eleven- and twelve-year-olds have been taught to mediate peer conflicts on the playground or in the lunchroom. Regardless of whether the mediator is an adult or older child, most conflict resolution models encompass similar steps. Let us turn our attention to a practical, systematic model that can be used to mediate children's disputes while teaching them appropriate problem-solving skills.

## ▼ A MODEL FOR CONFLICT MEDIATION

From the far end of the yard, Mrs. Woznawski, the after-school supervisor, hears Sarah shout, "Give me that pogo stick—I need it!" Bianca screams back: "Use something else! I'm not done." Alerted to the difficulty, the adult watches from a distance as the children continue their argument. However, as the dispute heats up, the children begin to grab and pull on the pogo stick. The time is ripe for Mrs. Woznawski to begin conflict mediation.

### Step One: Initiating the Mediation Process

The first step in approaching a conflict situation is for the adult to assume the role of mediator. This is accomplished by stopping the aggressive behavior, separating the combatants, and defining the problem: "You both want the pogo stick at the same time. It looks like you each have different ideas about what to do." The adult may have to position himself or herself between the children as he or she helps them focus on the mutual problem rather than on the object or territory they are defending. It is helpful to neutralize the object of contention by temporarily gaining control of it and assuring the children that it will be safe until the conflict is resolved: "I will hold the pogo stick until we can decide together what to do." This procedure stops the children from continuing to hit or grab, helps them to hear the adult and each other, and sets the stage for them to approach a highly emotional situation in a more objective manner.

### Step Two: Clarifying Each Child's Perspective

Clarifying the conflict based on the children's perspective is the primary focus of the second step. The adult asks each child in turn to state what he or she wants from the situation. It is important to allow each child ample opportunity, without interruption, to state his or her ultimate desire. This might involve possession of a toy or getting a turn. Some sample statements might include: "You both seem very angry. Sarah, you can tell me what you want. Bianca, you can tell me what you want when Sarah is finished." This step is critical. In order for the adult to be an effective mediator, the children must trust him or her not to make an arbitrary decision in favor of one child or the other. The adult establishes neutrality by withholding any evaluation of the merits of either child's position. Paraphrasing each child's view to the other child is also important in this step. This ensures that the adult correctly understands each child's point of view and helps the children to clarify both positions. Children who are very upset or quiet may require several opportunities to describe their position. It must be emphasized that, depending on the level of the children's distress, this step may take several minutes. Children may need help from the adult in articulating their desires. The adults should try to be as accurate as possible in paraphrasing, checking back with the children at each turn.

### Step Three: Summing Up

The third step occurs when the adult has gotten enough information to understand each child's perception of the conflict. The adult then defines the problem in mutual terms, implying that each child is responsible for both the problem and its solution: "Sarah and Bianca, you each want to play with the pogo stick all by yourself. We have a problem. It is important that we find a solution that will satisfy each of you." In other words, the adult states that a problem exists and that a solution must be found.

### Step Four: Generating Alternatives

Generating several possible alternative solutions is what happens in the fourth stage of mediation. Suggestions may be offered by the conflicted children themselves or may be volunteered by bystanders. Each time a possible solution is offered, the mediator paraphrases it to the children directly involved: "Jonathan says you could share." At this point, each child is asked to evaluate the merits of the recommendation: "What do you think, Sarah? What do you think, Bianca?" The mediator elicits as many divergent ideas as possible and should have no stake in which solution is eventually selected. Caregivers should be cautioned that each child should be a willing participant in the outcome and that no alternative should be forced on any child. It is typical during this procedure for children to reject certain possibilities that they may later find acceptable. Therefore, when a suggestion is repeated, the mediator should present it rather than assume it will be rejected again. If the children are not able to originate alternatives, the adult should help them out by saying something like: "Sometimes when people have this problem, they decide to use it together, take turns, or trade toys back and forth. What do you think?"

Sometimes during this step, children tire of the process and one or the other says something like, "I don't want it anymore" or "It's okay, she can have it." Other times, one of the children will simply walk away. If this happens, the mediator reflects and provides information, "This is hard work" or "You're getting tired of trying to solve this problem. Working things out can take a long time." If the child insists that he or she would like to solve the problem by giving up, respect his or her wishes. With practice, children increase their skills and are better able to tolerate the time involved in reaching a negotiated settlement. In the meantime, both children have witnessed the mediation process up to a certain point, and each will have a better idea of what to expect the next time it is used.

### Step Five: Agreeing on a Solution

Children will reject certain suggestions outright and will indicate that others seem more acceptable. The ultimate aim of the fifth step is to get the children to agree on a plan of action that is mutually satisfying. The role of the mediator is to help the children explore the possibilities that seem most acceptable to them. The plan should not include any alternatives that either child vehemently opposes. The final agreement usually involves some concessions on the part of each child and so may not represent the action the child would take if she or he did not have to consider another person's point of view. Eventually, the children will exhibit behaviors that indicate that each can find a way to accept one or a combination of ideas. The mediation process continues until the possibilities have been narrowed down to a workable solution. When this finally occurs, it is important for the mediator to identify that a resolution has been achieved. For example: "You think you can use the stick together. It sounds like you've solved the problem! Try out your idea."

### Step Six: Reinforcing the Problem-Solving Process

The purpose of the sixth stage of the mediation process is to praise the children for developing a mutually beneficial solution. The message to be conveyed is that the process of reaching the solution is as important as the solution itself. The way the mediator achieves this is to acknowledge the emotional investment each child had in the original conflict and the hard work involved in reaching an agreement: "It was important to each of you to have the pogo stick. You worked hard at figuring out how to do that without hurting each other."

### Step Seven: Following Through

The conclusion of the mediation process involves helping the children to carry out the terms of the agreement. This is accomplished by reminding the children what the terms were and, if necessary, physically assisting or demonstrating how to comply. At this point, adults should remain in the vicinity to determine the degree to which children carry out the agreement. If the plan begins to falter, the children should be brought together again to discuss possible revisions.

The seven steps involved in conflict mediation are summarized in Table 12–2.

### Conflict Mediation in Action

The following is a transcript of an actual conflict between two children, both five years old, in which the helping professional used the model just described.

#### Step one

*Angela:* Mr. Lewin, Evan and Aaron are fighting.

*Adult:* Aaron and Evan, you're both trying to put on that stethoscope. (Restrains the two children, who are pulling on the stethoscope, crouches to the children's level, and turns each child to face him) I'll hold it while we're deciding what to do about it. I'll hold it. I'll make sure it's safe. I'll hold on to it. (Removes the stethoscope from the children's grasp and holds it in front of him)

#### Step two

*Aaron:* I wanted that!

*Adult:* You wanted the stethoscope. How about you, Evan?

*Evan:* I want it.

▼ **Table 12–2    Summary of Conflict-Mediation Model**

| | |
|---|---|
| Step one: Initiating the mediation process | Establish the mediator role and neutralize object, territory, or right. |
| Step two: Clarifying each child's perspective | Clarify conflict based on each child's perspective. |
| Step three: Summing up | Define dispute in mutual terms; make clear each child has responsibility for both the problem and its solution. |
| Step four: Generating alternatives | Ask for suggestions from the children involved and from bystanders. |
| Step five: Agreeing on a solution | Help children create a plan of action that is mutually satisfying. |
| Step six: Reinforcing the problem-solving process | Praise children for developing a mutually agreed on solution and for working hard to achieve it. |
| Step seven: Following through | Help children carry out the terms of the agreement. |

*Adult:* You wanted the stethoscope, too. (Another child offers a stethoscope)

*Evan:* I don't like that kind.

*Aaron:* I want it.

*Adult:* Aaron says he really wants that stethoscope. What about you, Evan?

*Evan:* I want it!

**Step three**

*Adult:* You want it, too. Evan and Aaron both want to play with one stethoscope. We have a problem. What can we do about it? Anybody have any ideas?

**Step four**

*Aaron:* He can have Angela's.

*Adult:* You think he can have Angela's. It looks like Angela still wants hers. (Angela backs away).

*Evan:* I still want mine, too.

*Adult:* Evan, you want yours, too. Sometimes when we have a problem like this, we can figure out a solution. Sometimes we share it, sometimes we take turns. Anybody have any ideas?

*Another child:* Share it.

*Adult:* Shanna thinks you can share it. What do you think Aaron?

*Aaron:* Take turns.

*Adult:* Aaron thinks we should take turns. What do you think, Evan?

*Evan:* Unh uh. (Shaking his head from side to side).

*Adult:* You don't think we should take turns.

*Evan:* Then I just want it.

*Adult:* Then you just really want it, hmm. That's still a problem.

*Aaron:* I want it.

*Adult:* You really want a turn with it. How about you, Evan? What do you think?

**Step five**

*Evan:* No. Aaron can have one turn.

*Adult:* You think Aaron can have one turn.

*Evan:* Yes, guess so.

**Step six**

*Adult:* Thank you, Evan.

*Evan:* Not a long turn.

*Adult:* Not a long turn. You want to make sure that you get it back. Aaron, Evan said you could have one turn, and then you'll give it back to him.

*Evan:* A short turn.

*Adult:* A short turn. Aaron, you may have a short turn. Thank you very much, Evan and Aaron. That was really hard to do.

### Step seven

*Adult:* It's about five minutes till it's cleanup time. So Aaron can have a two-minute turn, and you can a two-minute turn.

*Adult:* (Two minutes later) Aaron, two minutes are up. Now, it is time for Evan's turn. Thank you, Aaron. You kept your part of the bargain, and Evan kept his.

## How Children Think about Conflict Resolution

Children are capable of generating a variety of solutions to conflicts. The nature of the solutions they select is determined largely by how they perceive conflict in general. Thus, children's concept of conflict resolution evolves as their understanding of relationships becomes more sophisticated.

Initially, very young children see force or withdrawal as the most likely solutions to a disagreement (Selman, 1980). This simplistic view can be summed up as "fight or flight." When two toddlers fight over a toy they might try grabbing or hitting to resolve the situation or simply give up if a peer refuses to give them a favored item.

As children mature, their ability to understand the needs of others increases. This helps them to take into account other children's perspectives when objects or rights are in dispute. However, they also expect peer interactions to be balanced (Berk, 1997; Hewitt, 1975). If a peer uses aggression to approach a problem, that aggression creates an imbalance, which must be resolved. Although children as young as five years old disapprove of random aggression, when arguments break out, their philosophy becomes "an eye for an eye and a tooth for a tooth." In the view of older preschoolers and some elementary-aged children, the most common equalizer is for the victim to return the aggression in kind. Thus, children justify aggressive solutions by saying things like, "He hit me first," or "I had it." Children's need for equity at this age also contributes to the feeling that victims must get some restitution from the offending party for the conflict to be ended satisfactorily. Successful resolution depends on the aggressor taking responsibility for restoring harmony. This can take the form of an apology or some action to reverse the hurtful words or deeds (Youniss, 1980). For instance, it is common to hear children shout "Say you're sorry" or "You take that back!" as evidence of this kind of thinking.

Eventually, children's reasoning evolves to where they recognize that both participants bear some responsibility for the conflict and will benefit from a mutually satisfying settlement (Carlsson-Paige and Levin, 1992). They also understand that more than one solution may be possible. Arrival at these notions depends on cognitive maturation and experience. The mediation model presented here helps children move in this direction: they have an opportunity to observe problem solving in action and experience the consequences of nonviolent resolution while benefiting from the guidance of a supportive adult.

When mediation models like this are used with preschoolers, most children suggest some form of alternative action as a solution. Taking turns, trading objects, replacing one object with another, and dividing the materials are the most common ideas offered. Grade-school children often decide to use materials simultaneously or to select an altogether new material. Older children sometimes forego their claim to a right or possession if the other child acknowledges the error of his or her aggressive approach (e.g., "I didn't mean to push you" or "I'm sorry I took it away before you were finished") (Kostelnik and Stein, 1986; Stein and Kostelnik, 1984).

### Does Conflict Mediation Work?

At this point, you may be wondering whether using a model like the one just described actually reduces children's aggression and expands their ability to resolve conflicts on their own. Studies do indeed show that children who participate in conflict mediation on a regular basis improve in their ability to engage in that process. Over time, children increase the number and variety of solutions they suggest and decrease the amount of time they need to negotiate a settlement (Crary, 1993; Stein and Kostelnik, 1984). In addition, as the negotiation process becomes more familiar, the number of onlookers increases. These children, along with the disputants, become more actively involved in suggesting ideas and reasons for a particular course of action. As a result, during none of some 500 documented conflicts did a second conflict erupt elsewhere in the room while mediation was going on (Kostelnik and Stein, 1986; Stein and Kostelnik, 1984). Gradually, children also become better able to resolve conflicts on their own without the help of a formal mediator (Johnson and Johnson, 1995). Finally, there is promising evidence that in groups in which mediation is used, not only does aggression diminish, but positive, prosocial behaviors increase (Carlsson-Paige and Levin, 1992; Holden, 1997). This type of instruction, combined with the other strategies suggested in this chapter, will go a long way toward decreasing children's aggressive social interactions.

The mediation model outlined here can be adapted for use with children as young as three or as old as twelve years of age. The steps the model includes are similar to many mediation programs currently available commercially as well as others described in the literature. It can be adapted for use by an adult in a single classroom, by an entire program staff, and by children serving as peer mediators in formal group settings. Conflict mediation is most effective for dealing with incidents of instrumental aggression. Hostile aggression requires additional skills.

## ▼ WHEN AGGRESSION BECOMES HOSTILE

Four-year-old Selena has developed a pattern of picking on Cammy, a younger, physically smaller child in her child-care home. The provider notes that Selena seems angry much of the time and that she hits anyone who disagrees with her; she is especially aggressive toward Cammy. Selena calls Cammy names and physically torments her. Cammy has begun to exhibit signs of anxious behavior, such as crying when her mother leaves in the morning and clinging to the caregiver throughout the day.

Tristan's parents are thinking about pulling him out of Elmwood school. The fourth-grader complains that a certain group of boys continually threaten him in the hallways and on the playground. They play cruel pranks such as trashing his locker or spilling food on him in the cafeteria. The boys tell him that he smells bad and warn other children not to associate with him. They make fun of his family, his culture, and his abilities. Their tactics have made life miserable for Tristan, yet his teacher does not feel comfortable intervening. She believes adult intervention will only make things worse and has told Tristan he will have to "work things out for himself."

All children have times when they exhibit aggressive behavior. However, some children routinely use hurtful actions such as rejection, name calling, or intimidation to exert power over others. Such incidents go beyond the simple altercations common among children; they represent prolonged misuse of influence by one person or group of persons over another. This form of hostile aggression is tradition-

ally called **bullying.** Bullying is most prevalent in the later elementary years, yet even preschoolers can exhibit early signs of hostile behavior (Reynolds, 1996; Tremblay, 1994). Such actions take their toll both on the victim and on the aggressor.

### Victims of Bullying

Any child can become the target of a bully. However, the most likely victims are children least able to respond effectively to taunts and physical assaults. This involves children possessing limited language abilities and few social skills, children who are socially isolated, and ones who are physically weak. Low self-esteem is another distinctive characteristic of victimized children. Most victims respond passively to their tormentors. They seldom initiate the hostile attack and rarely assert their rights when it happens. A few youngsters can be described as provocative victims. They incite aggressive reactions by crying easily; by becoming very defensive or angry when it is not appropriate or by misinterpreting joking or teasing as verbal aggression when that is not the intent (Roffen, Tarrant, and Majors, 1994). Regardless of the cause, each time victims become involved in aggressive incidents, their ineffective responses reinforce the bully's behavior, prompting the cycle of aggression to continue. Moreover, chronic victims of bullying are disliked and elicit little sympathy from peers who observe their predicament (Perry, Willard, and Perry, 1990). For instance, victims who provoke attack through ineffective or irritating behaviors are often viewed as "getting what they deserve" (Ferguson and Rule, 1988). In addition, both aggressive and nonaggressive children anticipate potential rewards from interacting with chronic victims in terms of getting what they want. In other words, classmates see victims as patsies who can be easily taken advantage of and made to give up coveted items. It is no surprise then that victims of bullying experience a severely diminished sense of competence and worth. They may express their discomfort through lack of appetite, disturbed sleep, real or imagined illnesses, inability to concentrate, increased fear of facing others, unexplained bouts of crying or extremely anxious behavior, reluctance to go to the formal group setting, or unusually aggressive behavior toward others (often younger peers, siblings, or pets).

### Bullies

Bullies are generally fearful, confused, and insecure. Bullies also value aggression. They expect it to get them what they want and feel justified using hostile acts to assert their will. A look into their background often reveals that they have been victims of bullying themselves in another time and place. Some bullies are youngsters who have experienced few boundaries, gaining an impression that they can do anything they like. Other children become bullies as a result of attributing hostile intent to peers, even when that intent is not real. They believe their hostile outbursts are justified as a means of maintaining their rights. A fourth scenario involves children who experience some overwhelming life event, which leaves them angry and confused. Unable to control the situation, they try to control the behavior of others through coercion. Rather than risk expressing their anger toward those close to them, such children find a "safe" target among their peers. Finally, children who are the product of a coercive home life often exhibit bullying behavior with peers (Coie, et al., 1991; Essa, 1995; Roffey, Tarrant, and Majors, 1994). Regardless of what has prompted it, bullying that goes unchecked in the preschool and early elementary years manifests itself as delinquency and academic failure by middle school (Offard, 1992; Tremblay, 1994). Moreover, children for whom bullying becomes a standard mode of conduct are four times more likely as adults to be involved in violent crime, be imprisoned, be involved in domestic violence, abuse their children, and be unable to hold down a job (Brendtro and Long, 1995; Eron, et al., 1987).

## The Role of Adults in Relation to Bullying

Both victims and bullies are unhappy people whose long-term prognosis for social and academic success is poor. Such destructive behavior must be taken seriously by the adults in children's lives. Children cannot be left to their own devices to "simply work things out." Proactive strategies can be enacted individually with victim and tormentor, as well as on a program-wide basis.

**Working with victims.** Children are less likely to be victimized if they possess verbal assertiveness skills with which to establish their desires and protect their rights (Slaby, et al., 1995). All children need support in developing these skills, but this is especially true for youngsters who lack general language proficiency and social awareness. Early evidence from continuing research would appear to suggest that assertiveness training is among the most effective types of intervention in reducing bullying behavior (Roffey, Tarrant, and Majors, 1994). Teaching children what they might do to appear

more confident can also reduce their vulnerability. Finally, victims often behave in ways consistent with the cue-distortion hypothesis described in the early pages of this chapter. Their misinterpretation of benign behavior as aggression may prompt a cycle of aggression from which it is difficult to extract themselves. Adult coaching regarding the accurate interpretation of social cues is an effective countermeasure (Goleman, 1995).

**Dealing with bullies.** Bullies cannot simply be shunned or ignored by adults in formal group settings. Such tactics push them beyond the bounds of normal social circles, confirming their poor opinion of themselves and reinforcing their defiant style. Thus, clear boundaries and consistent expectations are key ingredients for working with perpetrators of hostile aggression. Children must be told that such behavior will not be tolerated. Hostile youngsters must also be helped to control their angry impulses (Essa, 1995). Strategies such as self-talk, identification of emotions, deciphering behavioral cues that tell how others are feeling, and logical consequences have been described in previous chapters and are effective tools related to impulse control. Interestingly, aggressors also benefit from the same strategies that support victims—assertiveness training and coaching related to more accurate interpretations of social encounters. For instance, in one program, aggressive grade-schoolers benefited from targeted training in which they were taught to see how some of the social cues they interpreted as hostile (e.g., being jostled in the hall) were in fact neutral or friendly. They also practiced taking the perspective of other children, to get a sense of how they were being perceived when they resorted to coercion. Another facet of the training involved learning to monitor their angry feelings—to recognize what prompted those feelings and to find alternatives (such as humor, assertion, walking away, or counting to ten) rather than lashing out when those feelings arose. After only six weeks, their behavior showed significant signs of improvement. These positive results lasted well into their teenage years (Lochman, 1994).

**Program-wide solutions.** Working individually with victims and bullies has the potential for positive results. However, these outcomes can either be sabotaged or strengthened by the climate of the formal group setting overall. Programs are ripe for development of bully behavior when there are unclear expectations for children's behavior, lack of consistency among staff in dealing with behavioral difficulties, poor communication between home and program, and children spending time unsupervised. These negative conditions are exacerbated when adults in the setting manifest bullying themselves or when grown-ups fail to take children's complaints of bullying seriously or ignore the problem altogether (Roffey, Tarrant, and Majors, 1994). Such programs become "bully laboratories," in which both victims and aggressors suffer.

On the other hand, antibullying conditions are the same ones used in schools implementing alternatives to corporal punishment. These are listed on page 336 of this chapter. The emphasis in such programs is on positive discipline strategies that demonstrate respect for children and require them to take responsibility for their actions. Staff model the behaviors they wish children to adopt. Consistency among staff is also stressed. Strong home-program partnerships are characteristic of these programs as well. Most importantly, programs in which bullying is less likely to occur are ones in which children have a clear understanding that hostile aggression will be handled fairly and openly with concern for victims and perpetrators alike.

## SKILLS FOR HANDLING CHILDREN'S AGGRESSIVE BEHAVIOR

 **Dealing with Aggression in the Formal Group Setting**

*1.* **Model nonaggressive behavior.** Use the skills you have learned thus far to present a calm, rational demeanor for children to imitate. Even when confronting children or adults whose behavior angers or frustrates you, keep your voice level and firm, your movements controlled, and your gaze directed at them. Do not scream or make threatening gestures.

*2.* **Eliminate aggressive materials from your setting.** Forbid children to bring aggressive toys to the program. If youngsters arrive with toy weapons, slingshots, or BB guns, temporarily confiscate them and send them home with the child at the end of the day. Inform parents of this policy. In addition, monitor books, pictures, filmstrips, films, and other instructional aids. Avoid those that depict aggression as a preferred means of solving problems. Do not assume that materials are suitable just because they have won awards or are recommended by a friend.

*3.* **Manage classroom materials to minimize potential frustration among children.** Check equipment to make sure that it works. Ascertain whether materials are appropriate for the children's developmental stage. If they are not, revise them. Materials that are too simple or too challenging often are a source of frustration to children. If a piece of equipment does not function, repair it or replace it with something else. Have enough materials that youngsters do not have to wait for long periods of time to gain access to them. Simultaneously, allow children to have things long enough so that they feel satisfied. If there are too few items for either of these to happen, supplement the materials in some way. Reintroduce familiar materials on a regular basis so children can have repeated experience with them and expand on their skills.

*4.* **Manage the daily routine to minimize potential frustration among children.** Alert children to upcoming changes in routine so they are not taken by surprise when such changes occur. Warn them prior to transitions between activities so they can finish what they are doing before going on to the next thing. Keep rules to a minimum, and explain their purposes with personal messages. Provide options throughout the day so that children do not feel regimented and can gain a sense of autonomy. Periodically, present new things for youngsters to work with or revamp old activities so children perceive the program as interesting.

*5.* **Manage classroom space to minimize potential frustration among children.** Arrange classroom furniture to give children easy access to functional activity spaces. Make these areas large enough for more than one child to occupy comfortably. Provide walkways through the classroom and exits from one area to another so children can move about freely without acci-

*continued*

## SKILLS FOR HANDLING CHILDREN'S AGGRESSIVE BEHAVIOR—continued

dentally bumping into peers or objects or otherwise interfering with one another's activities.

**6. Remain alert to children for whom frustration is building.** Watch children for signs of frustration. When it is evident that a child is becoming distressed, intervene. Offer comfort, support, information, or guidance as befits the situation. If circumstances allow, ask the child in question what he or she can think to do—take a break, get help from another child, go to another resource for information, watch someone else for a while, and so on. Support children when they attempt one of these solutions. If the child is stumped, ask other children to suggest a way to resolve the dilemma: "Raul is feeling frustrated. The paint is soaking all the way through his paper and spoiling his picture. Sam and Carlos, what do you think Raul could do about this problem?" In this way children have a chance to turn frustrating situations into more positive encounters.

**7. Provide children with opportunities to feel competent.** Assign them age-appropriate responsibility: watering the plants, feeding the fish, checking that the computer is turned off at the end of the day, and so forth. Give children chances to make choices and to try a variety of tasks and experiences independently. Structure these so children feel challenged but not so overwhelmed that success is unlikely. Teach children the skills they need to achieve their goals: how to use tools, how to play games, how to work with others.

**8. Reinforce children's behaviors that are incompatible with aggression.** Acknowledge their helpful, cooperative, empathic responses. Make a special effort to note such behaviors in youngsters who are typically aggressive. Although all children benefit from positive reinforcement, more aggressive children particularly need to hear that they are capable of nonhurtful behavior. It is all too easy to get into the rut of expecting aggression from certain children and failing to recognize the more positive things they do. Avoid this by assigning yourself the task of purposely looking for

nonaggressive behaviors and telling children your favorable observations.

**9. Rechannel group play in which children are pretending to shoot one another with guns.** When you observe children pretending to use blocks, Tinker Toys, or their fingers as weapons, step in immediately and redirect the play. Say something like: "You're having fun. You're using the stick as a gun. It upsets me when you pretend to shoot someone else. Guns are dangerous. They are not toys. Use the stick to dig with. You may not use it as a weapon." Do not be sidetracked by children's protestations that they were "just pretending." Reflect their assertion: "You weren't shooting each other for real. That may be. It makes me feel sad when children even play at hurting others. There are better games to play. Let's figure one out."

**10. Help children learn the language of assertiveness.** Plan discussions and formulate activities to highlight sample words children might use when they want to express themselves or maintain their rights assertively. Take advantage of teachable moments throughout the day to teach these same lessons. Chapter 8 provides examples of how skits might be used to teach such scripts. Refer to Chapter 13 for guidelines about how to plan activities and use on-the-spot coaching with similar aims in mind. Sample scripts include: "No hitting," "Stop pushing me," "I'm still using this," "I want a turn," "When will I know that your turn is over?" "Stop calling me names," "Please stop grabbing," or "I'm not ready yet."

**11. Set consistent limits on children's aggressive behavior.** Stop aggressive behavior, relying on physical intervention if necessary. Acknowledge the aggressor's emotions, express your concern, and explain why the behavior is unacceptable. Suggest specific alternative behaviors for younger children to pursue; help older children generate their own ideas for a solution to the problem. Clearly state the consequences for continued aggression, and follow through immediately should children persist. This approach can be employed in response to acciden-

## SKILLS FOR HANDLING CHILDREN'S AGGRESSIVE BEHAVIOR—continued

tal, expressive, and instrumental aggression as well as those incidents of hostile aggression that obviously have been provoked by another child's actions. Given a case of accidental aggression, if the aggressor fails to desist after being told the victim's acts were unintentional, use the personal message, warning, and follow-through skills you have learned. Do the same if a child engaged in expressive aggression does not accept the preferred substitute. Implement similar strategies in response to cases of instrumental aggression in which children are developmentally unable to negotiate or there is no time to do so. Use the same tactic when you observe children using hostile aggression as a way to "save face." For example, children who shove in reaction to being jostled themselves, or those who get into a teasing interchange, are exhibiting signs of having been provoked and will benefit from having their point of view acknowledged while at the same time hearing that their behavior is forbidden.

**12. Attend to the victims of aggression.** Comfort the victim in front of the aggressor, and help the child generate ideas of how to respond to similar aggressive acts in the future. "You're upset. Jeanna hit you. The next time she tries that, put up your hand and say, '*Stop*'." In addition, whenever possible, involve the aggressor in helping the victim as well. Avoid humiliating the aggressor or coercing her or him to apologize in your attempt to assuage the victim's distress.

**13. Praise children when they attempt nonaggressive solutions to difficult situations.** Use positive personal messages and effective praise when you observe children settling a potential dispute, refraining from hitting to resolve a conflict, or coming to the aid of a victim of hostile aggression. Compliment children's efforts to be nonviolent even if their approach has been rebuffed by others. Offer comfort and suggestions for how their performance could improve in the future.

**14. Intervene when accidental aggression occurs.** Comfort the victim and explain the acci-

dental nature of the aggression. If the aggressor does not realize the results of his or her actions, point them out in concrete nonjudgmental ways: "Look at Susan. She is crying. When you knocked over the chair it hit her in the back. That hurt." Teach the aggressor to use phrases like "It was an accident," "I didn't mean it," or "It wasn't on purpose." When appropriate, assist the aggressor in finding ways to make restitution. This is a good time to teach the words, "I'm sorry" if the aggressor truly regrets his or her actions. Sometimes victims can contribute ideas for restitution as well, "Susan, what could Kathleen do to help you feel better?"

**15. Use substitution in response to children's expressive aggression.** When working with toddlers, acknowledge the aggressor's perspective. Point out firmly the inappropriateness of the behavior and provide a substitute object for his or her use: "Geoffrey, it's fun to crash blocks. Those are Brian's—here are some you can play with." Move the aggressor away from the victim to focus his or her attention on the substitute object. Comfort the victim and help him or her repair the damage.

When working with older children, include the aggressor in the reparations before offering the substitution. Help the victim articulate a reaction to the aggressive act as a way of making the perpetrator more aware of the inadvertent impact of his or her violent behavior.

**16. Mediate children's conflicts.** When incidents of instrumental aggression occur, utilize the conflict-mediation model described in this chapter. Carry out each step in order:
**a.** Initiate the mediation process.
**b.** Clarify each child's perspective.
**c.** Sum up the situation.
**d.** Assist children in generating alternatives.
**e.** Help children agree on a solution.
**f.** Reinforce the problem-solving process.
**g.** Aid children in following through on their agreement.
Make sure you allow yourself enough time to work through the entire process. If you have less than 5 minutes available, do not begin negotiation. Implement the strategies of the per-

*continued*

sonal message and negative consequence presented in Chapters 10 and 11 instead.

**17. Use physical restraint to calm young children whose aggressive actions are dangerous to themselves or others.** If young children begin to flail their arms and legs, hit wildly, or otherwise engage in physically hurtful behaviors, it may be necessary to carry out the crisis management technique of physical restraint (Gartrell, 1994; Hendrick, 1996). As described in the time-out section of Chapter 11, physical restraint involves holding children in a passive "bear hug." This will keep them from further injurious behavior. There are two safe ways to restrain young children. One is to wrap your arms around their arms and your legs around their legs. You may prefer to sit with the child on a chair or sit in a "pretzel" position on the floor. A second approach is to hold the child in on your lap sideways, clasping your arms tightly around his or her body, securing the child's arms. This latter position avoids the risk of having the child hit your face with the back of his or her head. Quickly slip off the child's shoes if you can, to avoid hard kicks. Depending on the child, soft words or singing quietly may be soothing. Other children do best in silence. Do not attempt to restrain older children or youngsters who are taller and weigh more than you do unless you have had special training. There are safe ways to restrain such youngsters, but the techniques must be modeled to be learned properly.

**18. Respond to children's unprovoked hostile aggression using parts two and three of the personal message only.** When children engage in deliberate acts of cruelty that have no obvious connection to personal efforts to maintain self-esteem, do not reflect. Instead, move immediately into a statement that outlines your emotion and the reason for your reaction, identifies the specific behavior that has prompted your ire, and directs the child to stop. Look directly at the child and deliver your message in a calm, matter-of-fact tone. For example, when Mary deliberately trips Justine for no apparent reason, you might say: "It really bothers me that you

tripped her. She could get hurt. Don't do that again." Similarly, when Mark calls William "four eyes" to embarrass him in front of a group, you could say: "It makes me angry when you taunt people. That's unkind. Stop." In both cases, if the behavior continues, proceed immediately to the warning and follow-through. Your goal in situations such as these is to limit the aggression without further embarrassing the victim or prompting unnecessary escalation of the incident.

Note that this is one of the few times in which a reflection is not advised. When a child is capriciously trying to damage another person's self-esteem, injure them, or destroy their property, their emotions are often unfathomable to the adult. Thus, either an affective or behavior reflection may sound accusatory, and a paraphrase reflection may inadvertently reinforce the negative features of the behavior.

**19. Teach hostile aggressors ways to control their angry impulses.** Talk with children about their strong feelings—what those feelings are and what prompts them. Work with children to recognize signs that their emotions are escalating beyond their control. Teach children self-talk to help them maintain their composure. Point out the feelings of victims to assist angry children in empathizing with people who are hurt, unhappy, or angry too. Teach children relaxation techniques. Consider short-term use of tangible rewards to assist children in recognizing and practicing nonaggressive responses in provocative circumstances. These strategies and others described in Chapter 5, Responding to Children's Emotions, and Chapter 6, Supporting Children in Stressful Situations, encourage children's development of impulse control.

**20. Teach hostile aggressors how to more accurately interpret social cues and respond with those cues in mind.** Provide children with practice recognizing social cues such as voice tone, facial expressions, and words that differentiate aggressive actions from nonaggressive ones. Pose hypothetical situations, enact short skits with puppets, or use role-playing to demonstrate these variations. Next, ask children to in-

## SKILLS FOR HANDLING CHILDREN'S AGGRESSIVE BEHAVIOR—continued

terpret what they have observed. Point out that there may be more than one interpretation for each event: "You think he bumped her because he didn't like her. Another reason might be that there were too many people crowded around the table. There wasn't room for everybody to stand without touching each other." Encourage children to practice taking the perspective of the victim, to get a sense of how aggressors are perceived when they resort to coercion: "How do you think Marvin felt when Geraldine shoved him and yelled at him?" Once they become somewhat accurate in their conclusions, invite children to generate nonaggressive reactions to the scenarios you pose. "When Marvin stepped on Geraldine's foot, what could she do instead of shoving him so hard?" or "What would happen if she did that?" or "What will happen next?" Make sure to have the children critically evaluate each proposed response. "Why do you think that is a good idea?" or "Why don't you think that will work?" or "Which of our ideas seems best?" This final step helps children move beyond generating random suggestions to consciously weighing the merits of disadvantages of each—a skill they must possess to be successful at controlling aggression in real-life circumstances.

After children have become relatively successful at interpreting and creating nonaggressive responses to hypothetical situations, help them transfer the skills they have learned to their daily interactions with peers (Slaby, et al., 1995). Use on-the-spot coaching in actual social situations to help typically aggressive children go through the steps just described (recognizing cues, interpreting them accurately, generating nonaggressive responses, choosing a response, enacting it). Refer to Chapter 8, Supporting Children's Friendships, for more information about such coaching. Notice when children put a check on initial aggressive impulses or react in nonaggressive ways at times when formerly they may have responded with aggression. Use effective praise to help children recognize the progress they are making.

21. **Explore alternatives to corporal punishment if it is practiced in your setting.** Most

schools and centers do not require that all helping professionals use corporal punishment, even though some on the staff may. Prior to accepting a position, ascertain whether you will be expected to paddle children. If this is a requirement of the job, consider seeking another. If it is not, discuss with your supervisor ways in which you can use your disciplinary approach within the confines of the system.

### Help Children Deal with Aggression Beyond the Formal Group Setting

1. **Provide accurate information when children assume that, because society condones aggression in one arena, it is permissible in all arenas.** Children often try to justify their own aggressive behavior by likening it to behaviors they attribute to sports figures, the police, or the military. For instance, a child might say that he or she was acting like a particular boxer when responding to an insult with a swift uppercut. If children fall back on arguments such as these, point out that the child's use of violence was outside the bounds society considers appropriate. The aggressive action of the boxer is confined to the boxing ring, is governed by rules, and requires special equipment and training. Moreover, although society permits a person to fight under these constraints, fighting in day-to-day interactions is not acceptable. Use similar reasoning regarding police or military use of force. Explanations such as these are more likely to garner children's attention than are absolute condemnations. Whether or not you personally agree with these forms of violence, they do exist, and children are exposed to them. Your job as a helping professional is to assist children in understanding the constraints society places on certain forms of violence.

2. **Point out to children that individuals can choose nonaggressive solutions to problems.** Children who see violence on television, read about it, and are exposed to it in their daily lives may assume that there is no alternative to aggression. Take advantage of group discussions and private conversations to explain that people can choose many different ways to solve prob-

*continued*

## SKILLS FOR HANDLING CHILDREN'S AGGRESSIVE BEHAVIOR—continued

lems; some are hurtful, and some are not. One reason people resort to the former is that they do not always know nonhurtful alternatives. Tell children that you would like them to learn nonaggressive solutions and will work with them to discover what some of these might be.

**3. Help children formulate ways to cope with aggressors beyond your jurisdiction.** Listen sympathetically when children talk about aggression to which they have been subjected in other settings. Reflect their concern, anger, frustration, or fear. Brainstorm with the child alternatives that would be both acceptable and feasible for her or him to implement. Allow the child to rehearse a chosen tactic with you prior to trying it out. Ask the child to let you know the eventual outcome. If more planning and practice are needed, offer it. For instance, if a child is being victimized by a bully, some alternative strategies to consider might include avoiding the bully, talking back, assuming an air of indifference to taunts, finding allies whose presence will make being singled out less likely, and improving his or her skill in the area that is the subject of derision.

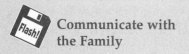 **Communicate with the Family**

**1. Communicate to parents how you intend to deal with aggression in the formal group setting.** Explain what you will do as well as what you will not do. Provide a rationale for your choices. Do not try to coerce parents into adopting your methods for themselves, but do make it clear that in your setting, certain adult practices are acceptable and others are inappropriate. If parents tell you to spank their children if they misbehave, say something like: "You're really anxious for your child to behave at school. That's important to me, too. I will be making it clear to children what the rules are, and I will be using consequences to enforce them. However, paddling is not one of my consequences." Briefly describe a sample disciplinary encounter, using the skills you have learned, to demonstrate what you mean.

**2. Provide parents with information about violence on television and its link to childhood aggression.** Educate parents regarding television's potentially harmful as well as positive effects. Do this by inserting relevant facts, figures, and guidelines into a classroom, school, or center newsletter. Send home short articles on the topic or present the information to parents in a workshop. Invite parents to gather informally to discuss the issues and to brainstorm for ideas how to make television a more positive nonaggressive influence in children's lives.

**3. Draw families' attention to your policy regarding the use of pretend guns in the classroom.** Provide information regarding what we know about children's play with gun-like toys, then make it clear that pretend guns will not be permitted in the program. This policy can be communicated at orientation sessions early in the year, in the parent handbook for your program, and/or in a newsletter sent home. Explain your rationale both in terms of reducing the potential for children getting poked, cut, or punctured as well as reducing aggression among children in the group. Be careful to avoid making judgmental statements about guns or gun owners. Remember that family members may be hunters, police officers, or military personnel, all of whom use guns for legitimate purposes. Instead, focus on the negative effects of children pretending to hurt each other.

**4. Listen thoughtfully if parents report that their child is being bullied by other children. Respond with appropriate action.** It has been reported that commonly when parents mention their child is being bullied, program personnel minimize the importance of this problem, maintain that such predicaments are beyond their jurisdiction, or shift the conversation to other difficulties the child might be having (Roffey, Tarrant, and Majors, 1994). The denial that surrounds bullying is detrimental to child development. That is, adults who pretend bullying is not happening or who think of it as mere child's play are not doing all they can to help bullies and victims develop more appropriate interaction strategies. If you become aware that a child

**SKILLS FOR HANDLING CHILDREN'S AGGRESSIVE BEHAVIOR—continued**

is being bullied, talk with parents about possible ways to address the issue, both at home and in the program. If a child or parent complains of bullying about which you have been unaware, promise to observe the situation more closely. Develop a plan for how you will respond using strategies outlined in this chapter. Address concerns related both to the victim and the bully. Ask family members for input and ways the plan might be generalized for home use. Carry out the plan, offering and getting periodic feedback from home. Support parents as they express their frustration or concern throughout the process. Keep family members apprised of children's progress.

5. **Talk with the parents of children who engage in bullying behavior.** If a child is beginning to establish a pattern of bullying behavior in the program, bring this to his or her parents' attention. Ask if they have observed similar actions at home. Using the strategies outlined in this chapter, work with family members to create a plan to address the child's aggression. Check in with parents periodically to discuss the child's progress. Maintain a helpful, supportive manner throughout the process.

6. **Remain alert to children who may witness or experience violence in their families.** Help children sort through the intense emotions such incidents elicit. If the aggression is vicarious (e.g., aimed at someone else or the result of violent television or older sibling play) work with the child to figure out coping strategies he or she can use. Whenever the child appears to be the victim of aggression, follow the procedures outlined in Chapter 15 regarding child abuse.

## ▼ PITFALLS TO AVOID

The major pitfalls in handling children's aggressive behavior have already been covered in the section on ineffective strategies. Hence, the following section focuses on the common mistakes adults make when mediating children's conflicts.

**Failing to lay the groundwork.** Prior to initiating conflict mediation, the adult must have established himself or herself in the children's eyes as someone who cares about them, who will keep them safe, and who is predictable in reacting to children's actions. It is on these primary elements of adult-child relationships that the model is founded. Failure to establish these conditions undermines the spirit of the process. Therefore, the mediation model is most effectively implemented only after children are comfortable and familiar with their caregivers, the surroundings, and the daily routines.

**Ignoring developmental considerations.** In order to successfully participate in conflict mediation, children must be able to indicate acceptance or rejection of proposed alternatives. Children whose age or development has not reached the point at which they can state their desires, or children who do not speak the same language as the mediator, are not yet ready to engage in this model. Children can communicate verbally or by using an effective substitute such as signing.

In addition, adults who try conflict mediation are cautioned to remain sensitive to children's tolerance for frustration. Not all children are ready to go through all of the steps at once. Most children calm down as mediation proceeds. Those whose behavior becomes increasingly agitated are demonstrating a lack of readiness. At that point, the procedure should be terminated, with the adult enforcing a limit to resolve the original conflict: "You both want the stethoscope. I can't let you hurt each other as a way to decide who gets it, so I will have to decide. Evan, you can have the stethoscope for 2 minutes, and then Aaron, you can have a 2-minute turn." At the same time, children should be praised for their hard work up to that point: "Evan and Aaron, you worked hard at telling me what you wanted. That helped a lot." Gradually, children will be able to proceed further in the process.

**Mandating rather than mediating.** Adults often neglect to use conflict mediation properly because they feel uncomfortable taking their attention away from an entire group in order to focus on only one or two children. They worry that the mediation process requires more time than they can spare.

Instead, they may separate children, remove the disputed toy, and dictate an expedient solution. This approach undoubtedly works in the short run. However, it does not provide an opportunity for children to practice problem-solving strategies. As a result, over time, the adult continues to bear the primary responsibility for conflict resolution rather than gradually transferring this responsibility to the children.

It is important to consider the fact that mediation takes place where the conflict occurs; disputing children are not removed from the group. As a result, children who are not directly involved in the conflict frequently participate as observers or advisors. In this way, the teaching that is taking place affects several children at once. Also, because children become so engrossed in the process, another conflict rarely erupts elsewhere in the room during this time.

**Denying children's legitimate claims.** In his or her zeal to reach a compromise, a helping professional may inadvertently deny a child's legitimate right to maintain possession of a desired object. The mediator may hear such statements as "I had it first," or "She took it from me." When this occurs, the focus then shifts to helping the perpetrator generate appropriate strategies, such as asking, trading, or bargaining, to achieve his or her goal. There also will be times when a child has used an acceptable strategy for obtaining the object and the child in possession refuses. When this occurs, the mediator can help the children develop a suitable time frame for the exchange to take place. If the mediator does not know who has the legitimate claim, this can be stated in a personal message that also stresses the inappropriateness of any violent solution to a difference of opinion.

**Affixing blame.** Sometimes, when adults hear a commotion, their first impulse is to say: "Okay, who started it?" or "Haven't I told you not to fight?" Children's responses to these queries frequently take the form of denial or accusation, neither of which leads to clarification or constructive problem solving. It is better to approach the conflict saying "You both seem very upset" or "It looks like you both want the stethoscope at the same time." These statements focus on the problem that exists between the children rather than attributing sole responsibility to either child.

**Taking sides.** In order to establish credibility and be accepted as a mediator, the adult must be perceived as impartial. For this reason, she or he should avoid indicating initial agreement or disagreement with any position that is stated. This means strictly avoiding giving nonverbal cues such as nodding, frowning, and finger tapping as well as refraining from verbal indications of support, sympathy, disdain, or revulsion.

**Denying a child's perspective.** There will be times during conflict mediation when a child expresses a point of view that seems ludicrous or untrue. In those circumstances, it is tempting for the adult to try to correct the child's perception: "You know you really don't hate John," or "You shouldn't be so upset about having to wait your turn," or "You should feel pleased that John wants to play with you at all after the way you've been acting." Although any one of these statements may seem accurate to the adult, they do not correspond to the child's perception of the situation. As a result, what began as mutual problem solving will end in fruitless argument. As hard as it may be, it is the adult's responsibility to exercise patience and allow children to work through their own feelings about the problem under discussion.

**Masterminding.** It is natural for adults to want to resolve conflicts quickly. Sometimes, to accelerate the mediation process, they step in with their own solution rather than permitting children to work out the problem themselves. A related tactic is to force children toward a preconceived conclusion by asking such questions as "Don't you think . . . ?" or "Doesn't it seem that you should . . . ?" or "Wouldn't it be nice if we . . . ?" If the teacher has chosen to initiate the mediation process, he or she should allow it to proceed to a mutual resolution. Otherwise, children become frustrated at being led to believe that they are responsible for reaching a decision when in reality, they must acquiesce to the teacher's conclusion. When this occurs, the chances for continued conflict are high because children do not feel a real commitment to an approach that is dictated to them. In addition, coercive strategies do not help children to practice the problem-solving skills they will need to reconcile future disagreements. Finally, the use of such autocratic techniques seriously jeopardizes the adult's credibility in subsequent attempts to mediate children's conflicts.

**Ignoring ripple effects.** There is a normal tendency for the adult to center his or her attention only on the children directly involved in the dispute, missing the effect the conflict has on other children in the vicinity. When children fight, it is common for a general sense of tension to pervade the group.

Children on the periphery feel quite relieved when the adult steps in to mediate, and they should be allowed to watch the process as it unfolds. In this way, they have an opportunity to see that disagreements can be resolved in safe, supportive ways. It is important to note that even when the conflict has been settled to the satisfaction of the two adversaries, other children may be reluctant to play with either of them or to enter the area in which the conflict occurred. The adult can remedy this situation by announcing, for example: "Evan and Aaron have figured out a way to share the stethoscope. They are going to take turns. There is plenty of room in this hospital for other children who would like to play." This proclamation provides a signal that the conflict is officially over and playful interactions may resume.

## ▼ SUMMARY

Aggression is any verbal or physical behavior that injures, damages, or destroys. Four types of aggression have been identified: accidental, expressive, instrumental, and hostile. The first three categories are unintentional by-products of an interaction; hostile aggression is a purposeful act. Assertiveness and aggressiveness are two different things. Although both involve exerting influence over others, assertion does not include any intent to injure or demean. There is no one factor that causes violent behavior in children. Current research shows that aggression is influenced by biology and is learned through modeling, direct instruction, and reinforcement as well. The way children express aggression changes over time due to cognitive maturation and experience. Hostile aggression becomes more evident as children mature. Both boys and girls demonstrate aggressive behavior, although the tactics they use are somewhat different. Males tend to be more direct and physically abusive, and females rely on indirect, verbal strategies. It has been difficult to ascertain whether these patterns depend more on biology or culture.

Adults have tried different ways to reduce children's aggression. Physical punishment, ignoring aggression, catharsis, displacement, and inconsistency actually increase children's antisocial behavior and should not be used. Effective preventive techniques include serving as a model of self-control and limiting the aggressive toys, films, books, pictures, or television programs to which children are exposed in the formal group setting. Helping children to recognize their own competence while reducing the frustration in their lives also is beneficial. When adults teach children prosocial behaviors and praise them for nonaggressive action, aggression is replaced with more appropriate conduct.

When children do exhibit aggression, adults can assist them in changing their behavior by explaining instances of accidental aggression, by using substitution to rechannel expressive aggression, by helping children learn the language of assertiveness, and by intervening to de-escalate aggressive play. At the same time, it is important for adults to create an environment in which children know that aggression is unacceptable. Setting limits on hurtful behavior and following through on those limits is an important tactic for accomplishing this aim. Children also benefit when they have an opportunity to explore potential responses to the aggression of others. It is difficult for some children to shift from violent to peaceful strategies all at once. Adults must gradually introduce a logical sequence of steps to help children move in this direction. Children can learn alternatives to aggression through planned activities. In addition, they can be taught to negotiate their differences through on-the-spot conflict mediation. When hostile aggression occurs, adults must be quick to respond with firm limits and strategies aimed at teaching children how to curb angry impulses, interpret social cues more accurately, and replace their aggressive reactions with less violent ones. Attention must be paid both to bullies and their victims. Program-wide strategies for dealing with hostile aggression are also important to develop. Finally, working with family members is essential for reducing childhood aggression of all kinds.

## ▼ DISCUSSION QUESTIONS

1. Describe the four types of aggression. Discuss behaviors that differentiate them from one another. Present examples of behavior you have witnessed that fit into a particular category.
2. Describe an interaction in which you have observed either a child or an adult being aggressive. Discuss what changes in that person's behavior would have made the actions assertive instead.
3. Choose a fictional character or a public figure you consider aggressive. In a small group, identify some of that person's characteristics. Apply your knowledge of learned aggression to offer some explanation for the person's behavior.

4. Describe the emergence of aggression in children. Discuss how maturity and experience influence the types of aggression children display at different ages.

5. In this book, we have taken a strong stand against corporal punishment. Discuss your reactions to that position.

6. Describe the differences between catharsis, displacement, and substitution. Identify instances from your own experience in which you have seen these techniques used. Talk about the outcomes you observed.

7. Describe an aggressive behavior exhibited by a child without revealing the child's identity to the group. Use the strategies and skills outlined in this chapter to assist you in formulating a plan for reducing the unwanted behavior.

8. Two children come to the program with toy light sabers they got over the weekend. They want to play with them in the classroom. Using the content of this chapter as background, discuss what you would do in this situation.

9. When Mr. Clark drops the children off at school, he mentions that he noticed some bruises on Timmy, one of the children in the carpool. The child told him his older brother had smacked him around when their parents were out. The teacher thanked Mr. Clark and then said, "Oh, I'm sure there's nothing to worry about. Timmy tends to exaggerate." Find the place in the NAEYC Code of Ethical Conduct (Appendix A) that offers professional guidelines in such a situation. Based on your understanding of the Code, decide whether the teacher's behavior was ethical or unethical.

10. Share with the group your experience in attempting the conflict-mediation model presented in this chapter. Describe children's reactions, your own reactions, and the eventual outcome. Brainstorm with classmates ways to improve your technique.

## ▼ Field Assignments

1. Describe an incident of childhood aggression that occurred in your field placement. Discuss how it was handled by another adult. Evaluate the effectiveness of the approach that was used. Next, describe how you handled an aggressive incident involving a child in your setting. Evaluate the effectiveness of your approach.

2. Interview two community professionals who work with young children. Obtain information from them regarding the strategies they use to help children who exhibit aggressive behavior. Report your findings.

3. Describe a situation in which you were involved in conflict mediation. Begin by discussing what prompted the conflict. Next, talk about the children's reactions to the mediation process and what final outcome occurred. Identify two things you did well during the process and one thing you would like to improve the next time such a situation arises. Conclude by discussing your reaction to your role as a mediator.

4. Watch a child's television show (cartoon) or movie and record the frequency of aggressive or violent acts. Discuss possible effects on children.

5. Review the parent handbook for the program in which you are participating. Identify policies and procedures aimed at reducing childhood aggression.

 ## ▼ Chapter 13

# Promoting Prosocial Behavior

## ▼ Objectives

*On completion of this chapter, you will be able to describe:*

▼ Examples of prosocial behavior.

▼ How children benefit when they act prosocially.

▼ Prerequisite abilities and skills related to prosocial behavior.

▼ Gender, age, cultural, and environmental factors that influence prosocial behavior.

▼ Strategies to increase children's prosocial behavior.

▼ Family communication strategies related to prosocial behavior.

▼ Pitfalls to avoid in promoting children's prosocial behavior.

| | | |
|---|---|---|
| Helping | Sympathizing | Rescuing |
| Sharing | Encouraging | Defending |
| Giving | Sacrificing | Reassuring |
| Cooperating | Aiding | Comforting |

All of these terms describe **prosocial behaviors.** They are the opposite of antisocial conduct, such as selfishness and aggression, and represent positive values of society. These acts of kindness assist, support, or benefit others and often are executed without the doer's anticipation of external rewards (Shaffer, 1994). At times, they also involve some risk to the individual performing them, such as when a person defends a friend in a situation that is either physically or socially dangerous. The disposition to engage in such actions is learned and practiced as a child, eventually carrying over into adulthood. Consequently, there is a tendency for caring, compassionate children to grow up into caring, compassionate adults. Whereas children who are less concerned with the well being of others demonstrate less positive attitudes in their adult lives (Clary and Miller, 1986; Rosenhan, 1972). Yet, evidence suggests that the roots of caring, sharing, helping, and cooperating are in every child (Hoffman, 1988). Al-

though older children demonstrate a wider range of prosocial behaviors, even very young children have the capacity to demonstrate prosocial responses in a number of different settings (Chapman, et al., 1987; Denham, 1995; Stockdale, Hegland, and Chiaromonte, 1989).

Regardless of age, children's interactions tend to be more positive than negative. For instance, data suggest that the ratio of children's prosocial behaviors to antisocial acts is no less than 3:1 and may be as high as 8:1 (Moore, 1982). This means that for every negative behavior, youngsters average three to eight positive actions. This proportion remains relatively stable throughout the preschool and elementary years. Thus, childhood is an optimal period for the development of prosocial attitudes and conduct. Although it is obvious that children benefit from acts of kindness directed toward them, youngsters who help, share, cooperate, comfort, or rescue also benefit.

### Values to Children of Acting Prosocially

Children who engage in prosocial behavior develop feelings of satisfaction and competence from assisting others. When youngsters help with the family dishes, share information with a friend, comfort an unhappy playmate, or work with others to achieve a final product, they come away thinking: "I am useful. I can do something. I am important." By helping, sharing, comforting, and cooperating, they have an impact on their world. The resulting perception of being capable and valuable contributes to a healthy self-image (Coopersmith, 1967; Trawick-Smith, 1997). Kindness also serves as a sign of affection and friendship. It contributes to positive feelings in both doers and receivers, providing entry into social situations and strengthening ongoing relationships (Hartup and Moore, 1990; Marcus and Leiserson, 1978). Children whose interactions are characterized by kindness maximize the successful social encounters they experience. They are viewed more positively by others than children whose actions are less thoughtful. This increases the likelihood that their kind acts will continue in the future and betters children's chances for receiving help or cooperation when they need it. Children who seldom help or cooperate frequently are left to their own devices when confronted with difficult situations (Horowitz and Bordens, 1995; Peterson, 1980). Table 13–1 lists the benefits of engaging in prosocial behavior.

In addition, when children are the beneficiaries of any type of prosocial action, they get a closer look at how such behaviors are carried out. Each episode serves as a model from which they derive useful information to apply to future encounters. If children are only infrequently on the receiving end of prosocial acts, they have fewer opportunities to learn about them. Recipients also have chances to learn how to respond positively to the kindness that others extend to them (Marcus and Leiserson, 1978). Individuals who never learn this skill eventually receive fewer offers of comfort and support. As a result, there are times when they suffer needlessly because they are unwilling or unable to seek

help or cooperation from those who are in a position to give it.

Besides benefiting the individual, prosocial behavior has advantages for groups as well. Group settings in which children are encouraged to be cooperative and helpful result in more friendly interactions and productive group efforts than settings in which little attention is paid to these values (Gazda, 1995). Moreover, routine or tedious chores, such as cleanup, are more easily managed. When everyone pitches in, tasks are quickly accomplished and no one person feels overly burdened. An added benefit is that youngsters begin to develop a positive group image in which they view both themselves and other group participants as genial and competent (Marion, 1994).

## Steps to Acting Prosocially

At one time, it was thought that if children could only be taught to think prosocially, the appropriate actions would automatically follow. Unfortunately, kind thoughts have not been significantly linked to prosocial acts. Although even preschoolers can explain that sharing, taking turns, and working together are good things to do, they do not necessarily act in these ways when doing so would be appropriate. Children must get beyond simply thinking about what is right; they have to go through a series of steps that move them from thought to action. These include (1) becoming aware that sharing, help, or cooperation is needed, (2) deciding to act, and (3) carrying out the prosocial behavior.

**Step one: awareness.** Youngsters must first become aware that someone would benefit from a prosocial response (Honig and Wittmer, 1996). To do this requires accurately interpreting what they see and hear. This means recognizing typical distress signals such as crying, sighing, grimacing, or struggling as well as correctly identifying verbal cues: "This is too much for me to do all by myself," or "If we work together, we'll finish faster." How easily children recognize such cues depends on how clear they are. Ambiguous or subtle signals are more difficult for children to interpret than direct ones (Horowitz and Bordens, 1995). For instance, if Patience observes Duwana fall and moan, it may not be clear to her that Duwana needs assistance. However, if Duwana cries and calls for help, Patience will comprehend her distress more easily. Likewise, Patience might enter the awareness phase of prosocial behavior if an adult pointed out to her the signs of distress exhibited by Duwana. In most

| ▼ Table 13–1 | Benefits of Engaging in Prosocial Behavior |
| --- |

1. Creates feelings of satisfaction
2. Builds perceptions of competence
3. Provides entry into social situations
4. Promotes on-going relationships
5. Increases chances of receiving help or cooperation
6. Leads to positive group atmosphere

cases, people who come upon a problem situation look both to the victim and the reactions of others nearby to determine if a real problem exists. This is especially true when the situation is ambiguous or vague. If onlookers appear unfazed, a potential helper may remain unaware that intervention is needed. This is illustrated when Abdul's Lego construction falls crashing to the floor. Abdul appears unhappy but makes no sound. Several children nearby look up, but seeing no tears or other overt signs of distress, return to their play. Roger, observing the entire scene may also assume that assistance is unnecessary because no one else made a move to help. He might think differently if an adult or other child said something like, "Are you okay?" or "That's too bad your tower fell." These comments prompt awareness that the situation could indeed be distressing to Abdul.

After children become aware of someone else's distress they often respond empathically. That is, they feel the distress or frustration of the person in need and then respond. Initially, young children's reaction is to mimic the distress signals by crying or sighing themselves. Later, preschoolers and school-age children become more adept at coupling their emotional response with some gesture of assistance (Eisenberg, et al., 1995; Zahn-Waxler, Friedman, and Cummings, 1983).

**Step two: decision.** Once children identify a person in need, they are faced with the decision of whether or not to act. Three factors that influence this decision include children's relationship to the person in need, their mood, and whether they think of themselves as basically prosocial beings.

*Relationship.* Children of all ages are most likely to respond prosocially to people they like and with whom they have established relationships (Birch and Billman, 1986; Jones, 1985). Although children may react compassionately to people they do not know, friends are more often kind to one another than they are to strangers. Prosocial acts such as sharing are also more likely to occur if the recipient is someone who has shared with the giver previously or if sharing will require the receiver to do likewise in the future (Damon, 1988). Under these circumstances, children feel obligated to one another based on their notions of fairness and reciprocity. In other words, children believe one good turn deserves another.

*Mood.* Mood also affects whether or not children decide to pursue a prosocial course of action (Cunningham, et al., 1990; Hoffman, 1982). Children of all ages who are in a positive frame of mind are more likely to act prosocially than those in a negative or neutral mood. When youngsters are happy, they become optimistic about the outcome of their efforts. They may even undertake difficult or costly prosocial actions with the expectation of ultimate success. On the other hand, children who are angry or sad often cannot see beyond their own unhappy circumstances to aid others or may believe that their actions will fail anyway. Exceptions to this rule occur when older children, who are in a bad mood, perceive that behaving prosocially will actually improve their state of mind. Their subsequent acts of kindness may be carried out in the hope of making themselves feel better. However, if they see no self-serving benefits to their actions, such children will decide not to engage in prosocial activities.

*Self-perception.* A child's decision of whether or not to behave prosocially may also hinge on how kind the child considers herself or himself to be. Children who frequently hear themselves described as cooperative or helpful believe they are and often choose to act in ways that support this self-image (Baron and Bryne, 1993; Grusec and Redler, 1980). Youngsters who have no such self-perceptions may shy away from deciding to carry out a prosocial act because such behaviors do not fit the way they see themselves in relation to others.

**Step three: action.** If children assume responsibility for sharing, helping, or cooperating, they must then select and perform a behavior they think is appropriate to the situation. Their conduct in such circumstances is influenced by two abilities: perspective taking and instrumental know-how (Berk, 1997; Moore, 1982).

In **perspective taking,** children recognize what would be useful to someone else whose needs may not mirror their own at the moment. Toddlers who offer Mommy their well-chewed cracker as a way to ease her distress over the mess made by the puppy mean well, but do not understand what is truly needed to rectify the situation. Their ineffectiveness is not surprising because they have limited role-taking skills. As these abilities emerge, preschoolers and youngsters in the lower elementary grades become better equipped to help and to cooperate in situations in which the setting is familiar or the circumstances of distress resemble something they themselves have experienced. Eventually, children ten years of age and older also become able to project appropriate responses in unfamiliar situations.

However, goodwill alone will not fix a damaged library book. One also must know something about the most appropriate tape with which to repair the binding or the best way to erase crayon marks from the pages. This is called **instrumental know-how** and involves having the knowledge and skills necessary to act competently (Goleman, 1991). Children who have many skills at their disposal are the most effective in carrying out their ideas. Those who have few skills may have good intentions, but their efforts often are counterproductive or inept. Moreover, younger children who are the most prosocial also are the most likely to engage in some antisocial behaviors. Due to their inexperience, they cannot always discriminate appropriate actions from inappropriate ones. Gradually, children become more aware of what differentiates these two types of behavior and become better able to initiate actions that are useful and appropriate.

Children may experience difficulty in proceeding through any one of the three steps just described. For instance, youngsters may overlook or misinterpret cues that convey another person's need for a prosocial response. They also may miscalculate when determining what behaviors are suited to the situation. A child who is trying to comfort may shove a favorite storybook in another child's face, hug so hard that it hurts, or say something lacking tact, like "Well you don't smell *that* bad." Young helpers may miss the mark by adding water to the acrylic paint to make it go further or by using toothpaste to scrub the windows because they have heard that it cleans so well. In a similar vein, youngsters attempting to defend someone may become aggressive or "catty" as a way to show their favor. At times, children may assume that cooperation means giving up all of one's own ideas or settling for mediocrity in an effort to please everyone or that dissent is totally inappropriate. These are all natural mistakes children make in learning how to be kind to one another. As children mature and gain experience, these become less frequent.

### The Influence of Gender and Age on Prosocial Behavior

As with many other areas of development, scientists have tried to determine whether a person's potential to be prosocial can be predicted by gender or age.

**Gender.** The majority of studies have shown no gender differences in children's willingness to engage in prosocial behavior. A few have yielded mixed results (Honig and Wittmer, 1992; Shaffer, 1994). It would seem that both boys and girls have an equal capacity to be prosocial. Age, on the other hand, does make a difference in the extent to which

children are prosocial and in the reasoning they use to guide their actions.

**Age.** Simply growing older does not guarantee that a person will become more prosocial. However, it generally can be said that children's capacity for prosocial behavior expands with age (Eisenberg, et al., 1995a). The first signs begin early in life. For instance, infants and toddlers seem to recognize and often will react to a companion who is crying or in obvious distress (Reynolds, 1996; Zahn-Waxler, Iannotti, and Chapman, 1982). However, such actions are not a dominant feature of toddlerhood. Sharing, helping, cooperating, comforting, and defending become much more common as children mature. This comes about as a result of their increased accuracy in recognizing signs of distress, their improved language abilities (e.g., potential helpers can ask someone what's wrong or offer verbal encouragement), their growing understanding of what deeds might be interpreted as supportive, and their greater range of potential responses. Sharing provides a good example of these age-related trends.

In a typical early childhood program that serves toddlers and preschoolers, you're bound to see examples of children sharing. Companions as young as two years old offer playthings to one another. However, they find sharing with adults easier, and their frequency of sharing is relatively low compared with older children. This is because younger children are by nature territorial and egocentric (Reynolds, 1996). They highly prize the possession of the moment, making it difficult for them to relinquish objects, even when they are no longer using them. This explains why four-year-old Michael, who rides the tricycle and then runs off to dig in the sand, protests loudly when another child gets on the tricycle. To Michael, the tricycle is his and he dislikes giving it up even though he had lost interest in it. Additionally, younger children don't have the verbal negotiation skills necessary to resolve disputes over possessions or to strike bargains with people that satisfy each party. Consequently, their initial reasons for sharing focus on self-serving interests, such as sharing now so the recipient will be obliged to share with them in the future or to appease a peer who threatens, "I won't be your friend if you don't gimme some" (Birch and Billman, 1986; Levitt, et al., 1985).

Throughout the later preschool and early elementary years, children come to realize that sharing leads to shared activity and that playing with another person is often more fun than playing alone (Reynolds, 1996). During this time children's peer interactions increase and their sharing abilities become greater. The most dramatic changes occur between six and twelve years of age (Honig and Wittmer, 1992; Staub, 1979). There are several reasons why older children share more easily. First, their more advanced intellectual abilities enable them to recognize that it is possible for two people to legitimately want the same thing at the same time, that possessions shared can be retrieved, and that sharing often is reciprocated (Berk, 1997). They also understand that there is a difference between sharing (which means temporary loss of ownership) and donating (which is permanent), and can understand, as well as make clear to others, which of the two is intended (Smith, 1982). In addition, they have more skills at their disposal that allow them to share in a variety of ways. If one approach, such as taking turns, is not satisfactory, they have such options to fall back on as bargaining, trading, or using an object together. These youngsters also have had the opportunity to learn that sharing is viewed favorably by those around them, so they may use this strategy to elicit positive responses (Eisenberg, Lennon, and Roth, 1983; Eisenberg, et al., 1995b). Finally, older children find it easier to part with some items because they differentiate among the values of their possessions. Something that is no longer their "pride and joy" or something that seems to have little value can be given away.

Children in the early elementary years are also motivated to share by a desire for acceptance from others. Prosocial acts such as sharing are seen as good, making it more likely that children who engage in such behavior will enjoy the approval of their peers. The self-sacrifice that comes with sharing is compensated for by that approval. Gradually, as children mature, their reasoning also becomes influenced by the principle of justice. Sharing becomes a way to satisfy that principle. At first children define justice as strict equity, meaning that everyone deserves equal treatment regardless of circumstance. When sharing is called for, children figure that each person must have the same number of turns, that each turn must last the same amount of time, and that everyone must receive the same number of pieces. There is much discussion among peers at this age about fairness. Eventually, children come to believe that equity includes special treatment for those who deserve it—based on extra effort, outstanding performance, or because of disadvantaged conditions (Damon, 1988). Under these circum-

stances, children decide that sharing does not have to be exactly the same to be fair. They recognize that a person who has fewer chances to play may require a longer turn or reason that someone who worked especially hard on a project deserves to go first. This reasoning is sometimes evident in children as young as eight years of age, but for others it appears much later. In either case, such thinking deepens children's understanding of prosocial behavior, leading to more frequent instances of kindness than is possible earlier in life.

The differences between older and younger children in their ability to share underscores changes in their general development and reasoning abilities. Readers will note that children gradually move from self-oriented rationales ("He'll like me better if I share") to other-oriented reasoning ("She'll be unhappy if she doesn't get a turn") and from concrete rationales ("I had it first") to more abstract ideals ("She needs it"). Ultimately, children become better able to "put themselves in another person's shoes" and do so to support their self-respect. The latter achievement tends to occur in later adolescence and is seldom seen in children younger than twelve years of age. Finally, there is evidence that the levels of reasoning described here relate to the actual behaviors children display (Eisenberg, Lennon, and Roth, 1983; Eisenberg, et al., 1995a). Youngsters who are more mature, moral reasoners display a bigger repertoire of prosocial skills and are more likely to engage in prosocial behavior than children who reason at less mature levels. Table 13–2 summarizes the influence of age on prosocial behavior. Children's maturity is determined by their own biological clock and by their cultural experiences.

## Cultural Influences on Prosocial Behavior

In most societies people endorse the norm of social responsibility, that is, behaving in ways that contribute to the common good. The fact that people come together to form groups such as families and communities is based on this ideal. However, cultures clearly differ in the emphasis they place on prosocial behaviors like sharing, helping, or cooperating. Some emphasize competition and individual achievement, whereas others stress cooperation and group harmony. Some have a high tolerance for violence; others do not. In any case, cultural influences play a role in the extent to which kindness is a factor in human interactions. These influences are expressed in laws, in economic policies, through the media, and in the institutions people create. The ways in which members of the society think about

▼ **Table 13–2    Influence of Age on Prosocial Behavior**

| YOUNGER (AGES TWO TO SIX) | OLDER (AGES SIX TO TWELVE) |
|---|---|
| 1. Self-oriented motives | 1. Other-oriented motives |
| 2. Recognize own claim | 2. Recognize legitimacy of others' claims |
| 3. Prize the possession of the moment | 3. Differentiate value among objects |
| 4. "Here and now" thinking | 4. Thinking of future benefits; past experience may be used to guide behavior |
| 5. Few verbal skills with which to bargain or negotiate | 5. Well-developed verbal skills |
| 6. Some difficulty seeing more than one option | 6. Many alternative solutions |

children, how children spend their time, what they see and hear, how they are treated at home and in the community, and the expectations people have for children's behavior are all culturally based. Children growing up in societies that value kindness, helpfulness, and cooperation are apt to internalize those values and display corresponding behaviors in their daily living (Konner, 1991; Whiting and Edwards, 1988). Additionally, cultures that promote warm, loving relationships between adults and children, as well as the early assignment of tasks and responsibilities are likely to produce prosocial children (Hoffman, 1984; Mussen and Eisenberg-Berg, 1977; Taylor and Machida, 1994). The most common place in which societies' youngest members encounter these cultural teachings is in the microsystems of home and formal group settings such as the school or child-care center. Adults are major players in these settings. In fact, adult influences most strongly impact whether children become more or less prosocial.

## Adult Influences on Prosocial Behavior

Adults have a major impact on the degree to which children learn to be helpful and cooperative. One way they do this is by creating an immediate environment that either facilitates or inhibits the development of children's prosocial behavior (Honig and Pollack, 1990; Honig and Wittmer, 1996). In group settings, the atmosphere most likely to promote nurturing, sharing, cooperating, and rescuing has the following characteristics (Cummings and Haggerty, 1997; Staub, 1978):

1. Participants anticipate that everyone will do his or her best to support one another.
2. Both adults and children contribute to decisions made, practices, and procedures.

3. Communication is direct, clear, and mutual.
4. Individual differences are respected.
5. Expectations are reasonable.
6. People like one another and feel a sense of belonging to the group.
7. There is an emphasis on group as well as individual accomplishments.

Adults shape such an environment by using an authoritative discipline style, by modeling prosocial behavior, by rewarding children's attempts at prosocial actions, and by instructing children in prosocial values or skills.

**Discipline strategies.** Nurturant adults who utilize an authoritative approach to discipline promote prosocial behavior in the children with whom they interact (Honig, 1982; Honig and Wittmer, 1996). For example, children of authoritative parents tend to collaborate with others to achieve goals, are more likely to share, and are sympathetic when other children need help (Baumrind, 1995). Such adults teach prosocial values by applying other-oriented reasoning and explaining why they consider this type of behavior desirable. These techniques promote development of the empathy, competence, and rationales children need in order to behave prosocially.

On the other hand, youngsters whose parents use withdrawal of love or assertion of power to discipline children are far less likely to act helpfully, generously, or sympathetically (Baumrind, 1995; Hoffman, 1977). Children of permissive parents tend to be self-indulgent; children of authoritarian parents are obedient, but seldom take the initiative to do something unless it is dictated. Neither of these attitudes fosters empathy, which is the prerequisite for prosocial behavior. Nor do they encourage youngsters to implement positive actions that may not result in a tangible reward.

**Modeling.** Hearing about prosocial behavior is effective, but seeing it in action makes the lesson more vivid. Youngsters who frequently observe people cooperating, helping, sharing, and giving are most likely to act in those ways themselves (Denham, 1995; Grusec and Arnason, 1982). Thus, adults who model such actions, either with other adults or with children help to increase children's prosocial conduct. Furthermore, there is evidence that the effects of such modeling is long-lasting. Investigations of prosocial behavior into adulthood indicate that those who were most prosocial were the most likely to have experienced the benefits of prosocial models as they were growing up. Subjects who were denied such models were also less prone to exhibit high levels of kindness (Clary and Miller, 1986).

Although everyone has the potential to be a prosocial model, certain people are more likely to be imitated than others. Children emulate those models in their lives who are skilled in their behavior, are considered to be of high status by the observer, are helpful and friendly, and are in a position to administer both rewards and consequences (McGinnis and Goldstein, 1984; Schickedanz, 1994). Models who are aloof, critical, directive, punitive, or powerless commonly are ignored. In addition, prosocial modeling has its greatest impact when what adults say is congruent with what they do (Yarrow, Scott, and Waxler, 1973). Researchers have found that when there is inconsistency between words and deeds, the model is less credible and may even prompt children to engage in fewer prosocial acts (Curry and Johnson, 1990; Midlarsky, Bryan, and Brickman, 1973). This follows the old adage "Actions speak louder than words."

Hence, adults who urge children to lend one another a hand but seldom offer assistance themselves show children that helping is not really a high priority. Likewise, if they lecture about the virtues of cooperating and sometimes do so, but grudgingly, youngsters are quick to learn that collaboration is distasteful. Furthermore, adults who insist that children always be truthful, yet tell "little fibs" when it is convenient for them, show children that lying is acceptable even when they say it is not. The result in all cases is that children become less inclined to help or cooperate. On the other hand, when children observe adults acting prosocially and deriving obvi-

ous pleasure from their actions, imitation becomes more likely (Bandura, 1989; Yarrow, Scott, and Waxler, 1973).

**Prosocial attribution.** As mentioned earlier, people's self-definition of how helpful they are is another factor that influences how prosocially they behave. Thus, the more kind, generous, or compassionate children believe themselves to be, the more kindly, generously, and compassionately they will behave toward others (Baron and Bryne, 1993; Grusec and Redler, 1980). Therefore, one way to promote prosocial acts is to encourage children to think of themselves in these ways. Adults who attribute prosocial behaviors to children say things like, "You shared because you like to help others" (Wittmer and Honig, 1994). Such **attributions** make it more likely that children will incorporate these actions and motivations into their images of who they are and what they can do. Attributions must be specific and closely related to what the child has done or said, rather than identifying the child as "a good helper" or saying, "You're a good person because you cleaned up."

**Rewarding prosocial behavior.** A prosocial environment is one in which such conduct is likely to be rewarded. Technically, all adults have to do is watch for instances of children being kind and then enact positive consequences. Yet, adults commonly fail to make the most of this strategy for one of three reasons. First, they may take children's prosocial behaviors for granted and not reward them adequately or often enough. Second, adults may inadvertently reward actions that actually counteract helpful or cooperative behavior. Finally, adults may try to reward children in tangible ways such as with candy or stickers.

In order to avoid these problems, adults must remember that prosocial behaviors are learned and are subject to the same conditions that characterize other learning episodes. That is, children must be motivated to learn and to feel successful. Neither of these criteria is met when adults ignore children who are trying to figure out what the positive expectations are or spend the majority of their time correcting them. Instead, adults must take as much care to enact positive consequences as they do to follow through with corrective ones. For instance, children's prosocial behavior is likely to continue when adults respond with effective praise and undivided attention (Grusec and Redler, 1980; Schickedanz, 1994).

**Competition.** Cooperation among children will be undermined if adults rely on competition as their primary means for motivating children. Youngsters are encouraged to compete rather than cooperate when they are told: "Let's see who can put the most blocks away," "Whoever gets the most words right gets a star," or "The nicest picture will go in the showcase." In each instance, youngsters are quick to determine that there will be only one winner and that helping or cooperating with someone else will sabotage their own chances for coming out on top. On the other hand, such situations could be modified to make it easier for the youngsters to cooperate by focusing on group accomplishments rather than on individual achievement: "Let's see how well we can all work together to put these blocks away," "I'll check the board to find out if the class got more words right today than it did yesterday," or "When you're finished painting your pictures, we'll go out and hang them in the hall." These conditions clear the way for youngsters to come to one another's assistance or to work together as appropriate. In addition, group-administered rewards encourage children to work as a team to achieve a common aim (Bryan, 1975). Putting a star up for each book read by the group or for each act of kindness helps keep track of the children's progress as a whole and directs their attention to what an entire group can achieve. Thus, it is effective to monitor the group's progress and then enact positive consequences when certain "benchmarks" are obtained rather than always rewarding youngsters individually. This approach has been found to lead to friendlier, more cooperative behavior among the participants (Fabes, et al., 1989).

When adults try to administer tangible rewards to encourage prosocial behavior among children, the results are usually counterproductive. Children who are bribed in these ways attribute their actions to the tangible rewards rather than to the needs of others or their own inclinations to treat others kindly.

**Direct instruction.** Children's prosocial behavior also increases when they have been trained to think and act prosocially (Cummings and Haggerty, 1997; Seefeldt, 1995). Such training focuses on the individual skills that lead to helping and cooperating. Recognizing prosocial behavior when it is displayed, identifying the needs of another, anticipating the consequences of acts, and generating multiple solutions to interpersonal problems are all prosocial skills.

A variety of strategies have been used to teach these to children of varying ages. Some include:

1. Discussing the value of prosocial behavior and giving examples of how children themselves can act prosocially.
2. Telling stories that illustrate prosocial principles.
3. Demonstrating prosocial behavior using small figures, dolls, puppets, televised vignettes, or live models.
4. Getting children to re-enact previously observed prosocial actions.
5. Having children role-play situations in which they take on the behaviors of helper and helpee.
6. Teaching children games that promote cooperation and awareness of others.
7. Creating opportunities for children to help or cooperate in real-life situations.

Youngsters who actively participate in tasks or situations that enable them to rehearse prosocial skills demonstrate the greatest instances of such behaviors in similar circumstances (Honig and Wittmer, 1996). These findings hold true from preschool through preadolescence, particularly for youngsters younger than six years of age. The opportunity to physically re-enact appropriate behaviors in relevant situations helps children better remember both the behavior and the cues that signal what conditions apply in a given circumstance. (McGinnis and Goldstein, 1990). For example, when Heidi watches a skit in which she must use a variety of cues to decide which puppet needs help, she is better equipped to recognize when help is needed in a real-life situation. Thus, the most productive approach for direct instruction is to combine verbal descriptions and explanations with practice of corresponding actions.

As can be ascertained from the preceding discussion, there are numerous ways for adults to promote prosocial behavior among children. Some of these, such as using an authoritative style of discipline and modeling and rewarding prosocial actions, are aimed at creating an environment in which helpfulness and cooperation are nurtured and expected. Formal instruction also can be used to teach children prosocial attitudes and behaviors. Specific techniques related to each of these are presented next.

## SKILLS FOR PROMOTING PROSOCIAL BEHAVIOR IN CHILDREN

 ### Create a Prosocial Environment

Using the skills you have learned in previous chapters will help you create an atmosphere that is conducive to the development of prosocial behavior. Some additional strategies include the following.

*1.* **Take advantage of naturally occurring opportunities to label children's prosocial acts.** When children clean the guinea pig's cage, tell them they are showing concern for the animal's well-being. When Theresa announces that she received a get-well card during her recent absence, point out that sending the card was the way someone chose to comfort her. Explain that youngsters who remain quiet while a peer gives a report are helping him or her to concentrate. When children take turns, mention that this is a way of cooperating with one another. All of these instances enable you to highlight prosocial behavior rather than lecturing or moralizing about it.

*2.* **Point out instances in which an unintentional lack of kindness was shown and describe an alternate, prosocial approach.** Through inexperience or thoughtlessness, people sometimes are inconsiderate, selfish, uncooperative, or uncharitable. When this happens, point out to children the effects that behavior had on the person to whom it was directed and describe a more appropriate action. Rather than labeling the child as "selfish," say, "When you didn't give her any, it hurt her feelings." Thus, if youngsters laugh when one of them trips and drops his or her lunch tray, they should be told that their response was unkind because it caused embarrassment and that it would have been more considerate to have helped the child get up and clean up ("It embarrassed Sam when you laughed. He feels really uncomfortable. Help him to pick up the tray.") Likewise, should children see an adult continually interrupt another person, the antisocial nature of this act could be discussed and alternatives suggested.

*3.* **Create opportunities for children to cooperate.** Each day, include projects and routines that require the efforts of more than one person. Assign children to work together to feed the animals rather than doing it yourself or having one child perform the task alone. Allow children to set up the science experiment together rather than having it ready beforehand. Ask several youngsters to collaborate on a mural rather than giving each his or her own section to paint.

*4.* **Create opportunities for children to help.** Give children some responsibility for the care and maintenance of their environment. Although it may be easier for adults to do some tasks themselves, children gain valuable helping experience if they have real work to do.

Periodically, assign youngsters to help one another. Make sure each child has a chance to be both helper and helpee. This can be done individually or in groups. For instance, in gymnastics, children could take turns "spotting" one another on the mat, or one group of youngsters could be taught a math game to teach to another group, who in turn could help them work a crossword puzzle. Encourage children to help one another as occasions arise.

When children ask you to help, try instead to find another child who could fulfill that role. Lifting a child to reach the glue for a playmate instead of getting it yourself, enlisting the aid of age-mates in comforting an unhappy child, or requesting information from a peer in response to a child's question are all examples of this strategy.

*5.* **Use prosocial reasoning when talking with children.** Offer explanations for classroom expectations that are prosocially motivated. For instance, explain that turn taking gives everyone a chance to try a new object or experience. Point out that comforting a friend in distress makes the unhappy child feel better and often makes the comforter feel better too. Focus on other-oriented rationales as well as benefits to the doer. Discuss the special needs represented by each child and how fairness requires taking into account individual circumstances. Ask children to talk about the prosocial reasons behind certain activities in the classroom, such as why people wait to tell their idea until after another

*continued*

person has finished. Set aside time to talk with children about specific incidents in which they and their peers were kind to one another. Reflect on these circumstances and encourage children to discuss how prosocial acts make people feel.

**6. Reward prosocial behavior.** Remain alert to children's attempts to be helpful, cooperative, or kind. Avoid taking these actions for granted or waiting for dramatic episodes before administering a reward. Instead, acknowledge small kindnesses, such as when children move out of the way, help to carry something, play together without bickering, share an idea, or offer encouragement to someone else. Show approval and appreciation by smiling and using positive personal messages.

**7. Administer group rewards.** Think of situations that have the potential for children to work together. These may be newly introduced conditions (such as a special project) or circumstances that traditionally have focused more on individual achievement. For instance, if you have emphasized each child taking care of his or her own area or materials, plan to change this routine to encourage youngsters to work together to clean up a larger area. Implement your plan. Afterward, praise children for their cooperation and helpfulness.

**8. Demonstrate a variety of prosocial behaviors.** Adults who share, help, cooperate, comfort, and rescue illustrate the importance of these behaviors as well as how to carry them out. In order to make the most of this method, carefully examine your own behavior with children and with other adults and then set an example for children to follow. Although it may seem easiest to comfort, rescue, or help children, do not forget to share and cooperate as well. Making a banner for the ward, picking a name for the volleyball team, or building with unit blocks are all situations that lend themselves to modeling cooperation. Allowing a child to borrow your book or distributing portions of a birthday cake made for you by a friend are ways for you to share.

**9. Demonstrate constructive ways of responding to other people's prosocial behavior.** Regardless of whether you are interacting with children or adults, and in spite of whether or not you want help, a positive response contributes to the prosocial environment. If you desire the help that is offered, say, "Thank you" with a pleased expression on your face. If you would rather do something on your own, or if the proposed assistance would not be helpful, do not simply brush the child or adult aside. Instead, acknowledge the kindness and explain that this is something you would like to do yourself or describe an action that would be more useful. In both cases, you are modeling appropriate ways of either accepting or declining help. These are important actions for children to observe.

**10. Be positive when engaging in prosocial behavior.** Because children tend to imitate adults who seem to enjoy giving help and cooperation, exhibit obvious pleasure in prosocial situations. Smile and say things like, "It makes me feel good to help you."

**11. Point out the prosocial behaviors modeled by yourself and others.** Children are better able to understand the prosocial models they see when their behavior is explained. Provide children with such information by saying things like: "Arthur was having a hard time coming up with words for his song, so Lamont is helping him by making a list of some that rhyme," "Sally is worried about getting her X ray, so I'm going to go in with her," or "Randi and Mike have decided to use the workbench together. Randi will use the hammer while Mike uses the saw. Then, they'll trade."

**12. Use positive attribution to increase children's prosocial self-images.** Say specific things, such as, "Elke, you were really helpful to Danielle when you reached up high for the dictionary she needed," or "Lonny and Javon, you were cooperative when you worked together on the diarama. That made the work easier for both of you," or "Jackson, you showed a lot of kind-

## SKILLS FOR PROMOTING PROSOCIAL BEHAVIOR IN CHILDREN—continued

ness when you wiped your sister's tears. It made her feel better knowing you were concerned about her."

 **Give Direct Instruction Related to Prosocial Behavior**

Receiving direct training in helping and cooperating leads to an increase in children's prosocial behavior. Such instruction can be provided through on-the-spot teaching in naturally occurring situations or through preplanned activities. In both cases, the role of the adult is to teach children basic facts about kindness, to demonstrate applications to real-life situations, and to give children a chance to rehearse related skills. Each approach has certain elements in common but also unique characteristics that must be understood in order to implement them successfully.

 **Provide On-the-Spot Instruction**

As you will recall, there are three steps involved in behaving prosocially: awareness, decision making, and action. The main focus of on-the-spot instruction is to assist children at any point beyond which they seem unable to proceed.

*1. Observe children for signs of prosocial behavior.* Watch children carefully. Take note when they show consideration for another person, when they attempt to assist someone, or when they join forces, even briefly. All too often, adults focus on children's negative behaviors; the one big fight Christopher had stands out in their mind and, as a result, they overlook that at one point in the day, he offered help to someone and later appeared distressed at the despair of a friend. Both of these behaviors are signs that Christopher is learning to think of people other than himself.

*2. Ask children directly to help you.* This is particularly important when working with preschoolers who have not yet developed the observational sills to accurately recognize when

help is needed. Pointing out your need for assistance gives them practice in recognizing situational cues and performing corresponding behaviors related to kindness.

*3. Make children aware when someone else needs help or cooperation.* There are times when children fail to recognize distress signals or other signs that indicate that help or cooperation is desired. Rectify this by giving children relevant information to assist them in becoming more attuned to the circumstances at hand. If Marianne seems oblivious to Barney's struggle to carry a heavy board, say: "Look at Barney. He's working awfully hard. He looks like he could use some help." Likewise, if children are outside trying to pick teams and several youngsters are laughing at a private joke, it may be difficult for others to hear whose name is being called. As a result, those who are straining to listen may try to elicit cooperation by telling the jokesters to "pipe down," or "shut up." Such language could easily be misinterpreted by those to whom it is directed or even seen as a challenge to continue. Information from you at this point would be useful: "You are having a good laugh. It's hard for other people to hear. They're just asking you to cooperate by being a little quieter."

*4. Teach children signals they might give to elicit help or cooperation from others.* In the preceding example, youngsters who were trying to get their loud age-mates to cooperate used an antagonistic strategy, which could have backfired. They, too, could benefit from some basic information, such as: "When you yelled at them, it just made them get louder. It might have been better to walk over and explain why you wanted them to be quiet." Toddlers and preschoolers, as well as youngsters in highly charged situations, respond best to direct suggestions. Offer these in the form of script or sample words that they might use: "Tell Marianne, 'This board's too big for me to carry alone.'" With your support and encouragement, most school-age children who are not passionately involved in a situation will be able to generate their own ideas for what to say.

*continued*

## SKILLS FOR PROMOTING PROSOCIAL BEHAVIOR IN CHILDREN—continued

**5. Point out situations in which people could decide to help or cooperate.** At times, children are aware that someone needs their help or cooperation, but don't know what to do next. This is when you can highlight that a prosocial decision can be made by saying something such as: "Janice looks like she needs your help. We can decide to help her," or "Mr. Crouch wants us all to work together on this project. We'll have to decide whether or not to do that."

**6. Discuss situations in which it would be best to decide not to cooperate.** Help children sort out the reasons for such decisions. These would involve circumstances in which people or property are endangered or moral codes are violated. For example, joining together for the purpose of stealing, cheating on an exam, or spray-painting the lavatory walls would be inappropriate cooperative efforts. With school-age children, discuss peer pressure and generate strategies and scripts children might use to cope in uncomfortable peer-related circumstances.

**7. Assist children in determining what type of help or cooperation is most suitable for a particular situation.** Once children show some signs of wanting to help or cooperate, aid them in deciding what action to take. Provide information for them to consider, such as: "Sometimes, when people are unhappy, it helps when someone hugs them or says nice things to them," or "Sometimes, people feel satisfaction from attempting to do something that is difficult, and their pleasure is spoiled if another person takes over." Demonstrations also are useful. Showing a child how to crank the foot of a hospital bed up and down, illustrating to children how one person can steady a mannequin while another puts the clothes on, or demonstrating how it takes two people to make the computer game work are all ways to make these types of discussions more concrete. In addition, discuss ways children can support another person's efforts without offering direct, physical assistance. Point out the importance of a reassuring smile, the "thumbs-up" sign, or cheering from the sidelines. These are all ways children can provide comfort and encouragement. Finally,

teach children to ask questions such as: "Do you want help?", "How can I help you?", "What do you need?", and "What would you like me to do?" This enables children to acquire information about what kind of behavior another person might perceive as helpful or cooperative in a given situation.

**8. Teach children how to share.** Teaching children how to share is not the same as telling them to do it. Use planned activities and on-the-spot instruction to acquaint children with many different ways to share materials and territory—taking turns, using an object/place simultaneously, dividing materials/territory, finding a substitute object/place, or compromising. Additional strategies include the following:

Demonstrating what sharing looks like
Suggesting multiple options from which children might choose
Pointing out instances of sharing as they occur
Reading stories that illustrate ways to share as discussion starters

Give children sample scripts to use in asking for something, as well as for expressing their desire to finish using something. Also, help children negotiate the sequence for using an item; for instance, "I get it next, then Mary gets a turn." Another strategy is to teach children who are waiting for a turn to ask, "How will I know when your turn is over?" This requires the child in possession of an item to designate a signal for completion and gives the waiting child something specific to look for. Older children appreciate being able to say, "Okay, but I get it next." Establishing their turn in the order of possession satisfies their need for some control in the situation. Finally, help children recognize legitimate instances in which sharing can be expected (e.g., using class materials) and other times when sharing cannot be expected (e.g., using someone else's private property). All of these techniques touch on nuances of sharing that cannot be conveyed by simply demanding that children "share."

**9. Work at increasing children's perspective-taking skills.** For children to understand

## SKILLS FOR PROMOTING PROSOCIAL BEHAVIOR IN CHILDREN—continued

when help or cooperation are needed or when an act of kindness is called for, they must learn to put themselves in the place of another person. This is a skill that can be taught to children who are as young as four and five years of age, and one that benefits people of all ages. Promote children's conscious understanding of prosocial behavior by using open-ended questions, such as "How did you know that would happen?" or "What made you think of trying that?" or "How did you know Carlos needed help?" Promote children's consequential thinking by asking such questions as, "What will happen if . . .?" or "What will happen next . . .?" or "If you did . . ., how might that make Roger feel?" Finally, promote children's alternative thinking with such statements as, "William wants to finish the project himself. What could you do to help him do that?" or "What's another way you could help?"

**10. Provide opportunities for children to increase their instrumental know-how.** While attitudes are very important in forming children's prosocial tendencies, knowing what to do in order to be effective is equally valuable. To enable children to develop these particular skills and knowledge, adults should teach children the following strategies. Help children put feelings into words so they are able to express their own emotions and understand the expression of other people's emotions. Provide numerous formal and informal opportunities for children to make decisions in the classroom. This gives children practice in generating alternatives to problems and in developing confidence in their abilities to find positive solutions. Finally, give children chances to learn useful skills. Sorting and organizing materials in the classroom, holding doors while others carry things, speaking on the telephone, accessing information, and using actual tools to fix broken toys are only some of the possibilities for learning. Other ideas will arise as the needs present themselves.

**11. Work with children to evaluate the results of their actions.** Children learn a lot from taking a retrospective look at what they have done as close to the event as possible:

"Did jumping on the box solve the problem?"
"Did Leslie feel better after you talked to her?"
"What happened when you let David finish on his own?"
"How could you tell that Celeste appreciated what you did?"
"Were there enough of you, or did you need more people to work on that project?"
"Were you able to give Raymond all the information he needed?"
"How do you think it worked out for everybody to have a 5-minute turn with the microscope?"

If children are unable to assess their own performances, offer some information yourself or help them glean information from others. This evaluation could be conducted during a private conversation with a child or as a group assessment of group effort. Regardless of how well their prosocial venture worked out, praise children for attempting it.

**12. Encourage children to accept kindness from others.** Sometimes, children are unaware of or misinterpret other children's attempts at prosocial behavior. Thus, Tricia may not realize that when Audrey takes over, she is actually trying to help, nor may she understand that Sam's apparent lack of decisiveness is his way of trying to cooperate. In situations like these, point out what is really taking place.

In addition, there are children who, wanting to be independent or self-sufficient, actively reject assistance, reassurance, or sympathy. Frequently, they neither cooperate nor expect cooperation from others. Their rationale is that they expect nothing and give nothing. In reality, such youngsters often fear rejection or "taking a chance on" someone. These children need to experience kindness before they can extend it to those around them. Because their actions put other children off, it is you who must reach out. Do not fail to provide unreceptive youngsters with the same courtesies or offers of help and encouragement that you might grant to a more appreciative child. This is the first step in help-

*continued*

## SKILLS FOR PROMOTING PROSOCIAL BEHAVIOR IN CHILDREN—continued

ing them become more accepting of prosocial behavior from someone else.

**13. Support children when their attempts at kindness are rebuffed.** At times, children's enthusiasm is dashed if their offer of help is refused or an action they thought was helpful turns out not to have been. If this happens, acknowledge the child's disappointment or frustration and discuss the situation. If you can, offer information that might assist the child in understanding the outcome. If you do not know why their attempt failed, be supportive and sympathetic.

All of the preceding strategies can be used individually, on separate occasions, or in combination. Which specific technique is called for depends on the particular circumstance in which you are involved. This is illustrated in the following real-life scenario:

**SITUATION:** Kenton and Josh, two six-year-olds, are playing with a construction toy that has many interconnecting pieces. Josh builds an elaborate vehicle, which Kenton admires.

*Kenton:* Make me one like yours.

*Josh:*  Well, if I make it, it'll be mine.

*Kenton:* But I want one. Make me one.

*Josh:*  Then it'll be mine!

*Kenton:* I can't get the pieces to fit.

At this point, it is obvious that Kenton is unsuccessfully trying to elicit Josh's help. Now is when the adult intervention is appropriate.

*Adult:*  Josh, Kenton is asking you for help. Sometimes, when people help, they do the job for someone. However, it sounds like you think if you make the car for Kenton, it will have to be yours. Another way people help is by showing someone how to do it. That way, Kenton can make his own car with your help. How does that sound to you?

*Josh:*  Okay.

*Kenton:* Yeah.

Josh demonstrated how his car went together. Once this was well under way, the adult com-

mented briefly on the boys' cooperative behavior as well as on Josh's willingness to help a friend.

In this situation, the adult enabled one child to become aware of another child's signals and provided information about a possible course of action. She also rewarded the children for demonstrating prosocial behavior. Later in the day, she could take a moment to informally talk with Kenton and Josh about their reactions to the helping episode. Another type of direct instruction involves teaching prosocial behavior through planned activities.

 **Coordinate Planned Activities**

Planned activities are lessons adults develop in advance and carry out with children individually or in groups. The best activities are not necessarily the most elaborate; rather, they are those that have been well prepared and then implemented in ways that are sensitive to children's interests and needs. The following illustrates how best to accomplish this.

**1. Decide what prosocial skill you want to teach.** Choose one of the skills described in this chapter, such as becoming aware that someone needs help, deciding to help, or taking action to help.

**2. Think of many different ways the prosocial skill you have chosen might be presented to children.** Lessons that include both discussion and active participation are the most effective. Active participation means getting children physically involved in the activity by handling props, moving about, and talking rather than simply listening. Some examples of successful activities include:

a. Reading and telling stories that have a prosocial theme. Stories might include such classics as *The Musicians of Bremen* (Scholastic Books), which tells the tale of how, through cooperation, several elderly animals were able to live long lives in peace. Another old tale is the ever popular *Three Little Pigs*, in which the pigs cooperate to defeat the hungry wolf. Older children might enjoy finding

## SKILLS FOR PROMOTING PROSOCIAL BEHAVIOR IN CHILDREN—continued

examples of prosocial behavior in chapter books, such as *Charlotte's Web*.

b. Dramatizing prosocial situations through skits, using puppets, dolls, or stand-up figures.

c. Discussing with the children prosocial events that have occurred in the formal group setting.

d. Role-playing prosocial episodes. Sample topics might include how to ask for help or cooperation, how to decide whether help or cooperation is needed, determining what type of action would be most helpful or cooperative, and how to decline unwanted help.

e. Discussing scenes from magazines, books, or posters. The discussion might involve identifying who was helped, who provided help, and how the help was carried out or pointing out cooperative and uncooperative behaviors.

f. Playing cooperative games such as ring-around-a-rosy with toddlers or carrying out a scavenger hunt with older children in which groups of children search for things as a team rather than competing as individuals.

g. Turning traditionally competitive games such as Bingo into cooperative group efforts. To adapt this game, have one card for every two or three children. The object is to help one another find the matching numbers or pictures, rather than competing to be the first to complete a card. When one group's card is complete, those youngsters may move to another group to help them. Several game books are on the market that emphasize cooperative efforts.

h. Creating group projects, such as a class book or mural, to which everyone contributes.

**3. Select one of your activity ideas to develop further.** Make a realistic assessment of what props are available, how much time you will have, the physical setting, and the number of children you will be working with at one time. For instance, do not choose a story that takes 20 minutes to read if you only have 10 minutes in which to work. Likewise, if the only setting available is a bustling waiting room, or the only time available is when children may be hungry or preoccupied with other responsibilities, it is not appropriate to plan activities that require intense concentration.

**4. Develop a plan of action that outlines the prosocial activity from start to finish.** Write this plan down as a way to remember it and further think it through. Include what you will say to introduce the activity, any instructions you may have to give, how you will handle materials, how you will have children use them, the sequence of steps you will follow, and how you will close. Anticipate what you will say or do if children seem uninterested or unable to carry out your directions.

**5. Gather the materials you will need.** Make any additional props that are necessary.

**6. Implement your plan.** Utilize skills you have learned in previous chapters related to nonverbal and verbal communication, reflecting, asking questions, playing, and developing skits to enhance your presentation.

**7. Evaluate your activity in terms of immediate and long-term prosocial outcomes.** Typical evaluation questions include: Who were the children who participated? What did children actually say or do in this activity? How did children demonstrate interest or lack of interest? Later in the day, did children refer either to the activity or the prosocial skill covered in the activity in their conversation or play? Over time, do children spontaneously demonstrate prosocial behaviors highlighted by the activity?

**8. Repeat the same prosocial activity, or a variation of it, at another time.** Children learn prosocial concepts through repeated exposure over time. Therefore, do not expect to see immediate behavior change or the adoption of prosocial skills in their everyday interactions after just one or two presentations of a particular skill.

 **Communicate with the Family**

Children's prosocial behaviors within the family setting can, and should, be encouraged by

*continued*

## SKILLS FOR PROMOTING PROSOCIAL BEHAVIOR IN CHILDREN—continued

family members. Following, are some strategies that will enable you to join forces with parents and other significant people in children's lives to promote children's prosocial behavior.

**1. Communicate your classroom philosophy of cooperation to families.** Cooperative activities, rather than competitive ones, group projects, and individual work give children a message that each person in the classroom has an important role in the smooth functioning of that setting. These are all ways of promoting a spirit of community cooperation and helpfulness. Use positive personal messages as a way of promoting these positive and growth-enhancing behaviors. Communicate your philosophy to parents in the form of a newsletter in which you describe what prosocial behavior is and how it is encouraged in the classroom.

**2. Initiate and model cooperative activities in the program that include family members.** There are many tasks to be done in a classroom such as special maintenance of computers, washing door and window frames, sterilizing toys, planting bushes or trees on school grounds, or fundraising for new play equipment that may provide logical opportunities to involve family members. Several publicly and privately funded programs in a small city in Michigan (and in many others throughout the nation) hold infrequent but regular "work parties," during which adult and child family members have important roles in classroom or school improvement. Such tasks as the ones described require varying degrees of expertise, thus providing opportunities for a wide range of participation. The work party time focuses on building community among the teachers, children, and their families, as well as accomplishing the necessary work. In all cases, families are actively involved in the planning and the execution stages of the project. Professionals work with family members to break down the tasks into manageable components, so that everyone can be successful and to ensure that all necessary materials and equipment are ready to be used. An essential feature of projects such as this one is that all the professionals are model-

ing the cooperative behavior they are asking of others. On a smaller scale, you may wish to choose one special project that will involve families in an active, cooperative way. Work with other professionals in your setting to select the project and to organize family involvement. Remember to point out to the children the helpful actions carried out by their family members. Be sure not to make invidious comparisons, but simply make children aware of the help that was offered.

**3. Invite parents and other family members to help in the formal group setting.** Expand the old concept of "room mothers" to include every member of the child's family. At the beginning of the program year, send out a "family interest survey" eliciting information about things adult family members are interested in doing, such as repairing toys, sewing, accompanying field trips, designing bulletin boards, or telling stories. Among the most valuable contributions families can make to the classroom are such activities as teaching songs or musical games that represent their cultural heritage, preparing foods that may be unfamiliar to many students, and so on. Families may be reluctant to respond in writing, so carry out conversations with parents at informal times as a way of both finding out information and encouraging them to participate. Some adults may be more comfortable helping "behind the scenes," whereas others may be able to take advantage of working directly with the children. Provide an opportunity for all kinds of participation, and be sure to acknowledge all help in writing and verbally. Children will benefit from sending a "thank you" note to the family, as well.

**4. Answer families' questions about the role of competition and cooperation in their children's lives.** At the same time that cooperation is being fostered in the classroom, some parents may express concern that in order to be "successful in life" their children need to feel competitive. Hold discussions with family members on this topic or introduce it as part of a newsletter to families. Encourage parents to

## SKILLS FOR PROMOTING PROSOCIAL BEHAVIOR IN CHILDREN—continued

express their views and acknowledge their perceptions. Point out some of the differences between "doing one's best" and "beating the opposition." For example, children's achievement may be measured in many ways:

Reviewing how much better they did this time than last

Monitoring the cumulative success of team members working together

Setting specific, individual goals and charting how close one comes to achieving the goal over time

Recording in some graphic or otherwise retrievable manner (e.g., audio or videotape) the achievement of individuals and/or groups of children

Keeping journal entries (either dictated or self-written) regarding the emotions of the individual upon working toward an identified goal

Help parents understand how to support their children through the disappointments and hard times that inevitably come with competition and comparisons. Rather than denying their children's perceptions of "failure," aid parents in understanding how to use affective reflections and continuing responses to encourage children to reveal and, therefore, better understand their emotions at such times. Point out developmental norms with regard to how children at various ages assess their success or failure. In addition, mention, if appropriate, that while some children become more motivated to do as the adult wishes when prompted by a competitive statement or challenge, friction among children also increases.

**5. Assist adults in figuring out how their children can be helpful at home.** In many families, certain routine chores are assigned to the youngest members. Jobs such as making one's own bed in the morning, clearing dishes from the table, meal planning, and even simple meal preparation are well within the abilities of most

children. Responsibility for these tasks gives children a sense of contributing to the life of their family, as well as increasing their self-perceptions of competence and worth. Encourage adult family members to have discussions with their offspring as to the ways in which the children can be helpful at home. Suggest that the family draw up a list of chores to be done and that young family members choose from among the list. Sometimes children prefer doing the same task over and over; at other times, they would rather change jobs frequently. Suggest the family make a decision about this, and explore the possibility that the same strategy need not necessarily apply to every child. In other words, some children in a family may hold the same responsibility, while others switch. Offer a visible means of letting everyone know that a job is done, such as a chart with stars or other stickers that the children are responsible for marking.

Caution parents against fostering competition among their children. Negative comparisons have the effect of discouraging rather than encouraging participation. Suggest instead, that some chores may be more efficiently handled when several people cooperate. Also include standards for completion in order to avoid misunderstandings. For example, in one family, eight-year-old Aaron was to sweep the kitchen after dinner. His father was cross with him for not returning the broom and dustpan to the closet. After some discussion, both parties realized that although the adult assumed that putting things away was part of the job, the child did not see that as part of his responsibility. As a consequence, the chore was changed to sweeping the floor *and* putting away the tools.

Finally, explain to adults the importance of not taking children's work for granted. Children are more likely to continue their efforts when their assistance has been acknowledged and the positive influence of their contributions on the operations of the family has been appreciated.

## Sample Activities

Table 13–3 presents five prosocial activities to give
you examples of how to formulate your own.

| ▼ Table 13–3 | Sample Activities |
|---|---|

### ACTIVITY 1

**Activity Name:** Sharing a Lump of Clay

**Goal:** To help children share

**Materials:** A two-pound lump of clay, a table with five chairs (one for an adult, four for children), one plastic knife, one pair of scissors, one 12-inch length of wire

**Procedure:**
1. Place a lump of clay in the center of the table.
2. Neutralize the clay by keeping one hand on it. Say: "I have one big ball of clay, and there are four children who want to use it. Tell me how everyone can have a chance."
3. Listen to children's ideas; elicit suggestions from everyone.
4. Clarify each child's perspective by paraphrasing his or her ideas to the group. Follow up with, "And what do you think of that?"
5. Remain impartial throughout this process. Do not show disapproval of any child's idea, regardless of its content.
6. Remind children as necessary that the first step in playing with the clay is deciding how that will take place.
7. If children become bogged down, repeat pertinent helping facts and principles.
8. Summarize the solution when it has been achieved.
9. Praise children.
10. Carry out the agreed-upon solution.

### ACTIVITY 2

**Activity Name:** Helping Decisions

**Goal:** To teach children to recognize situations in which people need help and to determine appropriate ways of helping

**Materials:** Eight to ten pictures selected from magazines that show people or animals who need help in some way or who are being helped in some way. These should be large enough for four or five children to be able to see them two or three feet away and should be mounted on cardboard. Pictures should depict a variety of ages, cultures, and helping situations.

**Procedure:**
1. Select one picture at a time for discussion. Keep other pictures face down.
2. Introduce the activity by saying: "I have several pictures here about helping. Look at this one; somebody needs help."
3. Prompt discussion with questions and statements such as: "Tell me who needs help? How did you know? Is there anyone in the picture who could help? What could they do? Who has another idea? What do you think this man will do if someone tries to help? Why might the man not want her to help him? What might you do if you had the same problem as the people in the picture?"
4. Paraphrase children's suggestions and ideas and elicit reactions from other youngsters in the group.
5. Accept all the children's suggestions and praise them for working so hard at figuring out who needs help, who could help, and what should be done.
6. Should the discussion falter, provide useful information by repeating pertinent helping terms, facts, and principles.
7. Repeat the procedure with additional pictures.

▼ **Table 13–3—continued** **Sample Activities**

### ACTIVITY 3

**Activity Name:** Helping Skits

**Goal:** To give children practice recognizing opportunities to help and in determining appropriate help

**Materials:** Two child-like puppets or dolls and a block or other "heavy" object

**Procedure:**
1. To a small or large group of children, introduce the following scenario: "Pretend these puppets/dolls are real children who are about your age and who attend a program like ours. Their names are Isaac and Reuben (or Nina and LaKeesha). This is a story about helping. Watch what these children do and we will talk about it afterward."
2. Present a situation in which one of the puppets/dolls is struggling to lift the heavy object. Have the puppet show signs of strain (grunting, groaning, etc.). The other puppet should stay within view but on the sidelines, looking on. Announce the end of the scene by saying, "The End."
3. Pose the following questions to the children:
   Who needed help?
   How could you tell?
   What did (character name) do or say that showed he/she needed help?
   What did the other person do or say?
   Did he/she know that help was needed?
   What could (the first character) do or say to show he/she needed help?
   What could (the second character) do or say to show he/she was helpful?
4. Replay the scene using children's suggestions. Help them evaluate the success or failure of the strategy by asking similar questions as above. Replay the episode a few times, using different suggestions made by children or using such ideas as: The second character recognizes help is needed, but declines to help, or the second character offers "help" that hinders rather than aids, and so on.

   After a time by which children are familiar with physical help (this may take days or weeks depending on children's experience and cognitive abilities), change the scenario to one that depicts alleviation of stress or upset. Such a scene might include a character upset at the loss of a pet or favorite writing implement. Carry this out much as you did the previous episodes, focusing on the recognition of distress and the helpful or nonhelpful responses of the second character. Remember to help children evaluate the strategy each time.

(Note: It is important that you switch the roles of the puppet/doll characters frequently so that children do not develop stereotypic notions of how certain people behave, whether as a result of gender, race, physical abilities, or other factors.)

As a follow-up on this activity, give children the opportunity to create their own scenarios around the theme of helping. Help them figure out which behavior to focus on and how they will determine which actions to portray. You will find that, over time, children may become quite skilled at this play.

### ACTIVITY 4

**Activity Name:** Group Box Sculpture

**Goal:** To give children the opportunity to cooperate spontaneously

**Materials:** Boxes, cartons, and containers of various sizes and shapes (these could be provided by the adult, or children could be asked to bring one or more to contribute to the project); glue; masking tape; staple gun; stapler; poster paint; brushes; newspapers; towels; sponges and buckets; scissors; markers; crayons; glitter; fabric swatches; wallpaper. There should be a wide variety of materials but a limited supply of each.

*continued*

▼ **Table 13-3—continued    Sample Activities**

| | |
|---|---|
| **Procedure:** | 1. Set up the activity prior to the children's arrival by placing all of the materials in the center of the project area—crayons in one bin, markers in another, scissors in another, and so on. This will encourage youngsters to share materials more than if each child had his or her own personal supply. |
| | 2. Introduce the activity by explaining that many people will work together to make a group sculpture. No one person will be in charge. Instead, everyone must work as a team. There are many materials available, and children may use any of them. |
| | 3. Stand back and allow children to figure out how to proceed. |
| | 4. Provide momentary help by giving relevant information related to the concepts or by mediating any conflicts that arise. Children should be allowed to work out their own disagreements if this can be accomplished without physical danger. |
| | 5. Point out instances of cooperation, compromises that are made, and other prosocial behaviors that are exhibited. |
| | 6. Keep the project and give children a chance to talk about their role and the role of others producing it. |

(Note: This project may take more than one day to complete.)

---

**ACTIVITY 5**

---

| | |
|---|---|
| **Activity Name:** | Classroom Fish Tank |
| **Goal:** | To enable children to experience three phases of cooperation: planning, implementing a plan, and sharing in the outcome. |
| **Materials:** | Several books about tropical fish and a large glass tank. As the project is planned, additional equipment will be purchased: gravel, filtering mechanism, plants, fish, fish food, etc. |
| **Procedure:** | 1. Introduce the project by explaining that the children, as a group, will have the opportunity to put together an aquarium. This will be a cooperative effort in which everyone will participate in planning what will be needed, setting up the fish tank, stocking it, caring for the fish, and enjoying it. |
| | 2. Divide the group into "investigation" teams, to study the written material on tropical fish. Explain that the fish tank should include fish that are compatible with one another, as well as fish and other animals that help clean the tank. Suggest that children explore bottom dwellers and surface dwellers. Older children can make use of the school or community library, as well as the sources you provide. Each group may assume responsibility for a different phase of the project (deciding on equipment, fish recommendations, cost of purchasing equipment, and so on) or each group may outline the entire project. |
| | 3. Once the lists are drawn up, correlate the suggestions as part of a large group discussion. Help the children establish a plan for proceeding. Part of this plan may include a field trip to a local pet store, in which case, this, too, must be planned. |
| | 4. With the children, carry out the steps of the plan. |
| | 5. Throughout the process, elicit ideas and help from as many children as possible and provide pertinent information by reiterating the cooperation facts and principles. Point out examples of cooperation in the group. Carry out discussions evaluating children's responses to the project, including changes that might be made in the future. |

(Note: The degree of complexity of this project is open-ended. The activity could be simplified by having all the materials on hand, by limiting the size of the groups, and minimizing the decisions to be made. It could be extended by having children generate a fund-raising project to pay for the materials).

## ▼ PITFALLS TO AVOID

Whether you are teaching children prosocial behavior by creating an atmosphere that is conducive to acts of kindness, providing on-the-spot instruction, or using planned activities, there are certain mistakes to avoid.

**Failing to recognize children's efforts to behave prosocially.** Children who are just learning to help and cooperate may be awkward in their attempts or may initially pursue a course of action that, at first, bears little resemblance to kindness. When this happens, adults may misinterpret these behaviors as purposefully uncooperative or unhelpful. Although limits on potentially harmful behavior are appropriate, children should receive support for their good intentions as well as information on how to improve their performance. This means it will be necessary to ascertain what a child was trying to achieve before taking corrective action. Thus, if children are adding water to the acrylic paint or scrubbing the window with toothpaste, don't automatically assume that their motives are to ruin the materials or to strike out at you. Instead, ask questions such as: "What were you trying to do?", "What did you think would happen?", or "Why are you . . .?" If they give an indication that their intent was to be helpful, acknowledge their efforts and explain why what they are doing is not as useful as it could be and what they could do instead. Make sure that your voice tone is sincerely questioning and not accusatory. These same strategies can be employed in any situation in which a child is attempting to help, cooperate, comfort, or rescue via some inappropriate means.

There will be occasions when you do set a limit or enforce a consequence only to discover later that the child truly was trying to help. If this happens, go back to the child, explain that you now understand what he or she was trying to do, and discuss why corrective action was necessary. Give the child specific ideas about what to do instead.

**Bringing a prosocial model's behavior to a child's attention through negative comparison or through competition.** As has been stated previously, children are more likely to imitate models whose behavior is pointed out to them. However, adults should not use these situations to make unfavorable comparisons between the model's behavior and that of the child. Statements like "Look at Roger. He's so polite. Why can't you be more like

that?" make the child feel defensive rather than receptive and do not make imitation likely. A better approach would be to say: "Roger accidentally bumped into Maureen, so he said, 'Excuse me.' That was a very polite thing to do." The first statement was an evaluative remark aimed at shaming the child; the second provides factual information in a nonjudgmental way.

**Coercing children to engage in insincere prosocial behavior.** It is not uncommon for adults who are trying to teach children consideration to manipulate them into expressions of kindness that the youngster's do not really feel. This is illustrated by the parent who insists that twelve-year-old Raymond "be nice" and give Aunt Martha a kiss, even though the child has protested that he doesn't like to do it. He complies, not to be kind to Aunt Martha, but to avoid trouble. Similar difficulties arise when children are prodded into saying they are sorry when, in fact, they are not. Again, youngsters learn that apologizing is the quickest way out of a dilemma rather than a sincere expression of remorse. Likewise, children who are urged to bestow false compliments on others as a way to charm them are learning that hypocrisy is acceptable. In order to avoid these undesirable outcomes, adults must refrain from being preoccupied with the outer trappings of kindness at the expense of helping children develop the empathy that is necessary for true kindness to occur. Hence, it would be better to give the child information about the other person that might prompt empathic feelings: "Aunt Martha is glad to see you. She loves you very much. It would make her feel good to know that you care about her, too," "When you were trying to practice with your crutches, you banged Jerry in the leg. That hurt a lot," or "You told me you thought Carrie's spider was neat. She'd probably like to hear that from you."

**Making children share everything, all the time.** There is no doubt that sharing is an important interpersonal skill that children should learn about. Unfortunately, there are times when adults promote this virtue too enthusiastically. They make children give up items that they have really not finished using as soon as other children want them. For instance, Elizabeth was using three grocery bags to sort the food in her "store." One bag was for boxes, one was for cans, and one was for plastic fruit. She needed all three bags. Helen approached and asked if she could have one of the bags to make a "dress." Elizabeth protested, but the adult insisted that Helen be given a bag. The adult dumped out the fruit and gave a sack to Helen. In this case, Elizabeth had a legitimate right to finish using the bag. It would have been easier for her to share it willingly once her game was over. A better approach would have been to say: "Elizabeth, when you are finished playing your game, Helen would like a chance to use a bag. Tell her when you are ready."

A variation of this problem occurs when adults arbitrarily regulate turn-taking as a way to get children to share. For example, as soon as a child gets on a tricycle, the adult admonishes, "Once around the yard, and then you'll have to get off so someone else can have a turn." This approach is utilized in a well-meaning effort to avoid conflict or to be fair. However, it often ends up with no child feeling truly satisfied. Furthermore, it requires constant adult monitoring. Instead, allow children to fully use the materials to which they have access. It would be better, if at all possible, to expand the amount of equipment available so that youngsters are not pressured into having to give up something with which they are deeply involved. If this is not possible, prompt empathic feelings by pointing out that others are waiting and would like a turn, too. Finally, remember to praise children when they finally relinquish what they have been using to someone else. Point out how their actions pleased the child who wanted to be next.

## ▼ SUMMARY
Youngsters who behave prosocially develop feelings of satisfaction and competence, have many successful encounters, and get help and cooperation from others in return. They learn to respond positively to offers of help and cooperation from others as well. Groups in which prosocial behavior is fostered are friendlier and more productive than those in which it is ignored.

To behave prosocially, children first must become aware of situations in which such acts would be beneficial. Then, they have to decide if and how they will act and finally, take the action (or lack of action) they have decided on. Desiring to act prosocially and knowing how best to do it are not necessarily learned at the same time. As children mature and gain experience, they become more proficient at matching their prosocial actions to the needs of others. Children's abilities to take on another's perspective also affect their prosocial behavior; that is, children with good role-taking abilities are generally more prosocially inclined. This link becomes stronger with age.

Age and culture influence children's prosocial behavior; gender may not. In our society, nurturing and sharing increase with age; rescuing and cooperating behaviors first increase and then show a downward trend. Children in cultures that value group living steadily increase in cooperativeness as they mature. Similarly, in many studies, rural children are more cooperative than urban children. Particular societal characteristics either promote or inhibit prosocial conduct.

The most profound influences on children's helpful and cooperative behavior are the discipline strategies adults use, the behaviors they model, the behaviors in children they reward, and the prosocial values and the skills they teach. Teaching children kindness can be accomplished through creating an atmosphere conducive to prosocial actions, through on-the-spot instruction, and through planned activities. Partnerships between the family and the professionals who work with the children enhance children's intentions and skills toward prosocial behavior.

## ▼ DISCUSSION QUESTIONS
1. Identify several aspects of prosocial behavior. Discuss their similarities and differences using examples from real life.
2. In small groups, talk about the benefits and risks of behaving prosocially. When appropriate, tell about some personal instances in which you did or did not behave prosocially and the consequences of those behaviors.
3. Geraldo is working hard at constructing a bridge out of tongue depressors. He seems to be having difficulty getting it to stay up. Patrick is watching.
   a. Describe the steps Patrick will go through in acting prosocially toward Geraldo.
   b. Discuss all the possible choices Patrick will have to make and the potential outcomes of each decision.

4. Describe the influence of age on children's prosocial behavior. Discuss the emergence and the increase or decline of particular types of prosocial behaviors as children get older. Give reasons based on your understanding of children's development.

5. Discuss cultural influences on children's prosocial behavior. Describe experiences in your own upbringing to illustrate. Describe particular family or social values that had an impact.

6. Describe the attributes of the atmosphere of a formal group setting that facilitate the development of children's prosocial behavior. Discuss specifically how the discipline strategies you have learned thus far contribute to this atmosphere.

7. Describe six ways in which adults can model cooperation in the formal group setting and in the home. Discuss how children can translate these techniques into their own behavior.

8. Using examples from the formal group setting in which you work, describe instances in which adults:
   a. Rewarded children's prosocial behavior.
   b. Overlooked children's prosocial behavior.
   c. Inadvertently punished children's prosocial behavior.
   Discuss any aftermath you observed, either immediately or within a short time.

9. Discuss the role of direct instruction on children's prosocial behavior. Relate specific skills that foster helping and cooperating to particular strategies for teaching these skills.

10. Referring to Appendix A, NAEYC Code of Ethical Conduct, find the principles and ideals to use in judging the ethics of the following situation: Two teachers in your program are excited about an activity they heard about at a recent workshop. Each time children do a kind act they earn a point. The child with the most points at the end of the week is named "kindness kid" for a day.

## ▼ FIELD ASSIGNMENTS

1. Choose a prosocial skill. In a few sentences, describe an activity you will use to teach children about the behavior you have selected. **Carry out your plan with children.** Describe how you carried out your plan and how the children responded. Briefly talk about how you might change or improve your plan for repetition in the future.

2. Identify a job you ordinarily carry out yourself in your field placement. Describe at least three ways you could get children involved in helping you. Implement one of your strategies. Then describe what actually happened. Discuss what it is about your plan you might repeat in the future and what you might change.

3. Focus on modeling prosocial behavior. Describe a prosocial behavior that you modeled and how you did it. Next, discuss a situation in which you pointed out prosocial modeling by yourself or by another person. Write out the words you used.

4. Select a prosocial skill to teach children. Use the on-the-spot strategies identified in this chapter. Document children's progress over time.

5. Describe a conversation between you (or another professional) and an adult family member in which a child's prosocial behavior was discussed. Outline the nature of the behavior as well as any strategies that were suggested to encourage the prosocial actions. Write a brief evaluation based on the material covered in this and earlier chapters.

# ▼Chapter 14

## Supporting Children's Development: Sexuality, Ethnicity, and Special Needs

## ▼ OBJECTIVES

*On completion of this chapter, you will be able to describe:*

▼ Children's psychosexual development.

▼ Outcomes related to the development of ethnic identity, preferences, and attitudes in young children.

▼ Issues surrounding inclusion of children with special needs in formal group settings.

▼ The impact of temperament on children's individuality.

▼ Skills for effective handling of developmental issues related to children's sexuality, ethnicity, special needs, and other differences.

▼ Strategies for communicating with families about children's individual differences.

▼ Pitfalls in the handling of issues related to variations in children's development.

---

A four-year-old boy in the housekeeping area of a large child-care center suddenly announces that the dolls are "going to make a baby." Putting one doll on top of the other, he tells two other children who are playing nearby, "Watch this!" and proceeds with a fairly demonstrative performance. The other two children watch with obvious fascination. As the teacher approaches, the child quickly picks up one of the dolls, purposefully ending the play episode.

Several young children begin arguing over selection of a variety of small dolls representative of different ethnic groups. The hands-down favorites are the white and Asian dolls. An adult cheerfully suggests that no one has chosen any of the black dolls lying on the bottom of the box. "We can't. They're dirty and bad," responds one of the children. The adult is particularly surprised because the statement is made by an African-American child.

Kathy, a student who is visually impaired is being mainstreamed into a fifth-grade classroom. She watches tensely as two teams are chosen for kickball during recess. When she is not chosen by either team, the teacher announces, "Kathy will want to play, too." There is an embarrassed silence, but no offer is made by either team to have Kathy join them.

---

At times, helping professionals may feel genuine embarrassment, irritation, discomfort, and uncertainty in handling sensitive situations such as these. Because of personal emotions that automatically arise in response to their own moral sensibilities and past experiences, adults may find themselves reacting too intensely, avoiding or ignoring negative behaviors, or feeling momentarily confused about what might be the most effective response. Occasionally, adults may misinterpret a child's intentions. For example, in 1996, a six-year-old boy in a North Carolina classroom gained national attention for kissing a classmate. He was charged with sexual harrassment and isolated by his teacher from other children, causing him to miss out on a coloring activity and an ice cream party as a consequence. When questioned about what he understood about sexual harrassment, the child was at a loss for an explanation, simply saying, "She's my friend."

A serious by-product of excessive adult anxiety, discomfort, or rejection in such situations is the deleterious effect such reactions or avoidance may have on children's development—primarily the production of guilt, loss of self-esteem, or the reinforcement of negative attitudes, misinformation, and maladaptive behavior.

Conversely, when adults are able to maintain a sensitive, nonreactive, and matter-of-fact approach in handling sensitive issues, positive psychosocial development and competence are promoted in the child. Supportive adults keep in mind the value and principles of a positive corrective experience and view the child's behavior in terms of what the child is trying to express, rather than simply focusing on the positive or negative qualities of the behavior.

In addition to responding appropriately to children's behavior in sensitive areas, helping professionals also have the responsibility of steering children away from developing harmful biases. They can do this by sharing children's literature that focuses on diversity, promoting cooperative learning and discussions, answering questions honestly and thoughtfully, and providing experiences that teach self-awareness and counter biases. Derman-Sparks (1989), in her excellent guide for developing anti-bias curriculum for young children admits that her suggestions are value based: "Differences are good; oppressive ideas and behavior are not." She suggests that children become aware very early that "color, language, gender, and physical ability differences are connected with privilege and power. They learn by observing the differences and similarities among people and by absorbing the spoken and unspoken messages about those differences. Racism, sexism, and handicapism have a profound influence on their developing sense of self and others."

## ▼ CHILDREN'S PSYCHOSEXUAL DEVELOPMENT

### The Development of Sexual Attitudes

From infancy, all human beings have sexual feelings. A positive attitude toward sexuality means accept-ing these sensual feelings and urges as natural rather than shameful. Children's subsequent ability to handle such feelings effectively will depend on their earliest experiences. Early encounters involving psychological intimacy with significant others teach a child that interpersonal involvement is safe or dangerous, pleasurable or unpleasurable, depending on the extent to which important people are nurturing, nonjudgmental, empathic, supportive, and committed to promoting the child's well-being.

Similarly, children develop positive or negative attitudes toward their own bodies and bodily functions depending on adults' verbal and nonverbal reactions as they help children with everyday functions such as bathing, dressing, and elimination. If adults use words such as "nasty" or "dirty" to describe genital areas or elimination, children are apt to develop feelings that there is something unacceptable about them.

**Masturbation.** Although childhood masturbation is a fairly universal human experience, it can elicit major concern in some adults. Most children discover their genital areas quite by accident during infancy as they become acquainted with their own bodies through poking into openings and exploring their own extremities. Briggs (1975) outlines three stages of normal development related to masturbation, the first occurring as the child experiences an overall pleasant sensation on contact with the sensitive nerve endings in the genitalia and then actively strives to repeat the experience. It should be pointed out that, although it is pleasurable, the masturbatory experience in the young child is not qualitatively the same as that experienced by a sexually mature individual. In fact, young children can be seen deriving comfort from and enjoying similar sensations by stroking other, less provocative body parts such as their noses and ears, twisting locks of their hair, or rubbing pieces of soft material between thumb and finger. Adults who view masturbatory behavior as abnormal or precocious sexual behavior and therefore "wrong" may actively attempt to discourage such exploration through shaming, threatening, or punishing the child.

The second stage of masturbatory play occurs between three and five years of age, when children experience growing emotional attachment to the opposite-sexed parent and find gratification for these feelings through self-manipulation. Residues of these feelings, and subsequent behavior, can be found in children who frequently lean their bodies against a favored adult or who spend increasing amounts of time sitting very close, touching the adult, combing or brushing his or her hair, or playing tickling games.

The third stage of normal masturbatory development occurs during preadolescence or adolescence in response to the emergence of hormonal surges and the appearance of secondary sexual characteristics, which invite renewed exploratory interest. Few persons today still believe old myths about the harmful consequences of masturbation; most regard them as misguided attempts to control natural impulses. Although many adults are uncomfortable seeing a child masturbate in public, more are becoming informed about the need to simply instruct the child that handling one's genitals should be a private act.

In any of these three stages, children may engage in masturbation consciously or unconsciously as a source of comfort when feeling tired, tense, anxious, stressed, bored, or isolated from others; when needing to go to the bathroom; when watching TV or listening to a story during group time; to get attention; or because it simply feels pleasurable. Young boys often unknowingly clutch at their genitals when worried, tired, or excited. Adults who grew up in environments in which such behavior was condemned may continue to carry with them a sense of shame that affects their adult sexuality. Such feelings usually tend to intensify their reactions to such behavior in others.

**Sex play.** This type of play can be disturbing to many adults and often accompanies the second stage of masturbatory play for three- to five-year-olds. By this age, children have learned that there is an opposite sex. Most also have discovered that this opposite sex is equipped with different genitalia, which are interesting not only because of their markedly different appearance but also because they are used in a different way for elimination.

Because children are curious beings as well as sexual beings, it should come as no surprise that they may want to explore these differences and that they commonly do so during the course of playing "house," "doctor," and other childhood games. At this stage of development, children show interest in adult heterosexual behavior and in play focused on genital behavior. Young children who have witnessed the actual birth of a younger sibling or who have watched representations of a birth on television sometimes extend sex play to act out the birth process. Those who are exposed to media depictions of sexuality or real-life encounters occasionally use dolls and other toys to reconstruct remembered acts.

A potentially serious problem can occur when children sometimes choose to insert objects into each other's genital openings as part of their sex play. Although adults should acknowledge children's curiosity in such situations, they also should explain the harm that can be caused by putting objects into body openings, including other openings such as the eyes, mouth, nose, and ears. Adults should calmly set limits about sex play and redirect inappropriate behavior to another activity.

Children's curiosity about the human body should not be dismissed, and adults can help satisfy children's natural desires to learn more about their bodies and the bodies of others by answering questions in a simple and forthright manner. Some excellent picture books that provide satisfactory answers to many of the questions children pose about sexual differences and where babies come from include Patricia Pearse's *See How You Grow* (1988), Angela Rayston's very simple *Where Do Babies Come From?* (1996), or the more explicit book by Peter Mayles, *Where Did I Come From?* (1995). These and others can be suggested for use by parents. Using correct terminology (e.g., "penis" rather than "weewee") is also an important part of teaching physiological facts and takes away the aura of secrecy about sexual differences.

**Peeping or voyeurism by children.** Often considered in the category of "sexual disturbances," voyeurism usually occurs when children's natural curiosity about sexual differences has been seriously stifled. Some children who do not have opposite-sexed siblings, a natural laboratory for learning about sex differences, may use the child-care center or school bathroom to satisfy some of their curiosity. For this reason, directors of preprimary centers often purposely choose to leave the doors off toilet stalls. This can be upsetting for some parents who feel that such practices promote precocious interest in sexuality, although there is evidence to the contrary. Also, young children who have been taught that toileting should take place in absolute privacy may be somewhat stressed. For this reason, at least one stall should have a door.

Peeping and other deviant behaviors also can occur in children who have been sexually abused or chronically overstimulated sexually by witnessing adult homosexual or heterosexual activity. These children may go beyond covert behavior and become more openly aggressive sexually. When such behavior occurs in very young children, it can be shocking to adults, particularly when they view such children as entirely "innocent" and incapable of such thoughts and actions. A child-care aide described the experience of having a four-year-old boy begin unbuttoning her blouse as he sat on her lap listening to a story she was reading. When she asked him to stop what he was doing, he grinned and matter-of-factly told her, "I want to see your breasts." She notes: "I was amazed *and* shaken that this little four-year-old knew exactly what he was saying and doing. I'm still having a hard time dealing with it, and I find myself avoiding him."

Similarly, school officials in a midwestern middle school found it necessary to indefinitely suspend a sixth-grade boy who, despite intensive efforts by staff to get him to alter his behavior, repeatedly grabbed at female classmates' breasts and genital areas. Accompanying the inappropriate intimate gestures were explicit descriptions of what he planned to do with the girls sexually.

A male teacher in an elementary-school classroom found himself in a professionally threatening situation when one of the girls in his class charged that he was making sexual advances toward her and other female students. Investigation revealed that, in reality, the student was struggling with a sexually abusive situation at home and had been substituting feelings about her father's behavior in a desperate attempt to end what had become an intolerable situation for her.

**Responding to unexpected behaviors.** Although adults can be thrown temporarily off balance when children unexpectedly display behaviors such as exhibitionism, peeping, public masturbation, homosexual acts, and sexually explicit language, several "rules of response" should be kept in mind:

1. It is important not to overreact. It must be determined whether the act is an isolated one on the child's part in innocent response to some information or misinformation about socially acceptable sexual behavior or a fairly serious symptom of emotional and/or pathogenic disturbance. The latter may require continued observation and, if the behaviors are repeated, more detailed evaluation by other professionals.
2. Inappropriate behavior on the part of the child should be addressed by correcting any misunderstandings and by expressing clear expectations for children's behavior.
3. When the child's behavior appears to be the consequence of a sexual disturbance rather than just normal development, helping professionals should make a genuine attempt to investigate negative influences on the child that may be taking place in the other environments in which the child plays and lives. If such influences are found, caring adults should make every effort to provide the child with necessary protection and safety to see that such dangers are minimized and/or eliminated.

## Troublesome Aspects of Children's Psychosexual Development

In addition to behaviors related to normal sexual development and those that appear to be outcomes of sexual disturbances in children, there may be aspects of psychosexual development or behavior in children that can be problematic for some adults. Perhaps most troublesome is the behavior of the effeminate boy or excessively tomboyish girl. At the other end of the continuum, however, are those children who seem to play extremely stereotypical and rigid sex roles at the expense of developing a wider range of androgynous behaviors, that is, behaviors that are viewed as non–sex-specific. For example, an androgynous male would not see child care as solely a woman's responsibility; similarly, an androgynous female would view learning how to change a tire as beneficial and appropriate rather than as "masculine." Adults who themselves hold more androgynous views and see these as appropriate may be uncomfortable seeing children developing what they feel are narrow psychosexual viewpoints. Shapiro (1990:58) indicates that no matter how carefully parents guard against their children developing traditional male/female stereotypes, four- and five-year-old children move in that direction anyway. Their determination seems fueled by gender stereotypes preserved "everywhere else: on television, in books, at child care and school, in the park, and with friends."

Myths about feminine and masculine psychological differences, such as that girls are more social or "suggestible" than boys, have lower self-esteem, are better at role learning, and are less analytical, have not been substantiated by research. Four psychosexual differences that *do* appear to hold up under scrutiny are the following (Berk, 1996; Maccoby and Jacklin, 1974):

1. Girls have greater verbal ability than boys, particularly beyond the age of eleven years.
2. Boys excel in visual-spatial ability, again, a finding more consistently present in adolescence and adulthood than in early childhood.
3. Boys excel in mathematical ability, particularly from age twelve on.
4. Males are more aggressive, both physically and verbally; girls are more emotionally sensitive, compliant, and dependent.

The difference in aggressive behavior seems to be the most troublesome to deal with. Adults who do not support such a viewpoint or who are particularly threatened by a lot of vigorous activity may tend to suppress boys' natural vigor rather than providing effective outlets for their energy (Hendrick, 1996). One third-grade teacher made wrestling and chasing games off-limit activities on the playground for the boys in her class. No other suggestions were made about what might replace such play, and when two of the boys in the class continued wrestling, she would order them to stand quietly against the building until they could think of something else to do other than "bully one another." Other children in the class who had been more compliant soon began to tease the two boys, who became labeled as the "bullies," with no intervention on the teacher's part. When one of the boys' parents expressed concern over the reputation her son was earning, the teacher countered with the explanation that "If other children could control themselves and find more acceptable outlets for their energy in using the playground equipment provided, so could the boys." In a study by Soderman and Phillips (1986), it was hypothesized that this unwillingness or inability of classroom teachers to deal with boisterous behavior has contributed to the overrepresentation of boys in special-education classes for the emotionally impaired and learning disabled. Males consistently outnumber girls in such programs by a ratio of 3:1 and, in some school districts, the ratio is as high as 20:0.

## Gender-Role Development

Inherent in a child's developing sense of self is the ability to feel good about his or her sexual roles related to procreation and childbearing (Hendrick, 1996). Here, we want to distinguish at the outset the difference between **gender identity** (biological, male-female identification) and **gender-role identification,** which refers to the behaviors and characteristics associated with a particular gender. Gender-role development is highly complex, with both cognitive and social variables highly influential. Parents play a particularly important role. Specifically, boys who interact more with their fathers and girls who interact more with both parents become more traditional with respect to developing gender roles. Conversely, girls whose mothers worked outside the house showed greater flexibility. Television viewing also appeared to influence development of gender-role knowledge and flexibility (Levy, 1989).

Children progress through a series of stages in acquiring gender role concepts. This sequence depends on experience and intellectual maturity. Ages may vary from child to child, but the sequence always remains the same and may be described as follows (note the overlapping of the last three stages):

**Stage one: general awareness of gender (birth to eighteen months of age).** The first stage of gender-role development begins the moment a child is born, a name is selected, and exuberant adults ooh and aah over the "sweet, dainty baby girl" or the "big, strapping baby boy." Children listen to themselves frequently described as a boy or a girl and then hear gender-typed attributes associated with those labels. Although children of this age are not capable of producing elaborate speech, they take in much of the conversation directed at them. By eight months of age, the normal infant differentiates self from others, and there is evidence that he or she also may recognize other specific categories, such as size and gender. Boys *may* acquire gender knowledge earlier than girls and at least partly in reaction to parental expectations and reinforcements for gender-stereotyped play. This is demonstrated in their very early preferences for same-gender toys and an increase in masculine toy play (O'Brien and Huston, 1985).

**Stage two: gender identity (eighteen months to three years of age).** By this time, children have learned the gender labels *boy, girl, he,* and *she* and have begun to apply them to others with increasing accuracy. Children at this stage distinguish between the sexes entirely on appearance, depending on visual cues such as hairstyle, clothing, or activities. Children do not yet understand that under all those clothes, people have either male or female genitalia, and that it is by such characteristics that maleness and femaleness are truly distinguished. Thus, toddlers may insist that a female with a deep voice is a man and a male with long hair is a woman. The labels they are taught do not match the attributes they see. Initially, children are more certain of others' gender than their own because it is easier to observe others than oneself. But, by two or three years of age, they have learned to label themselves as a girl or a boy. Once this has been established, the child's gender identification appears to be fixed and irreversible (Shaffer, 1995). As was pointed out earlier, it is at this stage that children realize that they and all other people are either male or female. Realization of this concept is called *gender identity*.

**Stage three: gender stability (four to six years of age).** The major milestone of this stage is for children to realize that boys always become men and girls always become women; boys cannot become women, and girls cannot become men. This is not something children inherently know; they must learn it. Few children attain this understanding prior to age six, and until a child gains this understanding, it is not uncommon for boys to say they can grow up to be a "mommy." Children demonstrate understanding when they can correctly answer questions such as "When you were a baby, were you a little boy or a little girl?" or "Two weeks from now, will you be a girl or a boy?" Those children who have well-established *gender stability* usually will react to such questions with a surprised look or retort that they find the questions silly.

**Stage four: gender constancy (four to eight years of age).** A more advanced concept is *gender constancy.* This involves children's recognition that gender is constant or permanent and does not vary despite changes in clothing, appearance, activity, or personal desire (Eaton and Von Vargen, 1981). Researchers have found that when they ask five- and six-year-olds questions such as "If Mary really wants to be a boy, can she?" or "If Mary cuts her hair short, would that make her a boy?" a majority of children fail to understand that because Mary is female, she will remain female regardless of how she feels about the prospect, what she wears, or how she looks. Although children may be aware of the difference between female and male genitalia, they often are confused about how outward appearances relate to basic masculinity and femininity (Kohlberg, 1966). Thus, this phase of development is a period of gender-role inflexibility. Children focus on the most obvious gender cues and therefore engage in what adults would interpret as stereotypical behavior. Numerous studies support the notion that rigid gender typing during this period is to be expected, and that attempts to minimize such behavior meet with only modest success.

**Stage five: gender-role identification (six to eight years of age and older).** Once children achieve gender constancy, it is to their advantage to be satisfied with their gender, whichever it is, and that usually is what happens. In this stage, children begin to imitate same-gendered adults and peers and gravitate toward gender-typed clothing, games, characteristics, and behavior. Lutz and Ruble (1995) believe this quest is sparked by children's newly found concept of gender constancy and attempts to behave in ways consistent with it.

As the identification process continues, many children will describe their own gender in positive terms and use negative descriptors for the opposite gender (Slaby and Frey, 1978). Girls say: "Girls look nice," "Girls give kisses," "Boys are mean," and "Boys like to fight." Boys, on the other hand, are inclined to say things like "Boys work hard," "Boys are strong," "Girls are crybabies," and "Girls are weak." Some behaviors are not so stereotyped. Boys and girls alike feel that both genders are able to run fast, not be scared, be the leader, or be smart. All these behaviors relate to children's attempts to accept and adopt the socially defined behaviors and attitudes associated with being male or female (Kostelnik, 1984).

Gender-role development has a major effect on children's understanding of their place in society as a male or female and also in the roles they take on to express their maleness or femininity. However, identity and role taking also are shaped by children's environments and their experiences within those environments. For example, there is evidence that abused children may develop significant difficulties in their gender identification. Segal and Yahraes describe such a child:

> Isolated from his peers and disinterested in the normal activities of typical boys . . . , he enjoyed making clothes for his Barbie dolls, with which he played for hours on end. In the laboratory he often folded his arms high on his chest in an attempt, he said, to imitate breasts. Like many of the other abused children, he appeared anxious, forlorn, and frightened. . . . Under an early barrage of abuse from the outside world, he—and many of the other young victims—seemed to have lost his sense of identity and to have entered a prolonged and unresolved sexual crisis. (1979:182)

In the same vein, the young girl described earlier who projected her father's sexual advances onto her teacher was described by the school principal as remarkably masculine in both her appearance and her behavior. There seemed to be a conscious effort on her part to reject her own gender identity and, in light of the stress she had been experiencing, that rejection became fully understandable.

## Effects of Parental Absence on Psychosexual Development

Whether children's gender identity is negatively affected by the absence of the same-gendered parent has received serious attention by researchers. Because the majority of children continue to be cared for by their mothers, almost all studies have examined the father's absence. Cross-cultural studies indicate that an early lack of opportunity for young boys to form an identification with their fathers was associated later with a higher frequency of aggression and violence and an almost total rejection of femininity in every form, almost as if these so-called masculine characteristics—physical strength, dominance, toughness, aggression—were being worn as badges in an "overboard" attempt to prove their masculine identity. The result is that boys today, who more frequently grow up in the absence of their fathers, may be substituting the traditional masculine attributes with more socially costly attributes such as dominance, toughness, aggression, daring behavior, and even violence (Hoffman, 1995; Thompson, 1986). Conversely, boys who spend considerable time involved with their fathers become significantly more empathic and compassionate adults than those males with little father involvement (Koestner, 1995; Pruett, 1993). Studies of girls whose fathers had been absent revealed a tendency for these girls to have trouble with later heterosexual behavior, manifested by extreme shyness and anxiety about sex or by sexual promiscuousness and inappropriately assertive behavior with male peers and adults. Shyness and anxiety were more likely to be found in girls whose fathers had died, and sexually assertive behavior was found more often in girls whose fathers were absent because of divorce (Cherlin, Kiernan, and Chase-Lansdale, 1995; Hetherington, 1985).

For children whose sexual behavior or gender-role identification seems to be on a divergent track, helping professionals must sort out those behaviors that seem to be consistent with normal development and those that are not. When behavior is inappropriate, the child will need understanding as well as supportive intervention. Adults who are unsure about how to evaluate a child's behavior objectively or provide necessary guidance need to consult professionals who have additional expertise in this area.

Although we are living in an era of significant change regarding sexual values and roles, the restructuring of male-female concepts does not call for the abandonment of all current social definitions constituting masculinity and femininity. Helping professionals must, however, be aware of how their own personal convictions may affect their responses to children and their program planning for them. They also must have a clear grasp of the difference between a nonsexist curriculum and one that attempts to deny or destroy a child's basic valuing of his or her own sexuality (Hendrick, 1998).

## ▼ ETHNIC IDENTITY, PREFERENCES, AND ATTITUDES IN CHILDREN

Just as gender-role development appears to be age- and stage-specific, so is the development of *ethnicity*, or cultural awareness and sensitivity. Adults sometimes are caught off guard by disparaging remarks children may make about a person of differing racial or ethnic origin. Such remarks can be quite innocent in nature, simply reflecting the child's lack of experience and information, or they may be more intentionally hostile, such as when they demonstrate the development of a style of "humor" that debases different races, nationalities, or religions. This type of humor depends on a negative conceptualization of the disparaged group and cannot succeed unless the child has learned to think in terms of "good guys" and "bad guys." There also are conscious slurs that result from a child's developing **ethnocentrism** (the exaggerated preference for one's own group and a concomitant dislike of other groups) (Aboud and Skerry, 1984; McGhee and Duffey, 1983).

Because of their own ethnocentrism, professionals may occasionally find themselves fighting feelings of mild dislike or even strong hostility toward children, parents, or colleagues who belong to other racial or ethnic groups. These feelings can also stem from socioeconomic differences. Whatever the source, such feelings affect our interactions, causing patronizing behavior, avoidance, or even aggressiveness. Polakow (1993) describes a scenario in which three African-American preschoolers were constantly and exclusively singled out as "Mrs. Naly's black (and deviant) troublemakers":

Jomo goes over to the piano and sounds a note. Mrs. Naly rushes over. "Can you tell me what that says?" she says, roughly pulling Jomo so that he turns and faces a hand-lettered sign which has a frowning face. "No playing," he says, squirming under her grasp. "Right," she responds and walks back to the art table. Danny and Ryan, who are playing on the floor, tickle Jomo and he falls on top of them laughing. The three boys roll on the floor giggling and tickling each other, and Ryan's foot catches a shelf with stacking blocks. The blocks fall on top of the boys, and more giggling ensues as Ryan says, "Quit it man—I'm building," and starts to build a structure on the floor. As the other two follow, Mrs. Naly approaches from the other side of the room. "You three are misbehaving again—you're just going to have to learn to settle down, and until you do, you'll be in trouble with me—no outside time today!" For the third day that week, the three "troublemakers" are kept inside while the other children go out. Mrs. Naly tells me that none of those three is ready for kindergarten: "They're real problem kids and their families are a mess." (p. 125)

Because children's developing self-concept is heavily influenced by the interactions they have with others, including peers and nonfamilial adults, the attitudes others hold about the child's racial group, social class, or religious sect will be critical. As soon as children achieve a basic sense of self as distinct from others (fifteen to eighteen months), they are capable of "being ashamed and feeling ashamed" (York, 1991:162). As a result, when children perceive they have negative social status, basic feelings of self-worth will suffer.

How we develop racial and ethnic preferences and dislikes has received a great deal of attention since the Supreme Court's 1950 desegregation efforts. It is believed that factors that lead to the development of racist attitudes clearly have their origin in early childhood and include elements of direct learning, personality, cognition, perception, communication from the media and the important people in children's lives, and reinforcement of behavior (Bernal and Knight, 1993). As early as two or three years of age, children begin to notice differences in the way people look and the way they behave. Early positive or negative attitudes tend to increase with age, clearly showing more consensus and reliability at four years of age than at three and becoming fairly well ingrained in all children by the age of six (see Table 14–1).

Once children have developed to the point at which they can place objects, people, and things into categories and have had labels provided to them for this classification, they experience both positive and negative perceptions of racial and ethnic concepts. As children respond to their observations, they receive verbal feedback from others that is both informational and evaluative. For example, Martin became very friendly with Eugene, a light-skinned African-American classmate. When he asked his mother if Eugene could come home to play after school, she responded negatively, saying she preferred that Martin not invite black children home. Martin, later appealing again to his mother, challenged her statement that Eugene was black, noting that he didn't have black skin. "Yes," replied his mother. "But that isn't the only way you can tell someone is black. He has very broad lips and a

black person's hair. He's black, all right. You just play with your own kind." Thereafter, Martin began looking at Eugene and children like Eugene in a different way.

Usually at about five years of age, the child begins to develop an established concept of "us" and "them" related to racial cues. Katz (1976) has referred to this as a stage of "perceptual elaboration," when children begin to expand their perception of the differences that characterize particular groups. At the same time, intragroup differences become less important. For example, children may focus on the general differences between African-Americans, Caucasians, and different Asian groups in terms of skin color, eye color and shape, hair texture, shape of lips, and other facial characteristics and become less discerning about the wide variations among individuals within these outgroups, helping to build later faulty perceptions that "they all look alike." It is also at this age that a "rejection" stage begins, when children begin to rationalize their feelings and preferences aloud. Children of this age can be very rule bound and rigid in their behavior (York, 1991). As a result, they tend to choose friends that are alike in gender and race. Verbal aggression increases but can be effectively moderated by engaging five- and six-year-olds in discussions about fairness.

It is difficult to gauge the ratio of prejudicial (i.e., preconceived hostile attitudes, opinions, feelings, or actions against another person or race) and nonprejudicial experiences a child may have in developing particular racial and ethnic concepts. Unless more opportunities for positive examples are actively provided, children can become victims of a pile-up of negative experiences. Because of young children's developing and immature cognition, these have the potential of translating later on into a tendency toward negative perceptions. Parents and other adults play a major role in helping children rethink values and beliefs that narrow perspectives or that create a lack of empathy and compassion for others. An African-American educator noted that "many black children spend all day long in environments where they feel they are not valued. But when they get home and back in their own neighborhoods, they know they're accepted, that they're all right." There is evidence that what goes on in the classroom in the relationships between teachers and certain students may either reinforce negative attitudes about minority-group membership or modify them in a positive direction.

Native American children may experience more difficulty. Research indicates that by the age of ten,

### ▼ Table 14–1    Acquisition of Racial Awareness

**Two- and Three-Year-Olds**

Notice and ask about other children's and adults' physical characteristics, although they are still more interested in their own.

Notice other children's specific cultural acts, for example, Elena speaks differently from me; Mei eats with chopsticks; Jamal's grandpa, not his mother, brings him to school.

May exhibit discomfort and fears about skin color differences and physical disabilities.

**Four-Year-Olds**

Are increasingly interested in how they are alike and different from other children; construct "theories" that reflect "preoperational thinking" about what causes physical and apparent cultural differences among the children and adults they know, societal stereotypes, and discomforts.

Although still focused on themselves and others as individuals, begin to classify people into groups by physical characteristics (same gender, same color, same eye shape) using the general classification schemes they apply to inanimate objects (for example, lack of class inclusion).

Are often confused about the meaning of adult categories for what "goes together." For example, how can a light-skinned child have a dark-skinned parent? Why are children called Black when their skin isn't black? Mexican people speak Spanish, so if I don't speak Spanish, then I am not Mexican. Girls are supposed to have girl names, so how can "Sam" be a girl? How can you be an "Indian" if you aren't wearing feathers?

Begin to become aware of and interested in cultural differences as they relate to the daily lives of children and adults they know (e.g., who makes up their family, who lives in their house, what languages they speak, what jobs family members have).

Show influence of societal norms in their interactions with others ("Girls can't do this; boys can") and learned discomforts with specific differences in their interactions with others ("You can't play; your skin is too dark").

**Five-Year-Olds**

Demonstrate continued interest in general, racial, ethnic, and ability differences and similarities, as well as an awareness of additional characteristics such as socioeconomic class, age, and aging.

Demonstrate heightened awareness of themselves and others as members of a family and curiosity about how families of other children and teachers live; for example, "Can Sara have two mommies?"

Continue to construct theories to classify or explain differences among classmates.

Continue to absorb and use stereotypes to define others and to tease or reject other children.

**Six-Year-Olds**

Have absorbed much of their family's classification systems for people, but still get confused about why specific people are put into one or another category by adults.

Use prevailing **biases,** based on aspects of identity, against other children.

Are beginning to understand that others also have an ethnic identity and various life-styles as they understand their own emerging group identity.

**Seven- and Eight-Year-Olds**

Demonstrate heightened curiosity about other people's life-styles, religion, and traditions, including people with whom they do not have direct contact.

Can begin to appreciate the deeper structural aspects of a culture, such as beliefs about humans' relationship to the land and the impact of different historical environments on people's ways of life.

Understand, through new cognitive tools, that there are different ways to meet common human needs.

Can begin to appreciate the past if history is presented concretely through stories about real people.

May experience heightened in-group solidarity and tension or conflict between children based on gender, race, ethnic identity, and socioeconomic class, and exclusion of children with disabilities because of interest in their own groups and because of the impact of societal biases on them.

Source: Reprinted by permission from Derman-Sparks. "Reaching Potentials through Antibias, Multicultural Curriculum." In *Reaching Potentials: Appropriate Curriculum and Assessment for Young Children,* Vol. 1, edited by S. Bredecamp and T. Rosegrant. Washington, D.C.: NAEYC, 1992, 119.

a third of the children still assert that they are white and evaluate themselves more negatively than do other minority cultures. It is thought that the subordinate role of the children's parents in white society, as well as negativity and repressed hostility in the parents, are "caught" by the children, who respond with self-deprecation and passive, apathetic, and ambivalent attitudes toward white people. Because most Native Americans do not believe in a "melting pot" theory, they struggle to remain separate but equal. As a result, their children often experience a conflict of cultures, knowing they must become part of the mainstream in order to be successful; at the same time, however, they must also respect their heritage in the Indian culture to affirm their own identity (Sample, 1993).

There is little research that looks at the effects of "transplanting" single children from one culture to another, as has been the case with many Korean children. Questions must be asked about the timing and effect of interrupting the sequence of development of ethnic identity and racial attitudes in such children, many of whom find themselves members of what ordinarily would constitute an outgroup. Increases in the numbers of adoption cases involving African-American children and their Caucasian adoptive parents raise similar questions.

In summary, the child's development of ethnic and racial identity and outgroup attitudes begins in infancy as soon as the child becomes perceptually aware of physical differences in people. It then proceeds through a sequence in which children label and classify people, develop opinions, and begin to value particular attributes, persons, or lifestyles over others. Prejudice can be the outcome as the child's attitudes and preferences grow more rigid. However, if children are challenged appropriately to examine their feelings and attitudes, remain open to new information, and have opportunities to become familiar with a variety of people, they can emerge into adolescence and young adulthood free of the limiting and distorted perspectives that ultimately lay the foundation for hurtful social behavior.

For our children who are made more vulnerable because of race, ethnicity and/or class, Weissbourd (1996) maintains that they can prosper *if* provided a continuous relationship with a consistently attentive and caring adult, opportunities in school and in the community for real achievement, and strong friendships with other adults and children. Those "other adults and children" can be found in the thousands of child-care and classroom settings across this country. Marge Scherer, editor of *Educational Leadership*, notes that in some of the poorest schools in the United States, "hundreds of teachers are seizing their power every day—the power to make school a safe and wonderful place for children. Unable to change world conditions except by

increments, they stand in the front lines, cherishing those who are in their care" (1997:5).

# ▼ INCLUSION OF CHILDREN WITH SPECIAL NEEDS

Another potentially vulnerable group of children in many educational and child-care settings are those who are disabled in one way or another, but not to a degree that would make them ineligible for membership in mainstream society. Although it has been estimated that approximately 10 percent of all children have special needs, disabilities, and/or developmental delays, it is difficult to determine an exact number. Some **disabling conditions,** such as Down's syndrome, cerebral palsy, missing body parts, severe visual or speech impairments, are easy to spot. Others, such as mild or moderate emotional impairment or learning disabilities, are more difficult to determine. When including children with special needs in the everyday classroom, it is often the latter disabilities—those that are more "invisible"—that are not as readily embraced by other children and adults in the setting.

With today's advances in medical technology, greater numbers of children born with disabling conditions are surviving and eventually entering our child-care and educational systems. Many of them require special services (Widerstrom, 1990). Although all children have unique needs, children with special needs are those whose well-being, development, and learning would be compromised if particular and expertly designed attention is not provided in the early years. A special focus must be directed toward specifically organized and adjusted environments. Moreover, these children need professionals who are sensitive to their general needs but also highly competent in promoting learning. Helping professionals must also have the skill to work effectively with a child's family if they are to foster optimal development (Wolery and Wilbers, 1994).

Given the comprehensive services provided today to children with disabling conditions, it is difficult to believe that prior to 1975, many American children with impairments were denied enrollment in public schools. Between 1960 and 1975, various states in the U.S. had begun to recognize the benefits of providing early intervention and were pushing for federal support. This came in the form of Public Act 94-142, the Education for All Handicapped Children Act (later renamed in 1990 as the Individuals with Disabilities Education Act or IDEA). It provided services for children between the ages of three and twenty-one but focused largely on children six years of age or older. In 1986, Public Law 99-457 was enacted, enlarging the scope of 99-142 with a downward extension that now ensures services for all children with disabilities, including at-risk infants and toddlers with handicapping conditions and special needs (Part H) and preschoolers in need of services (Part B).

Provisions of these laws mandate the following (Wolery and Wilbers, 1994:19–20):

▼ All preschool children (ages three through five), regardless of their disability are entitled to free, appropriate public education. No child can be excluded because of her or his disabling condition.
▼ Each preschool child with a disability must have an individualized education program (IEP) or, if younger than three years of age, an Individualized Family Service Program (IFSP).
▼ The procedures used to identify, classify, and place children in special early education programs must be nondiscriminatory—that is, the tests and measures must be used for the purpose for which they are intended and administered by adequately trained individuals, and all measures and assessment practices must be free of bias. Also, appropriate prior notification and consent must be obtained from parents before the administration of such measures for classification, planning, and placement.
▼ Children must be placed in the least restrictive appropriate environment. This means that services must be provided to the extent possible with nondisabled children.
▼ Parents have the right to question and challenge any actions taken by the school in relation to their child's education.
▼ Parents have the right to be involved in planning and developing the state and local educational policies and in developing and implementing their child's IEP or IFSP.

## Categories of Disabling Conditions

A disability is not necessarily a handicap and becomes one only when the child experiences a problem functioning or interacting in the environment because of the impairment. It should be emphasized that children with special needs are individuals with as much variety in ability and personality as typically developing children. Also, because they may have more than one disability, impairment, or compromised health condition, precise diagnosis is often difficult. Disabling conditions are categorized in various ways depending on whether the categorizing group is medically, educationally, or legislatively oriented. The major categories that seem most useful to teachers, parents, and child-care personnel are learning disabilities, developmental disabilities, mental retardation, serious emotional disturbance, speech and language disorders, and physical or sensory disabilities (Behrman, 1996). Descriptions of these categories are given in Table 14–2.

**Children with attention-deficit/hyperactivity disorder (ADHD).** Without a doubt, there has been a dramatic and troubling increase in the numbers of young children diagnosed in this category, with over 4 million children being seen in pediatric clinics and almost 2 million taking stimulant medication to control their behavior. Although ADHD is hypothesized to be a neurological disorder, a specific cause has *not* been firmly established, and it is not listed as a disability under the IDEA. A biochemical theory suggests that there may be a problem in the reticular activating system of the brain so that neurotransmitters fail to fire unless medication is given to stimulate them. Because it is often seen in parent *and* child, there is some evidence of a genetic link. Little evidence supports theories that diet is an important factor or that psychogenic or family dynamics cause the disorder. These children are twice as likely to be diagnosed as LD, making them eligible for special education, and others are made eligible for services under Section 504 of the Rehabilitation Act.

According to the American Psychiatric Association's *Diagnostic and Statistical Manual of Mental Disorders* (*DSM-IV;* 1994), the essential feature of ADHD is a "persistent pattern of inattention and/or hyperactivity-impulsivity that is more frequent and severe than is typically observed in individuals at a comparable level of development." Four criteria for diagnosis are:

▼ Some symptoms must have been present before age seven years.
▼ Some impairment must be present in at least two settings (e.g., home/school).
▼ There must be clear evidence of interference with developmentally appropriate social, academic, or occupational functioning.
▼ The disturbance does not occur exclusively during the course of other specific disorders.

Symptoms of inattention include difficulty in organizing task and activities, being easily distracted, or

| ▼ Table 14–2 | Major Categories of Disabling Conditions |
| --- | --- |
| CATEGORY | DESCRIPTION |
| Learning disabilities (LD) | Learning disabilities, although difficult to define, are said not to be due to visual, hearing, or physical disabilities, mental retardation, or emotional disturbance. Included conditions relate to brain injury, perceptual-motor impairment, dyslexia (difficulty in reading), or developmental aphasia (impaired ability to use or understand words). This category may include as many as 51 percent of K–12 students served under IDEA and 5 percent of all children in our public schools. Increased awareness of the existence of these disabilities, ambiguous definitions, and an inability of regular education to accommodate individual differences account for much of the steady growth in this category. |
| Developmental disabilities (DD) | As defined by federal legislation, the category of DD includes the following conditions:<br>▼ Mental retardation, cerebral palsy (CP), epilepsy, or other adverse neurological condition<br>▼ Treatment needed similar to that required for the mentally retarded<br>▼ Evidence of the disability before the age of eighteen<br>▼ Expectation that the disability is long term and will continue on indefinitely<br>Children with neurological impairments have specific, identifiable central nervous system disorders or damage. CP, a nonprogressive disorder, usually is characterized by motor or movement dysfunction and some impairment of intellectual and perceptual development. As many as 70 to 80 percent of children with cerebral palsy experience multiple disabling conditions, including speech and hearing problems and some aberration of motor dysfunction (spasticity, paralysis, muscle weakness, lack of coordination). Epilepsy is characterized primarily by seizures, either the more common and severe grand mal type, or the milder petit mal type, which is characterized by brief staring episodes, eyelid fluttering, or lapses in speech fluency. There may be frequent seizures, severe visual impairment, and/or other disabilities for some children, whereas others are only mildly disabled and able to function without help (Zigler and Finn-Stevenson, 1987).<br>Although children who are hyperactive or hyperkinetic often are classified as neurologically impaired, it should be noted that rarely do active children have CNS disorders or damage. |
| Mental retardation | Mental retardation is defined by significantly below-average intellectual functioning (an IQ score of 70 or below, divided into subcategories of moderate, severe, profound) existing concurrently with deficits in adaptive behaviors (developmentally appropriate skills displayed by a child in taking care of his or her own needs and carrying out social responsibilities). These children constitute 11 percent of IDEA-eligible children, and African-American children are twice as likely as Caucasians to be diagnosed because of poverty and cultural bias. |
| Serious emotional disturbance | Emotionally disturbed (approximately 9 percent of IDEA-served children) may display frequent or intense temper tantrums, inability to tolerate frustration, moodiness, and withdrawal, difficulty in making friends, or "school phobia." Severe emotional disturbance also includes the conditions of infantile autism (extreme withdrawal from normal interaction and exhibition of unusual or bizarre behaviors) and childhood schizophrenia (a cluster of psychotic or severely inappropriate or deranged behaviors). |
| Speech and language disorders | This category makes up an additional 22 percent of children eligible for services under IDEA. Most have a speech disorder involving articulation. Approximately half of the children have language impairments that include problems with comprehension, expression, word-finding, and/or auditory discrimination. |

Source: Data from Behrman, R. E. "Special Education for Students with Disabilities: Analysis and Recommendations." *The Future of Children* 6 (1996): 4–24.

| ▼ Table 14–2—continued     Major Categories of Disabling Conditions | |
|---|---|
| **CATEGORY** | **DESCRIPTION** |
| Physical or sensory disabilities | This category makes up another 7 percent of eligible children, including those with hearing or visual impairment, orthopedic impairment, or traumatic brain injury. Some children's vision is so limited that it cannot serve as a channel for learning. Although it is rare for a child to be totally blind, an individual is considered legally blind when keenness of vision does not exceed 20/200 in the better eye with correcting lenses. Hearing losses may be present that range from partial to severe. Individuals considered deaf are those whose hearing loss was so severe at birth or during the period of language development that normal language comprehension and expression have not been acquired. |

inability to sustain attention. To the degree that it is maladaptive and inconsistent with a child's developmental level, symptoms of hyperactivity may include such characteristics as constant "on the go" behavior, extreme restlessness or fidgeting, and talking excessively.

Medications for ADHD include stimulants (e.g., Ritalin, Dexedrine, and Cylert), antidepressants, and medications such as Mellaril and Tegretol, which are designed for children whose problem may not be in the lower brain but in the cortical area. According to the U.S. Drug Enforcement Administration (1996), a survey of pediatricians revealed that, on average, they spent less than an hour evaluating children before prescribing Ritalin. In 1996, the United Nations released a report critical of the dramatic increase in the use of a stimulant drug to temper the behavior of American children, noting that it is now prescribed for 3 to 5 percent of all children in the United States, with and estimated 10 to 12 percent of all boys between the ages of six and fourteen on the drug (Crossette, 1996). Consumption of Ritalin in states such as Georgia and Michigan are at an all-time high (1.36 and 2.32 grams per 100 population, respectively), compared with states such as Hawaii and California (0.25 and 0.58 grams, respectively). Concern about misdiagnosis of the condition is warranted, since there are a number of medication contraindications, including loss of appetite and weight; sleep difficulties; stomachaches; headaches; tics; Tourette's syndrome association; emotional lability and cloudy cognitive ability; height and growth impairments; generalized anxiety; and abuse of the drug.

Barkley (1990) indicates that where teachers have a "poor grasp of the nature, course, outcome, and causes of ADHD and misperceptions about appro-

priate therapies," prognosis for the child will be poor. Overall, in addition to the need for sensitive child-care practitioners, a child's future is more positive if hyperactivity and aggression are a minimal part of the condition, if IQ is higher, and if family strengths are well developed. Social skills will be an important and powerful predictor of the child's ability to cope and be successful. The National Association of School Psychologists (NASP, 1992) believes that effective classroom intervention must be tailored to the unique learning strengths and needs of each child. A "best practice" approach for dealing with children with attention deficit disorder is included in the skills section toward the end of this chapter.

The severity of any of these disabling conditions and the availability of community, school, and family resources will determine whether a child will attend a special school or be included in the social, recreational, and educational activities that other children experience. The purpose of inclusion is twofold: to promote the acceptance of children with disabilities through reduction and removal of social stigma, and enhancement of their social competence so they can later live more comfortably and successfully in the mainstream of society. Making this a reality requires a collaborative approach with constructive attention to ensuring access to services, developing and enforcing quality assurance standards, and training personnel and administrators in appropriate strategies for meeting the needs of extremely diverse populations of children (Sexton, et al., 1993).

Personnel in public school, child-care centers, and other programs for children have made great strides in making these mandated "least restrictive environments" as available as possible to children with a variety of disabling conditions. Architectural barriers and problems with transportation and toilet facilities have dramatically improved despite the expense involved. Formal preparation and inservice education for professionals who work primarily with nondisabled children now regularly include information and skill training regarding disabling conditions, strategies for supporting the social integration of children, and techniques for modifying curricula for children with special needs. Inservice programs to upgrade professional knowledge and skills are increasingly directed toward enhancing professional competencies in classroom management of children with special needs, screening and evaluation, interpretation of clinical reports, agency referral, and the structuring of IEPs and IFSPs.

The challenges encountered by helping professionals involved in the inclusion of children with disabilities often are similar to those attempting **racial integration**: successfully melding those who are different from the majority into the mainstream. Some children accomplish this with few problems; others experience increased conflict, isolation and accompanying loss of self-esteem. Placing students with special needs into the regular classroom can be:

> the beginning of an opportunity. But it carries the risk of making things worse as well as the possibility of making things better for the integrating child. If the [process] goes badly, [these] students will be more severely and directly stigmatized, stereotyped, and rejected. Even worse, they may be ignored or treated with the paternalistic care one reserves for pets. If [mainstreaming] goes well, however, true friendships and constructive relationships may develop. (Johnson and Johnson, 1980:90)

Additional concern evolves from observations that children who are disabled are often less assertive in the regular classroom and may experience more peer rejection. Conversely, when skilled professionals truly value inclusion, there is good evidence that all children in the setting—both with special needs and without special needs—have positive experiences in planning and learning with those who one day will be their co-workers and neighbors.

## Children's Perceptions of Disabling Conditions

Social acceptance by other children depends not so much on a child's limitations as on individual characteristics such as independence, friendliness, and other social skills. Successful integration also will depend on the helping professional's ability to

structure the environment, paying as much attention to the social dynamics of the integration as to physical facilitation and curricular aspects (Guinagh, 1980). As pointed out earlier, young children are keenly aware of differences in other children and react in a variety of ways when they encounter a child who acts, moves, looks, speaks, or thinks differently. Because young children are still learning the "rules" of life, and generalize about the rest of the world from their own experience, they often are strict conformists about what is acceptable and what is not. They tend to explain disabilities in terms of what they already know, and their attempts to resolve their own curiosity often involve the following (Ginsberg, 1976):

*Identification with the child who has a disabling condition.*  Children have been observed taking two long blocks and using them for crutches; asking a parent for a helmet "just like the one" worn by a classmate with a brain injury; and responding to a classmate born with only one finger on each hand with, "When I was a baby, I had only one finger, too."

*Creating explanations for a disability.*  In reference to a classmate who could not walk, a child was overheard saying, "Tommy is still a baby." Another child, while talking about a classmate with cerebral palsy, explained, "He didn't eat enough carrots." Another child told a teacher, "When Sally grows up, she's gonna hear real well."

*Fears about their own intactness.*  Children may express this concern by avoiding a child with a disability. Children also have been noted in dramatic play making such statements as, "My arm's gonna get chopped off."

*Recognition and observation of special characteristics.*  Children talk about and name the differences they notice in another child or person. Younger, preverbal children simply may point to a hearing aid, brace, or person in a wheelchair.

*Acceptance.*  Children sometimes choose the child who is physically or mentally challenged to play with, share with, or sit next to. They may show particular delight in a the child's achievements: "Look! Kenny got his own coat on."

## Children's Attitudes Toward Peers Who Are Disabled

Young children who have not learned negative social attitudes toward disabling conditions will not automatically reject a child simply on the basis of a disability. They are open to social models portrayed by adults and thus are able to learn positive attitudes toward disability when a positive model is provided through the adults' actions, words, nonverbal behaviors, and explanations.

Supporting the fact that individual differences and experiences cannot simply be ignored in the blending of human beings in social situations, Laing (1967:63) noted that "human beings relate to each other not simply externally, like billiard balls, but by the relations of the two worlds of experience that come into play when two people meet."

Negative attitudes toward atypical peers exhibited by children aged five and older often exist before these children have experiences with mainstreaming. These are natural responses to first impressions and to the labeling process that fosters stigmatization. The process that occurs in the actual interaction between children with disabling conditions and those without disabilities will determine whether this initial rejection will be reinforced or replaced by greater acceptance. Such acceptance results from mutual interaction and experiences where: (1) children have to depend on one another for assistance; (2) feelings of psychological safety are present and rejection and threat are absent; (3) differences are seen realistically and accepted as natural and okay; and (4) perceptions about working and playing with one another in the setting—no matter what the existing differences—are upbeat and generally rewarding, rather than distasteful and unpleasant.

An actual observation of the process of peer acceptance over a period of time was made by a researcher when Chris, a preschooler with a moderate-to-severe hearing loss, was being mainstreamed into a university preschool setting. To date, he had not been well accepted by the other children. Because he chanced to begin a spontaneous play episode that caught the interest of some of the children, he eventually "earned" his way into the group (Soderman, 1979:150–151):

> March 2. The subject spots a purple cape hanging in the dramatic-play area. He puts it on and begins pretending he is a vampire, moving about the room flapping his wings and "scaring" other children. He draws the attention of several other nondisabled children who decide they, too, want capes so they can be vampires.

"Vampire play" grew in popularity for several days afterward. The head teacher allowed the children to wear the capes about the room instead of confining their play to the dramatic-play corner, which usually was encouraged.

> March 7. Cameron takes Chris up to a student teacher, telling her, "I have a whole team of vampires. He's (pointing to Chris) on my team." Cameron then "attacks" a helping adult standing nearby. Chris copies him. Cameron spreads his "wings" over Chris, catching him and saying, "Gotcha, little vampire." He takes

him to a locker and puts him inside roughly. Chris tries to "break out." Cameron indicates the other children to Chris and says, "Let's suck their blood." They are joined by David. Cameron catches Chris again, saying to David, "I caught the little bat; I caught the little vampire!" He then lets Chris go, saying to Chris and David, "C'mon, team. We're a whole team."

The subject is definitely a member of the team and, thus, on his way to becoming an integrated, mainstreamed member of the class. Should the head teacher have insisted that the play be maintained in the dramatic-play area or asked the boys to play something else "nicer" than vampire play, the moment may have been lost. The fragile nature of the process, chance happenings, and sensitivity on the part of the supervising adults can be seen in a subsequent observation and example of "expectations for reworking future interaction with classmates":

> March 8. Chris has his "bat cape" on again. It is precious to him, and he searches for it as soon as he enters the room. It has been his key to getting into the group. When he attempts to climb on some larger equipment with it, a student teacher asks him to remove the cape because of safety. He declines to play on the equipment, rather than give up the cape. The student teacher is aware of the cape's importance and does not push the issue. If Chris takes the cape back to the dramatic-play corner while he climbs, someone else may take it, and he will have lost his key.

### Guidelines for Integrating Children with Disabling Conditions into Formal Group Settings

The quality of the integrative process will differ significantly depending on the extent to which helping professionals recognize the interdependence between special-education agency, and regular teaching staff; appreciate the long-range value of positive inclusion efforts; are able to collaborate with other professionals and adults who support the child's development; and are willing to make the additional effort needed to go beyond the mere maintenance of special needs students in the nonspecialized setting.

The skills every teacher must master in dealing with typical variations among nondisabled children are needed even more when dealing with those who have special needs. The tendency to view the child with a disability as a "collection of deficits to be corrected" is highly detrimental. Instead, the strengths of good early childhood educational strategies are most effective in encouraging growth in these children: providing group activities that foster peer interaction, allowing free play opportunities, and structuring a less controlled classroom atmosphere (Widerstrom, 1990:213). In addition, every teacher needs to educate himself/herself on the disability, perhaps seeking advice from a consultant teacher. The ability to provide specific enrichment and developmentally appropriate stimulation for these children requires classroom practices that are sensitive to the differences that exist between children, involve a close fit between the practicing professional's expectations and the children's developing abilities, and highlight the importance of each child's contributions to the group.

There is no set formula for successful inclusion. What is clear is that it must be made a priority by the administrators, parents, and professionals who are involved, entailing a major commitment and effort on the part of the staff if efforts are to yield more than simply maintenance of the exceptional children in nonspecialized settings. This commitment and effort must be actively geared toward providing the kinds of interactive and nurturing experiences that produce optimal growth in all areas of children's development.

## Other Differences

**Advanced and precocious children.** Over the years, Howard Gardner (1995) has made us more sensitive to children's multilearning capabilities and the fact that some children will be more highly developed than others in any one of the seven multiple intelligences, as described in Chapter 1. These individual differences may result in noticeable limitations, average abilities, or advanced development because of a rich variety of educational and family experiences, precocious development, or "gifted and talented" characteristics.

Giftedness has been defined as the ability to solve the most complex problems in effective, efficient, elegant, and economical ways (Maker, 1993; Maker and Nielson, 1996). Adults can use the following guidelines when trying to assess whether or not a child is truly gifted, talented, or has some kind of outstanding potential (Gage and Berliner, 1992:222):

▼ Talent in performing or creating
▼ A wide variety of interests and information
▼ Ability to concentrate on a problem, task, or activity for long periods
▼ Ability to engage in abstract thinking and to construct relationships between problems and solutions
▼ Independent thinking characterized by creative ideas

▼ Extensive curiosity
▼ Early reading ability
▼ Use of a large vocabulary
▼ Rapid learning of basic skills

Not all children who seem advanced are truly gifted or talented, but practitioners must be alert for children who excel or have special needs in any of the multiple intelligences outlined by Gardner. Moreover, because young children are in process of developing their abilities and capabilities in many areas, there is a real danger that children may be tagged as either "slow" or "advanced" when time and further observation of their development may prove the diagnosis is untrue (McAfee and Leong, 1997:213). In addition, cognitive "gifts" in one area may occasionally come at the cost of proficiency in other developmental areas. Some of the world's brightest and most talented individuals, including Albert Einstein, Thomas Edison, Lewis Carroll, Winston Churchill, and William Butler Yeats were, in fact, thought to be seriously "learning disabled" in their early years. None of these individuals' strong interests and needs as children were recognized; instead, they were overlooked by adults who equated intellectual prowess, giftedness, and talent with conformity, neatness, good behavior, rapid learning, and early maturation (West, 1991).

When children appear truly advanced in one area, there is always the temptation to believe they are generally advanced in all areas, and this may not be so. Children who are large for their age, have well-developed vocabularies, or who are more cognitively sophisticated than their peers are sometimes expected by adults to excel in *all* areas and reprimanded when they fall short.

Rather than placing advanced and precocious children in specialized settings, heterogeneous grouping that allows for diverse abilities and variety in developmental growth patterns, cultures, languages, temperaments, and individual needs is the strongest model for nurturing human development (Maker and King, 1996). The best approach for supporting the potential of any child with special needs, whether delayed or advanced, is to pair that child with a professional who is highly knowledgeable about child development and skill emergence in young children, and also well trained in developing effective programming for a range of abilities in a group of young children. Best practice—whether for children with special needs, average abilities, or advanced capabilities—involves providing engaging, interdisciplinary experiences in all areas of developing intelligences and respecting the experiential and developmental differences children bring with them into any context.

**Temperament and individuality.**  A pioneering work in the individuality of temperament was that of Thomas, Chess, and Birch (1968) who studied 136 children from infancy to preadolescence. On the basis of interviews with parents and direct observation, the researchers delineated nine characteristics of temperament: activity level; rhythmicity of biological functioning (i.e., regularity of functions such as hunger, excretion, sleep); approach and withdrawal (response to a new person or experience in terms of acceptance or withdrawal); adaptability (ease in adapting to change); intensity of reaction; threshold of responsiveness (sensory stimulation needed to evoke a response); quality of mood; attention span and persistence; and distractibility. These components were then clustered into three general types of temperament:

1. Forty percent of the sample were classified as "easy" children—those who were moderately low in intensity and who were adaptable, approachable, predictable with respect to bodily function, and positive in mood.
2. Ten percent were termed "difficult" children. These children often were negative in mood, demonstrated slow adaptability to change, were unpredictable with respect to biological functioning, and were given to intense reactions when stressed. They also had a tendency to withdraw when confronted with unfamiliar people, activities, or stimuli.
3. Fifteen percent of the sample were termed "slow-to-warm-up" children. Although they took considerably longer to adapt than did "easy" children, they eventually were responsive, although they demonstrated low activity levels and low intensity levels.

Of the sample, 35 percent of the children did not appear to fit into any of the three categories.

Those children in the "difficult" category have greater potential to be classified as having ADHD when, in fact, their behavior may be more the result of personality factors at more extremes ends of a normal continuum of behavioral responses. Charac-

teristics that are common in both ADHD-diagnosed children and "difficult" children include a negative response to new situations, greater amount of time in a negative mood, emotional intensity (even in infancy) and eating or sleeping disturbances.

Some scientists question the desirability of labeling children "difficult." They maintain that such identification may not be valid; it can, in fact, be damaging, given a caregiver's resulting expectations for such children. Reality reminds us, however, that although serious issues continue to surround valid assessment of difficult temperament, there is no question that certain children *are* more difficult to deal with than others (Soderman, 1985). Whether their difficulties are a reflection of their own constitutional characteristics, disturbed caregiver-child interactions, or other environmental stressors, the fact remains that difficult traits do appear early in some young children. Equally important is our knowledge that difficult behavior may be modified or intensified by life experiences. The child, as an active agent in his or her own socialization, plays an important part in flavoring those experiences. The important others in a child's life also play ongoing roles in the dynamic unfolding of his or her individual personality.

This concept of mutual influence is important. When children are difficult to handle, less confident caregivers often develop self-doubts, feelings of guilt, and anxiety over what the future holds for the child and their relationship with the child. Unless difficult behaviors, or caregivers' perceptions of those behaviors, can be satisfactorily modified, a sense of helplessness often begins to pervade all interactions with the child. Dreams of being a competent parent or teacher may yield to the hard reality that the child is unhappy, out of control, and moving in a negative direction developmentally. Attitudes toward the difficult behavior may move swiftly from early amusement or pride over a child's "assertiveness" to disapproval and even rejection by the adult. Adult responses, in turn, have a marked effect on whether additional stress will be imposed on the child or whether the child will be guided successfully toward developing more positive coping behaviors (Brier, 1995; Carlson, Jacobvitz and Stroufe, 1995; Soderman, 1985).

## SKILLS FOR SUPPORTING CHILDREN'S DEVELOPMENT RELATED TO SEXUALITY, ETHNICITY, AND SPECIAL NEEDS

 **Adapt Skills to Support Children's Development**

Positive results in the development of children's attitudes and behaviors related to sexuality, ethnicity, special needs, and personality differences can be accrued when adults adapt the following skills into their repertoire of interaction techniques:

**1. Educate yourself about persons of varying cultural, religious, racial, and developmental backgrounds.** Participate in community, social, or cultural events that represent different groups and find ways to become personally acquainted with at least one family of each racial and cultural group in your community. Go beyond seeking information only related to foods and holidays. Find out as much as possible about subtle social conventions that sometimes cause irritation when not understood: concepts of family, time, nature, gender roles, aesthetics, ecology, dress, and safety (DiMartino, 1989:32). Take advantage of opportunities to broaden your familiarity with other groups through ethnic festivals, community-awareness programs involving those with disabilities or open events sponsored by religious groups other than your own. In addition, seek out establishments in your area, such as stores and restaurants, that offer artifacts and food representative of particular cultures. There are organizations and institutions in many cities and in universities that focus on international programs. These organizations also schedule films and lectures and distribute newspapers and magazines from other countries. You can visit a medical-supply store that caters to the disabled and examine the different equipment that some individuals use to function more effectively. Finally, volunteer in programs in which you are likely to interact with people who are different from yourself. Look on these experiences not only as a way to help others who are different from you, but as an opportunity to broaden your own understanding.

**2. Evaluate your own responses to the individual differences described in this chapter.** Pay careful attention to your nonverbal behaviors as well. If you find yourself drawing away, making a face, or avoiding eye contact with a child who falls into any of the categories discussed or to one who brings up sensitive subjects, stop. Remember that in your professional role, you are obligated to treat all children with respect and sensitivity. Watch out for any tendency on your part to blame whole groups of people for what individuals do, and demand proof when you hear children repeat rumors that reflect on any group; do not tell stories, however funny, that reflect on any group, and do not laugh when others tell them. Show disapproval when others use hateful terms that slur any group. In addition, monitor your verbal responses, making sure you do not dismiss or deny children's feelings and verbal expressions of these feelings. It may also be useful to discuss situations that are difficult for you with a colleague or classmate as a way to clarify your own attitudes as well as to elicit further suggestions.

**3. Set curricular goals to include a multicultural approach to teaching.** Begin with what is familiar, most needed, and meaningful to children in the classroom. According to York (1991:24–25), this includes the following:

▼ Recognizing the beauty, value, and contribution of each child
▼ Fostering high self-esteem and a positive self-concept in children
▼ Teaching children about their own culture
▼ Introducing children to other cultures
▼ Providing children with a positive experience exploring similarities and differences
▼ Encouraging children to respect other cultures
▼ Increasing children's ability to talk to and play with people who are different from them
▼ Helping children to be group members
▼ Talking about racism and current events regularly with children
▼ Helping children live happily and cooperatively in a diverse world
▼ Helping children to notice and do something about unfair behavior and events

## SKILLS FOR SUPPORTING CHILDREN'S DEVELOPMENT RELATED TO SEXUALITY, ETHNICITY, AND SPECIAL NEEDS—continued

**4. Build a positive *social climate* in which both similarities and differences are valued.** It would be unrealistic, for example, to tell a child who has noticed a disability in another child that the child is "just like you." Rather, the helping professional needs to point out how they are different *and* the same (Derman-Sparks, 1989). Without criticizing a child for noticing a difference or belaboring the point, the helping professional needs to emphasize that each person has something valuable and unique to contribute to the group. Take advantage of the many children's books about individual differences as well as puppet play, films, videotapes, and filmstrips to promote growth in the understanding of others. Utilize resource people from the community, including those with varying racial and ethnic origins and disabling conditions. Take advantage of video technology to allow children to visit other countries and explore differing lifestyles without leaving the classroom (Winter, 1995). Foster positive attitudes and attitude changes in school-age children by role playing and disability simulations. For example, wheelchairs can be borrowed from equipment companies to allow students to understand the difficulty involved in maneuvering a wheelchair. Glasses can be made with layers of yellow cellophane to simulate visual impairment. In addition to focusing on the religious, racial and ethnic, and developmental differences that can be found in others, it is necessary also to discuss similarities between people: we all need friends, we all have similar emotions, and all people have both positive and negative qualities.

**5. Build a cooperative, rather than competitive, spirit within the group.** Encourage children to rely on one another and to seek each other's help in solving problems rather than depending on the adults in the setting. Use small, heterogeneous groups whenever possible, rather than competitive or individualistic learning activities, to foster the development of acceptance, rapport, and mutual understanding among children of different racial, ethnic, and developmental backgrounds. Structure activities in which children have opportunities to establish eye contact, talk with one another, and develop common goal structures. Provide needed support to guide these groups toward success and reasonable goal achievement, remembering that repeated failure by the group may result in discouragement and a tendency to blame lack of success on the weakest members of the group. Purposely plan activities that will highlight, at one time or another, the skills of all children in the program. For example, one paraprofessional had a student who was blind demonstrate her ability to get around the room and explain the kinds of cues in the room on which she relied for help. Students then were blindfolded and, with the help of another student to keep them safe, tried their luck at negotiating the same path, relying not on their sight but on the cues their classmates had identified.

**6. Identify youngsters who have health-related problems or developmental delays.** Observe whether or not children are physically healthy. Become acquainted with and use screening strategies such as the Early Screening Inventory (Meisels, 1989) and Denver Developmental Screening Test II (Frankenburg, 1992) that can identify children having problems with adaptive behavior, motor development, language delays, and verbal comprehension and expression. When indicated, follow up with more in-depth study with the help of the child's parents and other helping professionals. Practice developmental surveillance of children's progress by eliciting parents' concerns about their child through open-ended questions (e.g., "What do you find most difficult about caring for your child right now?"). Pay particular attention to a child's gross motor milestones in the first year of life and to language milestones in the second year. When in doubt, refer to the specialists dealing in early intervention (Solomon, 1995).

**7. Learn about what goes on in the children's lives away from the program and consider this when planning for them.** Find ways to build links between your program and other elements of the child's mesosystem. For example, a

*continued*

teacher working with Dominic, a child who was being included into her afternoon kindergarten class, decided to follow up on a comment by the bus driver that the child was falling asleep while being transported to the school. She discovered that Dominic, in addition to his disabling condition, was dealing with incredible role strain for a five-year-old. He was spending his mornings in a very structured, intensive special-education setting where, because of his relatively greater amount of residual hearing, he was considered by his peers to be a leader. Following lunch and the bus ride to kindergarten, he was thrust into a situation in which he was having difficulty being accepted by his nondisabled peers, who thought he "talked funny." In short, he was "at the top of the heap" in the morning and very much at the bottom in the afternoon. In addition to the psychological strain he was experiencing in dealing with his contrasting status in the two very different educational settings, it was observed that he frequently was expected to make up missed work in the special-education setting, which interrupted his valued free time with the other children. The problem was compounded when he went each day from the kindergarten class to a caregiver's home where he waited with his sister until 11:00 p.m. to be picked up by his mother, who was working evenings. The situation obviously called for a conference between parents and professionals and a restructuring of Dominic's schedule. In addition, the adults in each setting had to adjust their expectations to respond more appropriately to the child's needs.

**8. Respond thoughtfully to children's questions about sexuality, ethnicity, disabling conditions, and other differences.** Listen carefully to determine what it is they really want to know. Clarify the question by reflecting before answering. For example, if a child asks the question "Is Timmy still a baby?" about a seven-year-old who can't walk, you would want to clarify with, "You mean, 'How come Timmy can't walk yet?'" After determining the child's purpose, answer the question at a level he or she

can understand. Often, in an effort to be comprehensive, adults give children more information than they need or can manage. Give short, precise, clear answers in language that the child understands. Use simple phrases and familiar analogies. Then, check to see what the child thinks you have said by asking him or her to paraphrase your answer. "Tell me in your own words why Sandy talks the way she does." Work from there to expand the child's understanding, if necessary. Don't give more information than children ask for; allow them time to assimilate what already has been said.

In responding to preschooler's questions, remember this age group's "magical" and egocentric thinking processes. They are trying to make sense of a new and unfamiliar piece of information about other human beings. In doing so, they will rely on their own experiences, fears, and fantasies and directives from parents to assimilate the information. Be alert to what is behind children's questions. They may simply misunderstand an issue or want additional information, or they may genuinely fear some aspect of the situation. Reassure children when they seem to be overly concerned, and watch for evidence that the child is more comfortable once the explanations have been given.

You may have to answer the same question several times for very young or overly fearful children. When questions about another child's physical, ethnic, or developmental differences are repeatedly asked in that child's presence, redirect the curious child to discuss the issue with you privately.

**9. Use correct vocabulary when referring to body parts, cultural groups, or disabling conditions.** Words like *vagina, penis,* and *breast* describe specific parts of the body, which should be as accurately labeled as other body parts. To do otherwise demeans the body and teaches children that genital organs are not natural but are things to be ashamed of. Likewise, certain cultural groups prefer to be called by a particular name. For instance, some people prefer to be known as *Black Americans,* others as *African-Americans* or *people of color;* some as *Indians,*

## SKILLS FOR SUPPORTING CHILDREN'S DEVELOPMENT RELATED TO SEXUALITY, ETHNICITY, AND SPECIAL NEEDS—continued

some as *Native Americans*; and some prefer the term *Latino* whereas others favor *Hispanic* or *Mexican-American*. If you are not sure about the preferences of the families in your group, find out. Similarly, describe a child as hearing impaired rather than saying that her ears are broken. Point out that another youngster has cerebral palsy rather than the "shakes." In each of these situations, it is better to be truthful and precise when speaking with children than to try to sidestep the sensitive arenas through euphemisms or inaccurate terminology.

**10. React calmly to children's sex play.** Reflect children's interest in their own bodies and the bodies of others. Give them information that will satisfy their curiosity, such as the names of their body parts and how they function. Set limits on behavior that is inappropriate or dangerous, such as fondling another child's genitalia, masturbating in public, or putting something in a child's vagina or anus. For instance, a child who is masturbating might be told: "Touching yourself like that feels good. That's something that people wait to do when they are alone. I'm worried you're missing the other activities that we have. You can choose between playing at the art table or in the space station." Likewise, if in the course of playing doctor, a child tries to take the rectal temperature of a classmate by poking him with a pipe cleaner under his pants, step in immediately. Reflect, "You're pretending to be a doctor," and continue with a personal message: "I'm worried that you will hurt him with the pipe cleaner. It is important not to put objects inside of someone's body. You can pretend to take his temperature like this." (Demonstrate an appropriate alternative.)

**11. Provide natural opportunities for children to learn more about their sexual development.** For very young children, the bathroom at the preschool or child-care center is an ideal place to ask questions, observe similarities and differences, and learn that body parts and body functions do not have to be hidden behind closed doors. Allow preschoolers to use the bathroom in one another's presence if they wish. Also,

provide dolls with anatomically correct genitalia for them to play with. With parents' permission, use books to communicate information to older children. Act as a resource for answering their questions and clearing up misunderstandings. Avoid using plants and animals as a substitute for discussing human reproduction. The latter is quite different from the former, and children have difficulty inferring meaning from metaphorical information (Borland, 1984).

**12. In your day-to-day treatment of children, be as gender fair as possible and actively nurture "opposite gender" characteristics to encourage full human development—gentleness, nurturance, cooperation, and communication in males and courage, competence, and independence in females.** Be aware of and avoid adult tendencies that have been documented, that is, tendencies to interrupt girls more frequently when they are speaking and/or providing boys with more help, attention, information, and encouragement to solve problems. In order to encourage a wide range of development in both boys and girls, present important concepts in many diverse ways and repeatedly. Encourage visual-spatial activity and logico-mathematical experiences in early childhood for girls (mazes, maps, blocks, geo-boards and more practice in noting likenesses and differences). These may be helpful in shoring up abilities that are often needed later in fields where few women excel (Schlank and Metzger, 1997). Similarly, boys may benefit from more active involvement in language activities and experiences, as well as help in stress and conflict management, intrapersonal, and interpersonal skill-building.

**13. Remain alert for valuable learning experiences that may be created spontaneously by the children. Be flexible enough to let them progress without interruption.** At times, children's interactions with materials and with one another capture their interest to such an extent that our own best laid curricular plans are usurped. When this happens, assess whether allowing children to deviate from intended activ-

*continued*

## SKILLS FOR SUPPORTING CHILDREN'S DEVELOPMENT RELATED TO SEXUALITY, ETHNICITY, AND SPECIAL NEEDS—continued

ities will allow other learning or needed social adaptations to occur. Sometimes, as illustrated by the following example, a spontaneous event can be far more valuable than the planned one:

> A student teacher commented to her head teacher that, although the children were not very socially accepting of a young classmate with a hearing impairment, they certainly were curious about the hearing aid she wore. In response, the head teacher suggested that the student prepare a "lesson" for the children to teach them how a hearing aid worked.
>
> Subsequently, the student teacher set up on one of the tables a display of vibrating objects, including a tuning fork and xylophone, which she invited the children to examine. While she was working with some of the children and the tuning fork, the child with the hearing impairment began looking at the xylophone, which also was a wheeled toy that could be pulled with a string. Instead of using the striking mallet on the toy, the child put the xylophone on the floor and began pulling it across the room, marching as she went. Several nonhandicapped children fell in line after her, marching and singing, "Down by the station, early in the morning . . ." The children who had been observing the tuning fork activity also fell in line, leaving the student teacher and her carefully constructed display of vibrating objects in favor of the march.

Later, at a follow-up session in which the teachers were discussing the success of the lesson, the student teacher explained that the display had been somewhat dismantled with the loss of the xylophone and departure of her "audience" but that she felt the children had more to gain by joining the march. When asked to elaborate on the reasons why, the student noted that the social interaction of the child with a disability with her nondisabled peers, although a primary objective in the inclusion of the child, had not been going well. "I just thought it was a great opportunity to let the children take care of something that's had me stumped." Much to the student's relief, her head teacher congratulated her on her rationale and her ability to capture the "teachable moment."

**14. Help children develop appreciation for our diverse heritage as a society.** As a part of the daily routine, sing songs, tell stories, play games, and engage in other activities that relate to the cultures represented by the children and staff in your group. If your group is homogeneous, introduce other customs anyway. It may be best to begin with groups that can be found in the wider community rather than cultures with whom children are unlikely to interact. Paper folding is a common Asian pastime. Making a piñata provides opportunities for Hispanic children to explore and discuss this custom. Making and eating potato latkes for a snack acquaints children with a Jewish custom. Using currency from other countries can become an interesting counting activity in a math class. An activity in which children try to carry a bundle on their heads or backs allows them to become familiar with how people in different cultures solve the problem of carrying a load from one place to another. Similarly, the daycare center that has accumulated footwear common to many societies, such as a variety of slippers and sandals, exposes children to the fact that, although many people protect their feet, the manner in which they do so may vary. It is better to integrate such activities into the ongoing curriculum rather than to occasionally have a "Mexico day" or "Black American week." The latter approach sensationalizes and makes artificial what, to the culture itself, is just a natural part of living.

**15. Help children develop pride in their own cultural heritage.** Pronounce a child's name as his or her family pronounces it rather than Anglicizing it. Honor differences in language and traditions. Serve foods that are familiar to the children's particular backgrounds, asking for suggestions and recipes. Allow children to bring in articles that are used in family celebrations and to explain to the group how they are used. Include dress-up clothes from a variety of cultures. Encourage parents to share such items as dolls, pictures, books, and music. The purpose of including such activities and items in the children's everyday classroom experiences is to help each child feel included and valued and to encourage the development of friendly and re-

## SKILLS FOR SUPPORTING CHILDREN'S DEVELOPMENT RELATED TO SEXUALITY, ETHNICITY, AND SPECIAL NEEDS—continued

spectful attitudes toward all ethnic, racial, and cultural groups (Hendrick, 1998).

**16. Utilize rules and consequences to let children know that purposeful slurs and unkind references to particular children or groups will not be tolerated.** If youngsters seem to be using terms such as "homo" or "honky" without knowing what they mean, provide pertinent rationales for why such behavior is unacceptable to you. When children deliberately use such tactics to wound the self-esteem of another, they are engaging in hostile aggression. This should be stopped with a personal message, warning, and follow-through as necessary. Carry these out in a calm, firm tone.

**17. Monitor all teaching materials and activities for racial, cultural, gender-role, religious, and developmental stereotypes.** Continuously watch for ways in which the curriculum may inadvertently limit children's potential by socializing them to develop narrow perceptions of their own roles and abilities or those of others. Encourage boys and girls to participate in a wide range of enriching activities on the basis of their interests and developing skills rather than on outmoded ideas.

**18. Assess your classroom environment for antibias and culturally relevant materials (Carter, 1993:55):**

▼ What groups are represented by pictures and photographs displayed (e.g., race, culture, gender, family structures, life-styles, age, physical disabilities)? Is any one dominant? Do they represent real or stereotyped individuals? Are they contemporary or historical?

▼ What genders and cultures are included in music activities, displayed artwork (prints, sculpture, textiles, artifacts), dress-up area, and reading corner?

**19. Interview parents to explore their culture, asking about special days and family celebrations.** Ask how they guide behavior and recognize special achievement or rites of passage. Plan whole-family events such as potluck din-

ners. Provide child care so that grandparents or other relatives can attend. Ask if transportation is a problem. Plan activities that are nonthreatening and fun for all ages. Take pictures and display them where children and their parents can look at them together. Honor or highlight each family individually in your newsletter, providing them with an opportunity to share a favorite family story with others in the program.

**20. Respond immediately to children's verbal hostile aggression using parts two and three of the personal message.** Taunting, teasing, using slurs, or making unkind references to other people are forms of hostile aggression. Stop them instantly. Use a calm, matter-of-fact tone, then go on to the warning and follow-through, if necessary. Thus, if Madeline calls Victorio a "wop," approach her immediately and in a quiet, firm voice, say: "I get upset when you refer to people using derogatory words like wop. It's unkind and disrespectful. Stop." Note that this variation on the personal message is to be used *only* with older children whose unkind words are purposeful. Complete personal messages are more appropriate with younger children, who may not understand the significance of their remarks or their impact on others.

**21. Respond professionally and compassionately to children who are challenging (Stephens, 1996:47) and children with disabling conditions (Graves, Gargiulo, and Sluder, 1996:427):**

▼ Maintain a predictable daily schedule. Privately warn children of changes in routine, since problems are most likely to occur during transitions. Rehearse any changes that can be anticipated (e.g., role-play procedures that will be followed for a field trip). Adjust the schedule of the day to accommodate the specific differences in your group of children.

▼ Give children simple, step-by-step directions when guiding them through activities or routines. Allow ample time for completing tasks and be patient.

*continued*

## SKILLS FOR SUPPORTING CHILDREN'S DEVELOPMENT RELATED TO SEXUALITY, ETHNICITY, AND SPECIAL NEEDS—continued

▼ Establish a minimum of classroom rules that set limits and clearly define expectations in a positive fashion (usually focused on health and safety). Involve children in structuring these rules.

▼ Because some children become overwhelmed when given too many choices, limit the number of activities offered at one time. Work in small groups as much as possible. Make a concerted effort to keep the classroom from being overly stimulating. Rotate toys and materials, leave more white space on the walls, and keep noise and voice levels steady. If children begin losing control, provide more structure by offering fewer choices and more specific directions to follow.

▼ Make sure all activities are developmentally appropriate. Remember that successful experiences with hands-on materials are especially important. Use activities and materials relevant to the child's life experiences. Incorporate multisensory approaches to learning and include movement activities whenever possible.

▼ Document problematic behaviors in a daily log. Analyze log entries. Can you identify what triggers antisocial behavior such as hitting, kicking, or having tantrums? Can the classroom be further modified to eliminate or reduce the triggers?

▼ Create quiet, secluded corners so that children can remove themselves when necessary from the overstimulation of group living. Provide access to less distracting areas of the classroom when children are expected to complete tasks requiring close attending skills.

▼ Coach children toward self-control. Every child can be impulsive, but especially high-spirited children. Teaching them self-discipline is imperative. Helping them master language for expression of feelings and desires will help them gain positive social skills. Apply positive discipline techniques consistently, and provide numerous instances of positive reinforcement.

▼ Remember that establishing good rapport with children before implementing consequences is critical. Praise and other forms of positive attention, such as a smile, nod, or pat on the back are some of the most basic but powerful management tools.

▼ Involve parents; encourage them to be partners in their child's experience. Hold frequent conferences to coordinate classroom practices with home practices. Keep parents fully informed.

▼ Make and maintain connections to special-education personnel when a child's deficits impact negatively on classroom performance.

▼ When working with children diagnosed with ADHD, deliver rules and instructions in a clear, brief, and highly visible way (e.g., display on wall; have a child repeat out loud when following through). Provide consequences for negative behavior consistently and swiftly, since delays reduce or degrade efficiency.

▼ Teach to the child, not the disability label; instructional strategies appropriate for typical children are usually effective (with some modification) for special-needs children.

▼ When *you* become overwhelmed and drained, seek the counsel of a supportive friend or co-worker. Find someone you trust who will just listen and can give you the release you need to face the next day with an optimistic attitude.

 **Communicate with Families about Children's Individual Differences**

*1. Actively listen to parents to discover their agenda and wishes concerning their child's experience in the program.* For example, an African-American mother was concerned that there were no other minority children in the program. A father expressed worry about his young son's gender orientation because of the amount of time the child spent dressing up in feminine clothing in the pretend play area. Parents of a bright four-year-old asked what you were doing to teach her how to read. Be clear about their thoughts and feelings and what they believe your responsibility is in relation to their concerns. Find out their attitudes about education and educators.

## SKILLS FOR SUPPORTING CHILDREN'S DEVELOPMENT RELATED TO SEXUALITY, ETHNICITY, AND SPECIAL NEEDS—continued

**2. Respond with empathy and honesty to parents' concerns.** Realize that parents often are seeing a problem in terms of what it means for the future of a child, whereas you may be more concerned about the child's present functioning and behavior. For example, the two most common concerns of parents of children with disabilities are the social acceptance and future of the child (Montgomery, 1982). Professionals can gain a great deal of insight into how a child functions by learning more about the parents' feelings, thoughts, behaviors, and values. How do they feel about this child? Are they proud or disappointed? What are their hopes for him or her? Let parents know that their concerns are important to you before outlining intervention strategies you believe best match their child's needs. Follow through responsibly in giving parents the information they need on an ongoing basis.

**3. When integrating children with special needs, utilize parents as a primary resource.** With respect to at least one child in the program, each parent is an unqualified expert. You can make this concept work for you and the child by forming partnerships with parents. As well as providing advice to them when they ask, you can ask their advice when having a difficult time figuring out what to do with their child (e.g., "How do you get Jenny to hang up her coat? I'm having a tough time helping her re-member to do that!"). With especially shy children, most of the year could go by before you get a handle on the child's likes, dislikes, and interests. A parent often can provide a valuable shortcut to a workable strategy.

**4. Be supportive and responsive to parents of non–special-needs children who have questions and concerns about the presence of special-needs children in the group.** Such concerns are to be expected. Parents may worry that their own child may not get enough attention or may regress in his or her own development. If you become defensive or intimidating or make parents feel guilty for having "negative" feelings, you probably will construct unwanted barriers. Respond as honestly as possible to both open and hidden concerns. For example, a parent might ask, "Things going pretty smoothly this year with all the changes?" If you were to respond, "Not bad," leaving it there, you may cut off an opportunity to have the parent share his or her concerns. If, however, you respond: "Not bad. How are parents looking at the changes?" you leave an opening for the parent to bring up a concern with a general response. Make yourself available to answer questions and invite parents into the classroom to observe for themselves. Let parents know you are interested in their questions and feedback and that you value openness.

## ▼ PITFALLS TO AVOID

When utilizing the skills described, there are common pitfalls you must strive to avoid:

**Overprotecting the child who is atypical or from a minority group.** Whenever helping adults give special privileges to one child and not to others, they run the risk of alienating other children and hampering the potential development of the favored child. Rules should be changed to accommodate individual children only when there are safety issues involved, when the child's learning modes are inadequate for the task at hand, or when children are not emotionally able to meet the challenge set before them. When rule changes are necessary, simple, matter-of-fact explanations can be given to other children. In addition, they can be drawn into a discussion about how to make the rule change palatable, given the circumstances. Children's sense of fairness, particularly when they are asked their opinion about a problem, almost always inclines them toward helpfulness. When rules are changed arbitrarily, however, and without apparent fairness, children can become resentful, rejecting, and hostile toward the other child and/or the supervising adult.

**Failing to see negative interactions because they are not part of the success picture you have in mind.** It is tempting to ignore negativity or inappropriate behavior in the classroom because one feels it reflects on one's ability to adequately control the situation. The tendency is to overlook negative incidents or to make light of them when others who are concerned bring them to one's attention. Professionals may instead focus on superficial evidence that children are accepting one another when focused observation reveals a less positive picture. Incidents in which a child is being exploited, manipulated, isolated, or harmed (physically or psychologically) by children or adults in the setting must be addressed immediately by (a) interrupting the incident; (b) acknowledging the emotions of all individuals involved; (c) stating that exploitive and harmful behavior is not allowed under any circumstances; and (d) structuring alternatives that will lead not only toward promotive interaction and feelings of psychological safety but also toward positive acceptance of one another.

**Overreacting to children's mouthing of stereotypes.** When children parrot popular stereotypes, such as "She can't lift that; she's only a girl" or "Asians have no feelings," one's natural reaction is to become upset and to lecture children on the insensitivity or inaccuracy of what they have said. Although the intent of such admonishments is positive, the outcome often is negative. Children may become defensive, belligerent, or covert. A better approach is not to condemn but to quietly convey accurate information to children, such as "It would take a strong person to lift that box—a strong girl, or a strong boy" or "All people have emotions. Some people show their emotions more than others."

**Inadvertently using stereotypical language.** All people have phrases in their vocabulary that they use unthinkingly. Some of these may be unintentionally offensive. Referring to someone as an "Indian giver," describing the haggling process as "Jewing someone down," saying you'll go out "Dutch" with someone, or asking children to sit "Indian style" are examples. In addition, referring to workers as "firemen," "postmen," and "salesgirls" reinforces sex-role stereotypes. More egalitarian terminology would include "firefighters," "postal workers," and "salesclerks." Similarly, beware of segregating males and females unnecessarily. It is not constructive to pit boys against girls in games or have children retrieve their art projects by

having one gender go before the other. Use other attributes to designate subgroups, such as "Everyone with green socks may get their coats" or "All the people at this table may be dismissed."

**Failing to plan for and evaluate student progress effectively.** Although children's programs almost always have an evaluation component attached to them, occasionally these are summative in nature and based simply on how much the student was able to accomplish against a given standard in a given period of time. Too often, that standard is not based on the individual child's status or ability to achieve prior to the evaluation period but on predetermined, normative criteria. Thus, children who have ability deficits for one reason or another are certain to measure up poorly unless they are given reasonable mastery objectives based on their own ability. Similarly, children who consistently need more challenging activities than most of the children must have their progress evaluated more frequently. Because of the structuring of special-needs students' individualized education programs (IEPs), they are less likely than other children to experience such problems, although significant periods of time elapse between planning and re-evaluation of the plans. Although there is much discussion about the pros and cons of individualizing learning and evaluation, insufficient attention to this element can set into motion a no-win situation for children who have special needs.

**Failing to seek the support of administrators, parents, other professionals, and community members.** Just as children work within a team situation in the classroom, professionals are part of a larger team of adults who support, to greater or lesser degrees, what goes on in the program. Helping professionals working with children who require additional resources, such as more time, understanding, patience, staff, and materials, must be able to justify those needs to other adults who are in positions to help, depending on how they perceive the special needs of these children relative to the needs of all the other children in the program. It is probably a given that adults who work with children with special needs will need additional resources. When these are not forthcoming there is a tendency toward burnout in the professional who views the problem as a lack of support. What is needed is more effective communication between helping professionals and the other adults who are in positions to support the program.

**Responding only to the needs of parents with whom you feel comfortable and avoiding parents with different values or differing racial, ethnic, or cultural backgrounds.** Parents who are different from the majority of the other parents or who don't speak fluent English may shy away from becoming involved in the group setting because they feel they have little to offer or that what they have to offer will not be valued. Some may sense, fairly or unfairly, a condescending or standoffish attitude on the part of the professional. For example, one young woman who applied for a Head Start position was excited about working with "those" children. What she hadn't counted on was that her job also required her to work with "those" parents. Armed with some of her best ideas from a parent-teacher interaction class she had taken in college, she marched in the first evening to share some of her expertise. The parents hadn't come prepared to receive it and had other things on their minds. She said the next day to one of her colleagues, "All they wanted to do was sit and talk and drink coffee!" She and the parents never were able to get beyond that, and the young woman lasted only the rest of the year in that position. Instead of working to meet parents where they needed her to meet them, she indignantly waited for them to "show some interest in their kids." However, their need to talk to one another about their concerns had to come first. Professionals who have had few personal experiences with certain ethnic groups and cultures can gain new understandings by making a genuine effort to study ethnic groups and cultures different than their own. This can be done by taking classes, traveling, and taking advantage of social opportunities to interact with people who have different attitudes and value systems.

## ▼ SUMMARY

Sensitive issues surrounding children's sexuality, ethnicity, special needs, and personality differences sometimes can cause the helping professional discomfort, irritation, embarrassment, or confusion in choosing the most effective ways to support children and their families. When these feelings lead to avoidance, rejection, aggressiveness, or overprotectiveness on the part of helping adults, their ability to support children's development and competency building is significantly diminished.

Sexual behavior in children such as public masturbation, sex play, peeping, sex-oriented language, and sexually assertive moves toward an adult should be handled as matter-of-factly as possible, with the adult calmly guiding the child toward more appropriate behavior. Apparent deviations in psychosexual development, although sometimes troublesome to adults, may not be subject to alteration and call instead for understanding and a more thorough knowledge of the child's perspective. Severe sexual deviations should be handled by seeking the expertise of other professionals.

Children's attitudes toward other racial and ethnic groups, like gender-role development, appear to be age- and stage-specific. Adults who work with children and parents of other racial and ethnic origins or socioeconomic status occasionally may find themselves dealing with negative feelings based on their own ethnocentrism and experiences. Unless they can rise above these feelings, their professional effectiveness will be undermined or negatively affect children's self-esteem and developing ethnic attitudes. Conversely, positive behaviors on the part of the adult serve as an important prerequisite to prejudice prevention and reduction.

Inclusion of special-needs children into formal group settings also is an area requiring additional sensitivity on the part of the adult. The objective of integrating children with disabling conditions is twofold: to promote acceptance of atypical children through stigma reduction and removal, and to enhance their social competence so they can later live more comfortably and successfully in the mainstream of society. The challenge for professionals involved in inclusion efforts is similar to that encountered by those attempting racial integration, that is, melding those who are different from the majority successfully into the mainstream. This potential for qualitatively improving the lot of the child with special needs through inclusion carries a greater risk of increased stigmatization, stereotyping, and rejection if the helping professional is not able to facilitate supportive interaction between nondisabled and special-needs children in the group. Success will depend on the adult's own commitment to successful integration, his or her ability to structure the environment, and the attention she or he pays to the developing social dynamics in the learning context.

Respecting the uniqueness of all persons is a positive statement confirming our ability to be truly human toward one another. Adults who interact on a day-to-day basis with children have the responsibility to surround those children with an accepting, nurturant, growth-enhancing environment—one that allows children to see themselves and others as fully functioning, competently developing human beings.

## ▼ Discussion Questions

1. The parent board of an all-white cooperative nursery school is considering offering a scholarship to an African-American preschooler for the coming year. What advantages and disadvantages do you see in such an arrangement? What kinds of preparation do you feel should be made prior to implementing such a procedure?

2. You have a Korean-American child in your third-grade classroom and find that he is being harassed on the way home by three of the more popular boys in the classroom. You arrange to meet with the three boys. How do you begin your discussion with them? Role-play this situation with three classmates who can take the part of the students.

3. You are teaching in a large, urban middle school. An eleven-year-old girl approaches you during lunch hour, saying that a young male security guard in the school tried fondling her and has been asking her if he can take her home after school. How do you respond to her? What action, if any, do you take?

4. You are holding an open house for parents. The father of a five-year-old boy approaches you and asks you what you think about letting boys play with dolls. He also asks, "How early can you tell whether or not a male is going to be gay?" State your initial response to him exactly as you would make it. Review the normative sequence in the development of gender identity as you might relate it to the father.

5. You have observed that one of the parents who has volunteered to tutor children with reading problems appears to be highly impatient with Kevin, a second-grader. This morning, you overhear her saying to him: "Your problem is laziness. That's why a lot of you black children aren't able to ever finish school. Is that what you want to happen to you?" How do you handle this situation?

6. As you round the corner into the "quiet" area reserved for reading, you discover two five-year-old boys examining each other's genitals. What are your initial thoughts? What do you say to the boys? Do you take any further action? If so, what?

7. One of the boys in your Cub Scout group appears to be extremely nervous. On picking him up after a meeting, his mother notices him touching his genitals. In front of the other boys, she crudely quips: "For crying out loud, Terry, quit playing with yourself. You're going to make it fall off!" You ask her if you can talk privately with her for a moment. What do you say to her?

8. You see one of the white preschoolers vigorously rubbing the arm of a black aide. When you ask about it, the aide laughs and says, "He's trying to rub off the dark color of my skin." How do you respond?

9. In the middle of the morning's activity, one of the children unexpectedly has a grand mal seizure. Following the episode, the rest of the children are visibly shaken, and some are crying. What do you say to them? Afterward, with the potential of it happening again, how do you prepare the classroom and the children for the possibility?

10. Children in the child-care center are having a snack of raisin toast and peanut butter. The student teacher has been instructed to serve only one piece to each child until all children have been served. You notice that Kendra, a child with Down's syndrome, has been sitting at the table for quite a long time and is on her second piece of toast. When you ask the student about the situation, she says, "I know the rule, but I feel sorry for her." Verbalize your response exactly as you would make it to the student teacher.

11. Read the following ethical scenario. Refer to the NAEYC Code of Ethical Conduct presented in Appendix A. Find the section(s) that provides insight into the professional responsibilities related to the following situation:

    Jessica, a child with cerebral palsy, uses a wheelchair. She attends Maple Avenue Child Development Center. During outdoor time, she is wheeled into the teachers' lounge and left there to watch television, while the other children play outside. Her caregiver explains, "T.V. is a good activity for her because there's nothing for her to do on the playground. This way, she doesn't get hurt."

12. If you were to assess your own personality type based on the brief discussion of temperament in this chapter, would you say you were an *easy* child to raise, a *slow-to-warm-up* child, or a *difficult* one. If someone were to interview your family, what kinds of specific examples might they provide to support or dispute your conclusions?

## ▼ Field Assignments

1. In order to become more skillful in handling others' responses, it is important to examine your own feelings about the sensitive areas that are the focus of this chapter. Respond as honestly as possible to the following: With respect to your own sexuality, differing ethnic, religious, racial persons or groups, and disabled persons or populations:

   a. cite any negative childhood experiences you had.

   b. identify any faulty or stereotypic information you remember being given.

   c. on a scale of 1–10, 10 being most comfortable, describe how comfortable you are related to your own sexuality and interaction with people different from you.

   d. describe any negative adult experiences you have had related to these areas.

   e. have your beliefs and thinking about individual differences changed during your adult years? If so, how?

   f. what social changes do you think need to take place in order to have less biased behavior related to these issues?

2. Professionals who work on a day-to-day basis with children should become familiar with some of the screening tools used to assess growth and development. These are tools that can be simply administered without specialized knowledge or clinical experience. They are available through universities, colleges, intermediate school districts, hospitals, or clinics. The ESI (Early Screening Inventory) and DDST II (Denver Developmental Screening Test II) are two examples. Arrange to obtain one of these tools and use it to test three different children in the age range indicated. Obtain permission from the child's parents prior to testing the child. Since you are probably not experienced in assessment at this point, do not share the results of the test with the child, the child's parents, or other professionals. Remember to keep the results confidential.

3. We need to constantly monitor teaching materials and classroom activities for racial, cultural, gender-role, sexual, religious, and developmental stereotypes. Examine the materials and activities in your classroom for any unnecessary stereotyping that can be found in the following:

   ▼ Textbooks or children's books
   ▼ Assessment tools
   ▼ Religious holidays observed in programming
   ▼ Foods served
   ▼ Responsibilities delegated to children for care and management of the environment
   ▼ Activities planned on-site and off
   ▼ Rules and regulations
   ▼ Resource people invited to participate in the program
   ▼ Make-up of professional and paraprofessional staff

# ▼Chapter 15

## Making Judgments

## ▼ OBJECTIVES

*On completion of this chapter, you will be able to describe:*

▼ What is a judgment.

▼ Judgment questions related to goals, strategies, and standards.

▼ Variables that influence the judgments helping professionals make.

▼ The need for making ethical judgments.

▼ The priority principles involved in making a judgment.

▼ What constitutes extreme behavior and why it occurs.

▼ What constitutes child abuse and why it occurs.

▼ Judgment skills related to ethical codes of conduct, day-to-day decision making, children's extreme behavior, and child abuse.

▼ Family communication strategies.

▼ Pitfalls to avoid in making judgments.

---

The children in the hospital playroom are told that at the end of the session, everything must be put back where they found it. When cleanup time is announced, all the children pitch in to help. A few minutes later, they proclaim the job finished. As Mr. Walters, the childlife specialist, surveys the room, he notices that although tables are clean and everything has been put away, the cupboards are disheveled and not all of the markers have been capped. Looking at the children's beaming faces, he ponders, "Should I make them do more, or should I accept the job they've done?"

While observing children on the playground, Ms. Curtis notices that Alexandra, who frequently is the victim of classroom jokes, once again is being teased. She wonders, "Should I intervene, or will that make matters worse?"

The daycare provider, working at the sink, hears four-year-old Jonathan's cup fall. She turns to see milk all

over the floor. Jonathan blames the spill on his imaginary friend, Boo. The adult thinks, "Should I treat this as a deliberate lie, or should I go along with him?"

The teacher observes that over the past several days, Yuri has been pulling her hair out. The child's mother has witnessed the same behavior at home. Together they wonder, "Is this something serious or a passing phase?"

For the second time this month, Stuart comes to the center badly bruised. Again, he claims he fell down the stairs. The director muses, "Is this really the result of an accident, or could it be a sign of abuse?"

---

Every day, helping professionals are faced with making judgments such as these. That is, they must evaluate a particular state of affairs and then decide what to do. Some of the situations they encounter demand on-the-spot decision making; others allow time for longer deliberation. Some involve relatively minor incidents; others are much more serious. Some call for maximum intervention, others for only minimal interference or none at all. Yet, hurried or carefully planned, small or large, involving more or less direct action, all judgments affect the lives of children and adults.

The best judgments are those that helping professionals make consciously. For example, it is better for Mr. Walters, the childlife specialist, to praise the children for picking up the toys because he has *decided* this is the best course of action than to do so unthinkingly. In this way, his judgment becomes a deliberate response to a specific circumstance.

Essentially, all judgments involve the same series of steps found in any decision-making model:

1. Assessing the situation
2. Analyzing possible strategies in response to it
3. Selecting and implementing a strategy or combination of strategies
4. Evaluating the outcome

For Mr. Walters to reach his decision, he first would have to formulate a picture of what was happening. This would mean taking into account the children's lack of familiarity with the playroom, the anxiety many of them felt at being in a hospital setting, his supervisor's desire for neatness, how important were the things left undone, the children's display of pride, his knowledge that no one would be using the playroom again until tomorrow, and his own feelings of pleasure that the children had worked together.

Next, he would have to think about the possible responses available to him. Some of these include accepting the children's work without comment, having them redo the work, singling out particular children as being either more or less successful, scolding them all for not doing enough, and praising the children for working together willingly.

The next step of deliberately selecting one or more of these responses would be based on Mr. Walters' analysis of the potential outcomes of each. In this case, the analysis would probably occur on the spot and would involve trying to envision which response would best support his overall aim that children feel comfortable in the hospital environment. Making these kinds of predictions would be challenging because many of the prospective outcomes would be ambiguous. That is, some would be unknowable and some would include both positive and negative aspects that would be hard to weigh. For instance, Mr. Walters could not

be sure whether making the children redo the work would seem reasonable to them or would make them feel defeated. Nor could he be certain how youngsters with whom he was unfamiliar would react to a scolding. Similarly, even if he praised the children for their efforts, it is possible that some youngsters would view his words as false because they would recognize the discrepancy between their own performance and a really clean room.

From this discussion, it can be seen that formulating a judgment carries with it certain risks and no guarantees. Yet, as uncertain as the process is, going through these steps makes it more likely that the adult's actions will match his or her aims. Furthermore, evaluating the outcomes that actually occur once an option is carried out provides additional information that can be used as input for future judgments.

Because judgments are influenced both by the situation and by the person who is deciding how to proceed, any two persons faced with formulating a judgment about the same circumstance might make entirely different, yet equally good, decisions. Hence, judgments are so personal and so situation-specific that we will not attempt to present prescribed answers to a variety of scenarios. Rather, our aim is to point out what variables to consider when making a judgment as well as how to think through the judgment process.

## The What and Why of Judgments

The majority of judgments helping professionals make relate to goals, strategies, or standards. Consideration of each of these prompts certain questions that adults must answer and that affect the actions they take.

**Goals.** Adults in formal group settings have in mind certain **goals** aimed at enhancing children's social development. Typical goals include fostering children's sense of worth, promoting their consideration of others, improving their ability to make friends, and increasing their capacity for controlling impulsive behavior. Each of these represents a desired outcome, the achievement of which contributes to increased social competence. None are wholly attained within the setting or time period during which a helping professional works with a particular child. However, forward movement toward the goal represents progress.

When adults establish goals, their interactions with children gain purpose. That is, they have an end result to work toward, rather than operating haphazardly with no purpose in mind. Helping professionals differentiate their goals as general or specific, long range or short range, more or less important, and independent of or interdependent with other aims (Goldsmith, 1996). Furthermore, they develop goals for individual children as well as goals for the entire group. Sometimes these multiple aims are compatible; sometimes they are in direct opposition to one another. Therefore, adults must make many judgments regarding their goals. Some of the questions to be asked include:

What are the appropriate goals for each child?
Is a goal that is appropriate for one child also suited for another?
What should be done when pursuit of a goal for an individual runs counter to one established for the group?
Is a particular goal still valid?
What should be done when one goal for a child seems incongruent with another?
What factors necessitate changing a goal?
What makes one goal more important than another?

It is questions such as these that Mrs. Torez must consider when, during a class discussion, Jesse blurts out an answer without raising his hand. Her goal for the group has been for children to exercise greater impulse control and demonstrate it by waiting to be called on. Yet, Jesse is a shy child who Mrs. Torez has been encouraging to become more assertive. Should her response be geared toward supporting the group goal or the one established for Jesse? Is there a way to address both goals without compromising either? What Mrs. Torez does will be based on her judgment of the situation.

**Strategies.** In order to pursue their goals for children, adults implement particular **strategies.** These strategies may be obvious or more subtle, planned or spontaneous, and specific or general. At times, different techniques may be chosen to achieve the same goal; at other times, similar strategies may be utilized to pursue different goals. The judgments helping professionals make regarding strategies are many. Some of these involve determining:

Which strategy is best suited to achieving a particular goal.
Whether the potentially most effective strategy actually is feasible.
How compatible the strategies implemented for one goal are with those for another.

How long to continue implementing a strategy before judging its effectiveness.
Whether or not a planned strategy is being carried out as originally intended.
Whether a strategy can stand alone or whether it must be carried out in conjunction with other strategies.

A situation in which judgments about strategies must be made arises when Mr. Chvasta considers T. J.'s persistent misbehavior in the group. For the past several months, the adult has been trying to get T. J. to exhibit fewer instances of antisocial behavior. He has tried several options, none of which has had the desired effect. Recently, he has begun to wonder whether he has used too many different approaches, too rapidly. He also wonders whether his efforts to contend with T. J. have led him to neglect other children, prompting them to act out. The conclusions Mr. Chvasta reaches and what he will do about them depend on the judgments he makes.

**Standards.** Success in accomplishing goals is assessed using **standards.** People establish standards when they decide that a certain amount of a behavior or a certain quality of behavior represents goal attainment. Behaviors that do not meet these criteria are indications that the goal has not yet been achieved. The measurement of standards may be formal or informal, known by children or unknown by them, purposeful or intuitive on the part of the adult. Questions that focus on judgments about standards are as follows:

What standards should be established?
Should the same standard apply to all children?
When or why should a standard be changed?
When competing standards exist, which standards should prevail?
How well does a child's behavior meet a given standard?

Mr. Walters, the childlife specialist, is making a judgment about standards when he decides whether or not the children's definition of a clean room is good enough to accept. Ms. Heller is also thinking about standards when she tries to determine how many questions a child must answer correctly in order to receive a star. Her dilemma over whether rewards should be based on the percentage correct for the whole class or on the percentage of improvement of each child also is a question of standards. In each case, final determinations regarding an acceptable level of performance will come about as the result of adult judgments.

# ▼ Variables That Affect Judgments

Goals, strategies, and standards are fluid. Goals that are accomplished are replaced by other goals, and those that obviously are unattainable are revised; strategies that are outmoded or ineffective are changed; standards that no longer fit are altered (Nickell, Rice and Tucker, 1976). Because none of these remains constant forever, helping professionals continually make judgments about them. Their judgments are influenced by three variables: their values, their knowledge of how children learn and grow, and their assessment of the situation at hand. Let us examine each of these influences more closely.

## Values

Underlying each judgment a helping professional makes are his or her values. **Values** are the qualities and beliefs a person considers desirable or worthwhile (Berns, 1993). As such, values are deeply internalized feelings that direct people's actions. For instance, adults for whom honesty is a value set goals for children with that value in mind. Some of these might include telling the truth, not cheating on tests, and completing one's work without copying. To achieve these goals, these adults implement related strategies such as rewarding children who tell the truth, separating children who are taking tests, and teaching children appropriate sources for getting help as a substitute for copying. In addition, they apply related standards to determine how well their goals have been met. For instance, an adult might allow a preschooler to tell a "tall tale" but refuse to accept a fabrication from a fifth-grader. He or she might expect 100 percent of the students to keep their eyes on their own papers during an exam and monitor students' homework to determine that none of their answers were exactly the same. Not only do adults' values influence their goals for children, but they also affect how adults interpret and appraise children's behavior. As a result, an adult may view children who tell tall tales with less favor than children who refrain from such practices.

Because values cannot be seen, their presence can only be inferred from what people do (Goldsmith, 1996). For instance, Mary Gonzales frequently reminds children about the value of telling the truth and doing their own work. She often carries out activities in which children must discriminate between fact and fancy. She reveals her emotions

rather than hiding them, and she encourages children to describe their true reactions even when they are in opposition to her own. If a child copies another's work, he or she is told to do it over. Based on her actions, you might surmise that the value of honesty is important to her. On the other hand, were she to ignore minor incidents of cheating, tell fibs herself, or attempt to deny children's emotions, her behavior would indicate that honesty was not critical to her. Even if she were to say that it was, her actions would belie her words.

**How values develop.** Values are a product of socialization. Families, society, culture, teachers, religion, friends, professional colleagues and organizations, and the mass media all contribute to your belief system. In this way, every facet of a person's environment has a direct or indirect impact on his or her thinking. Because value acquisition starts in the cradle, it is the family that has the first, most immediate, and most profound influence on this process. Family members, through their day-to-day interactions, transmit to the young fundamental notions of living. As people mature, these beliefs are supplemented by inputs from their mesosystems, exosystems, and macrosystems. All of these combine to form a particular orientation that individuals internalize and that guides them throughout their lives (Bronfenbrenner, 1989).

Because each person's ecological milieu is unique, no two people have exactly the same value system. Values differ across cultures, between families in the same culture, and among individual family members. This means there is no one correct set of values to which all persons subscribe.

**Prioritizing values.** People develop a system of values that often is hierarchical, ranging from most critical to least important. The order of importance is determined by whether a person treats a particular value as *basic* (one that is absolute regardless of context) or *relative* (one that depends on context for interpretation). It is thought that basic values usually take priority over relative values, and relative values take on more or less importance depending on the situation (Deacon and Firebaugh, 1981). In Mary's case, the basic value of honesty pervades everything she does. Therefore, choices between being forthright, circumspect, or deceitful usually result in the former being selected.

However, a value's hierarchy is not always so linear, with each value being placed above or below another. Rather, several values may occupy the same level of importance at the same time. These values may be compatible or contradictory. The similar weight shared by a cluster of competing values explains why people sometimes experience value conflicts. For instance, a person may equally value honesty and kindness. At times, he or she may be caught in the dilemma of whether to tell the truth, perhaps hurting someone's feelings, or to be less than truthful in order to be kind. Which path is pursued will be based on the person's judgment in that particular circumstance.

**Recognizing your own values.** Becoming cognizant of your personal values enhances professional performance. Helping professionals who are consciously aware of their values are in a good position to examine them. They can better determine when conflicting values exist within themselves or between themselves and others and take systematic steps to resolve dilemmas. Additionally, it is possible for them to determine whether their actions are congruent with the values they espouse. This makes it more likely that they will be consistent in their interactions with children and their families. For all of these reasons, clarifying your values is an important facet of professional life.

**Knowing the values supported by your profession.** In addition to personal values, values espoused by the profession at-large provide useful guides for making judgments. Such values are usually identified in the ethical codes of conduct adopted by professional organizations or societies. A code of ethical conduct to which members are committed represents the collective wisdom of the field regarding common values, required practices that support those values, and prohibited practices that undermine them. In other words, a code of ethics provides a tangible framework for thinking about professional values and how those values might influence your behavior in the formal group setting. Helping adults who know what their professional code of ethics entails and those who keep that code in mind at all times have a credible foundation for the judgments they make.

**Respecting clients' values.** Helping professionals also must be sensitive to the differing values held by the children and families with whom they work. They cannot expect their clients' values to exactly mirror or always be compatible with their own. When educators, counselors, recreational leaders, social workers, or childlife specialists are confronted with dissimilarities between their values

and those of their clients, their task becomes one of finding ways to work with them that demonstrate respect for their belief systems. Regardless of what action is eventually taken, children, families, and professionals all must perceive that social rewards have been gained.

**Separating values from goals, strategies, and standards.** Although variations in values are common between helping professionals and their clients, there are times when professionals mistake differences in goals, strategies, and standards for value conflicts. In reality, it is possible for dissimilar goals, strategies, and standards to be applied in response to the same value. For example, Mrs. Williams values competence and has a goal for her son, Webster, to be able to handle social situations with greater proficiency. She teaches him to establish his rights through physical force and considers his winning a fight as a positive indication of his abilities. Mrs. Pritchard, his teacher, shares the same value and goal, but her tactics and standards differ. She teaches Webster to use words to establish his rights and views his avoidance of physical confrontation as a measure of achievement. In this case, the dissimilar approach between parent and teacher is based not on conflicting values, but on differing means. Although values are almost impossible to debate, strategies can be negotiated. The two adults do have common ground. If Mrs. Pritchard recognizes this, she will have a positive base from which to approach the parent. If she does not see this shared perspective, her efforts to influence the parent could result in failure.

In addition to an understanding of values, there are two other variables that affect the judgments helping professionals make. The first involves how well they take into account children's current level of functioning; the second is whether they look at each situation in context.

## Knowledge of Child Development and Learning

When adults make judgments about goals, strategies, and standards related to children's behavior, they must weigh such variables as the child's age, what the child's current level of comprehension might be, and what experiences the child has had. Although age is not an absolute measure of a youngster's capabilities and understanding, it does serve as a guide for establishing appropriate expectations. For instance, adults who know that preschoolers do not yet have a mature grasp of games with rules would not view a four-year-old who spins twice or peeks at the cards in a memory game as a cheater. Subsequently, they would not require very young children to adhere to the rules of a game in the same way they might expect grade-schoolers to. Likewise, awareness that seven- and eight-year-olds normally spend much time verbally designating who is "friends" with whom would keep adults from scolding youngsters who engage in this practice. Rather, their strategy for improving peer relations might consist of group discussions aimed at encouraging children to discover similarities with others in the group.

The kinds of previous knowledge and skills a child brings to a situation should also be taken into account. Obviously, children with little or no exposure to a particular situation or skill should not be expected to pursue exactly the same goals or perform at the same level of competence as youngsters whose backlog of experience is greater. For instance, goals for a field trip to a farm for children from the inner city would be different from those established for youngsters from a rural area. Standards related to dressing independently would be different for a two-year-old from those for a six-year-old, not only because of differences in age, but because the older child has had more practice. Furthermore, a child who has lived all her life in Florida would not initially be expected to demonstrate the same degree of skill in putting on a snowsuit as would a child from a northern climate, where such clothing is commonplace. In instances such as these, helping professionals use children's development and experience to guide their judgments.

### The Situational Context

Adult judgments do not take place in a vacuum. Rather, they are made within an ecological milieu, which is influenced by several factors. Some of these include time, human resources, material resources, the physical environment, and the specific details of the behavioral episode itself. The goals, strategies, and standards finally decided on are all affected by these constraints. For instance, under normal circumstances, Ms. Omura's goal is to foster independence among the children in her class. Ordinarily, children are given the time to make their own decisions, to repeat a task in order to gain competence, and to do as much as possible for themselves. However, these goals and strategies have to be modified during a tornado drill, when the goal of safety supercedes that of independence. Under such circumstances, children have no choice about taking shelter, nor can they take their time dressing themselves. As a result, slow dressers get more direct assistance than is customarily provided.

Similarly, Mr. Ogden might think that the best strategy for helping an impulsive child is constant, one-to-one monitoring by an adult. Yet, he concludes that he would be unable to implement this approach because of demands on his own time and the lack of other adults who might serve in this role.

The impact of contextual factors also is evident when a social worker who ordinarily advocates sharing, but who also knows that Michelle has recently become a big sister, allows her to keep all of the watercolors to herself one day. He realizes that this child already is sharing many things for the first time—attention at home, her room, and even some of her things. In his judgment, asking her to share on this occasion is unnecessarily stressful, so he does not oblige her to follow the rule for now.

Physical resources and available time also affect judgments. This explains why the presence of a huge mud puddle on the playground could be viewed as either a place to avoid or an area of exploration. Which judgment is made depends in part on what kind of clothing the children are wearing, whether soap and water are available for cleanup, whether it is warm enough to go barefoot, and whether there is enough time for children to both play in the mud and get cleaned up before the next activity period.

As you can see, values, knowledge of child development and learning, and the situational context all influence the kinds of judgments helping professionals make. Next we will explore how these variables affect judgments about ethical behavior, judgments involving one's priorities, judgments about extreme behavior, and judgments related to child abuse and neglect.

## ▼ Judgments About Ethical Behavior

Helping professionals continually confront ethical dilemmas in their daily work. A nationwide survey conducted by Feeney and Sysko (1986:16) identified typical examples such as these:

▼ Being asked to discuss a child or family in a nonprofessional setting such as the grocery store or at a social event

▼ Being required to implement policies that one believes are not good for children

▼ Seeing children engage in worthless or inappropriate activities

▼ Knowing that a program is in violation of state regulations

▼ Dealing with conflicting requests from divorced/separated parents

Such concerns arise from incidents professionals witness directly and ones they hear about. These predicaments affect children, families, colleagues, supervisors, or other community members. Whatever the circumstance, the basic judgment to be made is which actions are right and which ones are wrong. These are moral judgments, requiring the application of one's professional code of ethics. In this text, we have used the NAEYC Code of Ethical Conduct as a guide for professional behavior. Up until this point, however, our primary focus has been on recognizing circumstances addressed by the Code. Although familiarity with the Code is essential, it is not sufficient to ensure that the values embodied in the ethics document are actually translated into action. For the latter to occur, helping professionals must develop techniques for discussing dilemmas and expertise in reaching solutions that reflect knowledge of the profession's values and standards (Freeman and Brown, 1996). Utilizing the Code in these ways is a skill. It can be learned just as other skills are learned through direct instruction, modeling, and positive reinforcement. Personal reflection on ethical dilemmas (both hypothetical and real) and conversations with colleagues about such dilemmas are essential strategies. Currently, scenarios involving ethical behavior are regularly described in *Young Children,* the NAEYC professional journal. These provide excellent sources for discussion. Real-life encounters also offer good food for thought. Time set aside during preservice classes, staff meetings, or other training sessions to use the Code to illuminate such ethical problems is time well spent. Professionals in training as well as those already practicing in the field, must engage in this endeavor if they are to gain expertise in choosing actions that support professional values rather than simple expediency or intuition (Katz, 1991). Thus, ethical judgments provide the foundation on which all other professional judgments are made.

A second type of professional judgment involves establishing priorities from among competing interests. Some of these include self-interest versus children's interests, individual interests versus group interests, and the interests of one person versus those of another. People also may experience conflicts within their own value system that cloud their ability to make a definitive judgment. Although there are no absolute rules for distinguishing among these, there are some general principles helping professionals can use when faced with difficult decisions.

## Priority Principles

The following principles are arranged in a hierarchy from most to least important. Each one has higher priority than those that follow it. All of them serve as guideposts for which priorities take precedence in a given circumstance. These principles came about as a result of our experiences with families and children and through discussions with helping professionals representing a variety of backgrounds.

**PRINCIPLE A: Strategies that preserve children's safety take precedence over all others.** The overriding concern of every helping professional is children's physical and mental welfare. If you must choose between an option in which a child's health and well-being can be maintained and other, more efficient, easier, or less involved options in which safety is in question, there is no choice. You are ethically and morally obligated to pursue the safest alternative.

**EXAMPLE:** The fifth-grade science class is doing an experiment with heat that involves the use of Bunsen burners. The children, working in small groups, are running behind schedule in their task. Another class is due to arrive in a few minutes. While surveying the room, the teacher notices that a few children, still working, have taken off their protective goggles. The adult feels caught between wanting them to get the experiment over with in time and feeling that she should enforce the safety standards. Even though there are only a few minutes remaining, and making the children don the goggles will cause a delay, the appropriate course is clear, as mandated by principle A: safety first.

**PRINCIPLE B: Priority is given to the approach that promises the most positive and the least negative outcomes.** Although all goals, strategies, and standards have some benefits and some drawbacks, it is best to eliminate the most negative options and choose from among those that are most favorable. Sometimes, the best option has the largest number of benefits. Sometimes, an option is best because its negative aspects are less detrimental than the other alternatives under consideration.

**EXAMPLE:** During a conference with the director of the daycare center, Mrs. Leeper (one of the parents) reveals that her father is terminally ill and is not expected to live much beyond the new year. She has not yet shared the news with her children and has approached the center director for advice. Together, they identify the benefits of telling the children about the situation right away, such as giving the children lead time to deal with the tragedy, a chance to say goodbye to their grandfather, and an opportunity to share in a family experience; a chance for Mrs. Leeper to gain family support; and the relief of not having to keep it a secret. Drawbacks to telling the children include causing everyone to feel sad during the holiday as well as the difficulty of introducing a topic about which she feels uncomfortable and with which the children have had little experience. The two adults also explore the pros and cons of not telling. Favorable aspects of postponing the disclosure are that the children probably will have an uninterrupted holiday and that the mother will not have to deal with the issue right away. The negative impacts of this approach include the mother's heightening anxiety, her inability to share a very traumatic period of her life with loved ones, the potential shock to the children, and their probable distress over sensing that something is wrong but not knowing what it is.

Taking all of these factors into account, Mrs. Leeper makes the judgment that it is better to tell them than to remain silent. In her opinion, the benefits of telling right away outweigh both the benefits of not telling and the negative aspects of making the announcement.

**PRINCIPLE C:** When faced with a situation in which the child's needs and the adult's needs differ, priority is given to meeting the child's needs, unless doing so compromises the adult's basic values. In other words, when adults' and children's interests compete, children's interests have the higher priority; except when the adult would find pursuit of those needs unlivable.

**EXAMPLE:** Children at the Jefferson School are rehearsing for a spring concert. The music teacher is especially anxious for the youngsters to put on a good show because music teachers from several other districts will be in the audience. While listening to the opening number, she realizes that Sandra sings loudly and enthusiastically, but off key. She debates whether or not to allow the child to sing. She knows that other teachers have told such youngsters to mouth the words without making a sound. At the same time, she is aware of how much Sandra is anticipating singing at the concert. Based on her understanding of principle C, she rejects restricting Sandra's participation in favor of allowing her to sing. In this case, the adult permitted the child's needs to come before her own.

**EXAMPLE:** Kathy's brother was killed in a traffic accident by a car driven by a black woman. Although the accident happened over a year ago, Kathy still harbors great anger toward all black people. Today when she passes out the spelling papers, she calls each black child "nigger." The teacher recognizes Kathy's need to express her emotions, but interprets the child's actions as a violation of her own basic value of respect for people of all races. Thus, guided by principle C, she chooses to forbid Kathy to use derogatory language in her classroom.

**PRINCIPLE D:** When making a judgment that involves choosing one goal from among several contradicting goals of equal weight, priority is given to the goal that the adult has fewest opportunities to address in day-to-day encounters. Often, situations arise in which it is possible to concentrate on reinforcing only one of several competing goals. Pursuit of one goal would negate another goal. When this happens, it is best to pursue the goal that is less often addressed.

**EXAMPLE:** Jorge received $10 from his grandmother for his birthday. He took the entire amount and bought his mother a change purse painted with a half-naked woman in a suggestive pose. He is proud of his purchase and pleased to be giving his mother a gift. His mother is touched that he so selflessly used his money for someone other than himself, but also is concerned with his poor choice and lack of fiscal awareness. She realizes that she must focus on one aspect of the situation or the other. If she tries to deal with both by thanking him and then having him return the inappropriate purchase, she would, in fact, diminish the genuineness of her praise. She must choose between the value she places on prosocial behavior and her value related to money management. After much thought, following the premise of principle D, she thanks Jorge for the change purse and says nothing about the inappropriate image. She decided that she would have many future opportunities to teach fiscal responsibility but would have fewer chances to reward Jorge's gift giving.

**PRINCIPLE E:** When choosing between two strategies, one that supports a short-term objective but interferes with long-term goals and another that has the opposite effect, priority is given to pursuing long-term goals. At times, strategies that lead to either short- or long-term goals conflict. When this happens, choose those that best contribute to the long-range outcome.

**EXAMPLE:** The children from the center have been on a walking field trip. They are tired, and the adults are anxious to get back—it has been a long afternoon. The group has reached the middle of the block. The school building is right across the street, and there is no traffic in sight. The leader considers jaywalking, but realizes that such an action would detract from her long-range goal of teaching children the appropriate way to cross the street. Her decision to have the children walk several extra yards to the corner, thereby using the crosswalk, is based on her understanding of principle E.

**PRINCIPLE F: When faced with competing group and individual needs, priority is given to the approach that best satisfies each. Such solutions may involve a compromise that addresses both sets of needs simultaneously. If this is not possible to achieve, competing needs may be addressed sequentially. In either case, helping professionals strive to achieve win-win solutions as opposed to outcomes in which either the individual or the group is perceived as a "winner" or "loser."** On occasion, an option that would benefit a child at that point in time will be at odds with what would be optimal for the group as a whole. Sometimes, it is possible to blend these needs through a combination of strategies. At other times, this is not so feasible and a choice must be made between primary benefit for one or the other. Under these circumstances, helping professionals may address both sets of needs in sequence, knowing that the final result may not be completely satisfactory to all.

**EXAMPLE:** The children are seated in a group, listening to a story. Suddenly, the adult becomes aware that Leslie is sobbing quietly. The adult interrupts the story, saying: "Leslie, you look unhappy. What's wrong?" The child continues to cry without answering. The adult is torn between the group's desire to hear the story and the child's need to be comforted. In accordance with principle F, after offering a brief explanation to the other children, the adult postpones reading the story to comfort Leslie. Later, she takes time to read the story to the group.

**EXAMPLE:** Vito has little self-confidence. The one area in which he excels is building with blocks. Day after day, he builds elaborate structures and then begs that they remain standing, undisturbed. At first, the adult honors Vito's wishes, even though it limits other children's access to the blocks. She reasons that it is more important for Vito to feel good about an accomplishment than for the group to use the materials. However, over time, the adult notices that the youngsters are becoming increasingly upset about their lim-

ited opportunities to build. Although no one seems to resent Vito, children are really starting to feel short-changed. Using principle F, the adult decides to limit how long a structure can remain standing as well as Vito's monopolization of the blocks. She offers him a choice of using the blocks exclusively for a few minutes or using them for a longer time in conjunction with other children.

**PRINCIPLE G: When choosing between options that have equally positive and negative outcomes, priority is given to the one that is most personally satisfying.** At times, all of the alternatives you generate seem to have about the same number of benefits and drawbacks. There may be no particular option that is clearly the most or least desirable. In cases such as these, helping professionals should select the option with which they are most comfortable. This principle has been included so that adults have some guide for what to do when no alternative stands out. A decision based on this principle is preferable to remaining indecisive and avoiding a conscious judgment.

**EXAMPLE:** The adult is reading books to the group. There is time for one more story before they go home. Half of the children want a dinosaur story; half prefer one about space. Both are worthwhile tales, and selecting only one means that some children may be dissatisfied. The adult decides to read the dinosaur book because he finds it amusing. He has made his choice based on principle G.

Using the priority principles just described is an effective way of thinking through the judgment process. These principles can be applied to a wide range of scenarios involving both on-the-spot decision making and more long-term deliberations. Moreover, these principles are valid in dealing with issues of varying magnitude. For this reason, we feel they can be generalized to most of the day-to-day judgments helping professionals have to make. See Table 15–1 for a summary of priority principles.

However, some situations call for judgments that are so specialized that they must be addressed separately. Two such situations involve making judgments about children's extreme behavior and making judgments related to child abuse. In both cases, the essential judgment to be made is whether or not the condition exists. If the answer is no, the preceding principles apply. If the answer is affirmative, there are precise guidelines for what to do next. We will now focus on each of these special cases in turn.

| ▼ Table 15–1 | Priority Principles for Making Day-to-Day Judgments |
|---|---|
| Pursue safety first | Strategies that preserve children's safety take precedence over all others. |
| Weigh pluses and minuses | Priority is given to the approach that promises the most positive and the least negative outcomes. |
| Begin with child's needs | When faced with a situation in which the child's needs and the adult's needs differ, priority is given to meeting the child's needs, unless doing so compromises the adult's basic values. |
| Focus on "rare" opportunities | When making a judgment that involves choosing one goal from among several contradictory goals of equal weight, priority is given to the goal that the adult has the fewest opportunities to address in day-to-day encounters. |
| Choose long-term goals | When choosing between two strategies, one that supports an immediate objective but interferes with long-term goals, and another that has the opposite effect, priority is given to pursuing long-term goals. |
| Look for win-win solutions | When faced with competing group and individual needs, priority is given to the approach that best satisfies each. |
| Decide on personal satisfaction | When choosing between options that have equally positive and negative outcomes, priority is given to the strategy that is most personally satisfying. |

## ▼ JUDGMENTS ABOUT EXTREME BEHAVIOR

Sometimes, helping professionals find themselves in a dilemma, trying to decide whether a child's behavior merits the attention of additional behavioral or medical experts. On one hand, a child's actions may be so baffling or so dysfunctional that the adult fears that ignoring them could have serious consequences. On the other hand, he or she worries about alarming the family, offending them, or asking them to commit to what may be a significant outlay of time or money. Torn between both sides of issue, the helping professional may find it impossible to make a conscious decision. Fortunately, there are guidelines available to enable professionals to make such judgments with more assurance.

### What Constitutes Extreme Behavior

Dr. Louise Guerney, a clinical psychologist and professor emeritus at the Pennsylvania State University, has developed criteria for determining what behaviors should be considered extreme (1984, 1997). It is from her work that we have drawn the material for this portion of the chapter. Dr. Guerney notes that some behaviors are extreme by virtue of their mere presence. Others are designated as extreme because they exceed the normal boundaries you would expect in relation to a child's age. How intense a behavior is and how generalized it becomes are additional factors you must take into account when determining whether behavior is ex-

treme. Other variables that influence your judgment include the effect the behavior has on the child's present or future functioning and how resistant the behavior is to modification.

**Presence of self-destructive behaviors and cruelty to others/animals.** Self-destructive acts are danger signs. Their very appearance should prompt immediate intervention. Self-destructive acts are those that children inflict on themselves and that result in physical injury or mental damage. This is exemplified by the youngster who disfigures herself by scratching; by the child who bangs his head, causing contusions; and by the child who deliberately courts danger as a thrill-seeking device. In each case, the behavior is too serious to be allowed to continue.

Similarly, children who repeatedly engage in unprovoked acts of cruelty toward others and/or the animals in their lives are displaying antisocial behaviors that go beyond the powers of the adult in the formal group setting to deal with alone. This is especially true when children claim that such acts are accidental or put the blame on others, all the while seeming to enjoy the havoc that results. If such actions become customary, either at home or in the program, the child is exhibiting signs of extreme behavior.

**Sudden drastic changes in behavior patterns.** Another cause for concern is a child's normal behavior pattern changing suddenly or radically. A generally happy, responsive child who becomes withdrawn and fearful, a habitually mild-mannered child who overnight becomes volatile, and a child who begins complaining of unrelenting stomachaches are all showing evidence of extreme behaviors. Because these actions are so out of character, they signal a need for closer scrutiny.

**Age.** Frequently, a behavior is considered extreme if it reappears or continues to exist long after you would expect a child to have outgrown it. Although it is typical for two-year-olds to have temper tantrums, even frequent ones, nine-year-olds do not usually behave this way. Thus, if a nine-year-old repeatedly resorted to explosive outbursts, it would be obvious that the behavior should be categorized as extreme. Likewise, if an eight-year-old suddenly begins bed-wetting, a behavior more typical of infancy and toddlerhood, this turn of events would deserve serious attention.

**Intensity of the behavior.** The intensity of a behavior involves its frequency and duration. Problem behaviors are generally considered normal if they appear only occasionally or briefly. However, they are labeled extreme if they occur frequently or if they last for protracted periods of time. For instance, it is not unusual for preschoolers to periodically seek the comfort of blanket and thumb when frightened or tired. On the other hand, were three-year-old Michael to spend the majority of his waking hours pacifying himself in this manner, the behavior would be considered extreme. Likewise, everyone has times when they want to "sneak" an extra cookie or snack item. However, the child who regularly steals or hoards food is exhibiting signs of extreme behavior. Whether parents or the professional with whom the child comes in regular contact should seek outside help would depend on how long the problem lasts. There are times when extreme behaviors are short lived. That is, they appear for a few days, and then children gradually return to their original behavior patterns. Such instances are viewed as temporary crises that require adult support but not necessarily outside intervention. However, should the behavior endure, some serious exploration of the child's situation, with the help of an expert in such matters, would be in order.

**Breadth of the behavior.** Indiscriminate manifestations of behavior often are considered extreme. That is, certain actions that might be considered normal if their appearance were limited become abnormal when they pervade all aspects of a child's life. For instance, it is common for youngsters aged four through nine to tell untruths to protect themselves in incriminating situations or to make themselves seem more interesting. Although hardly exemplary, their resorting to lies under duress or in moments of self-expansiveness should not be categorized as extreme. On the other hand, there are a few children who rely on falsehoods in virtually all situations, regardless of whether they are in obvious trouble or in a circumstance in which absolute adherence to the facts is unimportant. These youngsters tend to lie about many things even when the truth would serve them better. Lying in this form is indiscriminate and should be examined in conjunction with a behavioral expert to determine how it could be modified.

**Effect on the child's present and future functioning.** Behaviors that have the potential to hamper children's growth or development should be treated as extreme. This is exemplified by children who repeatedly force themselves to throw up after eating, those who are so hostile or lacking in affect they do not let anyone get close to them, and youngsters who become so centered on getting good grades that they resort to cheating, lying, and sabotage of others' work to better their own standing. Likewise, diabetic children who deliberately avoid their medication or habitually eat forbidden foods fall into this category. Young people who are so shy or standoffish that they literally have no friends or acquaintances also are enmeshed in extreme, counterproductive patterns of behavior. In each case, consultation with parents and behavioral experts is recommended.

**Resistance of the behavior to change.** Resistance for more than a short time (usually several weeks) to *reasonable* efforts to correct a common, everyday problem is a sign that the behavior has become extreme. "Reasonable efforts" refer to adult use of relevant, constructive strategies aimed at eliminating negative actions while simultaneously promoting desirable alternate behaviors. It also implies consistency. That is, the problem behavior must receive attention on a predictable basis, and the strategies employed must be used often enough and long enough that a behavior change is likely. Within this definition, a child who periodically experiences negative consequences for being out of his seat, but who at other times is inadvertently rewarded for wandering, is not demonstrating resistant behavior but rather the effects of the adult's lack of predictability. On the other hand, were the child to experience appropriate consequences over a two-month span but still habitually wander the room, this could be taken as evidence that the behavior had become extreme.

Similarly, a developmental task for all young children is to become toilet trained. Although the optimal period for this to occur varies among individuals, it is accepted that by about three years of age, most children will have begun this training. Yet, some children resist learning to use the toilet. Initial resistance is common and should not be a signal for alarm. However, there are youngsters whose resistance continues to mount so that bladder or bowel control is still not achieved into the grade-school years. Under these conditions, the behavior can appropriately be described as extreme.

### Frequently Reported Sources of Extreme Behavior

When adults are confronted with children's extreme behavior, they often wonder where it comes from and why it occurs. Although the variables influencing any single child may differ widely, three of the most commonly reported sources include physiological factors, childhood fears, and childhood depression (Fitch, 1985; Goleman, 1995).

**Physiology.** It has been suggested that some children who exhibit extreme behavior do so as a result of protein, vitamin, or mineral deficiencies in their diet (Santrock, 1995). For instance, children who are deprived of essential B vitamins have impaired concentration, resulting in a shorter attention span and a lack of task commitment. Other researchers claim that biochemical irregularities, such as glandular disorders (Eames, 1962) and hypoglycemia (Roberts, 1969), are related to the maladaptive behavior patterns some children display. Over the past several years, scientists also have hypothesized that some genuinely extreme, noncompliant behavior is related to neurological dysfunction. Hyperactive behavior, sometimes diagnosed as Attention Deficit Disorder or Attention Deficit/Hyperactivity Disorder, which involves impulsive, uncontrolled behaviors as well as exceedingly active behavior not typical of the majority of children, are the most common of these. For instance, brain damage, which may result from birth complications or a later head injury, can make it difficult for a child to

sit still. Also, chemical imbalances in the brain may interfere with the transfer of signals from one cell to another. Either way, brain dysfunction may contribute to a child's need for constant motion and an inability to relax (Berger, 1996; Wender and Klein, 1986). Although not all overly active behavior is neurologically based, the preceding findings indicate that this may sometimes be the case. Another extreme behavioral problem that results from neurological difficulties is Tourette's syndrome. Children with this condition display many tics (repeated involuntary movements, such as eye blinking), which may be accompanied by the shouting of obscenities and the production of loud and/or strange noises. All of these behaviors are actually beyond the child's ability to control. Although it is not common, this condition has been included here to underscore the point that some extreme behaviors can be related to bioneurological dysfunctions. In cases such as these, assistance from specially trained professionals is necessary.

**Childhood fears.** Another source of extreme behavior in children is fear. All children at one time or another become afraid of certain places, people, things, or events. Even if extreme in intensity for days or sometimes weeks, these fearful episodes usually are of a relatively short duration. (Refer to Chapter 5 for a review of typical childhood fears and what to do about them.) Time, along with adult empathy and support, will dissipate most of these.

Yet, there are times when fears persist for such long periods and permeate so many areas of a child's life that they interfere with the child's ability to function. Such extreme fears are called **anxiety disorders.** They are persistent, unfounded, out of proportion to the actual danger or threat, and lead to maladaptive behavior (Berns, 1994). Most often, this maladaptation takes the form of extreme withdrawal. For example, seven-year-old Veronica reached a point where she was terrified at the mere prospect of coming in contact with anything fuzzy. Initially, Veronica had expressed a fear of mice. Gradually, her fear extended to encompass most fuzzy objects, such as stuffed animals, blankets, and the fur collar on her coat. As time went on, she became hysterical at the touch of a cotton swab and when asked to use yarn in a weaving project. Ultimately, her anxiety prompted her to resist leaving the sanctuary of her home, from which most of the offending items had been eliminated.

A common anxiety disorder during the grade-school years is known as school refusal, or **school phobia** (Papalia and Olds, 1993). Although many youngsters experience some anxiety about school, about 16 out of every 1,000 develop such severe anxieties that they become physically ill at the prospect of going to school each day (Gelfand, Jenson, and Drew, 1982). Their resistance to school becomes extreme: screaming, crying, and tantrums are common, as are severe stomachaches, headaches, and sore throats. The child's distress may be directly related to incidents at school (a scolding from a teacher, a bullying classmate, embarrassment over poor work) (Ambron and Salkind, 1984). It also may be caused by other factors not so easily discernible, such as fears that develop from a misunderstood conversation or the chance remark of a friend (Kostelnik, Stein, and Whiren, 1982). In either case, the child's reaction is to attempt to withdraw from all school contacts.

Occasionally, rather than trying to resolve fear through withdrawal, some youngsters try to master it directly. In the process, they often overreact, engaging in potentially harmful activities. For example, following a period of extreme fear of fire, some children set fires. They reason that their ability to produce a flame at will and to extinguish it themselves demonstrates their power over it.

Another worrisome way that some children cope with fear is to develop an obsession or a compulsion. Undesired, recurring thoughts are called **obsessions**. These are persistent preoccupations: ideas children cannot get out of their heads. Impulses to repeatedly perform certain acts are called **compulsions** (Berns, 1994). Everyone exhibits some obsessive or compulsive behavior at some time, and in their mildest forms, neither of these is a problem. For instance, the childhood chant "Step on a crack, break your mother's back; step on a line, break your mother's spine" prompts some children around the age of seven or eight to keep their eyes glued to the sidewalk, compulsively avoiding the fateful cracks and lines. This is a game involving great ritual into which children enter happily with no feeling of inner coercion (Kessler, 1972). They believe in the power of the chant enough to honor it, and yet, they do not really think a misstep will cause injury.

However, if a compulsion or obsession begins to interfere with a person's functioning and is one from which he or she derives no pleasure or social benefits, it is judged extreme. For instance, ten-year-old Jessica was obsessed with the thought of having to urinate even though there was no physical basis for her concern. Her obsession caused her to make as many as fifty trips to the bathroom each day. Often, once she got there, she was unable to produce even a drop. When Jessica was denied access to the bathroom as often as she wanted, her anxiety over a possible accident drove her to tears. She became so preoccupied with this one biological function that she was able to think of little else.

How a child's compulsion might disrupt his or her life is illustrated by Craig, whose elaborate rituals at mealtime prevented him from enjoying his lunch. It also made him seem "weird" to age-mates, causing them to avoid him. Before allowing himself to take a bite, Craig felt compelled to unfold his napkin a certain way and then refold it several times. Next, he spread it out with the corners in a particular position. Each corner was then carefully torn off and placed in a neat pile to the left. He had equally time-consuming routines for the preparation of his sandwich and milk. If the procedure was interrupted, Craig became quite upset and began over again.

All of the fear-related circumstances just described exceed the bounds of normalcy. When these kinds of episodes take place, the attention of behavioral experts is called for.

**Childhood depression.**   A source of extreme behavior that has become increasingly prevalent in the two-to-twelve age group is childhood depression (Goleman, 1995; Papalia and Olds, 1993). Behaviors associated with this phenomenon range from affective ones, like sadness, continual crying, withdrawal, inability to concentrate, lack of interest in life, and feelings of defeat, to physical manifestations such as severe and frequent stomachaches or headaches for which there seems to be no physiological basis.

Sometimes, extreme misbehavior can be a symptom of depression as well. It shows itself in such acting-out behaviors as stealing, fighting, or defiance. These and other destructive acts are characterized by excessive disobedience and unrelenting resistance to change. It must be remembered that all children occasionally disobey for a variety of reasons and that noncompliance does not, in and of itself, mean that a child is suffering from depression. Rather, outside help is warranted when unremitting, intense, hostile disobedience occurs over a long period of time.

## ▼ Judgments Regarding Child Abuse and Neglect

When helping professionals believe that a child in their care has suffered the trauma of child abuse or neglect, their emotions may run high. Initially, they may experience disbelief, horror, anger, or panic. If they allow these feelings to dictate their reaction, their response will not be constructive. Incredulity may cause them to ignore a serious problem; shock may immobilize them; rage may prompt them into a destructive mode of action; and panic could detract from their ability to deal with the situation coherently. At times like these, helping professionals must be able to control their emotions and make a calm, rational judgment about whether there is a possibility of child abuse. In order to make such a judgment, they first must understand the nature of child abuse and the signs to look for.

### Defining Abuse and Neglect

The mistreatment of children includes both **abuse**—actions that are deliberately harmful to a child's well-being—and **neglect**—failure to appropriately meet children's basic needs (Berger and Thompson, 1995). Legally, every state has its own definition of these acts. However, there is general agreement that abuse and neglect most often take the following forms:

*Physical abuse:* assaults on children that produce pain, cuts, welts, bruises, broken bones, and other injuries. Whipping children, tying them up, locking them in closets, throwing them against walls, scalding them, and shaking them violently are common examples.

*Sexual abuse:* includes molestation, exploitation, and intimidation. Children who are sexually abused are pressured into engaging in sexual activity through subtle deceits, bribes, or outright threats and force. Most incidents of child sexual abuse involve genital fondling, oral-genital contact, or sexual abuse of the breasts or anus. Sexual intercourse is another but less common, occurrence (Finkelhor, 1990). Sexually abused children may also be subjected to obscene phone calls or sexually explicit language; they may be made to exhibit themselves or to watch the exhibition of an adult.

*Physical neglect:* failure of adults to provide adequate food, clothing, shelter, medical care and supervision for children. Neglected children starve because they are not fed; freeze when they are left without clothing in frigid temperature, and may

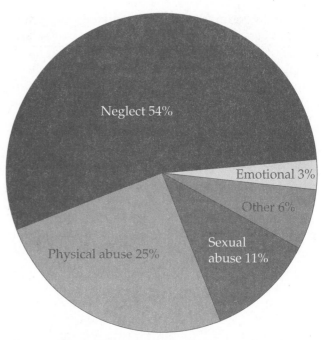

**Figure 15–1** 1995 Substantiated abuse and neglect cases. (Source: National Committee to Prevent Child Abuse, Annual Fifty States Survey Highlights, August 12, 1996.)

perish in fires, when left unsupervised (Papalia and Olds, 1993).

*Emotional abuse:* actions that deliberately destroy children's self-esteem. Such abuse is usually verbal and may take the form of scapegoating, ridiculing, humiliating, or terrorizing children.

*Emotional neglect:* failure of adults to meet children's needs for affection and emotional support. Emotionally neglected children are ignored or subjected to cold, distant relationships with adults.

In each of these cases, children's current levels of functioning are damaged and there is a potential threat to their future well-being. At one time it was thought that such negative acts occurred rarely and were perpetrated by a few "sick" people in our society. We now know better.

Figure 15–1 shows substantiated cases of abuse and neglect from a 1995 survey.

### Scope of the Problem

Child abuse is a very serious problem, which is more widely recognized today than ever before. In 1995 it was reported that approximately 3.1 million children in the United States were victims of child abuse. This represents about double the number reported ten years ago. Currently, in our country, at least five children a day die of some form of abuse, and every year 140,000 are so seriously injured that they are disabled for life (Children's Defense Fund, 1997). These figures are based on reported cases; the real numbers undoubtedly are higher because much abuse is never brought to the attention of the authorities. Such data suggest that at least one out of every ten young people will experience violation of their person during the childhood years. According to the law of averages, this means that a helping professional may come in contact with about two or three such children during a twelve-month period. This is not to say that an abused child will be found in every formal group setting. It does underscore the fact that sometime during their career, helping professionals will have to make a judgment that a child is a victim of abuse. In fact, the problem has become so widespread that all fifty states now have laws requiring that suspected cases of child abuse be reported by doctors, teachers, and other helping professionals who work with children. Furthermore, in most states helping professionals are legally responsible for any injury to a child that comes about because the professional failed to make such a report (Click, 1995).

## The Abusers

Who would beat, bash, burn, choke, neglect, starve, rape, sodomize, or otherwise assault a child? Are the perpetrators of such hideous deeds psychopathic monsters? Overwhelmingly, the evidence says, no. Rather, they are ordinary people who, for any number of reasons, subject children to humiliating or physically injurious acts. Child abuse cuts across all ages, both genders, all races, all social classes, all family structures, and all socioeconomic groups. There are no characteristics that infallibly separate abusers from nonabusers, victims from nonvictims. Although certain conditions may be more or less highly related to abuse, their existence alone is not an absolute indicator of whether or not abuse will occur. Rather, it is a combination of variables that determines actual outcomes.

**Physical abusers.** Physical abuse is most likely to occur at the hands of the natural parent (Belsky, 1993). Parents who physically abuse their children are not crazy people. Only 10 percent actually suffer from a serious psychotic disorder (Berger and Thompson, 1995; Steele, 1980). The remainder are adults who claim to care for their children, although the care they offer frequently is marred by violence or neglect.

Initially, scientists assumed that abusive parents would display specific personality traits that might distinguish them from their nonabusing counterparts. Over time, it was found that they were somewhat more impulsive, immature, self-centered, hypersensitive, and troubled (Leavitt, 1983; Zigler and Rubin, 1985). Yet, the investigations in which such findings were reported were not always conclusive or unanimous (Wolfe, 1985). More precise data have been generated by studies that focus more on the parents' behavior and attitudes toward their children. From these, it has been found that abusive parents often inaccurately assume intentionality in children's behavior and consider normal child behavior as "difficult" (Belsky, 1993; Egeland, Sroufe and Erickson, 1983). Thus, a mother may be convinced that a school-age child who fell down and scraped his knee did so deliberately just to upset her. These parents frequently have unreasonable expectations for children's behavior and distorted perceptions of what children should be able to do at a given age (Bavolek, 1989). For instance, a parent might become incensed when an infant does not stop crying on demand or when a three-year-old proves incapable of getting her own lunch. Physically abusive parents also tend to believe in physical punishment and are afraid that without it, their children will be spoiled (Steele, 1983; Trickett and Susman, 1988). They exhibit a low tolerance for stress, possess a poor repertoire of life skills, and express general dissatisfaction with the parental role (Bugental, Blue, and Cruzcosa, 1989). In an overwhelming number of cases, they have experienced poor relationships with their own parents, often having been abused as children themselves (Goleman, 1995; Steele, 1986).

Finally, situational factors within and outside the family play a significant role in the likelihood of abuse occurring (Garbarino, 1995). For example, abuse is most common in families in which finances are severely strained (regardless of socioeconomic status). Other stressful life events such as divorce, unemployment, family conflict, overcrowding, lack of a support system, or drastic changes in status and role create the conditions in which abuse may eventually take place (Berk, 1997). Most recently, the results of a nationwide survey by the National Committee to Prevent Child Abuse also linked child abuse with homelessness and substance abuse by parents (Children's Defense Fund, 1997). It also has been discovered that abusive families frequently are isolated families. That is, they have little access to parenting information that might be of use to them or to potential resource people and have no real means of social comparison, either for their children or for themselves. This isolation heightens, and sometimes causes, many of the problems they experience.

Increasingly, scientists believe that abuse occurs as a result of an interactive effect among all of the variables just described: the adult's personality, his or her lack of parenting skills, unrealistic expectations, situational characteristics, and lack of community support services (Papalia and Olds, 1993). The volatile nature of the encounter may be heightened by the child's own attributes, such as temperament or physical appearance. How and why this occurs will be discussed shortly.

**Sexual abusers.** For many years, parents and helping professionals have warned children to stay away from strangers. Most often, the child molester has been portrayed as a classic "scary person": an unfamiliar, middle-aged male in a raincoat who hangs around parks or schools waiting to tempt a lone child with candy. Unfortunately, this scenario does not cover the most common situations in which children are at risk. In reality, in 80 percent of child **sexual abuse** cases, the child knows the offender, and in over 50 percent, the offender is a member of the child's own household (AAPC, 1985). When sexual abuse by strangers does occur, it is most likely to happen in a single episode, during warm-weather months, outside, in an automobile or a public building. On the other hand, abuse perpetrated by family members or acquaintances is apt to occur repeatedly, at any time, and at home (Shaffer, 1994). In these cases, force or bribery seldom is used. Instead, the child may submit to the adult's requests in deference to the adult's perceived status in the family or from a desire to please.

Families in which the father or father figure abuses a daughter represent the most common incidents of abuse. These families often are plagued by dysfunctional relationships, especially between spouses. The adult male frequently has low self-esteem and is weak and resentful rather than virile or oversexed as is the common stereotype. Although some mothers do not recognize the situation, others are aware but unable to face their predicament and so must deny what is happening. In fact, once the abuse becomes known, it is not uncommon for family members to turn against the victim, blaming her for the disruption. Circumstances such as these can go on for years if no intervention is forthcoming.

**Neglectful parents.** Parents who fail to meet their children's basic physical and emotional needs are generally apathetic and irresponsible (Wolfe, 1985). They also lack the basic skills necessary to organize a safe, warm home environment. As a result they tend to ignore their children. Such parents are likely to have been poorly nurtured themselves and to have stressful relationships with other significant adults in their lives. Thus, they do not have access to models who could demonstrate more appropriate forms of engagement with children.

### The Victims

The majority of physical-abuse cases are initiated during the preschool years (Lang and Daro, 1996). This is a time when children have little power to retaliate and have fewer people to tell. Generally, parents do not physically abuse all of their children. Instead, one victim is singled out. It often is the child's own personal characteristics that contribute to his or her being selected. For instance, physically unattractive infants, premature or low-birth-weight infants, and children who began life unwanted are more likely to be abused than youngsters who were not born under these negative circumstances (Harter, Alexander, and Neimeyer, 1988; Newman and Newman, 1997). Likewise, physically or mentally handicapped youngsters, as well as those who are considered temperamentally difficult, are more likely to become victims, of abuse (Friedrich and Boriskin, 1976; Sherrod, et al., 1984). Finally, there is evidence that youngsters who are frequently disruptive and noncompliant are treated more abusively than those who are more passive.

Although 10 percent of all victims of sexual abuse are younger than five years of age, the majority are school children between the ages of nine and twelve (Santrock, 1995). Females are victimized at a much higher rate than males (the estimated ratio is 10:1). Overwhelmingly, victims are young girls, and perpetrators most often are adult males (Canavan, 1981). Although females are primary targets, it should not be forgotten that boys also are victims of abuse and that adult females can be abusers. Unlike physical abuse, child sexual abuse often extends to more than one victim within the same family. These sexual encounters frequently begin with innocent touching and progress to fondling and then to overt sexual stimulation. Forcible rape rarely occurs. Instead, there often are pleasurable overtones to the interactions, which contribute to children's confusion over what is happening to them. The most likely victims are those who lack information about sexual abuse and what to do if it occurs (Koblinsky and Behana, 1984). Children who have low self-esteem and those who are physically weak and socially isolated are the most likely candidates for victimization (Faller, 1990).

**Effects on victims.** An obvious outcome of either physical or sexual abuse is injury. For example, it has been reported that abusive acts are the fourth most common cause of death in children five years of age and younger (Children's Defense Fund, 1997). Other problems include fractures, lacerations, internal injuries, pregnancy, and venereal disease. Physical and sexual abuse have been correlated with truancy, running away, drug and alcohol abuse, sexual promiscuity, psychological distress, physical complaints, dramatic behavior changes, depression, suicidal tendencies, violent crime, inability to trust others, guilt, and anger (Adams-Tucker, 1982; Steele, 1986; Trickett, et al., 1991). In addition, we can only begin to calculate the cost to society of caring for victims, incarcerating perpetrators, and the loss of productive family functioning. Perhaps most significantly, this phenomenon has been tied to abuse in future generations. Having little experience with alternate ways of behaving, children who have been targets of abuse often enact similar violence on their own children. However, this is not the case for every victim. Individuals can break the cycle of maltreatment. This is most likely to happen when they receive support from a nonabusive adult during childhood, when they receive therapy at some point in their lives, and when they have a satisfying, nonabusive relationship with a spouse (Shaffer, 1994). All of these factors make early detection crucial.

Because of the close contact helping professionals enjoy with the children in their care, they play an important role in identifying victims of abuse.

### Signs of Abuse

Several signs may indicate possible child abuse. Some relate to the child's appearance, others to the child's behavior, and still others to what the child says. Certain family indicators also should be considered. The presence of one sign alone does not automatically signal abuse. However, if one or more are present, they should be interpreted as a warning that additional attention is warranted (Berk, 1997). These signs are summarized in Table 15–2. In Figure 15–2, a comparison of typical and suspicious locations of bruising on children's bodies is shown.

---

**▼ Table 15–2    Signs of Child Abuse and Neglect: Physical, Behavioral, Verbal, and Family Indicators**

**PHYSICAL ABUSE AND NEGLECT**

**Physical Indicators**

Bruises
  Bruises on the face, lips, or mouth; on large areas of the back, torso, buttocks, or thighs; on more than one side of the body
  Bruises of different coloration, indicating that they occurred at different times
  Bruises that are clustered
  Bruises that show the imprint of a belt buckle, coat hanger, strap, or wooden spoon
Welts
Wounds, cuts, or punctures
Burns
  Rope burns on arms, legs, neck, face, or torso
  Burns that show a pattern (cigarette, iron, radiator)
  Burns on the buttocks or genitalia
  Caustic burns
  Scalding-liquid burns
Fractures
  Multiple fractures in various stages of healing
  Any fracture in a child younger than two years of age
Bone dislocations
Human-bite marks
Neglect
  Child is consistently dirty, hungry, or inappropriately dressed for the weather

*continued*

**▼ Table 15–2—continued   Signs of Child Abuse and Neglect: Physical, Behavioral, Verbal, and Family Indicators**

Neglect—continued
  Child has been abandoned
  Child has persistent medical problems that go unattended

**Behavioral Indicators**
The child:
  Is wary of physical contact with adults
  Flinches when adults approach or move
  Exhibits a dramatic change in behavior
  Shows extreme withdrawal or aggression
  Indicates fear of parents or caregivers
  Consistently arrives early and stays late
  Is consistently tired or falls asleep during the day
  Is frequently late for school or absent
  Is under the influence of alcohol or drugs
  Begs or steals food
  Shows a limited capacity for experiencing pleasure or enjoying life

**Verbal Indicators**
The child:
  Reports injury by parents or caregiver
  Offers inconsistent explanations for injuries or condition
  Offers incredible explanations for injuries or condition
  Makes comments such as: "Can I come and live with you?", "Do I have to go home?", "My mom/dad doesn't like me"
  Reports not having a place to sleep and/or enough to eat

**Family Indicators**
The family:
  Maintains a filthy home environment
  Is socially isolated from the rest of the community
  Is extremely closed to contacts with school or child's friends
  Refuses to allow child to participate in normal school activities (physical education, social events)
  Offers inconsistent, illogical, or no explanation for child's injury or condition
  Shows lack of concern about child's injury or condition
  Attempts to conceal child's injury or condition
  Describes the child as evil, monstrous, or incorrigible
  Reports or uses in your presence inappropriate punishments (denial of food, prolonged isolation, beating)
  Consistently speaks demeaningly to the child
  Abuses alcohol or drugs
  Reacts defensively to inquiries regarding the child's health

## SEXUAL ABUSE

**Physical Indicators**
The child:
  Is pregnant
  Shows signs of venereal disease
  Has blood in urine
  Has genitals that are swollen or bruised
  Shows presence of pus or blood on genitals
  Has physical complaints with no apparent physical cause
  Has torn or stained underclothing
  Shows rectal bleeding

▼ Table 15–2—continued    Signs of Child Abuse and Neglect: Physical, Behavioral, Verbal, and Family Indicators

**Behavioral Indicators**

The child:

Persistently scratches genital area

Has difficulty sitting on chairs or play equipment (squirming, frequently readjusting position, frequently leaving seat)

"Straddle walks" as if pants were wet or chafing

Suddenly loses appetite

Suddenly reports nightmares

Shows extreme withdrawal or aggression

Shows wariness of contact with adults

Shows inappropriate seductiveness with adults or other children

Shows a sudden lack of interest in life

Withdraws into fantasy behavior

Regresses to infantile behavior such as bed-wetting, thumb sucking, or excessive crying

Shows limited capacity for enjoying life or experiencing pleasure

Is promiscuous

Runs away

Is frequently truant

Exhibits knowledge of sexual functions far beyond other children in his or her peer group

Suddenly withdraws from friends

**Verbal Indicators**

The child:

Complains of pain in the genital area

Reports incidents of sexual contact with an adult or older child

Reports having to keep secret a game with an adult or an older child

Expresses fear of being left alone with a particular adult or older child

Reports: "She/he fooled around with me," "She/he touched me," or "My mother's boyfriend/my father/my brother/my aunt does things to me when no one else is there"

**Family Indicators**

The family:

Exhibits an obvious role reversal between mother and daughter

Is socially isolated from the rest of the community

Is extremely closed to contacts with school or child's friends

Demonstrates extreme discord

Refuses to allow child to engage in normal social interactions

---

**EMOTIONAL ABUSE AND NEGLECT**

---

**Physical Indicators**

None

**Behavioral Indicators**

The child:

Does not play

Is passive and compliant or aggressive and defiant

Rarely smiles

Has poor social skills

Is socially unresponsive

Avoids eye contact

Seeks attention constantly and always seems to want and need more

Relates indiscriminately to adults in precocious ways

*continued*

▼ Table 15–2—continued    Signs of Child Abuse and Neglect: Physical, Behavioral, Verbal, and Family Indicators

Shows reluctance to eat or fascination with food
Is prone to rocking, thumb sucking

**Verbal Indicators**
The child:
Reports problems sleeping
Continually describes self in negative terms
Is reluctant to include family in program-related events

**Family Indicators**
The family:
Conveys unrealistic expectations for the child
Seems to rely on the child to meet own social and emotional needs
Shows indifference or lack of interest in child
Lacks basic knowledge and skills related to child rearing
Describes child in primarily negative terms
Seems focused more on meeting own needs than those of the children
Blames child

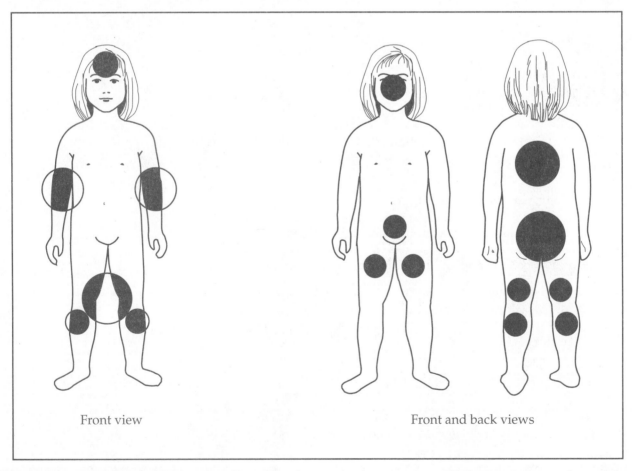

Front view                                        Front and back views

**Figure 15–2** Comparison of the location of typical and suspicious bruising areas. The bruises that typically result from children's play are depicted on the left. The bruises on the right seldom happen as a result of play. (Source: Head Start Bureau and Children's Bureau, U.S. Department of Health, Education and Welfare. *Child Abuse and Neglect: A Self-Instructional Text for Head Start Personnel.* Washington, D.C.: U.S. Government Printing Office, 1977.)

## Reporting Child Abuse

Early childhood professionals are required by law to report any evidence of suspected child abuse. Such reports signal only the suspicion that abuse has occurred. Helping professionals who, in good faith, document signs of abuse and relay them to the proper authorities are acting as an advocate for the child.

The reporting process is straightforward. Although particular institutions and government jurisdictions have their own individual procedures, most include:

1. A disclosure of the suspicion to a designated person within the program: social worker, principal, director.
2. A verbal report to the social agency responsible for children's protective services in a particular community. This report is conveyed either directly by the individual who has the suspicion or indirectly through a designated spokesperson. In either case, the identity of the person who originally suspected abuse is kept confidential and is revealed only with his or her consent.
3. A written report to the social agency with which verbal contact was initiated. This usually occurs within two to three days. The written statement contains essential information, usually is brief, and is written in the person's own words rather than in legalistic terms.
4. An interview with the child. This is most common when sexual abuse is suspected. Youngsters usually are interviewed in the presence of some-

one they trust; in many cases, this is the helping professional in whom they confided.
5. Continued investigation. From this point on, the case falls within the jurisdiction of a protective service worker. Although contact with the helping professional is desirable, the burden of responsibility has now shifted to the protective service worker.

## Child Abuse Prevention in the Formal Group Setting

Less than 2 percent of all substantiated cases of child abuse occur in formal group settings (Lung and Daro, 1996). Although this is a relatively small portion of the total cases, we must do all we can to reduce the possibility that abuse will happen when children are in our care. Hiring procedures for new staff and policies focused on day-to-day operations and family communication can all be designed with child abuse prevention in mind. A summary of strategies that make abuse less likely to occur on the job is presented in Table 15–3.

This chapter has focused on factors that influence judgments helping professionals make. We have concentrated on four distinct categories: ethical judgments, judgments in day-to-day encounters, judgments about children's extreme behavior, and judgments regarding child abuse and neglect. Specific skills associated with each of these now follow. The family communication strategies for this chapter are integrated within the category of judgment to which they pertain. Pitfalls that should be avoided are also described following the skills section.

---

▼ **Table 15–3    Preventative Strategies That Reduce the Probability of Child Abuse in Formal Group Settings**

**Hiring Practices**

Applicants are carefully screened. This includes all staff members, substitutes, and volunteers—people who work with the children directly and those who provide support services to the program such as cooks and custodians.

Screening strategies include signed written applications, personal interviews, on-site observations with children, verification of personal and professional references and education qualifications, criminal record checks, and signed declarations related to previous convictions of any crime against children or other violent crime. A person's failure to fully disclose previous convictions is cause for automatic dismissal.

New employees are oriented to the job and are informed of the child-abuse prevention procedures to follow.

Mandatory probation periods for new employees are instituted, during which time they are paired with seasoned employees who provide modeling and consultation. New employees are observed frequently to assess their interactions with children.

*continued*

▼ Table 15–3—continued     Preventative Strategies That Reduce the Probability of Child Abuse in Formal Group Settings

**Day-to-Day Operations**

The program's discipline policies are clearly defined.

Programs create conditions that alleviate staff fatigue and burn-out such as limiting the number of children for which each adult is responsible, keeping group sizes within established bounds, providing adequate breaks, and offering refresher training related to discipline, classroom management, parent relations, staff conflict, and child-abuse prevention.

Programs are structured to avoid the possibility of private, hidden opportunities for child abuse to occur. All early childhood spaces are regarded as public. Daily routines and the physical environment (both indoors and outdoors) are reviewed to eliminate the possibility that staff members have solitary access to children with no possibility of being observed by others. Program policies encourage parental drop-in visits and provide ongoing supervision by qualified personnel throughout the day.

**Family Communication**

Family members are welcome to the program at all times.

Staff members communicate with families regularly, establish warm caring relationships with parents and other family members, and explain the discipline strategies they use.

Children are only be released to parents, legal guardians, and the people parents have designated in writing.

Programs provide families with information about child abuse, child-abuse prevention measures taken by the program, and methods for reporting suspected child abuse.

Sources: Data from NAEYC Position Statement on the Prevention of Child Abuse in Early Childhood Programs and Responsibilities of Early Childhood Programs to Prevent Child Abuse, 1996; Click, P. M. *Administration of Schools for Young Children*. Albany, N.Y.: Delmar Publishers, 1996; and National Committee for the Prevention of Child Abuse. *Intervening with New Parents: An Effective Way to Prevent Child Abuse*. Chicago: NCPCA, 1996.

## SKILLS FOR MAKING JUDGMENTS

### How to Make Ethical Judgments

**1. Become familiar with the NAEYC Code of Ethical Conduct.** Review the Code. Know what it contains. Refer to it often when faced with perplexing situations that challenge your personal and professional values.

**2. Identify situations that have ethical implications.** This may encompass both hypothetical and real circumstances. Refer to the journal *Young Children* for sample cases illustrating ethical dilemmas. Think about ways to approach these. Refer to the sample answers in each issue, comparing your response to those of others in the field. In addition, keep a journal of your experiences with children and families. Catalog examples from real life to discuss with colleagues in an appropriate setting.

**3. Practice using the NAEYC Code of Ethical Conduct in response to ethical dilemmas.**

Some circumstances are easily categorized as ethical or unethical because they clearly support or run counter to the Code. Others are not so obvious. This may be due to their complexity or the subtle nature of the incident. In either case, practice will improve your skills and confidence using the Code. Both students in training and practitioners in the field report that such practice is most beneficial when carried out regularly and in small groups of colleagues.

▼ First, decide what makes a troubling situation an ethical dilemma. Remember, not all worrisome situations are ethical in nature. Ethics implies right and wrong: support or lack of support for the professional standards are outlined in the Code. Identify signals that alert you to potential ethical issues. Listen carefully to the signals other people say they use. Compare these to your own and add or subtract ones that would be helpful for future use.

## SKILLS FOR MAKING JUDGMENTS—continued

▼ Next, sort out matters that must be addressed by different people. The response to an ethical dilemma may require varying actions by more than one person. Explore what these responses might be.

▼ Finally, refer to the Code for help in thinking about priorities and responsibilities in determining a plan to address the situation. The point is not to achieve unanimous agreement on a single course of action, but to generate one or more strategies that support ethical approaches to the problem. Identify those strategies that seem most congruent with your own thinking. Consider what you would say and do to carry out your plan. Keep a record of typical responses to hypothetical circumstances. In real-life situations in which you are involved, carry out your plan. Then make note of the outcomes for future reference.

**4. Refer to the Code when talking about why you carry out certain practices in your work and why you refrain from using others.** Such conversations may be with parents, colleagues, or lay persons. Explaining to others that we have a code of ethics is a valuable sign of professionalism. It also provides justification for judgments and decision making that goes beyond intuition. For instance, the reason early childhood professionals do not deprive children of food or use of the toilet as a means of punishment is that such behavior is unethical according to principles set forth in the Code. As a profession we have agreed that ethical behavior requires us to inform parents of accidents involving their child and to maintain family confidentiality. These expectations are outlined in the Code. Referencing the Code periodically is a good way to keep its standards in the forefront of your thinking.

 **How to Make Day-to-Day Judgments**

**1. Become aware of values that are important to you.** Think about decisions you have made in your own life in terms of the values they represent. Try to determine what basic beliefs govern your interactions with children and their fami-

lies. Figure out if there are discernible patterns to the kinds of choices you make. Discuss your ideas with friends and colleagues. Compare your reactions with theirs, and try to articulate why you have chosen a particular path. Take advantage of formalized opportunities to engage in values clarification.

**2. Comprehensively assess situations in which a judgment must be made.** Make an initial survey that includes the following factors: recognition of the child's perspective, awareness of your own affective state, consideration of the child's age and past experiences, and an analysis of the situational context.

**SITUATION:** Brian approaches the lunch table with dirty hands. When you remind him to wash, he says, "But I already washed my hands three times."

*Child's emotions:* Frustration, annoyance, discouragement, surprise

*Your reactions:* Disbelief, uncertainty about what to do next, concern about the child's health, apprehension about the example being set for others, sympathy for the child's efforts

*Other factors to consider:*
a. Brian has had several unhappy interactions today.
b. Brian usually forgets to wash his hands altogether.
c. Children in the group have been questioning some of the rules.
d. Your last interaction with Brian involved a confrontation.
e. The cook is signaling that lunch is on the table.

Because this type of analysis covers so much territory, you may think it can only be incorporated in judgments that allow time for long-term deliberation. Actually, this process also can be applied to on-the-spot decision making as well. At first, you may feel so pressured in a situation that you think of some, but not all, of the critical variables. However, as you gain experience, you will become more adept at quickly considering multiple factors when making a judgment.

*continued*

## SKILLS FOR MAKING JUDGMENTS—continued

If you are in a situation in which you are an observer and in which safety is not in question, take a few moments to sort out the issues prior to acting. Should you be in a circumstance in which an immediate response is expected, use an affective reflection and the middle portion of the personal message (that is, your emotions and the reasons for them) to identify aloud the child's perspective and your own. If, at that point, you need a few more moments to think, tell the children so: "You're anxious to go in swimming. I'm in a real quandary; I know it's hot, but I'm not sure how to keep an eye on all of you. Let me think about it for a minute, and then I'll decide what to do.

**3. Consider alternative strategies in terms of their potential outcomes.** Imagine various responses to a particular situation. Predict the possible impact of each on the child, on yourself, and on others. Think about how each outcome would either support or impede your current goals for all parties. The following illustrates this process in relation to the preceding example about Brian.

*Possible actions to take:*

1. Acknowledge Brian's effort and let him proceed to lunch.

2. Acknowledge Brian's efforts, explain your own concerns, and tell him to rewash his hands.

3. Acknowledge Brian's efforts, acknowledge the difficulty of the task, and offer to help.

*Possible outcomes:*

1.a Brian will feel successful and therefore will be more likely to remember the rule in the future.
1.b Other children may notice that Brian didn't have to wash as thoroughly as they did and will not have faith in your rules.
1.c Brian will feel successful, but you may still feel uncomfortable about the dirt on his hands.
1.d You and Brian will get to lunch on time.
1.e You will avoid another confrontation with Brian.

2.a Brian may feel discouraged that his efforts were not good enough.
2.b Brian's pride in having washed his hands may be replaced with resentment.
2.c You will be involved in another confrontation with Brian.
2.d Children will perceive that your standards are the same for everyone.
2.e You and Brian will be late for lunch.
2.f Brian's hands may become cleaner.
2.g Brian may interpret that you think he's lying.

3.a All of the outcomes identified for option (2),
3.b Brian's feelings of incompetence may be reduced by your support.
3.c Brian will have the opportunity to learn more about how to wash his hands properly.

▼▼▼▼▼

**SKILLS FOR MAKING JUDGMENTS—continued**

**4. Select and implement a strategy or combination of strategies that supports your overall goals for children and that is based on your priorities for the situation.** Keep in mind the goals you are working toward for each child and for the group as a whole. In addition, use the priority principles outlined in this chapter to help you sort out what is most important in a given instance. Use the goals and priorities you identify as the basis for action.

In regard to Brian's case, were the adult to determine that safety was not a major issue, other considerations would have to be made. For instance, the professional's long-range goal for Brian might be to help him to feel more confident. A goal for the entire group might be individualism. Thus, the adult may interpret that this is a situation in which priority principles C and E are relevant. Based on all these factors, he or she would be led to judge that acknowledging Brian's efforts and letting him proceed to lunch is the most appropriate action.

On the other hand, were the adult to interpret the situation as one involving safety, then priority principle A would prevail, signaling the necessity of implementing options (b) or (c) (having the child rewash, either alone or with help). Selection of the former or the latter would depend on whether the adult judged the situation to be one of noncompliance or lack of knowledge.

**5. Include nonintervention as a strategy option.** Taking no action in a situation can be the result of a considered judgment on your part. For example, on the playground, Myron drops a hard line drive. "Oh damn," he says. Miss Delmar, who overhears this, considers many options: lecturing Myron, having him apologize for using a curse word, sending him off the field, or ignoring the incident. She surveys the situation. Myron looks surprised and chagrined that he dropped the ball. He is seemingly unaware of the epithet. The adult does not really feel offended because his words were more an exclamation of surprise than true profanity. Also, it is unlikely that anyone else heard him. Considering the excitement of the situation, Myron's embarrassment over his fielding error,

and the context of the game, she judges that the best goal for Myron is to have another chance catching. Every option other than ignoring the episode probably would impede achievement of this goal, so she makes a second judgment not to intervene.

**6. Adopt standards that take into account children's age and experience.** Apply your understanding of child development and learning to your expectations for children's performance. Do not expect children to perform perfectly the first few times. Allow them to make mistakes. Observe youngsters carefully to determine what they can and cannot do, then set your standards accordingly. As they become more adept, increase your expectations gradually. It is with this in mind that the adult may have judged Brian's "almost-clean" hands as "clean enough" for the time being. However, several days hence, the standard could be raised because Brian would have had additional opportunities to increase his skill.

**7. Reassess situations in light of new information.** Remember that you can make different judgments regarding your goals, strategies, and standards as you acquire new knowledge. This may mean selecting an option you had previously discarded or developing an entirely new one. For instance, the judgment to allow Brian to proceed to lunch might be changed if you overheard him bragging to a friend that on his way out of the bathroom, he saw a dime at the bottom of the toilet, which he reached in to get.

**8. Evaluate the judgments you make.** Take time to assess the effectiveness of your thinking and of corresponding actions. Consider whether the potential outcome became reality. If so, ask yourself whether it contributed to progress toward a desired goal. If the anticipated effect did not occur, reflect on what contributed to the incongruous result and what might be done instead. Discuss your deliberations with a colleague or supervisor.

**9. Learn from judgment errors.** Sooner or later, you will make a judgment that you will come to

*continued*

## SKILLS FOR MAKING JUDGMENTS—continued

regret. When this happens, mentally review the circumstances under which you made it. Consider what prompted your response and what other options were available to you at the time. Try to determine what went awry, and figure out what you might do if you had the decision to make again. Sometimes, you will conclude that you made a bad judgment and that another option would have been better. On other occasions, you will deduce that the judgment was right at the time, even though the outcome was negative or stressful. Mentally catalogue relevant information for future use. Then, move on. It is counterproductive to unceasingly agonize over a past judgment.

**10. Support colleagues who have made poor judgments.** When fellow staff members have made a judgment and it has turned out poorly, offer comfort and encouragement. Be available as a sounding board and listen to their evaluation of what went into their decision. Help them sort out what went wrong and brainstorm remedial strategies or alternate approaches for the future.

**11. Identify values you and colleagues or parents hold in common when differences in goals, strategies, and/or standards exist.** Talk over conflicts in approach that arise. Explore thoroughly the other person's perceptions by asking him or her to describe his or her understanding of the situation and overall purpose within it. Listen carefully and quietly, avoiding jumping to conclusions, interrupting, or giving your opinion prematurely. Use the reflective listening skills you have learned to convey interest and acceptance. Look beyond the details of what people are saying to the essence of their message. Find common aims at this level. Then, proceed to negotiate the goals, strategies, and standards that might be acceptable to both of you.

In most cases, this type of clarification should contribute to mutual understanding and a more unified approach. If you recognize that you have a true conflict in values, acknowledge this state of affairs. Then, determine what you will have to do to make the situation livable.

 **How to Deal with Children's Extreme Behavior**

**1. Get to know the children in your group prior to making a judgment that any one of them is exhibiting extreme behavior.** Although the mere presence of some behaviors is enough to signal a problem, most can be identified as extreme only because they represent a major deviation from the child's customary pattern. For this reason, it is important that you give yourself enough time to determine what is typical for each child. Thus, the loud outbursts from a child that initially were startling may seem less unusual over time or may represent a brief episode rather than a prevailing mode of interaction for the child. Similarly, the extremely quiet behavior of one youngster might be normal and functional for him or her; the same demeanor in a usually exuberant child could be seen as a legitimate cause for concern.

**2. Make a concerted effort to change a behavior by using appropriate guidance techniques before judging it extreme.** Use the skills you have learned in previous chapters as your initial means of addressing problematic behavior. Be consistent in your approach, and allow enough time (usually several weeks) for your strategies to have a fair chance of success. Ask a colleague to review your plan and/or to observe its implementation in order to judge whether it is appropriate and whether you are carrying it out effectively. If you discover that a child's continued exhibition of a problem behavior is the result of a faulty plan or ineffective implementation, make the corresponding revisions.

**3. Confirm your judgment that a child's behavior is extreme.** Make an objective record of the child's behavior over time. Then, refer to books that describe age norms. If the behavior is not categorized as appropriate for the child's age, check to see if it is typical of other ages, particularly younger ones. If the latter turns out to be the case, remember that children under stress often regress. Although you should continue to monitor such behavior, do not consider it extreme unless it persists over a long period of

## SKILLS FOR MAKING JUDGMENTS—continued

time. However, should the child's activity not be described for any age group, it is possible that it falls outside appropriate limits, irrespective of age. To determine if this is the case, carefully observe other children of comparable age while they are both active and quiet. If no other children manifest the behavior in question, talk to an experienced and trusted colleague who has worked with many children effectively. Also, consult your supervisor or other co-workers whose job responsibilities encompass this type of consultation. Check to see if they agree that the behavior is outside of that considered acceptable for the child's age and circumstances. If others agree that the behavior seems extreme, seek out a reputable professional for consultation.

**4. Communicate to the family your concern that their child's behavior is extreme.** When making the initial contact, whether in person, by telephone, or by written message, express your concern matter-of-factly and request a meeting with the parent(s). On one hand, avoid going into elaborate detail; on the other hand, avoid sounding secretive and mysterious. Both tactics can only serve to alarm the parents or make them feel defensive. You might say something like: "I've been observing Charles for the last several days and have become concerned about his sudden lack of interest in interacting with the other children. Normally, he's quite outgoing, and his withdrawal has persisted for some time. I'd like to set up a time to discuss this with you in more detail."

When the meeting takes place, be prepared to provide concrete examples of the behavior in question. Find out if the same behavior occurs at home and whether or not the parent considers it atypical. If, as the conference proceeds, you reach the conclusion that indeed, the behavior is extreme, share this observation with the parent(s) and provide a rationale for your judgment. Be prepared to suggest specific courses of action the parent(s) could take.

**5. Seek out or recommend the type of professional who could deal most appropriately with a particular problem.** Determine with the fam-

ily who will contact the consulting professional. If the behavior may be physically based, as in problems with eating, elimination, sleeping, too much or too little energy, or obvious depression, first contact a physician. If no physical difficulties are found, consult next with a behavioral specialist.

If an extreme behavior is obviously unconnected to physical sources, begin with a behavioral expert, such as someone trained in speech therapy or learning disabilities. These people are more likely to be familiar with behavioral problems than would many physicians. Further, reputable, competent behavioral specialists would be aware of conditions to which physical difficulties could contribute and would suggest medical consultation in such instances.

Check on potential community resources such as child-guidance clinics, college psychological clinics, school guidance counselors, community mental health agencies, social-service agencies in your area, intermediate school districts (umbrella agencies that offer special services across school districts), and programs specializing in youngsters whose problems are similar to the one you have tentatively identified for a particular child. Even when an individual program may not exactly suit your needs, personnel there may be able to direct you to a more appropriate source.

**6. Provide emotional support to families who are seeking outside help for their child's extreme behavior.** The referral process often takes a long time, resulting in anxiety or frustration for families. Offer words of encouragement or sympathy, and be willing to listen to familial complaints and lamentations. Use reflective listening skills to communicate your understanding. Take additional action, if possible, to speed up the process.

**7. Follow up on your recommendation that a child or family receive outside services.** If you have agreed to contact a medical or behavioral expert, do so promptly. Make the contact directly or through the channels dictated by your agency or program. Periodically check on the progress of your referral and make sure that

*continued*

contact actually is made. Should the family assume primary responsibility for seeking help, communicate with them regularly to find out what has happened.

**8. Provide accurate, relevant information to the consulting professional.** Share your observations of the child's behavior, either verbally or in writing. Make available records you have kept regarding his or her behavior pattern, or summarize them in a report. Invite the outside expert to observe the child within the formal group setting. Offer to meet with him or her and the family.

**9. Coordinate the way you deal with the child's extreme behavior in the formal group setting with the way it is being handled by the family and by the consultant to whom the child has been referred.** Find out what action has been recommended. Discuss with the consultant and the family the feasibility of adapting your program to the consultant's recommendations as well as ways in which your actions can complement theirs. For instance, if it has been decided that certain behaviors will be rewarded and others ignored at home and in the therapy session, follow the same guidelines, if possible. Provide feedback to all adults involved in the plan regarding the child's progress in your setting. Make relevant suggestions for changes and revisions in the plan. Also, ask for feedback regarding your own performance. Maintain periodic contact with both the consultant and the family throughout this time.

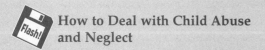 **How to Deal with Child Abuse and Neglect**

**1. Find out the appropriate procedures for reporting child abuse and neglect.** Read the laws of your state regarding child abuse and neglect, including what constitutes abuse, the persons or agencies to whom such cases should be referred, who is legally obligated to report abuse, and what safeguards exist for those reporting. Although all fifty states mandate reporting suspected cases and protect helping professionals

from legal prosecution when making reports in good faith, the specifics of who is bound to report, who is notified, and how it is done vary. For example, the Michigan Child Protection Law requires all school administrators, teachers, counselors, social workers, nurses, physicians, dentists, audiologists, law-enforcement officers, and duly regulated child-care providers to make an oral report of *suspected* child abuse or neglect to the local department of social services.

In addition to obtaining this legal knowledge, find out the reporting protocol of the formal group setting in which you are employed. If you are required to make a report through a designated person, determine how you will be appraised that your report has been filed. Also, ask what role you are expected to play in subsequent action. Should the policy require that you report your suspicions directly to the authorities, find out who they are. (Often, these are described as "children's protective services.") If you are unable to locate the authorities in your community, contact one of the nationwide emergency numbers provided in Appendix B.

**2. Watch for signs of child abuse and neglect.** Use the physical, behavioral, verbal, and family indicators outlined in Table 15–2. Pay attention to children. Look at them. Listen to what they say. Be alert for changes in a child's physical condition or demeanor. Believe children when they persistently complain that they are hungry, that they "hurt down there," or that cousin Billy beat them with a strap (Hendrick, 1996). Most children do not make up stories about abuse or molestation.

**3. Document your suspicions.** Keep written notes about the sign that caused you to suspect child abuse or neglect and the date on which it occurred. If more than one sign is present, record each of them.

**4. Promptly report suspected cases of child abuse or neglect.** Should a child or family display a combination of signs that you have been trained to recognize as indicative of child abuse, report it. Do not delay in the hope that conditions will change or that you were wrong. Do not vacillate about what to do. Once the suspicion is there, the subsequent action is clear.

**5. Reassure children who have revealed that they are victims of abuse or neglect.** Say something like: "It was hard for you to tell me about this" or "You're upset your momma knocked your tooth out. I'm really glad you told me." Let them know that you believe what they have said and that no harm will come to them from you for reporting the incident. Reflect their feelings of confusion, worry, anger, or guilt. Allow them to talk out their feelings and to describe individual incidents with as much or as little detail as they want. Remain receptive and supportive of abused children no matter how uncomfortable or distressed you may feel. On the other hand, avoid pumping children for details that are beyond their capacity or willingness to reveal at a given time. Express your sympathy about what has happened, but at the same time, do not berate the child's family. Even youngsters who have been ill treated often feel a loyalty to family members. They may withdraw if they perceive that they must defend their family to you.

Many children feel guilty regarding their role in the abusive situation. They may conclude that because they are "no good" or "ugly" or "so bad," the adult had no choice but to abuse them. Attempt to rectify these misperceptions by stating that what happened was not the child's fault. Instead, it was the adult's behavior that was inappropriate. Explain that sometimes, adults become angry, confused, or lonely, but that beating children, tricking them, or subjecting them to unwanted fondling is wrong.

**6. Talk to children about physical touching.** Begin with infants, and continue throughout the childhood years, to use feeling words to describe physical interactions. Provide children with information about how touching affects them and others. Say things like: "A hug feels good," "Pinching hurts," "You were happy when Jeremy scratched your back," or "You didn't like it when Marion hit you." Such statements form the foundation for a "touch vocabu-

lary" that can be expanded as children develop. Familiarizing children with these specialized words is the first step in teaching personal safety.

**7. Teach children personal safety.** It is widely believed that children benefit when they are taught ways to avoid exploitive touching. Refer to the personal safety terms, facts, and principles in Appendix C for ideas on relevant and accurate facts to present to children. Use these facts and principles as the basis for discussions with children and to give you ideas about appropriate material for activities and skits. Review Chapters 8 and 13 for guidelines on how to construct these. Adapt your presentation to match children's understanding and experience. For example:

a. Initiate a discussion in which children talk about touches that make them feel good and touches that make them feel bad. Introduce the idea of confusing touches: those that start out feeling good but that eventually become uncomfortable (tickling, bear hugs, petting). Point out that no one has the right to use bad touch or confusing touch with another person. Tell children that if someone tries to touch them in ways they do not like, they can say "No," get away, and then tell someone they trust.

b. Set up a skit in which one character tries to trick another character into doing something. With very young children or older youngsters who have had little prior training, begin with obvious tricks unrelated to sexual abuse. As the children begin to understand the notion of a trick, introduce skits that address inappropriate touching (e.g., bribery, keeping a "secret," or flattery). Emphasize the point that it is not okay for people to force children to touch them or to trick children into touching them. Teach children that if a person tries to trick them into touching him or her or into doing things the child does not understand, the child can say, "No," get away, and tell someone he or she trusts.

c. Play the "What if . . . ?" game as a way to check children's understanding of how to respond in dangerous situations. Make up pre-

*continued*

## SKILLS FOR MAKING JUDGMENTS—continued

tend episodes, such as "What if the man down the street asks you to come in and see the new puppies?", "What if your babysitter asks you to keep a secret, especially from your mom and dad?", or "What if you have a fight with your friends in the park and a nice lady you don't know offers you a ride home?" Reflect children's answers and provide accurate information as appropriate. Ask open-ended questions to further extend the discussions.

**8. Treat families with sensitivity even when child abuse is suspected or has occurred.** If you have been the source of a child-abuse report, contact the family after it has been made. Inform them that you suspect that their child has been subjected to physical or sexual abuse. Explain that you are legally bound to report such suspicions and that you wanted them to know you had done so. Indicate that you would like to be supportive of the family in any way they might find acceptable. Expect a hostile or incredulous reaction, particularly if the parents themselves have been involved in the abuse. Avoid berating the family or spending a great deal of time trying to justify your actions to them. The purpose of this contact is not to humiliate them or to try to get them to repent, but to indicate that you respect them enough that you would not do something behind their backs.

Should parents choose to respond to you, either in defense of their actions, to explain extenuating circumstances, or to accuse you of misrepresenting them, listen nonjudgmentally. Use the reflective listening skills you have learned to accomplish this.

Keep confidential all matters related to the case. Do not gossip or disclose tantalizing tidbits to other parents or to staff members who are not directly involved. Refuse to answer questions from curious people who have no legitimate right to the information.

If you are in a situation that requires continued contact with the family, treat them casually and civilly. Acknowledge their presence, speak to them, and be genuine in your interactions. This means not being effusive or more friendly than you have been in the past. Talk about day-to-day affairs rather than "the case."

**9. Be aware of help available in your community for parents who indicate they are on the brink of abuse.** Promising studies show that many abusing parents can be helped so that they no longer resort to physical violence (Shaffer, 1995). This is an indication of how important it is to refer parents to people and programs designed to assist them. Find out as much as you can about such support programs in your area. Identify short-term alternatives such as hot lines, sources of respite care, parent groups, educational opportunities, and workshops. In addition, keep a file of long-term options including local individual and family therapists, mental-health agencies, and religious and social-service programs, as well as such nationally recognized groups as Parents Anonymous and the National Committee to Prevent Child Abuse (see Appendix B).

## ▼ PITFALLS TO AVOID

There are many guidelines to remember in deciding how to make a judgment. The skills just covered describe the behaviors you should exhibit. The pitfalls that follow describe behaviors you should avoid.

**Failing to make a conscious judgment because of time pressures.** Sometimes, helping professionals are so rushed that they think they cannot take the time to figure out what to do. Instead, they react instinctively. Occasionally, their intuitive responses are correct and fit well into a comprehensive approach to the child and the group. More often, they satisfy short-term ends but do not comprehensively address long-term goals. Although it is not always feasible to ponder over what to do, it is possible to incorporate the judgment process somewhere in the situation. Even if this can be done only in retrospect, assessing your judgment is a valuable professional skill. Moreover, unless safety is the issue, it is better to postpone your reaction in order to think it out than to respond haphazardly. Frequently, time spent in an initial assessment that leads to a successful approach is less than that accumulated over time in failed efforts.

**Staying with a poor judgment too long.**  At times, people become "wedded" to a selected option because they have invested so much time and energy in making that judgment. They fail to recognize signs that a goal or standard does not fit, that a strategy useful under other circumstances is not effective in this instance, or that a plan simply is not working. If they continue to ignore these cues, the situation will deteriorate. The best way to avoid this pitfall is to keep alert to changes in the situational context and to remain receptive to new information. Continual re-evaluation of judgments made also is essential, as is a willingness to let go of unproductive approaches.

**Failing to recognize your limitations.**  Helping professionals err when they imagine themselves as the only person capable of helping a child even when the child's problems call for skills beyond their own. This mind-set can be the result of any of the following:

1. They may think they are the only ones who care enough to handle the child appropriately or who understand the child well enough to know what to do.
2. They may jealously guard their role in the child's life and perceive other helping professionals as interlopers.
3. They may not recognize the seriousness of the child's situation.
4. They may interpret consultation with an outside expert as an indication of their own inadequacy.
5. They may think they possess skills that, in fact, they do not.

In any case, this type of thinking is not conducive to creating the most favorable climate for the child's development. Helping professionals who find themselves resisting making a referral, even when all signs indicate that doing so is in the best interest of the child, must examine their attitudes. If they find that their lack of enthusiasm relates to any of the reasons just described, reconsideration is in order.

**Neglecting to clarify your own role in relation to the consulting professional.**  Working with an outside consultant requires a coordination of efforts. Children benefit most when they are handled consistently throughout their mesosystem. This means that professionals in the formal group setting must have a clear understanding of what expectations, if any, the consultant has for their performance. It is not enough to have a vague picture of what is required. Instead, you must develop a precise list of expectations. It is therefore important to clarify mutual goals and the strategies and standards that will support them.

**Not following the recommendation of a consultant long enough to allow it to work.**  One of the most common pitfalls in working with an outside consultant is to prematurely abandon a mutually agreed-on plan. Having finally taken the step of calling in an outsider, the helping professional may expect instant results. When these are not forthcoming, he or she gives up in disappointment. To avoid succumbing to this form of disillusionment, it is best to formulate, in conjunction with the consultant, a time line along which progress will be measured. Knowing that a particular approach might have to be employed for several weeks or even months before a change can be expected increases your patience and makes setbacks easier to bear.

**Ignoring signs of abuse.**  Sometimes, in an effort to avoid dealing with a difficult situation or because they wish it were not so, helping professionals overlook obvious cues that abuse has occurred. If a child exhibits bruises and reports that his mother beat him, the professional may think, "Oh, all children get paddled sometimes." When a youngster's vagina is raw and bleeding, the adult attributes it to masturbation. Should a child continually be dirty and smell bad, the adult passes it off as typical of that cultural group or social class. Children are not served well when adults reach these conclusions, which are based not on the facts but on their own psychological and emotional defenses. Every sign that could indicate abuse must be taken seriously. Children should not be made to suffer because adults are afraid to face reality.

**Threatening families you suspect of child abuse.**  Occasionally, rather than reporting a case of probable child abuse, helping professionals try to intervene directly with the family. They confront family members, saying things like: "If you do this again, I'll have to report you" or "Promise me you'll stop, and I won't report you." Their motives may be self-serving (wishing to avoid legal entanglements) or well-meaning (hoping to save the family embarrassment). In either case, these tactics are ill advised and should not be used. Rather, helping professionals should follow the procedures outlined in the child abuse section of this chapter.

**Purposely frightening children as a way to teach personal safety.** Adults who are trying to teach children to be careful about strangers and exploitive touching may deliberately overgeneralize their warnings so that youngsters become fearful of everyone and all forms of physical contact. Describing in lurid detail horrible incidents of abuse, treating all situations as unsafe, and failing to distinguish "good touch" from "bad touch" contributes to this negative perception. It is not healthy for young people to feel always in jeopardy. Instead, they must be exposed to a balanced view in which caution is promoted, but complete terror and distrust is avoided.

**Assuming personal safety training will automatically protect children from sexual abuse.** Even with personal safety training, many children will have trouble saying, "No" to adults, especially people with whom they have a close relationship. Young children should not be expected to handle the full burden of protecting themselves. Treat personal safety training as one potential tool children have at their disposal, not as a one-time inoculation against all potential abuse. Throughout childhood, children continue to need the support of caring adults. Remain alert to signs of sexual abuse regardless of whether or not children have had any training in this regard.

## ▼ SUMMARY

Helping professionals continually make judgments for and about the children with whom they work. These encompass long- or short-range judgments, judgments adults have time to evaluate carefully and those that must be made immediately, and judgments that have profound or relatively minor effects. All judgments must be made consciously.

In making any judgment, helping professionals go through several steps. First, they assess the circumstance; next, they think about possible actions in response; eventually, they must select one or a combination of strategies, which they then put into action. Finally, helping professionals evaluate the results of their decisions and use this information to guide future judgments. Although no outcome can be guaranteed, following this process makes a measured judgment more likely. Furthermore, the prob-

ability is greater that the adult's goals, strategies, and standards for children will be congruent.

Goals represent milestones on the path toward achieving social competence. Strategies are the specific practices adults employ to pursue their goals for children. Standards are used to determine the degree to which goals have been achieved. Developing, implementing, and evaluating goals, strategies, and standards calls for a multitude of judgments.

Several variables affect the judgments people make. Among these are their values. Values are not directly observable but are inferred from an individual's behavior. People acquire values through the socialization process. They develop a value hierarchy in which values are prioritized. This can be a complex process, and it explains why individuals experience value conflicts. Understanding your own values leads to more conscious behavior and helps individuals to respect the values of others as well as to separate values from goals, strategies, and standards.

A second variable that affects judgments helping professionals make is their knowledge of child development and learning. A third is the context of the situation in question. Deciding which professional behaviors are right and which ones are wrong is a function of ethical judgment. Helping professionals refer to their ethical codes of conduct in making such determinations. Other judgments involve establishing priorities from among a range of possibilities; it is important to adopt and follow principles for how to set these priorities. Such principles range from putting safety first to making choices based on personal preferences.

The preceding discussion has dealt with everyday kinds of judgments. Two arenas require specialized judgments: children's extreme behavior and child abuse or neglect. The judgment to be made in each case is whether or not the condition exists. Once this is determined, there are specific actions helping professionals should follow. The factors that go into a judgment of whether children's behavior is extreme are: the presence of self-destructive acts or a sudden shift in a child's functioning; inappropriate behavior for the child's age; persistently intense behavior; indiscriminate evidence of particular behaviors; impairment of a child's present or future functioning; and resistance of the behavior to change. Extreme behavior often can be attributed to physiological causes, children's fears, and childhood depression.

Judgments about suspected child abuse or neglect are critical for children's health and well-being. Physical abuse is a nonaccidental injury that results from acts of omission or commission by a parent, guardian, or caregiver. Sexual abuse exists when youngsters are forced or persuaded to engage in sexual activity by an older child or adult. There are differences between the victims of physical and sexual abuse as well as between the perpetrators of these two forms. Some of the effects of abuse on its victims are injury, truancy, dramatic behavior changes, psychological distress, guilt, and anger. The need for early intervention is critical, so helping professionals must become familiar with the signs of abuse. For each type, there are physical, behavioral, verbal, and family indicators. All states have specific reporting guidelines that helping professionals must learn.

There are specific skills helping professionals can learn to enable them to make ethical judgments, day-to-day judgments, judgments involving children's extreme behavior, and judgments about child abuse and neglect. In addition, there are behaviors that helping professionals should avoid when making these types of judgments.

## ▼ DISCUSSION QUESTIONS

1. Discuss the relationship between helping professionals' values and their goals, strategies, and standards for children. Give some examples from your own life.
2. In a small group, discuss a value that you hold. As best you can, trace its origin and how it has affected a judgment you have made.
3. Consider the following cases. Use the NAEYC Code of Ethical Conduct (Appendix A) to help you make a judgment about the ethics or lack of ethics displayed. First, identify parts of the Code that pertain to each case. Next, determine whether the person(s) acted in an ethical or unethical way. Finally, discuss possible responses.

   Akim Shakcez was recently hired as assistant teacher in the three-year-old room at the McMillan Child-Care Center. His room is next to the toddler room. He notices that although the legal ratio is one adult for every four toddlers, the twelve children are frequently left with one adult in attendance. When he mentions this concern to the director, she says, "You pay attention to what goes on in your room. I'll worry about the rest." Akim observes no change in the supervision pattern for toddlers over the next several weeks.

   The parent council for a cooperative nursery school decides not to interview James Beck for the job of head teacher in the toddler group because they believe women are the best caregivers for children that age.

   The State of Michigan is reviewing Public Act 116—the State Regulations for Child Care. Mr. Kowalski, a second-grade teacher, volunteers to be on the review panel.

4. Discuss the priority principles outlined in this chapter. Make comments either in support of or in opposition to:
   a. The order in which they are presented.
   b. A specific principle or principles.
   c. How they should or should not be applied.
5. Define what is meant by extreme behavior. Describe four factors that must be taken into account when making a judgment about whether or not a behavior is extreme. Discuss three pitfalls to avoid in making this kind of judgment.
6. Discuss how a child's fear may result in extreme behavior. Describe the judgments a helping professional must make in such a case.
7. Define what is meant by physical abuse and neglect. Discuss who are the most likely victims and the most likely perpetrators. Discuss what you would do if you suspected physical abuse.
8. Define what is meant by sexual abuse. Discuss who are the most likely victims and the most likely perpetrators. Discuss what to do if you suspect sexual abuse.
9. You help a three-year-old with toileting and notice what appear to be welt marks on her buttocks and legs. Find the place in the NAEYC Code of Ethical Conduct (Appendix A) that offers professional guidelines in such a situation. What should you do, based on the Code?
10. Discuss the similarities and differences in judgments you would make on a day-to-day basis and those you would make when dealing with extreme behavior or child abuse.

## ▼ FIELD ASSIGNMENTS

1. Interview an early childhood professional about ethical decisions he or she has made. Without betraying the rule of confidentiality, ask the person to describe a situation requiring an ethical judgment in which he or she was involved. Ask: What made it an ethical dilemma? How was the situation handled? Looking back on the outcome, would he or she do anything differently if the same circumstance arose again?

2. Describe at least two situations that occurred during your field placement in which you made a conscious judgment using the priority principles identified earlier in this chapter. Describe each situation and what you did. Identify the priority principle(s) you used. Discuss your response with classmates. Would you handle the situation the same way again? Why or why not?

3. Name the person in your field placement to whom you would report a suspected case of child abuse. Outline the child-abuse reporting procedures required in your agency or state. Name the governmental agency responsible for dealing with child abuse in your community. Identify at least three agencies, services, or programs available to parents who are on the brink of child abuse or who have committed child abuse.

4. Look up the law of your state regarding the reporting of child abuse and neglect.

# ▼Appendix A

# The National Association for the Education of Young Children Code of Ethical Conduct

## PREAMBLE

NAEYC recognizes that many daily decisions required of those who work with young children are of a moral and ethical nature. The NAEYC Code of Ethical Conduct offers guidelines for responsible behavior and sets forth a common basis for resolving the principal ethical dilemmas encountered in early childhood education. The primary focus is on daily practice with children and their families in programs for children from birth to eight years of age: infant/toddler programs, preschools, child-care centers, family daycare homes, kindergartens, and primary classrooms. Many of the provisions also apply to specialists who do not work directly with children, including program administrators, parent educators, college professors, and child-care licensing specialists.

Standards of ethical behavior in early childhood education are based on commitment to core childhood education deeply rooted in the history of our field. We have committed ourselves to:

▼ Appreciating childhood as a unique and valuable stage of the human life cycle

▼ Basing our work with children on knowledge of child development

▼ Appreciating and supporting the close ties between the child and family

▼ Recognizing that children are best understood in the context of family, culture, and society

▼ Respecting the dignity, worth, and uniqueness of each individual (child, family member, and colleague)

▼ Helping children and adults achieve their full potential in the context of relationships that are based on trust, respect, and positive regard

The Code sets forth a conception of our professional responsibilities in four sections, each addressing an arena of professional relationships: (1) children, (2) families, (3) colleagues, and (4) community and society. Each section includes an introduction to the primary responsibilities of the early childhood practitioner in that arena, a set of ideals

This Code of Ethical Conduct and Statement of Commitment was prepared under the auspices of the Ethics Commission of the National Association for the Education of Young Children. The Commission members were Stephanie Feeney (Chairperson), Bettye Caldwell, Sally Cartwright, Carrie Cheek, Josué Cruz, Jr., Anne G. Dorsey, Dorothy M. Hill, Lilian G. Katz, Pam Mattick, Shirley A. Norris, and Sue Spayth Riley.
Reprinted with permission from the National Association for the Education of Young Children.

pointing in the direction of exemplary professional practice, and a set of principles defining practices that are required, prohibited, and permitted.

The ideals reflect the aspirations of practitioners. The principles are intended to guide conduct and assist practitioners in resolving ethical dilemmas encountered in the field. There is not necessarily a corresponding principle for each ideal. Both ideals and principles are intended to direct practitioners to those questions which, when responsibly answered, will provide the basis for conscientious decision making. While the Code provides specific direction for addressing some ethical dilemmas, many others will require the practitioner to combine the guidance of the Code with sound professional judgment.

The ideals and principles in this Code present a shared conception of professional responsibility that affirms our commitment to the core values of our field. The Code publicly acknowledges the responsibilities that we in the field have assumed and in so doing supports ethical behavior in our work. Practitioners who face ethical dilemmas are urged to seek guidance in the applicable parts of this Code and in the spirit that informs the whole.

# SECTION I: ETHICAL RESPONSIBILITIES TO CHILDREN

Childhood is a unique and valuable stage in the life cycle. Our paramount responsibility is to provide safe, healthy, nurturing, and responsive settings for children. We are committed to supporting children's development by cherishing individual differences, by helping them learn to live and work cooperatively, and by promoting their self-esteem and resiliency.

## Ideals

I-1.1—To be familiar with the knowledge base of early childhood education and to keep current through continuing education and in-service training.

I-1.2—To base program practices upon current knowledge in the field of child development and related disciplines and upon particular knowledge of each child.

I-1.3—To recognize and respect the uniqueness and the potential of each child.

I-1.4—To appreciate the special vulnerability of children.

I-1.5—To create and maintain safe and healthy settings that foster children's social, emotional, intellectual, and physical development and that respect their dignity and their contributions.

I-1.6—To support the right of each child to play and learn in inclusive early childhood programs to the fullest extent consistent with the best interests of all involved. Usually, children with disabilities should be served in the same programs they would have attended if they did not have disabilities.

## Principles

P-1.1—Above all, we shall not harm children. We shall not participate in practices that are disrespectful, degrading, dangerous, exploitative, intimidating, psychologically damaging, or physically harmful to children. *This principle has precedence over all others in this Code.*

P-1.2—We shall not participate in practices that discriminate against children by denying benefits, giving special advantages, or excluding them from programs or activities on the basis of their race, religion, gender, national origin, ability or the status, behavior, or beliefs of their parents. (This principle does not apply to programs that have a lawful mandate to provide services to a particular population of children.)

P-1.3—We shall involve all of those with relevant knowledge (including staff and parents) in decisions concerning a child.

P-1.4—When, after appropriate efforts have been made with a child, the family, and appropriate specialists if needed, the child still does not appear to be benefiting from a program, we shall communicate our concern to the family in a positive way and offer them assistance in finding a more suitable setting.

P-1.5—We shall be familiar with the symptoms of child abuse, including verbal or emotional abuse, and neglect and know community procedures for addressing them.

P-1.6—When we have evidence of child abuse or neglect, we shall report the evidence to the appropriate community agency and follow up to ensure that appropriate action has been taken. When possible, parents will be informed that the referral has been made.

P-1.7—When another person tells us of their suspicion that a child is being abused or neglected but we lack evidence, we shall assist that person in taking appropriate action to protect the child.

**P-1.8**—When a child protective agency fails to provide adequate protection for abused or neglected children, we acknowledge a collective ethical responsibility to work toward improvement of these services.

# SECTION II: ETHICAL RESPONSIBILITIES TO FAMILIES

Almost all children grow up in families. Families are of primary importance in children's development. (The term *family* may include others, besides parents, who are responsibly involved with the child.) Because the family and the early childhood educator have a common interest in the child's welfare, we acknowledge a primary responsibility to bring about collaboration between the home and school in ways that enhance the child's development.

## Ideals

**I-2.1**—To develop relationships of mutual trust with the families we serve.

**I-2.2**—To acknowledge and build upon strengths and competencies as we support families in their task of nurturing children.

**I-2.3**—To respect the dignity of each family and its culture, language, customs, and beliefs.

**I-2.4**—To respect families' child-rearing values and their right to make decisions for their children.

**I-2.5**—To interpret each child's progress to parents within the framework of a developmental perspective and to help families understand and appreciate the value of developmentally appropriate early childhood practices.

**I-2.6**—To help family members improve their understanding of their children and to enhance their skills as parents.

**I-2.7**—To participate in building support networks for families by providing them with opportunities to interact with program staff and families, and other community resources.

## Principles

**P-2.1**—We shall not deny family members access to their child's classroom or program setting.

**P-2.2**—We shall inform families of program philosophy, policies, and personnel qualifications, and explain why we teach as we do—in accordance with our ethical responsibilities to children (see Section I).

**P-2.3**—We shall inform families of and, when appropriate, involve them in policy decisions.

**P-2.4**—We shall involve families in significant decisions affecting their child.

**P-2.5**—We shall inform the family of accidents involving their child, of risks such as exposures to contagious disease that may result in infection, and of occurrences that might result in emotional stress.

**P-2.6**—Families shall be fully informed of any proposed research projects involving their children and shall have the opportunity to give or withhold consent without penalty. We shall not permit or participate in research that could in any way hinder the education or development of the children in our programs.

**P-2.7**—We shall not engage in or support exploitation of families. We shall not use our relationship with a family for private advantage or personal gain, or enter into relationships with family members that might impair our effectiveness in working with children.

**P-2.8**—We shall develop written policies for the protection of confidentiality and the disclosure of children's records. The policy documents shall be made available to all program personnel and families. Disclosure of children's records beyond family members, program personnel, and consultants having an obligation of confidentiality shall require familial consent (except in cases of abuse or neglect).

**P-2.9**—We shall maintain confidentiality and shall respect the family's right to privacy, refraining from disclosure of confidential information and intrusion into family life. However, when we are concerned about a child's welfare, it is permissible to reveal confidential information to agencies and individuals who may be able to act in the child's interest.

**P-2.10**—In cases where family members are in conflict we shall work openly, sharing our observations of the child, to help all parties involved make informed decisions. We shall refrain from becoming an advocate for one party.

P-2.11—We shall be familiar with and appropriately use community resources and professional services that support families. After a referral has been made, we shall follow up to ensure that services have been adequately provided.

# SECTION III: ETHICAL RESPONSIBILITIES TO COLLEAGUES

In a caring, cooperative workplace, human dignity is respected, professional satisfaction is promoted, and positive relationships are modeled. Our primary responsibility in this arena is to establish and maintain settings and relationships that support productive work and meet professional needs.

## A—Responsibilities to Co-Workers

### Ideals

I-3A.1—To establish and maintain relationships of trust and cooperation with co-workers.

I-3A.2—To share resources and information with co-workers.

I-3A.3—To support co-workers in meeting their professional needs and in their professional development.

I-3A.4—To accord co-workers due recognition of professional achievement.

### Principles

P-3A.1—When we have concern about the professional behavior of a co-worker, we shall first let that person know of our concern in a way that is respectful of cultural diversity among staff and attempt to resolve the matter collegially.

P-3A.2—We shall exercise care in expressing views regarding the personal attributes of professional conduct of co-workers. Statements should be based on firsthand knowledge and relevant to the interests of children and programs.

## B—Responsibilities to Employers

### Ideals

I-3B.1—To assist the program in providing the highest quality of service.

I-3B.2—To maintain loyalty to the program and uphold its reputation.

### Principles

P-3B.1—When we do not agree with program policies, we shall first attempt to effect change through constructive action with the organization.

P-3B.2—We shall speak or act on behalf of an organization only when authorized. We shall take care to note when we are speaking for the organization and when we are expressing a personal judgment.

## C—Responsibilities to Employees

### Ideals

I-3C.1—To promote policies and working conditions that foster competence, well-being, and self-esteem in staff members.

I-3C.2—To create a climate of trust and candor that will enable staff to speak and act in the best interests of children, families, and the field of early childhood education.

I-3C.3—To strive to secure an adequate livelihood for those who work with or on behalf of young children.

### Principles

P-3C.1—In decisions concerning children and programs, we shall appropriately utilize the training, experience, and expertise of staff members.

P-3C.2—We shall provide staff members with working conditions that permit them to carry out their responsibilities, timely and nonthreatening evaluation procedures, written grievance procedures, constructive feedback, and opportunities for continuing professional development and advancement.

P-3C.3—We shall develop and maintain comprehensive written personnel policies that define program standards and, when applicable, that specify the extent to which employees are accountable for their conduct outside the workplace. These policies shall be given to new staff members and shall be available for review by all staff members.

P-3C.4—Employees who do not meet program standards shall be informed of areas of concern and, when possible, assisted in improving their performance.

P-3C.5—Employees who are dismissed shall be informed of the reasons for their termination. When a dismissal is for cause, justification must be based on evidence of inadequate or inappropriate behavior that is accurately documented, current, and available for the employee to review.

**P-3C.6**—In making evaluations and recommendations, judgments shall be based on fact and relevant to the interests of children and programs.

**P-3C.7**—Hiring and promotion shall be based solely on a person's record of accomplishment and ability to carry out the responsibilities of the position.

**P-3C.8**—In hiring, promotion, and provision of training, we shall not participate in any form of discrimination based on race, religion, gender, national origin, culture, disability, age, or sexual preference. We shall be familiar with laws and regulations that pertain to employment discrimination.

## SECTION IV: ETHICAL RESPONSIBILITIES TO COMMUNITY AND SOCIETY

Early childhood programs operate within a context of an immediate community made up of families and other institutions concerned with children's welfare. Our responsibilities to the community are to provide programs that meet its needs and to cooperate with agencies and professions that share responsibility for children. Because the larger society has a measure of responsibility for the welfare and protection of children, and because of our specialized expertise in child development, we acknowledge an obligation to serve as a voice for children everywhere.

### Ideals

**I-4.1**—To provide the community with high-quality, culturally sensitive programs and services.

**I-4.2**—To promote cooperation among agencies and interdisciplinary collaboration among professions concerned with the welfare of young children, their families, and their teachers.

**I-4.3**—To work, through education, research, and advocacy, toward an environmentally safe world in which all children are adequately fed, sheltered, and nurtured.

**I-4.4**—To work, through education, research, and advocacy, toward a society in which all young children have access to quality programs.

**I-4.5**—To promote knowledge and understanding of young children and their needs. To work toward greater social acknowledgment of children's rights and greater social acceptance of responsibility for their well-being.

**I-4.6**—To support policies and laws that promote the well-being of children and families. To oppose those that impair their well-being. To participate in developing those that are needed. To cooperate with other individuals and groups in these efforts.

**I-4.7**—To further the professional development of the field of early childhood education and to strengthen its commitment to realizing its core values as reflected in this Code.

### Principles

**P-4.1**—We shall communicate openly and truthfully about the nature and extent of services that we provide.

**P-4.2**—We shall not accept or continue to work in positions for which we are personally unsuited or professionally unqualified. We shall not offer services that we do not have the competence, qualifications, or resources to provide.

**P-4.3**—We shall be objective and accurate in reporting the knowledge upon which we base our program practices.

**P-4.4**—We shall cooperate with other professionals who work with children and their families.

**P-4.5**—We shall not hire or recommend for employment any person who is unsuited for a position with respect to competence, qualifications, or character.

**P-4.6**—We shall report the unethical or incompetent behavior of a colleague to a supervisor when informal resolution is not effective.

**P-4.7**—We shall be familiar with laws and regulations that serve to protect the children in our programs.

**P-4.8**—We shall not participate in practices which are in violation of laws and regulations that protect the children in our programs.

**P-4.9**—When we have evidence that an early childhood program is violating laws or regulations protecting children, we shall report it to persons responsible for the program. If compliance is not accomplished within a reasonable time, we will report the violation to appropriate authorities who can be expected to remedy the situation.

**P-4.10**—When we have evidence that an agency or a professional charged with providing services to children, families, or teachers is failing to meet its obligations, we acknowledge a collective ethical responsibility to report the problem to appropriate authorities or to the public.

**P-4.11**—When a program violates or requires its employees to violate this Code, it is permissible, after fair assessment of the evidence, to disclose the identity of that program.

# ▼Appendix B

## Organizations That Address Child Abuse and Related National Helplines

*Child Help USA*
840 Guadalupe Parkway
San Jose, CA 95110
(800) 422-4453

A resource for sexual-abuse victims, perpetrators, and their families to call for referrals to local affiliates in 50 states and Canada.

*EPOCH USA*
Center for Effective Discipline
155 W. Main Street, Suite 100-B
Columbus, Ohio 43215

This organization advocates an end to parental use of physical punishment in the United States. Provides information and sample materials.

*National Clearinghouse of Child Abuse and Neglect Information*
P. O. Box 1182
Washington, D.C. 20013-1182
(800) FYI-3366

*National Committee to Prevent Child Abuse*
332 S. Michigan Ave., Suite 1600
Chicago, IL 60604
(312) 663-3520
www.childabuse.org

Provides information for people who want to find solutions to child abuse, including sexual abuse. Stresses preventive efforts, gives referrals and offers volunteer opportunities.

*Service of U.S. Department of Health and Human Services, Administration on Children, Youth and Families*
www.calib.com/nccanch/

This national directory is designed to give helping professionals a starting point when looking for referrals.

*Parents Anonymous*
(National office and affiliate of the National Committee for the Prevention of Child Abuse)
520 S. Lafayette Park Place
Los Angeles, CA 90057

A crisis-intervention program for parents who abuse their children. Operates a hot line and provides referrals to local chapters.

## Helplines

| Organization | Toll-free Number |
| --- | --- |
| Child Find | 800-292-9688 |
| Child Find Hotline (parents reporting lost children) | 800-I-AM-LOST (800-426-5678) |
| Childhelp National Child Abuse Hotline | 800-4-A-CHILD (800-422-4453) |
| Haven from Domestic Violence | 800-249-4789 |
| Immunization Hotline (English) | 800-232-2522 |
| Immunization Hotline (Spanish) | 800-232-0233 |
| Just for Kids Hotline | 888-594-KIDS |
| National Center for Missing and Exploited Children | 800-843-5678 |
| National Child Safety Council | 800-327-5107 |
| Nationwide Domestic Violence Hotline | 800-799-SAFE |
| National Runaway Hotline | 800-621-4000 |
| National Youth Crisis Hotline | 800-442-4673 |
| Operation Lookout, National Center for Missing Youth | 800-782-7335 |
| Runaway Hotline | 800-231-6946 |
| Youth Crisis Hotline | 800-448-4663 |

# ▼Appendix C

# Personal Safety Terms, Facts, and Principles

## Beginning Terms, Facts, and Principles

1. Your body is your own.
2. You have a right to the privacy of your body in dressing, bathing, and sleeping.
3. When anyone touches you in a way you don't like, you can say, *"No!"*
4. There are many kinds of touch: some touches make you feel good; some touches make you feel bad.
5. No one has the right to touch you in a way that hurts or feels frightening or confusing.
6. No one has the right to force or trick you into touching them. Some kinds of hurtful tricks include:
   a. Telling children something that isn't true.
   b. Pretending to know you or your parents.
   c. Promising you treats.
   d. Offering to give you a ride.
7. When anyone touches you in a way that you don't like, tell someone you trust about it right away, even if you've been told to keep it a secret.
8. It's not fair for an adult or older child to touch you in a way that you don't like. If an adult or older child touches you in a way that's not fair, it is not your fault.
9. Sometimes, people try to trick children into doing things that aren't good for them. Sometimes, people who try to trick children seem nice at first.
10. If someone tries to trick you, tell someone else about it right away, even if you've been told to keep it a secret.
11. Good secrets are about happy surprises and can be fun to keep for a little while.

12. Bad secrets are about things that make you uncomfortable, confused, scared, or unhappy. If someone wants you to keep a bad secret, tell someone you trust right away.
13. People you trust are the people with whom you always feel safe.
14. A stranger is a person whose name you don't know; you don't know where they live, and your parents don't know them either.
15. If someone you don't know does anything that seems strange or frightening, you can:
   a. Run
   b. Yell or scream, "Leave me alone—you're not my father (mother)!"
16. If someone you *do* know does something that seems frightening or confusing, you can:
   a. Yell or scream, "Leave me alone!"
   b. Run and find someone you trust and tell them what happened.
   c. If the person you tell doesn't believe you, find someone else to tell right away.

## Intermediate Terms, Facts, and Principles

1. Sometimes, pleasant touches become unpleasant or confusing:
   a. Holding someone's hand feels good, but it hurts if your hand is squeezed too hard.
   b. Tickling can be fun, but tickling too hard or for too long can be upsetting.
2. Sometimes, you feel like being hugged or kissed; sometimes, you don't. You can tell someone how you feel.
3. When you feel like giving a hug or a kiss, first ask if it's okay. If someone says, "Yes," give

them a hug or kiss. If someone says, "No," don't give them a hug or kiss.

4. Parents worry when they don't know where their children are. It's important to always be where your parents think you are.

5. Being lost is a scary feeling. When your parents can't find you, they worry too.

6. When you're lost, there are some strangers you can ask for help:

 a. Ask a mother with children.

 b. Ask another child to take you to his or her mom or dad. Tell them you're lost.

 c. Tell a salesclerk or cashier that you can't find your mom or dad.

 d. Tell a person wearing a uniform, such as a police officer or a mail carrier.

 e. Tell one of these people your phone number so they can call home for you.

7. Parents often have private code words that they tell only the people who are allowed to take you away with them.

8. If you have a code word, your mom or dad will never send a stranger to get you who doesn't know your family's special code word.

9. If someone says your parents sent them and doesn't say the code word, don't go with them. Tell someone you trust what happened.

---

These terms, facts, and principles were developed by Donna Howe, Instructor, Department of Family and Child Ecology, Michigan State University, 1985.

# ▼References

Aboud, F. E., and S. A. Skerry. "The Development of Ethnic Attitudes." *Journal of Cross Cultural Psychology* 15, no. 1, 3 (1984): 3–34.

Acredolo, L. P., and J. L. Hoke. "Infant Perception." In *Handbook of Developmental Psychology,* edited by B. B. Walman and G. Struker. Englewood Cliffs, N.J.: Prentice-Hall, 1982.

Adams-Tucker, C. "Proximate Effects of Sexual Abuse in Childhood: A Report on 28 Children." *American Journal of Psychiatry* 139 (1982): 1252–1256.

Adamson, L. *Communication Development During Infancy.* Dubuque, IA: Brown & Benchmark, 1995.

Adler, A. *Practice and Theory of Individual Psychology,* New York: Harcourt, Brace and Company, 1923.

Ainsworth, M. D. S. "The Development of Infant-Mother Attachment." In *Review of Child Development Research,* Vol. 3, edited by B. M. Caldwell and H. N. Riccuti, Chicago: University of Chicago Press, 1973.

Aldis, O. *Play Fighting.* New York: Academic Press, Inc., 1975.

Alexander, K. L., and D. R. Entwistle. "Achievement in the First Two Years of School: Patterns and Processes." *SRCD Monographs* 53, no. 2 (1988).

Alexander, T., P. Roodin, and B. Gorman. *Developmental Psychology.* New York: Van Nostrand Reinhold Co., Inc., 1980.

Allen, K. E. "The Parent-Teacher Partnership in Programs for Young Children." *Resources in Education* 7 (1983).

Altman, K. "Effects of Cooperative Response Acquisition on Social Behavior During Free Play." *Journal of Experimental Psychology* 12 (1971): 385–395.

Alward, K. R. *Arranging the Classroom for Children.* San Francisco: Far West Laboratory for Educational Research and Development, 1973.

Ambron, S. R., and N. J. Salkind. *Child Development.* New York: Holt, Rinehart & Winston, 1984.

American Association for Protecting Children. *Highlights of Official Child Neglect and Abuse Reporting.* Denver, Colo.: AAPC, 1985.

American Medical Association. *Physicians' Guide to Media Violence.* Chicago: AMA, 1996.

American Psychiatric Association. *Diagnostic Criteria from DSM-IV.* Washington, D.C.: APA, 1994.

Anderson, H. H., and J. E. Brewer. "Studies of Teachers' Classroom Personalities." *Applied Psychology Monographs* (1945): 6.

Anthony, V. D. *Michigan Task Force on Drug Exposed Infants. Executive Summary.* Lansing, Mich.: Michigan Department of Health, 1992.

Anziano, M. C., et al. *Approaches to Preschool Curriculum.* New York: McGraw-Hill, 1995.

Ard, L. "Using Space." In *Room to Grow: How to Create Quality Early Childhood Environments,* edited by L. Ard and M. Pitts. Austin: Texas Association for the Education of Young Children, 1990, 1–10.

Ard, L., and M. Pitts, eds. *Room to Grow: How to Create Quality Early Childhood Environments.* Austin: Texas Association for the Education of Young Children, 1990.

Asher, S. R. "Children's Peer Relations." In *Social and Personality Development,* edited by M. E. Lamb. New York: Holt, Rinehart & Winston, 1978.

Asher, S. R., S. L. Oden, and J. M. Gottman. "Children's Friendships in School Settings." In *Current Topics in Early Childhood Education,* Vol. 1, edited by L. G. Katz. Norwood, N.J.: Ablex Publishing Corp., 1977.

Asher, S. R., and P. Renshaw. "Children without Friends: Social Knowledge and Social Skill." In *The Development of Children's Friendships,* edited by S. R. Asher and J. M. Gottman. New York: Cambridge University Press, 1981.

Ashton, R. "The State Variable in Neonatal Research: A Review." *Merrill-Palmer Quarterly* 19 (1973): 3–20.

Bach, G. R., and H. Goldberg. *Creative Aggression.* New York: Avon Books, 1974.

Bakeman, R., and J. Brownlee. "The Strategic Use of Parallel Play: A Sequential Analysis." *Child Development* 51 (1980): 873–878.

Baker v. Owen, 39 F. Suppl. 294 (M.D.N.C. 1975), Off'd U.S.—96 S. Cet. 210.

Balaban, N. *Starting School.* New York: Teachers College Press, 1985.

Baldwin, C. P., and A. L. Baldwin. "Children's Judgements of Kindness." *Child Development* 41 (1970): 29–47.

Ball, J. "The National PTA's Stand on Corporal Punishment." *PTA Today* (February 1989): XIV: 15–17.

Bandura, A. "The Role of the Modeling Process in Personality Development." In *The Young Child: Reviews of Research,* Vol. 1, edited by W. W. Hartup and N. L. Smothergill. Washington, D.C.: National Association for the Education of Young Children, 1967.

Bandura, A. *Aggression: A Social Learning Analysis.* Englewood Cliffs, N.J.: Prentice-Hall, Inc., 1973.

Bandura, A. *Social Foundations of Thought and Action: A Social Cognitive Theory.* Englewood Cliffs, N.J.: Prentice-Hall, Inc., 1986.

Bandura, A. "Social Cognitive Theory." In *Annals of Child Development,* Vol. 6, edited by R. Vasta. Greenwich, CT: JAI Press, Inc., 1989, 1–60.

Bandura, A., and W. Mischel. "Modification of Self-Imposed Delay of Reward Through Exposure to Live and Symbolic Models." *Journal of Personality and Social Psychology* 2 (1965): 698–705.

Bandura, A., D. Ross, and S. A. Ross. "Imitation of Film-Mediated Aggression." *Journal of Abnormal and Social Psychology* 66, no. 1 (1963): 3–11.

Bandura, A., and R. H. Walters. *Social Learning and Personality Development.* New York: Holt, Rinehart & Winston, 1963.

Bandura, A., and R. H. Walters. *Social Learning Theory.* Englewood Cliffs, N.J.: Prentice-Hall, Inc., 1977.

Banks, M. S. "The Development of Early Infancy." *Child Development* 51 (1980): 646–666.

Barfield, C., E. M. Simpson, and B. M. Groves. *How Community Violence Affects Children, Parents and Practitioners.* Washington, D.C.: National Center for Clinical Infant Programs, Fall 1992.

Barkley, R. A. *Attention Deficit Hyperactivity Disorder.* New York: The Guilford Press, 1990.

Baron, R. A., and D. Byrne. *Social Psychology.* Boston: Allyn and Bacon, Inc., 1991.

Baron, R. A., and D. Byrne. *Social Psychology: Understanding Human Interaction.* 5th ed. Newton, Mass.: Allyn and Bacon, 1993.

Bates, J. E. "Temperament as Part of Social Relationships: Implications of Perceived Infant Difficulties." Paper presented at the International Conference on Infant Studies, Austin, TX, 1982.

Bateson, G. "The Message 'This Is Play'." In *Child's Play.* edited by R. E. Herron and B. Sutton-Smith. New York: John Wiley & Sons, Inc., 1971.

Baumrind, D. Effects of Authoritative Parental Control on Child Behavior." *Child Development* 37 (1966): 887–907.

Baumrind, D. "Child Care Practices Anteceding Three Patterns of Preschool Behavior." *Genetic Psychology Monographs* 75 (1967): 43–88.

Baumrind, D. "Socialization and Instrumental Competence in Young Children." *Young Children* 26, no. 2 (December 1970): 104–119.

Baumrind, D. "Socialization and Instrumental Competence in Young Children." In *The Young Child: Review of Research,* Vol. 2, edited by W. W. Hartup. Washington, D.C.: National Association for the Education of Young Children, 1972.

Baumrind, D. "Current Patterns of Parental Authority." *Developmental Psychology Monographs* 4 (1973): 1.

Baumrind, D. "Socialization Determinants of Personal Agency." Paper presented at the biennial meeting of the Society for Research in Child Development, New Orleans, April 1977.

Baumrind, D. "Some Thoughts About Childrearing." In *Child Development: Contemporary Perspectives,* edited by S. Cohen and T. J. Comiskey, Itasca, Ill.: F. E. Peacock, Publishers, Inc., 1977.

Baumrind, D. "Parental Disciplinary Patterns." *Youth and Society* 9 (1978): 223–276.

Baumrind, D. Familial Antecedents of Social Competence in Middle Childhood. Unpublished manuscript, 1988.

Baumrind, D. "The Influence of Parenting Style on Adolescent Competence and Substance Use." *Journal of Early Adolescence* 11 (1991): 56–95.

Baumrind, D. *Child Maltreatment and Optimal Caregiving in Social Contexts.* New York: Garland Publishing, 1995.

Bavelas, J. B., et al. "Gestures Specialized for Dialogue." *Personality and Social Psychology Bulletin* 21, no. 4 (1995): 394–405.

Bavolek, S. J. "Assessing and Treating High-Risk Parenting Attitudes." *Early Child Development and Care.* 42 (1989): 99–111.

Beal, E. W., and G. Hochman. *Adult Children of Divorce: Breaking the Cycle and Finding Fulfillment in Love, Marriage, and Family.* New York: Delacorte, 1991.

Beane, J. "Middle School: Natural Home of Integrated Curriculum." *Educational Leaderships* 49 (1991): 2, 9–13.

Beardslee, W. R. "Youth and the Threat of Nuclear War." *The Lancet* (September 10, 1988): 618–620.

Becker, W. C., S. Engelmann, and D. R. Thomas. *Teaching: A Course in Applied Psychology,* Chicago: Science Research Associates, 1971.

Beckwith, L. "Relationships Between Infants' Vocalizations and Their Mothers' Behaviors." *Merrill-Palmer Quarterly* 17 (1971): 211–226.

Bee, H. *The Developing Child.* 8th ed. New York: Harper and Row, Publisher, 1996.

Beebe, B., and D. Stern. "Engagement-Disengagement and Early Object Experiences." In *Communicative Structures and Psychic Structures,* edited by N. Friedman and S. Grand. New York: Plenum Publishing Corporation, 1977.

Begley, S. "Your Child's Brain." *Newsweek* (February 1996): 55–62.

Behrman, R. E., ed. "Special Education for Students with Disabilities: Analysis and Recommendations." *The Future of Children* 6 (1996): 4–24.

Bell, S. M., and M. D. Ainsworth. "Infant Crying and Maternal Responsiveness." *Child Development* 43 (1972): 1171–1190.

Belsky, J. "Child Maltreatment: An Ecological Integration." *American Psychologist* 35 (1980): 320–335.

Belsky, J. "Etiology of Child Maltreatment: A Developmental Ecological Analysis." *Psychological Bulletin* 114 (1993): 413–434.

Belsky, J., and L. Steinberg. "The Effects of Day Care: A Critical Review." *Child Development* 49 (1978): 929–949.

Bem, S. L. "Androgyny and Gender Scheme Theory: A Conceptual and Empirical Integration." In *Nebraska Symposium on Motivation,* Vol. 32, edited by T. B.

Sondergregger. Lincoln: University of Nebraska Press, 1985, 1–71.

Benson, H. *The Relaxation Response*. New York: William Morrow & Co., Inc., 1976.

Berclay, C. J. *Parent Involvement in the Schools*. Washington, D. C.: National Education Association, 1977.

Berg, W. K., C. D. Adkinson, and B. D. Strock. "Duration and Frequency of Periods of Alertness in Neonates." *Development Psychology* 9 (1973): 434.

Berger, K. S. *The Developing Person*. New York: Worth Publishers, Inc., 1996.

Berger, K. S., R. A. Thompson. *The Developing Person: Through Childhood and Adolescence*. New York: Worth Publishers, 1995.

Berk, L. *Child Development*. 4th ed. Boston: Allyn and Bacon, 1997.

Berk, L. E., and A. Winsler. *Scaffolding Children's Learning: Vygotsy and Early Childhood Education*. Washington, D.C.: National Association for the Education of Young Children, 1995.

Berkowitz, L. "Control of Aggression." In *Review of Child Development Research*, edited by B. Caldwell and H. Riccuti. Chicago: University of Chicago Press, 1973, 95–141.

Berkowitz, L. *Aggression: Its Causes, Consequences and Control*. New York: McGraw-Hill, 1993.

Bernal, M. E., and G. P. Knight, eds. *Ethnic Identity: Formation and Transmission among Hispanics and Other Minorities*. Albany, N.Y.: State University of New York Press, 1993.

Bernard, S., and L. W. Sontag. "Fetal Reactivity to Tonal Stimulation: A Preliminary Report." *Journal of Genetic Psychology* 70 (1947): 205–210.

Berndt, T. J. "Developmental Changes in Conformity to Peers and Parents." *Developmental Psychology* 15 (1979): 608–616.

Berns, R. M. *Child, Family, Community*. New York: Holt, Rinehart & Winston, 1993, 1996.

Berns, R. M. *Topical Child Development*. Albany, N.Y.: Delmar Publishers, 1994.

Bernstein, B. "Social Class and Linguistic Development: A Theory of Social Learning." In *Education, Economy and Society*, edited by A. Halsey, J. Floud, and C. Anderson. New York: Prentice-Hall, Inc., 1961.

Berreth, D., and S. Berman. "The Moral Dimensions of Schools." *Educational Leadership* 54, no. 8 (May 1997): 24–27.

Berry, D. B. *Domestic Violence Sourcebook*. New York: Brunner/Mazel, 1995.

Bertenthal, B., and K. W. Fischer. "Development of Self-Recognition in the Infant." *Developmental Psychology* 14 (1978): 44–50.

Bessell, H. *Methods in Human Development: Theory Manual*. San Diego, Calif.: Human Development Training Institute, 1970.

Birch, L. L., and J. Billman. "Preschool Children's Food Sharing with Friends and Acquaintances." *Child Development* 57 (1986): 387–395.

Bishop, N. "A Systems Approach Toward the Functional Connections of Attachment and Fear." *Child Development* 46, (1977): 801–817.

Bivens, J. A., and L. E. Berk. "A Longitudinal Study of the Development of Elementary School Children's Private Speech." *Merrill-Palmer Quarterly* 36 (1990): 443–463.

Blanck, P., and R. Rosenthal. "Developing Strategies for Decoding 'Leaky' Messages: On Learning How and When to Decode Discrepant and Consistent Social Communications." In *Development of Nonverbal Behavior in Children,* edited by B. S. Feldman. New York: Springer-Verlag New York, Inc., 1982.

Blau, M. *Families Apart*. New York: Berkley Publishing, 1993.

Block, J. "Personality Development in Males and Females: The Influence of Differential Socialization." *Socialization Influencing Personality Development*. Berkeley, Calif.: University of California Press, 1979.

Blom, G. E., Cheney, B. D., and Snoddy, J. E. *Stress in Childhood*. New York: Teachers College Press, 1986.

Bloom, L., K. Lifter, and J. Brazelton. "What Children Say and What They Know: Exploring the Relations Between Product and Process in the Development of Early Words and Early Concepts." In *Language Behavior in Infancy and Early Childhood*, edited by R. Stark. New York: Elsevier/North Holland, 1981.

Blurton-Jones, N. "Categories of Child-Child Interaction." In *Ethological Studies of Child Behavior*, edited by N. Blurton-Jones, Cambridge, England: Cambridge University Press, 1972, 97–128.

Blurton-Jones, N. "Rough-Tumble Play Among Nursery School Children." In *Play: Its Role in Development and Evolution*, edited by J. Bruner, A. Jolly, and K. Sylva. New York: Basic Books, Inc., Publishers, 1976, 352–363.

Bodrova, E., and D. Leong. *Tools of the Mind: The Vygotskian Approach to Early Childhood Education*. Englewood Cliffs, N.J.: Prentice-Hall, Inc., 1996.

Boggs, S. T. "The Meaning of Questions and Narratives to Hawaiian Children." In *Functions of Language in the Classroom*, edited by C. B. Cazden, V. P. John, and D. Hymes. New York: Teachers College Press, 1972.

Bolin, G. G. "Ethnic Differences in Attitude Towards Discipline Among Day Care Providers: Implications for Training." *Child & Youth Care Quarterly* 18, no. 2 (Summer 1989): 111–117.

Boneau, C. A. "Paradigm Regained: Cognitive Behaviors Restated." *American Psychologist* 29 (1974): 297–309.

Borland, D. C. "Human Sexuality in the Home." *Two to Twelve* 2, no. 1 (1984): 1–4.

Boss, P. "Normative Family Stress: Family Boundary Changes Across the Life Span." *Family Relations* 29 (October 1980): 445–450.

Boukydis, C. F. Z. "Perception of infant crying as an interpersonal event." In *Infant Crying: Theoretical and Research Perspectives*, edited by B. M. Lester and C. F. Z. Boukydis. New York: Plenum, 1985.

Bower, G. "Mood and Memory." *American Psychologist* 36 (1981): 128–148.

Bowlby, J. *Attachment and Loss. Vol. 1: Attachment.* New York: Basic Books, Inc., Publishers, 1969.

Brackbill, Y. "Obstetrical Medication and Infant Behavior." In *Handbook of Infant Development,* edited by J. D. Osofsdy. New York: John Wiley & Sons, Inc., 1979, 76–125.

Brazelton, T. B. "Early Mother-Infant Reciprocity." In *The Family—Can It Be Saved?* edited by V. C. Vaughn III and T. B. Brazelton. Chicago: Yearbook Medical Publishers, 1976.

Brazelton, T. B. *To Listen to a Child: Understanding the Normal Problems of Growing Up.* New York: Addison-Wesley, 1984.

Brazelton, T. B., Koslowski, B., and Maen, M. "The Origins of Reciprocity: The Early Mother-Infant Interactions." In *The Origins of Behavior,* edited by M. Lewes and J. Rosenblum. New York: Wiley, 1974.

Bredekamp, S., and C. Copple. *Developmentally Appropriate Practice in Early Childhood Programs: Revised Edition.* Washington, D.C.: NAEYC, 1997.

Brendtro, L., and N. Long. "Breaking the Cycle of Conflict." *Educational Leadership* 52, no. 5 (February 1995): 52–56.

Brenner, A. *Helping Children Cope With Stress,* Lexington, Mass.: D.C. Heath & Company, 1984.

Bretherton, I. "Representing the Social World in Symbolic Play: Reality and Fantasy." In *Symbolic Play,* edited by I. Bretherton. New York: Academic Press, Inc., 1984, 1–41.

Bretherton, I., et al. "Learning to Talk about Emotions: A Functionalist Perspective." *Child Development* 57 (1986): 529–548.

Brewer, J. A. *Early Childhood Education.* 2d ed. Boston: Allyn and Bacon, 1995.

Brier, N. "Predicting Antisocial Behavior in Youngsters Displaying Poor Academic Achievement: A Review of Risk Factors." *Journal of Developmental and Behavioral Pediatrics* 16 (1995): 271–276.

Briggs, B. A. "Measuring Effective Early Childhood Teaching Behaviors." *Child and Youth Care Quarterly* 16, no. 3, (1987): 196–209.

Briggs, D. C. *Your Child's Self-Esteem.* New York: Doubleday & Company, Inc., 1975.

Broberg, A. "Inhibition in Children's Experiences of Out-of-Home Care." In *Social Withdrawal, Inhibition, and Shyness in Childhood,* edited by K. Rubin and J. Asendorph. Hillsdale, N.J.: Lawrence Erlbaum Associates, Inc., 1993.

Brody, J. E. "Reports Link PCB Exposure with Children's Development." *The New York Times* (September 12, 1996): A–8.

Bronfenbrenner, U. "Who Needs Parent Education?" Paper presented at the Working Conference on Parent Education, Mott Foundation, Flint, Mich., 30 September 1977.

Bronfenbrenner, U. "Ecological Systems Theory." In *Annals of Child Development,* edited by R. Vasta. Greenwich, CT: JAI Press, Inc., 6 (1989): 187–249.

Bronfenbrenner, U. "The Ecology of Cognitive Development Research Models and Fugitive Findings." In *Development in Context,* edited by R. H. Wozniak and K. W. Fischer. Hillsdale, N.J.: Erlbaum, 1993, 3–44.

Brooks, J. B. *The Process of Parenting.* Palo Alto, Calif.: Mayfield Publishing Co., 1991, 1996.

Brophy, J., and J. Putnam. "Classroom Management in the Elementary Grades." In *Classroom Management. Yearbook for the National Society for the Study of Education,* edited by D. Duke. Chicago: NSSE, 1979, 182–216.

Brown, B. "Slim Talk: A Strange Mirror of the Mind." *Psychology Today* 8 (1974): 8.

Brown, R., and U. Bellugi. "Three Processes in the Child's Acquisition of Syntax." *Harvard Educational Review* 34 (1964): 133–151.

Bryan, J. H. "Children's Cooperation and Helping Behaviors." In *Review of Child Development Research,* Vol. 5, edited by E. M. Hetherington. Chicago: University of Chicago Press, 1975, 127–180.

Bryant, B. K. "An Index of Empathy for Children and Adolescents." *Child Development* 53 (1982): 413–425.

Bubolz, M. M., and M. S. Sontag. "Human Ecology Theory." In *Sourcebook of Family Theories and Methods: A Contextual Approach,* edited by P. G. Boss, et al. New York: Plenum Publishing Corp., 1993, 419–448.

Buck, R. "Spontaneous and Symbolic Nonverbal Behavior and the Ontogeny of Communication." In *Development of Nonverbal Behavior in Children,* edited by R. S. Feldman, New York: Springer-Verlag New York, Inc., 1982, 28–62.

Bugental, D. "Interpretations of Naturally Occurring Discrepancies Between Words and Intention; Models of Inconsistency Resolution." *Journal of Personality and Social Psychology* 30 (1974): 125–133.

Bugental, D., J. Blue, and M. Cruzcosa. "Perceived Control over Caregiving Outcomes: Implications for Child Abuse." *Developmental Psychology* 25 (1989): 532–539.

Bugental, D., L. Caporael, and W. A. Shennum. "Experimentally Produced Child Uncontrollability: Effects on the Potency of Adult Communication Patterns." *Child Development* 51 (1980): 520–528.

Bugental, D., J. W. Kaswan, and L. R. Love. "Perception of Contradictory Meanings Conveyed by Verbal and Nonverbal Channels." *Journal of Personality and Social Psychology* 16 (1970): 647–655.

Bugental, D., L. Love, and R. Gianetto. "Perfidious Feminine Faces." *Journal of Personality and Social Psychology* 17 (1971): 314–318.

Bugental, D., et al. "Child Versus Adult Perception of Evaluative Messages in Verbal, Vocal and Visual Channels." *Developmental Psychology* 2 (1970): 367–375.

Bukatko, D., and M. Daehler. *Child Development: A Thematic Approach.* Boston, Mass.: Houghton Mifflin, 1995.

Bukatko, D., and M. W. Daehler. *Child Development: A Topical Approach.* New York: Houghton Mifflin, 1995.

Bukowski, W. J. "Age Differences in Children's Memory of Information about Aggressive, Socially Withdrawn, and

Prosocial Boys and Girls." *Child Development* 61 (1990): 1326–1334.

Bukowski, W. M., L. K. Sippola, and M. Boivin. "Friendship Protects 'At Risk' Children from Victimization by Peers." Paper presented at the meeting of the Society for Research in Child Development, Indianapolis, March 1995.

Burgoon, J. K., and L. Saine. "A Communication Model of Personal Space Violations: Explanation and an Initial Test." *Human Communication Research* 4, no. 2, (1978): 129–142.

Burton, R. V. "A Paradox in Theories and Research in Moral Development." In *Morality, Moral Behavior, and Moral Development,* edited by W. M. Kurtines and J. L. Gewirtz. New York: Wiley, 1984.

Burts, D., C. Hart, and R. Charlesworth. *Integrated Curriculum and Developmentally Appropriate Practice.* New York: State University of New York Press, 1997.

Buss, A. H., and R. Plomin. *A Temperament Theory of Personality.* New York: John Wiley & Sons, Inc., 1975.

Butterfield, R., and G. N. Siperstein. "The Mouth of the Infant." In *Third Symposium on Oral Sensation and Perception,* edited by J. F. Bosma. Springfield, Ill.: Charles C. Thomas, Publisher, 1972.

Byrne, D., and W. A. Griffit. "A Developmental Investigation of the Law of Attraction." *Journal of Personality and Social Psychology* 4 (1966): 699–702.

Cairns, R. B. *Social Development: The Origins and Plasticity of Interchanges.* San Francisco: W. H. Freeman & Company, Publishers, 1979.

Caldera, Y., A. Huston, and M. O'Brien. "Social Interactions and Play Patterns of Parents and Toddlers with Feminine, Masculine, and Neutral Toys." *Child Development* 60 (1989): 70–76.

Caldwell, B. M. "Aggression and Hostility in Young Children."*Young Children* 32 (January 1977): 4–13.

Calkins, S. "Origins and Outcomes of Individual Differences in Emotion Regulation." In *The Development of Emotion Regulation: Biological and Behavioral Considerations,* edited by N. A. Fox. Monographs of the Society for Research in Child Development, 240 (59), nos. 2–3 (1994): 53–61.

Campos, J. J., et al. "Socioemotional Development." In *Handbook of Child Psychology,* Vol. 2, edited by P. H. Hussen, New York: John Wiley & Sons, Inc., 1983.

Canavan, J. W. "Sexual Child Abuse." In *Child Abuse and Neglect: A Medical Reference,* edited by N. S. Ellerstein. New York: John Wiley & Sons, Inc., 1981, 233–253.

Canter, L. and M. Canter. *Assertive Discipline.* Santa Monica, Calif: Canter and Associates, Inc., 1983.

Carkhuff, R. R. *Helping and Human Relations: A Primer for Lay and Professional Helpers. Vol. I: Selection and Training.* New York: Holt, Rinehart & Winston, 1969.

Carlson, E. A., D. Jacobvitz, and L. A. Stroufe. "A Developmental Investigation of Inattentiveness and Hyperactivity." *Child Development* 66 (1995): 37–54.

Carlsson-Paige, N., and D. Levin. "Young Children and War Play." *Educational Leadership* (1988): 80–84.

Carlsson-Paige, N., and D. Levin. "Making Peace in Violent Times: A Constructionist Approach to Conflict Resolution." *Young Children* 48, no. 1 (1992): 4–13.

Carroll, J. J., and M. S. Steward. "The Role of Cognitive Development in Children's Understanding of Their Own Feelings." *Child Development* 55 (1984): 1486–1492.

Carson, D., et al. "Temperament and Communicative Competence as Predictors of Young Children's Humor." *Merrill Palmer Quarterly* 32, no. 4, (1986): 415–426.

Carter, D. B., and G. D. Levy. "Cognitive Aspects of Early Sex Role Development: The Influence of Génder Schemas or Preschoolers' Memories and Preferences for Sex-Typed Toys and Activities." *Child Development* 59 (1988): 782–792.

Carter, M. "Developing a Cultural Disposition in Teachers." *Exchange* 5 (1993): 52–55.

Case, R., and Y. Okamoto. *The Role of Central Conceptual Structures in the Development of Children's Thought.* Monographs of the Society for Research in Child Development. Vol. 61, no. 2, serial no. 246. Chicago: University of Chicago Press, 1996.

Casey, M., and M. Lippman. Learning to Play through Play. *Young Children* 46 (1991): 52–58.

Cassidy, D. J. "Questioning the Young Child: Process and Function." *Childhood Education* 65 (1989): 146–149.

Cavallaro, S., and R. Porter. "Peer Preferences of At-Risk and Normally Developing Children in A Preschool Mainstream Classroom." *American Journal of Mental Deficiency* 84 (1980): 357–366.

Cazden, C. B. *Language in Early Childhood Education.* Washington, D.C.: National Association for the Education of Young Children, 1972.

Center to Control Handgun Violence. *Personal Communication.* Washington, D.C., 1991.

Center for Disease Control. *AIDS Monthly Surveillance Report,* 1996.

Center for the Study of Social Policy. The Challenge of Change: What the 1990 Census Tells Us about Children. Washington, D.C., Center for the Study of Social Policy, 1992.

Cernock, J., and R. H. Porter. "Recognition of maternal axillary orders by infants." *Child Development* 56 no. 6, (1985): 1593–1598.

Chaikin, A. L., and U. J. Derlega. *Self-Disclosure.* Morristown, N.J.: General Learning Press, 1974.

Chance, P. *Learning Through Play.* New York: Gardner Press, Inc., 1979.

Chandler, L. A. *Assessing Stress in Children.* New York: Praeger, 1985.

Chang, H. N. L., A. Muckelroy, and D. Pulido-Tobiassen. *Looking In, Looking Out.* San Francisco: California Tomorrow Publications, 1996.

Chapman, M., et al. "Empathy and Responsibility in the Motivation of Children's Helping." *Developmental Psychology* 23 (1987): 140–145.

Charles, C. M. *Elementary Classroom Management,* New York: Longman, Inc., 1983.

Charles, C. M. *Building Classroom Discipline*. White Plains, NY: Longman, 1996.

Cherlin, A. J., K. E. Kiernan, and P. L. Chase-Lansdale. "Parental Divorce in Childhood and Demographic Outcomes in Young Adulthood." *Demography* 32 (1995): 99–318.

Children's Defense Fund. *The State of America's Children Yearbook, 1996*. Washington, D.C.: Children's Defense Fund, 1996.

Children's Defense Fund. *The State of America's Children*. Washington, D.C.: Children's Defense Fund, 1997.

Children's Rights Council. "Speak Out for Children." *Children's Rights Council, Inc.,* 11, no. 3 (Summer 1996): 9.

Chomsky, N. *Syntactic Structures*. The Hague: Mouton Publishers, 1957.

Chukovsky, K. "The Sense of Nonsense Verse." In *Play: Its Role in Development and Evolution*, edited by J. S. Bruner, A. Jolly, and K. Sylva. New York: Basic Books, Inc., Publishers, 1976, 596–602.

Clarizio, H. *Toward Positive Classroom Discipline*. New York: John Wiley & Sons, Inc., 1980.

Clarizio, H. *Contemporary Issues in Educational Psychology*. Boston: Allyn and Bacon, Inc., 1981.

Clarke-Stewart, A. *NEA Today* (January, 1989): 60–64.

Clarke-Stewart, A., S. Friedman, and J. Koch. *Child Development: A Topical Approach*. New York: John Wiley & Sons, Inc., 1985.

Clarke-Stewart, A., and J. B. Koch. *Children: Development through Adolescence*. New York: John Wiley & Sons, Inc., 1983.

Clary, E. G., and J. Miller. "Socialization and Situational Influences on Sustained Altruism." 57 (1986): 1358–1369.

Claussen, A. H., and P. M. Crittenden. "Physical and Psychological Maltreatment: Relations among Types of Maltreatment." *Child Abuse and Neglect* 15 (1991): 5–18.

Clewett, A. S. "Guidance and Discipline: Teaching Young Children Appropriate Behavior." *Young Children* 43, no. 4, Washington, D.C.: NAEYC, 1988, 26–31.

Click, P. M. *Administration of Schools for Young Children*. Albany, N.Y.: Delmar Publishers, 1995.

Clymen, R. B., et al. "Social Referencing and Social Looking among Twelve-Month-Old Infants." In *Affective Development in Infancy*, edited by T. B. Brazelton and M. W. Youeman. Norwood, N.J.: Abex, 1986, 75–94.

Cohen, B., J. S. De Loache, and M. S. Strauss. "Infant Visual Perception." In *Handbook of Infant Development*, edited by J. D. Osofsky. New York: John Wiley & Sons, Inc., 1979, 393–438.

Coie, J. D. "The Adolescence of Peer Relations." Paper presented at the biennial meeting of the Society for Research in Child Development, New Orleans, March 1993.

Coie, J. D., and K. A. Dodge. "Continuities and Changes in Children's Social Status: A Five-Year Longitudinal Study." *Merrill-Palmer Quarterly* 29 (1983): 261–282.

Coie, J. D., K. A. Dodge, and J. B. Kupersmidt. "Peer Group Behavior and Social Status." In *Peer Rejection in Childhood*, edited by S. R. Asher and J. D. Coie. New York: Cambridge University Press, 1990, 17–59.

Coie, J. D., and G. K. Koeppl. "Adapting Intervention to the Problems of Aggressive and Disruptive Rejected Children." In *Peer Rejection in Childhood*, edited by S. R. Asher and J. D. Coie. New York: Cambridge University Press, 1990.

Coie, J. D., et al. "The Role of Aggression in Peer Relations: An Analysis of Aggression Episodes in Boys' Play Groups." *Child Development* 62 (1991): 812–826.

Coleman, J. S. "Families and Schools." *Educational Researcher* 16 (1987): 32–38.

Coletta, A. J. "Positive Discipline: Effective Alternative Practices." Paper presented at the National Association for the Education of Young Children, Atlanta, GA, 1994.

Combs, M. L., and D. A. Slaby. "Social Skills Training with Children." In *Advances in Clinical Child Psychology*, edited by B. Lakey and A. Kazdin. New York: Plenum Publishing Corporation, 1978.

Comstock, G. "New Emphases in Research on the Effects of Television and Film Violence." In *Children and the Faces of Television: Teaching, Violence Selling*, edited by E. L. Palmer and A. Dorr. New York: Academic Press Inc., 1980, 129–144.

Coopersmith, S. *The Antecedents of Self-Esteem*. Princeton, N.J.: Princeton University Press, 1967.

Crary, E. *Without Spanking or Spoiling: A Practical Approach to Toddler and Preschool Guidance*. Seattle, Wash.: Parenting Press, 1993.

Crockenberg, S. B. "Infant irritability, mother responsiveness and social support influences on the security of infant-mother attachment." *Child Development* 52 (1981): 856–865.

Cross, J. F., and J. Cross. "Age, Sex, Race, and the Perception of Facial Beauty." *Developmental Psychology* 5 (1971): 433–439.

Crosser, S. "Managing the Early Childhood Classroom." *Young Children* 47, no. 2 (1992): 23–29.

Crossette, B. "Agency Sees Risk in Drug to Temper Childhood Behavior." *New York Times* 145 (February, 29, 1996): 7, 14.

Crow, G. A. *Children at Risk*. New York: Schocken Books, Inc. 1978.

Cryan, J. R. "The Banning of Corporal Punishment in Child Care, School and Other Educative Settings in the United States." *Childhood Education* (February 1987): 146–153.

Cummings, C., and K. Haggerty. "Raising Healthy Children." *Educational Leadership* 54, no. 8 (May 1997): 28–30.

Cunningham, M. R., et al. "Separate Processes in the Relation of Elation and Depression to Helping: Social Versus Personal Concerns." *Journal of Experimental Social Psychology* 26 (1990): 13–33.

Curry, N., and S. Arnaud. "Dramatic Play as a Degenerative Aid in the Preschool." In *The Puzzling Child*, edited by M. Frank. New York: Haworth, 1982, 37–48.

Curry, N., and D. Bergen. "The Relationship of Play to Emotional, Social, and Gender/Sex Role Development." In *Play As a Medium for Learning and Development: A Handbook for Theory and Practice,* edited by D. Bergen. Portsmouth, N.H.: Heinemann, 1987.

Curry, N. E., and C. N. Johnson. *Beyond Self-Esteem: Developing a Genuine Sense of Human Value.* Washington, D.C.: Research Monograph of the National Association for the Education of Young Children, Vol. 4, 1990.

Cushman, J. H. "Children's Health Is to Guide E.P.A." *The New York Times* (September 12, 1996): A-8.

Damon, W., ed., *New Directions for Child Development: Moral Development.* Vol. 2. San Francisco: Jossey-Bass, Inc., Publishers, 1978.

Damon, W. *Social and Personality Development.* New York: W. W. Norton & Company, 1983.

Damon, W. "The Moral Child." *New York Free Press,* 1988.

Damon, W. "Self Concept, Adolescent." In *Encyclopedia of Adolescence,* Vol. 2, edited by R. M. Lerner, A. C. Petersen, and J. Brooks-Gunn. New York: Garland, 1991.

Damon, W., and D. Hart. "The Development of Self-Understanding from Infancy Through Adolescence." *Child Development* 53 (1982): 841–864.

Damon, W., and D. Hart. *Self-Understanding in Childhood and Adolescence.* New York: Cambridge University Press, 1988.

Danish, S. J., and A. L. Hauer. *Helping Skills: A Basic Training Program.* New York: Behavioral Publications, 1984.

Darville, D., and J. A. Cheyne. "Sequential Analysis of Response to Aggression: Age and Sex Effects." Paper presented at the Biannual Meeting of the Society for Research in Child Development, Boston, 1981.

Davies, D. "Schools Reaching Out." *Phi Delta Kappan* 72, no. 5, (January, 1991): 376–382.

Dayton, G. O., et al. "Developmental Study of Coordinated Eye Movements in the Human Infant. I. Visual Acuity in the Newborn Human: A Study Based on Induced Optokinetic Nystagmus Recorded by Electro-oculography." *Archives of Ophthalmology* 71 (1964): 865–870.

Deacon, R., and F. Firebaugh. *Family Resource Management: Principles and Applications.* Boston: Allyn and Bacon, Inc., 1981.

DeAngelis, T. "Homeless Families: Stark Reality of the '90s." *APA Monitor* 1, no. 38 (May 1994).

DeCasper, A. J., and W. P. Fifer. "Of Human Bonding: Newborns Prefer Their Mothers' Voices." *Science* 208 (1980): 1174–1176.

Delaphenha, L. B. *Strategies for Teaching Young Children at Risk and/or Prenatally Exposed to Drugs.* Tampa, Fla.: Hillsborough County Public Schools, 1993.

Denham, S. A. "Scaffolding Young Children's Prosocial Responsiveness: Preschoolers' Responses to Adult Sadness, Anger, and Pain." *International Journal of Behavioral Development* 18, no. 3 (September 1995): 489–504.

Derman-Sparks, L. *Anti Bias Curriculum: Tools for Empowering Young Children.* Washington, DC: National Association for the Education of Young Children, 1989.

Desor, J. A., O. Maller, and L. S. Green. "Preference for Sweet in Humans: Infants, Children, and Adults." In *Taste and Development: The Genesis of Sweet Preference,* edited by J. M. Wuffenback, Bethesda, Md.: U.S. Department of Health, Education, and Welfare, 1977, 161–172.

deVogue, K. "Conflict Resolution with Children in Grade School." Presentation to Forest View Elementary School Teachers, Lansing, Mich., March 1996.

Dillon, J. T. "Using Questions to Depress Student Thought." *School Review* 87 (November 1978): 50–63.

Dillon, J. T. "To Question and Not to Question During Discussion: Non-Questioning Techniques." *Journal of Teacher Education* B, no. 6 (1981): 15–20.

DiMartino, E. C. "Understanding Children from Other Cultures." *Childhood Education* 66, no. 1 (1989): 30–32.

Dinkmeyer, D. *Developing Understanding of Self and Others (DUSO).* Circle Pines, Minn.: American Guidance Service, Inc., 1970.

Dinkmeyer, D., and G. D. McKay. *Systematic Training for Effective Parenting.* Circle Pines, Minn.: American Guidance Service, Inc., 1988.

Dittrichova, J., and K. Paul. "Behavioral States in Infants." *Ceskoslovensko Psychologie* 15 (1971): 529–538.

DiVesta, F. J. *Language, Learning, and Cognitive Processes.* Monterey, Calif.: Brooks/Cole Publishing Company, 1974.

DiVesta, F. J., and J. P. Richards. "Effects of Labeling and Articulation on the Attainment of Concrete, Abstract, and Number Concepts." *Journal of Experimental Psychology* 88 (1971): 41–49.

Dobson J. *Dare to Discipline.* Wheaton, Ill.: Tyndale House Publishers, 1987.

Dodge, D. T., A. L. Dombro, and D. G. Koralek. *Caring for Infants and Toddlers, Vol. II.* Mt. Ranier, Md.: Gryphon House, Inc., 1991.

Dodge, K. A. "Behavioral Antecedents of Peer Social Status." *Child Development* 54 (1983): 1386–1399.

Dodge, K. A. "Facts of Social Interaction and the Assessment of Social Competence in Children." In *Children's Peer Relations: Issues in Assessment and Interventions,* edited by B. H. Schneider. New York: Springer-Verlag, 1985, 3–22.

Dodge, K. A. "A Social Information Processing Model of Social Competence in Children." In *Minnesota Symposia on Child Psychology,* Vol. 18, edited by M. Perlmutter. Hillsdale, N.J.: Erlbaum, 1986.

Dodge, K. A., and Frame, C. L. "Social Cognitive Biases and Deficits in Aggressive Boys." *Child Development* 53 (1982): 620–635.

Dodge, K. A., R. R. Murphy, and K. Buchsbaum. "The Assessment of Intention-Cue Detection Skills in Children: Implications for Psychopathology." *Child Development* 55 (1984): 163–173.

Dodge, K. A., et al. *Social Competence in Children.* Monographs for the Society for Research in Child Development. 515 (2, Serial No. 213), 1986.

Doherty-Derkowski, G. *Quality Matters: Excellence in Early Childhood Programs.* New York: Addison-Wesley Publishers Ltd., 1995.

Dolgin, K. "The Importance of Playing Alone: Differences in Manipulative Play Under Social and Solitary

Conditions." In *Play As Context*, edited by A. Cheska. West Point, N.Y.: Leisure Press, 1981, 238–247.

Dollard, J., et al. *Frustration and Aggression*. New Haven, Conn.: Yale University Press, 1939.

Donovan, W., and L. Leavitt. "Physiology and Behavior: Parents' Response to the Infant Cry." In B. M. Lester and C. F. Z. Boukydis (Eds.) *Infant Crying: Theoretical and Research Perspectives*. New York: Plenum, 1985.

Dornbusch, S. M., et al. "The Relation of Parenting Style to Adolescent School Performance." *Child Development* 58 (1987): 1244–1257.

Dorr, A. "Contexts for Experience With Emotion, With Special Attention to Television." *The Socialization of Emotion*, edited by M. Lewis and C. Saarni. New York: Plenum, 1985, 55–85.

Doyle, P. "The Differential Effects of Multiple- and Single-Niche Play Activities on Interpersonal Relations Among Pre-schoolers." In *Play As Context*, edited by A. Cheska. West Point, N.Y.: Leisure Press, 1981.

Drake, J. D. *Interviewing for Managers: Sizing Up People*. New York: American Management Association, 1972.

Dreikurs, R. *The Challenge of Child Training: A Parent's Guide*. New York: Hawthorn Books, Inc., 1991.

Dreikurs, R., and P. Cassel. *Discipline Without Tears*. New York: Hawthorn Books, Inc., 1992.

Dreikurs, R., and L. Grey. *Logical Consequences*. New York: Dutton, 1990.

Dreikurs, R., and V. Soltz. *Children: The Challenge*. New York: Hawthorn Books, Inc., 1964.

Du Pont, R. L. "Phobias in Children." *Journal of Pediatrics* 102, no. 6 (1983): 999–1002.

Duffy, R. "Time-Out: How It Is Abused." *Child Care Information Exchange* 3 (September 1996): 61–62.

Dunn, J., J. R. Brown, and M. Maguire. "The Development of Children's Moral Sensibility: Individual Differences in Emotion Understanding." *Developmental Psychology* 31 (1995): 649–659.

Dunne, J. "Clear Creek ISD Trustee Margaret Snook Speaks Out." *P.O.P.S. News* Houston, Tex: Newsletter of People Opposed to Paddling Students, Inc., Spring 1990, 3.

Eames, T. H. "Physical Factors in Reading." *The Reading Teacher* 15 (1962): 427–432.

Eaton, W. O., and D. Von Vargen. "Asynchronous Development of Gender Understanding in Preschool Children." *Child Development* 52 (1981): 1020–1027.

Eckerman, C. "The Attainment of Interactive Skills: A Major Task of Infancy." Colloquium address given at the University of Virginia, Charlottesville, October 1978.

Eddy, J. M., and W. F. Alles. *Death Education*. St. Louis: The C.V. Mosby Company, 1983.

Edelman, M. W. "Testimony Prepared for the Joint Senate-House Hearing on Keeping Every Child Safe: Curbing the Epidemic of Violence." 103rd Congress, 1st session, March 10, 1993.

Educational Products, Inc. *Good Talking to You*. Portland, Ore.: EPI, 1988.

Egan, G. *The Skilled Helper*. Pacific Grove, Calif.: Brooks/Cole Publishing Co., 1994.

Egeland, B., L. A. Sroufe, and M. Erickson. "The Developmental Consequences of Different Patterns of Maltreatment." *International Journal of Child Abuse and Neglect* 7 (1983): 459–469.

Eiferman, R. "Social Play in Childhood." In *Child's Play*, edited by R. Herron and B. Sutton-Smith. New York: John Wiley & Sons, Inc., 1971, 270–297.

Eisenberg, N. "Sex-Typed Toy Choices: What Do They Signify?" In *Social and Cognitive Skills: Sex Roles and Children's Play*, edited by M. Liss. New York: Academic Press, Inc., 1983, 45–74.

Eisenberg, N. *Altruistic Emotion, Cognition and Behavior*. Hillsdale, N.J.: Lawrence Erlbaum Associates, Inc., 1986.

Eisenberg, N., R. Lennon, and K. Roth. "Prosocial Development: A Longitudinal Study." *Developmental Psychology* 19 (1983): 846–855.

Eisenberg, N., et al. "The Relations of Emotionality and Regulation to Children's Anger-Related Reactions." *Child Development* 65 (1994): 109–128.

Eisenberg, N., et al. "The Role of Emotionality and Regulation in Children's Social Functioning: A Longitudinal Study." *Child Development* 66 (1995a): 1360–1384.

Eisenberg, N., et al. "Prosocial Development in Late Adolescence: A Longitudinal Study." *Child Development* 66 (1995b): 1179–1197.

Ekman, P., and R. Davidson, eds. *Fundamental Questions About Emotions*. New York: Oxford University Press, 1994.

Ekman, P., and W. Friesen. "The Repertoire of Nonverbal Behavior: Categories, Origins, Usage, and Coding." *Semiotica* 1 (1969): 49–98.

Ekman, P., W. Friesen, and P. Ellsworth. *Emotion in the Human Face: Guideline for Research and Integration of Findings*. New York: Pergamon Press, Inc., 1972.

Elkind, D. *The Hurried Child—Growing Up Too Fast Too Soon*. Reading, Mass.: Addison-Wesley Publishing Company, Inc., 1981.

El 'Konin, D. "Symbolics and Its Functions in the Play of Children." In *Child's Play*, edited by R. Herron and B. Sutton-Smith. New York: John Wiley & Sons, Inc., 1971, 221–230.

Ellis, M. J. *Why People Play*. Englewood Cliffs, N.J.: Prentice-Hall, Inc., 1973.

Emde, R. N., T. J. Gaensbauer, and R. J. Harmon. "Emotional Expression in Infancy: A Biobehavioral Study." *Psychological Issues* 10, no. 1 (1976): 3–198.

Emde, R. N., et al. "The Moral Self of Infancy. Affective Core and Procedural Knowledge." *Developmental Review* 11 (1991): 251–270.

Engen, T., and L. P. Lipsitt. "Decrement and Recovery of Responses to Olfactory Stimuli in the Human Neonate." *Journal of Comparative and Physiological Psychology* 59 (1965): 312–316.

Epstein, J. L. "Paths to Partnership." *Phi Delta Kappan* 72, no. 5 (January 1991): 344–349.

Erikson, E. H. *Childhood and Society*. Rev. ed. New York: W. W. Norton & Co., Inc., 1950, 1963.

Eron, L. D., and L. R. Huesmann. "The Control of Aggressive Behavior By Changes in Attitudes, Values and the Conditions of Learning." In *Advances in the Study of Aggression*, Vol. 2, edited by R. J. Blanchard and C. Blanchard. New York: Academic Press, 1984.

Eron, L. D., et al. "Aggression and Its Correlates over 22 Years." In *Childhood Aggression and Violence*, edited by D. H. Crowell, I. M. Evans, and C. P. O'Connell. New York: Plenum Press, 1987.

Essa, E. *A Practical Guide to Solving Preschool Behavior Problems*. Albany, N.Y.: Delmar Publishing, 1995.

Everett, C., and S. Everett. *Healthy Divorce*. San Francisco: Jossey-Bass Publishers, 1994.

Evers, W. L., and J. C. Schwarz. "Modifying Social Withdrawal in Preschoolers: The Effects of Filmed Modeling and Teacher Praise." *Journal of Abnormal Child Psychology* 1 (1973): 248–256.

Fabes, R. A. "How Children Learn Self-Control." *Two to Twelve* 2, no. 5 (May 1984): 1–3.

Fabes, R. A., et al. "Effect of Rewards on Children's Prosocial Motivation: A Socialization Study." *Developmental Psychology* 25 (1989): 509–515.

Fagen, R. *Animal Play Behavior*. New York: Oxford University Press, 1981.

Fagot, B. "Consequences of Moderate Cross Gender Behavior in Preschool Children." *Child Development* 48 (1977): 902–907.

Fagot, B. "Reinforcing Contingencies for Sex Role Behaviors: Effect of Experience with Children." *Child Development* 49 (1978): 30–36.

Fagot, B., and R. Hagan. "Hitting in Toddler Groups: Correlates and Continuity." Paper presented at the Annual Meeting of the American Psychological Association, Washington, D.C., 1982.

Faller, K. C. *Understanding Child Sexual Maltreatment*. Newbury Park, Calif.: Sage, 1990.

Farrington, D. P. "Childhood Origins of Teenage Antisocial Behavior and Adult Social Dysfunction." *Journal of the Royal Society of Medicine* 86 (1993): 13–16.

Feeney, S., and L. Sysko. "Professional Ethics in Early Childhood Education: Survey Results." *Young Children* 45, no. 1 (1986): 24–29.

Feldman, R. S., L. Jenkins, and O. Popoola. "Detection of Deception in Adults and Children via Facial Expressions." *Child Development* 50 (1979): 350–355.

Feldman, R. S., J. B. White, and D. Lobato. "Social Skills and Nonverbal Behavior." In *Development of Nonverbal Behavior in Children*, edited by R. Feldman. New York: Springer-Verlag New York, Inc., 1982, 257–278.

Ferguson, T. J., and B. G. Rule. "Children's Evaluations of Retaliatory Aggression." *Child Development* 59 (1988): 961–968.

Feshbach, N. D., "Empathy Training: A Field Study of Affective Education." Paper presented at the annual meeting of the American Educational Research Association, March, 1978.

Feshbach, N. D., and S. Feshbach. "Children's Aggression." In *The Young Child: Review of Research*, Vol 2, edited by W. H. Hartup. Washington, D.C.: National Association for the Education of Young Children, 1976.

Feshbach, N., and S. Feshbach. "Empathy Training and the Regulation of Aggression: Potentialities and Limitations." *Academic Psychology Bulletin* 4 (1982): 399–413.

Feshbach, S. "Aggression." In *Carmichael's Manual of Child Psychology*, edited by P. Mussen. New York: John Wiley & Sons, Inc., 1970, 159–259.

Feshbach, S. "Child Abuse and the Dynamics of Human Aggression and Violence." In *Child Abuse: An Agenda for Action*, edited by G. Gerbner, C. J. Ross, and E. Zigler. New York: Oxford University Press, 1980.

Feyereisen, P., and J. deLannoy. *Gestures and Speech: Psychological Investigations*. Cambridge: Cambridge University Press, 1991.

Field, T. M., and E. Ignatoff. "Interaction of Twins and Their Mothers." Unpublished manuscript, University of Miami, 1980. As referred to by Campos, et al., "Socioemotional Development." In *Handbook of Child Psychology*, Vol 2, edited by P. Mussen. New York: John Wiley & Sons, Inc., 783–916.

Fields, M. V., and C. Boesser. *Constructive Guidance and Discipline: Preschool and Primary Education*. Columbus, Ohio: Merrill, 1994.

Finkelhor, D. "Early and Long-Term Effects of Child Sexual Abuse: An Update." *Professional Psychology: Research and Practice* 21, no. 5 (October 1990): 325–330.

Fitch, S. K. *The Science of Child Development*. Homewood, Ill.: The Dorsey Press, 1985.

Fitch, S. K. *Insights into Child Development*. Redding, Calif.: C.A.T. Publishing, 1995.

Flavell, J. H. *The Developmental Psychology of Jean Piaget*. New York: Van Nostrand Reinhold Co., Inc., 1963.

Flavell, J. H. *Cognitive Development*. Englewood Cliffs, N.J.: Prentice-Hall, Inc., 1977.

Flavell, J. H. *Cognitive Development*. 2nd ed. Englewood Cliffs, N.J.: Prentice-Hall, 1985.

Flavell, J. H., and J. F. Wohlwill. "Formal and Functional Aspects of Cognitive Development." In *Studies in Cognitive Development: Essays in Honor of Jean Piaget*, edited by D. Elkind and J. H. Flavell. New York: Oxford University Press, 1969, 67–120.

Forbes, D. "Recent Research on Children's Social Cognition: A Brief Review." In *New Directions for Child Development*, edited by W. Damon. San Francisco: Jossey-Bass, Inc., Publishers, 1978.

Fox, J., and R. Tipps. "Young Children's Development of Swinging Behaviors." *Early Childhood Research Quarterly* 10 (1995): 491–504.

Fox, N. A., ed. "The Development of Emotion Regulation: Biological and Behavioral Considerations." *Monographs of the Society for Research in Child Development* 240, no. 59 (1994): 2–3.

Fraiberg, S. *The Magic Years*. New York: Charles Scribner's Sons, 1968.

Frankenburg, W. K. *Denver II Training Manual*. 2nd Ed. Denver: DDM, Inc., 1992.

Franz, C. E., D. C. McClelland, and R. L. Weinberger. "Childhood Antecedents of Conventional Social Accomplishment in Mid-Life Adults: A 36-Year Prospective Study." *Journal of Personality and Social Psychology* 60 (1991): 586–595.

Frauenglass, M. H., and R. M. Diaz. "Self-Regulatory Functions of Children's Private Speech: A Critical Analysis of Challenges to Vygotsky's Theory." *Developmental Psychology* 21 (1985): 357–364.

Freeman, N. K., and M. H. Brown. "Ethics Instruction for Preservice Teachers: How Are We Doing in ECE? The Public's and Our Profession's Growing Concern with Ethics." *Journal of Early Childhood Teacher Education.* 17, no. 2 (Spring/Summer 1996): 5–18.

French, J. H. A Historical Study of Children's Heros and Fantasy Play. (ERIC Document) Boise State University, ID: School of Education, 1987.

Freud, S. *A General Introduction to Psychoanalysis.* Garden City, N.Y.: Doubleday & Company Inc., 1938.

Freud, S. *Jokes and Their Relation to the Unconscious.* New York: W. W. Norton & Co., Inc., 1960.

Friedrich, L. K., and A. H. Stein. "Aggressive and Prosocial Television Programs and the Natural Behavior of Preschool Children." *Monographs of the Society for Research in Child Development* 38 (151), 1973.

Friedrich, L. K., and A. H. Stein. "Prosocial Television and Young Children: The Effects of Verbal Labeling and Role-Playing on Learning and Behavior." *Child Development* 46 (1973): 27–38.

Friedrich, W. N., and J. A. Boriskin. "The Role of the Child in Abuse: A Review of the Literature." *American Journal of Orthopsychiatry* 46 (1976): 580–590.

Fromm, E. *The Art of Living.* New York: Harper & Row, Publishers, Inc., 1956.

Frost, J. *Play and Playscapes.* Albany, NY: Delmar Publishers Inc, 1992.

Frye, D. "Developmental Changes in Strategies of Social Interaction." In *Infant Social Cognition: Empirical and Theoretical Considerations,* edited by M. Lamb and L. Sherrod. Hillsdale, N.J.: Lawrence Erlbaum Associates, Inc., 1981.

Fuchs, D., and M. H. Thelen. "Children's Expected Interpersonal Consequences of Communicating Their Affective State and Reported Likelihood of Expression." *Child Development* 59 (1988): 1314–1322.

Furman, R. A. "Helping Children Cope with Stress and Deal with Feelings." *Young Children* 50, no. 2 (January 1995): 33–41.

Gage, N. L., and D. C. Berliner. *Educational Psychology.* Boston: Houghton Mifflin, 1992.

Galambos-Stone, J. *A Guide To Discipline.* Washington D.C.: National Association for the Education of Young Children, 1994.

Gall, M. *Minicourse Nine: Higher Cognitive Questioning, Teachers' Handbook.* Beverly Hills: Macmillan Educational Services, Inc., 1971.

Gallahue, D. "Transforming Physical Education Curriculum." *Reaching Potentials: Transforming Early Childhood Curriculum and Assessment,* vol. 2, edited by S. Bredekamp and T. Rosegrant. Washington, D.C.: NAEYC, 1995, 125–144.

Garbarino, J. "An Ecological Approach to Child Maltreatment." In *The Social Context of Child Abuse and Neglect,* edited by L. Pelton. New York: Human Services Press, 1981.

Garbarino, J. *Children and Families in the Social Environment.* 2d ed. New York: Aldine de Gruyter, 1992.

Garbarino, J. *Raising Children in a Socially Toxic Environment.* San Francisco: Jossey-Bass Publishers, 1995.

Garbarino, J., and G. Gilliam. *Understanding Abusive Families.* Lexington, Mass.: D. C. Heath & Company, 1980.

Garber, J., et al. "Depression in Preschoolers: Reliability and Validity of Behavioral Observation Measure." Paper presented at the Society for Research in Child Development, Toronto, 1985.

Garber, J., and M. E. P. Seligman. *Human Helplessness: Theory and Applications.* New York: Academic Press, 1980.

Gardner, H. "Reflections on Multiple Intelligences: Myths and Messages." *Phi Delta Kappan,* 77, no. 2 (1995).

Gardner, J. K. *Developmental Psychology.* Boston: Little, Brown & Company, 1981.

Gardner, R. A. *The Parent's Book About Divorce.* Toronto: Bantam Books, Inc., 1977.

Gareau, M., and C. Kennedy. "Structure Time and Space to Promote Pursuit of Learning in Primary Grades." *Young Children* 46, no. 4 (1991): 46–51.

Gargiulo, R. M., and S. B. Graves. "Parental Feelings." *Childhood Education* 67, no. 3 (Spring 1991): 176–178.

Garner, P. W., D. C. Jones, and J. L. Miner. "Social Competence Among Low-Income Preschoolers: Emotion Socialization Practices and Social Cognitive Correlates." *Child Development* 65 (1994): 622–637.

Gartrell, D. *A Guidance Approach to Discipline.* Albany, New York: Delmar Publishers, 1994.

Garvey, C. *Play.* Cambridge, Mass.: Harvard University Press, 1977.

Garvey, C., and R. Berndt. "Organization of Pretend Play." *JSAS Catalog of Selected Documents in Psychology* 1, ms. no. 1589 (1977).

Gazda, G. M. *Human Relations Development—A Manual for Educators.* 5th ed. Boston: Allyn and Bacon, Inc., 1995.

Gazda, G. M., W. Childers, and R. Walters. *Interpersonal Communication: A Handbook for Health Professionals.* Rockville, Md.: Aspen Systems Corp., 1982.

Gecas, V., J. M. Colonico, and D. L. Thomas. "The Development of Self-Concept in the Child: Mirror Theory Versus Model Theory." *Journal of Social Psychology* (1974): 466–482.

Geldhard, F. "Some Neglected Possibilities of Communication." *Science* 131 (1960): 1583–1584.

Gelfand, D. M., W. R. Jenson, and C. J. Drew. *Understanding Child Behavior Disorders.* New York: Holt, Rinehart & Winston, 1982.

Gelman, D. "The Miracle of Resiliency." In *Human Development—Annual Editions,* edited by K. L. Freiberg. Guilford, Conn.: Dushkin Publishing Group, 1997.

Gerbner, G., and N. Signorielli. "Violence on Television: The Cultural Indicators Project." *Journal of Broadcasting and Electronic Media* 39, no. 2 (1995): 278–283.

Gilligan, C. "Joining the Resistance: Girl's Development in Adolescence." Paper presented at the Symposium on Development and Vulnerability in Close Relationships, Montreal, May 1992.

Ginott, H. G. *Between Parent and Child.* New York: Avon Books, 1972.

Ginsberg, H. "And We Can Learn Together: Some Special Thoughts on Mainstreaming Children with Special Needs." Integration Project. East Lansing, Mich., Michigan State University, 1976.

Glasser, W. *Control Theory in the Classroom.* New York: Perennial Library, 1985.

Gnagey, W. "Controlling Classroom Misbehavior." What Research Says to the Teacher Series. Washington, D.C.: National Education Association, 1975.

Gnepp, J., and J. Klayman. "Recognition of Uncertainty in Emotional Inferences: Reasoning About Emotionally Equivocal Situations." *Developmental Psychology* 28 (1992): 145–158.

Goelman, H. "Conclusion: Emerging Ecological Perspectives on Play and Child Care." In *Children's Play in Child Care Settings,* edited by G. Goleman and E. Jacobs. Albany: State University of New York, 1994, 214–222.

Goffin, S. G. "How Well Do We Respect the Children in Our Care?" *Childhood Education* 66, no. 2 (1989): 68–74.

Goffman, E. *Interaction Ritual.* Chicago: Aldine Publishing Co., 1967.

Goldsmith, E. B. *Resource Management for Individuals and Families.* Minneapolis/St. Paul: West Publishing Co., 1996.

Goleman, D. *Psychology Updates.* New York: Harper-Collins, 1991.

Goleman, D. *Emotional Intelligence: Why It Can Matter More Than IQ.* New York: Bantam Books, 1995.

Gonzalez-Mena, J., and D. W. Eyer. *Infants, Toddlers and Caregivers.* Mountain View, CA: Mayfield Publishing, 1997.

Goossens, F., and M. Ijzendoorn. "Quality of Infants' Attachments to Professional Caregivers: Relation to Infant-Parent Attachment and Day-Care Characteristics." *Child Development* 61, no. 3 (1990): 832–837.

Gootman, M. "Discipline Alternatives that Work: Eight Steps Toward Classroom Discipline Without Corporal Punishment." *The Humanist* 48 (Nov./Dec. 1988): 11–14.

Gordon, J. "Teaching Kids to Negotiate." *Newsweek* (April 23, 1990): 65.

Gordon, T. *P.E.T. in Action.* Toronto: Bantam, 1978.

Gordon, T. *Discipline That Works: Promoting Self-Discipline in Children.* New York: Plume Books, 1992.

Gottman, J., J. Gonso, and B. Rasmussen. "Social Interaction, Social Competence and Friendship in Children." *Child Development* 46 (1975): 709–718.

Gottman, J., and J. Parkhurst. "A Developmental Theory of Friendship and Acquaintanceship Processes." In *Minnesota Symposia on Child Psychology,* Vol. 13, edited by W. A. Collins. Hillsdale, N.J.: Lawrence Erlbaum Associates, Inc., 1979.

Gould, R. *Child Studies Through Fantasy.* New York: Quadrangle Books, 1972.

Graves, S. B., R. M. Gargiulo, and L. C. Sluder. *Young Children: An Introduction to Early Childhood Education.* Minneapolis, Minn.: West Publishing Co., 1996.

Green, K., R. Forehand, and R. MacMahon. "Parental Manipulation of Compliance and Noncompliance in Normal and Deviant Children." *Behavior Modification* 3, no. 2 (1979): 245–266.

Greenberg, J. "Seeing Children Through Tragedy: My Mother Died Today—When Is She Coming Back?" *Young Children* 51, no. 6 (September 1996): 76–77.

Greenberg, P. "How to Institute Some Simple Democratic Practices Pertaining to Respect, Rights, Roots and Responsibilities in Any Classroom (without Losing Your Leadership Position)." *Young Children* 47, no. 5 (1992): 10–17.

Greenspan, S. "An Integrative Model of Caregiver Discipline." *Child Care Quarterly* 14, no. 1 (Spring 1985): 30–47.

Greenspan, S. I. *The Challenging Child.* New York: Addison-Wesley Publishing Company Inc., 1995.

Gregory, D. *Nigger: An Autobiography.* New York: E. P. Dutton, Inc., 1964.

Griffin, H. "The Coordination of Meaning in the Creation of a Shared Make Believe. "In *Symbolic Play,* edited by I. Bretherton. Orlando: Harcourt Brace Jovanovich, Inc., 1984.

Gronlund, N. E. *Sociometry in the Classroom.* New York: Harper & Row, Publishers, Inc., 1959.

Gross, I., E. Crandall, and M. Knoll. *Management for Modern Families.* Englewood Cliffs, N.J.: Prentice-Hall, Inc., 1980.

Gruendel, J. M. "Referential Extension in Early Language Development." *Child Development* 48 (1977): 1567–1576.

Grusec, J. E., and L. Arnason. "Consideration for Others: Approaches to Enhancing Altruism." In *The Young Child: Reviews of Research,* Vol. 3, edited by S. G. Moore and C. R. Cooper. Washington, D.C.: National Association for the Education of Young Children, 1982.

Grusec, J. E., and Mills, R. "The Acquisition of Self-Control." In *Psychological Development in the Elementary Years,* edited by J. Worrell. New York: Academic Press, 1982, 151–186.

Grusec, J. E., and Redler, E. "Attribution, Reinforcement, and Altruism: A Development Analysis." *Developmental Psychology* 16 (1980): 525–534.

Grusec, J. E., et al. "Learning Resistance to Temptation through Observation." *Developmental Psychology* 15 (1979): 233–240.

Guddemi, M. "Television and Young Children. The Effects of Television on Dramatic Play." Paper presented at the annual conference of the Southern Association on Children Under Six, March 5–8, 1986. ERIC document Ed. (1986): 267–929.

Guerney, L. *Foster Parent Training: A Manual for Parents.* University Park, Pa.: The Pennsylvania State University, 1975.

Guerney, L. *Parenting: A Skills Training Manual.* 2d ed. State College, Pa.: Ideals, 1980.

Guerney, L. "Understanding Children's Extreme Behaviors." *Two to Twelve: Current Issues in Children's Development* 2, no. 5 (May 1984): 7–9.

Guerney, L. Personal Communication, 1997.

Guinagh, B. "The Social Integration of Handicapped Children." *Phi Delta Kappan* 52, no. 1, 9 (1980): 27–29.

Guralnick, M. J. "The Value of Integrating Handicapped and Nonhandicapped Preschool Children." *American Journal of Orthopsychiatry* 46 (1976): 236–245.

Haeuser, A. A. "Swedish Parents Don't Spank." National Committee for the Prevention of Child Abuse, 1997, htp://www.cei.net/%Ercox/haeuser.html.

Halberstadt, A. "Toward an Ecology of Expressiveness." In *Fundamentals of Nonverbal Communication,* edited by P. Ekman and K. Scherer. Cambridge: Cambridge University Press, 1991.

Hale J. *Black Children: Their Roots, Cultures and Learning Styles.* Keynote address, presented at the Michigan Association for the Education of Young Children Annual Conference, Grand Rapids, Mich., March 1992.

Hall, E. T. *The Silent Language.* Garden City, N.Y.: Anchor Press/Doubleday, 1959, 1981.

Hall, E. T. *The Hidden Dimension.* Garden City, N.Y.: Doubleday & Company, Inc., 1966.

Hall, J. "Touch, Status, and Gender at Professional Meetings." *Journal of Nonverbal Behavior* 20, no. 1 (Spring 1996): 23–44.

Harris, M. "Children with Short Fuses." *Instructor* (November 1980): 170–171.

Harris, P. L. *Children and Emotion: The Development of Psychological Understanding.* New York: Basil Blackwell, Inc., 1989.

Harrison, A., and L. Nadelman. "Conceptual Tempo and Inhibition of Movement in Black Preschool Children." *Child Development* 43 (1972): 657–668.

Harter, S. "A Cognitive-Developmental Approach to Children's Expression of Conflicting Feelings and a Technique to Facilitate Such Expression in Play Therapy." *Journal of Consulting and Clinical Psychology* 45, no. 3 (1977): 417–432.

Harter, S. "Children's Understanding of Multiple Emotions: A Cognitive-Developmental Approach." Address given at the ninth annual meeting of the Piaget Society, Philadelphia, Pa., 1979.

Harter, S. "The Perceived Competence Scale for Children." *Child Development* 53 (1982): 87–97.

Harter, S. "Developmental Perspectives on the Self-System." In *Handbook of Child Psychology,* Vol. 4, edited by P. H. Mussen. New York: John Wiley & Sons, Inc., 1983.

Harter, S. "Competencies as a Dimension of Self-Evaluation: Toward a Comprehensive Model of Self-Worth." In *The Development of Self,* edited by L. Leahy. Orlando, FL: Academic Press, 1985.

Harter, S. "Cognitive-Developmental Processes in the Integration of Concepts about Emotions and the Self." *Social Cognition* 4 (1986): 119–151.

Harter, S. "Causes, Correlates, and the Functional Role of Global Self-Worth: A Life-Span Perspective." In R. J. Sternberg and J. Kelligan (Eds.), *Competence Considered.* New Haven, N.J.: Yale University Press, 1990, 67–97.

Harter, S. "Self and Identity Development." In *At the Threshold: The Developing Adolescent,* edited by S. S. Feldman and G. R. Elliott. Cambridge, Mass.: Harvard University Press, 1990.

Harter, S., P. C. Alexander, and R. A. Neimeyer. "Long-Term Effects of Incestuous Child Abuse in College Women: Social Adjustment, Social Cognition and Family Characteristics." *Journal of Consulting and Clinical Psychology* 56 (1988): 5–8.

Harter, S., and B. J. Buddin. "Children's Understanding of the Simultaneity of Two Emotions: a Five-Stage Developmental Acquisition Sequence." *Developmental Psychology* 23 (1987): 388–399.

Harter, S., and D. B. Marold. "Psychological Risk Factors Contributing to Adolescent Suicide Ideation." In *Child and Adolescent Suicide,* edited by G. Noam and S. Borst. San Francisco: Jossey-Bass Publishers, 1992.

Hartup, W. W. "Peer Interaction and Social Organization." In *Carmichael's Manual of Child Psychology,* Vol. 2, edited by P. H. Mussen. New York: John Wiley & Sons, Inc., 1970.

Hartup, W. W. "Aggression in Childhood: Developmental Perspectives." *American Psychologist* 29 (1974): 336–341.

Hartup, W. W. "Children and Their Friends." In *Issues in Childhood Social Development,* edited by H. McGurk. London: Methuen, Inc., 1978.

Hartup, W. W. "Peer Relations and Family Relations: Two Social Worlds." In *Scientific Foundations of Developmental Psychiatry.* London: Heinemann Medical Books, 1980.

Hartup, W. W. "Peer Relations." In *The Child Development in a Social Context,* edited by C. B. Kopp and J. B. Krakow. Reading, Mass: Addison-Wesley Publishing Co., Inc., 1982.

Hartup, W. W. "Peer Relations." In *Handbook of Child Psychology,* Vol. 4, edited by P. H. Mussen. New York: John Wiley & Sons, Inc., 1983.

Hartup, W. W. "Having Friends, Making Friends, and Keeping Friends: Relationships as Educational Contexts." *ERIC Digest.* Urbana, IL: ERIC Clearinghouse on Elementary and Early Childhood Education, 1991, 345–854.

Hartup, W. W., and S. G. Moore. "Early Peer Relations: Developmental Significance and Prognostic Implications." *Early Childhood Research Quarterly,* 5, no. 1 (1990): 1–18.

Havighurst, R. J. *Developmental Tasks and Education.* New York: Longman, Inc., 1954.

Hay, D., H. Ross, and B. D. Goldman. "Social Games in Infancy." In *Play and Learning,* edited by B. Sutton-Smith. New York: Gardner Press, Inc., 1979, 83–108.

Hay, D. F., and H. S. Ross. "The Social Nature of Early Conflict." *Child Development* 53 (1982): 105–113.

Hazen, N. L., and B. Black. "Preschool Peer Communication Skills: The Role of Social Status and Interaction Content." *Child Development* 60, no. 4 (1989): 867–876.

Heath, S. B. "Oral and Literate Traditions among Black Americans Living in Poverty." *American Psychologist* 44 (1989): 367–373.

Hegland, S. M., and M. K. Rix. "Aggression Assertiveness in Kindergarten Children Differing in Day Care Experiences." *Early Childhood Research Quarterly* 5 (1990): 105–116.

Hendrick, J. "Where Does It All Begin? Teaching Principles of Democracy in the Early Years." *Young Children* 47, no. 3 (1992): 51–53.

Hendrick, J. *The Whole Child.* Columbus, OH: Charles Merrill, 1996.

Hendrick, J. *Total Learning.* New York: Macmillan, 1998.

Henley, N. *Body Politics: Power, Sex and Nonverbal Communication.* Englewood Cliffs, N.J.: Prentice-Hall, Inc., 1977.

Herman, J., and J. P. Yeh. "Some Effects of Parent Involvement in Schools." *Resources in Education* 2 (1982).

Hetherington, E. M. "Divorce: A Child's Perspective." *American Psychologist* 10, no. 34 (1979): 851–858.

Hetherington, E. M., M. Stanley-Hagan, and E. R. Anderson. *Child Growth and Development—Annual Editions.* Guilford, Conn.: Dushkin Publishing Group, 1996.

Hetherington, M. "Long-Term Effects of Divorce and Remarriage on the Adjustment of Children." *Journal of the American Academy of Child Psychiatry* 24, no. 5 (September 1985): 515–530.

Hetherington, M. "Changes in and Stability of Cardiovascular Responses to Behavioral Stress: Results from a Four-Year Longitudinal Study of Children." *Child Development* 61 (1990): 1134–1144.

Hewitt, L. S. "The Effects of Provocation, Intentions and Consequences on Children's Moral Judgments." *Child Development* 46 (1975): 540–544.

Hicks, D. "Imitation and Retention of Film-Mediated Aggressive Peer and Adult Models." *Journal of Personality and Social Psychology* 2 (1965): 97–100.

Hildebrand, V. *Guiding Young Children.* 5th ed. New York: MacMillan Publishing Company, 1994.

Hitz, R., and A. Driscoll, "Praise or Encouragement?" *Young Children* 43, no. 5 (1988): 6–13.

Hoffman, C. D. "Pre- and Post-Divorce Father-Child Relationship and Child Adjustment: Non-Custodial Fathers' Perspectives." *Journal of Divorce and Remarriage* 23, nos. 1 and 2 (1995): 3, 20.

Hoffman, L. W. "Empathy, Its Limitations, and Its Role in a Comprehensive Moral Theory." In *Morality, Moral Behavior and Moral Development,* edited by W. M. Kurtines and J. L. Gewirtz. New York: Wiley, 1984.

Hoffman, M. "Affective and Cognitive Processes in Moral Internalization." In *Social Cognition and Social Behavior: Developmental Perspectives,* edited by E. T. Higgins, D. N. Ruble, and W. W. Hartup. New York: Cambridge University Press, 1983.

Hoffman, M. L. "Parent Discipline and the Child's Consideration of Others." *Child Development* 34 (1963): 573–585.

Hoffman, M. L. "Moral Internalization, Parental Power, and the Nature of the Parent-Child Interaction." *Developmental Psychology* 5 (1967): 45–57.

Hoffman, M. L. "Moral Development." In *Carmichael's Manual of Child Psychology,* Vol. 2, edited by P Mussen. New York: John Wiley & Sons, Inc., 1970, 262–360.

Hoffman, M. L. "Personality and Social Development." *Annual Review of Psychology* 28 (1977): 295–321.

Hoffman, M. L. "Development of Prosocial Motivation: Empathy and Guilt." In *The Development of Prosocial Behavior,* edited by N. Eisenberg-Berg. New York: Academic Press, Inc., 1982.

Hoffman, M. L. "Moral Development." In *Developmental Psychology: An Advanced Textbook,* edited by M. H. Bornstein and M. E. Lamb. Hillsdale, N.J.: Lawrence Erlbaum Associates, Inc., 1988.

Hoffman, M. L. "Empathy and Justice Motivation." *Motivation and Emotion* 14 (1990): 151–172.

Hoffner, C., and D. M. Badzinski. "Children's Integration of Facial and Situational Cues to Emotion." *Child Development* 60 (1989): 411–422.

Hohmann, M., and D. Weikart. *Educating Young Children: Active Learning Practices for Preschool and Child Care Programs.* Ypsilanti, Mich.: High Scope Educational Research Foundation, 1995.

Holden, G. "Changing the Way Kids Settle Conflicts." *Educational Leadership* 54, no. 8 (May 1997): 74–76.

Holmes, T., and R. Rahe. "The Social Readjustment Rating Scale." *Journal of Psychosomatic Research* 11 (1967): 213–218.

Holzman, M. "The Use of Interrogative Forms in the Verbal Interaction of Three Mothers and Their Children." *Journal of Psycholinguistic Research* 1, no. 4 (1972): 311–336.

Hom, H. L., Jr., and S. L. Hom. "Research and the Child: The Use of Modeling, Reinforcement/Incentives, and Punishment." In *Aspects of Early Childhood Education: Theory to Research to Practice,* edited by D. G. Range, J. R. Layton, and D. L. Roubinek. New York: Academic Press, Inc., 1980.

Honig, A. "Mental Health for Babies: What Do Theory and Research Teach Us?" Paper presented at the Annual Meeting of National Association for the Education of Young Children, New Orleans, La., November 12–15, 1992.

Honig, A. "Toddler Strategies for Social Engagement With Peers." Paper presented at the Biennial National Training Institute of the National Center for Clinical Infant Programs, Washington, D.C., December 1993.

Honig, A. S. "Prosocial Development in Children." *Children* 37, no. 5 (July 1982): 51–62.

Honig, A. S. "Compliance, Control and Discipline." *Young Children* 40, no. 3 (March 1985): 47–51.

Honig, A. S. "Stress and Coping in Children." *Young Children* 41, no. 5 (July 1986): 47–59.

Honig, A. S., and B. Pollack. "Effects of a Brief Intervention Program to Promote Prosocial Behaviors in Young Children." *Early Education and Development* 1, no. 6 (October 1990): 438–444.

Honig, A. S., and D. S. Wittmer. *Prosocial Development in Children: Caring, Sharing, and Cooperating: A Bibliographic Resource Guide.* New York: Garland, 1992.

Honig, A. S., and D. S. Wittmer. "Helping Children Become More Prosocial: Ideas for Classrooms, Families, Schools and Communities." *Young Children* 51, no. 2 (1996): 62–70.

Horowitz, I. A., and K. S. Bordens. *Social Psychology.* Mountain View, Calif.: Mayfield Publishing Co., 1995.

Hoversten, G. H., and J. P. Moncur. "Stimuli and Intensity Factors in Testing Infants." *Journal of Speech and Hearing Research* 12 (1969): 687–702.

Howe, N., et al: "The Ecology of Dramatic Play Centers and Children's Social and Cognitive Play." *Early Childhood Research Quarterly* 8 (1993): 235–251.

Howes, C. "Peer Interactions of Young Children." *Monographs of the Society for Research in Child Development* 53, serial no. 217 (1988): 1.

Hrncir, E. "Antecedents and Correlates of Stress and Coping in School Age Children." William T. Grant Foundation Fifth Annual Faculty Scholars Program in Mental Health of Children, 1985.

Humphreys, A., and P. K. Smith. "Rough-and-Tumble Play, Friendship and Dominance in School Children: Evidence for Continuity and Change With Age." *Child Development* 58 (1987): 201–212.

Hunziker, U. A., and R. G. Barr. "Increased Carrying Reduces Infant Crying: A Randomized Controlled Trial." *Pediatrics* 77, no. 5 (1986): 641–647.

Hutchinson, J. "What Crack Does to Babies." *American Educator* (Spring 1991): 31–32.

Hutt, C. "Exploration and Play in Children" In *Child's Play,* edited by R. Herron and B. Sutton-Smith. New York: John Wiley & Sons, Inc., 1971.

Hutt, S., H. G. Lenard, and H. F. Prechtl. "Psychophysiology of the Newborn." In *Advances in Child Development,* edited by L. P. Lippsett and H. W. Reese. New York: Academic Press, 1969.

Hyde, J. S. "How Large Are Gender Differences in Aggression? A Developmental Meta-Analysis." *Developmental Psychology* 20 (1984): 722–736.

Hyman, I. A. *Reading, Writing and the Hickory Stick: The Appalling Story of Physical and Psychological Violence in American Schools.* Boston, Mass.: Lexington Books, 1990.

Hyman, I. A., and J. D'Alessandro. "Good, Old-Fashioned Discipline: The Politics of Punitiveness." *Phi Delta Kappan* 66 (September 1984): 39–45.

Hyman, R. T. *Questioning in the Classroom.* Urbana, Ill.: Document Reproduction Service, 1977, 1-14 (catalog. no. ED 138–551).

Ingraham v. Wright, 95 S. Ct. 1401, at 1406, Citing 525 F.2d. 909 (1977), at 917.

Insko, C. A., and J. E. Robinson. "Belief Similarity Versus Race As Determinants of Reactions to Negroes by Southern White Adolescents: A Further Test of Rokeach's Theory." *Journal of Personality and Social Psychology* 7 (1967): 216–21.

International Coalition Against Violent Entertainment. *Press Release.* P. O. Box 2157, Champaign, IL 61820, (November 27, 1985).

Irwin, D. M., and S. G. Moore. "The Young Child's Understanding of Social Justice." *Developmental Psychology* 5, no. 3 (1971): 406–10.

Isabella, R., and Belsky, J. "Interactional synchrony and the origins of infant-mother attachment: A replication study." *Child Development* Vol 62, 2. (1991): 373–384.

Isberg, R. S., et al. "Parental Contexts of Adolescent Self-Esteem." *Journal of Youth and Adolescence* 18 (1989): 1–23.

Ivancevich, J. M., J. H. Donnelly, and J. L. Gibson. *Managing for Performance.* Plano, Tex.: Business Publications, Inc., 1983.

Izard, C. E. *Human Emotions.* New York: Plenum Publishing Corporation, 1977.

Izard, C. E. "The Primary of Emotion in Human Development." Paper presented at the biennial meeting of the Society for Research in Child Development, Boston, April 1981.

Izard, C. E. *The Psychology of Emotions.* New York: Plenum Publishing Corp., 1991.

Izard, C. E., and C. Z. Maltesta. "Differential Emotions Theory of Early Emotional Development." In *Handbook of Infant Development,* edited by J. D. Osofsky. New York: Wiley, 1987.

Jabs, C. "Is that Baby Scowling? Smiling? Crying?" *McCalls* 112, no. 10 (July 1985): 78–113.

Jacklin, C. N. "Male and Female: Issues of Gender." *American Psychologist* 44 (1989): 127–133.

Jackson, N., H. Robinson, and P. Dale. *Cognitive Development in Young Children.* Monterey, Calif.: Brooks/Cole Publishing Company, 1977.

Jarratt, C. J. *Helping Children Cope with Separation and Loss.* New York: Harvard Common Press, 1994.

Jason, J.M. "Abuse, Neglect, and the HIV-Infected Child." *Child Abuse and Neglect* 15, no. 1 (1991): 79–88.

Javernik, E. "Johnny's Not Jumping: Can We Help Obese Children?" *Young Children* (1988): 18–23.

Jensen, L. C., and K. M. Hughston. *Responsibility and Morality.* Provo, Utah: Brigham Young University Press, 1979.

Johnson, D. W., and R. T. Johnson. "Integrating Handicapped Students into the Mainstream." *Exceptional Children* 47, no. 2, 10 (1980): 90–98.

Johnson, D. W., and R. T. Johnson. *Reducing School Violence through Conflict Resolution.* Alexandria, VA: Association for Supervision and Curriculum Development, 1995.

Johnson, K. R. "Black Kinesics: Some Nonverbal Communication Patterns in Black Culture." *Florida FL Reporter* 57 (1971): 17–20.

Jones, D. C. Persuasive Appeals and Responses to Appeals Among Friends and Acquaintances." *Child Development* 56 (1985): 757–763.

Jones, E. *Dimensions of Teaching-Learning Environments.* Pasadena, Calif.: Pacific Oaks, 1981.

Jones, S. J., and H. A. Moss. "Age, State, and Maternal Behavior Associated with Infant Vocalizations." *Child Development* 42 (1971): 1039–1051.

Jordan, E., A. Cowan, and J. Roberts. "Knowing the Rules: Discursive Strategies in Young Children's Power Struggles." *Early Childhood Research Quarterly* 10 (1995): 339–358.

Jourard, S. M. "An Exploratory Study of Body-Accessibility." *British Journal of Social and Clinical Psychology,* no. 5 (1966): 221–231.

Kagan, J. *Change and Continuity in the First Two Years: An Inquiry into Early Cognitive Development.* New York: John Wiley & Sons, Inc., 1971.

Kagan, J. *Personality Development.* New York: Harcourt Brace Jovanovich, 1971.

Kagan, J. "The Effect of Day Care on the Infant." In *Policy Issues in Day Care. Summary of 21 Papers.* Washington, D.C.: U.S. Department of Health, Education, and Welfare, 1977.

Kagan, J. "The Psychological Requirements for Human Development." In *Family in Transition,* edited by A. S. Skolnick and J. H. Skolnick, Boston: Little, Brown & Company, 1977.

Kagan, J. "On the Nature of Emotion." In "The Development of Emotion Regulation: Biological and Behavioral Considerations," edited by N. A. Fox. *Monographs of the Society for Research in Child Development* 240, no. 59 (1994): 2–3, 7–24.

Kamii, C. "Viewpoint: Obedience is Not Enough." *Young Children* 39, no. 4 (1984): 11–14.

Kaplan, H. B., and A. D. Pokorny. "Self-Derogation and Psychosocial Adjustment." *Journal of Nervous and Mental Disease* 149 (1969): 421–434.

Kaplan, L. J. *Oneness and Separateness: From Infant to Individual.* New York: Simon & Schuster, Inc., 1978.

Kastenbaum, R. J. *Death, Society, and Human Experience.* St. Louis, Mo.: The C.V. Mosby Company, 1981.

Katz, L. G. "What Is Basic for Young Children?" *Childhood Education* 54, no. 1 (1977): 16–19.

Katz, L. G. "The Professional Early Childhood Teacher." *Young Children* 39, no. 5 (July 1984); 3–10.

Katz, L. G. "Where Is Early Childhood Education as a Profession?" In *Early Childhood Teacher Preparation,* edited by B. Spodek, O. Saracho, and D. Peters. New York: Teachers College Press, 1988, 192–208.

Katz, L. G. "Ethical Issues in Working with Young Children." In *Ethical Behavior in Early Childhood Education (Expanded Edition),* edited by L. G. Katz and E. H. Ward. Washington, D.C., NAEYC, 1991, 1–16.

Katz, L. G., and S. C. Chard. *Engaging Children's Minds: The Project Approach.* Norwood, N.J.: Ablex Publishing, Corp., 1989.

Katz, P. A. "The Acquisition of Racial Attitudes in Children." In *Towards the Elimination of Racism,* edited by R. A. Katz. New York: Pergamon Press, Inc., 1976.

Keeshan, B. "Banning Corporal Punishment in the Classroom." *The Humanist XLVIII* (Nov./Dec. 1989): 6–8.

Keller, A., L. H. Ford, Jr., and J. A. Meachum. "Dimensions of Self-Concept in Preschool Children." *Developmental Psychology* 14 (1978): 483–489.

Kelly, J. A. *Treating Child Abusive Families: Intervention Based on Skills Training Principles.* New York: Plenum Publishing Corporation, 1983.

Kelman, H. C. "Compliance, Identification and Internalization: Three Processes of Attitude Change." In *Groups and Organizations: Integrated Readings in the Analysis of Social Behavior,* edited by B. L. Hinto and H. J. Reitz. Belmont, Calif.: Wadsworth, Inc., 1958.

Kenden, A. "Some Functions of Gaze Direction in Social Interaction." *Acta Psychologia* 26 (1967): 22–63.

Keniston, K. "Do Americans Really Like Children?" *Childhood Education* 52, no. 1, 10 (1975): 4–12.

Kessler, J. W. "Neurosis in Childhood." In *Manual of Child Psychopathology,* edited by B. Wolman. New York: McGraw-Hill, Inc., 1972.

Key, M. R. *Paralanguage and Kinesics.* Metuchen, N.J.: Scarecrow Press, Inc., 1975.

Klein, C. *The Myth of the Happy Child.* New York: Harper Collins, 1975.

Klein, H. A. "Early Childhood Group Care: Predicting Adjustment from Individual Temperament." *Journal of Genetic Psychology* 13, no. 7 (1980): 125–131.

Klineberg, O. *Race Differences.* New York: Harper & Brothers, 1935.

Klinnert, M. D. "Infants' Use of Mothers' Facial Expressions for Regulating Their Own Behavior." Paper presented at the biennial meeting of the Society for Research in Child Development, Boston, April 1981.

Knopczyk, D. R., and P. G. Rodes. *Teaching Social Competence: A Practical Approach for Improving Social Skills for Students At-Risk.* Pacific Grove, Calif.: Brooks/Cole Publishing Co., 1996.

Koblinsky, S., and N. Behana. "Child Sexual Abuse, The Educator's Role in Prevention, Detection, and Intervention." *Young Children* 39, no. 6 (September 1984): 3–15.

Koestner, R. "A Multifactorial Approach to the Study of Gender Characteristics." *Journal of Personality* 63, no. 3 (1995): 681–710.

Kohlberg, L. "Development of Moral Character and Moral Ideology." In *Review of Child Development Research,* Vol. 1, edited by M. L. Hoffman and L. W. Hoffman. New York: Russell Sage Foundation, 1964.

Kohlberg, L. "Moral Stages and Moralization: The Cognitive-Developmental Approach." In *Moral Devel-*

opment and Behavior, edited by T. Lickona. New York: Holt, Rinehart & Winston, 1976.

Kohlberg, L. A. "A Cognitive Developmental Analysis of Children's Sex Role Concepts and Attitudes." In *The Development of Sex Differences,* edited by E. E. Maccoby. Stanford, Calif.: Stanford University Press, 1966.

Konner, M. *Childhood.* Boston: Little Brown Co., 1991.

Kontos, S., and Wilcox-Herzog, A. "Teacher's Interactions with Children: Why Are They So Important?" *Young Children* 52, no. 2 (1997): 4–12.

Korner, A. F. "The Effect of the Infant's State, Level of Arousal, Sex and Centogenetic Stage on the Caregiver." In *The Effects of the Infant on Its Caregiver,* New York: John Wiley & Sons, Inc. 1974, 105–121.

Korner, A. F., and E. B. Thoman. "Visual Alertness in Neonates As Evoked by Maternal Care." *Journal of Experimental Child Psychology* 10 (1970): 67–68.

Korner, A. F., and E. B. Thoman. "The Relative Efficacy of Contact and Vestibular Proprioceptive Stimulation in Soothing Neonates." *Child Development* 43 (1972): 443–453.

Korner, A. F., et al. "Characteristics of Crying and Non-Crying Activity of Full Term Neonates." *Child Development* 45 (1974): 953–958.

Kostelnik, M. J. "An Evaluation of a Program to Teach Young Children a Feeling Word Vocabulary." Master's thesis, The Pennsylvania State University, 1977.

Kostelnik, M. J. "Evaluation of a Communication and Group Management Skills Training Program for Child Development Personnel." Ph.D. diss., The Pennsylvania State University, 1978.

Kostelnik, M. J. "Evaluation of an In-Service Multi-Media Training Program in Discipline Skills for Teachers of Young Children." Paper presented at the annual meeting of the National Association for the Education of Young Children, Atlanta, Georgia, November 1983.

Kostelnik, M. J. "Children and Sex Stereotypes." *Two to Twelve* 2, no. 1 (January 1984): 4–7.

Kostelnik, M. "Developmental Practices in Early Childhood Programs." Keynote Address, National Home Start Day, New Orleans, LA, 1987.

Kostelnik, M. J., and P. D. Kurtz. *Communication and Positive Guidance Skills for Teachers of Young Children.* 3d ed. East Lansing, Mich.: Michigan State University Press, 1986.

Kostelnik, M. J., A. K. Soderman, and A. P. Whiren. *Developmentally Appropriate Programs in Early Childhood Education.* Columbus: Prentice-Hall, Inc., In press.

Kostelnik, M. J., and L. C. Stein. "Effects of Three Conflict Mediation Strategies on Children's Aggressive and Prosocial Behavior in the Classroom." Paper presented at the annual meeting of the National Association for the Education of Young Children, Washington, D.C., 14 November 1986.

Kostelnik, M., and L. C. Stein. "Social Development: An Essential Component of Kindergarten Education." In *The Developing Kindergarten: Programs, Children, and Teachers,* edited by J. S. McKee, MI: MiAEYC, 1990.

Kostelnik, M. J., L. C. Stein, and A. P. Whiren. "Mid-Year Crisis: What to Do When Children Don't Want to Come to the Center Anymore." *Day Care and Early Education* 1, no. 2 (1982): 42–45.

Kostelnik, M., L. C. Stein, and A. P. Whiren. "Children's Self-Esteem: The Verbal Environment." *Childhood Education.* 65, no. 1 (1989): 29–32.

Kostelnik, M. J., A. Whiren, and L. Stein. "Living with He-Man: Managing Superhero Fantasy Play." *Young Children* 41, no. 4 (1986): 3–9.

Krasner, L., and M. Krasner. "Token Economics and Other Planned Environments." In *Behavior Modification in Education: The Seventy-Second Yearbook of the National Society for the Study of Education, Part 1,* edited by C. C. Thoresen. Chicago: University of Chicago Press, 1972.

Kuczen, B. *Childhood Stress: Don't Let Your Child Be a Victim.* New York: Delacorte Press, 1982.

Kupersmidt, J. B., J. D. Coie, and K. A. Dodge. "The Role of Poor Peer Relationships in the Development of Disorder." In *Peer Rejection in Childhood,* edited by S. R. Asher and J. D. Coie. New York: Cambridge University Press, 1990, 274–308.

Kupersmidt, J. B., and C. Patterson. "Developmental Patterns of Peer Relations and Aggression in The Prediction of Externalizing Behavior Problems." Paper presented at the biennial meeting of the Society for Research in Child Development, New Orleans, March 1993.

Kuykendall, J. "Is Gun Play OK Here???" *Young Children* 50, no. 1, 1995: 56–59.

Labov, W. *The Study of Nonstandard English.* Urbana, Ill.: National Council of Teachers of English, 1970.

Ladd, G. W. "Effectiveness of a Social Learning Method for Enhancing Children's Social Interaction and Peer Acceptance." *Child Development* 52 (1979): 171–178.

Ladd, G. W. "Having Friends, Keeping Friends, Making Friends, and Being Liked by Peers in the Classroom: Predictors of Children's Early School Adjustment." *Child Development* 61 (1990): 1081–1100.

Ladd, G. W., and C. C. Coleman. "Young Children's Peer Relationships: Forms, Features, and Functions." In *Handbook of Research on the Education of Young Children,* edited by B. Spodek. New York: Macmillan, Inc., 1993, 54–76.

Ladd, G. W., and S. L. Oden. "The Relationship Between Peer Acceptance and Children's Ideas About Helpfulness." *Child Development* 50 (1979): 402–408.

Ladd, G. W., S. Profilet, and C. H. Hart. "Parents' Management of Children's Peer Relations: Facilitating and Supervising Children's Activities in the Peer Culture." In *Family-Peer Relationships: Modes of Linkage,* edited by R. D. Parke and G. W. Ladd. Hillsdale, N.J.: Erlbaum Associates, Inc., 1992, 215–254.

LaFrance, M., and C. Mayo. "Racial Differences in Gaze Behavior During Conversations: Two Systematic Observational Studies." *Journal of Personality and Social Psychology* 33 (1976): 547–552.

Laing, R. *The Politics of Experience,* New York: Ballantine Books, Inc., 1967.

Lamb, M. "Infant Care Practices and the Application of Knowledge." In *Applied Developmental Psychology,* edited by C. B. Fisher and R. M. Lerner. New York: McGraw-Hill, Inc., 1994.

Lamb, M. E. "Developing Trust and Perceived Effectance in Infancy." In *Advances in Infancy Research,* Vol. 1, edited by L. P. Lipsitt. Norwood, N.J.: Ablex Publishing Corp., 1981, 107–127.

Lamb, M. E., and J. Campos. *Development in Infancy.* New York: Random House, Inc., 1982.

Lamb, M. E., and M. A. Easterbrooks. "Individual Differences in Parental Sensitivity: Origin, Components and Consequences. In *Infant Social Cognition: Theoretical and Empirical Considerations,* edited by M. E. Lamb and L. R. Sherrod. Hillsdale, N.J.: Lawrence Erlbaum Associates, Inc., 1981, 127–154.

Lamovec, T. "Trust in Interpersonal Relationships." *Anthopos* 20 nos. 3–4 (1989): 181–193.

Lane, D. M., and D. A. Pearson. "The Development of Selective Attention." *Merrill-Palmer Quarterly* 28 (1982): 317–337.

Langlois, J. H. "From the Eye of the Beholder to Behavioral Reality: The Development of Social Behaviors and Social Relations As a Function of Physical Attractiveness." In *Physical Appearance, Stigma and Social Behavior,* edited by C. P. Heiman. Hillsdale, N.J.: Lawrence Erlbaum Associates, Inc., 1985.

Lansky, B. *The Best Baby Name Book.* Deephaven, Minn.: Meadowbrook Press, Inc., 1984.

Leahy, R. "Development of Conceptions of Prosocial Behavior: Information Affecting Rewards Given for Altruism and Kindness." *Developmental Psychology* 15 (1979): 34–37.

Leathers, D. G. *Nonverbal Communication Systems.* Boston: Allyn and Bacon, Inc., 1976.

Leavitt, J. E. "Helping Abused and Neglected Children." In *Early Childhood Education,* edited by J. S. McKee. Guilford, Conn.: Dushkin Publishing Group, Inc., 1983, 49–51.

Lee, L., and J. Charlton. *The Hand Book.* Englewood Cliffs, N.J.: Prentice-Hall, Inc., 1980.

Lefkowitz, M. M., et al. *Growing Up to Be Violent: A Longitudinal Study of the Development of Aggression.* New York: Pergamon Press, Inc., 1977.

LeFrancois, G. R. *Of Children.* Belmont, Calif.: Wadsworth, 1992.

Leiter, M. P. "A Study of Reciprocity in Preschool Play Groups." *Child Development* 48 (1977): 1288–1295.

Lenneberg, E. H. "Speech As a Motor Skill with Special References to Monophasic Disorders." In "The Acquisition of Language." *Monographs of the Society for Research in Child Development* 29, no. 1 (1964): 115–127.

Lepper, M. R. "Social Control Processes, Attributions of Motivation and the Internalization of Social Values." In *Social Cognition and Social Behavior: Developmental Perspectives,* edited by E. T. Higgins, D. N. Ruble, and W. W. Hartup. New York: Cambridge University Press, 1983.

Lerner, R. M., and J. V. Lerner. "Effects of Age, Sex, and Physical Attractiveness on Child-Peer Relations, Academic Performance, and Elementary School Adjustment." *Developmental Psychology* 13 (1977): 585–590.

Levenstein, P. "Cognitive Development Through Verbalized Play: A Mother-Child Home Program." In *Play: Its Role in Development and Evolution,* edited by J. Bruner, A. Jolly, and K. Sylva. New York: Basic Books, Inc., Publishers, 1976, 286–299.

Levin, D. E. *Teaching Young Children in Violent Times.* Cambridge, MA: Educators for Social Responsibility, 1994.

Levin, D. E. "Understanding and Responding to the Violence in Children's Lives." *Child Care Information Exchange* 102 (March/April 1995): 34–38.

Levinger, G., and J. D. Snoek. *Attraction in Relationships: A New Look at Interpersonal Attraction.* New York: General Learning Press, 1973.

Levitt, M. J., et al. "Reciprocity of Exchange in Toddler Sharing Behavior." *Developmental Psychology* 21 (1985): 122–123.

Levy, G. D. "Relations Among Aspects of Children's Social Environments, Gender Schematization, Gender Role Knowledge, and Flexibility." *Sex Roles* 21, nos. 11/12 (1989): 803–823.

Lewis, M. "State As an Infant-Environment Interaction: An Analysis of Mother-Infant Interaction As a Function of Sex." *Merrill Palmer Quarterly* 18 (1972): 95–121.

Lewis, M. "What Do We Mean When We Say Emotional Development?" In L. Cirillo, B. Kaplan, and S. Wapner (Eds.), *Emotions in Ideal Human Development.* Hillsdale, N.J.: Erlbaum, 1989.

Lewis, M. *Shame: The Exposed Self.* New York: The Free Press, 1992.

Lewis, M., and J. Brooks-Gunn. *Social Cognition and the Acquisition of Self.* New York: Plenum Publishing Corporation, 1979.

Lewis, M., and C. Michalson. "The Child's Social World." In *Emotion and Early Interaction,* edited by T. Field and A. Fogel. Hillsdale, N.J.: Lawrence Erlbaum Associates, Inc., 1982.

Lewis, M., and C. Saarni (Eds.). *The Socialization of Emotions,* New York: Plenum, 1985.

Lewis, M, et al. "Self Development and Self-Conscious Emotions." *Child Development* 60 (1989): 146–156.

Lewis, W. C., R. N. Wolman, and M. King. "The Development of the Language of Emotions: II. Intentionality in the Experience of Affect." *Journal of Genetic Psychology* 120 (1972): 303–316.

Liebert, R. M., and Sprafkin, J. *The Early Window: Effects of Television on Children and Youth* (3rd ed. New York: Pergamon, 1988.

Lochman, J. "Social-Cognitive Processes of Severely Violent, Moderately Aggressive, and Nonaggressive Boys." *Journal of Clinical and Counseling Psychology* 62 (1994): 366–374.

Loeb, R. C., L. Horst, and P. J. Horton. "Family Interaction Patterns Associated with Self-Esteem in Preadolescent Boys and Girls." *Merrill Palmer Quarterly* 26 (1980): 203–217.

Lorenz, K. *On Aggression.* Translated by M. K. Wilson. New York: Harcourt Brace Jovanovich, Inc., 1966.

Lowe, M. "Trends in the Development of Representational Play in Infants from One to Three Years: An Observational Study." *Journal of Child Psychology* 16 (1975): 33–48.

Lung, C. T., and D. Daro. *Current Trends in Child Abuse Reporting and Fatalities: The Results of the 1995 Annual Fifty States Survey,* Chicago: National Committee to Prevent Child Abuse, 1996.

Luria, A. R. *The Role of Speech in the Regulation of Normal and Abnormal Behavior.* London: Pergamon Press, Inc., 1961.

Lutz, S. E., and D. N. Ruble. "Children and Gender Prejudice: Context, Motivation and the Development of Gender Conception." In *Annals of Child Development,* Vol. 10, edited by R. Vasta. London: Jessica Kingsley, 1995.

Lytton, H. "Disciplinary Encounters Between Young Boys and Their Mothers and Fathers: Is There a Contingency System?" *Developmental Psychology* 15 (1979): 256–268.

Maccoby, E. "The Role of Parents in the Socialization of Children: An Historical Overview." *Developmental Psychology* 28 (1992): 1006–1018.

Maccoby, E., and J. A. Martin. "Socialization in the Context of the Family: Parent-Child Interaction." In *Handbook of Child Psychology.* 4th ed. Vol. 4, edited by P. H. Mussen. New York: Wiley, 1983.

Maccoby, E. E. *Social Development-Psychological Growth and the Parent-Child Relationship.* New York: Harcourt Brace Jovanovich, Inc., 1980.

Maccoby, E. E. "Socialization and Developmental Change." *Child Development* 55 (1984): 317–328.

Maccoby, E. E., and C. N. Jacklin. *The Psychology of Sex Differences.* Stanford, Calif.: Stanford University Press, 1974.

Maccoby, E. E., and C. N. Jacklin. "Sex Differences in Aggression: A Rejoinder and Reprise." *Child Development* 51 (1980): 964–980.

MacFarlane, A. *The Psychology of Childbirth.* Cambridge, Mass.: Harvard University Press, 1977.

Machotka, P., and J. Spiegel. *The Articulate Body.* New York: Irvington Publishers, Inc., 1982.

Madsen, C. H., Jr., and C. K. Madsen. *Teaching Discipline: Behavioral Principles Toward a Positive Approach.* Boston, Mass.: Allyn and Bacon, Inc., 1981.

Magid, K., and C. A. McKelvey. *High Risk: Children without a Conscience.* New York: Bantam Books, 1987.

Mahler, M., S. Pine, and A. Bergman. *The Psychological Birth of the Human Infant.* New York: Basic Books, Inc., Publishers, 1975.

Maker, C. J. "Creativity, Intelligence, Problem Solving: A Definition and Design for Cross-Cultural Research and Measurement Related to Giftedness." *Gifted Educational International* 9 (1993): 68–77.

Maker, C. J., and M. A. King. *Nurturing Giftedness in Young Children.* Reston, VA: Council for Exceptional Children, 1996.

Maker, C. J., and A. B. Nielson. *Curriculum Development and Teaching Strategies for Gifted Learners.* Austin, TX: Pro-Ed, 1996.

Marcus, R. F., and M. Leiserson. "Encouraging Helping Behavior." *Young Children* 33, no. 6 (September 1978): 24–34.

Marion, M. "Child Compliance: A Review of the Literature with Implications for Family Life Education." *Family Relations: Journal of Applied Family and Child Studies* 32, no. 4 (October 1983): 545–555.

Marion, M. *Guidance of Young Children,* 4th ed. New York, New York: Macmillan, 1995.

Markus, H. J., and P. S. Nuruis. "Self-Understanding and Self-Regulation in Middle Childhood." In *Development During Middle Childhood: The Years from Six to Twelve,* edited by W. A. Collins. Washington, D.C.: National Academy Press, 1984, 147–183.

Marshall, H. "The Development of Self Concept." *Young Children* 44, no. 5 (1989): 44–51.

Martin, H. "A Child-Oriented Approach to Prevention of Abuse." In *Child Abuse: Prediction, Prevention, and Follow-Up,* edited by A. W. Franklin. London: Churchill Livingstone, Inc., 1978, 9–20.

Maslow, A. H. *Motivation and Personality.* New York: Harper & Row, Publishers, Inc. 1954.

Matias, R., and J. F. Cohn. "Are MAX-Specified Infant Facial Expressions During Face-to-Face Interactions Consistent with Differentia Emotions Theory?" *Developmental Psychology* 29 (1993): 524–531.

Matson, J. L., and T. H. Ollendick. *Enhancing Children's Social Skills: Assessment and Training.* New York: Pergamon, 1988.

Mattick, I. "The Teacher's Role in Helping Young Children Develop Language Competence." *Young Children* 27 (1972): 133–139.

Maurer, D., and L. Heroux. "The Perception of Faces by Three-Month-Old Infants." Paper presented at the International Conference on Infant Studies, New Haven, Conn., 1980.

May, R. *Power and Innocence: A Search for the Sources of Violence.* New York: W. W. Norton & Co., Inc., 1972.

Mayle, P. *Where Did I Come From?* New York: Coral Publishing Group, 1995.

Mc Donald, K. "The Secrets of Animal Play." *Chronicle of Higher Education* (January 13, 1995): 8–9, 12–13.

McAfee, O., and D. Leong. *Assessing and Guiding Young Children's Development and Learning.* 2nd Ed. Boston: Allyn and Bacon, 1997.

McBride, S. "The Culture of Toy Research." In *Play as Context,* edited by A. Cheska. West Point, N.Y.: Leisure Press, 1981, 210–218.

McCarthy, P. R., and N. E. Betz. "Differential Effects of Self-Disclosing Versus Self-Involving Counselor Statements." *Journal of Counseling Psychology* 25, no. 4 (1978): 251–256.

McDavid, J. W., and H. Harari. "Stereotyping of Names and Popularity in Grade School Children." *Child Development* 37 (1966): 453–459.

McGee, B. H. "Forum: When a Kid Has Cancer." *Early Years* (October, 1982): 24–67.

McGhee, P. *Humor: Its Origin and Development.* San Francisco: W. H. Freeman & Company, Publishers, 1979.

McGhee, P. E., and N. S. Duffey. "Children's Appreciation of Humor Victimizing Different Racial-Ethnic Groups." *Journal of Cross-Cultural Psychology* 14, no. 1 (1983): 29–40.

McGinnis, E., and A. P. Goldstein. *Skillstreaming the Elementary School Child: A Guide for Teaching Prosocial Skills.* Champaign, IL: Research Press, 1984.

McGinnis, E., and A. P. Goldstein. *Skillstreaming in Early Childhood: Teaching Prosocial Skills to the Preschool and Kindergarten Child.* Champaign, IL: Research Press, 1990.

McGroarty, M. "The Societal Context of Bilingual Education." *Educational Researcher* 21, no. 2 (March 1992): 7–9.

McNiel, D. *The Acquisition of Language.* New York: Harper & Row, Publishers, Inc., 1970.

Mead, D. E. *Six Approaches to Child Rearing.* Provo, Utah: Brigham Young University Press, 1976.

Meers, J. "The Light Touch." *Psychology Today* 19, no. 9 (1985): 60–67.

Mehrabian, A. *Nonverbal Communication.* Chicago: Aldin-Atherton, 1972.

Mehrabian, M. *Silent Messages.* Belmont, Calif.: Wadsworth, Inc., 1971.

Mehrabian, M. *Public Places and Private Spaces: The Psychology of Work, Play and Living Environments.* New York: Basic Books, Inc., Publishers, 1976.

Meichenbaum, D. *Cognitive Behavior Modification: An Integrative Approach.* New York: Plenum Publishing Corporation, 1977.

Meichenbaum, D. H., and J. Goodman. "Training Impulsive Children to Talk to Themselves: A Means of Developing Self-Control." *Journal of Abnormal Psychology* 77 (1971): 115–126.

Meisels, S. J. "Can Development Screening Tests Identify Children Who Are Developmentally At Risk?" *Pediatrics* 83 (1989): 578–585.

Mellonie, B., and R. Ingpen. *Lifetimes.* New York: Bantam Books, Inc., 1983.

Mendler, A. N., and R. L. Curwin. *Taking Charge in the Classroom.* Reston, Va.: Reston Publishing Co., Inc., 1988.

Meriwether, H. "Why Doctors Worry about Media Influence on Kids." *Detroit Free Press* (September 15, 1996): 3F.

Meyer, J. "The Collaborative Development of Power in Children's Arguments." *Argumentation and Advocacy* 29 (Fall 1992): 77–88.

Meyers, A., and Weitzman, M. "Pediatric HIV Disease: The Newest Chronic Illness of Childhood." In *The Pediatric Clinics of North America*, edited by P. J. Edelson. Philadelphia: W. B. Saunders Co, 1991.

Michalson, L., and M. Lewis. "What Do Children Know About Emotions and Why Do They Know It?" In *The Socialization of Emotions*, edited by M. Lewis and C. Saarni. New York: Plenum, 1985, 117–140.

Midlarsky, E., J. H. Bryan, and P. Brickman. "Aversive Approval: Interactive Effects of Modeling and Reinforcement on Altruistic Behavior." *Child Development* 44 (1973): 321–328.

Miller, C. S. "Building Self Control: Discipline for Young Children." *Young Children.* Vol. 40, No. 1, Washington, DC: NAEYC, 1984, 15–19.

Miller, D. F. *Positive Child Guidance.* Albany, N.Y.: Delmar Publishers, Inc., 1996.

Miller, L. C. "Fears and Anxiety in Children." In *Handbook of Clinical Child Psychology*, edited by C. E. Walker and M. C. Roberts. New York: John Wiley & Sons, Inc., 1983.

Miller, P., and C. Garvey. "Mother-Baby Role Play: Its Origins in Social Support." In *Symbolic Play: The Development of Social Understanding*, edited by I. Bretherton. New York: Academic Press, Inc., 1984, 101–130.

Miller, P. A., et al. "Assessing Empathy and Prosocial Behaviors in Early Childhood: Development of a Parental Questionnaire." Paper presented at the bi-annual meeting of the Society for Research in Child Development, Indianapolis, Ind., March 1995.

Mischel, W. "How Children Postpone Pleasure." *Human Nature* 1 (1978): 51–55.

Mischel, W. *Personality.* New York: Rinehart & Winston, 1987.

Mischel, W., and C. J. Patterson. "Substantive and Structural Elements of Effective Plans for Self-Control." *Journal of Personality and Social Psychology* 34 (1976): 942–950.

Mize, J., and G. W. Ladd. "A Cognitive Social-Learning Approach to Social Skill Training with Low-Status Preschool Children." *Developmental Psychology* 26, no. 3 (1990): 388–397.

Mohr, D. M. "Development of Attributes of Personal Identity." *Developmental Psychology* 14 (1978): 427–428.

Monahon, C. *Children in Trauma: A Guide for Parents and Professionals.* San Francisco, Calif.: Jossey-Bass Publishers, 1993.

Montemayer, R., and M. Eisen. "The Development of Self-Conceptions from Childhood to Adolescence." *Developmental Psychology* 13 (1977): 314–319.

Montgomery, E. "To Parents of Children with Learning Disabilities—Some Insights from a Teacher's Perspective." *Journal of School Health* 52, no. 2, 2 (1982): 116–117.

Moore, N. V., C. M. Everton, and J. E. Brophy. "Solitary Play: Some Functional Reconsiderations." *Developmental Psychology* 10 (1974): 830–834.

Moore, S. G. "Prosocial Behavior in the Early Years: Parent and Peer Influences." In *Handbook of Research in Early Childhood Education*, edited by B. Spodek. New York: Free Press, 1982, 65–81.

Moore, S. G. "Socialization in the Kindergarten Classroom." In *Today's Kindergarten*, edited by B. Spodek. New York: Teachers College Press, 1986, 110–136.

Moore, S. G., and F. Olson. "The Effects of Explicitness of Instruction on the Generalization of a Prohibition in Young Children." *Child Development* 40 (1969): 945–949.

Morris, D. *Bodytalk: The Meaning of Human Gestures.* New York: Crown Trade Paperbacks, 1994.

Morris, J. B. "Indirect Influences on Children's Racial Attitudes." *Educational Leadership* 1 (1981): 286–287.

Morris, R., and T. Kratochwill. *Treating Children's Fears and Phobias: A Behavioral Approach.* Elmsford, New York: Pergamon, 1983.

Morrow, R. D. "Southeast Asian Child-rearing Practices: Implications for Child and Youth Care Workers." *Child & Youth Care Quarterly* 18, no. 4 (Winter 1989): 273–287.

Mueller, E., and T. Lucas. "A Developmental Analysis of Peer Interaction Among Toddlers." In *Friendship and Peer Relations,* edited by M. Lewis and L. Rosenblum. New York: John Wiley & Sons, Inc., 1975.

Muir, D., and J. Field. "Newborn Infants Orient to Sounds." *Child Development* 50 (1979): 431–436.

Mullen, J. K. "Understanding and Managing the Temper Tantrum." *Child Care Quarterly* 14, no. 3 (1983): 171–189.

Murphy, D. M. "Fears in Preschool-Age Children." *Child Care Quarterly* 14, no. 3 (1985): 171–189.

Murphy, J., et al. "Substance Abuse and Serious Child Maltreatment: Prevalence, Risk, and Outcome in a Court Sample." *Child Abuse and Neglect* 15 (1991): 197–211.

Murphy, K., and B. Schneider. "Coaching Socially Rejected Early Adolescents Regarding Behaviors Used by Peers to Infer Liking: A Dyad-Specific Intervention." *Journal of Early Adolescence,* 14 (1994): 83–95.

Murray, A. D., et al. "The Effects of Epidural Anesthesia on Newborns and Their Mothers." *Child Development* 52 (1981): 71–82.

Murray, J. P. *Television and Youth: 25 Years of Research and Controversy.* Boys Town, Nebraska: Boys Town Center for the Study of Youth Development, 1980.

Mussen, P., and N. Eisenberg-Berg. *Roots of Caring, Sharing, and Helping: The Development of Prosocial Behavior in Children.* San Francisco: W. H. Freeman & Company, Publishers, 1977.

Mussen, P. H., et al. *Child Development and Personality.* 7th ed. New York: Harper and Row, Publisher Inc., 1990.

Musson, S. *School-Age Care: Theory and Practice.* New York: Addison-Wesley Publishing Co., Inc., 1994.

Nabuzoka, D., and P. Smith. "Identification of Expressions of Emotions by Children With and Without Learning Disabilities." *Learning Disabilities Research & Practice* 10, no. 2 (1995): 91–101.

NAEYC Position Statement on Media Violence in Children's Lives. *Young Children* 45, no. 5 (1990): 18–21.

NAEYC. NAEYC Position Statement Responding to Linguistic and Cultural Diversity Recommendations for Effective Early Childhood Education. Washington, D.C.: NAEYC, 1996.

NAEYC. "Time Out for Time-out." *Early Years Are Learning Years* 15 (1996): 1.

National Association of School Psychologists. "Position Statement on Students with Attention Deficits." *Communique* 20 (1992): 5.

National Center for Children in Poverty. 6, no. 2 (1996–1997): 1–7.

National Coalition to Abolish Corporal Punishment in Schools. *Corporal Punishment Fact Sheet* Columbus, Ohio: NCACPS, 1994.

National Rifle Association. "A Parent's Guide to Gun Safety." Washington, D.C.: NRA, 1988.

National Safety Council. *Accident Facts.* Chicago: NSC, 1989.

Nelson, R. E. "Facilitating Children's Syntax Acquisition." *Developmental Psychology* 13 (1977): 101–107.

Neuspiel, D. R., and S. C. Hamel. "Cocaine and Infant Behaviors." *Developmental and Behavioral Pediatrics* 12, no. 1 (February 1991): Calif.: 55–64.

Newman, P. R., and B. M. Newman. *Childhood and Adolescence.* Pacific Grove, Calif.: Brooks/Cole Publishing Co., 1997.

Ney, P. G. "Transgenerational Child Abuse." *Child Psychiatry and Human Development.* 18, no. 3 (Spring 1988): 151–155.

Nickell, P., A. Rice, and S. Tucker. *Management in Family Living.* New York: John Wiley & Sons, Inc., 1976.

Noble, L. "The Face of Foster Care." *Educational Leadership* 54, no. 7 (April 1997) 26–28.

Nottelmann, E. D., et al. "Gonadal and Adrenal Hormone Correlates of Adjustment in Early Adolescence." In *Biological-Psychosocial Interactions in Early Adolescence: A Life-Span Perspective,* edited by R. M. Lerner and T. T. Fochs. Hillsdale, N.J.: Lawrence Erlbaum Associates, Inc. 1987, 303–320.

Nourot, P. M., and J. Van Hoorn. "Symbolic Play in Preschool and Primary Settings." *Young Children* 46, no. 6 (1991): 40–51.

O'Brien, M., and Huston, A. C. "Development of Sex-Typed Play Behavior in Toddlers." *Developmental Psychology,* 21, no. 5 (1985): 866–871.

O'Connor, R. D. "Relative Efficacy of Modeling, Shaping and the Combined Procedures for Modification of Social Withdrawal." *Journal of Abnormal Psychology* 79, no. 3 (1972): 327–334.

Offard, D. "Outcome, Prognosis, and Risk in a Longitudinal Follow-up Study," *Journal of the American Academy of Child and Adolescent Psychiatry* 31 (1992): 55–63.

O'Hair, D., and G. Friedrich. *Strategic Communication.* Boston: Houghton-Mifflin, 1992.

O'Hair, M. J., and E. Ropo. "Unspoken Messages: Understanding Diversity in Education Requires Emphasis on Nonverbal Communication." *Teacher Education Quarterly* 21, no. 3 (Summer 1994): 91–112.

Olds, A. R. "Why Is Environmental Design Important to Young Children?" *Children in Contemporary Society* 1, Special Issue 11 (1977): 5–8.

O'Leary, S. "Parental Discipline Mistakes." *Current Directions in Psychological Science* 4 (1995): 11–13.

Olweus, D. "Testosterone, Aggression, Physical and Personality Dimensions in Normal Adolescent Males." *Psychosomatic Medicine* 42 (1980): 253–269.

Olweus, D. "Schoolyard Bullying: Grounds for Intervention." *School Safety* (Fall 1987): 4–11.

Openshaw, D. K. "The Development of Self-Esteem in the Child: Model Theory Versus Parent-Child Interaction." Ph.D. diss., Brigham Young University, Provo, Utah, 1978.

Opler, M. K. "Cultural Induction of Stress." In *Psychological Stress,* edited by M. H. Appley and R. Trumbull. New York: Appleton-Century-Crofts, 1967, 209–241.

Oppenheimer, L. "The Nature of Social Action: Social Competence Versus Social Conformism." In *Social Competence in Developmental Perspective,* edited by B. H. Schneider. Dordrecht, the Netherlands: Kluwer Academic Publishers, 1989, 41–69.

Orlick, T. *Winning Through Cooperation.* Washington, D.C.: Acropolis Books, Ltd., 1978.

Orton, G. L. "A Comparative Study of Children's Worries." *Journal of Psychology* 110 (1982): 153–162.

Osofsky, J. D., and K. Conners. "Mother-Infant Interaction: An Integrative View of a Complex System." In *Handbook of Infant Development,* edited by J. D. Osofsky. New York: Wiley-Interscience, 1981, 519–548.

Ostwald, P. F. *Soundmaking: The Acoustic Communication of Emotion.* Springfield, Ill.: Charles C. Thomas, Publisher, 1963.

Packard, V. *Our Endangered Children.* Boston: Little, Brown & Company, 1983.

Papalia, D. E., and S. W. Olds. *Child's World.* New York: McGraw-Hill, Inc., 1993.

Papalia, D. E., and S. W. Olds. *A Child's World: Infancy through Adolescence.* New York: McGraw-Hill, Inc., 1996.

Papousek, H., and M. Papousek. "Mothering and the Cognitive Head Start: Psychobiological Considerations." In *Studies in Mother-Infant Interaction,* edited by H. R. Schaffer, London: Academic Press, Inc., 1977.

Park, K. A., and E. Waters. "Security of Attachment and Preschool Friendships." *Child Development* 60 (1989): 1076–1081.

Parke, R. D. "Some Effects of Punishment on Children's Behavior." In *The Young Child,* Vol. 2, edited by W. W. Hartup. Washington, D.C.: National Association for the Education of Young Children, 1972.

Parke, R. D. "Rules, Roles, and Resistance to Deviation: Explorations in Punishment, Discipline, and Self-Control." In *Minnesota Symposia on Child Psychology,* Vol. 8, edited by A. Pick. Minneapolis: University of Minnesota Press, 1974.

Parke, R. D. "Punishment in Children: Effects, Side Effects and Alternate Strategies." In *Psychological Processes in Early Education,* edited by R. Hom and R. Robinson. New York: Academic Press, Inc., 1977.

Parke, R. D. "Some Effects of Punishment on Children's Behavior—Revisited." In *Contemporary Readings in Child Psychology,* edited by R. D. Parke and E. M. Hetherington. New York: McGraw-Hill, Inc., 1977, 208–219.

Parke, R. D., and J. L. Duer. "Schedule of Reinforcement and Inhibition of Aggression in Children." *Developmental Psychology* 7 (1972): 266–269.

Parke, R. D., and Slaby, R. G. "The Development of Aggression." In *Handbook of Child Psychology,* Vol. 4, edited by P. Mussen. New York: Wiley, 1983.

Parker, J. G. and Asher, S. R. "Peer Relations and Later Adjustment: Are Low-Accepted Children 'at Risk'?" *Psychological Bulletin* 102 (1987): 357–389.

Parker, J. G., and Gottman, J. M. "Social and Emotional Development in a Relational Context: Friendship Interaction from Early Childhood to Adolescence." In *Peer Relations in Child Development,* edited by T. J. Berndt and C. W. Ladd. New York: Wiley, 1989.

Parmelee, A. H., W. H. Werner, and H. R. Schultz. "Infant Sleep Patterns from Birth to 16 Weeks of Age." *Journal of Pediatrics* 65 (1964): 576–582.

Parsons, J. E., C. M. Kaczala, and J. L. Meece. "Socialization of Achievement Attitudes and Beliefs: Classroom Influences." *Child Development* 53 (1982): 322–339.

Parfen, M. B. "Social Participation Among Preschool Children." *Journal of Abnormal and Social Psychology* 27 (1932): 243–269.

Parten, R. L. "How Effective Are Your Questions?" *The Clearing House* 52 (February 1979): 254–256.

Patterson, G. R. *Coercive Family Process.* Eugene, Oregon: Castalia Publishing, 1982.

Patterson, G. R., R. A. Littman, and W. Bucker. "Assertive Behavior in Children: A Step Toward a Theory of Aggression." *Monographs of the Society for Research in Child Development* 32 (1967): 1–42.

Patterson, G. R., and Stouthamer-Loeber. "The Correlation of Family Management Practices and Delinquency." *Child Development* 55 (1984): 1299–1307.

Peake, T. H., and D. Egli. "The Language of Feelings." *Journal of Contemporary Psychotherapy* 13, no. 2 (Fall/Winter 1982): 162–174.

Pearsall, P. "De-Stressing Children: Wellness for Children." *Offspring* 25, no. 2 (1983): 2–9.

Pearse, P. *See How You Grow.* Hauppage, New York: Barron's, 1988.

Peck, C. A., et al. "Teaching Retarded Preschoolers to Imitate the Free-Play Behavior of Nonretarded Classmates: Trained and Generalized Effects." *Journal of Special Education* 12 (1978): 195–207.

Pellegrini, A. "A Longitudinal Study of Popular and Rejected Children's Rough and Tumble Play." *Early Education and Development* 2 (3) (1991): 205–213.

Peller, L. "Models of Children's Play." In *Child's Play,* edited by R. Herron and B. Sutton-Smith. New York: John Wiley & Sons, Inc., 1971, 110–125.

Perry, D. G., J. C. Willard, and L. C. Perry. "Peers' Perceptions of the Consequences That Victimized Children Provide Aggressors." *Child Development* 61 (1990): 1310–1325.

Peters, D. L., and J. Belsky. "The Day Care Movement: Past, Present, and Future." In *Child Nurturance,* Vol. 2, edited by M. Kostelnik, et al. New York: Plenum Publishing Corporation, 1982.

Peters, D. L., and M. J. Kostelnik. "Day Care Personnel Preparation." In *Advances in Early Education and Day*

*Care,* Vol. 2, edited by S. Kilmer. Greenwich, Conn.: JAI Press, Inc., 1981.

Peterson, K. S. "Quest for Superkids: When Does Push Come to Shove?" *USA Today* (August 22, 1988): Sect. D.

Peterson, L. "Developmental Changes in Verbal and Behavioral Sensitivity to Cues of Social Norms of Altruism." *Child Development* 51 (1980): 830–838.

Peterson, R., and V. Felton-Collins. *The Piaget Handbook for Teachers and Parents.* New York: Teachers College Press, 1991.

Pettit, G., and A. Harrist. "Children's Aggressive and Socially Unskilled Behavior with Peers: Origins in Early Family Relations." In *Children on Playgrounds: Research Perspectives and Applications,* edited by C. Hart. Albany: State University of New York, 1993, 14–42.

Phyfe-Perkins, E. *Effects of Teacher Behavior on Preschool Children: A Review of Research.* Urbana, Ill.: ERIC Document Reproduction Service, 1982 (catalog no. 194).

Piaget, J. *The Origins of Intelligence in Children.* New York: W. W. Norton & Co., Inc., 1962.

Piaget, J. *Play, Dreams and Imitations in Childhood.* New York: W. W. Norton & Co., Inc., 1962.

Piaget, J. *The Moral Judgment of the Child.* New York: Free Press, 1965. (Originally published in 1932.)

Piaget, J. "The Rules of the Game of Marbles." In *Play: Its Role in Development and Evolution,* edited by J. Bruner, A. Jolly, and K. Sylva. New York: Academic Press, Inc., 1976, 411–441.

Polakow, V. *Lives on the Edge: Single Mothers and Their Children in the Other America.* Chicago: University of Chicago Press, 1993.

Polloway, A. M. "The Child in the Physical Environment: A Design Problem." In *Alternative Learning Environments,* edited by G. Coates. Stroudsburg, Pa.: Dowden, Hutchinson and Ross, 1974.

Postman, N. *The Disappearance of Childhood.* New York: Dell Publishing Co., Inc., 1982.

Potts, R., A. C. Huston, and J. C. Wright. "The Effects of Television Form and Violent Content on Boys' Attention and Social Behavior." *Journal of Experimental Child Psychology* 41 (1986): 1–17.

Powell, D. R. *Families and Early Childhood Programs.* Washington, D.C.: National Association for the Education of Young Children, 1989.

Prechtl, H., and M. O'Brien. "Behavioral States of the Full Term Newborn: The Emergence of the Concept." In *Psychobiology of the Human Newborn,* edited by E. Stratton. New York: Wiley, 1982, 53–74.

Pruett, K. D. "The Paternal Presence. Special Issue on Fathers." *Families in Society* 74, no. 1 (January 1993): 46–50.

Pulkkinen, L. "Self-Control and Continuity from Childhood to Adolescence." In *Life-Span Development and Behavior,* Vol. 4, edited by P. B. Battes and O. G. Brim, Jr. Orlando, FL: Academic Press, 1982.

Raffini, J. P. *Discipline: Negotiating Conflicts with Today's Kids.* Englewood Cliffs, N.J.: Prentice-Hall, Inc., 1980.

Rayston, A. *Where Do Babies Come From?* New York: DK Publishing, 1996.

Reed, D. F. "Preparing Teachers for Multicultural Classrooms." *The Journal of Early Childhood Education* 38, no. 12:2 (1991): 16–21.

Reganick, K. A. "Prognosis for Homeless Children and Adolescents." *Childhood Education* 73, no. 3 (Spring 1997): 133–135.

Reichenbach, L., and J. C. Masters. "Children's Use of Expressive and Contextual Cues in Judgments of Emotions." *Child Development* 54 (1983): 993–1004.

Reifel S., and J. Yeatman. "From Category to Context: Reconsidering Classroom Play." *Early Childhood Research Quarterly* 8 (1993): 347–367.

Resnick, L. "Teacher Behavior in an Informal British Infant School." *School Review* 81, no. 1 (1972): 63–83.

Reynolds, E. *Guiding Young Children: A Child Centered Approach.* Mountain View, CA: Mayfield Publishing Co. 1996.

Rheingold, H., and K. Cook. "The Contents of Boys' and Girls' Rooms As an Index of Parents' Behavior." *Child Development* 46 (1975): 459–463.

Riak, J. *Plain Talk about Spanking.* Alamo, Calif.: Parents and Teachers Against Violence in Education, 1994.

Rich, J. M. "Discipline, Rules and Punishment." *Contemporary Education* 55, no. 2 (1984): 110–112.

Rich, J. M. *Innovative School Discipline.* Springfield, IL: C. C. Thomas, 1985.

Richmond, V. and J. McCroskey. *Nonverbal behavior in interpersonal relations.* 2d ed. New York: Prentice Hall, 1995.

Ridley, C. A., and S. R. Vaughn. "The Effects of a Preschool Problem Solving Program on Interpersonal Behavior." *Child Care Quarterly* 12, no. 3 (Fall 1984): 222–230.

Riley, S. S. "Pilgrimage to Elmwood Cemetery." *Young Children,* 44, no. 2 (January, 1989): 33–36.

Ritchie, F. K., and I. J. Toner. "Direct Labeling, Tester Expectancy, and Delay Maintenance Behavior in Scottish Preschool Children." *International Journal of Behavioral Development* 7, no. 3 (1985): 333–341.

Ritchie, K., and Z. Johnson. "From Scooby-Doo to Skeletor: Evolving Issues in Superhero Play." Paper presented at the Annual Conference for the National Association for the Education of Young Children. Nov. 13–16, 1988. ERIC Document ED 280 574 PS016-396.

Rivara, F. P., et al. "Risk of Injury to Children Less Than 5 Years of Age in Day Care versus Home Care Settings." *Pediatrics* 84, no. 6 (December, 1989): 1011–1016.

Roberts, H. A. "A Clinical and Metabolic Reevaluation of Reading Disability." *Selected Papers on Learning Disabilities, Fifth Annual Convention, Association for Children with Learning Disabilities.* San Rafael, Calif.: Academic Therapy Publications, Inc., 1969.

Roedell, W. C., R. G. Slaby, and H. B. Robinson. *Social Development in Young Children: A Report for Teachers.* Washington, D.C.: National Institute for Education, U.S. Department of Health, Education, and Welfare, 1976.

Roff, M., S. B. Sells, and M. M. Golden. *Social Adjustment and Personality Development in Children.* Minneapolis: University of Minnesota Press, 1972.

Roffey, S., T. Tarrant, and K. Majors. *Young Friends: Schools and Friendships.* New York: Cassell Publishing Co., 1994.

Rogers, C. R. "The Necessary and Sufficient Conditions of Therapeutic Personality Change." *Journal of Consulting Psychology* 21 (1957): 95–103.

Rogers, C. R. *On Becoming a Person.* Boston: Houghton Mifflin Company, 1961.

Rohrer, J. C. "We Interrupt This Program to Show You a Bombing: Children and Schools Respond to Televised War." *Childhood Education* 72, no. 4 (1996): 201–205.

Rosenberg, M. *Conceiving the Self.* New York: Basic Books, 1979.

Rosenberg, M., and R. G. Simmons. *Black and White Self-Esteem: The Urban School Child.* Boston: American Sociological Association, 1971.

Rosenblith, J. *In the Beginning: Development from Conception to Age Two.* Newbury Park: Sage Publications, 1992.

Rosenhan, D. L. "Prosocial Behavior of Children." In *The Young Child: Reviews of Research,* Vol. 2, edited by W. W. Hartup. Washington, D.C.: National Association for the Education of Young Children, 1972, 340–360.

Rosenthal, M. S. "A Three-Year Report." *Phoenix House.* New York: Phoenix House Foundation, 1970, 5.

Roskos, K. "A Taxonomic View of Pretend Play Activity Among 4- and 5-Year-Old Children." *Early Childhood Research Quarterly* 5, no. 4 (1990): 495–512.

Rowe, M. B. "Pausing Phenomena: Influence on the Quality of Instruction." *Journal of Psycholinguistic Research* 3 (1974): 203–233.

Rubin, K. H., T. Maconi, and M. Hornung. "Free Play Behaviors in Middle and Lower Class Preschoolers: Parten and Piaget Revisited." *Child Development* 47 (1976): 414–419.

Rubin, K. H., and L. R. Rose-Krasnor. "Interpersonal Problem Solving and Social Competence in Children." In *Handbook of Social Development: A Lifespan Perspective,* edited by V. B. Hasselt and M. Hersen. New York: Plenum Publishing Corp., 1992, 283–323.

Rubin, Z. *Children's Friendships.* Cambridge, Mass.: Harvard University Press, 1980.

Ruble, D. "The Development of Social Comparison Processes and Their Role in Achievement-Related Self-Socialization." In *Social Cognitive Development: A Social-Cultural Perspective,* edited by E. Higgins, D. Ruble, and W. Hartup. New York: Cambridge University Press, 1983.

Ruble, T. L. "The Acquisition of Self-Knowledge: A Self-Socialization Perspective." In *Contemporary Topics in Developmental Psychology,* edited by N. Eisenberg. New York: Wiley-Interscience, 1987.

Rutter, M. "Psychosocial Resilience and Protective Mechanisms." *American Journal of Orthopsychiatry* 57, no. 3 (1987): 316–331.

Safier, G. A. "A Study of Relationships Between Life and Death Concepts in Children." *Journal of Genetic Psychology* 105 (1964): 283–294.

Salovey, P., and J. D. Mayer. "Emotional Intelligence." *Imagination, Cognition, and Personality* 9 (1990): 185–211.

Saltz, E., and J. Brodie. "Pretend-Play Training in Childhood: A Review and Critique." In *The Play of Children: Current Theory and Research,* edited by D. Pepler and K. Rubin. New York: S. Karger, 1982, 97–113.

Sample, W. "The American Indian Child." *Exchange* 3 (1993): 39–40.

Santrock, J. W. *Children.* 4th ed. Dubuque, IA: William C. Brown, Publishers, 1995.

Santrock, J. W. *Child Development.* Dubuque, IA: Brown and Benchmark Publishers, 1996.

Sayles, L., and G. Strauss. *Managing Human Resources.* Englewood Cliffs, N.J.: Prentice-Hall, Inc., 1981.

Scarr, S. *Mother Care—Other Care.* New York: Basic Books, Inc., Publishers, 1984.

Schacter, R., and C. S. McCauley. *When Your Child is Afraid.* New York: Simon & Schuster, Inc., 1989.

Schaefer, E. S. "Parents and Educators: Evidence from Cross-Sectional, Longitudinal, and Intervention Research." *Young Children* 4 (1972): 227–239.

Scheflen, A. *Body Language and the Social Order.* Englewood Cliffs, N.J.: Prentice-Hall, Inc., 1972.

Scherer, M. "Perspectives/Negotiating Childhood." *Educational Leadership* 54, no. 7 (April, 1997): 5.

Schickedanz, J. A. "Helping Children Develop Self-Control." *Childhood Education* 70, no. 5 (1994): 274–278.

Schickedanz, J. A., D. I. Schickedanz, and P. D. Forsyth. *Toward Understanding Children.* Boston: Little, Brown & Company, 1982.

Schickedanz, J., et al. *Curriculum in Early Childhood.* Boston: Allyn and Bacon, 1997.

Schlank, C. H., and B. Metzger. *Together and Equal.* Boston: Allyn and Bacon, 1997.

Schlichter, C. L. "The Answer Is in the Question." *Science and Children* 20, no. 5 (February 1983): 8–10.

Schorr, L. B. *Within our Reach,* New York: Doubleday, 1988.

Schultz, E. W., and C. M. Heuchert. *Child Stress and the School Experience.* New York: Human Sciences Press, Inc., 1983.

Seefeldt, C. "Transforming Curriculum in Social Studies." In *Reaching Potentials: Transforming Early Childhood Curriculum and Assessment,* edited by S. Bredekamp and T. Rosegrant. Washington, D.C.: NAEYC, 1995, 109–124.

Seefeldt, V., and J. Haubenstricker. "Patterns, Phases, or Stages: An Analytical Model for the Study of Developmental Movement." In *The Development of Movement Control and Coordination,* edited by J. A. Kelso and J. E. Clark. New York: John Wiley & Sons, Inc., 1982, 309–318.

Segal, J., and H. Yahraes. *A Child's Journey.* New York: McGraw-Hill, Inc., 1979.

Seligman, M. E. P. *The Optimistic Child.* Boston, Mass.: Houghton Mifflin Co., 1995.

Selman, R. L. "Social-Cognitive Understanding." In *Moral Development and Behavior: Theory, Research and Social Issues,* edited by T. Lickona. New York: Holt, Rinehart & Winston, 1976.

Selman, R. L. *The Growth of Interpersonal Understanding.* New York: Academic Press, Inc., 1980.

Selman, R. L. "The Child As Friendship Philosopher." In *In the Development of Children's Friendships,* edited by J. M. Gottman. Cambridge, England: Cambridge University Press, 1981.

Sexton, D., et al. "Infants and Toddlers with Special Needs and Their Families." *Childhood Education, Annual Theme Issue* (1993): 278–286.

Selye, H. *Stress without Distress.* New York: The New American Library, Inc., 1974.

Serbin, L. A. "Sex-Differentiated Free Play Behavior: Effects of Teacher Modeling, Location, and Gender." *Developmental Psychology* 17, no. 5 (September 1981): 640–646.

Serbin, L. A., I. J. Tonick, and S. H. Sternglanz. "Shaping Cooperative Cross-Sex Play." *Child Development* 48 (1977): 924–929.

Shaffer, D. R. *Social and Personality Development.* Pacific Grove, Calif.: Brooks/Cole Publishing Co., 1994.

Shaffer, D. R. *Developmental Psychology: Childhood and Adolescence.* Pacific Grove, CA: Brooks/Cole Publishing Co., 1995.

Shanab, M. E., and K. A. Yahya. "A Behavioral Study of Obedience." *Journal of Personality and Social Psychology* 35 (1977): 550–586.

Shantz, C. U. "The Development of Social Cognition." In *Review of Child Development Research,* Vol. 5, edited by E. M. Hetherington. Chicago: University of Chicago Press, 1975.

Shantz, C. U. "Conflicts Between Children." *Child Development* 58 (1987): 283–305.

Shantz, D. W. "Conflict, Aggression and Peer Status: An Observational Study." *Child Development* 57 (1986): 1322–1332.

Shapiro, L. "Gun and Dolls." *Newsweek* (May, 1990): 56–65.

Shapiro, L. *How to Raise a Child with a High EQ.* New York: Harper Collins Publishers, 1997.

Sharp, C. *Let's Talk: First Steps to Conversations.* Portland, OR: Educational Productions, 1987a.

Sharp, C. *Now You're Talking: Techniques that Extend Conversations.* Portland, OR.: Educational Productions, 1987b.

Sharp, C. "Between You and Me: Facilitating Child-to-Child Conversations." Portland, OR: Educational Productions, 1988.

Shaw, M. E. "Changes in Sociometric Choices Following Forced Integration of an Elementary School." *Journal of Social Issues* 29 (1973): 143–157.

Shay, S. W., and S. L. Murphy. "Scary People: When Touching Is Not Okay." *Two to Twelve: Current Issues in Children's Development* 2, no. 1 (January 1984): 7–9.

Sheppard, W. C., and R. H. Willoughby. *Child Behavior.* Chicago: Rand McNally & Company, 1975.

Sherman, J. A., and D. Bushell, Jr. "Behavior Modification As an Educational Technique." In *Review of Child Development Research,* Vol. 4, edited by F. D. Horowitz. Chicago: University of Chicago Press, 1975, 409–462.

Sherrod, K. B., et al. "Child Health and Maltreatment." *Child Development* 55 (1984): 1174–1183.

Sherrod, L. "Issues in Cognitive-Perceptual Development: The Special Case of Social Stimuli." In *Infant Social Cognition: Empirical and Theoretical Considerations,* edited by M. E. Lamb and L. Sherrod. Hillsdale, N.J.: Lawrence Erlbaum Associates, Inc., 1981, 11–36.

Shonkoff, J., and P. Hauser-Cram. "Early Intervention for Disabled Infants and Their Families: a Quantitative Analysis." *Pediatrics* 80 (1987): 650–658.

Shotwell, J., D. Wolf, and H. Gardner. "Exploring Early Symbolization: Styles of Achievement." In *Play and Learning,* edited by B. Sutton-Smith. New York: Gardner Press, Inc., 1979, 127–156.

Shure, M. B., and G. Spivack. *Problem-Solving Techniques in Childrearing.* San Francisco: Jossey-Bass, Inc., Publishers, 1978.

Shure, M. B., and G. Spivak. "Interpersonal Problem Solving as a Mediator of Behavior Adjustment in Preschool and Kindergarten Children." *Journal of Applied Developmental Psychology* 1 (1980): 35–39.

Siegal, M., and J. Cowen. "Appraisals of Intervention: The Mother's versus the Culprit's Behavior as Determinants of Children's Evaluations of Discipline Techniques." *Child Development* 55 (1984): 1760–1766.

Sifianou, M. "Do We Need to Be Silent to Be Extremely Polite? Silence and FTAs." *International Journal of Applied Linguistics* 5, no. 1 (1995): 95–110.

Singer, J. L. *The Child's World of Make Believe: Experimental Studies of Imaginative Play.* New York: Academic Press, Inc., 1978.

Singleton, L. "The Effects of Sex and Race on Children's Sociometric Choices for Play and Work." Urbana, Ill.: University of Illinois Press, 1974. (ERIC Document Reproduction Service catalog no. ED 100520.)

Slaby, R. G., and K. S. Frey. "Development of Gender Constancy and Selective Attention to Same-Sex Models." In *Social Issues in Developmental Psychology,* 2d ed., edited by H. Bee. New York: Harper & Row, Publishers, Inc., 1978.

Slaby, R. G., et al. *Early Violence Prevention.* Washington, D.C.: NAEYC, 1995.

Slife, B. D. "Role of Affective Assessment in Modeling Aggressive Behavior." *Journal of Personality and Social Psychology* 43 (1982): 861–868.

Smilansky, S. *The Effects of Sociodramatic Play of Disadvantaged Preschool Children.* New York: John Wiley & Sons, Inc., 1968.

Smith, A. I. "Nonverbal Communication Through Touch." Ph.D. diss., Georgia State University, 1970.

Smith, C. A. *Promoting the Social Development of Young Children.* Palo Alto, Calif.: Mayfield Publishing Co., 1982.

Smith, P. K. "A Longitudinal Study of Social Participation in Preschool Children: Solitary and Parallel Play Reexamined." *Developmental Psychology* 14 (1978): 517–523.

Smith, P. K., and M. Green. "Aggressive Behavior in English Nurseries and Play Groups: Sex Differences and Response of Adults." *Child Development* 46, no. 1 (1975): 211–214.

Smith, S. T. "Personality Traits, Values, Expectations and Managerial Behavior." Master's thesis, The Pennsylvania State University, 1971. As quoted in I. Gross, E. Crandall, and M. Knoll, *Management for Modern Families.* Englewood Cliffs, N.J.: Prentice-Hall, Inc., 1980, 32.

Soderman, A. "Interaction Within a Typical and Hearing-Impaired Preprimary Setting: An Intensive Study." Ph.D. diss., Michigan State University, 1979.

Soderman, A. "Dealing with Difficult Young Children: Strategies for Teachers and Parents." *Young Children* 40, no. 5, 7 (1985): 15–20.

Soderman, A. "Helping the School-Age Child Deal with Stress." *Focus* 10, no. 1 (1985): 17–23.

Soderman, A. "Contemporary Stressors in Kindergarten Children." In *The Developing Kindergarten: Programs, Children, and Teachers,* edited by J. S. McKee. MiAEYC, 1990.

Soderman, A. K. "Prevention of Conflict in Divorcing Families. SMILE." *Michigan Family Review.* Williamston, Mich.: Michigan Council on Family Relations, 1996.

Soderman, A., and M. Phillips. "The Early Education of Males: Where Are We Failing Them?" *Educational Leadership* 44, no. 3 (November 1986): 70–72.

Soderman, R. "Getting Ready for Middle School." *Two to Twelve* 2, no. 8, 8 (1984): 8–9.

Solomon, R. "Pediatricians and Early Intervention: Everything You Need to Know But Are Too Busy to Ask." *Infants and Young Children* 7, no. 3 (1995): 38–51.

Solomon, Z. P. "California's Policy on Parent Involvement." *Phi Delta Kappan* 72, no. 5 (January, 1991): 359–362.

Sommer, R. *Tight Spaces: Hard Architecture and How to Humanize It.* Englewood Cliffs, N.J.: Prentice-Hall, Inc., 1974.

Soroka, S. M., C. M. Corter, and R. Abramovitch. "Infants' Tactile Discrimination of Novel and Familiar Stimuli." *Child Development* 50 (1979): 1251–1253.

Spivack, G., J. Platt, and M. Shure. *The Problem-Solving Approach to Adjustment.* San Francisco: Jossey-Bass, Inc., Publishers, 1976.

Spivack, G., and M. B. Shure. *Problem-Solving Techniques in Childrearing.* San Francisco: Jossey-Bass, Inc., Publishers, 1974.

Sroufe, A. *Emotional Development.* Boston: Cambridge University Press, 1996.

Sroufe, L. A. "Wariness of Strangers and the Study of Infant Development." *Child Development* 48 (1977): 731–746.

Sroufe, L. A. "Social Emotional Development." In *Handbook of Infant Development,* edited by J. Osofsky. New York: John Wiley & Sons, Inc., 1979.

Sroufe, L. A., and Cooper, R. G. *Child Development: Its Nature and Course.* New York: Alfred A. Knopf, 1996.

Sroufe, L. A., and M. J. Ward. "Seductive Behavior of Mothers of Toddlers: Occurrence, Correlates and Family Origins." *Child Development* 51 (1980): 1222–1229.

Staub, E. "A Child in Distress: The Influence of Age and Number of Witnesses on Children's Attempts to Help." *Journal of Personality and Social Psychology* 14 (1970): 130–140.

Staub, E. "The Learning and Unlearning of Aggression." In *The Control of Aggression and Violence,* edited by J. L. Singer. New York: Academic Press, Inc., 1971, 93–124.

Staub, E. *Positive Social Behavior and Morality: Social and Personal Influences.* Vol. 1. New York: Academic Press, Inc., 1978.

Staub, E. *Positive Social Behavior and Morality: Socialization and Development.* Vol. 2. New York: Academic Press, Inc., 1979.

Stayton, D. J., R. Hogan, and M. D. S. Ainsworth. "Infant Obedience and Maternal Behavior: The Origin of Socialization Reconsidered." *Child Development* 42 (1971): 1057–1069.

Steele, B. "Psychodynamic Factors in Child Abuse." In *The Battered Child,* 3d ed., rev., edited by C. H. Kempe and R. E. Helfer. Chicago: University of Chicago Press, 1980.

Steele, B. F. "A Psychiatric Study of Parents Who Abuse Infants and Small Children." In *The Battered Child,* edited by R. E. Helfer and C. H. Kempe. 43, no. 12 (1983): 103–147.

Steele, B. F. "Notes on the Lasting Effects of Early Child Abuse Throughout the Life Cycle. Sixth International Congress of the International Society for Prevention of Child Abuse and Neglect." *Child Abuse and Neglect* 10, no. 3 (1986): 283–291.

Stein, L. C., and M. J. Kostelnik. "A Practical Problem Solving Model for Conflict Resolution in the Classroom." *Child Care Quarterly* 13, no. 1 (Spring 1984): 5–20.

Steiner, J. E. "Facial Expressions in Response to Taste and Smell Stimulation." In *Advances in Child Development and Behavior.* Vol. 13, edited by H. W. Reese and L. P. Lepsitt. New York: Academic Press, Inc., 1979, 257–296.

Stengel, S. R. "Moral Education for Young Children." *Young Children* 37, no. 6 (1982): 23–31.

Stephens, K. "Responding Professionally and Compassionately to Challenging Children." *Child Care Information Exchange* 9 (1996): 44–48.

Stern, D. *The First Relationship: Infant and Mother.* Cambridge, Mass.: Harvard University Press, 1977.

Stewig, J. W. "Reaching for Links That Foster Strength and Stability." *Phi Delta Kappan* 66, no. 9, 5 (1985): 640–642.

Stockdale, D. F., S. M. Hegland, and T. Chiaromonte. "Helping Behaviors: An Observational Study of Preschool Children." *Early Childhood Research Quarterly* 4, no. 4 (1989): 533–543.

Stocking, S. H., D. Arezzo, and S. Leavitt. *Helping Kids Make Friends.* Allen, Tex.: Argus Communications, 1980.

Stone, L. J., and J. Church. *Childhood and Adolescence.* New York: Random House, Inc., 1973.

Strayer, J. "A Naturalistic Study of Empathic Behaviors and Their Relation to Affective States and Perspective-Taking Skills in Preschool Children." *Child Development* 51 (1980): 815–822.

Streissguth, A. P., et al. "Fetal Alcohol Syndrome in Adolescents and Adults." *Journal of American Medical Association* 265, no. 15 (April, 1991): 1961–1967.

Stringer, B. R., and H. T. Hurt. "To Praise or Not to Praise. Factors to Consider Before Utilizing Praise as a Reinforcing Device in the Classroom Communication Process." Paper presented at the annual meeting of the Southern Speech Communications Association, Austin, TX, April 1981, 8–10.

Sullivan, H. S. *Concepts of Modern Psychiatry.* Washington, D.C.: William Alanison White Psychiatric Foundation, 1957.

Suomi, S. "The Perception of Contingency and Social Development." In *Infant Social Cognition: Theoretical and Empirical Considerations,* edited by M. E. Lamb and L. Sherrod. Hillsdale, N.J.: Lawrence Erlbaum Associates, Inc., 1981, 177–204.

Sutton-Smith, B., and S. Sutton-Smith. *How to Play with Your Child and When Not To.* New York: Hawthorn Books, Inc., 1974.

Sutton-Smith, B. *Toys As Culture.* New York: Gardner, 1986.

Swiniarsky, L. "Toys: Universals for Teaching Global Education." *Childhood Education* (Spring 1991): 161–163.

Swartzman, H. *Transformations: The Anthropology of Children's Play.* New York: Plenum Publishing Corporation, 1978.

Swaze, M. C. "Self-Concept Development in Young Children." In *The Self-Concept of the Young Child,* edited by T. D. Yawkey. Provo, Utah: Brigham Young University Press, 1980.

Swick, K. J., M. Brown, and S. Robinson. *Toward Quality Environments for Young Children.* Champaign, Ill.: Stripes Publishing Company, 1983.

Sylva K., S. Bruner, and P. Genova. "The Role of Play in the Problem-Solving of Children 3–5 Years Old." In *Play: Its Role in Development and Evolution,* edited by J. Bruner, A. Jolly, and K. Sylva. New York: Basic Books, Inc., Publishers, 1976, 244–261.

Sylwester, R. *A Celebration of Neurons: An Educator's Guide to the Human Brain.* Alexandria, Va.: Association for Supervision and Curriculum, 1995.

Taylor, A. R., and S. Machida. "Parental Involvement: Perspectives of Head Start Parents and Teachers." Paper presented at the American Educational Research Association, New Orleans, April 1994.

Taylor-Brown, S. "The Impact of AIDS in Foster Care: A Family-Centered Approach to Services in the United States." *Child Welfare* LXX:2 (April 1991): 193–209.

Thibault, J. W., and H. H. Kelley. *The Social Psychology of Groups.* New York: John Wiley & Sons, Inc., 1959.

Thomas, A., and S. Chess. *Temperament and Development.* New York: Brunner/Mazel, Inc., 1977.

Thomas, A., S. Chess, and H. Birch. *Temperament and Behavior Disorders in Children.* New York: New York University Press, 1968.

Thomas, R. M. *Comparing Theories of Child Development.* 2d ed. Belmont, Calif.: Wadsworth, Inc., 1985.

Thompson, D. C. "A New Vision of Masculinity." *Educational Leadership* 43, no. 4 (1986): 53–56.

Thompson, D. F., and L. Meltzer. "Communication of Emotional Intent by Facial Expression." *Journal of Abnormal and Social Psychology* 68, no. 2 (1964): 129–135.

Tien, G., and M. Rivkin. *The Young Child at Play: Reviews of Research,* Vol. 4. Washington, D.C.: NAEYC, 1986.

Tietjen, A. M. "Prosocial Reasoning Among Children and Adults in a Papua New Guinea Society." *Developmental Psychology* 22 (1986): 861–868.

Tisak, M. S., and J. H. Block. "Preschool Children's Evolving Conceptions of Badness: A Longitudinal Study." *Early Education and Development.* Vol. 4. (1990): 300–307.

Toner, I. J. "Punitive and Non-Punitive Discipline and Subsequent Rule-Following in Young Children." *Child Care Quarterly* 15, no. 1 (1986): 27–37.

Toner, I. J., R. D. Parke, and S. R. Yussen. "The Effect of Observation of Model Behavior on the Establishment and Stability of Resistance to Deviation in Children." *Journal of Genetic Psychology* 132 (1978): 283–290.

Tonkova-Yampolskaya, R. V. "On the Question of Studying Physiological Mechanisms of Speech." *Pavlov Journal of Higher Nervous Activity* 12 (1962): 82–87.

Tracy, R. L., and M. D. S. Ainsworth. "Maternal Affectionate Behavior and Infant-Mother Attachment Patterns." *Child Development* 52 (1981): 1341–1343.

Trad, P. V. "The Psychosocial Model Applied to Pediatric Care." *Psychosocial Scenarios for Pediatrics.* New York: Springer-Verlag, 1988.

Trause, M. A. "Stranger Responses: Effects of Familiarity, Strangers' Approach and Sex of Infant." *Child Development* 48 (1977): 1657–1661.

Trawick-Smith, J. "The Effects of Realistic versus Nonrealistic Play Materials on Young Children's Symbolic Transformation of Objects." *Journal of Research in Childhood Education* 5, no. 1 (1990): 27–36.

Trawick-Smith, J. *Early Childhood Development: A Multicultural Perspective.* Columbus, Ohio: Merrill, 1997.

Tremblay, R. "Predicting Early Onset of Male Antisocial Behavior from Preschool Behavior." *Archives of General Psychiatry* 51 (September 1994): 732–739.

Trepanier-Street, M. L. "The Developing Kindergartner: Thinking and Problem Solving." In *The Developing Kindergarten: Programs, Children, Teachers,* edited by J. S. McKee. East Lansing, MI: Michigan Association for the Education of Young Children, 1991.

Tribe, C. *Profile of Three Theories.* Dubuque, Iowa: Kendall/Hunt Publishing Co., 1982.

Trickett, P. K., and E. J. Susman. "Parental Perceptions of Child-Rearing Practices in Physically Abusive and Nonabusive Families." *Developmental Psychology* 24 (1988): 270–276.

Trickett, P. K., et al. "Relationship of Socioeconomic Status to the Etiology and Developmental Sequelae of Physical Child Abuse." *Developmental Psychology* 27 (1991): 148–158.

Tronick, E. "Emotions and Emotional Communication in Infants." *American Psychologist* 44, no. 2 (1989): 112–119.

Tronick, E., et al. "The Infant's Response to Entrapment between Contradictory Messages in Face-to-Face Interaction." *Journal of the American Academy of Child Psychiatry* 17 (1978): 1–13.

Turiel, E. "The Development of Concepts of Social Structure: Social Convention." In *The Development of Social Understanding,* edited by J. Glick and A. Clarke-Stewart. New York: Gardner Press, Inc., 1978.

Turner, C. W., and D. Goldsmith. "Effects of Toy Guns and Airplanes on Children's Anti-Social Free Play Behavior." *Journal of Experimental Psychology* 21 (1976): 303–315.

Turner, P. "Teacher Level of Questioning and Problem Solving in Young Children." *Home Economics Research Journal* 8, no. 6 (July, 1980): 399–404.

U.S. Bureau of the Census. *Statistical Abstract of the United States.* 15th ed. Washington, D.C.: U.S. Government Printing Office, 1995.

U.S. Bureau of the Census. *Current Population Reports.* Washington, D.C.: U.S. Government Printing Office, 1996.

U.S. Drug Enforcement Administration. *Conference Report: Stimulant Use in the Treatment of ADHD.* San Antonio, TX, December 10, 1996.

U.S. National Center on Child Abuse and Neglect. *Child Abuse and Neglect Report 7.* Washington, D.C.: Department of Health, Education, and Welfare, February 1977.

Vandell, D. L., and M. A. Corasaniti. "Variations in Early Childcare: Do They Predict Subsequent Social, Emotional and Cognitive Differences?" *Early Childhood Research Quarterly* 5 (1990): 555–572.

Van Dyke, H. T. "Corporal Punishment in Our Schools." *Education Digest* 57, no. 5. (1984): 296–300.

Vander Zanden, J. W. *Human Development.* New York: Alfred A. Knopf, 1989.

Vasta, R., M. M. Haith, and S. A. Miller. *Child Psychology: The Modern Science.* New York: Wiley, 1992.

Visher, E. D., and J. S. Visher. *How to Win as a Stepfamily.* New York: Brunner/Mazel, 1991.

Volkmar, F. R., and A. E. Siegel. "Responses to Consistent and Discrepant Social Communications." In *Development of Nonverbal Behavior in Children,* edited by R. Feldman. New York: Springer-Verlag. New York, Inc., 1982, 231–256.

Vuorenkoski, U., et al. "The Effect of the Cry Stimulus on the Temperament of the Lactating Breast of Primipara: A Thermographic Study." *Experientia* 25 (1969): 1286–1288.

Vuorenkoski, U., et al. "Cry Score: A Method for Evaluating the Degree of Abnormalities in the Pain Cry Response of the Newborn Young Infant." *Quarterly Progress and Status Report.* Stockholm: Speech Transmission Laboratory, Royale Institute of Technology, April 1971.

Vygotsky, L. *Mind in Society: The Development of Higher Psychological Processes.* Cambridge, Mass.: Harvard University Press, 1978.

Vygotsky, L. S. *Mind in Society: The Development of Higher Mental Processes.* Cambridge, Mass.: Harvard University Press, 1978.

Walden, T. A., and T. A. Ogan. "The Development of Social Referencing." *Child Development* 59 (1988): 1230–1240.

Walker, L. J., B. de Vries, and S. D. Trevarthan. "Moral Stages and Moral Orientations in Real-Life and Hypothetical Dilemmas." *Child Development* 58 (1989): 842–858.

Wall, P. "Children of Chemical Dependency: Respecting Complexities and Building on Strengths." *Preventing Forum* 11, no. 1 (February 1990): 1–2.

Wallerstein, J. S., and S. Blakeslee. *Second Chances.* New York: Ticknor and Fills, 1989.

Wallerstein, J. S., and J. K. Kelly. *Surviving the Breakup—How Children and Parents Cope with Divorce.* New York: Basic Books, Inc., Publishers, 1980.

Waters, B., et al. "The Psychological Consequences of Childhood Infection with Human Immunodeficiency Virus." *Medical Journal of Australia* 149 (August 1988): 198–202.

Waters, E., B. E. Vaughn, and B. England. "Indifferences in Mother-Infant Attachment Relationships at Age One: Antecedents in Neonatal Behavior in an Urban, Economically Disadvantaged Sample." *Child Development* 51 (1980): 208–216.

Watson, M. W., and K. W. Fisher. "Development of Social Roles in Elicited and Spontaneous Behavior During the Preschool Years." *Child Development* 18 (1980): 483–494.

Waxman, S. *What is a Girl? What is a Boy?* New York: Crowell, 1989.

Waxman, S. "Linguistic and Conceptual Organization in 30-Month-Old Children." Paper presented at a meeting of the Society for Research in Child Development, Baltimore, in April 1987.

Weilbacher, R. "The Effects of Static and Dynamic Play Environments on Children's Social and Motor Behaviors." In *Play As Context,* edited by A. Cheska. West Point: N.Y.: Leisure Press, 1981, 248–258.

Weinberger, L., and P. Starkey. "Pretend Play by African American Children in Head Start." *Early Childhood Research Quarterly* 9 (1994): 327–343.

Weiss, B., et al. "Some Consequences of Early Harsh Discipline: Child Aggression and Maladaptive Social Information Processing Style." *Child Development* 63 (1992): 1321–1335.

Weissbourd, R. *The Vulnerable Child: What Really Hurts America's Children and What We Can Do about It.* Reading, Mass.: Addison-Wesley, 1996.

Wender, P., and D. Klein. *Mind, Mood and Medicine: A Guide to the New Psychology.* New York: Farrar, Straus and Giroux. (1986): 11, 16.

Werner, E., and R. Smith. *Overcoming the Odds: High Risk Children from Birth to Adulthood.* Ithaca, N.Y.: Cornell University Press, 1992.

West, T. G. *In the Mind's Eye: Visual Thinkers, Gifted People with Learning Difficulties, Computer Images, and the Ironies of Creativity.* Buffalo: Prometheus Books, 1991.

Weston, D. R., and E. Turiel. "Act-Rule Relations: Children's Concepts of Social Rules." *Developmental Psychology* 16 (1980): 417–424.

Whiren, A. P. "The Preschool Planning for a New Day." *Parent Cooperative Preschool, International* 12, no. 1 (Spring 1970).

Whiren, A. P. "Establishing Routines for Young Children As a Framework for Learning." *Early Childhood Newsletter.* Michigan State University, Cooperative Extension Service, January-February 1977.

Whiren, A. P. "Table Toys: The Underdeveloped Resource." In *Ideas That Work with Young Children,* Vol. 2, edited by L. Adams and B. Garlick. Washington, D.C.: National Association for the Education of Young Children, 1979.

White, B. *The First Three Years of Life.* Englewood Cliffs, N.J.: Prentice-Hall, Inc., 1975.

Whitesell, N. R., and S. Harter. "Children's Reports of Conflict Between Simultaneous Opposite—Valence Emotions." *Child Development* 60 (1989): 673–682.

Whiting, B. B., and C. P. Edwards. *Children of Different Worlds.* Cambridge, Mass.: Harvard University Press, 1988.

Wickelgren, L. W. "Convergence in the Human Newborn." *Journal of Experimental Child Psychology* 5 (1967): 74–85.

Widerstrom, A. "Mainstreaming Handicapped Preschoolers." *Childhood Education* 58, no. 3 (January-February 1982): 172–177.

Widerstrom, A. "Educating Young Handicapped Children." In *Early Childhood Education Annual Editions,* edited by J. McKee and K. Paciorek, Guilford, CT: Dushkin Pub. Group, Inc., 1990.

Wieder, S., and S. I. Greenspan. "The Emotional Basis of Learning." In *Handbook of Research on the Education of Young Children,* edited by B. Spodek. New York: Macmillan, Inc., 1993, 77–104.

Williams, C., and J. Bybee. "What Do Children Feel Guilty About? Developmental and Gender Differences." *Developmental Psychology* 30, no. 5 (1994): 617–623.

Wing, L. "Play is Not the Work of the Child: Young Children's Perceptions of Work and Play." *Early Childhood Research Quarterly* 10 (1995): 223–247.

Winter, S. M. "Diversity: A Proposal for All Children." *Childhood Education* 71, no. 2 (1994/95): 91–95.

Wintre, M. G., and D. D. Vallance. "A Developmental Sequence in the Comprehension of Emotions: Intensity, Multiple Emotions, and Valence." *Developmental Psychology* 30, no. 4 (1994): 509–514.

Withall, J., and W. W. Lewis. "Social Interaction in the Classroom." In *Handbook of Research on Teaching,* edited by N. L. Gage. Chicago: Rand McNally & Company, 1963.

Wittmer, D. S., and A. S. Honig. "Encouraging Positive Social Development in Young Children." *Young Children* 4 (July 1994): 4–12.

Wolery, M., and J. S. Wilbers. *Including Children with Special Needs in Early Childhood Programs.* Washington, D.C.: NAEYC, 1994.

Wolfe, D. A. "Child Abusive Parents: An Empirical Review and Analysis." *Psychology Bulletin* 97, no. 3 (1985): 462–482.

Wolfe, L. "Reaching Potentials through Bilingual Education." In *Reaching Potentials: Appropriate Curriculum and Assessment for Young Children,* Vol. 1, edited by S. Bredekamp and T. Rosegrant. Washington, D.C.: NAEYC, 1992, 139–144.

Wolff, P. H. "Observations on the Early Development of Smiling." In *Determinants of Infant Behavior.* Vol. 2, edited by B. Foss. London: Methuen, 1963.

Wolff, P. H. "The Causes, Controls, and Organization of Behavior in the Neonate." *Psychological Issues* 5, no. 1 (1966): 7–11.

Wolff, P. H. "The Role of Biological Rhythms in Early Psychological Development." *Bulletin of the Menninger Clinic* 31 (1967): 197–218.

Wolff, P. H., S. R. Levin, and E. T. Longobardi. "Motoric Mediation in Children's Paired Associate Learning: Effects of Visual and Tactual Contact." *Journal of Experimental Child Psychology* 64 (1972): 176–183.

Wolfgang, C. H. *Solving Discipline Problems: Methods and Models for Today's Teachers.* Boston: Allyn and Bacon, Inc., 1995.

Woll, P. "Children of Chemical Dependency: Respecting Complexities and Building on Strengths." *Prevention Forum* 11, no. 1 (Fall 1990): 1.

Wunderlich, R. C. "Treatment of the Hyperactive Child." *Academic Therapy* 8 (1973): 375–390.

Yamamota, K., et al. "Voices in Unison: Stressful Events in the Lives of Children in Six Countries." *Journal of Child Psychology and Psychiatry* 28, no. 6 (1987): 855–864.

Yarrow, L. "Should Children Play with Guns?" *Parents* 58 (January 1983): 50–52.

Yarrow, M. R., P. Scott, and C. Z. Waxler. "Learning Concern for Others." *Developmental Psychology* 8 (1973): 240–260.

Yinger, J. *Problem Solving with Children.* San Francisco: Far West Laboratory for Educational Research and Development, 1975.

York, S. *Roots and Wings.* St. Paul, Minn.: Redleaf Press, 1991.

Yorker, B. "Corporal Punishment and Constitutional Law." Paper presented at the National Association for the Education of Young Children, Atlanta, GA, 1994.

Youniss, J. *Parents and Peers in Social Development.* Chicago: University of Chicago Press. 1980.

Zahn-Waxler, C., S. L. Friedman, and E. M. Cummings. "Children's Emotions and Behaviors in Response to Infants' Cries." *Child Development* 54 (1983): 1522–1528.

Zahn-Waxler, C., R. Iannotti, and M. Chapman. "Peers and Prosocial Development." In *Peer Relationships and Social Skills in Childhood,* edited by K. H. Rubin and H. S. Ross. New York: Springer-Verlag New York, Inc., 1982.

Zahn-Waxler, C., M. Radke-Yarrow, and J. Brady-Smith. "Perspective Taking and Prosocial Behavior." *Developmental Psychology* 13 (1977): 87–88.

Zahn-Waxler, C., M. Radke-Yarrow, and R. A. King. "Child Rearing and Children's Prosocial Initiations Toward Victims of Distress." *Child Development* 50 (1979): 319–330.

Zifferblatt, S. M. "Architecture and Human Behavior: Toward Increased Understanding of a Functional Relationship." *Educational Technology* 12 (1972): 54–57.

Zigler, E., and N. Rubin. "Why Child Abuse Occurs." *Parents* 60 (November 1985): 102–218.

Zigler, E. F., and M. Finn-Stevenson. *Children: Development and Social Issues.* Lexington, Mass.: Heath and Co., 1987.

Zimbardo, P. G., and S. L. Radl. *The Shy Child.* Garden City, N.J.: Doubleday & Company, Inc., 1982.

Zirpoli, T. J. "Physical Abuse: Are Children with Disabilities at Greater Risk?" *Intervention* 25, no. 1 (1990): 6–11.

Zuckerman, M., et al. "Controlling Nonverbal Cues: Facial Expressions and Tone of Voice." *Journal of Experimental Social Psychology* 17 (1981): 506–524.

Zuckerman, J., R. Driver, and N. Guadagno. "Effects of Segmentation Patterns on the Perception of Deception." *Journal of Nonverbal Behavior* 9, no. 3 (1985): 160–168.

Page numbers followed by *t* refer to tables.

# License Agreement for Delmar Publishers
## an International Thomson Publishing company

### Educational Software/Data

You the customer, and Delmar incur certain benefits, rights, and obligations to each other when you open this package and use the software/data it contains. BE SURE YOU READ THE LICENSE AGREEMENT CAREFULLY, SINCE BY USING THE SOFTWARE/DATA YOU INDICATE YOU HAVE READ, UNDERSTOOD, AND ACCEPTED THE TERMS OF THIS AGREEMENT.

Your rights:

1. You enjoy a non-exclusive license to use the enclosed software/data on a single microcomputer that is not part of a network or multi-machine system in consideration for payment of the required license fee, (which may be included in the purchase price of an accompanying print component), or receipt of this software/data, and your acceptance of the terms and conditions of this agreement.

2. You own the media on which the software/data is recorded, but you acknowledge that you do not own the software/data recorded on them. You also acknowledge that the software/data is furnished "as is," and contains copyrighted and/or proprietary and confidential information of Delmar Publishers or its licensors.

3. If you do not accept the terms of this license agreement you may return the media within 30 days. However, you may not use the software during this period.

There are limitations on your rights:

1. You may not copy or print the software/data for any reason whatsoever, except to install it on a hard drive on a single microcomputer and to make one archival copy, unless copying or printing is expressly permitted in writing or statements recorded on the diskette(s).

2. You may not revise, translate, convert, disassemble or otherwise reverse engineer the software/data except that you may add to or rearrange any data recorded on the media as part of the normal use of the software/data.

3. You may not sell, license, lease, rent, loan, or otherwise distribute or network the software/data except that you may give the software/data to a student or and instructor for use at school or, temporarily at home.

Should you fail to abide by the Copyright Law of the United States as it applies to this software/data your license to use it will become invalid. You agree to erase or otherwise destroy the software/data immediately after receiving note of Delmar Publishers' termination of this agreement for violation of its provisions.

Delmar Publishers gives you a LIMITED WARRANTY covering the enclosed software/data. The LIMITED WARRANTY can be found in this product and/or the instructor's manual that accompanies it.

This license is the entire agreement between you and Delmar Publishers interpreted and enforced under New York law.

### Limited Warranty

Delmar Publishers warrants to the original licensee/purchaser of this copy of microcomputer software/data and the media on which it is recorded that the media will be free from defects in material and workmanship for ninety (90) days from the date of original purchase. All implied warranties are limited in duration to this ninety (90) day period. THEREAFTER, ANY IMPLIED WARRANTIES, INCLUDING IMPLIED WARRANTIES OF MERCHANTABILITY AND FITNESS FOR A PARTICULAR PURPOSE ARE EXCLUDED. THIS WARRANTY IS IN LIEU OF ALL OTHER WARRANTIES, WHETHER ORAL OR WRITTEN, EXPRESSED OR IMPLIED.

If you believe the media is defective, please return it during the ninety day period to the address shown below. A defective diskette will be replaced without charge provided that it has not been subjected to misuse or damage.

This warranty does not extend to the software or information recorded on the media. The software and information are provided "AS IS." Any statements made about the utility of the software or information are not to be considered as express or implied warranties. Delmar will not be liable for incidental or consequential damages of any kind incurred by you, the consumer, or any other user.

Some states do not allow the exclusion or limitation of incidental or consequential damages, or limitations on the duration of implied warranties, so the above limitation or exclusion may not apply to you. This warranty gives you specific legal rights, and you may also have other rights which vary from state to state. Address all correspondence to:

Delmar Publishers
3 Columbia Circle
P. O. Box 15015
Albany, NY 12212-5015